KGB

By Christopher Andrew

Théophile Delcassé and the Making of the
Entente Cordiale

The First World War: Causes and Consequences

France Overseas: The Great War and the
Climax of French Imperial Expansion
WITH A.S. KANYA-FORSTNER

The Missing Dimension: Governments and
Intelligence Communities in the Twentieth Century
WITH DAVID DILKS

Her Majesty's Secret Service: The Making of
the British Intelligence Community

Codebreaking and Signals Intelligence

CHRISTOPHER ANDREW AND OLEG GORDIEVSKY

KGB

THE INSIDE STORY

Of Its Foreign Operations from Lenin to Gorbachev

HarperCollins*Publishers*

The publishers thank Faber & Faber Ltd. for permission to
reproduce lines from W. H. Auden's *Spain*.

Unacknowledged photographs are taken from private collections. The publishers have attempted to trace copyright owners.
Where inadvertent infringement has been made they apologize
and will be happy to make due acknowledgment in future editions.

Designed by Cassandra J. Pappas

Library of Congress Cataloging-in-Publication Data

Andrew, Christopher M.
    KGB : the inside story / Christopher Andrew, Oleg
Gordievsky.—1st ed.
        p.   cm.
    Includes index.
    ISBN 0-06-016605-3
    1. Soviet Union. Komitet gosudarstvennoĭ bezo-
pasnosti—History.   2. Intelligence service—Soviet
Union—History.   I. Gordievsky, Oleg.   II. Title.
JN6529.I6A53   1990
327.1'247'009—dc20
                                                    90-55525

To Leila, Maria, and Anna in Moscow
and to Darcy and Ken, Louisa and John in Washington,
in the hope that the spread of human rights
in the Soviet Union will, very soon,
enable them to meet.

Contents

Illustrations follow pages 232, 424, and 616

The Evolution
of the KGB

December 1917	Cheka
	↓
February 1922	Incorporated in NKVD (as GPU)
	↓
July 1923	OGPU
	↓
July 1934	Reincorporated in NKVD (as GUGB)
February 1941	NKGB
	↓
July 1941	Reincorporated in NKVD (as GUGB)
	↓
April 1943	NKGB
	↓
March 1946	MGB
	↓

October 1947– **November 1951**	Foreign intelligence transferred to K1

↓

March 1953	Combined with MVD to form enlarged MVD
	↓
March 1954	KGB

[*The term KGB is used in this book to denote the Soviet State Security
organization throughout its history, since its foundation as the Cheka in
1917 as well as, more specifically, to refer to State Security since 1954
when it adopted its present name.*]

Abbreviations
Used in Text

AEC	Atomic Energy Commission (USA)
AFSA	Armed Forces Security Agency (USA): predecessor of NSA
AK	Polish Home Army (World War II)
ANC	African National Congress
ASA	Army Security Agency (USA): predecessor of AFSA
AVO	Hungarian security service: predecessor of AVH
BfV	FRG security service
BND	FRG foreign intelligence agency
Cheka	All-Russian Extraordinary Commission for Combating Counter-Revolution and Sabotage (Soviet security service, 1917–22)
CIA	Central Intelligence Agency (USA)
CND	Campaign for Nuclear Disarmament (UK)
Comintern	Communist International
COMSUBLANT	Commander (U.S.) Atlantic submarine forces
CPUSA	Communist Party of the USA
CUSS	Cambridge University Socialist Society
DA	American Department (Cuban intelligence agency independent of DGI)

DGSE	French foreign intelligence service
DGSP	Rumanian security service (Securitate)
DIE	Rumanian foreign intelligence agency
DISA	Angolan security service
DLB	Dead letter box
DS	Bulgarian security service
DST	French security service
EC	European Community
ECCI	Executive Committee of Communist International
FBI	Federal Bureau of Investigation
FCD	First Chief (Foreign Intelligence) Directorate of KGB
FNLA	National Front for the Liberation of Angola
FRELIMO	Front for the Liberation of Mozambique
FRG	Federal Republic of Germany
GC & CS	Government Code & Cypher School (UK): predecessor of GCHQ
GCHQ	Government Communications Headquarters (UK)
GDR	German Democratic Republic
Gehlen Org	FRG semiofficial foreign intelligence agency: predecessor of BND
GKES	Soviet State Committee for External Economic Relations
GKNT	Soviet State Committee for Science and Technology
GPU	State Political Directorate (Soviet security service incorporated in NKVD, 1922–23)
GRU	Soviet military intelligence agency
GUGB	Main Administration of State Security (Soviet security service within NKVD, 1934–43)
Gulag	Labor camps directorate
Humint	Intelligence derived from human sources
HVA	GDR foreign intelligence agency
IADL	International Association of Democratic Lawyers
IB	Intelligence Branch (India)
ID	International Department of Soviet Communist Party Central Committee
INO	Foreign Intelligence Department of Cheka/GPU/OGPU/GUGB, 1920–41: predecessor of INU
INU	Foreign Intelligence Directorate of NKGB/GUGB/MGB, 1941–54: predecessor of FCD
IRA	Irish Republican Army

IRD	Information Research Department (UK)
IWA	International Workers Aid
JIC	Joint Intelligence Committee (UK)
K-5	East German security service, 1947–49: predecessor of SSD
KGB	Committee of State Security (Soviet security service, established 1954)
KHAD	Afghan security service
KI	Committee of Information (Soviet foreign intelligence agency initially combining foreign directorates of MGB and GRU, 1947–51)
KOR	Polish Workers' Defense Committee
KPD	German Communist Party
KR Line	Counterintelligence department in KGB residencies
KRO	Interwar counterespionage department of Cheka/GPU/OGPU/GUGB, predecessor of the KGB Second Chief Directorate
LPG	London Processing Group, transcription service of GCHQ
LSR	Left Socialist Revolutionary
MGB	Soviet Ministry of State Security, 1946–54
MGIMO	Moscow State Institute for International Relations
MI5	British security service
MOR	Monarchist Association of Central Russia ("The Trust")
MPLA	Marxist Popular Movement for the Liberation of Angola
MVD	Soviet Ministry of Internal Affairs, 1946–
NEP	New Economic Policy
NKGB	People's Commissariat of State Security (Soviet security service, 1941 and 1943–46: predecessor of MGB)
NKVD	People's Commissariat for Internal Affairs (incorporated State Security 1922–23, 1934–43): predecessor of MVD
NSA	National Security Agency (USA)
NSZRiS	The People's Union for Defense of Country and Freedom (anti-Bolshevik organization)
NTS	National Labor Alliance (Soviet émigré Social-Democratic organization)
OAU	Organization for African Unity
OGPU	Unified State Political Directorate (Soviet security service, 1923–34)
Okhrana	Tsarist security service, 1881–1917

OMS	International Liaison Department of Communist International
OSS	Office of Strategic Services (wartime predecessor of the CIA)
OUN	Organization of Ukrainian Nationalists
OZNA	Yugoslav security service: predecessor of UDBA
PCC	Cuban Communist Party (since 1975)
PDPA	Afghan Communist Party
PDRY	People's Democratic Republic of Yemen
PLO	Palestine Liberation Organization
POUM	Workers' Unification Party (Spanish Marxist/Trotskyist Party during 1930s)
PPR	Polish Workers' [Communist] Party: predecessor of PZPR
PRC	People's Republic of China
PR Line	Political intelligence department in KGB residencies
PROD	NSA Production Office
PSP	Cuban Communist Party: predecessor of PCC
PZPR	Polish United Workers' [Communist] Party
RENAMO	Mozambique National Resistance
ROVS	Russian Combined Services Union (White Russian émigré group)
RPC	Russian Political Committee (anti-Bolshevik organization)
SACP	South African Communist Party
SAS	Special Air Service (UK)
SB	Polish security service
SDECE	French foreign intelligence agency: predecessor of DGSE
SDI	Strategic Defense Initiative ("Star Wars")
SDKPiL	Social Democratic Party of Poland and Lithuania
SDP	Social Democratic Party (UK)
SED	East German Socialist Unity [Communist] Party
Sigint	Intelligence derived from intercepting, analyzing and decrypting signals
SIM	Spanish Republican security service
SIS	Secret Intelligence Service (UK)
SMA	Soviet Military Administration (East Germany)
Smersh	"Death to Spies!" (Soviet military counterintelligence, 1943–46)
SNASP	Mozambique security service
SOE	Special Operations Executive (UK)
Sovnarkom	Soviet Council of People's Commissars
SPD	German Social-Democratic Party
SR	Socialist Revolutionaries
SS	Nazi "protection squad"/security service
SSD	GDR security service ("Stasi")
S&T	Scientific and technical/technological intelligence

Stavka	Wartime Soviet GHQ/high command
StB	Czechoslovak security service
TUC	Trades Union Congress (UK)
UB	Polish security service, predecessor of SB
UDBA	Yugoslav security service
UNITA	Union for the Total Liberation of Angola
USC	Unitarian Service Commission
U-2	American spy plane
VMS	Supreme Monarchist Council (White Russian émigré group)
VPK	Soviet Military Industrial Commission
WES	West European Secretariat (Comintern)
WiN	"Freedom and Independence" (last active remnant of Polish Home Army)
WPC	World Peace Council
X Line	Scientific and technological intelligence department in KGB residencies
ZANU	Zimbabwe African National Union
ZAPU	Zimbabwe African People's Union
ZOMO	Polish paramilitary police

Transliteration of Russian Names

In transliterating Russian names, we have followed a simplified version of the method used by the U.S. Board on Geographic Names and BBC Monitoring Service. Simplifications include the substitution of "y" for "iy" in surnames (not Bokiy, Gorskiy, Agranovskiy, but Boky, Gorsky, Agranovsky), and of "i" for "iy" in first names (not Georgiy, Valeriy, Yuriy, but Georgi, Valeri, Yuri). The apostrophe ordinarily used to signify a soft sign is omitted. The "y" between the letters "i" and "e" (in all possible combinations) is omitted too (not Ageyev, Dmitriyevich, but Ageev, Dmitrievich).

In a few cases where a mildly deviant spelling of a well-known Russian name has become firmly established in Western publications, we have retained that version, e.g.: Khrushchev, Beria, Evdokia (Petrova), Joseph (Stalin), *Izvestia,* Zinoviev, and the names of Tsars.

Europe 1942

FINLAND

NORWAY

SWEDEN

NORTH SEA

ESTONIA

LATVIA

DENMARK

BALTIC SEA

LITHUANIA

E. PRUSSIA

NETHERLANDS

• Berlin

GERMANY

POLAND

BELGIUM

FRANCE

SLOVAKIA

SWITZERLAND

AUSTRIA

HUNGARY

RUMANIA

ITALY

ADRIATIC SEA

YUGOSLAVIA

BULGARIA

SPAIN

ALBANIA

GREECE

MEDITERRANEAN

SICILY

SEA

ALGERIA

TUNISIA

SOVIET ANNEXATIONS
1939 – 1940

FINLAND

SWEDEN

Leningrad

BALTIC SEA

ESTONIA

LATVIA

LITHUANIA

E PRUSSIA

U.S.S.R.

Berlin

POLAND

EASTERN
POLAND

U.S.S.R.

GERMANY

EASTERN
GALICIA

SLOVAKIA

BUKOVINA

BESSARABIA

HUNGARY

RUMANIA

BLACK
SEA

URKEY

Leningrad

```
0                    200 Miles
0                    300 Km
```

Greater Germany

Area occupied
by Germans

```
0                                200 Miles
0                                300 Km
```

Postwar Europe
Political boundaries after 1948

NORTH SEA

SWEDEN

FINLAND

NORWAY

BALTIC SEA

DENMARK

NETHERLANDS

BELGIUM

WEST GERMANY

EAST GERMANY

Warsaw
POLAND

CZECHOSLOVAKIA

FRANCE

SWITZERLAND

AUSTRIA

HUNGARY

RUMANIA

ITALY

ADRIATIC SEA

YUGOSLAVIA

BULGARIA

SPAIN

ALBANIA

GREECE

MEDITERRANEAN

SICILY

SEA

ALGERIA

TUNISIA

THE SOVIET UNION
& EASTERN EUROPE
1945-1948

ANNEXED TERRITORY
1939-40

ANNEXED TERRITORY
1945

COMMUNIST REGIMES
ESTABLISHED 1945-48

SOVIET OCCUPATION
ZONES

IRON CURTAIN 1948

FINLAND

Leningrad

U. S. S. R.

ESTONIA

LATVIA

LITHUANIA

NETHERLANDS

EAST
GERMANY

Warsaw.
POLAND

BELGIUM

WEST
GERMANY

CZECHOSLOVAKIA

FRANCE

AUSTRIA

SWITZERLD

HUNGARY

RUMANIA

YUGOSLAVIA

BULGARIA

ITALY

ALBANIA

Leningrad

U. S. S. R.

0   200 Miles

0   300 Km

BLACK
SEA

TURKEY

0   200 Miles

0   300 Km

KGB

Introduction

Most authors can expect, sooner or later, to make an accurate prediction, though they should not expect it to happen often. Christopher Andrew's turn arrived in October 1985 with the publication of his book *Secret Service: The Making of the British Intelligence Community.* While writing *Secret Service,* he had come to disbelieve the widespread assumption, largely derived from worldwide media interest in the Soviet moles educated at Cambridge University (where Andrew teaches history), that high-level penetration and defection remained more of a problem for the West than for the Kremlin. The career of Oleg Penkovsky, the Anglo-American mole in the GRU (Soviet military intelligence agency) who played a vital role in the Cuban missile crisis of 1962, was, he suspected, far from unique. In what Andrew's family assures him was an uncharacteristic moment of clairvoyance, he wrote in the first edition of *Secret Service:* "It is unsafe to conclude that there have been no Penkovskys since, simply because their names have yet to appear in the newspapers."[1] Just before *Secret Service* was published, news broke of another and even more successful Penkovsky, this time in the KGB. His name was Oleg Gordievsky.

A few months before he escaped from Russia in the summer of 1985, Gordievsky had been appointed KGB resident (head of station) in London. Since 1974 he had been working for SIS, the British Secret Intelligence Service (also known as MI6), as a penetration agent inside the KGB. In the summer of 1986 Gordievsky read *Secret Service* and got in touch with Andrew. As their discussions progressed over the next year, Andrew and Gordievsky were struck by the similarity of their interpretations of KGB operations. The recurrent obsession of the KGB, since its foundation as the Cheka six weeks after the October Revolution, with imaginary conspiracies as well as with real opponents had become a major theme in Andrew's research. It was an obsession that Gordievsky had experienced at first hand. The most dramatic period in his career as a KGB officer had occurred in the early 1980s when the Kremlin became seriously alarmed by a nonexistent Western plan for a nuclear first strike. Gordievsky was closely involved in the largest intelligence operation in Soviet history, an unprecedented worldwide collaboration between the KGB and the GRU, code-named RYAN, which sought to uncover the West's nuclear plot by such bizarre methods as monitoring the stocks in British blood banks, the number of animals killed in slaughterhouses, and the frequency of meetings between Mrs. Thatcher and the Queen.

The main problem confronting all historians who, like Andrew, had tried to research the history of KGB foreign operations had been the total inaccessibility, even in the Gorbachev era, of the records of its foreign intelligence arm, the First Chief Directorate (FCD). Gordievsky's access to many of these records over a period of twenty-three years offered a way around that apparently insuperable problem. As Andrew discovered at their first meeting, Gordievsky had long had a deep interest in KGB history as well as in its current operations. In 1980 he had been responsible for preparing the sections of a highly classified in-house history of the First Chief Directorate, dealing with KGB operations in Britain, Ireland, Scandinavia, and Australasia. He had found the research more interesting than the writing. There were many things that it was politically impossible to say about foreign intelligence operations even in a classified KGB history. No such inhibitions apply to the present volume, on which Andrew and Gordievsky began collaborating in the late summer of 1987. KGB officers will find it a good deal franker than their own in-house histories and, the authors hope, more informative.

Though this history has been written by Andrew, it is based on combined research, follows interpretations arrived at together in many detailed discussions, and represents the authors' joint conclusions. It draws on the secret archives of the KGB, on other source material in a wide variety of Western libraries and archives, and on Gordievsky's long experience of the FCD and KGB residencies abroad. After a year's training in 1962–63, Gordievsky spent nine years at the Center, the KGB's Moscow headquarters (1963–65 and 1970–72) and the Copenhagen residency (1966–70) organizing operations by KGB illegals (agents operating under false identities and not protected by diplomatic immunity). For the next thirteen years he worked in political intelligence (PR) in Copenhagen (1973–78), the Center (1978–82), and London (1982–85).

The decisive moment in Gordievsky's growing alienation from both the KGB and the Soviet system came in the summer of 1968 with the invasion of Czechoslovakia by forces of the Warsaw Pact and the crushing of the freedoms that had begun to flower in the Prague Spring. His ideas were similar to those that swept through Eastern Europe twenty years later, in the 1989 year of revolutions: the belief that the Communist one-party state leads inexorably to intolerance, inhumanity, and the destruction of liberties. Like every Soviet dissident in the Brezhnev era, however, Gordievsky had to face the dilemma of how to fight for democracy within a political system that had become expert at rendering its opponents impotent. By the time he returned for his second tour of duty in Copenhagen in 1973, he had decided that for him, as a KGB officer, the best way to carry on that fight was to work for the West. Gordievsky began to look for contacts with Western officials. After a period of mutual sounding-out, he began full-time collaboration with SIS late in 1974.

In the course of Gordievsky's work for the West, he delved as widely and as deeply into FCD records as was possible without unacceptable risk. His detailed research on KGB battle order has made possible the unprecedented lists of KGB residents in major Western capitals that appear as appendices to this volume. He also had many long discussions with senior KGB officers, diplomats, and Party officials. Gordievsky was frequently surprised at how much he learned simply by sitting in the offices of important *apparatchiks.* All had desks covered with the serried ranks of telephones that had become a much-prized Soviet status symbol.

In the early 1980s Gordievsky paid regular visits to the office of the deputy head of the FCD responsible for European intelligence operations, Viktor Fyodorovich Grushko. In order to speak to Grushko for ten minutes, Gordievsky sometimes had to spend over an hour in his office while the great man dealt with major problems of the day over several of his dozen telephones. The most senior Party leader whom Gordievsky briefed on current problems was Mikhail Sergeevich Gorbachev. During Gorbachev's first visit to Britain in December 1984, three months before becoming general secretary of the Soviet Communist Party, he was given three or four intelligence reports a day, most of them prepared by Gordievsky. Gorbachev also gave his views on some of the priorities affecting the future work of both the Soviet embassy and the KGB residency in London. He must later have reflected on the irony of being briefed for his first talks in Western Europe by an intelligence officer working for SIS.

Among the aspects of KGB history that had most interested both Andrew and Gordievsky before their collaboration began were the careers of the Cambridge moles. Cambridge University, at which Andrew teaches, has the unique though dubious distinction of having provided some of the ablest twentieth-century recruits to both the British intelligence community and its main opponent, the KGB. (Contrary to the impression given by some accounts, however, British recruits have been far more numerous.) After the release of the popular Western film *The Magnificent Seven* in 1960, the leading Cambridge recruits to the KGB became known in the Center as the "Magnificent Five." Portraits of the recruiters and the first controllers of the Cambridge moles have a place of honor in the secret "Memory Room" where the FCD commemorates its heroes.

Gordievsky followed with particular interest the career of the most successful of the Magnificent Five, Kim Philby, who defected to Moscow in January 1963 while he was in the middle of his first-year intelligence training course. When stationed in Copenhagen ten years later, Gordievsky bought a copy of a book by Patrick Seale and Maureen McConville, *Philby: The Long Road to Moscow,* and sent it to Philby via a friend in the Center, Albert Ivanovich Kozlov. Philby read it and returned it to Gordievsky with the handwritten dedication in English on the flyleaf:

To my dear colleague Oleg:
Don't believe anything about me
which you see in print!
                                        Kim Philby

Gordievsky's view of Philby was indeed quite different from the glamorous image of the master spy that the KGB sought to popularize in print. While on leave in Moscow in 1977, Gordievsky attended Philby's first lecture at the Center, given to an audience of about three hundred. Philby spoke in English. "This year," he began, "is a very special one. Not only does it mark the sixtieth anniversary of the Great October Revolution; it also sees the fiftieth anniversary of the Soviet Football Association." There were two bursts of laughter from the audience: immediately from those who understood English, after the translation from the remainder.

Having disarmed his audience, Philby then went on to make an oblique but devastating criticism of his treatment by the KGB during the fourteen years since his defection. "In the course of my career," he said, "I have visited the headquarters of some of the world's leading intelligence services. And now, at last, after fourteen years in Moscow, I am visiting yours for the first time."

During his spasmodic meetings with Western journalists, even on the rare occasions when he criticized the KGB's neglect of his talents, Philby never revealed the full extent of his hurt. He sought to give the impression that he held senior rank in the KGB. During his last interview with Phillip Knightley a few months before his death, he confirmed a report that he already held the rank of colonel at the time of his defection. But when asked by Knightley later in the same interview whether he had since become a KGB general, he gave a more equivocal reply. "Strictly speaking," he told Knightley, "there are no military ranks in the KGB, but I do have the privileges of a general." As Philby was well aware, there *are* military ranks in the KGB (Gordievsky was a colonel at the time of his defection), and there are KGB generals.[2] But to his personal chagrin, Philby, though he led a privileged existence, never rose above the rank of "agent." When he arrived in Moscow in January 1963, he confidently expected to be given a senior post at the Center. He was dismayed to discover for the first time that Western agents, however successful, were never allowed officer rank in the KGB. They remained, like Philby, simple agents. Up to his death in 1988, Philby's code name in the Center was Agent Tom.

As Philby discovered too late, the KGB never fully trusts its Western agents. When he defected in January 1963, his closest friend in Moscow, Guy Burgess, whose bizarre lifestyle upset the KGB even more than the Foreign Office, was dying from alcoholism. Despite repeated requests to the Center, Philby was not allowed to see him before his death in August 1963. In his will Burgess left Philby his library, his winter overcoats, some furniture, and £2000. Philby himself was always closely watched when he traveled to other Soviet Bloc countries. When he visited Cuba, he was required to travel by ship to eliminate the minimal risk that he might change planes in transit.

During his early years in Moscow, Philby was able to suppress some of his disappointment as he went through the lengthy, elaborate process of debriefing, recording every detail of every intelligence officer and operation he had ever encountered, and dealing with supplementary questions. He was also encouraged to help ghostwrite the memoirs of the leading Soviet illegal in postwar Britain, Konon Molody (*alias* Gordon Lonsdale), published in the West in 1965, and to prepare his own propagandist memoirs, eventually published after long deliberation at the Center in 1969. To compensate for his lack of officer rank, he was given the consolation of a series of awards from the intelligence services of the Soviet Bloc, beginning with the Order of Lenin in 1965. This made him, he told Knightley, in effect a Soviet knight: "Of course there are different sorts of Ks, but the Order of Lenin is equivalent to one of the better ones."

By 1967, however, with his debriefing complete, Philby had fallen into a deep depression, convinced "that the KGB had no idea what my real potential was." His private life too was falling apart. After arriving in Moscow he formed a friendship with Donald Maclean, whom he had scarcely met since leaving Cambridge. That friendship ended in 1965 when Philby's third wife left him and Melinda Maclean moved in. Within a year or so that relationship too was on the rocks. Philby roamed around Russia on a series of almost suicidal drinking bouts, which sometimes left him oblivious of where he was, uncertain whether it was night or day. Unlike Donald Maclean, who eventually drank himself to death (though much more slowly than Burgess), Philby was rescued from alcoholic oblivion by Rufa, "the woman I had been waiting for all my life." They were married in 1971.

Contacts with Philby merely confirmed Gordievsky in his decision during the early 1970s to begin working for the West. Philby tried desperately to persuade himself, as he looked over Moscow from the windows of his flat, that he could, as he claimed in his memoirs, "see the solid foundations of the future I glimpsed at Cambridge."[3] To Gordievsky it seemed, on the contrary, that the gulf between the myth image of the Soviet just society that had inspired Philby when he graduated from the university and the somber, stagnant reality of

Brezhnev's Russia was unbridgeable. There were moments when Philby himself seemed to recognize the immensity of the gulf. When he criticized failings of the Soviet system, KGB officers would commonly reply: "I'm not responsible," thus provoking the retort from Philby: "You're not responsible? Every Soviet citizen says he's not responsible. The truth is you're all responsible!"

Though the Center sought to popularize Philby's career in the West, it did not welcome the public exposure of Anthony Blunt, the fourth member of the Magnificent Five, in 1979. During the 1980s it watched in bemusement the highly publicized hunt by the British media for the Fifth Man along a series of false trails. Imaginary moles, as well as genuine Soviet agents, multiplied alarmingly in a series of bestselling books. Among those mistakenly accused were Frank Birch, Sefton Delmer, Andrew Gow, Sir Roger Hollis, Guy Liddell, Graham Mitchell, and Arthur Pigou, all deceased; Sir Rudolf Peierls who, despite claims that he too was dead, turned out to be alive and sued successfully for libel; Lord Rothschild, the victim until his death in 1990 of innuendo rather than open accusation, in case he also sued; and Dr. Wilfred Mann, who did not sue but published a convincing explanation of his innocence. By the end of the 1980s, the hunt for the Fifth Man had begun to resemble Monty Python's quest for the Holy Grail.[4]

Had the KGB been less addicted to conspiracy theory, it might have welcomed the confusion generated by the media mole hunt and the damage done by it to the reputation of MI5, which became the butt of numerous jokes suggesting that it was an outstation of the KGB. Instead, there were frequent suggestions in the Center that the whole mole hunt was some sinister British plot. Gordievsky had just moved to the British desk in the Third Department in 1981 when Chapman Pincher's sensational allegation that the Fifth Man was Sir Roger Hollis, director-general of MI5 from 1956 to 1965, burst onto the front pages of the British press.[5]

Gordievsky already knew the true identity of the Fifth Man from his research for the 1980 FCD official history. After the accusations against Hollis, however, Gordievsky spent hours discussing the case with Ivan Aleksandrovich Shishkin, head of Faculty Number Two (Counterintelligence) at the FCD training school, the Andropov Institute. Shishkin was one of the FCD's leading British specialists and had served in London as deputy resident and head of the KR (counterintelligence) line in London from 1966 to 1970. He was adamant that there was not a word of truth in the allegations against Hollis. One of Gordievsky's friends in the Center, Albert Kozlov, section chief in the Third Department, had also investigated the Hollis case. He too dismissed it as absurd.

In 1984 the Hollis story once again hit British headlines after the charges against him were repeated in a television interview by Peter Wright, a retired MI5 officer with a penchant for conspiracy theory, who had been the main source for Chapman Pincher's allegations three years earlier. At the time Gordievsky was on leave in Moscow in the middle of his London posting. He read a KGB telegram about Wright's allegations when visiting the head of the British desk, Igor Viktorovich Titov, formerly in charge of the PR line (Political Intelligence) in London and deputy resident there until his expulsion in the previous year. "The story is ridiculous," Titov told him. "There's some mysterious, internal British intrigue at the bottom of all this." Dmitri Andreevich Svetanko, consultant and a former deputy head of the FCD Third Department, agreed.

Gordievsky found it deeply ironic that British media interest in an imaginary Soviet mole should reach its peak at the very moment when the level of real KGB penetration in Britain was lower than for over half a century. The London residency files indicated that the KGB had had no source inside either MI5 or SIS since the arrest of George Blake in 1961. It seems never to have occurred to Peter Wright that one of the reasons why the government dismissed the charges against Hollis with such confidence was that SIS had its own well-placed source inside the KGB.

Gordievsky's career as an intelligence officer reached an astonishing climax in 1985. He had completed eleven years as an SIS penetration agent. And yet at the same time his reputation in Moscow Center had never stood higher. As head of the PR line and deputy resident in London since 1983, his political reporting had won high praise. The briefings he provided during Gorbachev's visit in December 1984 set the seal on his success in London. In January 1985 he was summoned to the Center and told that he had been appointed London resident to take over when the acting resident, Leonid Yefremovich Nikitenko, returned to Moscow in May. During his visit to the Center, Gordievsky was initiated into the resident's personal ciphers needed for top-secret communications with Moscow.

On Friday, May 17, 1985, Gordievsky received a telegram in London, summoning him back to Moscow to be officially confirmed as

London resident. But for his ability to surmount the crisis that followed, Gordievsky would not have survived, and this book could not have been written. On the face of it, despite the short notice, there was nothing suspicious about the telegram. It informed Gordievsky that he was to have discussions with Viktor Mikhailovich Chebrikov, chairman of the KGB and member of the Politburo, and with General Vladimir Aleksandrovich Kryuchkov, long-serving head of the First Chief Directorate, who was to succeed Chebrikov as chairman in 1988.

Viktor Ivanovich Popov, the irascible Soviet ambassador in London, was clearly impressed. On reading the telegram, Popov was all smiles. Despite earlier clashes with Gordievsky, he gave him avuncular advice on how to handle the important meetings that awaited him in Moscow. Gordievsky's sixth sense as an intelligence officer, however, told him that something was wrong. As he read the telegram, he felt a cold sweat in his palms, and his vision briefly clouded over. Soon after his talk with Popov a second telegram arrived briefing Gordievsky on the subjects Chebrikov and Kryuchkov would want to discuss with him. Gordievsky had the sense of a carefully baited trap awaiting him in Moscow. He told himself that the stress of his double life must be making him oversuspicious. Professional pride as a dedicated British penetration agent in the KGB persuaded him to suppress his doubts and return to Moscow.

Saturday, May 18, was one of the most hectic days in Gordievsky's three years at the London residency. As well as making arrangements for his departure and preparing briefings for Chebrikov and Kryuchkov, he had to deliver £5,000 to a KGB illegal. A residency technician had constructed an imitation brick with a hollow center just big enough to contain a plastic packet stuffed with 250 £20 notes. Gordievsky placed the brick in a plastic carrier bag and took his two small daughters, Maria and Anna, to play in Coram's Fields in Bloomsbury, near the Great Ormond Street Hospital for Sick Children. While playing with the girls, Gordievsky dropped the brick on a grassy verge between a path and a fence on the northern edge of the park.

On Sunday morning, May 19, Gordievsky was picked up from his apartment in Kensington High Street by a Soviet embassy Ford Granada and driven to Heathrow to catch the Aeroflot flight to Moscow. Since the trip was supposed to be a short one, his family stayed in London. At Moscow's Sheremetyevo Airport he had his first clear indication that something was wrong. The KGB immigration officer took some time checking his diplomatic passport, then in Gordievsky's presence made a telephone call to report his arrival. It also seemed mildly ominous that there was no KGB car to meet him, though he later discovered that a car had been sent but had gone to the wrong terminal. Gordievsky took a taxi instead. The driver already had two other passengers, who turned out to be West German diplomats returning to their Moscow flat. When Gordievsky identified himself as a Soviet diplomat, the West Germans became visibly agitated, apparently fearing some sort of trap, and asked to be driven straight to their embassy. Gordievsky wondered whether the KGB watchers outside the embassy would find it suspicious that he was in a taxi with two West German diplomats.

When he got back to his apartment at 109 Leninsky Prospekt, he knew even before opening the door that it had been searched. He and his wife Leila used only two of the three locks on the door. This time he found all three locked. "Typical," thought Gordievsky. KGB house-breakers were technically highly proficient but notoriously heavy drinkers and given to lapses in concentration. A first inspection revealed no sign of disturbance. On a second look around the bathroom, however, he found a small hole in the cellophane covering an unopened box of tissues, where a probe had been inserted. Gordievsky knew that the search of the apartment would have uncovered no clues except a pile of books purchased in the West (including virtually the complete works of Solzhenitsyn) and hidden beneath his bed; though still officially seditious, they were of the kind purchased unofficially by many Soviet diplomats. Before going to bed, he called the head of the Third Department in the First Chief Directorate, Nikolai Petrovich Gribin, to announce his return. Gribin said little, but his tone of voice seemed cooler than usual.

Next morning, Monday, May 20, a junior KGB officer, Vladimir Chernov, who had been expelled from Britain two years earlier, arrived at the apartment in his Lada to drive Gordievsky to the First Chief Directorate building at Yasenevo, near the Moscow ring road. Gordievsky was given a vacant room in the Third Department. When he asked about the promised meetings with Chebrikov and Kryuchkov, he was told to wait. "You'll be informed when they're ready to see you." For a week nothing happened. Gordievsky waited each day until about 8 P.M. for a telephone call to fix the meetings but was given only a series of excuses. Kryuchkov, he was told, had a very busy week with a series of conferences at KGB headquarters and at the Central Committee; Chebrikov could not see him until he had first met Kryuchkov.

Gordievsky filled in the time improving his briefs on Britain and KGB operations, and checking statistics on the British economy and armed forces.

Gribin tried to persuade Gordievsky to spend the weekend with him and his wife at a KGB dacha. To Gribin's visible irritation Gordievsky insisted on staying in his Moscow apartment instead so that he could see his mother and sister. Most of the weekend conversation was about his family in London. Maria was in her first year at the Church of England primary school in Kensington High Street, and Gordievsky was proud of her English. He told his mother and sister how she had come home one day and recited, in perfect English, the Lord's Prayer.

Gordievsky's second week back in Moscow was more eventful than the first. At about noon on Monday, May 27, he received a phone call in his room at the Third Department from General Grushko, deputy head of the First Chief Directorate, to tell him he was being summoned to an important meeting to discuss a new strategy for Soviet penetration of Britain with high-level agents. They were driven in Grushko's black Volga limousine to a KGB dacha a few miles away, where a sandwich lunch was waiting for them. "What about a drink?" asked Grushko. Gordievsky hesitated for a moment, remembering Gorbachev's anti-alcohol campaign. But since Grushko seemed to expect it, he accepted. A servant produced a half-liter bottle of Armenian brandy and poured them a glass each.

To Gordievsky's surprise, Grushko began asking questions about his family. In the middle of the sandwiches, they were joined by General Golubev and Colonel Budanov of Directorate K (Counterintelligence), whose responsibilities included the investigation of internal leaks. A second bottle of Armenian brandy was produced, and Gordievsky's glass filled from it. Almost immediately, he realized that he had been drugged. "I felt," he recalls, "that I was a different man." He began talking quickly and garrulously, conscious that one part of his mind was urging him not to lose control while another part told him the effort might be beyond him. As his head spun, he noticed Grushko leave the room while Golubev and Budanov began to fire questions at him.

Gordievsky was asked for his assessment of previous Soviet defectors, in particular about a French mole, code-named Farewell by the French, in the FCD Directorate T (responsible for scientific and technological espionage), who had been executed two years earlier. Then the questioning became more personal. "How could you listen to your daughter saying the Lord's Prayer?" he was suddenly asked. "I know I'm drugged and finding it hard to think straight," Gordievsky told himself, "but that means they listened in on my conversation with my mother and sister on the weekend. So my flat must be bugged." Next, Gordievsky was challenged about the works of Solzhenitsyn and Western publications beneath his bed. "How could you bring those anti-Soviet books over the border?" he was asked.

The next stage of the interrogation was much more aggressive. Gordievsky was directly accused of working for the British. He was given the name of a British diplomat. "That's the man who recruited you, isn't it?" demanded Golubev. "You saw your British friends before you returned to Moscow, didn't you?" Then Gordievsky was left by himself. Some time later Golubev returned. "Confess now!" he told Gordievsky. "Don't you remember? You confessed a moment ago. Confess again!" Gordievsky felt his head reeling, and heard himself as if from a distance, denying that he had any confession to make. "No, I didn't," he repeated mechanically. "No, I didn't." He remembered nothing more until he woke up next morning with a splitting headache in one of the dacha bedrooms.

Two dacha servants, one male, one female, were ready with coffee. Gordievsky drank cup after cup, but the headache remained. As he began to recall the events of the previous day his first thought was: "I'm done for. There's no way out." Gradually, however, a glimmer of hope returned. At about 9:30 A.M. Golubev and Budanov arrived at the dacha, acting as if the interrogation on the previous day had been simply an after-dinner conversation. Golubev soon departed but Budanov remained.

Though Gordievsky remembers Budanov as one of the most sinister KGB officers he ever met, his first questions seemed relatively harmless. At some point in his career Budanov had evidently been stationed in Britain. "What parts of England have you visited?" he asked. Gordievsky replied that because of the usual restrictions on Soviet diplomats (or KGB officers posing as diplomats) traveling outside London, his trips had been largely confined to party conferences in Blackpool, Brighton, and Harrogate. "Harrogate?" said Budanov. "Never heard of it." Then his tone changed. "You were arrogant and overconfident last night," he said. Gordievsky apologized. Budanov continued: "You also told us that we are recreating the atmosphere of the purges, renewing the witch hunt and spy mania of 1937. That is not true. In time I shall prove to you that you are wrong. A car will come shortly to drive you home."

Back in his apartment, Gordievsky telephoned Grushko. "I'm sorry I'm not well enough to come into the department today," he began. Grushko accepted his excuse. "I'm also sorry if I said anything out of turn yesterday," he continued, "but those two men who came along were very strange." "On the contrary," replied Grushko, "they're very nice people." The phrase sounded stilted but, Gordievsky reflected, Grushko knew that their conversation was being recorded. Gordievsky spent the rest of Tuesday and the whole of Wednesday recovering at home and, in his own words, "thinking, thinking, thinking." By Wednesday evening, his depression had lifted slightly. The events of the last two days and his success so far in resisting the charges against him suggested that he might be given a breathing space before sentence of death was passed on him. "Maybe, after all," he thought, "I can find some way out." A generation earlier he would simply have been liquidated. Nowadays the KGB had to have evidence.

On Thursday, May 30, Gordievsky returned to his room in the Third Department. Soon he was summoned to Grushko's office, where he found Grushko flanked by Golubev and a glum-looking Gribin, Gordievsky's department head. Grushko told him:

> Yesterday we discussed your case almost all day with Comrade Kryuchkov. You know that you've been deceiving us for a long time. That's why your mission in Great Britain will be terminated. Your family is returning to Moscow immediately. But we've decided you can continue to work in the KGB, though probably not in the First Chief Directorate. What's your reaction to that?

Gordievsky had no doubt that the proposal was simply a ruse intended to give him just enough rope to hang himself. He was under suspended sentence of death but, since the interrogation in the dacha had been a failure, was being put under surveillance and given a period at liberty in which it was hoped he would be detected trying to contact British intelligence or would provide other compromising evidence. With the advantage of hindsight, he saw that the emphasis put by General Golubev on trivia such as Maria's Lord's Prayer and the books beneath his bed seemed to show that the case against him rested so far chiefly on circumstantial evidence.

Since his only chance of survival was to play for time, Gordievsky decided to show himself as cooperative as possible. He apologized for falling asleep during his questioning in the dacha. "I think," he said, disingenuously, "that there must have been something wrong with the food." General Golubev, whose sense of the absurd was defective even by the standards of the KGB, indignantly disagreed. He defended the quality of the dacha lunch sandwich by sandwich. "The ham was good," he maintained. "The salmon roe was also very good. So was the cheese." Gordievsky did not challenge Golubev's eulogy of the sandwiches. "As for accusations about my work," he continued, "I don't know what you're talking about. But if you decide my work in the First Chief Directorate is to be terminated, I'll take it like an officer and a gentleman." In retrospect, he found his use of that final phrase, like Golubev's defense of the sandwiches, a mildly comic interlude in a desperate struggle for survival.

General Grushko seemed relieved by Gordievsky's response and glad to avoid the embarrassment of either an open admission or a vigorous denial of treason in his office. "Thank you, thank you," he told Gordievsky and shook his hand. He did, however, instruct Gordievsky to deliver the "anti-Soviet books" beneath his bed to the First Chief Directorate library. Had Gordievsky been brought to trial, they would no doubt have been featured as an exhibit. Gribin, the Third Department chief who a few months before had been full of praise for Gordievsky's work, avoided shaking his hand. "I don't know what to suggest," he said. "Just take it in a philosophical way." After his escape to England, Gordievsky thought of calling Gribin to tell him, "I took your advice. I took it in a philosophical way."

Gordievsky was given leave until August 3. He calculated that the cat-and-mouse game would continue at least until the end of his leave. He spent a bittersweet fortnight during June with Leila, Maria, and Anna in their Moscow apartment, his enjoyment of family life made more intense by knowledge of the separation that would follow. The rest of the family planned to leave for Leila's father's dacha in Transcaucasia on June 20. Gordievsky longed to go with them. But, knowing that he would need time to organize his escape, he accepted instead a place that was offered him in a KGB "sanatorium" (a kind of holiday hotel) at Semyonovskoye, once the location of Stalin's second dacha, a hundred kilometers south of Moscow. Shortly before he left, a former colleague from the same block of apartments, Boris Bocharov, asked him: "What happened in London, old chap? We had to recall all the illegals. Our operations are ruined. I heard a rumor that your deputy has defected." Next time he met Gordievsky, Bocharov had clearly been warned and avoided speaking to him.

Gordievsky spent his time at the KGB sanatorium taking gentle exercise, reading, and planning his escape. Most guests at the sanatorium had to share their rooms. By accident or design, Gordievsky's roommate was a KGB border guard. The surveillance carried out by local KGB personnel was a good deal less sophisticated than in the capital. Whenever Gordievsky went jogging, he noticed the same watchers pretending to urinate into the same bushes and using other conspicuous forms of concealment. He privately nicknamed one local KGB man with an apparently inexhaustible bladder Inspector Clouseau. In the sanatorium library Gordievsky studied what maps and guides he could of the frontier region that he planned to cross, but he did so standing at the shelves in order not to attract attention by taking them to read in his room. He made a point of borrowing books entirely unrelated to his escape plans. The last KGB officer to speak to him before he left the sanatorium asked him what on earth he was doing reading a book on the Russo-Turkish War of 1877–78. Gordievsky replied that he was filling gaps in his historical knowledge. Since his escape that book will have been searched in vain for clues by Moscow Center.

Gordievsky's family's departure for the Transcaucasus was unexpectedly postponed until June 30, and his children were able to visit him for a day. It was the last time he saw Maria and Anna. When the day came to an end and he put them on the train back to Moscow, he hugged them for so long that he only just managed to squeeze through the train's sliding doors as it left the station.

Twice during his stay in the sanatorium Gordievsky found pretexts to visit Moscow in order to contact SIS. He covered the ten miles to the nearest station on foot, using the long walk to plan the even longer walk on the frontier that would be part of his escape route. Remarkably, his contacts with SIS in Moscow seem to have gone unobserved by the KGB. On the first of his visits he saw his wife for the last time before his escape (Maria and Anna were spending the day in his mother's dacha near Moscow). He said goodbye to Leila in a Moscow supermarket, where they went shopping before Gordievsky caught the train back to the sanatorium. It was one of the most poignant moments in Gordievsky's life. What made it almost unbearable was that Leila could not know the significance it held for them both.

She kissed him briefly on the lips. Gordievsky tried to smile. He found himself saying softly, "That might have been a bit more tender." Gordievsky has remembered those words many times since his escape. So, no doubt, has Leila. The hardest part of the preparations for his escape was his inability to take his family into his confidence, and the knowledge that his escape might be followed by several years of separation. The alternative to separation, however, was a few more weeks of freedom followed by execution as a traitor and even greater heartbreak for his family.

On Wednesday, July 10, Gordievsky returned from the KGB sanatorium to his Moscow apartment. During the fortnight or so before his escape to the West he laid a series of false trails intended to confuse KGB surveillance, arranging several meetings with his friends and relatives for the week following his intended departure from Moscow. He also spent a good deal of time working on his unreliable Lada car to prepare it for a compulsory technical inspection. Gordievsky's watchers were used to seeing him leave his apartment on Leninsky Prospekt to go jogging and did not usually follow him on his runs. At 4 P.M. on Friday, July 19, he went jogging, wearing his usual old trousers and a sweatshirt, and carrying a plastic bag whose contents must later have caused intense speculation at the Center. Gordievsky never returned from his run. A few days later, after a complicated journey, he crossed the Soviet frontier. Since others may have to leave the Soviet Union by the same route, he is unwilling to identify it.

Gordievsky compares his sensation on reaching safety in the West to the moment in *The Wizard of Oz* when the film changes from black-and-white to Technicolor. Against all the odds, he had escaped certain execution by the KGB. For the first time in Soviet history, a KGB officer already identified as a Western mole had escaped across the Russian border. But even as Gordievsky was being congratulated by his friends, his first thoughts were for the family he had had to leave behind. The KGB still takes hostages. As this book goes to press, Leila, Maria, and Anna are among them. They are remembered in the authors' dedication.

1

Tsarist Origins
(1565–1917)

Russia's first political police, the distant ancestor of today's KGB, was the Oprichnina, founded in 1565 by Ivan the Terrible, the first Grand Duke of Muscovy to be crowned Tsar. The six thousand Oprichniki dressed in black, rode on black horses, and carried on their saddles the emblems of a dog's head and a broom, symbolizing their mission to sniff out and sweep away treason. As in Stalin's Russia, most of the treason that they swept away existed only in the minds of the Oprichniki and their ruler. Their victims included whole cities, chief among them Novgorod, most of whose inhabitants were massacred in a five-week orgy of cruelty in 1570. Ivan himself oscillated between periods of barbarous sadism and periods of prayer and repentance. After a seven-year reign of terror, the Oprichnina was abolished in 1572. Almost four centuries later the victims of Stalin's NKVD sometimes called their persecutors Oprichniki behind their backs. Stalin praised the "progressive role" of the Oprichnina in centralizing state power and reducing the power of the boyar aristocracy, but criticized Ivan for wasting time at prayer that could have been better spent liquidating more boyars.[1]

The next powerful organization founded to deal with political crime was Peter the Great's Preobrazhensky Prikaz, set up so surreptitiously at the end of the seventeenth century that the exact date of its

foundation still remains a mystery. Like the Oprichnina, the Preobrazhensky Prikaz foreshadowed, on a smaller scale, the climate of fear
and denunciation engendered by Stalin's Terror. Those who perished
in its cellars and torture chambers ranged from nobles who had tried
to evade state service to insignificant drunks who had dared to make
jokes about the Tsar.[2] Peter is chiefly remembered today both inside and
outside the Soviet Union as the modernizer of the Russian state, whose
new capital of St. Petersburg (now Leningrad) was intended "to open
a window onto Europe." But he was also a ruler of fearsome cruelty.
His son and heir, the Tsarevich Aleksei, who fled abroad, was lured
back to Russia and tortured to death.

Like Ivan's Oprichnina, Peter's Preobrazhensky Prikaz did not
survive its creator. Though political persecution continued intermittently, there was no further attempt to found a specialized political
police until after the unsuccessful Decembrist Rising of 1825, a century
after Peter's death. The Decembrists were Russia's first revolutionary
movement. Unlike earlier rebels, they aimed not simply at replacing the
Tsar but at creating a new political system—either a republic or a
constitutional monarchy—in which serfdom would be abolished. In
1826, in order to forestall further risings, Tsar Nicholas I (1825–55)
established the Third Section of his Imperial Chancellery as his political
police.[3]

Both Nicholas and the Third Section's first head, Count Benckendorff, sought to distance themselves from the brutal precedents of the
Oprichnina and Preobrazhensky Prikaz. The incongruous symbol of
the Third Section was a handkerchief allegedly presented by the Tsar
and preserved in a glass case in its archives. According to a pious but
plausible tradition, Nicholas told Benckendorff, "Here is your whole
directive. The more tears you wipe away with this handkerchief, the
more faithfully will you serve my aims." This eccentric metaphor suited
both the Tsar's grandiloquent self-image as "father-commander" of his
people and the Third Section's view of itself as the "moral physician"
of the nation. But the major preoccupation of the Third Section was
what the KGB later called "ideological subversion": political dissent in
all its forms. Like the KGB today, in order to keep track of dissent, it
believed it necessary to monitor public opinion. Benckendorff prepared
annual Surveys of Public Opinion, later entitled "The Moral and Political Situation in Russia." "Public opinion," declared the 1827 survey,
"is for the government what a topographical map is for an army command in time of war."

In addition to employing a large network of informers, the head of the Third Section also had under him a Corps of Gendarmes, several thousand strong, charged with safeguarding state security and immediately recognizable by their blue tunics and white gloves. Yet, by KGB standards, the Third Section was a small organization. Its headquarters *apparat* grew slowly from sixteen at its founding to forty by Nicholas I's death in 1855. The Third Section's heads lacked the personal brutality of earlier political police chiefs. Alexander Herzen, the leading political dissident of the post-Decembrist generation, was "ready to believe . . . that Benckendorff did not do all the harm he might have done as head of that terrible police, being outside the law and above the law, which had the right to interfere in everything. . . . But he did no good either; he had not enough will-power, energy or heart for that." When summoned into Benckendorff's presence in 1840, Herzen found his face "worn and tired," with "that deceptively good-natured expression which is often found in evasive and apathetic persons."[4] Count Aleksei Orlov, who succeeded Benckendorff after his death in 1844, was the brother of the leading Decembrist, General Mikhail Orlov. It is difficult to imagine Stalin a century later allowing any relative of Trotsky or Bukharin even to enter the NKVD, let alone to become its head.

Of the 290,000 people sentenced to Siberian exile or hard labor between 1823 and 1861, only 5 percent had been found guilty of political offenses, and many of these were not Russian dissidents but Polish patriots opposed to Russian rule. Within Russia political dissidence was still virtually confined to a disaffected section of the educated upper class. The reign of Nicholas I nonetheless institutionalized political crime. The 1845 Criminal Code laid down draconian penalties for all "persons guilty of writing and spreading written or printed works or representations intended to arouse disrespect for Sovereign Authority, or for the personal qualities of the Sovereign, or for his government." That code, writes Richard Pipes, is "to totalitarianism what the Magna Carta is to liberty." From 1845 to 1988, save for the period between the failed revolution of 1905 and the Bolshevik seizure of power in October 1917, it remained a crime to question the existing political order. The Criminal Code of 1960 punished "agitation or propaganda for the purpose of subverting or weakening Soviet authority" by prison terms of up to seven years, with up to five further years of exile. Tsarism bequeathed to Bolshevism both a political culture and a legal system in which only the state had rights.[5]

The Third Section prided itself on the fact that during 1848, the main nineteenth-century year of revolution in Western Europe, Russia remained "somnolent and at rest." The ferment in the countryside that followed the emancipation of the serfs in 1861 by Tsar Alexander II (1855–81) persuaded a generation of young upper-class Populists that the peasants were at last ripe for revolution. But the failure of the 1874 Pilgrimage to the People, in which earnest radical idealists toured the countryside striving vainly to rouse the peasants against Tsarism, turned some disillusioned Populists to terrorism. The advocates of terror argued that assassination of Tsarist notables would both demoralize the regime and demonstrate its vulnerability to the peasants in a form they could understand. The hard core of terrorists, who by 1879 had banded themselves together as the Executive Committee of the People's Will, were only about thirty strong. But in a three-year campaign of bombing and assassination from 1878 to 1881 they brought the regime close to panic, and in so doing exposed the inadequacies of the Third Section. In 1878 General Mezentsov, chief of the gendarmes and head controller of the Third Section, was stabbed to death in broad daylight in one of the main streets of St. Petersburg. His escort, Lieutenant Colonel Makarov, was so ill-prepared that he succeeded only in striking the assassin with his umbrella. The assassin escaped. After several further assassinations and attempts on the life of the Tsar, who was formally condemned to death by the People's Will, an investigation into the functioning of the Third Section revealed so many lapses in security that the Tsar "could not consider himself safe in his own residence."[6]

In August 1880 the discredited Third Section was abolished and replaced by a new Department of State Police (renamed in 1883 simply the Department of Police), responsible for all aspects of state security. Political crime was made the responsibility of a Special Department (Osobyi Otdel) within Police Headquarters and of a regional network of Security Sections (Okhrannoye Otdelenie), the first of which were set up in 1881. Henceforth the political police system became collectively known as the Okhrana. The reorganization failed, however, to save Alexander II, who was assassinated in 1881 with a crudely constructed hand grenade.

The Okhrana was unique in the Europe of its time in both the extent of its powers and the scope of its activities. Other European police forces operated under the law. The Okhrana, however, was a law unto itself. In matters of political crime it had the right to search, to imprison, and to exile on its own authority. The basic difference between Russia and the rest of Europe, wrote the liberal convert from Marxism, Peter Struve, in 1903, was "the omnipotence of the political police" on which Tsarism depended for its survival. Tsarist Russia, however, never became a full-fledged police state. By subsequent Soviet standards, the enormous powers of the Okhrana were used on only a modest scale. Even during the repression of the 1880s, only seventeen people were executed for political crimes—all actual or attempted assassinations. Among the terrorists who went to the scaffold was Alexander Ulyanov, condemned to death for his part in an unsuccessful plot to kill Alexander III on March 1, 1887, the sixth anniversary of Alexander II's assassination. Ulyanov's seventeen-year-old brother Vladimir (better known by his later alias, Lenin) is said to have sworn vengeance against the Tsarist regime. By 1901, 4,113 Russians were in internal exile for political crimes, 180 of them at hard labor.[7]

By far the most persecuted group in the Russian Empire was the Jews. Popular anti-Semitism, state-encouraged pogroms, disabling laws, and multiple forms of discrimination during the reigns of Alexander III (1881–94) and Nicholas II (1894–1917) led to the exodus of several million Russian Jews, mainly to the United States. The regime, from the Tsar downward, found the Jews a convenient scapegoat on whom to focus popular discontents. The sudden expulsion of almost thirty thousand Jews from Moscow at Passover 1891 set a precedent for Stalin's much larger-scale deportation of other ethnic minorities. Though the Okhrana did not originate state-sponsored anti-Semitism, it helped to implement it. The Okhrana official Komissarov received an official reward of 10,000 rubles for inciting anti-Jewish riots with pamphlets printed on Police Department presses.[8] The last head of the Okhrana, A. T. Vasilyev, self-righteously condemned as "base slander" "excited newspaper articles" in the West that accused the Tsarist government and the Okhrana of conniving at the pogroms. He explained in his memoirs that the "core of the evil" was the "unfortunate inaptitude of the Jews for healthy productive work":

> The government would never have had the slightest reason to adopt measures directed against the Jews had not these been rendered imperative by the necessity for protecting the Russian population, and especially the peasants. . . . There was a certain kind of oppression of the Jews in Russia, but, unfortunately, this was far from being as effective as it ought

to have been. The Government did seek to protect the peasants from the ruthless exploitation of the Jews; but its action
bore only too little fruit.[9]

State-sponsored anti-Semitism helps to explain why Marxism spread
more rapidly among the Jews than among any other ethnic group in
the Russian Empire. The first Marxist party with a mass following
was the Jewish Bund, founded in 1897. Jews were prominent also
among the founders of both the Russian Social Democratic Workers'
Party, the main Marxist grouping, in 1898, and the Socialist Revolutionary Party, the successor of the Populists, in 1902. The growing
Jewish presence in the revolutionary leadership further fueled the Okhrana's anti-Semitism.[10]

   Despite the Jewish origins of many "Old Bolsheviks," anti-
Semitism was to reemerge, usually in disguise, under Stalin. Unlike the
Okhrana, the KGB has promoted no pogroms. But it remains the most
anti-Semitic section of the Soviet establishment. Though the *nomenklatura* as a whole is almost closed to Jews, the Foreign Ministry and
Central Committee are normally prepared to consider candidates of
half-Jewish descent. The KGB is not. Behind the recurrent obsession
of some KGB officers with Zionist conspiracies and "ideological subversion" lurk remnants of the anti-Semitic myths propagated by the
Okhrana. In January 1985, L. P. Zamoysky, deputy head of the FCD
Directorate of Intelligence Information, a man with a reputation for
both intelligence and good judgment, solemnly assured the London
KGB residency, in Gordievsky's presence, that the Freemasons, whose
rites, he was convinced, were of Jewish origin, were part of the great
Zionist conspiracy.[11]

   KGB training manuals and lecture courses are understandably
reluctant to acknowledge any continuities between the Okhrana and
KGB in their treatment of political criminals or Jewish dissidents.
Rather greater recognition is given to the Okhrana's foreign intelligence
work.[12] The main priority of the Okhrana abroad was the surveillance
of Russian émigrés, nowadays conducted by KR (Counterintelligence)
line officers in each KGB residency. The emigration of political dissidents, which had begun with Herzen's exile in 1847, gathered pace
among the Populist generation of the 1870s. By the reign of Nicholas
II there were almost five thousand revolutionary émigrés preparing for
the overthrow of Tsarism by methods ranging from making bombs to
research in the Reading Room of the British Museum.[13]

The headquarters of the Okhrana's Foreign Agency (Zagranichnaya Agentura), set up for the surveillance of the émigrés, was located in the Russian embassy in Paris, the main émigré center.[14] According to French Sûreté records, the Foreign Agency began work in Paris, probably on a small scale, in 1882.[15] By 1884 it was fully operational, under the direction of the formidable Pyotr Rachkovsky. During the Populist era Rachkovsky had been a minor civil servant with revolutionary sympathies. In 1879 he was arrested by the Third Section and given the option of exile in Siberia or a career in the political police. Rachkovsky chose the latter and went on to become the most influential foreign intelligence officer in the history of Tsarist Russia. Unlike later KGB residents in Paris, he was also a prominent figure in Parisian high society, accumulating a fortune by speculation on the Bourse, entertaining lavishly in his villa at St. Cloud, and numbering directors of the Sûreté, ministers, and presidents among his intimates. A writer in the newspaper *Écho de Paris* said of him in 1901:

> If ever you meet him in society, I very much doubt whether you will feel the slightest misgivings about him, for nothing in his appearance reveals his sinister function. Fat, restless, always with a smile on his lips . . . he looks more like some genial, jolly fellow on a spree. . . . He has one rather noticeable weakness—that he is passionately fond of our little Parisiennes—but he is the most skillful operator to be found in the ten capitals of Europe.[16]

Rachkovsky and his successors as heads of the Foreign Agency enjoyed much the same status as the heads or deputy heads of the Okhrana in St. Petersburg, as well as considerable freedom of action. Like the Okhrana within Russia, the Foreign Agency employed both "external" surveillance (by plainclothes detectives, concierges, and others) and "internal" penetration (by police spies, some of whom had begun as genuine revolutionaries) against Russian émigrés.[17] So, far from objecting to Foreign Agency operations on French soil, the Sûreté welcomed them as a means of extending its own intelligence gathering. A Sûreté report concluded on the eve of the First World War:

> It is impossible, on any objective assessment, to deny the usefulness of having a Russian police operating in Paris,

whether officially or not, whose purpose is to keep under
surveillance the activities of Russian revolutionaries.

In order to maintain the good will of the French authorities, the Foreign Agency made a habit of exaggerating the revolutionary menace.
The Sûreté put the number of Russian revolutionaries in the Paris area
alone in 1914 at over forty thousand—almost ten times the real total
for the whole of Western Europe.[18]
      The willingness of other European police forces to cooperate
with the Foreign Agency was increased by a spate of anarchist assassinations. Among the assassins' leading victims were President Carnot of
France in 1894; Antonio Cánovas del Castillo, the Spanish prime minister, in 1897; the Empress Elizabeth of Austria-Hungary in 1898; King
Umberto of Italy in 1900; President McKinley of the United States in
1901; and a succession of prominent Russians: N. P. Bogolepov, the
minister of education in 1901; D. S. Sipyagin, minister of the interior
(and thus responsible for the Okhrana), in 1902; Sipyagin's successor,
V. K. Plehve, in 1904; Grand Duke Sergei Aleksandrovich, governor-
general of Moscow in 1906; and P. A. Stolypin, prime minister and
minister of the interior, in 1911. In 1898 an international conference of
security agencies in Rome approved a resolution that "The Central
Authorities responsible in each country for the surveillance of anar-
chists establish direct contact with one another and exchange all relevant information."[19]
      From Paris the Foreign Agency ran small groups of agents who
kept watch on Russian émigrés in Britain, Germany, and—from
1912—Italy. In Switzerland, an increasingly important center of the
revolutionary diaspora, it had three Geneva policemen on its payroll to
obtain information directly from police files and provide a check on
intelligence sent by the Swiss authorities. Surveillance of émigrés in
Belgium and Scandinavia was carried out by a mixture of the local
police and Foreign Agency agents sent from Paris on special assignments.[20] During the few years before the First World War, however, the
Foreign Agency was assailed by protests from socialist and radical
deputies for its activities on French soil.
      In 1913 the Russian embassy thought it prudent to announce
that the agency had been discontinued. Its work was officially taken
over by a private detective agency, the Agence Bint et Sambain, headed
by Henri Bint, a former French employee of the Agency. In reality, the
agency continued to operate, though with greater discretion than in the

past. But its official, if fictional, abolition damaged its close cooperation with the Sûreté, which complained in 1914 that "the French government will no longer be able to know as precisely as in the past what dangerous foreign refugees in France are doing."[21]

The Foreign Agency did not limit itself to intelligence collection. It also pioneered a wide variety of what the KGB later called "active measures," designed to influence foreign governments and public opinion, and "special actions" involving various forms of violence. In 1886 Rachkovsky's agents blew up the People's Will printing shop in Geneva, successfully making the explosion look like the work of disaffected revolutionaries. In 1890 Rachkovsky "unmasked" a bomb-making conspiracy by Russian émigrés in Paris. At a sensational trial some of the plotters were sentenced to imprisonment (one named Landezen, who had fled abroad, in absentia) and others exiled. The Okhrana then arrested sixty-three revolutionaries in Russia who were alleged to have links with the Paris bomb makers. In reality the plot had been inspired, on Rachkovsky's instructions, by Landezen, who was an agent provocateur of the Foreign Agency and provided the money for the bomb factory from agency funds.[22]

During his eighteen years in Paris (1884–1902) Rachkovsky managed to cover the tracks of his involvement in this and other cases of alleged émigré bomb factories and bombings. Raytayev, his successor as head of the Foreign Agency (1903–1905), was less fortunate. He was recalled to Russia after the Sûreté had discovered his involvement in an unsuccessful bomb attack in Paris against Prince Trubetskoi and the bombing of a French protest meeting against Tsarist repression of the 1905 revolution, during which two *gardes républicains* were wounded. In 1909, a revolutionary journalist named Vladimir Burtsev at last revealed Rachkovsky's role in the 1890 bomb-making conspiracy. He also alleged that the agent provocateur Landezen, who had escaped in 1890, was none other than the current Foreign Agency chief in Paris, Harting. The Sûreté concluded that Harting's "precipitate flight and disappearance" tended to prove the truth of Burtsev's revelations. Curiously, the Sûreté seemed little concerned about such episodes. The intelligence provided by the agency was, in its view, *"des plus précieux,"* and clearly outweighed the crimes of its agents provocateurs.[23]

Rachkovsky specialized in forgery as well as the use of agents provocateurs. There is a strong probability that he was responsible for the fabrication of the famous anti-Semitic forgery *The Protocols of the Elders of Zion,* which purported to describe a Jewish plot for world domination. The *Protocols* had limited influence before the First World War. For a time Nicholas II believed they provided the key to an understanding of the 1905 revolution but was then persuaded that they were a forgery and complained that they "polluted the pure cause of anti-Semitism." Between the wars, however, the *Protocols* reemerged as one of the central texts in Nazi and fascist anti-Semitism, becoming perhaps the most influential forgery of the twentieth century.[24]

Rachkovsky's role was not limited to intelligence collection and "active measures." He also sought to influence Russian foreign policy. Rachkovsky arrived in Paris in 1884 as a committed advocate of an alliance with France, diplomatically isolated since her defeat in the Franco-Prussian War of 1870–71. He was regularly used as secret intermediary in negotiations both for the Franco-Russian Dual Alliance in 1891–94 and for its modification in 1899. Among Rachkovsky's closest contacts in Paris was Théophile Delcassé, who became from 1898 to 1905 the longest-serving foreign minister in the seventy-year history of the French Third Republic. In arranging his own visit to St. Petersburg to modify the terms of the Dual Alliance in 1899, the Tsar's state visit to France in 1901, and President Loubet's return visit to Russia in 1902, Delcassé bypassed the French ambassador, the Marquis de Montebello, and worked instead through Rachkovsky. The Russian foreign minister, Count Muraviev, informed the unfortunate Montebello, "We have the fullest confidence in Monsieur Rachkovsky and he appears to have gained that of the French government." Rachkovsky eventually overreached himself and was recalled from Paris in 1902. What led to his downfall, however, was not his increasing intrusion into Franco-Russian diplomacy but the outrage of the Tsarina at his incautious revelation that a French "doctor" employed by her was an unqualified charlatan.[25]

The most important contribution by the Okhrana to the making of Tsarist foreign policy was its pioneering role in the development of sigint—the signals intelligence derived from intercepting and where possible decrypting other governments' communications. Like most major powers of the *ancien régime,* eighteenth-century Russia had possessed *cabinets noirs,* or "black chambers," which secretly intercepted both private and diplomatic correspondence. In Western Europe the development of the *cabinets noirs* was disrupted in varying degrees during the nineteenth century by public and parliamentary protests at interference with the mail service. In Britain, for example, the Decyphering Branch was abolished in 1844 after a Commons row over the opening of the correspondence of the exiled Italian nationalist Giuseppe Mazzini. British sigint did not resume until the First World War.[26] In autocratic Russia, however, the development of sigint was undisturbed by parliamentary protests. The Okhrana had black chambers working for it in the post offices of St. Petersburg, Moscow, Warsaw, Odessa, Kiev, Kharkov, Riga, Vilna, Tomsk, and Tiflis. The last head of the Okhrana, A. T. Vasilyev, virtuously insisted that their work was directed only against subversives and criminals: "The right-minded citizen certainly never had any reason to fear the censorship, for private business was, on principle, completely ignored."[27] In reality, as under the *ancien régime,* letter opening was a source of gossip as well as of intelligence. The coded correspondence of the Archbishop of Irkutsk disclosed, when decrypted, that he was having an affair with an abbess.[28]

The Okhrana's chief cryptanalyst, Ivan Zybin, was a code breaker of genius. According to the Okhrana chief in Moscow, P. Zavarzin, "He was a fanatic, not to say a maniac, for his work. Simple ciphers he cleared up at a glance, but complicated ciphers placed him in a state almost of trance from which he did not emerge until the problem was resolved." The original priority of the Okhrana's cryptanalysts was the coded correspondence of revolutionaries inside and outside Russia, but the Okhrana extended its operations to include the diplomatic telegrams sent and received by St. Petersburg embassies. Intercepted diplomatic dispatches had been an irregular source of foreign intelligence ever since the 1740s. In 1800 the foreign minister N. P. Panin wrote to his ambassador in Berlin:

> We possess the ciphers of the correspondence of the King [of Prussia] with his chargé d'affaires here: should you suspect Haugwitz [the Prussian foreign minister] of bad faith, it is only necessary to find some pretext to get him to write here on the subject in question. As soon as his or his King's despatch is deciphered, I will not fail to apprise you of its content.[29]

During the early nineteenth century, the increasing use of couriers rather than the mails for diplomatic traffic steadily reduced the number of dispatches intercepted by *cabinets noirs.* The growing use of the electric telegraph in the latter part of the century, however, greatly simplified both the transmission and interception of diplomatic communications. In France, diplomatic traffic at the end of the century was decrypted in *cabinets noirs* at both the foreign ministry and the Sûreté.[30] Similarly, in Russia diplomatic cryptanalysis was shared between the Okhrana and a *cabinet noir* in the foreign ministry. Under Aleksandr Savinsky, head of the foreign ministry's *cabinet noir* from 1901 to 1910, its status was enhanced and its organization improved.[31] The Okhrana, however, probably remained the dominant partner in the cryptanalytic cooperation with the foreign ministry.

The breaking of high-grade code and cipher systems usually depends not simply on the skill of code breakers but also on assistance from espionage. The Okhrana became the first modern intelligence service to make one of its major priorities the theft of embassy codes and ciphers as well as plain-text versions of diplomatic telegrams, which could be compared with the coded originals. In so doing it set an important precedent for the KGB. As British ambassador in St. Petersburg from 1904 to 1906, Sir Charles Hardinge discovered that the head Chancery servant had been offered the then enormous sum of £1,000 to steal a copy of one of the diplomatic ciphers.[32] In June 1904 Hardinge reported to the Foreign Office what he termed "a disagreeable shock." A prominent Russian politician had said he "did not mind how much I reported in writing what he told me in conversation, but he begged me on no account to telegraph as all our telegrams are known!"[33] Hardinge discovered three months later that Rachkovsky had set up a secret department in the ministry of the interior (which was responsible for the Okhrana), "with a view to obtaining access to the archives of the foreign missions in St. Petersburg."[34]

Efforts to improve the British embassy's rather primitive security were unavailing. Cecil Spring Rice, the embassy secretary, reported in February 1906: "For some time past papers have been abstracted from this Embassy. . . . The porter and other persons in connection with the Embassy are in the pay of the Police department and are also paid on delivery of papers." Spring Rice claimed to have "established" that the operation against the British embassy was run by Komissarov, the Okhrana official who had recently received an award for his successes in promoting anti-Semitic propaganda. On Komissarov's instructions, "Emissaries of the police are constantly waiting in the evening outside the Embassy in order to take charge of the papers procured." Despite the installation of a new embassy safe, the fitting of padlocks to the filing cabinets, and instructions to diplomatic staff not to let the Chancery keys out of their possession, the theft of papers continued. Two months later Spring Rice obtained proof "that access has been obtained to the archives of the Embassy, which have been taken off to the house of the Agent Komissarov, where they have been photographed." The probable culprit was a bribed embassy servant who had taken wax impressions of the padlocks to the filing cabinets, and had then been provided with duplicate keys by the Okhrana. The American, Swedish, and Belgian embassies all reported similar experiences.[35]

By the turn of the century, if not before, the diplomatic intelligence derived from sigint and stolen embassy documents was having an important (though still almost unresearched) influence on Tsarist foreign policy.[36] From 1898 to 1901 Russia made repeated attempts to persuade Germany to sign a secret agreement on spheres of influence in the Turkish Empire that would recognize her age-old ambitions in the Bosporus. The attempts were abandoned at the end of 1901 because, as the Russian foreign minister Count Lamsdorf informed his ambassador in Berlin, decrypted German telegrams showed that the German government had no real intention of signing an agreement.[37]

Throughout the reign of Nicholas II, Russia remained the world leader in diplomatic sigint. Britain, Germany, the United States, and most minor powers had no sigint agencies at all until the First World War. Austrian sigint seems to have been limited to military communications.[38] Tsarist Russia's only serious competitor in diplomatic sigint was her ally, France. During the twenty years before the First World War the *cabinets noirs* at the Quai d'Orsay and the Sûreté had some success in breaking the diplomatic codes and ciphers of most major powers. But whereas Russia broke some French diplomatic codes and ciphers, France was unable to decrypt any Russian diplomatic traffic at all (though she did have some success with Foreign Agency codes and ciphers).

In the summer of 1905, during the closing stages of, simultaneously, the Russo-Japanese War and the Franco-German crisis over Morocco, there was a brief period of sigint cooperation between Russia and her French ally. In June 1905 the Russian ambassador, on the orders of his government, handed the French prime minister, Maurice Rouvier, a copy of a decrypted German telegram dealing with the Moroccan crisis. Rouvier considered the telegram so important that he ordered the Sûreté to pass on to the Foreign Agency all the Japanese diplomatic traffic its *cabinet noir* was able to decrypt. The telegrams sent to St. Petersburg by the acting head of the Foreign Agency, Manuilov, transmitting the Japanese decrypts, were themselves decrypted by the *cabinet noir* at the Quai d'Orsay. Unaware that the decrypts had been given to the Russians on the orders of the prime minister, the Quai d'Orsay concluded instead that there had been a serious breach of sigint security and ordered its own cryptanalysts to break off all contact with those at the Sûreté. As a result of the farcical misunderstanding generated in Paris by the brief period of Franco-Russian sigint cooperation, the *cabinets noirs* at the Quai d'Orsay and the Sûreté continued independently for the next six years to decrypt substantial amounts of diplomatic traffic—sometimes the same diplomatic traffic—without ever communicating the results to each other. There seems to have been no further exchange of sigint between Russia and France.[39]

The intermittent confusion in France's handling of sigint had one major adverse consequence for Russian cryptanalysts. Russia continued until the eve of the First World War to decrypt significant, but still unquantifiable, amounts of the diplomatic traffic of all but one of the major powers. The exception, from 1912, was Germany.[40] The changes in German diplomatic code and cipher systems that seem to have defeated Russian cryptanalysts during the two years before the outbreak of war in 1914 stemmed directly from French indiscretions during the Franco-German Agadir crisis of 1911. In the course of that crisis the French foreign minister, Justin de Selves, discovered from German telegrams decrypted by his *cabinet noir* that the prime minister, Joseph Caillaux, had negotiated with the Germans behind his back. The decrypts were used by de Selves and some of his officials to start a whispering campaign accusing Caillaux of treachery. Angered by the campaign against him, Caillaux took the extraordinary step of calling on the German chargé d'affaires and asking to see the original text of telegrams that referred to him in order to compare them with the decrypted versions. "I was wrong," he later admitted to the president of the Republic, "but I had to defend myself." The Germans, not surprisingly, introduced new diplomatic ciphers, which defeated the French as well as their Russian allies.[41]

In Russia, as in France, foreign intelligence collection and analysis suffered from interdepartmental rivalry. Military intelligence was the responsibility of the first section of the General Staff. Though intelligence about the German army before 1914 was mediocre, that about Russia's other main opponent, Austria, was excellent.[42] Military intelligence's main source, Colonel Alfred Redl, a senior Austrian intelligence officer, was probably the most important agent anywhere in Europe during the generation before the First World War. During the winter of 1901–1902, Colonel Batyushin, head of Russian military intelligence in Warsaw, discovered that, unknown either to his superiors or to his friends, Redl was a promiscuous homosexual. By a mixture of blackmail and bribery of the kind sometimes later employed by the KGB, he recruited Redl as a penetration agent. With the money given him by the Russians, Redl was able to purchase cars not merely for himself but for one of his favorite lovers as well, a young Uhlan officer, to whom he also paid 600 crowns a month. Among the voluminous intelligence he provided during the decade before his exposure and suicide in 1913 were the Austrian mobilization plans against both Russia and Serbia.[43]

Tsarist diplomats and consuls also dabbled in intelligence, occasionally collecting material of military value. But military and diplomatic intelligence were poorly coordinated, reflecting the general lack of communication between the ministries of war and foreign affairs. Despite the army's interest in humint (human intelligence), it failed to grasp the importance of sigint. The first great German victory on the Eastern Front, at Tannenberg in August 1914, owed much to the Russian forces' remarkable foolishness in sending its radio messages unenciphered, in clear text. German radio operators initially began listening to enemy signals simply out of curiosity, but the German operations officer, Colonel Max Hoffmann, who became the architect of victory, quickly grasped their importance. Tannenberg became the first military victory made possible by sigint. Thanks to sigint, wrote Hoffmann later, "We knew all the Russian plans." Almost as in a war game, the Russians found themselves surrounded by an enemy who had followed their every movement.[44]

Just as the Okhrana had no monopoly on foreign intelligence collection, so it had no monopoly either on "active measures." Russia's most numerous agents of influence were foreign journalists who were bribed by the ministry of finance to support the massive foreign loans required by the Tsarist regime and the Russian economy, and to calm the anxieties of foreign investors about the safety of their investments. In much of pre-1914 Europe it was regarded as perfectly normal for governments to "subsidize" friendly foreign newspapers. A French parliamentary report in 1913, though critical of some aspects of intelligence work, described the need for such subsidies as "incontestable."[45] Russian "subsidies" were the largest in Europe.

Since France was by far the biggest foreign investor in prewar Russia, the chief target of the ministry of finance was the French press.

Artur Raffalovich, the ministry's representative in Paris, bribed every French newspaper of note with the single exception of the Socialist (later Communist) *L'Humanité*. By March 1905 the confidence of French investors had been so shaken by both the abortive Russian revolution and Russian reverses in the war against Japan that with the support of Delcassé, the French foreign minister, Raffalovich was distributing bribes to the tune of 200,000 francs a month. As usual in the case of agents of influence, it is difficult to assess the importance of the press support purchased in this way. In March 1905 even Raffalovich's largess failed to prevent French banks from breaking off negotiations for a further loan. By 1914, however, 25 percent of France's foreign investment was in Russia (four-fifths of it in government loans)—as compared with only 9 percent in the vast French Empire. Without press support, the kind of crisis of confidence that prevented the conclusion of a loan in March 1905 would surely have been more frequent.[46]

Though Tsarist Russia's foreign intelligence system was diffuse and poorly coordinated, it established a series of important precedents for the Soviet period. It engaged in a wide variety of "active measures" as well as in intelligence collection. It led the world in sigint and in the use of espionage to assist its code breakers. And in Alfred Redl it had the prototype of the more numerous foreign penetration agents (or "moles") who in the 1930s were to become the chief asset of Soviet foreign intelligence. There was, however, another Tsarist precedent that did even more than Redl to persuade Soviet intelligence services of the potential of penetration agents as a weapon against their opponents. The Bolsheviks discovered from Okhrana files after the February Revolution that almost from the moment the Russian Social Democratic Labor Party split into Bolsheviks and Mensheviks in 1903 they had been more successfully penetrated than perhaps any other revolutionary group.[47] Okhrana knowledge of Bolshevik organization and activities was so detailed and thorough that, despite the destruction of some of its records in the aftermath of the February Revolution, what survived has since become one of the major documentary sources for early Bolshevik history.

Some Okhrana files must later have been a source of embarrassment to Stalin, who, once in power, posed as the most loyal of Lenin's followers. In reality, as late as 1909, he criticized Lenin for a number of theoretical "blunders" and for an "incorrect organizational policy." A letter intercepted by the Foreign Agency in Paris in December 1910 reveals the moment when Stalin finally decided to throw in his lot with

Lenin. Lenin's line, he wrote, was "the only correct one," and he described Lenin himself as a "shrewd fellow" *(umnyi muzhik).* [48]

It is unlikely that Stalin was ever, as has been suggested, an Okhrana agent, though the Okhrana may well have tried to recruit him. The Okhrana had, however, no shortage of other agents in the Bolshevik Party. Of the five members of the Bolshevik Party's St. Petersburg Committee in 1908–1909, no fewer than four were Okhrana agents.[49] Other anti-Tsarist groups were also penetrated to varying degrees. Among those in the Social Revolutionary Party in the pay of Okhrana was the head of its "Fighting Section" from 1904 to 1909, Yevno Azev, who was responsible for organizing assassinations and terrorist attacks. Among his victims was the minister of the interior Vyacheslav von Plehve, blown to pieces by a Fighting Section bomb. Azev, however, was a confused figure who scarcely knew in the end "whether he was a terrorist spying upon the government or a police agent spying upon the terror."[50]

The most successful mole recruited by the Okhrana in 1910, from the Tsarist viewpoint, was a Moscow worker named Roman Malinovsky, who in 1912 was elected as one of the six Bolshevik deputies in the Duma, the Tsarist parliament. "For the *first* time," wrote Lenin enthusiastically, "we have an *outstanding leader* [Malinovsky] from among the workers representing us in the Duma." In a party dedicated to proletarian revolution but as yet without proletarian leaders, Lenin saw Malinovsky, whom he brought onto the Bolshevik Central Committee, as a portent of great importance: "It is really possible to build a workers' party with such people, though the difficulties will be incredibly great!" The Bolshevik and Menshevik deputies elected in 1912 sat for a year as members of a single Social Democratic group in the Duma. But when the group split in 1913 Malinovsky became chairman of the Bolshevik fraction.[51]

By 1912 Lenin was so concerned by the problem of Okhrana penetration that, on his initiative, the Bolshevik Central Committee set up a three-man "provocation commission"—one of whose members was Malinovsky. After the arrest of Stalin and his fellow member of the Central Committee, Yakov Sverdlov, in February 1913, as the result of information supplied by Malinovsky, Lenin discussed with Malinovsky what could be done to forestall further arrests. In July 1913 Lenin again discussed the problem of Okhrana penetration with Malinovsky and two of his chief lieutenants, Lev Kamenev and Grigori Zinoviev. Only Malinovsky saw the irony of their conclusion that there must be an

Okhrana agent near to the six Bolshevik deputies whose chairman he was. He was instructed to be "as conspiratorial as possible" in order to minimize the dangers of police penetration. S. P. Beletsky, the director of the Police Department, described Malinovsky as "the pride of the Okhrana."

But the strain of his double life eventually proved too much. Even Lenin, his strongest supporter, became concerned about his heavy drinking. In May 1914 the new deputy minister of the interior, V. F. Dzhunkovsky, possibly fearing the scandal that would result if Malinovsky's increasingly erratic behavior led to the revelation that the Okhrana employed him as an agent in the Duma, decided to get rid of him. Malinovsky resigned from the Duma and fled from St. Petersburg with a 6,000-ruble payoff, which the Okhrana urged him to use to start a new life abroad. Rumors rapidly spread that he had been an Okhrana agent. Yuli Martov, the Menshevik leader, wrote in June "We are all certain without the slightest doubt that he is a provocateur . . . but whether we will be able to prove it is another matter." Though accepting that Malinovsky had committed "political suicide," Lenin dismissed the charges against him.

When Malinovsky reemerged in a German prisoner-of-war camp, spreading Bolshevik propaganda among his fellow POWs, Lenin resumed correspondence with him and continued to defend him against the charge of having worked for the Okhrana. That charge, Lenin repeated in January 1917, was "absolute nonsense." When proof began to emerge from Okhrana files opened after the February Revolution, Lenin at first refused to believe it. Malinovsky's career came to a tragically bizarre end eighteen months later. In October 1918 he returned to Russia, insisting that "he could not live outside the revolution" and apparently hoping to rehabilitate himself. He was tried by a revolutionary tribunal and shot in the gardens of the Kremlin on November 6, 1918.

Malinovsky's ability to deceive Lenin for so long had much to do with Lenin's sense of guilt, like that of some other upper-class revolutionaries, at his own privileged upbringing. Malinovsky's supreme merit, in Lenin's eyes, was his lower-class origin. He was the prototype of the working-class organizers and orators who were in disappointingly short supply in Bolshevik ranks. Malinovsky's criminal record and sometimes violent habits only emphasized, in Lenin's view, his authentic working-class credentials. Lenin's initial attraction to Stalin, of which he was also later to repent, had a similar origin. Stalin's humble origins and rough manner, free from all trace of bourgeois refinement, once again triggered Lenin's feelings of guilt at his own class origins.

The penetration of the Bolshevik Party had, paradoxically, advantages as well as disadvantages for Lenin. Beletsky, the prewar police director, later admitted that "the whole purpose" of his prewar policy had been to prevent, at all costs, the unification of Russian socialism. "I worked," he said, "on the principle of divide and rule." The man most likely to keep Russian Socialists divided was Lenin. Though many Bolsheviks hoped for reunion with the Mensheviks, Lenin stood out resolutely against it. Beletsky actually smoothed Lenin's path on a number of occasions by conveniently arresting both his more difficult Menshevik opponents and those Bolsheviks most anxious for the reunification of the Russian Social Democratic Labour Party.

But whereas the Okhrana was convinced that a disunited party would necessarily mean a weaker socialist movement, Lenin believed that, on the contrary, the existence of a separate Bolshevik Party was the key to victory. Only a disciplined, doctrinally pure, "monolithic" élite of hardened revolutionaries could lead the Russian people to the promised land. Though the promised land was never reached, the chaotic conditions that followed the overthrow of Tsarism in February 1917 proved Lenin's strategy of revolution right. In the aftermath of the February Revolution the Bolsheviks were fewer in number than either of their main rivals, the Mensheviks and the Socialist Revolutionaries. But it was the Bolsheviks who took power in October. The remarkable tactical victory of the Okhrana in penetrating the Bolsheviks thus ended in 1917 in strategic defeat and its own extinction.

The February Revolution (March 8–12, 1917, by today's calendar) took most revolutionaries by surprise. Only six weeks earlier the forty-six-year-old Lenin, in exile in Switzerland, had predicted: "We the old will probably not live to see the decisive battles of the coming revolution." The Okhrana probably had a more accurate sense of the mood in Petrograd (as St. Petersburg was renamed on the outbreak of war) than any of the revolutionary groups. One of its agents predicted on the eve of revolution: "The underground revolutionary parties are preparing a revolution, but a revolution, if it takes place, will be spontaneous, quite likely a hunger riot." Those closest to revolution, he reported, were the mothers of large families, "exhausted from standing endlessly at the tail of queues, and having suffered so much in watching their sick and half-starved children": "they are stockpiles of inflammable material, needing only a spark to set them afire."[52] Sure enough, the Revolution was sparked by demonstrations among women queuing for bread on March 8. By the 10th the whole of Petrograd was on strike.

The decisive factor at this point was the attitude of the Petrograd garrison. In 1905 the Revolution had been broken by the army. In March 1917 the army joined the Revolution. Once again, the Okhrana had detected the way the wind was blowing. A political rally by striking workers had been broken up by Cossacks on February 27, but, reported the Okhrana, "in general there was an impression that the Cossacks were on the side of the workers."[53] On March 12 a section of the Petrograd garrison mutinied and the success of the Revolution was assured. Three days later Tsar Nicholas II abdicated in favor of his brother the Grand Duke Mikhail. When Mikhail renounced the throne the next day, March 16, over four centuries of rule by the Romanov dynasty came to an end. Power passed to a Provisional Government mainly composed of liberal politicians, coexisting uneasily with a Petrograd Soviet of Workers' and Soldiers' Deputies, which became the model, and in some sense the spokesman, for local soviets all over Russia.

With Tsarism into what Trotsky termed "the dustbin of history" went its political police. On March 12 the crowd broke into Okhrana headquarters. According to the outraged director of police, A. T. Vasilyev:

All the archives of the Special Investigation Branch, with records of finger-prints, photographs, and other data concerning thieves, forgers, and murderers, were dragged down into the courtyard and there solemnly burned. Further, the intruders also broke open my desk and appropriated 25,000 rubles of public money, which I had had in my keeping.

Though Vasilyev virtuously protested that he "could not recall a single illegal action" for which he was responsible, he soon found himself in the Peter and Paul fortress, complaining of having to sleep on "straw mattresses and pillows stuffed with hens' feathers," eat "dreadful, evil-smelling soup and an equally repulsive hash made of all sorts of unspeakable offal," and of being allowed to have a bath only once a fortnight in a freezing bathroom with "drafts in every direction."[54] The imprisonment of the head of the Okhrana, like the reduction of the Tsar

Nicholas II, Emperor of All Russia, to the rank of Citizen Romanov, seemed to symbolize the birth of a new democratic order and the final victory over despotism. In the aftermath of revolution both the Provisional Government and the Petrograd Soviet believed that Russia would never again have a political police.

2

The Cheka, Counterrevolution, and the "Lockhart Conspiracy" (1917–21)

The Cheka, the ancestor of today's KGB, was founded on December 20, 1917. When the KGB was established in 1954 it adopted the Cheka emblems of the shield and the sword: the shield to defend the Revolution, the sword to smite its foes. By the time Gordievsky escaped in 1985, his KGB identity card carried only the emblem of a shield; the sword had been dropped in an attempt to soften the KGB's ruthless reputation.[1] Today's KGB officers, however, still style themselves Chekisty and receive their salaries on the twentieth of each month ("Chekists' Day") in honor of the Cheka's birthday.[2]

Like British income tax on its introduction in 1799, the Cheka was originally intended only as a temporary expedient. Lenin little dreamed that it would rapidly become both the largest political police force and the largest foreign intelligence service in the world. Before the Bolshevik Revolution of October 1917 (November 7 by the Western calendar adopted afterward) Lenin had foreseen no need for either political police or foreign intelligence. When he returned to Petrograd (since renamed Leningrad) two months after the February Revolution had overthrown Tsarism, he hailed the coming of world revolution. The Bolsheviks confidently expected their own revolution to spark an international revolutionary movement that would overthrow world capitalism. In the new postrevolutionary world order there would be no place for conventional diplomats, let alone for spies. Leon Trotsky declared confidently on his appointment as People's Commissar for Foreign Affairs after the October Revolution: "I will issue a few revolutionary proclamations to the peoples of the world and then shut up shop." He ordered the publication of Tsarist Russia's secret treaties with its allies, then announced: "The abolition of secret diplomacy is the primary condition of an honorable, popular, really democratic foreign policy."[3]

Lenin's prerevolutionary vision of life in Bolshevik Russia was similarly utopian. In *State and Revolution,* written in the summer of 1917, he claimed that there would be no place even for a police force, still less for a secret police. He acknowledged that in the transition from capitalism to communism it would be necessary to arrange for "the suppression of the minority of exploiters by the majority of wage slaves of yesterday." But such suppression would be "comparatively easy":

> Naturally, the exploiters are unable to suppress the people without a highly complex machine for performing this task, but *the people* can suppress the exploiters even with a very simple "machine," almost without a "machine," without a special apparatus, by the simple *organization of the armed people.*

The people, Lenin believed, would mete out class justice on the street as the need arose.[4] The October Revolution, however, ushered in a world very different from the utopian vision of *State and Revolution.* Crucial to the legitimacy of the Soviet state that emerged from the Revolution is the Communist myth that, as "the vanguard of the proletariat," the Bolsheviks led a popular rising that expressed the will not merely of themselves but of the Russian people as a whole. The reality of the October Revolution, which neither Lenin nor his successors could ever admit even to themselves, was a coup d'état by a revolutionary minority against the moribund provisional government that had succeeded the Tsarist regime. By first opposing and then overthrowing an increasingly unpopular government, the Bolsheviks won mass, but not majority, support. In the postrevolutionary elections to the Constituent Assembly, their main rivals on the left, the Socialist Revolutionaries (SRs), gained an absolute majority while the Bolsheviks won less than a quarter of the vote. Even with the support of the Left Socialist Revolutionaries (LSRs), they remained in a minority. When the Assembly met in January 1918, the Bolsheviks broke it up.

The problem of opposition, both at home and abroad, to the new Bolshevik government, the Council of People's Commissars (Sovnarkom), proved vastly greater than Lenin had anticipated. He quickly concluded that "a special apparatus" to deal with it was necessary after all. Convinced of their monopoly of Marxist wisdom, the Bolshevik leaders tended from the outset to classify all opposition, whatever its social origin, as counterrevolution. On December 4 the Military Revolutionary Committee, which had carried out the October Revolution, created the Commission for Combating Counterrevolution and Sabotage under Feliks Dzerzhinsky. The news on December 19 of an impending strike by all state employees persuaded Sovnarkom, under Lenin's chairmanship, that still more drastic action was needed. Dzerzhinsky was instructed "to establish a special commission to examine the possibility of combating such a strike by the most energetic revolutionary measures." The next day, December 20, Lenin wrote to Dzerzhinsky: "The bourgeoisie is intent on committing the most heinous of crimes." Addressing Sovnarkom the same evening, Dzerzhinsky declared:

> Do not think that I seek forms of revolutionary justice; we are not now in need of justice. It is war now—face to face, a fight to the finish. Life or death! I propose, I demand an organ for the revolutionary settlement of accounts with counterrevolutionaries.

Sovnarkom approved the creation under Dzerzhinsky's leadership of the All-Russian Extraordinary Commission for Combating Counterrevolution and Sabotage, better known as the Cheka (one of several abbreviations of Vserossiiskaya Chrezvychainaya Komissiya po Borbe s Kontrrevolyutsiei i Sabotazhem).[5]

Feliks Dzerzhinsky is nowadays the object of a KGB-inspired personality cult, which showers on him greater adulation than the combined total of that bestowed on all his successors (an embarrassingly high proportion of whom are now officially acknowledged as major criminals). "Knight of the Revolution . . ." writes the Soviet historian V. Andrianov, "There were many people deserving this title. Even so, whenever these words are spoken, the mind turns primarily to Feliks Edmundovich Dzerzhinsky. . . . His entire heroic life paved the road to immortality."[6]

Like a majority of the early Cheka leadership, Dzerzhinsky was of non-Russian origin. He was born in 1877 into a well-to-do family of Polish landowners and intelligentsia, and believed in childhood that he had a vocation as a Catholic priest.[7] Instead he became a schoolboy convert to Marxism, and in 1895 joined the Lithuanian Social Democratic Party. A year later he abandoned his formal education in order "to be closer to the people" and "to learn from them." By his own later account, he quickly became "a successful agitator and got through to the completely untouched masses—at social evenings, in taverns and wherever workers met together." Dzerzhinsky was also, in his own words, "the fiercest enemy of nationalism." In 1900 he became a founding member of the Social Democratic Party of the Kingdom of Poland and Lithuania (SKDPiL), led by Rosa Luxemburg, which campaigned for proletarian internationalism and cooperation with Russian Marxists, not for an independent Poland. Compromise of any kind was alien to Dzerzhinsky's personality. He wrote in 1901: "I am not able to hate in half measures, or to love in half measures, I am not able to give up half my soul. I have either to give up my whole soul or give up nothing." At no point during his career as a revolutionary in Tsarist Russia or Poland was Dzerzhinsky at liberty for longer than three years. He was arrested for the first time in 1897 after a young worker "seduced by ten rubles from the gendarmes" informed on him. When his prison career ended twenty years later with his liberation from Moscow Central Prison after the February Revolution, he had spent eleven years in jail, exile, or penal servitude, and escaped three times.[8] On his release Dzerzhinsky joined forces with the Bolsheviks, initially as an SDKPiL delegate, was elected to the Bolshevik Central Committee at the summer Party conference, and took a prominent part in the October Revolution.[9]

During his first year as head of the Cheka, Dzerzhinsky worked, ate, and slept in his office in the Lubyanka. His powers of endurance and Spartan lifestyle earned him the nickname Iron Feliks.[10] The "Old Chekist" Fyodor Timofeevich Fomin later eulogized Dzerzhinsky's determination to refuse any privilege denied to other Chekists:

> An old messenger would bring him his dinner from the common dining room used by all the Cheka workers. Sometimes he would try to bring Feliks Edmundovich something a bit tastier or a little bit better, and Feliks Edmundovich would squint his eyes inquisitively and ask, "You mean that

everyone has had this for dinner tonight?" And the old man, hiding his embarrassment, would rush to answer, "Everyone, everyone, Comrade Dzerzhinsky."[11]

Like Lenin, Dzerzhinsky was an incorruptible workaholic, prepared to sacrifice both himself and others for the cause of the Revolution. "My strength," he claimed in his final speech before his death, "comes from never sparing myself."[12] After his death these qualities were used to construct a portrait of Dzerzhinsky resembling a feeble parody of the hagiography of a medieval saint. According to Viktor Chebrikov, chairman of the KGB from 1982 to 1988:

> Feliks Edmundovich whole-heartedly sought to eliminate injustice and crimes from the world and dreamed of the times when wars and national enmity would vanish forever from our life. His whole life was in keeping with the motto which he expressed in these words: "I would like to embrace all mankind with my love, to warm it and to cleanse it of the dirt of modern life."

St. Feliks would have been unlikely to appreciate Chebrikov's mildly comic eulogy, for his gifts did not include a sense of humor. Since, by the 1980s, "lofty humanists" such as Dzerzhinsky were supposed to have a sense of humor, however, Chebrikov made a humorless attempt to defend him against the charge of being humorless. Dzerzhinsky was not, Chebrikov insisted, "the ascetic that some people thought him. He loved life in all its manifestations and in all its richness, knew how to joke and laugh, and loved music and nature."[13]

The cult of St. Feliks within the KGB began immediately after his death in 1926. In a conference room in the KGB officers' club an effigy of Dzerzhinsky, incorporating death masks of his face and hands and wearing his uniform, was placed in a glass coffin as an object of veneration similar to Lenin's embalmed remains in the Red Square mausoleum.[14] Dzerzhinsky's reputation survived unscathed into the Stalinist era, though it became increasingly overshadowed by Stalin's own alleged genius for intelligence as for almost everything else. On the Cheka's twentieth anniversary in December 1937 Dzerzhinsky was eulogized as "the indefatigable Bolshevik, the steadfast knight of the Revolution": "Under his leadership on many occasions the Cheka staved off deadly dangers which threatened the young Soviet republic."[15] But as the Stalin period progressed, portraits of Dzerzhinsky became smaller and fewer. Shortly after the Second World War, the Dzerzhinsky effigy was thrown out of the KGB officers' club and apparently destroyed.[16]

The revival and expansion of the Dzerzhinsky cult during the 1960s was a product of de-Stalinization and the attempt by the KGB to take refuge from the horrendous reality of its involvement in the atrocities of the Stalinist era by creating a mythical past of its own imagining, in which St. Feliks, "knight of the Revolution," slew the dragon of Counterrevolution. The most frequently repeated quotation in KGB texts is Dzerzhinsky's insistence that Chekists require "a warm heart, a cool head, and clean hands." In the late 1950s a huge statue of Dzerzhinsky was unveiled outside KGB headquarters in Dzerzhinsky Square. The main object of veneration within the First Chief (Foreign Intelligence) Directorate today is a large bust of Dzerzhinsky on a marble pedestal constantly surrounded by fresh flowers. All young officers in the FCD at some stage in their early careers have to lay flowers or wreaths before their founder's bust then stand silent for a moment with head bowed much as if they were war veterans at the tomb of the unknown soldier. By such rituals today's KGB officers succeed in strengthening their self-image as Chekisty and suppressing, at least in part, the uneasy awareness of their far more direct links with Stalin's NKVD.[17]

The original weapons approved by Sovnarkom on December 20, 1917, for use by Dzerzhinsky and the Cheka against the forces of counterrevolution were "seizure of property, resettlement, deprivation of [ration] cards, publication of lists of enemies of the people, etc."[18] The Cheka's main weapon, however, was to be terror. As Lenin woke up rapidly to the reality of opposition on a scale he had considered inconceivable before the Revolution, he concluded that "a special system of organized violence" would be necessary to establish the dictatorship of the proletariat. In the class war the Bolsheviks could not afford to be constrained by outmoded notions of "bourgeois" legality or morality. The greatest revolutionary rising of the nineteenth century, the Paris Commune of 1871, had been defeated, Lenin argued, because it placed too much faith in conciliation and too little in force. Its failure to suppress the bourgeoisie by force had led directly to its downfall. Lenin spoke scathingly of "the prejudices of the intelligentsia against the death penalty."[19] The masses, he believed, had healthier instincts. As early as December 1917 he encouraged them to practice lynch law ("street justice") against "speculators," and generally to terrorize their "class enemies."[20]

Like Lenin, Dzerzhinsky, though not personally a brutal man, burned with ideological hatred for the class from which he had sprung. He told his wife that he had trained himself to be "without pity" in defending the Revolution. One of his chief lieutenants, Martyn Ianovich Latsis, wrote in the Cheka periodical *Krasny Terror (Red Terror):*

> We are not waging war against individuals. We are exterminating the bourgeoisie as a class. During investigation, do not look for evidence that the accused acted in word or deed against Soviet power. The first questions that you ought to put are: To what class does he belong? What is his origin? What is his education or profession? And it is these questions that ought to determine the fate of the accused. In this lies the significance and essence of the Red Terror.[21]

While Dzerzhinsky and his lieutenants were converted to Red Terror only by what they saw as the objective needs of class war, some of the Cheka rank and file, especially in the provinces, showed a less high-minded enjoyment of brutality. Yakov Khristoforovich Peters, the most important of Dzerzhinsky's early deputies, later acknowledged that "many filthy elements" had tried to attach themselves to the Cheka.[22] He omitted to mention that some of them succeeded. Cheka atrocities, though on a smaller scale than those of Stalin's NKVD, were every bit as horrific.

Until the summer of 1918 the Cheka's use of terror was moderated by the Left Socialist Revolutionaries (LSRs), on whose support the Bolsheviks initially relied. In January 1918 despite opposition from Lenin and Dzerzhinsky, the LSRs in Sovnarkom successfully demanded representation in the Cheka. One of the four LSRs appointed to the Cheka Collegium, Vyacheslav Alexeevich Aleksandrovich, became Dzerzhinsky's deputy. In March 1918 the LSRs left Sovnarkom in protest against the peace of Brest-Litovsk with Germany. The Bolshevik Party changed its name to Communist, and Sovnarkom, henceforth wholly Communist, moved its seat of government and the Russian capital from Petrograd to Moscow. But though the LSRs had left the government, remarkably they remained in the Cheka. Indeed, according to the LSR version of events, Dzerzhinsky pleaded with them to stay, telling their leader Maria Spiridonova that, without their support, he would "no longer be able to tame the bloodthirsty impulses in [Cheka] ranks." So long as the LSRs remained in the Cheka, there were no executions for political crimes. Dzerzhinsky had such confidence in his LSR deputy, Aleksandrovich, that after the move to Moscow he surrendered to him the main responsibility for day-to-day administration so that he could concentrate on operational work.[23]

The Cheka established its Moscow headquarters at Bolshaia Lubyanka 11, previously occupied by the Yakor (Anchor) Insurance Company and Lloyd's of London. (Later it moved to number 2, formerly the home of the Rossia Insurance Company, now the headquarters of the KGB and renamed Ulitsa Dzerzhinskogo 2.[24]) What Dzerzhinsky called the "bloodthirsty impulses" among the Cheka rank and file inevitably made their arrival in Moscow unwelcome. Among the Chekists' first Moscow victims was the celebrated circus clown Bim-Bom, whose repertoire included jokes about the Communists. Like the KGB, the Cheka was not noted for its sense of humor about ideological subversion. When stern-faced Chekists advanced on Bim-Bom during one of his performances, the circus audience assumed at first that it was all part of the fun. Their mood changed to panic as Bim-Bom fled from the ring with the Chekists firing after him.[25]

Besides terror, the main weapon used by the Cheka against counterrevolution was agent penetration. Though Dzerzhinsky denounced the Tsarist tradition of agents provocateurs, he quickly became expert at using them.[26] By the beginning of 1918, according to a Soviet official history, Chekists were already "regularly undertaking such dangerous operations" as agent penetration: "The situation of the tense class struggle demanded quick action in exposing the nests of counterrevolution. Any careless step could cost the Chekist his life. But courage and valor were his natural traits." According to the KGB version of events, the first major success of Cheka penetration was achieved against the organization called Union of Struggle against the Bolsheviks and the Dispatch of Troops to [General] Kaledin, based in Petrograd. A Chekist named Golubev, posing as a former Tsarist officer, "succeeded in quickly penetrating the Union, exposing many members of the White officers' underground, and in finding out the location of their secret meetings." As a result, during January and February, the whole Union, about four thousand strong, "was exposed by the Chekists and rendered completely harmless, with aid from the Red Guards."[27] Much expanded during the 1930s, the Cheka's two most effective techniques in destroying opposition to the Bolsheviks, terror and agent penetration, formed the basis of the two most striking achievements of Stalin's NKVD: the greatest peacetime Terror in European history and the largest-scale penetration of foreign government bureaucracies ever achieved by any intelligence service. The first major expansion of both terror and agent penetration, however, occurred during the Civil War of 1918–20.

The young Soviet regime faced a bewildering variety of threats to its survival. The October Revolution and its aftermath had left it in initial control only of Petrograd, Moscow, and a fluctuating area within roughly a three-hundred-mile radius of Moscow (rather more to the east, less to the south). Most of the rest of Russia was in administrative chaos. The dispersal of the democratically elected Constituent Assembly effectively destroyed the Bolsheviks' claims, in the eyes of most of the world (but not, of course, their own), to be the legitimate government of Russia. Their problems were compounded by the draconian peace settlement that the Germans demanded and which Lenin insisted Soviet Russia had no option but to accept. "If you are not inclined to crawl on your belly through the mud," Lenin told the many doubters in the Bolshevik leadership (who included Dzerzhinsky), "then you are not a revolutionary but a chatterbox."

By the peace of Brest-Litovsk on March 3, 1918 (nullified eight months later by the Allied victory on the Western Front), the Bolsheviks were forced to consent to the dismemberment of western Russia. In May the revolt in Siberia of the Czechoslovak Legion recruited by the former Tsarist army marked the beginning of two and a half years of civil war. By July there were eighteen anti-Bolshevik governments in what remained of the old Tsarist Empire. Recognized only by its German conqueror (until it in turn was conquered in November), the Soviet regime was an international pariah. By the summer of 1918 the remaining Allied diplomats stranded in Soviet Russia were conspiring with the Bolsheviks' opponents, and the British, French, American, and Japanese governments had begun military intervention.[28]

The Bolsheviks saw the Civil War from the beginning as part of a great Allied plot. In reality the revolt of the Czechoslovak Legion had been prompted not by the Allies but by fears for its own survival after attempts by Leon Trotsky, now commissar for war, to disarm it.[29] To Lenin and Sovnarkom, however, it seemed evident that the Czechs were the tools of "the Anglo-French stockbrokers." "What we are involved in," said Lenin in July, "is a systematic, methodical and evidently long-planned military and financial counterrevolutionary campaign against the Soviet Republic, which all the representatives of Anglo-French imperialism have been preparing for months."[30] The KGB still tends to interpret all plots and attacks against the young Soviet regime as "manifestations of a unified conspiracy" by its class enemies at home and the "imperialist powers" abroad.[31] The reality was very different. Had there been a "unified conspiracy," the Bolshevik regime could never have survived.

During 1919 the Bolsheviks faced three great military threats: the spring attack by the forces of the former Tsarist naval commander Admiral Kolchak from Siberia, and the summer offensives by the White generals Denikin and Yudenich from, respectively, the Caucasus and the Gulf of Finland. Yudenich reached the outskirts of Petrograd and almost succeeded in cutting the railway linking it with Moscow. That the Bolsheviks survived these attacks was due, in part, to Trotsky's brilliant leadership of the Red Army. Their survival owed even more, however, to the divisions of their opponents. Had the separate offensives of Kolchak, Denikin, and Yudenich been part of a coordinated onslaught on Petrograd and Moscow, the counterrevolution would probably have triumphed. Instead, each of the White armies acted independently of the others. Each of the main anti-Bolshevik commanders was anxious to reserve for himself the honor of defeating the Soviet regime, and each in isolation failed. The Red Army portrayed itself as fighting not for a minority government but for the people of Russia against White generals whose only program was reaction and whose only interest was the restoration of their own former privileges.

The chaos of the Civil War offered Western governments an opportunity that was never to return to undo the October Revolution. They failed to take it. Until victory over Germany had been secured in November 1918, the main aim of Allied intervention was not ideological, as Soviet historians have traditionally claimed, but military: to ease the pressure on the Western Front at a critical moment in the war. The peace of Brest-Litovsk enabled the Germans to transfer large numbers of troops from the Eastern Front and launch their biggest offensive in the West since the beginning of the war. To the British commander-in-chief Field Marshal Haig it seemed that the supreme crisis of the war had come. He told his troops in a famous order of the day on April 11: "Every position must be held to the last man: there must be no retirement. With our backs to the wall, and believing in the justice of our cause, each one of us must fight on to the end." By June 1918 the

Germans were on the Marne and threatening Paris. The fate of the
Bolshevik regime in the East was, by comparison, of only minor importance. Though the tide of war in the West turned rapidly in the course
of the summer, the speed of the final German collapse in the autumn
took the Allies by surprise.

The inept plots against the Soviet regime devised by Western
diplomats and intelligence officers in Russia during the summer of 1918
never posed any serious threat to the Bolsheviks. Indeed, the Cheka
seemed positively anxious to encourage the plotters to enlarge their
plots in order to win a propaganda victory by exposing them. Even after
the armistice with Germany, when Western governments gave more
serious attention to overthrowing the Bolshevik regime, their attempts
to do so were at best half-hearted. Two or three Allied divisions landed
in the Gulf of Finland in 1919 could probably have forced their way
to Moscow and overthrown the Soviet government. But in the aftermath of the First World War not even two or three divisions could be
found. Those troops that were sent served mainly to discredit the White
cause and thus actually to assist the Bolsheviks. They were too few to
affect the outcome of the Civil War but sufficient to allow the Bolsheviks to brand their opponents as the tools of Western imperialism.
Most Bolsheviks, however, imagined themselves facing a determined
onslaught from the full might of Western capitalism.

The Cheka proudly claimed, and the KGB still believes, that
it played a crucial part in defending the young Soviet state against a
gigantic conspiracy by Western capital and its secret services. In 1921
Lenin paid tribute to the Cheka as "our devastating weapon against
countless conspiracies and countless attempts against Soviet power by
people who are infinitely stronger than us":

> Gentlemen capitalists of Russia and abroad! We know that
> it is not possible for you to love this establishment. Indeed,
> it is not! It has been able to counter your intrigues and your
> machinations like no one else when you were smothering us,
> when you had surrounded us with invaders, and when you
> were organizing internal conspiracies and would stop at no
> crime in order to wreck our peaceful work.[32]

Though the conspiracies of Western diplomats and intelligence services
were far feebler than Lenin alleged or the KGB still supposes, the
Cheka did indeed achieve a series of successes against them. Its most

successful weapon was the use of penetration agents ("moles") and agents provocateurs of the kind pioneered by the Okhrana. The Cheka's first major penetration of a Western embassy, however, went badly wrong.

The only power with whom the Bolshevik regime had formal diplomatic relations was Imperial Germany, with whom it exchanged envoys after Brest-Litovsk. On April 23, 1918, a German embassy under Count Wilhelm Mirbach installed itself in Moscow. Six days later a member of Mirbach's mission wrote in his diary: "Here we must be ever on the alert for approaches by agents and provocateurs. The Soviet authorities have rapidly revived the former Tsarist Okhrana . . . in at least equal size and in more merciless temper, if in somewhat different form." Penetration of the German embassy was made the responsibility of a counterespionage section set up in May 1918 within the Cheka's Department for Combating Counterrevolution. In 1921–22 the counterespionage section was to be expanded to form the Counterespionage Department or KRP, the ancestor of today's Second Chief Directorate in the KGB. The first head of the section, a twenty-year-old Left Socialist Revolutionary (LSR) named Yakov Blyumkin, was probably the youngest section chief in KGB history. Blyumkin successfully penetrated the German embassy by recruiting Count Robert Mirbach, who was an Austrian relative of the German ambassador and had become a Russian prisoner of war. In June Blyumkin extracted from Mirbach a signed undertaking to supply the Cheka with secret intelligence on Germany and the German embassy.[33]

Dzerzhinsky, however, had been unwise to entrust the penetration of the German embassy to Blyumkin, for the LSRs remained bitterly opposed to the treaty of Brest-Litovsk. On July 4 the LSR Central Committee approved a plot to assassinate the German ambassador, in the belief that they would thus dramatically bring to an end Bolshevik "appeasement" of the Germans, renew the war on the Eastern Front, and advance the cause of world revolution. The assassination was entrusted to Blyumkin and an LSR photographer working under him in the Cheka, Nikolai Andreev.

On the morning of July 6 Blyumkin prepared a document on Cheka notepaper with the forged signatures of Dzerzhinsky and the Cheka secretary authorizing himself and Andreev to hold talks with the German ambassador. Dzerzhinsky's LSR deputy, Aleksandrovich, was then brought into the plot by Blyumkin and he added the official Cheka seal. The same afternoon Blyumkin and Andreev drove to the German embassy and secured a meeting with the ambassador on the pretext of discussing the case of his relative Count Robert Mirbach. Blyumkin later claimed that he himself fired the revolver shots that killed the ambassador. According to the evidence of embassy staff, however, Blyumkin's three shots all missed their target and Count Wilhelm Mirbach was gunned down by Andreev.[34]

The Cheka's early career as "the shield and sword of the Revolution" thus almost ended in disaster. Instead of defending the new Communist state, in July 1918 it nearly became the instrument of its destruction. Lenin telegraphed Stalin that Mirbach's assassination had brought Russia within "a hair's-breadth" of renewed war with Germany. The assassination was followed by an LSR rising, in which the Cheka's Lubyanka headquarters was seized and Dzerzhinsky taken prisoner. But the LSRs had no clear plan of campaign and their rising was crushed within twenty-four hours by Lettish troops loyal to the Communists. On July 8, Dzerzhinsky stepped down from the Cheka leadership at his own request while a commission of inquiry investigated the circumstances of the rising and the Cheka was purged of LSRs. By the time Dzerzhinsky was reinstated as chairman on August 22, the Cheka had become an exclusively Communist agency, whose use of terror against its political opponents was no longer restrained by the moderating influence of the LSRs. "We represent in ourselves organized terror," said Dzerzhinsky. "This must be said very clearly."[35]

Lenin took an active, if naïve, interest in the application of technology as well as terror to the hunt for counterrevolutionaries. He was attracted by the idea that a large electromagnet could be devised that would detect concealed weapons in house-to-house searches, and pressed the idea on the Cheka. Dzerzhinsky, however, was unimpressed. "Magnets," he told Lenin, "are not much use in searches. We have tested them." But he agreed as an experiment to take large magnets on house searches in the hope that counterrevolutionaries would be frightened into handing over their weapons themselves.[36] The experiment was soon abandoned.

The Cheka's penetration of Allied missions and intelligence networks in Russia ended more successfully than its operations against the German embassy. The KGB still regards as one of its great past triumphs the Cheka's uncovering in the summer of 1918 of the so-called "Lockhart plot," involving British, French, and American diplomats and secret agents. Robert Bruce Lockhart, formerly acting British consul-general in prerevolutionary Moscow, was an able but erratic member of the consular service, whose career had twice been interrupted by his complicated love affairs. At the beginning of 1918, after the withdrawal of the British ambassador, Lockhart was sent back to Russia to make unofficial contact with the Bolshevik regime. He achieved little. The original aim of his mission—to persuade the Bolsheviks to continue the war with Germany by promising them Allied aid—ended in failure.

Even after the peace of Brest-Litovsk, however, Lockhart did not immediately lose hope. He reported to London that, despite the peace treaty, there were "still considerable opportunities of organizing resistance to Germany." Trotsky, the commissar for war, and Georgi Chicherin, his successor as commissar for foreign affairs, both anxious to keep open communications with London, encouraged Lockhart to believe that Brest-Litovsk might not last long. Lockhart, however, had lost the ear of his government. "Although Mr. Lockhart's advice may be bad," commented one Foreign Office official acidly, "we cannot be accused of having followed it."[37]

Once Lockhart himself lost hope of reviving the war on the Eastern Front, he changed rapidly from pro-Bolshevik diplomat to anti-Bolshevik conspirator. By mid-May he was in contact with agents of the anti-Bolshevik underground led by the former Socialist Revolutionary terrorist Boris Savinkov, organizer of the prewar assassinations of Plehve and the Grand Duke Sergei. In his memoirs Lockhart later denied giving Savinkov any encouragement. His telegrams to London tell a different story. On May 23, 1918, he forwarded without comment to the Foreign Office a plan supplied by one of Savinkov's agents "to murder all Bolshevik leaders on night of Allies landing and to form a Government which will be in reality a military dictatorship." By now Lockhart had become an ardent supporter of Allied military intervention to help overthrow the Communist regime. As yet the British government, still preoccupied by the problems of winning the war with Germany, was not.

The Secret Intelligence Service, then known as MI1c, added further to the confusion caused by Lockhart. In addition to the MI1c station commander, Lieutenant Ernest Boyce, who remained nominally in charge of secret-service work in Russia, several other officers arrived to try their luck in the early months of 1918. Lockhart formed "a very poor opinion" of their work. "However brave and however gifted as linguists," they were, in his opinion, "frequently incapable of forming a reliable political judgment." They were deceived by forged documents alleging that the Communist leaders were in the pay of the Germans and by false reports of regiments of German prisoners of war in Siberia armed by the Bolsheviks. MI1c was still a peripheral element in British foreign policy rather than, as the Cheka persuaded itself, the powerful arm of a secret strategy drawn up at the very center of Whitehall's corridors of power.

The modern British secret service, the forerunner of today's SIS, was founded only in 1909. Until the outbreak of war it remained a tiny, underfunded agency unable to afford a single full-time station chief abroad. As a secret report later acknowledged, because of its shortage of funds, until 1914 "use had to be made of casual agents whose employment as a class has by war experience been clearly demonstrated to be undesirable." During the First World War MI1c underwent both a considerable expansion and a partial professionalization. By the beginning of 1918 it controlled a network of over four hundred Belgian and French agents reporting regularly and accurately on German troop movements in occupied Belgium and northern France.

Both MI1c's priorities and its main successes were on the Western Front. Russia, by comparison, was still a sideshow. MI1c officers in Russia had a good deal in common with the enthusiastic amateurs and serving officers used for secret service work in Victorian and Edwardian Britain in the days before the founding of a professional secret service. Their swashbuckling adventures had little discernible influence on British policy to Communist Russia. The Cheka, however, saw their sometimes eccentric exploits as evidence not of confusion or amateurism but of a deep-laid, labyrinthine plot by Western intelligence services.[38]

Though Lockhart had a low opinion of MI1c operations in Russia, the sheer audacity of its most extrovert agent, Sidney Reilly, took his breath away. Reilly had been born Sigmund Rosenblum, the only son of a wealthy Jewish family in Russian Poland, in 1874. During the 1890s he broke off contact with his family and emigrated to London. Thereafter he became a self-confident, intrepid international adventurer, fluent in several languages, expert in sexual seduction, who wove around his cosmopolitan career a web of fantasy that sometimes deceived Reilly himself and has since ensnared most of those who have written about him. Though a fantasist, Reilly possessed a flair for intelligence tradecraft combined with an indifference to danger that won the admiration of both Sir Mansfield Cumming, the first head of the Secret

Intelligence Service, and Winston Churchill. Lockhart described Reilly's flamboyant personality as a mixture of "the artistic temperament of the Jew with the devil-may-care daring of the Irishman."[39]

Reilly, claims one bestselling history of the British Secret Service, "wielded more power, authority and influence than any other spy," was an expert assassin "by poisoning, stabbing, shooting and throttling," and possessed "eleven passports and a wife to go with each."[40] The facts of Reilly's career, though on a somewhat less epic scale, are still remarkable. Before the First World War, he had established himself in St. Petersburg as a successful businessman and bigamist, who was also employed by Cumming as a part-time "casual agent." When Reilly returned to Russia in the spring of 1918 with the code name ST 1, his exploits sometimes crossed the border from high adventure to low farce. The Cheka, not surprisingly, failed to see the joke.

Reilly announced his arrival in Moscow on May 7 with characteristic bravado by marching up to the Kremlin gates, telling the sentries he was an emissary from Lloyd George, and demanding to see Lenin personally. Remarkably, he managed to get as far as one of Lenin's leading aides, Vladimir Bonch-Bruyevich, who was understandably bemused. The Commissariat for Foreign Affairs called Lockhart to inquire whether Bonch-Bruyevich's visitor was an impostor. Lockhart later admitted that he "nearly blurted out that [Reilly] must be a Russian masquerading as an Englishman or else a madman." On discovering from Boyce, the MI1c station chief, that Reilly was a British agent, Lockhart lost his temper, summoned Reilly to his office, "dressed him down like a schoolmaster and threatened to have him sent home." But, recalled Lockhart, Reilly was "so ingenious in his excuses that in the end he made me laugh." Reilly then adopted a new disguise as a Levantine Greek, recruited further mistresses to assist him in his work, and began plotting Lenin's overthrow in earnest.[41]

Reilly still tends to bemuse Soviet intelligence specialists who study his bizarre career. According to a 1979 official Soviet history of Military Chekists, "rich with heroic deeds," but guaranteed to "contain nothing sensational or imaginary," Reilly was born in Odessa of an "Irish captain" and a Russian mother. The same "strictly documentary" account also misidentifies him as the MI1c "main resident" (head of station) in Russia, a post actually held by Ernest Boyce.[42] Reilly's career has a particular fascination for the present chairman of the KGB, General Vladimir Aleksandrovich Kryuchkov. In 1979, while head of the First Chief (Foreign Intelligence) Directorate, his interest probably stimulated by a recent in-house history of the KGB, Kryuch- kov summoned all the books on Reilly from the FCD library. "And," said one of the librarians, "he seems to be reading them."[43]

The most celebrated of Reilly's colleagues in MI1c's Russian operations, Captain (later Brigadier) G. A. Hill, code-named IK 8, was, in Lockhart's opinion, "as brave and as bold as Reilly" and "spoke Russian just as well."[44] "Jolly George Hill," as Kim Philby later de- scribed him,[45] considered his days as a British spy in Russia "a joyful adventure in the pages of my life." His boyhood travels with his father, "an English pioneer merchant of the best type" whose business interests had stretched from Siberia to Persia, gave him what he considered better preparation for espionage than any amount of professional train- ing. Hill arrived in Russia two months before the Bolshevik Revolution to join a Royal Flying Corps mission, but began working for MI1c in the spring of 1918. Like Lockhart, he hoped at first that the treaty of Brest-Litovsk would break down and that the Bolsheviks could be persuaded to rejoin the war against Germany. Hill's memoirs, grandly entitled *Go Spy the Land,* describe with an exuberant lack of modesty how he won Trotsky's confidence and helped to mastermind the early development of both Soviet military intelligence and the Cheka:

> Lectures to Trotsky, theater and supper parties did not inter-
> fere with the work I had planned. First of all I helped the
> Bolshevik military headquarters to organize an Intelligence
> Section for the purpose of identifying German units on the
> Russian Front and for keeping the troop movements under
> close observation. . . . Secondly, I organized a Bolshevik
> counterespionage section to spy on the German Secret Ser-
> vice and Missions in Petrograd and Moscow.[46]

Hill's contemporary reports to MI1c and the War Office tell a less sensational, though still impressive tale. He "got the Moscow District Military Commander to organize a Bolshevik identifications section [for German units], and promised them every assistance from En- gland." But there is no evidence that, as Hill claimed in his memoirs, he personally helped to found the section. Nor is it likely that Hill played any part in founding the Cheka's Counterespionage Section in May 1918.[47] He later admitted that he never met its first head, Yakov Blyumkin.[48] But there may well have been some limited exchange of

German intelligence between Hill and the Cheka. When Anglo-Soviet intelligence collaboration was established on a more substantial scale during the Second World War, Hill returned to Moscow as liaison officer for the Special Operations Executive. According to Kim Philby, "The Russians hailed him with delight. They knew all about him."[49] By the summer of 1918 Hill's first brief experience of cooperation with Soviet intelligence had come to an end. Having despaired, like Lockhart, of persuading the Communist regime to reenter the war with Germany, he set up a network of his own to identify German and Austrian units on the Eastern Front and, with the help of "patriotic Russian officers," to prepare for sabotage against them.[50]

By July 1918 Lockhart himself, despite his later denials, was also deeply involved in supporting plots to overthrow the Communist regime. Together with the French consul-general in Moscow, Fernand Grenard, he handed over ten million rubles to the counterrevolutionary National Center group in Moscow, loosely linked to Savinkov in the Northeast and the White Army of the Tsarist General Alekseev in Kuban. But neither Lockhart nor Grenard was any match for Dzerzhinsky. In June Dzerzhinsky dispatched two Chekists of Lettish origin, Yan Buikis and Yan Sprogis, using the aliases Shmidken and Bredis, to Petrograd, where they posed as representatives of the Moscow counterrevolutionary underground seeking Allied support. There they obtained an introduction to Captain Cromie, R.N., naval attaché at the British embassy, who had stayed on in Petrograd after the ambassador's recall with the principal aim of blowing up the Russian Baltic Fleet if there was any danger of its falling into German hands. Cromie in turn introduced Buikis and Sprogis to Reilly, who was deeply impressed by their reports of disaffection among the Lettish troops in Moscow. Reilly saw in the Letts the key to the overthrow of the Communist regime.

> The Letts were the only soldiers in Moscow. Whoever controlled the Letts controlled the capital. The Letts were not Bolsheviks; they were Bolshevik servants because they had no other resort. They were foreign hirelings. Foreign hirelings serve for money. They are at the disposal of the highest bidder. If I could buy the Letts my task would be easy.

Buikis and Sprogis allowed themselves to be persuaded by Cromie and Reilly to call on Lockhart in Moscow.[51]

Preparations for an anti-Bolshevik coup in Moscow coincided with the beginning of British military intervention against the Bolsheviks in northern Russia. A company of marines commanded by Major General Frederick Poole had landed at the Arctic port of Murmansk on March 6, only three days after the treaty of Brest-Litovsk. But the marines had not been sent to overthrow the Bolsheviks. Their landing was intended instead to prevent the Germans from getting the vast quantities of Allied war materials shipped to Murmansk for use on the Eastern Front.

Allied intervention changed in character when Poole made a second landing at Archangel on August 2 with a detachment of Royal Marines, a French battalion, and fifty American sailors. The ostensible purpose of the Archangel landing was, once again, to prevent war supplies from falling into German hands, but it was timed to coincide with an anti-Bolshevik coup. Two groups of Allied agents, landed secretly a fortnight before the arrival of the marines, were caught and imprisoned by the Bolsheviks. But a successful coup was carried out on the night of August 1 by Captain Georgi Chaplin, a Russian naval officer formerly attached to the Royal Navy, who was almost certainly acting in concert with Poole's intelligence chief, Colonel C. J. M. Thornhill (formerly of MI1c). When Poole's troops landed next day, they did so at the invitation of a self-styled anti-Bolshevik "Supreme Administration of the Northern Region."[52]

Curiously, the Allied landing at Archangel, where Poole established himself as a virtual viceroy ruling by decree, did not immediately cause an open breach between Britain and the Bolsheviks. The Foreign Office cabled Lockhart on August 8: "You should so far as possible maintain existing relations with the Bolshevik Government.[53] Rupture, or declaration of war, should come, if come it must, from Bolsheviks not from the Allies." During the second week of August the Cheka's Lettish agents provocateurs, Buikis and Sprogis, called on Lockhart at his Moscow office and presented a letter from Cromie. Lockhart, who claimed to be "always on my guard against agents provocateurs," inspected the letter carefully. He was quickly reassured. Both the writing and the spelling were unmistakably Cromie's: "The expression that he was making his own arrangements to leave Russia and hoped 'to bang the dore [sic] before he went out' was typical of this very gallant officer."[54]

Shortly afterward Buikis brought along to a second meeting with Lockhart another agent provocateur, Colonel Eduard Berzin, described by Lockhart as "a tall, powerfully-built man with clear-cut features and hard, steely eyes, . . . in command of one of the Lettish regiments which formed the Praetorian Guard of the Soviet Government."[55] This time Reilly and Grenard, the French consul-general, were present as well. All were persuaded by Berzin that the Lettish troops were ready to join an anti-Bolshevik revolt and that "everything could be arranged in the space of about five to six weeks." At Lockhart's proposal, it was agreed that Reilly should "take charge" of all negotiations with the Letts, conducted from about August 20 onward in a safe house provided by the Cheka.[56] To finance the coup, Reilly provided 1,200,000 rubles, which Berzin passed on to the Cheka.[57]

French and American agents were also involved, like MI1c, in assisting anti-Bolshevik groups. On August 25, at a meeting of Allied agents at the Moscow office of the United States consul-general, de Witt Poole, also attended by the French military attaché General Lavergne (but not by Lockhart), it was agreed that after the impending departure of the remaining Allied diplomatic staff from Russia, espionage and sabotage would be conducted by stay-behind Allied agents: Reilly for Britain, Colonel Henri de Vertement for France and Xenophon de Blumental Kalamatiano (an American of Russian-Greek descent) for the United States. Among those present at the meeting, however, was a Cheka agent: René Marchand, a journalist attached to the French mission, who had become a secret supporter of the Bolsheviks and later became a founder member of the French Communist Party.[58]

On August 28 Reilly left for Petrograd to hold secret meetings with anti-Bolshevik Letts in company with the Cheka agent provocateur Colonel Berzin.[59] For the moment Dzerzhinsky preferred to bide his time and give the Allied conspirators in Moscow and Petrograd enough rope to hang themselves. This leisurely game of cat and mouse was cut short on August 30 when the head of the Petrograd Cheka, M. Uritsky, was assassinated by a military cadet, and Lenin himself was shot and seriously wounded by a possibly deranged Socialist Revolutionary named Fanya (Dora) Kaplan. These two unconnected incidents unleashed a reign of terror. In Petrograd alone over five hundred political prisoners were executed in two days.[60]

In the early hours of August 31, according to the Soviet version of events, "Cheka agents started the liquidation of the Lockhart conspiracy." Though the Cheka failed to catch Reilly, it caught the American agent Kalamatiano, then posing as a Russian engineer under the alias Serpovsky, and discovered in a hollow cane in his apartment a list of the money he had distributed to Russian agents.[61] Though Lockhart, unlike Reilly and Kalamatiano, could claim diplomatic immunity, he was awakened in his apartment at about 3:30 A.M. on August 31 by "a rough voice ordering me to get up at once." He opened his eyes, "looked up into the steely barrel of a revolver," and discovered about ten armed Chekists in his bedroom.

He was driven with his assistant Captain Hicks to the Lubyanka to be interrogated by Dzerzhinsky's assistant, the Lett Yakov Peters, "his black hair, long and waving as a poet's . . . brushed back over a high forehead," his expression "grim and formidable." "Do you know the Kaplan woman?" asked Peters. Though Lockhart had never met her, according to his account of the interrogation he claimed diplomatic immunity and replied that Peters had no right to question him. "Where is Reilly?" Peters continued. Again Lockhart made no reply. Then Peters produced from a folder a pass to General Poole in Archangel, which Lockhart had given the Cheka's Lettish agents. "Is that your writing?" he asked. For the first time Lockhart realized that Buikis and Sprogis were agents provocateurs, but he still failed to grasp that Colonel Berzin was also part of the Cheka plot. Once again, he informed Peters "with studious politeness" that he could answer no questions.[62]

Peters later gave a rather different account of the interrogation of Lockhart, who, he claimed, "was so frightened that he did not even present his diplomatic papers. Probably the poor English diplomatic representative thought he was being accused of Lenin's murder, and he probably had a bad conscience."[63] Lockhart himself believed that the main purpose of Peters's questions was to link him with Fanya Kaplan's attempt on Lenin's life. His immediate anxiety, however, was the notebook in his breast pocket. The Cheka agents who arrested him ransacked his apartment but failed to notice the notebook in his jacket, which recorded "in cryptic form" the money disbursed by Lockhart— no doubt including the funds given to Savinkov and Reilly. Expecting to be searched at any moment, Lockhart asked to go to the lavatory. With two armed guards standing over him, he coolly tore the embarrassing pages from his notebook and used them as toilet paper.[64]

At about 6 A.M. a woman dressed in black, with black hair and "great black rings under her eyes," was brought to join Lockhart and Hicks in their room in the Lubyanka.

We guessed it was Kaplan. Doubtless the Bolsheviks hoped
that she would give us some sign of recognition. Her composure was unnatural. She went to the window and leaning her
chin upon her hand, looked out into the daylight. And there
she remained, motionless, speechless, apparently resigned to
her fate, until presently the sentries came and took her away.

Fanya Kaplan was shot four days later in a Kremlin courtyard, still
uncertain whether her attempt on Lenin's life had succeeded.

At 9 A.M. Lockhart and Hicks were freed from the Lubyanka,
and left to make their own way home. Back at Lockhart's flat, they
discovered that his mistress, Mura Beckendorff, had been arrested by
the Cheka.[65]

Reilly, meanwhile, was in Petrograd, probably unaware of
Lockhart's arrest. At midday on August 31, three hours after Lockhart's release, he arrived at the apartment of Ernest Boyce, the MI1c
station chief. There he outlined the plan for a rising by the Lettish
troops guarding the Kremlin. According to Reilly's account of their
discussion, Boyce described the plan as "extremely risky" but "worth
trying." If it failed, however, he said that the responsibility would be
Reilly's. Boyce then left for the British embassy, intending to bring
Captain Cromie back to his apartment to be briefed by Reilly.[66] By the
time he arrived, Cromie was dead. A crowd led by Cheka agents,
enraged by a rumor that Uritsky's assassin had been given shelter in the
embassy, stormed into the building. Cromie confronted the mob, was
told to get out of the way or "be shot like a dog," opened fire, and was
killed in the gunfight that followed.[67]

A Cheka raid in the early hours of September 1 on the apartment of the French agent de Vertement, probably after information had
been supplied by the Cheka informant René Marchand, led to the
discovery of explosives intended for use in sabotage operations.[68]
Though de Vertement himself escaped capture, Sovnarkom announced
triumphantly next day:

Today, September 2, the conspiracy organized by Anglo-
French diplomats, at the head of which was the chief of the
British Mission, Lockhart, the French consul-general Grenard, the French General Lavergne, and others, was liquidated. The purpose of this conspiracy was to organize the

capture of the Council of People's Commissars and the proc-
lamation of a military dictatorship in Moscow; this was to
be done by bribing Soviet troops.

The statements made no mention of the fact that the plan to use Soviet
troops (the Lettish battalions) in a military coup had been devised by
Cheka agents provocateurs. It also sought to excuse the violation of
Lockhart's diplomatic immunity by claiming implausibly that his identity had not been clear when he was arrested:

> At the secret headquarters of the conspirators an English-
> man was arrested who after being brought before the Special
> Investigating Commission, said that he was the British diplo-
> matic representative, Lockhart. After the identity of the ar-
> rested Lockhart had been established, he was immediately
> released.

The Sovnarkom statement did, however, correctly reveal that Reilly,
identified as "one of Lockhart's agents," had provided 1,200,000 rubles
to finance the plot. It also correctly claimed that other Allied missions
were involved. Though René Marchand was not publicly identified as
a Cheka informant, he gave an account of the meeting of Allied agents
held on August 25 to discuss espionage and sabotage in a letter of
protest to the French president, Raymond Poincaré. A copy of the
letter was conveniently discovered, no doubt by prior arrangement, in
the course of a Cheka search and published in the Communist press.[69]

In the Sovnarkom statement of September 2, as in subsequent
Soviet pronouncements, Lockhart was presented as the ringleader of
the Allied conspiracy. Lockhart's own main concern at this stage in the
crisis, however, was for the safety of his imprisoned mistress. On September 4 he went to the Commissariat of Foreign Affairs to plead,
without success, for Mura's release. Then, impulsively, he decided to
appeal directly to Peters and walked to the Lubyanka, where he was
immediately aware that his arrival "caused some excitement and much
whispering among the guards in the entrance hall." Peters listened
patiently to Lockhart's plea for Mura and told him that his assurance
that she had been involved in no conspiracy would be carefully considered. "You have saved me some trouble," he continued. "My men have
been looking for you for the past hour. I have a warrant for your
arrest." Despite opposition from the Commissariat for Foreign Affairs,

which paid greater heed than the Cheka to the principle of diplomatic immunity, Lockhart was arrested on the spot and spent the next month in captivity.[70]

On September 5, presumably in an attempt to justify the re-arrest of Lockhart on the previous day, *Izvestia* published a statement signed by Dzerzhinsky and Zinoviev, the Petrograd Party boss, that went much further than the Sovnarkom statement of the 2nd. The English and French were accused of being the "organizers" of the attempt on Lenin's life and the "real murderers" of Uritsky: "They have murdered Comrade Uritsky because he brought together the threads of an English conspiracy in Petrograd."[71] In reality the Cheka's agents provocateurs had been trying without much success to persuade English agents to organize an assassination plot, which could then have been publicly exposed. On about August 22 Berzin tried to persuade Reilly that, for the anti-Bolshevik coup to succeed, there were two pressing reasons why Lenin and Trotsky would have to be assassinated:

1. Their marvelous oratorical powers would so act on the psychology of the men who went to arrest them that it was not advisable to risk [arrest].
2. The assassination of two of the leaders would create a panic so that there would be no resistance.

Reilly told Hill that "he had been very firm in dissuading [Berzin] from such a course and that he would in no way support it." The right policy, he insisted, was "not to make martyrs of the leaders but to hold them up to ridicule before the world."[72] The particular form of ridicule Reilly had in mind was to remove Lenin's and Trotsky's trousers, parade them in their underpants through the streets of Moscow, and so make them public laughingstocks.[73] Not surprisingly, it did not suit the Cheka to publicize a plot to remove Lenin's and Trotsky's trousers. This eccentric scheme was thus never included in the list of real and imaginary plots of which British agents were accused. Ernest Boyce, the MI1c station chief in Petrograd, may have been less hostile than Reilly and Hill to the idea of assassination. One of his Russian agents claimed that Boyce had inquired, probably speculatively, "if he was prepared to do away with one or two prominent members of the Soviet government." When the agent threatened blackmail on September 6 and demanded money not to reveal Boyce's inquiry, it was thought "advisable to pay up rather than having anything fresh brought up against us."[74]

By the time of the attempted blackmail, MI1c operations in Russia had virtually collapsed. Boyce had been arrested and thrown into a hideously overcrowded jail. The Cheka arrested several of Reilly's mistresses but Reilly himself obtained a forged passport from Hill and was smuggled out of Russia on board a Dutch freighter. Hill too avoided capture but, after eighteen of his agents and couriers had been caught and executed, concluded that he would have to seek further instructions and funds in London in order to "start afresh with new personnel and new headquarters." Lockhart, unlike Boyce, spent most of his captivity in the relative comfort of the apartment of a former lady-in-waiting in the Kremlin. In the course of his imprisonment his mistress, Mura, was released and allowed to visit him. Berzin was briefly lodged in the same apartment as a stool pigeon, but Lockhart "was afraid to exchange a word with him." In October Lockhart, Boyce, and Hill were allowed to return home together with other Allied personnel in exchange for the release of Soviet officials held in London.

Lockhart's farewell to Peters was strangely amicable. When Peters came on September 28 to announce that Lockhart was to be set free, he gave him a signed photograph, showed him photographs of his English wife in London, and asked him to deliver a letter to her. Then Peters had second thoughts. "No," he said, "I shan't trouble you. As soon as you're out of here you'll blaspheme and curse me as your worst enemy." Lockhart told him not to be a fool: "Politics apart, I bore him no grudge. I would remember his kindness to Mura all my life. I took the letter." Peters told Lockhart he would do better to stay in Russia: "You can be happy and make your own life. We can give you work to do, capitalism is doomed anyway."[75] What Peters omitted to tell Lockhart was that he had evidence that Mura was a German spy. He later claimed that he did not mention this even at the trial of "the Lockhart conspiracy" in December for fear that it would damage Lockhart's career. Peters eventually published this allegation in 1924, however, in protest against what he called the "rabid anti-Soviet campaign" being conducted by Lockhart in England.[76]

After his release, Lockhart returned to London. So did Boyce and Reilly. Hill, however, on reaching Finland, was ordered by Cumming, chief of MI1c, to return to Russia for a few weeks to assist anti-Bolshevik groups in sabotage operations. On Cumming's recommendation, Hill was awarded the DSO and Reilly the MC for their Russian exploits. In December Lockhart, Reilly, Grenard, and de Vertement were sentenced to death in absentia by the Supreme Revolutionary Tribunal in Moscow. Kalamatiano, the American agent arrested on August 31, remained in jail in Moscow. He was twice told he was being taken out to be shot, in unsuccessful attempts to make him talk, then reprieved and finally allowed back to the United States in 1921.[77]

The Cheka regarded its "liquidation of the Lockhart conspiracy" as a triumph of heroic proportions. The KGB still does. "One could say without exaggeration," claims an official history, "that the shattering blow dealt by the Chekists to the conspirators was equivalent to victory in a major military battle."[78] In reality, the Cheka had won only a minor skirmish. Its opponents had been not a determined coalition of capitalist governments but a group of adventurous, politically naïve Western diplomats and secret agents left largely to their own devices in the chaotic early months of Bolshevik rule. By far the most sophisticated part of the Lockhart conspiracy—the plan for a revolt by Lettish troops in Moscow—had been mounted by the Cheka itself. The Cheka's mastery of the use of penetration agents and agents provocateurs demonstrated during "the Lockhart conspiracy," however, was to make possible a more decisive victory over the British Secret Intelligence Service in the course of the 1920s.[79]

By the beginning of 1920 the White forces, though not yet finally defeated, no longer posed a serious threat to the Bolshevik regime. A decree signed by Lenin and Dzerzhinsky on January 17 announced the end of the death penalty for "enemies of the Soviet authorities." Within three weeks Lenin had had second thoughts. On February 6 he told a conference of provincial Chekas that the death penalty was simply "a matter of expediency" and likely to be needed to deal with further "counterrevolutionary movements and revolts."[80] The Polish invasion of the Ukraine in April 1920 and the six-month Russo-Polish war that followed led to the ruthless stamping out by the Cheka of another wave of real and imaginary conspiracies. According to a KGB official history: "The decisive struggle of the organs of the Cheka . . . foiled the plans of the White Poles and their Entente inspirers to undermine the fighting ability of the Red Army through espionage, sabotage and banditry."[81]

By the end of 1920, Dzerzhinsky's lieutenant Martyn Latsis was asserting the Cheka's right to total supervision of Soviet society: "Counterrevolution has developed everywhere, in all spheres of our life, manifesting itself in the most diverse forms. It is therefore clear that there is no sphere of life exempt from Cheka coverage." Latsis's totalitarian vision contained in embryo the Stalinist police state that emerged in the 1930s.[82]

The total of Cheka executions during the period 1917–21 was probably well over 250,000.[83] By 1921, however, with the Bolshevik victory in the Civil War now secure, many in the Party believed that the Cheka had outlived its usefulness. The Cheka predictably disagreed. Though its growth was temporarily stunted and its powers briefly curtailed, it survived in slightly different form. The Ninth All-Russian Congress of Soviets resolved on December 28, 1921, that "the strengthening of Soviet authority at home and abroad permits the narrowing of the functions of the [Cheka] and its agencies."[84] On February 8, 1922, the Cheka was replaced by the State Political Directorate (Gosudarstvennoye Politicheskoye Upravlenie or GPU), which was incorporated in the Internal Affairs Commissariat (NKVD). Dzerzhinsky had been commissar for internal affairs as well as head of the Cheka since March 1919, and thus retained control of the GPU.

On paper at least the powers of the GPU were drastically reduced by comparison with those of the Cheka. Its sphere of influence was strictly limited to political subversion; ordinary criminal justice was to be the responsibility of the law courts and revolutionary tribunals. The GPU was given the power only to investigate; it lost the power of summary justice and confinement to concentration camp by administrative order. Gradually, however, the GPU recovered most of the Cheka's powers. It did so with Lenin's blessing; he wrote in May 1922, "The law should not abolish terror: to promise that would be self-delusion or deception." Decrees of August and October 1922 gave the GPU the power to exile, imprison, and in some cases execute counterrevolutionaries, "bandits," and certain categories of criminal.

On the formation of the U.S.S.R. in 1923 the GPU was raised in status to a federal agency, the Unified State Political Directorate (Obyeddinenoye Gosudarstvennoye Politicheskoye Upravlenie or OGPU). A "judicial collegium" was attached to the OGPU to mete out summary justice to counterrevolutionaries, spies, and terrorists. Whereas the Cheka had been intended as only a temporary expedient to defend the Revolution in its hour of peril, the GPU, OGPU, and their successors were solidly established at the center of the Soviet state.[85]

3

Foreign Intelligence and "Active Measures" in the Dzerzhinsky Era (1919–27)

Soviet Russia embarked on an ambitious program of covert action beyond its frontiers even before it began systematic foreign intelligence collection. While the Cheka during the Civil War was defending the Bolshevik regime against a series of real and imaginary conspiracies at home, the work of Soviet agents abroad was geared first and foremost to spreading the Revolution. The organizer of most of the covert action, however, was not the Cheka but the Comintern, the Soviet-dominated Communist International, whose executive committee (the ECCI) considered itself "the general staff of world revolution."

After October 1917 most of the Bolshevik leadership lived in constant expectation that their own revolution would advance across Europe, then spread around the globe. The crumbling of the great empires of Central Europe during the final stages of the war on the Western Front raised Lenin's hopes to fever pitch. He wrote on October 1, 1918: "The international revolution has come so close within the course of one week that we may count on its outbreak during the next few days. . . . We shall all stake our lives to help the German workers in expediting the revolution about to begin in Germany."[1] On November 9, two days before the Armistice, Germany was proclaimed a republic, and workers' and soldiers' councils were formed on the Soviet model.

Lenin's early hopes, however, were quickly dashed. In January 1919 a Berlin rising supported, though not initiated, by the newly founded German Communist Party (KPD) was crushed, and its two charismatic leaders, Rosa Luxemburg and Karl Liebknecht, were brutally murdered by right-wing army officers. Though the murders destroyed the KPD's already slender prospects of replacing the socialist SPD as the main party of the left, they made dictation to it by Moscow much easier. By the time of her death Rosa Luxemburg had emerged as the most powerful Marxist critic of the Bolshevik regime, accusing Lenin of creating not dictatorship by the proletariat but dictatorship over the proletariat. She was perhaps the one foreign Communist capable of standing up to Lenin and offering more than token opposition to the transformation of the Communist International into a tool of Soviet foreign policy.[2]

The founding congress of the Comintern held at Moscow early in March 1919 was a mostly fraudulent piece of Russian revolutionary theater. Only five delegates arrived from abroad. Most of the remainder were handpicked by the Bolshevik Central Committee from its foreign supporters in Moscow. Some had never been to the countries they were supposed to represent, and some of the parties of which they were delegates did not yet exist. But for much of the European left such technicalities scarcely mattered. For countless left-wing militants Moscow had become the socialist New Jerusalem, and the birth of the Comintern only strengthened their enthusiasm. The French Communist Louis-Oscar Frossard spoke for many of them:

Assailed by a world of enemies, half starving amid anarchy and turmoil, Russia was struggling to build that land of justice and harmony that we had all dreamed of. Outlawed and hated everywhere else, there Socialism was triumphant. What the Socialists of every country had been wishing for, wanting, preparing for, waiting for in vain, the Socialists of Russia, driven by an implacable will, were achieving. Over the ancient empire of the Tsars waved the red flag of the International. No more exploitation of man by man! Capitalism had at last been throttled, floored, dispossessed! . . . Onward! Mankind was not doomed, for over Russia a new day was dawning![3]

The Comintern's continued faith in world revolution was matched by the foreboding of some Western statesmen. A fortnight after its first congress had dispersed, Lloyd George warned the French prime minister Georgi Clemenceau:

> The whole of Europe is filled with the spirit of revolution.
> . . . The whole existing order in its political, social and economic aspects is questioned by the masses of the population from one end of Europe to the other.

For a few heady weeks the Revolution seemed to be spreading even before the Comintern had begun to export it. Without prompting from Moscow, soviet republics were declared in Hungary on March 21 and in Bavaria on April 7. Grigori Zinoviev, the president of the Comintern, forecast that within a year all Europe would be Communist. But the Bolsheviks were forced to stand helplessly by as the Bavarian Soviet was crushed after less than a month by a combination of regular and irregular troops, and again in August as the Hungarian Soviet Republic was overthrown by a Rumanian invasion.[4]

In October 1919 the Comintern established two secret Western European outposts to assist the spread of revolution: the Western European Secretariat (usually abbreviated to WES) in Berlin and the Western Bureau (usually unabbreviated) in Amsterdam. Their heads—Yakov Reich (alias Comrade Thomas) in Berlin, Sebald Rutgers in Amsterdam—were personally selected by Lenin in preference to more prominent German and Dutch Communists whom he considered less likely to follow instructions from Moscow. Lenin briefed Reich and Rutgers individually on their clandestine missions, finances, and initial contacts.

The Western Bureau in Amsterdam, however, quickly came under police surveillance.[5] On the second day of its first secret conference in February 1920, the Russian delegate, Mikhail Markovich Borodin, found the Dutch police recording the proceedings on a Dictaphone in an adjoining apartment. He rushed into the conference room to shout a warning, hotly pursued by the police, who arrested all the delegates.[6] Though the delegates were subsequently released, the British contingent returned home without the Comintern funds on which they had been counting.[7] In April 1920 the Western Bureau was discontinued.

The WES in Berlin was more successful. Comrade Thomas established an elaborate secret network, which sent couriers to Moscow and elsewhere on diplomatic passports, supplied false papers for Communist militants, and distributed funds to the German and other West European Communist parties. Since the police paid less attention to women than to men, a number of his couriers were female Party workers, among them the sister of Iosif Stanislavovich Unshlikht, who in April 1921 became Dzerzhinsky's deputy. Thomas demonstrated his technical virtuosity by renting two aircraft and a boat to carry delegates, all supplied with false papers or diplomatic passports, to the Second Comintern Congress in Petrograd.[8]

The Petrograd Congress adopted "twenty-one conditions," mostly drafted by Lenin, which imposed what amounted to military discipline on its members. All Communist parties were required to operate illegally as well as legally, and "to create a parallel illegal organization which at the decisive moment will help the party to do its duty to the revolution."[9] Karl Radek, one of the Russian members of the ECCI, declared, "Since Russia is the only country where the working class has taken power, the workers of the whole world should now become Russian patriots."[10] Most foreign Communists agreed. Labour Party leaders in Britain fairly described the British Communist Party as "intellectual slaves of Moscow." But it was a servitude freely, even joyously, entered into. One of the more critical British delegates to the Comintern Congress wrote after his return from Petrograd: "It is fairly evident that to many Communists Russia is not a country to learn from, but a sacrosanct Holy of Holies to grovel before as a pious Mohammedan faces the Mecca in his prayers."[11]

Zinoviev told the Comintern Congress that the ECCI had not merely the right but the obligation "to 'meddle' in the work of parties that belong or wish to belong to the Communist International."[12] The principal instruments of such "meddling" were the representatives, nicknamed "eyes of Moscow," sent by the ECCI to member parties and Communist groups. Paul Levi, the president of the KPD and head of the German delegation at the Congress, wrote after breaking with the Comintern in 1921:

> [These representatives] never work with the leadership of individual Communist parties, but always behind their backs and against them. They enjoy the confidence of Moscow but the local leaders do not. . . . The Executive Committee [of the Comintern] acts as a Cheka projected outside the Russian borders.[13]

The "eyes of Moscow" sat on the central committees of the parties to which they were accredited and sent back secret reports, which, according to Comrade Thomas, were seen only by Lenin and the Comintern's Little Bureau (in effect its Politburo).[14] Comintern representatives abroad acted as what the Italian socialist Giacinto Serrati called "grey eminences" in helping to organize splits in socialist parties, which in 1920–21 led to the foundation of new Communist parties in France, Italy, Czechoslovakia, and elsewhere. The French socialist André Le Troquer complained in 1920 at the socialist congress at Tours that prompted the foundation of the French Communist Party: "Though I do wish to join the Third International [Comintern], I am not willing to put up with the clandestine surveillance that is going on, surveillance even of this congress."[15]

The Comintern emissaries also helped to impose on other Communist parties the conspiratorial methods practiced by the Bolsheviks in Tsarist Russia. One of their emissaries' most important functions was to transmit funds from Moscow to Communist parties and the pro-Soviet press, often in the form of jewels confiscated from the Tsarist aristocracy and bourgeoisie. Exiled grand dukes in Paris and other European capitals sometimes claimed (probably mistakenly) to recognize in jewelers' shop windows remnants of the imperial crown jewels.[16] The Finnish Communist Aino Kuusinen, wife of Otto Kuusinen, who in 1921 became the Comintern's secretary-general, later recalled how in the winter of 1920 he financed a secret mission to London by another Finnish Communist, Salme Pekkala:

> Suddenly Kuusinen produced four large diamonds from his waistcoat pocket and showed them to us all, saying: "Each of these is worth forty thousand." I can no longer remember which currency this referred to. Then he handed the diamonds to Pekkala's wife and said with a smile: "Here's some money for the journey."[17]

Another courier used to smuggle Tsarist jewels into Britain was Francis Meynell, a young director of the socialist *Daily Herald.* Though Meynell was sometimes searched on his return to England, he was never caught. During one "jewel trip" he smuggled two strings of pearls buried in a jar of Danish butter. On another occasion he posted from abroad a large and expensive box of chocolate creams, each containing a pearl or a diamond, to his friend the philosopher Cyril Joad (later star of the BBC radio program *Brains Trust*). Once back in London, Meynell was taken to Scotland Yard but searched in vain. Two days later Meynell and his wife recovered the chocolate creams from Joad and "spent a sickly hour sucking the chocolates and so retrieving the jewels."[18]

The enthusiastic amateurism with which Tsarist jewels were used to finance international revolution led, unsurprisingly, to some serious cases of embezzlement. In 1919 Borodin was sent with Tsarist jewels sewn in the lining of two leather suitcases to deliver to Communists in the United States. Probably fearing that he was under surveillance during the journey, he entrusted the suitcases to an Austrian whom he met on board ship. Though the Austrian promised to deliver the bags to Chicago, they never arrived. For a time Borodin himself came under suspicion of jewel theft.[19]

During the Comintern's first two years its program of covert action went little beyond instructing and financing non-Russian revolutionaries and Bolshevik sympathizers. In March 1921 in Germany it made its first attempt to launch a revolution. The main initiative for the German "March Action" came from Béla Kun, then the most celebrated non-Russian Communist, a veteran of the October Revolution as well as the former leader of the Hungarian Soviet Republic, and a member of the Comintern's Little Bureau. "The bourgeois governments," Kun believed, "were still weak. Now was the time to hit them, again and again, with a chain of uprisings, strikes and insurrections." Germany, the birthplace of Marxism, was also, he argued, capitalism's most vulnerable point. Lenin was less enthusiastic. His own faith in imminent world revolution was on the wane. After the devastation of the Civil War, he believed that Soviet Russia needed a period of internal recuperation and détente abroad with her imperialist foes. But Kun seems to have won Lenin over by arguing that a successful insurrection in Germany would reduce international pressure on the Soviet regime.

Early in March Kun and a secret Comintern delegation arrived in Berlin to plan the German revolution. Comrade Thomas, the existing Comintern representative in Germany, was appalled. "I protested violently," he later claimed, "and demanded that Kun be recalled. I sent them proof that the preconditions for any uprising simply did not exist in Germany. Moscow remained silent." By March 17, however, Kun had won over the KPD leadership. "The workers," it instructed, "are herewith called into battle." Representatives from the French, British,

Czech, and other Communist parties were summoned to witness and learn from the forthcoming German revolution.

On March 21 and 22 strikes and insurrections began. On the 24th the KPD ordered a general strike and urged the workers to seize arms.

The great majority of the German labor force, however, took no part in the struggle. By April 1 the few insurgent areas had been crushed, and the KPD called off the general strike. One hundred forty-five workers had been killed, an unknown number wounded and 3,470 arrested.

Levi, who had resigned as KPD leader in February, blamed the Comintern for forcing the KPD into attempting a revolution opposed by the German workers themselves: "Thanks to the Executive Committee and its role, the existence of the German Communist Party, hitherto Europe's only Communist-led mass party, is in grave danger." Heinrich Brandler, Levi's successor as KPD leader, denounced the claim that either the ECCI "or persons close to it" had anything to do with bringing about the "March Action" as "the slyest, dirtiest piece of slander." This allegation, repeated the Comintern president, Zinoviev, was "an infamous lie." But in 1926 the "lie" was officially confirmed. It was finally admitted in Béla Kun's official biography that "In 1921 the Communists sent him on a mission to Germany, where he directed the March Action undertaken by the proletariat."[20]

Though neither Lenin nor the Comintern could bring themselves to accept responsibility for the March action, its failure marked a watershed in Soviet policy. The priority now was not the spread of the Revolution but the consolidation of the Soviet regime at home. At the Tenth Party Congress in March 1921, when announcing his intention "to put an end to opposition, to put the lid on it," and establish a one-party Communist state purged of the remnants of the Mensheviks and SRs, Lenin admitted: "We have failed to convince the broad masses." Large areas of the Russian countryside were swept by famine, industry was close to collapse, and peasant uprisings continued in the Ukraine and Central Asia.

While the Party Congress was in session, the sailors of the Kronstadt garrison, formerly described by Trotsky as "the beauty and pride" of the Revolution, rebelled against the political repression and economic hardship imposed by the Bolshevik regime. The manifesto of the Kronstadt rebels, "What We Are Fighting For," singled out as one of its main targets the Cheka, which it likened to the Oprichniki of Ivan the Terrible: "The power of the police-gendarme monarchy passed into the hands of the Communist usurpers who, instead of bringing freedom to the workers, instilled in them the constant fear of falling into the torture-chambers of the Cheka, which in their horrors far exceeded the police rule of the Tsarist regime."[21] The Cheka's predilection for conspiracy theory predictably made it quick to detect the long arm of Western imperialism behind the Kronstadt rising. Dzerzhinsky reported to Lenin that the rebellion was part of a plot orchestrated by French agents in Riga, working in collusion with the SRs, "to carry out a coup in Petrograd, with the support of the sailors and the discontented working masses, upon which France intends to send her fleet into the Baltic." Lenin noted his agreement.[22] On March 17, just as the KPD was preparing for the "March action" in Germany, the Kronstadt rebellion was brutally suppressed by fifty thousand Red Army troops, including Cheka detachments.

Kronstadt hastened, though it did not cause, a major shift in Bolshevik policy. At the Tenth Party Congress Lenin announced the introduction of the New Economic Policy (NEP). Food requisitioning was stopped, private trading and small-scale private enterprise were restored, and attempts were made to persuade foreign businessmen to provide Russia with their skills and capital. The major priorities of Soviet diplomacy henceforth were to negotiate trade agreements and secure diplomatic recognition from the capitalist world. The beginning of this process was the arrival of a Soviet trade mission in London in May 1920, headed by the commissar for foreign trade, Leonid Krasin, who began protracted negotiations for an Anglo-Soviet trade treaty.[23] Krasin's principal assistant and translator was a Cheka officer, N. K. Klyshko. The Special Branch reported that, immediately on his arrival in England, Klyshko made contact with "Communist elements."[24] A further sign of the growing priority of foreign intelligence collection was Dzerzhinsky's decision to found a Foreign Department (Inostrannyi Otdel, better known as INO) on the Cheka's third anniversary, December 20, 1920.[25]

INO's main diplomatic target was Great Britain, regarded by Soviet leaders as still the greatest of the world powers and the key to Bolshevik Russia's acceptance by the capitalist world. Within little more than a year of the signature of the Anglo-Soviet trade agreement in March 1921, Russia negotiated similar accords with Germany, Italy, Sweden, Norway, Austria, and Czechoslovakia. At the time of the signature of the Anglo-Soviet agreement, the infant INO still had little reliable intelligence on British foreign policy. In a report to Lenin the Cheka correctly identified the most influential supporter of the agreement as the prime minister himself, David Lloyd George. The main opposition, it reported, came from "the Conservative Party of Curzon and Churchill, which is based on the Foreign Office and its surrounding circles."[26]

It did not, however, require secret intelligence to identify Lord Curzon, the foreign secretary, and Winston Churchill, then colonial secretary, as the two most committed anti-Bolsheviks within the cabinet. When Krasin met the cabinet at 10 Downing Street at the beginning of Anglo-Soviet trade negotiations in May 1920, Churchill stayed away rather than "shake hands with the hairy baboon." Curzon reluctantly attended the reception, but when Krasin held out his hand, at first declined to accept it. Only when the prime minister exclaimed, "Curzon! Be a gentleman!" did the foreign secretary take Krasin's still-outstretched hand.[27] Apart from identifying Curzon and Churchill as leading British opposition to the trade treaty, the Cheka showed only a crude grasp either of British politics or of the influences on British foreign policy in March 1921. Churchill was still a coalition Liberal and not, as the Cheka alleged, a Conservative; he crossed the floor of the House of Commons only in 1924.

The Cheka's main, perhaps only, secret source on British policy to Russia, cited several times in its report, was the journalist Arthur Ransome,[28] later famous as a children's novelist, best known as the author of the *Swallows and Amazons* adventure stories of boating in the Lake District. Ransome was both a distinguished man of letters and a perpetual schoolboy. As wartime correspondent of the (London) *Daily News* in revolutionary Russia he had displayed a curious blend of shrewdness and naïveté. He became captivated by the "dear good wild mad practical impractical credulous suspicious purblind clear-sighted infernally energetic Bolsheviks," and full of a confused admiration for their revolutionary vision of a new society:

> Every man is in some sort, until his youth dies and his eyes harden, the potential builder of a New Jerusalem. . . . And even if this thing that is being builded here with tears and blood is not the golden city that we ourselves have dreamed, it is still a thing to the sympathetic understanding of which

each one of us is bound by whatever he owes to his own youth.[29]

Ransome got to know many of the Bolshevik leaders personally, eventually marrying Trotsky's secretary after long and embittered divorce proceedings with his English first wife. He admired both Dzerzhinsky and his deputy Peters:

> [Dzerzhinsky] is a calm, cool-headed fanatic for the revolution with absolute trust in his own conscience and recognizing no higher court. He has been much in prison where he was remarkable for his urgent desire to take upon himself unpleasant labour for other criminals such as cleaning cells and emptying slops. He has a theory of self-sacrifice in which one man has to take on himself the unpleasantness that would otherwise be shared by many. Hence his unwillingness to occupy his present position.

Even when confronted by evidence of Cheka atrocities, Ransome still sought to justify its existence as the only alternative to chaos. In 1921 he even contrived to defend the suppression of the Kronstadt rebellion.[30] Both the Cheka and SIS were much interested in Ransome. Though some SIS officers regarded him as a Bolshevik agent, others were anxious to exploit his remarkable range of contacts with the Russian leadership. Tentative SIS approaches to Ransome, however, came to nothing. Ransome's biographer concludes that Ransome and SIS both tried and failed "to exploit the other."[31] If Ransome had mentioned his dealings with SIS—and he was generally anxious to impress the Bolshevik leadership with his influential British contacts—he would certainly have raised the Cheka's estimate of his importance. The Cheka may also have known of Ransome's postwar meetings with Sir Basil Thomson, head of both the Special Branch and the postwar Directorate of Intelligence responsible for monitoring civil subversion.[32]

In 1919 Ransome moved from Moscow to Riga in Latvia but continued for several years to make regular trips to Russia as correspondent for the Manchester *Guardian*. His brief and fragmentary diary records meetings during these visits with such senior Cheka figures as Dzerzhinsky's deputies, Peters and Unshlikht.[33] Ransome's other Cheka contacts included N. K. Klyshko, the Cheka representative with the Soviet delegation that negotiated the Anglo-Soviet trade agreement.[34]

The Cheka inaccurately singled out *The Times* journalist Harold Williams (who in 1922 became foreign editor) and the SIS officer Sir Paul Dukes as the main influences on Curzon's and Churchill's opposition to the Anglo-Soviet trade treaty.[35] This error reflected in part the Cheka's tendency, in common with some other foreign observers, to overestimate the influence of both *The Times* and the secret service within the Whitehall corridors of power. But the malign influence attributed to Williams and Dukes also probably derived, in part, from Ransome's comments on them. Ransome had quarreled violently with Williams, once a close friend, over Williams's hostility to the Bolsheviks.[36] And he had a similar contempt for Dukes's clandestine missions for SIS, which, he maintained, gave him "much the same sort of view of Russia as a hunted fox gets of a fox-hunt."[37] The Cheka also inaccurately described Williams as a baronet. He was, it added, "married to a certain Tyrkova, who is thought to be the daughter of the famous statesman of a conservative-Cadet [Constitutional Democratic Party] tendency." On this point Lenin himself corrected the Cheka report. Williams's wife, he wrote to Dzerzhinsky, was not Tyrkova but Tyrtova ("My wife knew her well personally in her youth") and was, in her own right, "a very prominent Cadet."[38]

Ransome's tendency to overstate his own influence and contacts in Whitehall was probably responsible for leading the Cheka to the inaccurate conclusion that his visit to Russia early in 1921 was part of a special mission entrusted by Lloyd George to himself and a businessman named Leith to further the cause of a trade agreement. Ransome told the Cheka that "the Soviet Union has a greater influence on the East [than Britain] and that the Muslim world is more inclined to Russian influence than it is to English." The Cheka wrongly concluded that "the spread of Soviet influence to the East, to which England is unable to set any serious obstacles" was one of the motives inclining England to sign a trade treaty. Ransome also told the Cheka that reports in the English press of the Kronstadt rebellion and opposition to the Bolsheviks in Petrograd and Moscow were evidence of "organized pressure on English public opinion" designed to wreck the trade treaty. The Cheka reported: "Ransome considers that the time might be opportune for the Soviet Government to publish the true state of affairs."[39]

Lenin wrote to Dzerzhinsky after reading the Cheka report: "In

my opinion it is very important and, probably, fundamentally true."[40]
Lenin and the Cheka attached so much importance to Ransome's ill-
informed views on British policy partly because he told them what they
expected to hear and tended to confirm their existing conspiracy theories. Ransome had few, if any, British secrets to betray, but he had a
passionate commitment to helping the Bolsheviks gain diplomatic recognition in the West. After the conclusion of the first step in that
process, the Anglo-Soviet trade treaty of March 1921, Ransome's usefulness to the Cheka increased. He became the friend and, on occasion,
the confidant of the head of the British trade mission, Robert Hodgson,
who must certainly have been unaware of his contacts with the Cheka.

In May 1923 the trade treaty was threatened by the so-called
"Curzon ultimatum," accusing the Soviet government of subversion
and hostile propaganda in India and among India's neighbors. Ransome, by his own account, spent many hours discussing the ultimatum
with Chicherin, his deputy Litvinov, and, though his memoirs do not
mention it, probably the GPU as well. He argued that while Curzon
remained implacably hostile to Soviet Russia, the British government
as a whole did not want to break off relations. "I have," wrote Ransome, "seldom drunk so much tea in the Kremlin in so short a time."[41]
His diary records four meetings with Litvinov, three with Chicherin,
two with Hodgson, and one each with Bukharin and Zinoviev, all in
the space of four days.[42]

Hodgson had instructions not to discuss the Curzon ultimatum
with the Commissariat for Foreign Affairs but was persuaded by Ransome to agree to an "accidental" meeting with Litvinov in woods
outside Moscow.[43] Eight months later Ransome at last achieved his
ambition of seeing the Soviet Union break out of its diplomatic isolation. He was present at the ceremony in Moscow in January 1924 when,
following the election of Britain's first Labour government under Ramsay MacDonald, Hodgson presented an official note to Chicherin formally recognizing the Soviet regime as the de jure government of
Russia. "It was," wrote Ransome, "a very happy day for me. 'My war,'
which had lasted for more than five years after the Armistice of 1918,
was over."[44]

During the early 1920s British intelligence on Soviet foreign policy was
clearly superior to the Cheka's on Britain. Soviet Russia did not yet
possess the sigint that had provided the Tsarist foreign ministry with
its most important diplomatic intelligence. During their first decade in

power the Bolsheviks suffered from two serious sigint handicaps. The first was their fear of relying on the relatively sophisticated codes and ciphers that they had inherited from the Tsarist regime, and their introduction of less secure systems based at first on simple forms of letter transposition. The second was the dispersion of the Tsarist code breakers, who had given prerevolutionary Russia the world lead in cryptanalysis. Worse still, from the Bolshevik point of view, some of the best had fled abroad.[45]

The head of the Russian section at Britain's interwar sigint agency, the Government Code and Cypher School (GC & CS, the ancestor of today's GCHQ), Ernst ("Fetty") Fetterlein, was a refugee from the Tsarist *cabinet noir,* who had escaped with his wife to Britain by hiding aboard a Swedish ship, which was unsuccessfully searched before it left Russia. Fetterlein claimed to have been the leading cryptanalyst of Tsarist Russia, with the rank of admiral. His colleagues in GC & CS found that "on book ciphers and anything where insight was vital he was quite the best."[46] The great American cryptographer, William Friedman, who met Fetty soon after the end of the war, was struck by the large ruby ring on the index finger of his right hand: "When I showed interest in this unusual gem, he told me that the ring had been presented to him as a token of recognition and thanks for his cryptanalytic successes while in the service of Czar Nicholas, the last of the line."

Ironically, those successes had included decrypting British diplomatic traffic.[47] His main achievement during the decade after the Revolution was to help decrypt Russian diplomatic traffic for the British. Though he spoke English with a thick Russian accent, Fetterlein was a fine linguist. Much of his English, however, had been learned from *Sexton Blake* and other popular detective novels; he sometimes amused his colleagues in GC & CS with remarks such as "Who has boned my pencil?" or "He was a rotter!" Fetterlein said little about prerevolutionary Russia. Occasionally a fellow cryptanalyst would draw him out by making a disingenuous comment with which he was known to disagree. "And the Tsar, Mr. Fetterlein, I believe he was a very strong man with good physique?" Fetty usually rose to the bait and replied indignantly: "The Tsar was a weakling who had no mind of his own, sickly and generally the subject of scorn."[48]

Thanks to Fetterlein and his British colleagues, GC & CS was able to decrypt most high-grade Russian diplomatic traffic during the negotiation of the Anglo-Soviet accord. The Soviet intercepts made dramatic reading. Lenin advised Krasin at the outset of negotiations in June 1920: "That swine Lloyd George has no scruples or shame in the way he deceives. Don't believe a word he says and gull him three times as much." Lloyd George took such insults philosophically. Some of his ministers did not. Curzon and Churchill used the evidence in the intercepts of subsidies to the *Daily Herald* and British Bolsheviks, and of other forms of Soviet subversion in Britain and India, to demand that the trade delegation be expelled and the trade negotiations abandoned.

Though determined not to sacrifice the prospect of a trade agreement, Lloyd George felt it prudent to respond to the outrage with which most of his ministers reacted to the evidence of subversion in the Soviet intercepts. On September 10 the prime minister accused the head of the Moscow Communist Party, Lev Kamenev, who had arrived in August to lead the trade delegation with Krasin as his deputy, of "gross breach of faith" and various forms of subversion. Though Krasin was allowed to remain, Kamenev, who was due to return to Russia for consultation the next day, was told that he would not be permitted to come back. Lloyd George claimed "irrefutable evidence" for his charges but declined to say what it was. The Soviet delegation should, however, have realized that their telegrams had been decrypted.

In August the cabinet had agreed to release a selection of the Soviet intercepts. Eight intercepted messages concerning Soviet subsidies to the *Daily Herald* were given to all national newspapers except the *Herald* itself. In order to mislead the Russians into believing that the messages had leaked from the entourage of Maxim Litvinov in Copenhagen, the press was asked to say that they had been obtained from "a neutral country." *The Times,* however, failed to play the game. To Lloyd George's fury, *The Times* began its story with the words: "The following wireless messages have been intercepted by the British government." Klyshko, the Cheka resident (station chief) with the trade delegation, however, was clearly a novice in sigint. Either he failed to read *The Times* attentively or he wrongly assumed that, save for the "Marta" cipher used to transmit the eight published messages, Soviet ciphers were still secure. Nor did he grasp the significance of leaks to the *Daily Mail* and *Morning Post* in September based on further Soviet intercepts. The extent of British penetration of Soviet code and cipher systems was first realized not by the trade delegation but by Mikhail Frunze, commander-in-chief of the Southern Red Army Group, which defeated the forces of the White general, Baron Wrangel, in the Crimea. Frunze reported to Moscow on December 19, 1920:

> It emerges from a report furnished to me today by Yam-
> chenko, former head of the Wrangel radio station at Sevas-
> topol, that absolutely all our ciphers are being deciphered by
> the enemy in consequence of their simplicity. . . . The overall
> conclusion is that all our enemies, particularly England, have
> all this time been entirely in the know about our internal,
> military-operational and diplomatic work.[49]

A week later the trade delegation in London was instructed to conduct
as much of its correspondence as possible by courier "until the establishment of new cipher systems." These new systems, when introduced
early in 1921, defeated Fetterlein and his British colleagues for several
months. By the end of April, however, GC & CS had begun once again
to decrypt substantial amounts of Soviet diplomatic traffic. The celebrated "Curzon ultimatum" of May 1923 denouncing Soviet subversion, not only merely quoted a series of Soviet intercepts, but repeatedly—and undiplomatically—taunted the Russians with the successful
interception of their communications:

> The Russian Commissariat for Foreign Affairs will no doubt
> recognize the following communication dated 21st February,
> 1923, which they received from M. Raskolnikov. . . . The
> Commissariat for Foreign Affairs will also doubtless recog-
> nize a communication received by them from Kabul, dated
> the 8th November, 1922. . . . Nor will they have forgotten
> a communication, dated the 16th March, 1923, from M.
> Karakhan, the Assistant Commissary for Foreign Affairs, to
> M. Raskolnikov.

In the summer of 1923 Moscow again introduced new code and cipher
systems, which for a time defeated Fetterlein and his colleagues. But,
probably by the end of 1924, GC & CS succeeded once again in decrypting significant amounts of Soviet diplomatic traffic.[50]

Though Soviet sigint still lagged behind Britain's at the time of
the Curzon ultimatum, the INO (foreign intelligence department) network abroad was already larger, more ambitious, and more aggressive
than that of SIS, whose budget had been drastically cut back after the
end of the First World War. The spread of Soviet trade missions and
embassies after the Anglo-Soviet trade agreement of March 1921 gave
INO the opportunity to establish a network of "legal residencies"

headed by "residents" (station chiefs) operating under diplomatic cover within Soviet missions.[51] As in Britain, the issue of diplomatic cover gave rise to recurrent friction between diplomats and intelligence officers. SIS station commanders abroad between the wars tended to live an underprivileged existence as "passport control officers" on the fringes of British embassies, where they were commonly regarded as an embarrassment rather than an asset by ambassadors, who preferred to keep intelligence at arm's length from diplomacy.[52] INO residents were far more powerful figures than SIS station commanders, and their intermittent clashes with Soviet ambassadors were correspondingly greater. According to Georgi Agabekov, an OGPU resident who defected in 1930:

> Theoretically the OGPU resident is subordinate to the ambassador, of whom he is officially the second secretary or something of the sort. But, in fact . . . his authority often exceeds that of the ambassador. Greatly feared by his colleagues, even by the ambassador, he holds over their heads the perpetual fear of denunciation. Sometimes the ambassador . . . lodges a complaint against the resident in his capacity as embassy secretary. Then you'll see an embassy divided into two camps, resident and ambassador each with his own partisans, till Moscow recalls one or the other and his partisans will soon follow.[53]

The head of the INO, the foreign section of the Cheka and its successors, responsible for running the residencies abroad, from August 1921 until late in 1929 was Mikhail Abramovich Trilisser, a Russian Jew who had become a professional revolutionary in 1901 at the age of only eighteen. Before the First World War he had specialized in tracking down police spies among the Bolshevik émigrés. Even Stalin's one-time secretary, Boris Bazhanov, who defected in 1928 hotly pursued by the OGPU, described Trilisser as "a clever and intelligent Chekist."[54] Like most other senior INO officers of his generation, Trilisser was liquidated during the Terror of the late thirties, only to be posthumously rehabilitated after Stalin's death. His portrait hangs today in a place of honor in the Memory Room of INO's successor, the First Chief Directorate of the KGB.[55]

For his first two years as head of the INO Foreign Section, Trilisser seems to have delegated most of the day-to-day management of the section to his Estonian assistant, Vladimir Andreevich Styrne. Besides being notable for his youth (he was only twenty-two when he joined the Foreign Section in 1921), Styrne also brought with him a blood-curdling reputation for ruthlessness. Though the story is impossible to corroborate, he was believed within the Cheka to have had his own parents liquidated.[56]

At about the time when Trilisser took over the INO in 1921, the Comintern set up a secret international liaison department, the OMS (Otdel Mezhdunarodnykh Svyazey), to run its clandestine network of agents abroad.[57] The OMS performed a valuable service for INO by drawing into secret-service work foreign Communists and fellow travelers (Communist sympathizers) who were more likely to respond to an appeal for help from the Communist International than to a direct approach from Soviet intelligence. Many of the best OGPU and NKVD foreign agents in the 1930s believed initially that they were working for the Comintern.[58]

OMS also pioneered the development of the "front organizations" that were later to become an important instrument of Soviet "active measures" (influence operations). The greatest virtuoso of the front organizations set up with OMS funds was the German Communist deputy Willi Münzenberg, affectionately described by his "life partner," Babette Gross, as "the patron saint of the fellow-travellers."[59] During the Russian famine of 1921 Münzenberg set up International Workers' Aid (IWA) with headquarters in Berlin, and quickly established himself as the Comintern's most effective propagandist. According to Babette Gross:

> His magic word was solidarity—at the beginning solidarity with the starving Russians, then with the proletariat of the whole world. By substituting solidarity for charity Münzenberg found the key to the heart of many intellectuals; they reacted spontaneously. . . . When he spoke of the "sacred enthusiasm for the proletarian duty to help and assist" he touched on that almost exalted readiness for sacrifice that is found wherever there is faith.[60]

Each act of 'solidarity with the Russian people' forged an emotional bond between the donor and the idealized version of the Soviet worker-peasant state presented by Comintern propaganda.

The IWA became known in Party slang as the "Münzenberg Trust." According to Arthur Koestler, who was sent to work for him in 1933, Münzenberg had acquired "a greater measure of independence and freedom of action in the international field than any other Comintern leader. . . . Undisturbed by the stifling control of the party bureaucracy," his imaginative propaganda campaigns were "in striking contrast to the pedantic, sectarian language of the official Party Press."[61] The Münzenberg Trust quickly gained the support of a galaxy of "uncommitted" writers, academics, and scientists. The portrait of a large-eyed hungry child stretching out a hand for food in Käthe Kollwitz's poster, produced for Münzenberg in 1923, became one of the most powerful and best-remembered images of the century. In the course of the 1920s, the Münzenberg Trust established its own newspapers, publishing houses, book clubs, films, and theatrical productions. As far away as Japan, according to Koestler, the Trust controlled directly or indirectly nineteen newspapers and magazines. Remarkably, Münzenberg even managed to make most of his ventures pay.[62]

The IWA was the progenitor of a series of what Münzenberg privately called "Innocents' Clubs,"[63] founded to "organize the intellectuals" under covert Comintern leadership in support of a variety of voguish causes. He had a friendly contempt for the "innocent" bourgeois intellectuals whom he seduced by the lure of spiritual solidarity with the proletariat. Though his main preoccupation was propaganda, Münzenberg also used the "Innocents' Clubs" as a cover for OMS intelligence networks, which included some of the intellectuals he had seduced.[64]

At the operational level there was, inevitably, recurrent friction between the overlapping networks of OMS and the more powerful INO. At the Center, however, the friction between the two secret agencies was lessened by the personal friendship between Mikhail Trilisser, the head of INO, and Iosif Aronovich Pyatnitsky, head of OMS from its foundation in 1921 until he was purged in the mid-thirties. Like Trilisser, Pyatnitsky was Jewish and had begun a career as a professional revolutionary in his late teens. Before the First World War he had specialized in smuggling both revolutionaries and revolutionary propaganda in and out of Tsarist Russia.[65] INO was usually the dominant partner in the relationship with OMS. While Trilisser had a seat on OMS, Pyatnitsky had no position in INO.[66]

The most ambitious covert action involving both OGPU and Comintern was the final attempt to launch a revolution in Germany.

Though approved by the Politburo, the initiative on this occasion came from the Comintern. In March 1923 Lenin suffered a third stroke, which ended his active political life. The Comintern's leaders were determined to spread the revolution to at least one other country before his death. If Communism triumphed in Germany, they were convinced that it would sweep across Europe.[67] On August 15 Zinoviev interrupted his summer holiday to instruct the German Communist Party (KPD) to prepare for the coming revolution.[68] On August 23 the Politburo held a secret meeting to hear a report from the Comintern German specialist, Karl Radek. "Here at last, Comrades," said Trotsky, "is the tempest we had been expecting impatiently for so many years. It is destined to change the face of the earth. . . . The German revolution means the collapse of world capitalism."

Though less euphoric than Trotsky, the Politburo decided to send a secret four-man mission on false papers to Berlin to prepare for the German revolution. Radek was to transmit to the KPD the instructions of the Comintern (decided for it by the Soviet Politburo) and direct its Central Committee accordingly. Unshlikht, Dzerzhinsky's OGPU deputy, was to organize and arm the "Red Hundreds" who would carry out the revolution and to set up a German OGPU afterward to stamp out counterrevolution. Vasya Schmidt, the Soviet commissar for labor, who was of German origin, was to organize revolutionary cells within the unions, which in the aftermath of revolution would become German soviets. Yuri Pyatakov, a member of the Russian Communist Party's Central Committee, was to coordinate the work of the others and be responsible for liaison between Moscow and Berlin.[69]

There was in reality never any serious prospect of a German revolution in 1923. The KPD had only a fraction of the support among the German working class enjoyed by its socialist rival, the SPD, and the German government was far less feeble than Kerensky's provisional government in October 1917. The Soviet secret mission, however, remained determinedly optimistic. Pyatakov's reports to Moscow, though contemptuous of the KPD leadership, insisted that the German proletariat was ready for revolution. A special meeting of the Politburo late in September gave the go-ahead. Its conclusions were considered so secret that its minutes, instead of being circulated to the Party's Central Committee, as was usual at this period, were locked in the safe of the Politburo secretary.

According to the plan approved by the Politburo, following

demonstrations to celebrate the anniversary of the Bolshevik Revolution, Unshlikht's Red Hundreds would begin armed conflicts with the police. The resulting mayhem, and the official repression it was calculated to provoke, were expected to lead to a general working-class insurrection, in the course of which Unshlikht's detachments would seize the key centers of power, as the Red Guards had done in Petrograd six years before.[70] Arms for the Red Hundreds were smuggled by cargo steamer from Petrograd to Hamburg, where they were unloaded by Communist dockers.[71]

The German revolution was due to begin in the early hours of October 23. Iosif Pyatnitsky, the head of OMS, Dmitri Manuilsky of the Communist Party's Central Committee, and Otto Kuusinen, the Comintern's Finnish secretary-general, sat up all night in Kuusinen's study, smoking and drinking coffee while they waited for a telegram from Radek in Berlin to tell them the revolution had begun. Throughout the night a direct telephone line was kept open to Lenin's sickbed at Gorky, where other Soviet leaders were assembled. Lenin himself could mumble only a few syllables, though his mind remained alert for news of the revolution he had predicted five years before. The news, however, never came. At dawn on October 23 a telegram was sent to ask Radek what had happened. A few hours later came his one-word reply: "Nothing." At the last minute Radek and the KPD leadership had called off the planned insurrection because of lack of working-class support. Though a rising went ahead in Hamburg, it was quickly crushed. Bitter recriminations followed.[72] The KPD was heavily criticized in Moscow for having thrown away a "favorable opportunity."[73] The blame more properly belonged to Moscow for having persuaded itself, in defiance of the evidence, that the opportunity had ever existed.[74]

Thenceforth the Comintern's main hopes for the spread of revolution moved from Europe to Asia, especially to India and to China. Within Europe the failure of the 1923 "German October" confirmed the shift of emphasis that had followed the failure of the German "March Action" in 1921 away from sponsoring revolutionary insurrections to establishing trade and diplomatic relations with the capitalist powers. For some years the Cheka and its successors had greater success against Western diplomatic targets in Moscow than in Western capitals. The trade missions and embassies established in Moscow from 1921 onward proved far easier to penetrate than the major foreign ministries abroad. Surveillance of foreign missions was the responsibility of the Cheka's counterintelligence department, the KRO, headed for most of the 1920s by Artur Khristyanovich Artuzov. Born in 1891, Artuzov was the son of an Italian-Swiss cheese maker, who had settled in Russia, and the nephew of M. S. Kedrov, head of the NKVD Department of Forced Labour.[75] He later succeeded Trilisser as head of INO from late 1929 until 1934. His portrait hangs today in the Memory Room of the First Chief Directorate, together with a eulogy of his work as head of both KRO and INO.[76]

The classified history of the FCD praises Artuzov chiefly as an ideas man. He pioneered a variety of penetration techniques against foreign missions, ranging from the "honey trap" to less subtle methods of intimidation later employed by the KGB. Foreign diplomatic couriers were followed from the moment, and sometimes even before, they crossed the Soviet border in the hope of gaining access to the contents of their diplomatic bags. When couriers traveled, as they frequently did, on the night sleeper between Petrograd and Moscow, a special carriage was added to the train, fitted out as a photographic laboratory, in the hope of gaining access to their diplomatic bags while the couriers were asleep.[77] One courier employed by the Finnish trade delegation in Moscow during 1921 had to resist seduction on the night sleeper by an attractive Cheka female agent anxious to separate him from his bag.[78] Shortly afterward another Finnish courier was put to sleep with the help of drugged tea from a train samovar and the contents of his bag photographed in the laboratory carriage— the first recorded case of the use of drugs by Soviet intelligence against a diplomatic target.[79]

Unlike INO during the 1920s, KRO had its own laboratory, which ran training courses on the art of opening diplomatic bags, forging official seals, making secret inks and using drugs.[80] Probably the most striking of the KRO's early successes against foreign diplomats was with the Estonian Roman Birk, who fell heavily into debt while playing cards in Moscow with a Cheka agent. Birk not only made available the contents of his diplomatic bag but was himself recruited by the Cheka, later taking part in the "Trust" deception, the most successful Soviet intelligence operation of the 1920s.[81]

In 1922 the KRO seems to have devised an even more sinister plan to deal with Robert Hodgson, the head of the British Trade Delegation. A former Tsarist official claimed, probably reliably, that the Commissariat for Foreign Affairs had offered him a job if he agreed to spy on the British mission. Hodgson reported to the Foreign Office:

Roller [head of the British section of the KRO] proposed
that he should entice me to his house, that I should there be
drugged and my pockets searched; it was thought that by this
means valuable information could be secured. My acquaintance urged the obvious objections to this genial suggestion;
the Mission motor car would be standing outside the house,
inquiries as to my prolonged absence would be made from
the Mission and complications must ensue which could
hardly be agreeable to the Soviet government.

Artuzov agreed and the plan was dropped.[82]

The commonest KRO operations against foreign missions in
Moscow were the intimidation of their Russian employees and other
contacts. In May 1924 Hodgson sent Litvinov, the commissar for foreign affairs, who he correctly believed disapproved of at least some
OGPU excesses, two "perfectly friendly" letters giving examples of the
harassment of his mission over the previous two years. Several of the
cases concerned an OGPU officer using the name Anatoli Vladimirovich Jurgens, who, said Hodgson, "appears to have specialized in terrorizing women and young girls." Early in 1922 Jurgens summoned one
of the maids at the trade mission named Theresa Koch and threatened
to jail her for life unless she signed a document agreeing to spy on the
mission and report to the Cheka once a week:

Finally, being completely terrorized, she signed. She was
threatened with condign punishment should she reveal the
incident to me. . . . For months afterwards she did not dare
to leave the Mission premises. Later, when she wished to
leave the country, permission was systematically refused, the
reason being that she had been connected with some incident
at Ekaterinoslav—where she has never been in her life.

Early in 1923 Jurgens tried similar pressure on an old woman named
Maria Nikolayevna Schmegman, who had become acquainted with
Hodgson through selling antique furniture to him. Jurgens told her that
she would never leave the Lubyanka alive unless she signed an agreement to steal documents from Hodgson and spy on his embassy.

Finally, she signed the undertaking. For a considerable time
afterwards she was persecuted by Jurgens. She was also

threatened with the severest punishment if she spoke of the matter to anyone.

Early in 1924 the girlfriend of a trade-mission employee, Tatiana Romanovna Levitskaya, was also asked to spy on the mission. When she refused, she was sentenced to three years' exile in the Narim region as a British spy.[83]

"In comparison with other missions," Hodgson told the Foreign Office, the British mission was "treated with relative decency." After protests by the Polish legation at harassment by the OGPU, it received a formal apology from the Commissariat for Foreign Affairs.[84] Unlike the Poles, Hodgson received no formal apology. But he reported in August 1924 that OGPU intimidation had ceased (only temporarily, as it later turned out) since his protest in May: "M. Chicherin has obviously taken the matter much to heart, and is extremely anxious that repetition of such obnoxious episodes should be avoided in the future."[85]

The Cheka and its successors frequently found it easier to penetrate European diplomatic missions outside Europe than in Europe itself. In the early 1920s the mistress of the British consul at Resht, Persia, supplied a Cheka officer named Apresov with the consul's secret papers. On moving to become OGPU resident at Meshed in 1923, Apresov also obtained from the British consulate copies of the consul's reports to the British embassy in Teheran as well as correspondence between the military attaché in Teheran and the high command in India.[86]

The non-European capital in which European missions were most vulnerable to Soviet penetration in the pre-Stalin era was probably Beijing (Peking). A police raid on the Soviet Embassy in Beijing in April 1927 recovered copies of a number of highly secret British diplomatic documents. They included, according to a Foreign Office minute, "probably the two most important despatches" written by the British ambassador, Sir Miles Lampson, over the previous few months. Lampson himself claimed that "leakage" from the Italian and Japanese legations had been even more serious:

Documents obtained from Italian [Legation] consist mainly of decyphers of all important telegrams between Peking and Rome and vice versa, and those from Japanese [Legation] are comprehensive and even include such details as seating ar-

rangements at official dinners and record of conversations
held between officials of Legation and visitors thereto.

Lampson reported that both the head chancery servant and another
member of the Chinese staff at the British legation had been discovered
to be working for the Russians.[87] The Foreign Office failed to learn the
lessons of the legation leaks. Throughout the interwar years it possessed
not merely no security department but not a single security officer.
Security at British missions continued to be inadequate, sometimes
outrageously so. Leaks of documents from the Rome embassy, involving at least one local employee, began in 1924 and continued until the
Second World War.[88]

　　　Though most Soviet espionage against foreign missions in Beijing was organized by military intelligence rather than by the OGPU,
the documents seized during the raid on the Soviet embassy provide a
revealing insight into some of the methods used by both intelligence
agencies. One set of instructions for the recruitment of "lower grade"
Chinese staff in foreign legations ("office boys, watchmen, house coo-
lies, etc.") suggested: "Very suitable recruiting agents may prove [to be]
those [Communist] Party workers who are sufficiently trained to carry
out the enlisting of secret agents on the basis of idealistic considera-
tions." The agents recruited were to collect torn-up documents from
embassy wastepaper baskets, "spoiled typewritten sheets, first proof
sheets from all kinds of duplication machines, etc." Special attention
should be paid to the stencils used in duplicating machines:

> The agents who steal material of this kind should be encour-
> aged with pecuniary rewards. These rewards, however, must
> be small for two reasons:
>
> a.　A large amount of money in the hands of agents may
> 　　arouse suspicion in other Chinese servants of the office
> 　　in question and through them become known to their
> 　　masters.
> b.　On no account should the agent have any chance to
> 　　suspect that he is supplying us with valuable material for
> 　　which as soon as an opportunity occurs he may bargain
> 　　with us. On the contrary, we must always point out to
> 　　him that we are waiting for something more important
> 　　from him, and if we pay him extra it is only because we

hope he will be more successful in future. Hence it is clear that the salary of such agents must be only very little more than the salary which they are getting from their masters.

For good work by the secret agents, the recruiting agents must be given rewards as they are, properly speaking, the moving power behind this work.

Secret agents should be instructed to show "industry, punctuality and outward devotion and attachment" to their masters, and generally do their utmost to avoid suspicion. Those handling them needed "always to be on guard against false information" and alive to the possibility that an agent might be discovered by his legation and used to supply bogus information.[89]

The documents stolen from foreign diplomatic missions, when compared with the ciphered versions, were of great assistance to Soviet code breakers. On occasion, as in the Tsarist period, cipher material was stolen as well.[90] By the mid-twenties sigint was once again emerging as an important source of Russian diplomatic intelligence. Within the OGPU sigint was the responsibility of a Special Section (Spets Otdel) headed by Gleb Ivanovich Boky. The Special Section was already functioning within the Cheka in 1921 but its functions at that stage seem to have been rather assorted and largely concerned with labor camps. Gradually, however, it came to specialize in sigint. Its head, Boky, born in 1879, the son of a Ukrainian schoolteacher and an old Bolshevik, had an exemplary revolutionary record, which included twelve spells in Tsarist jails, two Siberian exiles, and participation in the revolutions of 1905 and October 1917. He headed the Special Department for sixteen years, from 1921 until he was purged in 1937 during the Stalinist terror.[91] By the mid-twenties the Special Section had succeeded in bugging some Moscow embassies as well as breaking their codes. Boky was believed to have given Chicherin a dramatic demonstration of his section's technical virtuosity by inviting him to listen to a live relay of the Afghan ambassador in Moscow making love to an opera singer who was also employed as an OGPU "swallow."[92]

In March 1921, when Soviet Russia began to emerge from diplomatic isolation after the Anglo-Soviet Trade Treaty, her diplomatic intelligence had been feeble. The infant INO's only intelligence on the foreign policy of the "Main Adversary," Great Britain, derived

from the misleading analysis of Arthur Ransome. By the time of Dzerzhinsky's death in July 1926, the situation had been transformed. Soviet
sigint, though not yet in the Tsarist class, was once again a major source
of diplomatic intelligence. The penetration of Western embassies in
Moscow and elsewhere gave Russia probably the best diplomatic humint in the world. Moscow, by contrast, had become too hostile an
environment for most Western intelligence services to operate in at all.
At no point between the wars did SIS even possess a Moscow station.
Like most other Western intelligence services, it sought with decreasing
success to penetrate Russia from across its frontiers, chiefly from Finland and the Baltic States.[93]

Britain's lack of diplomatic humint, however, was offset in the
mid-twenties by its continuing superiority in sigint and by its access to
Comintern communications. High-grade Tsarist diplomatic ciphers, at
least during the generation before the First World War, seem to have
defeated all foreign cryptanalysts. Soviet diplomatic and intelligence
ciphers, by contrast, remained vulnerable for a decade after the Revolution.[94] The Comintern at this period was probably at least as porous as
Western embassies in Moscow. The Comintern leadership was well
aware that "many of its secrets were penetrated by agents of foreign
governments."[95] MI5 and the Special Branch in London and the Intelligence Bureau of the British Raj in Delhi successfully intercepted a
stream of Comintern communications to and from British and Indian
Communists. Indian Communists now use these intercepts as an important source for their own history.[96] The Comintern sometimes sought
to cover up its own security lapses for fear that OGPU would insist that
it be more closely supervised.[97]

Documents were not the only Comintern property that were
found to be missing. Vasili Kolarov, the Bulgarian representative on the
ECCI, once went by night sleeper to represent the Comintern at a
military celebration at Minsk. When he awoke, his clothes as well as
his briefcase had been stolen. Peeping out of the window he saw a
welcoming party of officers standing stiffly to attention while a military
band struck up martial music. Tension mounted as the band continued
to play and Kolarov failed to appear. Eventually his predicament was
discovered and he was smuggled off the train in borrowed overcoat and
boots. The Italian representative on the ECCI, Palmiro Togliatti, alias
Ercoli, suffered a similar fate. Aino Kuusinen later recalled calling on
Togliatti and his wife in their Moscow hotel:

I knocked at the door. Togliatti answered, but said he could not open it as he had nothing on. All their things had been stolen during the night. . . . Evidently the thieves had climbed in by way of the balcony and the open window as the occupants of the room lay fast asleep.[98]

Rather more serious was the fact that Comintern funds intended for foreign Communists continued to be embezzled by corrupt couriers or Communist officials. The leading Indian Communist, M. N. Roy, lived in some style in Paris and traveled freely, apparently on misappropriated Comintern funds, while other Indian Communists complained of large sums that, as they euphemistically put it, had gone "astray." In order to account for his misappropriated funds, Roy on at least one occasion presented the Comintern with a list of nonexistent Indian Communists whom he had subsidized.[99]

The Comintern suffered a particular embarrassment during the British general strike in 1926. Allan Wallenius, the English-speaking Comintern librarian, was given £30,000 to deliver to Communist leaders of the London dockers. He set out for Stockholm with a forged Swedish passport, boarded a British ship bound for England, and made friends with a stoker who explained that as well as being a good Communist himself he knew personally the Communists to whom the money was to be delivered. On his return, Wallenius explained to Otto Kuusinen that the stoker had agreed to deliver the money himself. Kuusinen's wife later recalled the sequel:

"What was the stoker's name?" asked Otto drily.
"He told me his name, but I've forgotten it."
Speechless with fury, Otto pointed to the door. Needless to say, the money never got to its destination.[100]

Western governments found, however, that profiting from the Comintern's regular lapses of security was attended by a number of pitfalls. Genuine intercepted Comintern communications were an intelligence source sometimes muddied by forged documents. White Russian forgers in Berlin, Reval, and Warsaw were constantly producing forged Soviet and Comintern documents of varying plausibility as a means both of earning money and of discrediting the Bolsheviks. From time to time Western governments and intelligence services were taken in. In September 1921 the Foreign Office suffered the extreme embarrassment of citing in an official protest note to Moscow a series of Soviet and Comintern documents which it later discovered to have been forged in Berlin. Sir Wyndham Childs, assistant commissioner in charge of the Special Branch from 1921 to 1928, found the forgers "an intolerable nuisance," for "they gave the Russians an opportunity to shout 'forgery' when a genuine document was being dealt with."[101]

The charge that genuine intercepted documents were in fact all forgeries rapidly became one of the most successful forms of OGPU and Comintern disinformation. The most celebrated example of such disinformation concerns the so-called "Zinoviev letter" dated September 15, 1924, intercepted by SIS and published in the press during the general election campaign of October 1924. This document, which instructed British Communists to put pressure on their Labour sympathizers, intensify "agitation-propaganda work in the armed forces" and generally prepare for the coming of the British revolution, was widely— though wrongly—believed at the time to have won the election for the Conservatives and ended the life of Britain's first Labour government.

The original of the Zinoviev letter has since disappeared, and it is now impossible to be certain whether it was genuine or not. There was no shortage of forged Comintern documents on offer, but there was no shortage either of genuine Comintern intercepts. The incoming Conservative government claimed substantial corroboration for the Zinoviev letter from other intelligence sources, which are now known to have included a "trusted" MI5 agent at the British Communist Party headquarters who regularly provided reliable intelligence on other Comintern communications.[102] The British Communist Party was formally rebuked by the Comintern at the end of 1924 for its carelessness in handling secret documents.[103] Two possibilities remain. Either the Zinoviev letter was genuine or, if it was forged, the instructions it contained were sufficiently close to those in a genuine Comintern communication for the MI5 agent to confuse the two.[104]

Whether or not the Comintern was right to claim that the Zinoviev letter was a forgery, there is no doubt that it built upon that claim a successful campaign of disinformation designed to demonstrate that it never sent instructions to member parties of a kind which in reality it sent quite regularly. The centerpiece of its campaign was a Moscow visit in November 1924 by a naïve three-man TUC delegation sent from London to inspect Comintern files in order to establish the truth about the Zinoviev letter. Aino Kuusinen later described the "three days and nights of feverish activity" necessary to remove secret instructions to British Communists and other "compromising documents" from the Comintern archives before the delegates arrived. Even the register of daily correspondence was entirely rewritten in a sanitized form:

> The result was that the trio were completely misled and the Comintern was absolved of any subversive and secret activities in England. After the delegation had left, there was general relief and everyone had a good laugh over the fact that they had been able to pull the wool so easily over the Englishmen's eyes.[105]

One of the results of the Zinoviev letter affair was that the secret work of the Comintern's OMS was thenceforth subject to greater control by the OGPU and, on military matters, by Soviet military intelligence (then the Fourth Bureau of the General Staff, later the GRU).[106] The OGPU increased the number of its own agents within the OMS network to monitor its secret work. OMS simultaneously took steps to improve the security of its communications. In 1925 Abramov, Pyatnitsky's chief assistant in OMS, founded a secret school in the Moscow suburb of Mytishchi to train foreign Comintern radio operators to communicate with OMS by coded radio messages. After Wallenius's bungled attempt to send funds to Communist dockers during the British general strike of 1926, a more reliable courier system using Communist merchant seamen was set up under the supervision of military intelligence, with the help of Edo Fimmen, head of the Hamburg Seamen and Transport Workers' Union. The reliability of the couriers chosen was tested in a series of trial runs with dummy packages before they were used in earnest.[107]

Despite the growing success of Soviet espionage during the 1920s, its main target remained not capitalist governments but, as at the foundation of the Cheka, counterrevolution. Until the end of the Civil War the chief counterrevolutionary threat had been located on Russian soil. With the evacuation of the last of the White armies in November 1920, the main bases of counterrevolution moved abroad. On December 1, 1920, Lenin instructed Dzerzhinsky to devise a plan to neutralize these bases. Four days later Dzerzhinsky proposed a multipronged attack: more hostage taking from among the families in Russia of prominent émigrés, special detachments to attack émigré leaders in their foreign bases, and an expansion of the deception techniques using agents provocateurs that had defeated the Lockhart plot.[108] "For the detection of foreign agencies on our territories," Dzerzhinsky proposed to "organize pretended White Guard associations."[109] The threat to the Bolshevik regime from the White Guards after their defeat in the Civil War was always slight, but in Lenin's mind it assumed enormous proportions. He told the Third Comintern Congress in July 1921:

> Now, after we have repulsed the attack of international counterrevolution, there has been formed abroad an organization of the Russian bourgeoisie and of all the Russian counterrevolutionary parties. The number of Russian émigrés, who are scattered through all foreign countries, might be counted at from one and a half to two million. . . . We can observe them all working jointly abroad irrespective of their former political parties. . . . They are skillfully taking advantage of every opportunity in order, in one form or another, to attack Soviet Russia and smash her to pieces. . . . In certain respects we must learn from this enemy. These counterrevolutionary émigrés are very well informed, excellently organized, and good strategists. . . . There is an old proverb that a beaten army learns much. They are learning with the greatest avidity and have achieved great successes.

Lenin appealed to "our foreign comrades" to keep the White Guards in their countries under surveillance.[110]

The KGB still numbers among its greatest past triumphs the deception operations against the White Guards after the Civil War. Two such operations—code-named Sindikat and Trest (Trust)—figure prominently in the training courses on "active measures" at the FCD Andropov Institute.[111]

Sindikat was targeted against the man believed to be the most dangerous of all the White Guards: Boris Savinkov, former Socialist Revolutionary terrorist and deputy minister of war to Kerensky. During the Russo-Polish War of 1920 Savinkov had headed the anti-Bolshevik Russian Political Committee (RPC) in Warsaw and was largely responsible for recruiting the Russian People's Army, which fought under Polish command against the Red Army. In January 1921 Savinkov formed from the remnants of the RPC a new organization dedicated to the overthrow of the Bolsheviks: the People's Union for

Defense of Country and Freedom (NSZRiS), which ran an agent network in Soviet Russia to collect intelligence and prepare for risings against the regime.[112] According to the Soviet version of events, "nearly all Savinkov's agents were simultaneously on Poland's payroll, with the Polish police helping to put them across the border."[113] Despite Polish assistance and smaller subsidies from the French, British, and Czechs, Savinkov hovered on the brink of bankruptcy. The SIS station chief in Warsaw reported to "Head Office" in June 1921: "The position is becoming desperate. The balance in hand today amounts to 700,000 Polish Marks, not even sufficient to pay [Savinkov's] staff their salaries for the month of July."[114]

Savinkov's most serious problem, though he did not realize it, was not his shortage of Western funds, but Soviet penetration. In December 1920, just as Savinkov was organizing the NSZRiS, he received a visit in Poland from the deputy chief of staff of the Soviet Internal Service Troops in Gomel, Aleksandr Eduardovich Opperput, who claimed to belong to an anti-Bolshevik underground and brought with him a suitcaseful of fabricated secret documents. Opperput's real name was Pavel Ivanovich Selyaninov and he was to prove himself one of the Cheka's most successful agents provocateurs.[115] His unusual name should itself have aroused some suspicion at a time when the Soviet regime was introducing so many abbreviations into the Russian language. "Opperput" looks suspiciously like an abbreviated combination of Operatsiya (Operation) and Putat' (Confuse): "Operation Confuse." Neither Savinkov nor the Western intelligence services with whom Opperput came into contact grasped the significance of his name, and he continued to confuse both for a number of years. Savinkov recruited Opperput as one of his chief lieutenants, thus enabling him to identify the leading members of the NSZRiS on Soviet soil. Most were rounded up by the Cheka and forty-four were given a show trial in August 1921. In order to preserve his cover, it was reported that Opperput himself had been arrested.[116]

The intelligence supplied by Opperput provided the basis for an official Soviet protest to the Polish government against Savinkov's attempts to provoke anti-Soviet risings from his Warsaw base. In October 1921, at Polish insistence, Savinkov left to establish a new base first in Prague, then in Paris.[117] The second stage of the Cheka operation, Sindikat-2, now began, designed to disrupt what remained of Savinkov's organization in both Russia and the West, and finally to lure Savinkov himself back to a show trial in Moscow. The operation was simplified by Savinkov's increasingly unstable hold on reality. Late in 1921 he visited England, renewed his acquaintance with Winston Churchill, and began a high-level round of visits. Remarkably, he even visited the Russian trade delegation in London. He claimed after his visit that its head, Krasin, deeply impressed by his vision of a post-Bolshevik Russia, had suggested that he join the Soviet government. Sir Mansfield Cumming, chief of SIS, told the Foreign Office, probably on the basis of Krasin's intercepted telegrams, not to trust Savinkov's account: he had in reality "met with a far from favorable reception" by the trade delegation. Shortly before the Christmas holidays Churchill motored down to Chequers with Savinkov to see the prime minister. They found Lloyd George surrounded by Free Church ministers and a Welsh choir, who sang hymns in Welsh for several hours. When the hymns were over, Savinkov tried and failed to win Lloyd George over to his visionary schemes. Savinkov, however, later gave a quite different version of the meeting, in which the hymns sung by the Welsh choir became transformed into a rendering of "God Save the Tsar" by Lloyd George and his family.[118]

Though increasingly a fantasist, Savinkov remained a charismatic figure for his dwindling band of followers. Even Churchill retained some admiration for him. "When all is said and done," he wrote, "and with all the stains and tarnishes there be, few men tried more, gave more, dared more and suffered more for the Russian people."[119] In the summer of 1922 Savinkov's aide, L. D. Sheshenya, a former Tsarist officer, was captured by Soviet border guards as he crossed the Russo-Polish frontier. On GPU instructions, Sheshenya wrote to Savinkov's émigré supporters in Poland reporting that he had made contact in Russia with a well-organized anti-Bolshevik underground. A senior KRO officer, A. P. Fyodorov, then paid several visits to Poland posing as A. P. Mukhin, one of the leaders of the imaginary Moscow underground, and persuaded the head of the Savinkov organization in Vilno, Ivan Fomichov, to return with him to Russia. In Moscow Fomichov held talks with a group of GPU agents provocateurs posing as leaders of the underground, and agreed to ask Savinkov to assume leadership of their group.[120]

In July 1923 "Mukhin" met Savinkov in Paris. The Moscow underground, he told him, was deeply divided over tactics and desperately needed his experienced leadership. Instead of going to Moscow himself, however, Savinkov sent his aide, Colonel Sergei Pavlovsky. On his arrival in Moscow in September, Pavlovsky was arrested and, according to the KGB's sanitized account of the case, after being initially "very aggressive," "he too agreed to help and the GPU assigned him a role to play." Pavlovsky's part in the deception was to send a series of messages urging Savinkov to come to Moscow too.[121] In July 1924 Savinkov at last fell for the bait, decided to return to Russia, and telegraphed to his old friend and collaborator Sidney Reilly to come over from New York and help him plan his secret mission to his homeland. On August 15, after three weeks' discussion with Reilly, Savinkov crossed the Russian border with some of his supporters and walked straight into an OGPU trap.[122] Under interrogation his resistance rapidly collapsed. At a show trial on August 27 Savinkov made a full confession:

> I unconditionally recognize Soviet power and none other. To every Russian who loves his country I, who have traversed the entire road of this bloody, heavy struggle against you, I who refuted you as none other did, I tell him that if you are a Russian, if you love your people, you will bow down to worker-peasant power and recognize it without any reservations.

In return for his recantation Savinkov escaped the death sentence and was given ten years in prison. According to the official KGB version of events, he threw himself to his death from an unbarred prison window in May 1925.[123] In reality, as the current KGB leadership is well aware, Savinkov was pushed to his death down a stairwell in the Lubyanka. The site was several times pointed out to Gordievsky by a number of KGB veterans. All were convinced Savinkov had been pushed.

Even more successful than Sindikat was the Cheka's invention of a fictitious monarchist underground, the Monarchist Association of Central Russia (MOR), better known by its cover name *Trest* (Trust), which for six years was one of the classic peacetime deception operations in modern intelligence history. The Trust's chief targets were two of the principal White Russian émigré groups: the Supreme Monarchist Council (VMS) based in Berlin, and the Russian Combined Services Union (ROVS), headed by General Aleksandr Kutepov in Paris. The existence of the nonexistent MOR was first revealed in the late autumn of 1921 to the VMS delegate in Reval, Yuri Artamonov, by a KRO officer, Aleksandr Yakushev, who claimed to be a secret member of the

Trust able to travel abroad as a Soviet trade representative. Through Artamonov the KRO was able to make contact with the VMS. In 1922 Artamonov moved to Warsaw, where he became the ROVS representative and provided a channel of communication with General Kutepov in Paris. Over the next few years Yakushev and other Trust representatives supplied by the KRO paid a series of visits to Germany, France, and Poland, expanding their contacts with the White Russian émigré communities. On some trips Yakushev was accompanied by General Nikolai Potapov, a former Tsarist officer who had sided with the Bolsheviks soon after the Revolution but now claimed to be military chief of staff in the MOR.[124]

The main role in winning the confidence of General Kutepov, who was more alert than most White Guards to the possibility of Soviet deception, was played by Maria Zakharchenko-Schultz, the widow of two Tsarist officers. After her first husband's death in the Great War Maria left her baby with friends and joined the army at the front as a volunteer. Her second husband was killed fighting in the Civil War, after which Maria retreated with White forces into Yugoslavia. In 1923 she joined Kutepov's organization, was given the code name Niece and traveled to Russia to make contact with the Trust. Pepita Reilly, last wife of the celebrated British agent, described Zakharchenko-Schultz as "a slender woman with plain yet attractive, capable face, steady, honest, blue eyes, obviously well-bred, and answering very well to Sidney's description of her as a school ma'rm." Zakharchenko-Schultz contributed so effectively to the Trust's success that she has inevitably been accused of being a conscious agent of it.[125] The version of the operation taught at the FCD Andropov Institute, however, portrays her, probably correctly, as an unconscious agent cleverly manipulated by Aleksandr Opperput, who seduced her during her visit to Moscow and continued an affair with her over the next few years.[126] Zakharchenko-Schultz's mixture of passion and naïveté, combined with her ability to win the confidence of both Kutepov and Reilly, made her one of the Trust's most important assets.

The Trust provided the KRO with a means both of penetrating the main White Guard émigré groups and of flushing out their remaining sympathizers in Russia itself. It also deceived in varying degrees the intelligence services of Finland, the Baltic States, Poland, Britain, and France. Roman Birk, the Estonian trade official blackmailed by the KRO, acted as one of the couriers between the White Guards and the nonexistent MOR. Polish diplomats allowed MOR messages to be sent in their diplomatic bags.[127] The passage of Trust representatives across the Russian frontier was supposedly facilitated by an NCO in the Soviet border guards, Toivo Väha, who, though in the pay of Finnish military intelligence, was in reality working for KRO.[128] According to a Soviet official history, no fewer than eight members of the Trust received rewards of various kinds from the Western intelligence services they had deceived.[129] There is some corroboration for this claim: at least one Trust agent appears to have received a gold watch from Polish intelligence.[130]

The Trust's most spectacular coup was its success in luring to his destruction the alleged British "master spy" Sidney Reilly, wrongly believed by the KRO to be its most dangerous foreign opponent. Ever since his Moscow adventures in 1918, Reilly had regarded the "salvation of Russia" from the Bolsheviks as "a most sacred duty." "I also venture to think," he told the SIS chief, Sir Mansfield Cumming, at the end of the war, "that the state should not lose my services. I would devote the rest of my wicked life to this kind of work." But Cumming, and still more the Foreign Office, had become wary of Reilly's erratic talent and fondness for bizarre operations, such as the attempted removal of Lenin's and Trotsky's trousers. He was refused a job on Cumming's peacetime staff and retained only a loose connection with SIS.[131]

For several years after the war Reilly plunged into a variety of business ventures on both sides of the Atlantic, ranging from Czech radium exports to an allegedly miraculous new medicine named "Humagsolan," none of which made him the fortune he had expected. Simultaneously he pursued a series of sometimes fantastic schemes to bring down the Bolsheviks. His chief confederate in the early 1920s was Boris Savinkov. It was Reilly who in 1922 brought Savinkov to Britain, in defiance of instructions from both Cumming and the Foreign Office, for the round of visits that ended with his bizarre encounter with Lloyd George at Chequers. Reilly's hold on reality became increasingly uncertain. According to one of his secretaries, Eleanor Toye, "Reilly used to suffer from severe mental crises amounting to delusion. Once he thought he was Jesus Christ."[132] Soviet intelligence, however, interpreted Reilly's eccentric schemes to overthrow the Bolshevik regime as evidence not of his declining hold on reality but of an elaborate conspiracy by SIS approved at the highest level within Whitehall. By 1924 it had become a major priority of the Trust operation to neutralize Reilly by luring him across the Russian frontier. Even today Reilly still retains within the KGB his undeserved reputation as a British master spy.

The OGPU's plans to capture Reilly were unwittingly assisted by his friend Commander Ernest Boyce, who had been SIS station chief in Russia during Reilly's 1918 adventures. Boyce had been deeply impressed by Reilly's flair and bravado. Politically naïve himself, he failed to grasp the impracticality of Reilly's schemes to overthrow the Bolsheviks. In 1919 Boyce became SIS station chief in Helsinki, the main base for British intelligence operations against Russia. His enthusiasm for the Trust rivaled his admiration for Reilly. Even after Savinkov's show trial in August 1924, Boyce remained convinced that the Trust was growing in strength and even had secret supporters within the Soviet government. Despite instructions from the SIS head office not to become involved in Reilly's schemes, Boyce wrote to him in January 1925 asking him to meet representatives of the Trust in Paris. Reilly, then in New York with his American business ventures collapsing about him, replied in March that though his personal affairs were in "a hellish state . . . I am, at any moment, if I see the right people and prospects of real action, prepared to chuck everything else and devote myself entirely to the Syndicate's [Trust's] interests."[133]

After a number of delays caused by Reilly's "hellish" debt-ridden business dealings, he arrived in Paris on September 3, where he had talks with Boyce and General Kutepov, and decided to proceed to Finland to meet representatives of the Trust. Kutepov, however, tried to discourage Reilly from visiting Russia itself.[134] The Trust, meanwhile, sought to provide additional evidence of its reliability by smuggling out of Russia Boris Bunakov, the brother of Boyce's "head agent," Nikolai Bunakov. Another Trust courier subsequently brought out Boris Bunakov's violin, to which he was much attached. Even then, neither Boyce nor Reilly smelled a rat. Reilly arrived in Helsinki on September 21, then traveled with Nikolai Bunakov and Maria Zakharchenko-Schultz to Viborg for a meeting with the Trust's chief representative, Yakushev. Reilly had originally intended to go no further than Viborg. Yakushev, however, successfully appealed to Reilly's vanity and delusions of grandeur, persuading him that it was vital for him to meet the Trust leadership in Russia. Reilly was assured that he would be back in Finland in time to catch a boat leaving Stettin on September 30.[135] He left for the Russian border with Yakushev, leaving Bunakov with a letter for his wife, Pepita, "only for the most improbable case of a mischance befalling me." Even if "the Bolshies" were to question him, Reilly assured his wife, it was inconceivable that they would realize his true identity: "If by any chance I should be arrested in Russia it could be only on some minor, insignificant charge and my new friends are powerful enough to obtain my prompt liberation."[136]

Reilly was due to return from Russia on the night of September 28–29. He failed to do so. Instead the OGPU staged a dramatic piece of theater designed to impress Finnish military intelligence and SIS. That night shots were heard near the village of Allekul on the Soviet side of the border, and a man was seen being carried away on a stretcher by frontier guards. When Toivo Vähä, the Soviet frontier guard who had helped to smuggle Trust emissaries and couriers across the border in apparent collaboration with the Finns (but in reality on OGPU instructions), failed to renew contact with Finnish military intelligence, both SIS and the Finns concluded, as the OGPU had intended, that he and Reilly had been killed or captured during the frontier crossing.[137]

According to the current, probably embroidered, Soviet version of how Reilly met his end, he was not arrested immediately he crossed into Russia on September 25. Instead he was taken by Yakushev to a dacha near Moscow to meet a group of OGPU officers masquerading as the "political council" of the Trust. Reilly was asked to put forward his plan of action and, according to the Soviet account, proposed financing the Trust's activities by burglarizing Russian museums and selling their art treasures in the West. He was then arrested. After interrogation Reilly was told that the death sentence passed on him in absentia at the end of the "Lockhart plot" trial in December 1918 would be carried out. Soviet accounts allege that in a vain attempt to save himself he sent a personal appeal to Dzerzhinsky:

> After prolonged deliberation, I express willingness to give you complete and open acknowledgment and information on matters of interest to the OGPU concerning the organization and personnel of the British Intelligence Service and, so far as I know it, similar information on American Intelligence and likewise about Russian émigrés with whom I have had business.

Had Reilly really been prepared to cooperate with the OGPU, however, he would doubtless have been given a show trial like Savinkov's. Instead, according to the Soviet version of events, he was shot on November 3, 1925.[138]

Several years after Reilly had been lured back to Russia, the OGPU was still spreading mystification and disinformation about his fate. The Trust deception continued until 1927. Pepita Reilly, who traveled first to Paris then to Helsinki to seek news of her husband, became one of its victims. Before meeting Maria Zakharchenko-Schultz in Helsinki, Mrs. Reilly "had very little doubt but that she was a provocation agent." As soon as she met her, however, all Pepita's doubts dissolved:

> At my first glance I decided that I could trust her. At my second I knew that I was going to like this woman.
> Seeing me thus, looking very mournful, very desolate, very lonely, Mme. Schultz embraced me with great emotion, telling me that she felt herself entirely responsible for my husband's death, and that she would not rest until all the circumstances had been discovered and a rescue effected if he were still alive, or a revenge secured if he were in truth dead.

But, added Zakharchenko-Schultz, there was little doubt that Sidney Reilly was dead. She produced a clipping from *Izvestia* that gave the authorized version of the bogus gun battle at Allekul on the night of September 28–29, and reported that "four smugglers" had been caught trying to cross the border; two had been killed, one taken prisoner, and the fourth had died of his wounds while being taken to Petrograd. According to the evidence she had collected, it was Reilly who had died of his wounds on the way to Petrograd without the Bolsheviks' realizing who he was.[139]

Despite Pepita Reilly's confidence in Maria Zakharchenko-Schultz herself, she was highly skeptical of her story. Though Reilly had a false passport and a borrowed suit, he was wearing a specially tailored shirt and underwear carrying his initials as well as a watch with an inscription in English. In his pocket was a signed photograph of Pepita. The OGPU could thus hardly have failed to realize that they had captured the celebrated British master spy and would, in his wife's view, certainly have shouted their triumph from the housetops. Zakharchenko-Schultz admitted that all this had not occurred to her but promised to work with Pepita in discovering "the truth."[140] Before long Mrs. Reilly came close to a nervous breakdown:

I called for revenge. . . . Mme. Schultz stood over me, kind, capable, sensible, sympathetic. She asked me to trust her completely. I took her hand dumbly. She asked me to join the organization. I trusted her. With the approval of the Moscow center I joined the "Trust" under the party name of "Viardo." And thus it was that I stepped into my husband's place in the ranks of anti-Bolshevism.

With the encouragement of the Trust Mrs. Reilly placed a notice of her husband's death in *The Times* (London): "Sidney George Reilly killed September 28th by G.P.U. troops at the village of Allekul, Russia." Though she did not believe that Reilly was still alive, she naïvely hoped that it would force the Bolsheviks to reveal her husband's fate. But the Soviet press simply confirmed the fact of Reilly's death and later published "horrible lies" about him. She was consoled by the belief that "The whole power, influence, intelligence of the Trust was being employed to find out the truth of what had happened to Sidney." Early in 1926 Mrs. Reilly received a letter from the leaders of the Trust (including Yakushev and Opperput) encouraging her to visit Russia once she had learned some Russian "so that you could take an active part in the work and so that we could introduce you to the members of our group." In the meantime Maria Zakharchenko-Schultz told Pepita that she was "devoting her life to finding out what had really happened to Sidney Reilly." She sent letters in secret ink to Pepita in Paris from Petrograd, Helsinki, and Warsaw: "True to her promise," wrote Mrs. Reilly, "she was leaving no stone unturned."[141]

The Trust's main problem in dealing with Western intelligence services was in responding to the requests it received to provide military intelligence. The OGPU was happy to provide political disinformation but found it more difficult to concoct bogus but plausible intelligence on the Soviet armed forces and arms industry. The Trust thus usually fended off approaches from SIS and other intelligence services by insisting that it was dedicated to preparing the overthrow of the Bolshevik regime and that this objective might be prejudiced by the search for military intelligence.[142] What was probably its first major foray into military disinformation ended in near disaster. Soon after Marshal Pilsudski became Polish minister of war (and, in effect though not in name, head of government) in 1926, he instructed his general staff to ask the Trust to obtain the Soviet mobilization plan. Yakushev was approached and, after some hesitation, agreed to supply the plan for $10,000. The document provided by the Trust, however, contained patently false data on the Russian railways just across the Polish border. After examining the alleged Soviet mobilization plan, Pilsudski returned it to his general staff with the one-word comment "Forgery."[143] Following the suspicions aroused by the traps set for Savinkov and Reilly, the failure of probably the Trust's first major exercise in military disinformation clearly indicated that its days were numbered.

In the spring of 1927 Zakharchenko-Schultz wrote a tearful letter to Mrs. Reilly (and doubtless also to Kutepov) reporting her discovery that the Trust was "full of provocateurs": 'All is lost. . . . It is impossible to go on living with what I have just learned after four years' work to which I gave everything so joyfully." The Allekul ambush had been "all lies and acting":

> Your husband was killed in a cowardly and ignoble fashion. He never reached the frontier. This whole comedy was staged for the rest of us. He was captured at Moscow, and imprisoned in the Lubyanka as a privileged prisoner. Each day he was taken out for exercise in a car and on one of these occasions he was killed from behind on the orders of one of the chiefs of the GPU—Artuzov, an old personal enemy of his who thus took his revenge in such a base manner. . . . The fact that I did not know this does not diminish my responsibility. His blood is upon my hands, it will remain there all my life. I shall wash them by avenging him in a terrible manner or by dying in the attempt.

Mrs. Reilly's first reaction was one of sympathy for Zakharchenko-Schultz:

> It must have been terrible for Marie to have the realization forced upon her that for all these years she had been the dupe of the Soviets and that through her so many people, including the husband of her dearest friend, had been killed or captured.

Pepita did not believe her friend's version of Reilly's death but assumed that she had been taken in by another deception. Zakharchenko-Schultz ended her letter by asking for "one more favor." Would Pepita send her everything she could discover about Opperput?[144]

Unaware that Maria was Opperput's mistress, Pepita replied by sending a dossier on Opperput which, she naïvely believed, "would have surprised the worthy gentleman had he known." Zakharchenko-Schultz replied that Opperput had now admitted everything to her, but said he had been forced to become an agent provocateur after being tortured in 1921:

> Now he is unfolding everything, he is helping the representatives of the other countries who are being fooled and surrounded by Bolshevik agents to escape from this terrible position.[145]

By the time she wrote this letter Zakharchenko-Schultz was with her lover Opperput in Finland, where he was ostensibly engaged in exposing the work of the Trust. Opperput's public confessions to the press, as well as his private briefings to White Russian émigrés and Western intelligence services, were, however, simply the final stage in the deception. Since the deception could clearly no longer be continued, the OGPU had decided to end it in a manner that would both enhance its own reputation and demoralize its opponents. While apparently denouncing the OGPU, Opperput constantly emphasized its omnipotence and the impossibility of fighting against it. And he exaggerated the failings of its opponents, claiming for example that the Polish intelligence service had been practically taken over by Soviet agents.[146] One Scandinavian intelligence officer later claimed that after Opperput's disclosures the intelligence services of Finland, the Baltic States, Poland, Britain, and France "were for some time scarcely on speaking terms."[147]

In May 1927 Zakharchenko-Schultz and Opperput returned to Russia. Before leaving they tried to persuade Pepita Reilly, like her husband two years earlier, to cross the border with them. But the telegram sent to Paris asking her to join them was handed by American Express to the wrong Mrs. Reilly and reached Pepita a fortnight late. Had it reached her in time, she would have tried to persuade Zakharchenko-Schultz that Opperput was "a transparent provocateur," whose "diabolical cunning" was luring her to her doom.

General Kutepov believed that Zakharchenko-Schultz's discovery of the Trust's deception had "unhinged her mind": "She seemed bent on returning to Russia to wreak her vengeance on the people who had duped her, and thus to cleanse herself of the blood of the many whom unwittingly she had sent to their death." Not long after her return, Kutepov and Mrs. Reilly received the news they had been expecting. Zakharchenko-Schultz had shot herself rather than be captured. "And thus," wrote Mrs. Reilly, "died the bravest of all Russian women, who fought against the tyrants of their country." Kutepov probably agreed.[148] Genrikh Grigoryevich Yagoda, deputy head of the OGPU, claimed in an interview with *Pravda* that both Zakharchenko-Schultz and Kutepov were long-standing SIS agents.[149]

Nowadays the KGB publicly celebrates Sindikat and Trest as two of its greatest victories over counterrevolutionary conspiracy and Western intelligence services. But at the same time it continues part of the deception plans on which they were based. The Cheka agents provocateurs who launched both operations, Opperput and Yakushev, are still alleged to have begun as, respectively, "a follower of Savinkov" and "a monarchist" before seeing the light and agreeing to cooperate with the OGPU.[150] Twenty years after the Trust was exposed it was to become the model for a further series of deception operations against both SIS and the CIA.

4

Stalin and Spy Mania
(1926–38)

Among the most pious passages in KGB literature are those that chronicle the final hours of its first chairman, Feliks Dzerzhinsky. "On July 20, 1926," writes Fyodor Fomin, the most senior of the early Chekists to survive the Stalinist purges, "he fell at his post of duty, fighting the enemies of the Party." Only three hours before his death Dzerzhinsky addressed a plenum of the Central Committee and the Central Control Commission and in a flaming speech aimed at deviators from the Leninist Party line, inquired of his audience with, according to Fomin, "complete justification":

> Do you really know where my strength lies? I never spare myself. (Voices from various places saying: "Right.") That is the reason why everybody here trusts and likes me. I never speak against the dictates of good conscience, and if I see disorder I attack it with all my strength.

Dzerzhinsky's remarkable tribute to himself was swiftly followed by a fatal heart attack. His death provoked an even more fulsome eulogy from the plenum that had heard his final speech:

In the most trying times of endless plots and counterrevolutionary uprisings, when the Soviet land was turning to ashes
and the bloody circle of the enemy surrounded the proletariat which was fighting for its freedom, Dzerzhinsky displayed superhuman energy; day and night, night and day,
without sleep, without food, and without the slightest rest he
stayed at his post of duty. Hated by the enemies of the
workers, he won even their respect. His princely figure, his
personal bravery, his penetrating comprehension, his directness, and his exceptional nobility, invested him with great
authority.[1]

Dzerzhinsky's death came at a convenient moment for Joseph Stalin,
whose victory in the prolonged succession struggle that followed
Lenin's death was now almost complete. "Iron Feliks" would almost
certainly have resisted (even if in the end unsuccessfully) the OGPU's
use against dissent within the Party of the weapons of provocation
and deception that he had no compunction in using against non-
Communists. Since Lenin's death Dzerzhinsky had been chairman of
the Supreme Council of the National Economy (Vesenkha) as well as
head of the OGPU. He would surely have opposed both the attack on
"bourgeois specialists" in industry and the ferocious class war in the
countryside that Stalin was to launch within a few years.[2] In the
"flaming speech" delivered three hours before his death he uttered his
most savage criticism yet of the Party apparatus: "When I look at our
apparatus, at our system of organization, our incredible bureaucracy
and our utter disorder, cluttered with every sort of red tape, I am
literally horrified."[3]

Dzerzhinsky's chosen successor, Vyacheslav Rudolfovich
Menzhinsky, a tall, slender man with gold-rimmed pince-nez, was more
pliant than his predecessor. Superficially, the two men had a good deal
in common. Both were old Bolsheviks of well-to-do Polish ancestry.
Menzhinsky had joined the Cheka Collegium soon after its foundation
and became Dzerzhinsky's first deputy chairman on the foundation of
the OGPU. He was probably the most intellectual of all KGB heads.
Even the OGPU defector Georgi Agabekov, who took an uncharitable
view of his former colleagues, described him as "a man of profound
culture" and "complete education." According to Fomin, Menzhinsky
was already fluent in twelve languages when he joined the Cheka and
later mastered Chinese, Japanese, Persian, and Turkish. He was a

polymath as well as a polyglot, whose interests included physics, chemistry, astronomy, and mathematics.[4]

But Menzhinsky was also a far less powerful figure than his predecessor. Even Fomin's officially approved eulogy acknowledges that "He did not have a commanding voice"; for many of those who worked with him "it was strange to hear an order from the OGPU chairman which usually began with: 'I humbly request . . .' "[5] Trotsky, whose persecution by the OGPU began in the Menzhinsky era, found him strangely colorless: "The impression he made on me could best be described by saying that he made none at all. He seemed more like the shadow of some other unrealized man, or rather like a poor sketch for an unfinished portrait."

Menzhinsky was no Stalinist. During the Civil War he had visited Trotsky at the Front to warn him that Stalin was conducting "a very complicated intrigue" against him. But he put up no serious resistance to Stalin's growing power.[6] Even before he succeeded Dzerzhinsky, Menzhinsky already suffered from angina. He commonly received visitors stretched out on a couch in his room in the Lubyanka. "The doctors," he explained, "have ordered me to lie down." In April 1929 a serious heart attack put Menzhinsky out of action for two years. He returned to part-time work in 1931, but by 1933 was no longer able to climb the stairs to his apartment in the Kremlin and went into virtual retirement at a dacha outside Moscow.[7]

Because of Menzhinsky's failing health and passive style of leadership, power within the OGPU passed increasingly to his more aggressive deputy chairman, the Jewish Genrikh Grigoryevich Yagoda. Thick-set, with a ruddy complexion, Yagoda contrasted strikingly with Menzhinsky in manner as well as appearance. Even within the KGB he is nowadays remembered only with embarrassment. Few memoirs of the Stalin era mention his name without execration. "As manifestly as Menzhinsky is a man of complete education," wrote Agabekov, "so is Yagoda brutal, uncultivated, and gross." His coarseness and brutality cannot have been evident when Dzerzhinsky appointed him as second deputy chairman in 1923. To Dzerzhinsky he probably seemed simply an efficient, energetic, ambitious bureaucrat. Yagoda became a classic example of a bureaucrat corrupted by excessive power, with a growing pretentiousness that matched his increasing brutality.[8] On the eve of his fall from power in the summer of 1936, one of his officers found him absorbed in designing for himself a new full-dress uniform: white woolen tunic decorated with gold braid, a small gilt dagger of the kind once worn by Tsarist naval officers, light blue trousers, and shoes of imported patent leather.[9]

Stalin never wholly trusted Yagoda, partly because of his own anti-Semitism, partly because of Yagoda's ideological sympathy with the "Right Opposition" and its charismatic leader Nikolai Bukharin. In 1928 Bukharin told Kamenev that both Yagoda and Trilisser, second deputy chairman of the OGPU and head of INO, were "with us." Yagoda, he said, had secretly given him information on peasant risings.[10] But Bukharin also predicted that Yagoda was an opportunist whose support could not be relied on. In 1931 Stalin tried to strengthen his influence in the OGPU by sending a Party *apparatchik,* A. I. Akulov, to be joint first deputy chairman with Yagoda. Within a year Akulov had been frozen out.[11] Stalin, however, reached an accommodation with Yagoda while waiting for an opportunity to place his own man at the head of the OGPU.

Yagoda was a careerist rather than an ideologue, prepared to throw in his lot with Stalin to further his career but never willing to give him unconditional support. Trilisser was a more committed supporter of the Right Opposition; as early as 1923 he had joined with Bukharin in attacking the Trotskyist line.[12] But at the end of 1929, Yagoda, seeing Trilisser as a potential rival, successfully intrigued with the Central Committee to oust him from the OGPU. Trilisser was succeeded as head of INO by the former KRO (Counterespionage) chief Artur Artuzov.[13]

The OGPU's successful winding-up of the Trust deception during the first year of the Menzhinsky-Yagoda leadership was overshadowed by an embarrassing series of foreign intelligence failures. The security of the rapidly expanding network of OGPU and military intelligence residencies was threatened by the vulnerability of Soviet cipher systems and their inexperience in running enthusiastic but sometimes amateurish local Communists as agents. In the spring of 1927 there were sensational revelations of Soviet espionage in eight different countries.

In March a major spy ring was revealed in Poland, headed by the White Russian general turned OGPU agent, Daniel Vetrenko; a leading official in the Soviet-Turkish trade corporation in Istanbul was found engaged in espionage on the Turkish-Iraqi border; and the Swiss police announced the arrest of two members of a Soviet spy ring. In April a police raid on the Soviet consulate in Beijing uncovered a mass of documents on Soviet espionage; and the French Sûreté arrested eight members of a Soviet spy ring run by Jean Cremet, a Politburo member of the French Communist Party. In May officials of the Austrian foreign ministry were found supplying secret information to the OGPU residency, and there was a Special Branch raid in London on the premises of the All-Russian Co-operative Society (Arcos) and the trade delegation, following the discovery of what the excitable British home secretary, Sir William Joynson-Hicks, denounced with some degree of hyperbole as "one of the most complete and one of the most nefarious spy systems that it has ever been my loss to meet."[14]

The two most traumatic shocks for Soviet foreign espionage were the police raids in Beijing and London, both followed by the publication of some of the intelligence documents seized. The documents published in China provided a wealth of embarrassing detail on Soviet secret operations (mostly by military intelligence), including instructions from Moscow "not to shrink from any measures, even including looting and massacres" when promoting conflicts between the Chinese population and Westerners. There were also names of agents, instructions to Chinese Communists to assist in intelligence operations, and details of munitions smuggled into China.[15] The documents published in England were fewer and far less dramatic, but accompanied by the equally embarrassing revelation that Britain had once again broken Soviet diplomatic codes. The prime minister, foreign secretary, and home secretary all read decrypted extracts from intercepted Soviet telegrams to the House of Commons.[16]

The impact on the Kremlin and the OGPU of the sensational revelations in Beijing and London was all the greater because they came at turning points in Russian relations with both China and Britain. Since 1922 Soviet policy in China had been based on an alliance with the Nationalist Kuomintang. In April 1927 a Communist-led rising delivered Shanghai into the hands of the Kuomintang general Chiang Kai-shek. Chiang, said Stalin, "should be squeezed like a lemon and then thrown away." In the event it was the Communists who became the lemon. Having gained control of Shanghai, Chiang began the systematic massacre of the Communists who had captured it for him. The Communists, on Stalin's instructions, replied with a series of armed risings. All were disastrous failures.[17]

Revelations of Soviet espionage also led to a break, though of a less brutal kind, in relations with Britain, still regarded in the Soviet Union as the leading world power. Ever since the British general strike in May 1926, which conspiracy theorists in the Conservative Party had wrongly attributed to a Russian plot, pressure had been mounting on Stanley Baldwin's government to break off diplomatic relations with the Soviet Union. Dramatic new evidence of Soviet espionage in the armed services in the spring of 1927 was the last straw. On May 26, 1927, Sir Austen Chamberlain informed the Soviet chargé d'affaires, Arkadi Rosengolts, that His Majesty's Government was breaking off diplomatic relations because of "anti-British espionage and propaganda." He gave his message an unusually personal point by quoting a decrypted Soviet telegram sent by Rosengolts to Moscow on April 1 "in which you request material to enable you to support a political campaign against His Majesty's Government."

On his way home by train Rosengolts stopped at Warsaw Central Station to breakfast with the Soviet ambassador Pyotr Voikov in the railway buffet. Just before Rosengolts's train left, Voikov was shot several times by a White Russian émigré, who shouted, "This is for Nationalist Russia, not for the International!" The Soviet government was quick to claim that "a British arm directed the blow which killed Voikov."[18] Ironically, during the last of the prewar show trials in 1938, Rosengolts was himself forced to confess to working for British intelligence from 1926 onward.[19]

The Soviet intelligence disasters in the spring of 1927 had two immediate consequences. The first was a drastic overhaul of the security of Soviet embassies, OGPU residencies, and cipher systems. An urgent circular to Soviet missions and trade delegations ordered the destruction of all documents whose capture might cause fresh embarrassment. Even in Teheran, where the risk of attack on the embassy was insignificant, the huge bonfires of OGPU archives in the diplomatic compound alarmed the local fire brigade. OGPU residencies were ordered to keep on file correspondence for the past month only, and to make plans for its immediate destruction in the event of a raid. New regulations for running local Communists as agents were intended to ensure that no future trace survived of their contacts with the OGPU.[20]

To protect the security of diplomatic and OGPU communications the Kremlin ordered the adoption of the laborious but (when correctly used) unbreakable "one-time pad" cipher system. As a result, between 1927 and the Second World War Western cryptanalysts were able to decrypt virtually no high-grade Soviet communications, though GC & CS in Britain continued to have some success with coded Comintern messages and low-level Russian military traffic. A. G. Denniston, the operational head of GC & CS, wrote bitterly that the result of the publicity given by the British government to the breaking of Soviet codes had been "to compromise our work beyond question."[21]

These intelligence disasters had a profound effect on Stalin. Characteristically he saw them as evidence of a deep-laid imperialist plot:

> It is hardly open to doubt that the chief contemporary question is that of the threat of a new imperialist war. It is not a matter of some indefinite and immaterial "danger" of a new war. It is a matter of a real and material threat of a new war in general, and a war against the U.S.S.R. in particular.

The leader in creating "a united imperialist front" against the Soviet Union, Stalin alleged, was its chief enemy, "the English bourgeoisie and its fighting staff, the Conservative Party": "English capitalism always has been, is, and will continue to be the most ferocious suppressor of popular revolutions." Stalin detected three main stages to the plot orchestrated by the Conservative government. The first was the raid on the Soviet embassy in Beijing, which was intended to "reveal 'awful' documents about the disruptive work of the U.S.S.R., thereby creating an atmosphere of general indignation." The second stage in the plot was the Arcos raid in London and the breach in Anglo-Soviet diplomatic relations, designed to "start a diplomatic blockade of the U.S.S.R. throughout Europe" as a prelude to war. The third stage was the murder of Voikov in Warsaw, "organized by the agents of the Conservative Party" in imitation of the assassination of the Archduke Franz Ferdinand at Sarajevo in 1914, which had sparked off the First World War.[22]

Though this British "plot" had miscarried, there would inevitably be others. Britain was continuing to finance "espionage-terrorist groups in the U.S.S.R." and trying to foment revolts in collusion with White émigrés and other imperialist powers. Stalin denounced "all those leaders of the workers' movement who 'consider' the threat of a new war an 'invention,' who soothe the workers with pacifist lies, who shut their eyes to the bourgeoisie's preparations for a new war." There were two urgent priorities in order to counter the imperialist threat. The first was "strengthening the defensive capacity of our country" by economic growth, especially in war industries, and improving the vigilance of the Soviet people. The second priority was "strengthening our rear" by a determined onslaught on alleged internal enemies: terrorists, industrial wreckers, and other "rubbish." The "rubbish," Stalin implied, included the opposition within the Communist Party: "What can we say after all this of our wretched opposition and its new attacks on the party in face of the threat of a new war? What can we say about the same opposition finding it timely, when war threatens, to strengthen their attacks on the party?"[23]

By 1927 the only significant resistance to Stalin's growing personal power came from within the Bolshevik Party. There is no doubt that the war scare came at a convenient moment as Stalin prepared to consolidate his own leadership. But there is equally little doubt that Stalin, the most "sickly suspicious" (to use Khrushchev's phrase) of all Communist leaders, believed his own conspiracy theory. So, in one form or another, did most of the Party hierarchy. Indeed their ideology almost obliged them to do so. It was an article of Bolshevik faith that international capitalism could not tolerate the consolidation of Soviet power. Imperialist governments and their secret services must necessarily be plotting the overthrow of the "worker-peasant state." It was the responsibility of the OGPU as "the shield and sword of the Revolution" to uncover the inevitable imperialist plots and nip them in the bud. Since no major Western leader from the end of the Civil War until the rise to power of Adolf Hitler in 1933 gave any serious thought to toppling the Bolshevik regime, it followed that the only plots that the OGPU could uncover were imaginary ones. Stalin became increasingly obsessed by imaginary plots. During the decade after the war scare of 1927 he gradually constructed a steadily more comprehensive conspiracy theory, which in its final form was almost as grotesque, though not as venomous, as the myth of the Jewish world conspiracy that obsessed Hitler. The two greatest dictators in modern European history, Stalin and Hitler, were both conspiracy theorists who ended by seeing mass murder as the only way to liquidate the imaginary plots that threatened them. Their chief accomplices were their security forces.

The first use to which Stalin put the OGPU was to strengthen his own personal authority within the Communist Party. Like the Cheka's, the OGPU's principal duty remained to combat counterrevolution. But the definition of counterrevolution changed. Under Lenin it had meant opposition to the Communist Party. Under Stalin it increasingly meant opposition to Stalin. Since the only significant opposition to Stalin came from other Communists, the OGPU began to use within the Party the techniques of infiltration and provocation formerly reserved for the Party's opponents. The first victims were the "Left Opposition" led by Trotsky and Zinoviev.

In September 1927 an OGPU agent provocateur in the Left Opposition uncovered an illegal "printing shop" (in reality little more than a duplicating machine) on which the opposition planned to print its program. According to the OGPU defector Aleksandr Orlov, when Yagoda reported the discovery, Stalin replied: "Good! Now promote your secret agent to the rank of an officer of General Wrangel and indicate in your report that the Trotskyites collaborated with a Wrangelian White Guardist."[24] Stalin duly reported to the Central Committee and Central Control Commission that the Left Opposition was guilty of collusion with the Whites. In November 1927 Trotsky, Zinoviev, and almost a hundred of their followers were expelled from the Party. Zinoviev agreed to recant, denounced "Trotskyism," and was readmitted to the Party. Trotsky refused and in January 1928 was sentenced by the OGPU to internal exile in a remote corner of Kazakhstan on the Chinese border.[25]

Less than a decade later Trotsky became the object of the most determined manhunt in KGB history. In 1928, however, the anti-Trotskyist witch hunt was still in its infancy and the great heretic's removal from Moscow had about it an element of black comedy, which would have been unthinkable only a few years later. When the OGPU came to his Moscow flat on the morning of January 17 to take him into exile, Trotsky was still in his pajamas. As in prerevolutionary days when the police came to arrest him, he locked himself in his room. After unsuccessful negotiations through the locked door, the officer leading the OGPU detachment ordered his men to force an entry. Trotsky was surprised to recognize the officer as one of his former bodyguards during the Civil War. On seeing his former commissar in his pajamas the officer broke down and sobbed, "Shoot me, Comrade Trotsky, shoot me!" Trotsky refused, successfully pacified his one-time bodyguard and persuaded him of his duty to obey orders, reprehensible though they were. He then resumed his posture of passive disobedience and refused either to dress or to leave. The OGPU detachment removed Trotsky's pajamas, put on his clothes, and then carried him, amid the protests of his family, to a car waiting to transport him to the Trans-Siberian Express.[26]

When Trotsky was forced into foreign exile in Turkey in February 1929, the OGPU did its best to ensure that this time there were no witnesses of his departure in case he resorted once again to passive resistance. Together with his wife, elder son Lev Sedov, and an escort of two OGPU officers, he boarded the *Ilyich* in Odessa harbor, and found no other passengers on board. Even the crew were warned to keep out of sight and avoid contact with Trotsky's group. As the *Ilyich* entered the Bosporus, one of Trotsky's OGPU escorts handed him $1,500 "to enable him to settle abroad." Penniless, Trotsky swallowed his pride and took the money. He spent the first six weeks of his foreign exile in the Soviet embassy at Istanbul, then moved to the Turkish island of Prinkipo.[27]

The witch hunt conducted by the OGPU in the late 1920s was directed against economic as well as political subversion. In March 1928 the OGPU announced the discovery of a "counterrevolutionary plot" in the Shakhty coal mines of the Donbass basin. According to the most persuasive account, the plot was first uncovered late in 1927 by the OGPU chief in the northern Caucasus, Y. G. Yevdokimov, who reported to Menzhinsky that a group of engineers in the town of Shakhty had conspired with former mine owners in the White Russian diaspora and with Western imperialists to wreck the mines. When Menzhinsky demanded evidence, Yevdokimov produced a series of intercepted letters written to the engineers from abroad. Though the letters appeared relatively harmless, Yevdokimov claimed that they contained "wrecking" instructions in a code known only to the engineers. Menzhinsky was skeptical and gave Yevdokimov a fortnight to break the code. At this point Yevdokimov appealed directly to Stalin, who authorized him to arrest the engineers. At a special meeting of the Politburo Stalin was authorized to take personal charge of the case.[28]

Out of a series of incidents involving industrial accidents, faulty machinery, inebriated workers, inefficient managers, bourgeois engineers, foreign businessmen, and—probably—a limited number of cases of genuine vandalism, the OGPU then constructed a "far-reaching international intrigue" orchestrated from Warsaw, Berlin, and Paris. After two months' denunciations by the Soviet media of "dastardly saboteurs, plotters and spies," the whole fantastic conspiracy theory was set out in a 250,000-word indictment of fifty Russian and three German technicians and engineers accused of sabotage and espionage. Their long-drawn-out show trial, which opened in May beneath the immense crystal chandeliers of the Moscow House of Trade Unions (the prerevolutionary Nobles' Club), had a new audience at every session. In all, over a hundred thousand factory workers, peasants, schoolchildren and other groups of selected spectators witnessed parts of the proceedings. The United Press correspondent, Eugene Lyons, a former Communist fellow traveler, wrote afterward:

> The few who insisted their innocence . . . provided the biggest thrills for spectators. To see them at bay, their backs arched, panic in their voices, turning from a stinging question by the prosecutor to ward off a statement by a fellow-prisoner, swinging around to meet a judge's admonition—spinning, flailing, stumbling over their own words—finally standing still, exhausted and terror-stricken, staring into the auditorium as though aware of spectators for the first time, was indeed keen sport: lucky shock-brigadiers who drew such a session!

The macabre drama played out in the House of Trade Unions was somewhat less brutal than the later show trials of the Stalin era. Only eleven of the alleged Shakhty saboteurs were sentenced to death, and six were reprieved as a reward for good performances in the roles assigned to them by the OGPU. The great majority both of the spectators and of Soviet newspaper readers found the drama presented for their edification convincing. "The class enemy in our midst" conspiring with counterrevolutionaries abroad provided convenient scapegoats for shortages and privations that might otherwise have been blamed on the leadership.[29]

At the April 1928 plenum of the Central Committee Stalin himself spelled out the enormous ramifications of the conspiracy allegedly uncovered at Shakhty:

> It would be stupid to assume that international capital will leave us in peace. No, comrades, that is not true. Classes exist, international capital exists, and it cannot calmly watch the development of the country which is building socialism. Formerly international capital thought of overthrowing the Soviet power by means of direct military intervention. The attempt failed. Now it is trying, and will try in the future, to weaken our economic power by means of invisible economic intervention, not always obvious but fairly serious, organizing sabotage, planning all kinds of "crises" in one branch of industry or another, and thus facilitating the possibility of

future military intervention. It is all part and parcel of the class struggle of international capital against the Soviet power, and there can be no talk of any accidental happenings.[30]

Those KGB officers with whom Gordievsky discussed the Shakhty trial half a century later recognized that it was a product of wreckermania and spy fever. In Gordievsky's time, however, the KGB could not bring itself to admit as much officially. Even the classified in-house history of the KGB completed in 1978 under the direction of the head of the Second Chief (Counterintelligence) Directorate, Grigori Fyodorovich Grigorenko, maintained, without conviction, that there had been a real conspiracy.[31] In public, at the beginning of the Gorbachev era, the KGB was still sticking rigidly to the interpretation of the Shakhty affair given by Stalin in 1928. According to an unclassified official history published in 1979:

It is undoubted that the wreckers, spies, and diversionists who came forth in the late 1920s in a unified anti-Soviet formation represented a serious threat to the development of socialism and the strengthening of the defensive might of our nation. The exposure of this hostile underground by the OGPU organs, including special sections, helped the Party and government to thwart the anti-Soviet plans of international reaction.[32]

In 1928 this conspiracy theory was taken seriously—very probably even by most of the OGPU officers who manufactured the evidence at the Shakhty trial. Stalin's Russia suffered from a variant of the spy fever that had swept much of Europe during the First World War. During the first weeks of the war "many thousand" suspected German spies were reported to the London police. Not one proved genuine. Spy mania, wrote the head of the Metropolitan Special Branch, Basil Thomson, "assumed a virulent epidemic form accompanied by delusions which defied treatment." For the remainder of the war some ministers and a section of public opinion suffered from the recurrent delusion that industrial unrest and other hindrances to the war effort were the result of subversive conspiracies funded by the enemy. In a celebrated case for criminal libel in 1918 the jury was persuaded that the German secret service possessed a "black book" listing 47,000 British sexual perverts, mostly in high places, who were being blackmailed to sabotage the war effort.[33]

Spy mania returned at the beginning of the Second World War. In 1940, after the fall of France and the Low Countries to the Germans, Britain was swept by fears of a "fifth column" of enemy subversives not much less extravagant than the spy mania of the First World War. A Home Intelligence report in June concluded: "Fifth Column hysteria is reaching dangerous proportions." For a time even Winston Churchill and his chiefs of staff believed that "the most ruthless action" was required to root out what was in reality an almost nonexistent menace.[34]

The wartime delusions in the Western democracies about large fifth columns, like the Cold War witch hunt against frequently imaginary Communists in the United States led by Senator Joseph McCarthy, make it easier to understand the origins of the Stalinist obsession with anti-Soviet subversion at a time when the regime felt under simultaneous threat from class enemies at home and imperialists abroad. But the Stalinist witch hunt was different both in kind and in scale from anything experienced in the West. Churchill's alarmism at the menace of a fifth column in 1940 was short lived. By the end of the year he had concluded that "witch-finding activities" were counterproductive. The American administration during the Cold War was one of the targets rather than one of the instigators of McCarthy's witch hunts.

By contrast, the witchfinder-general in the Soviet Union was Stalin himself. In the West the persecution of imaginary spies and subversives during the two world wars and of imaginary Communists during the Cold War produced only a handful of fatalities. In the Soviet Union during the 1930s imaginary enemies of the people were liquidated in the millions. Stalin and his supporters used the imaginary conspiracy revealed at the Shakhty trial to call for an end to the NEP era of tolerance to bourgeois interests and the beginning of a determined assault on the class enemies wrecking the economy, bourgeois specialists in industry and kulaks (better-off peasants) in the countryside.

Having disposed of the Left Opposition, Stalin felt free to appropriate its radical policies for a dramatic socialist transformation of the Soviet economy. Bukharin and the Right Opposition, who favored less radical policies based on conciliation rather than class conflict, were swept aside even more easily than the Left. In January 1929 Bukharin lost his place on the Politburo. High among the reasons that impelled the Stalinist leadership to embark during the next year on a crash program of industrialization under the First Five-Year Plan and compulsory collectivization in the countryside designed "to liquidate the kulaks as a class" was a chronic sense of insecurity at the combined menace of class enemies within and imperialist foes abroad. In a speech to the Central Committee in November 1928 Stalin insisted that the survival of socialism in one country depended on the ability of the Soviet economy to overtake the West: "Either we do it, or we shall be crushed." He repeated the same warning in February 1931:

> One feature in the history of old Russia was the continual
> beatings she suffered because of her backwardness. . . . We
> are fifty or a hundred years behind the advanced countries.
> We must catch up this distance in ten years. Either we do it
> or we go under.[35]

The Stalinist transformation of the Soviet economy was born in idealism as well as in insecurity. The prospect of a great leap forward into a fully socialist economy kindled among the new generation of Party militants much the same messianic fervor that had inspired Lenin's followers in 1917. Fifty years later, the dissident Soviet general Petro Grigorenko still recalled "the enthusiasm and passion" of himself and other young Communists as Stalin hailed 1929 as "The Year of the Great Change":

> Bread was in dreadfully short supply, there were queues,
> rationing and famine were just around the corner, and yet we
> were carried away by Stalin's [message] and rejoiced: "Yes,
> a great change indeed, the liquidation of peasant small-hold-
> ings, the destruction of the very soil from which capitalism
> might re-emerge. Let the sharks of imperialism just try to
> attack us now. Now we are on the high road to the triumph
> of socialism."[36]

Many of Trotsky's Russian supporters were won over by Stalin's economic vision. Yuri Pyatakov, president of the State Bank and a former close associate of Trotsky, declared in an impassioned speech to the Council of People's Commissars in October 1929: "The heroic period of our socialist construction has arrived."[37]

But if the "heroic period" of socialist construction galvanized the enthusiasm of many Party militants, it also required the coercive power of the OGPU. In November 1929 all prisoners serving sentences of over three years, whether for political offenses or not, were transferred to the jurisdiction of the OGPU, whose vast network of labor camps *(gulag)* rapidly developed during the 1930s into a major source of forced labor for the Soviet economy. The mixture of visionary idealism and brute force during the first Five-Year Plan transformed the Soviet industrial economy. More was accomplished by setting unrealistic production targets in the conviction that there were "no citadels which Bolshevism cannot storm" than realistic but less inspiring estimates could ever have achieved. Great new industrial centers were created in the Urals, Kuzbass, and the Volga, the cities of Magnitogorsk and Komsomolsk-on-the-Amur rose from the virgin soil; new technology was taken to remote areas in Kazakhstan and the Caucasus, the mighty Dnieper dam was constructed, and the output of electricity almost trebled. And all this was achieved in the early 1930s at a time when the depression in the West sparked by the Wall Street Crash of July 1929 was at its nadir. Soviet spokesmen confidently contrasted the successes of socialist construction with the insoluble contradictions of international capitalism.[38]

The depression did not, in Soviet eyes, make capitalism less dangerous. Stalin warned in June 1930:

> Every time that capitalist contradictions begin to grow acute the bourgeoisie turns its gaze towards the U.S.S.R. as if to say: "Cannot we settle this or that contradiction of capitalism, or all the contradictions taken together, at the expense of the U.S.S.R., the land of the Soviets, the citadel of the revolution, which by its very existence is revolutionizing the working class and the colonies . . . ?" Hence the tendency to adventurist assaults on the U.S.S.R. and to intervention, a tendency which is found to be strengthened as a result of the developing crisis.

With the Conservative defeat in the British general election of June 1929, the return of Ramsay MacDonald's second Labour government, and the resumption of Anglo-Soviet diplomatic relations, Britain ceased to be the chief menace. The main threat of war, said Stalin, now came from France, "the most aggressive and militarist country of all aggressive and militarist countries."[39] Soviet fear of attack was heightened by a French campaign against Russian "dumping" on Western markets.

In October 1930 the French Ministry of Commerce and Industry ordered restrictions on Soviet imports and tried to persuade France's allies in Eastern Europe to follow suit. The Soviet Union retaliated with a total ban on French imports and public warnings at the aggressive designs of French imperialism.[40] The French plan, claimed Vyacheslav Molotov, chairman of Sovnarkom and future commissar for foreign affairs, was "to organize an economic blockade of the U.S.S.R." as a preparation for an armed attack.[41]

The renewed threat of foreign aggression intensified the hunt for internal saboteurs in league with foreign, especially French, imperialists. On September 22, 1930, the press announced that the OGPU had uncovered a "counterrevolutionary society" of forty-eight professors, agronomists, and food administrators, headed by Professor Alexander Ryazantsev, who were accused of a plot to sabotage the country's food supply. Next day the papers were filled with editorials and workers' resolutions calling for the counterrevolutionary conspirators to be executed. On September 24 it was announced that all forty-eight villains had been shot, and extracts were published of their confessions to mostly imaginary crimes. At hundreds of workers' meetings, according to the Soviet press, "the proletariat fervently thanked the glorious OGPU, the unsheathed sword of the revolution, for its splendid work in liquidating this dastardly plot."[42]

Behind almost every shortage and major industrial accident the OGPU uncovered further "dastardly plots." The most remarkable imaginary conspiracy uncovered during the first Five-Year Plan was that of an underground "Industrial Party" comprising two thousand engineers and official planners who for some time had been planning the overthrow of the Soviet regime. They were in collaboration with the general staffs of a dozen nations, led by the French, the leading French statesmen Raymond Poincaré and Aristide Briand, assorted foreign celebrities, including Lawrence of Arabia and the oil magnate Sir Henry Deterding, and a White Russian provisional government in Paris (two of whose members turned out to be dead), waiting to return to Russia and restore capitalism.[43] The opening of the show trial of the Industrial Party's eight-man executive committee amid the faded splendors of the former Nobles' Club was accompanied by a gigantic parade of more than half a million factory and office workers tramping through the snow to chants of "Death! Death! Death!" A warning was issued during the trial that bands of imperialist agents might at any time attempt to rescue the accused and unleash a massive campaign of sabotage. But after an eloquent appeal by the aging Maxim Gorky to the workers, peasants, and intellectuals of the entire world, the agents failed to materialize and the imaginary threat of foreign war was averted.[44]

Half a century after the trial the KGB still absurdly maintained that the Industrial Party had been a genuine "underground espionage centre . . . directed and financed by Western secret agents, as well as by . . . former major Russian capitalists located in Paris."[45] Gordievsky knew no one in the KGB who took this nonsense seriously. It is tempting to conclude that the OGPU attitude to the trial was as cynical in 1930 as that of the KGB fifty years later, and that the whole Industrial Party affair was a deliberate deception from beginning to end. The truth is not so simple. The OGPU had no doubt discovered disaffected engineers and officials who despised the Soviet regime and had links of various kinds with the vast White Russian diaspora abroad. But the OGPU's incurable addiction to conspiracy theory convinced it that it was dealing with a highly organized counterrevolutionary plot in which imperialist agents must necessarily have a part. It then felt free to use its collective imagination in scripting and staging a dramatic reconstruction of the conspiracy for the edification of the Soviet people, their friends in the Communist International, and other progressive forces abroad.

Most of the evidence required for these Stalinist morality plays was provided by the confessions of the "conspirators." In 1967 one of the victims of the early show trials gave this written deposition to the procurator of the Soviet Union, explaining how the OGPU obtained the confessions:

> Some . . . yielded to the promise of future benefits. Others, who tried to resist, were "made to see reason" by physical methods. They were beaten—on the face and head, on the sexual organs; they were thrown to the floor and kicked, choked until no blood flowed to the head, and so on. They were kept on the *konveier* without sleep, put in the *kartser* (half-dressed and barefoot in a cold cell, or in an unbearably hot and stuffy cell without windows), and so on. For some, the mere threat of such methods, with an appropriate demonstration, was enough.[46]

Very few indeed of those for whose edification the show trials were intended had serious doubts about them. Even the Trotskyists, despite their own persecution by the OGPU, had no doubt about the reality of the Industrial Party conspiracy. Trotsky insisted that "specialist wreckers" had been "hired by foreign imperialists and émigré Russian compradores." An underground Trotskyist in Moscow saw the workers' anger at the "specialist wreckers" as encouraging evidence of their "genuine revolutionary enthusiasm." A worker at the Red Proletarian Factory in Moscow recalled forty years later: "The anger and indignation of the workers condemning the traitors' acts have remained in my memory for life."[47]

The Industrial Party trial ended, unexpectedly, in anticlimax. Five death sentences were delivered by the judges to cheers and a storm of applause in the courtroom. Then, two days later, it was announced that the death sentences had been commuted to ten years' imprisonment. Some were surreptitiously rehabilitated.[48] The reasons for the change of heart were economic. Despite the training of a new generation of proletarian technocrats, the rapid progress of the first Five-Year Plan had revealed industry's continuing dependence on the skills of "bourgeois specialists."

At a conference of managers early in 1931 Sergo Ordzhonikidze, who had become head of the Supreme National Economic Council during the Industrial Party trial, emphasized the need for "a careful approach" toward specialists who "work honestly." During spring the council reviewed a number of cases of exiled and imprisoned engineers who requested rehabilitation. Stalin himself hypocritically declared in June 1931: "We have always regarded and still regard 'specialist baiting' as a harmful and disgraceful phenomenon"; he called for "maximum care for those specialists, engineers and technicians of the old school who are definitely turning to the side of the working class." Menzhinsky underlined the wisdom of Stalin's speech in a rare article in *Pravda,* emphasizing that Dzerzhinsky had made frequent use of the OGPU "to protect specialists from all kinds of oppression."[49]

The moratorium on "specialist baiting" did not end wrecker mania. Stalin and many in the OGPU remained convinced that part of the counterrevolutionary conspiracy hatched by domestic traitors and foreign enemies involved a long-term plan to sabotage the Soviet economy. In March 1933 six British electrical engineers working for the Metropolitan-Vickers Company on projects in Russia were arrested together with a larger number of Russian wreckers on charges of sabotage and espionage. Though some of the British engineers had obtained what the Metro-Vic managing director described as "general information" on the Soviet economy (probably of a kind that would have been freely available in the West), the sabotage was, as usual, imaginary. By now the routine of the show trial in the former Nobles' Club was well established. The Russian defendants duly confessed their imaginary crimes:

> All of them watched for the flick of Proseecutor Vyshinsky's whip and obeyed with the frightened alacrity of trained animals. In their "last words" they begged for their lives and promised to do penance in the tones and the words that had become a familiar refrain since the Shakhty trial.

The British engineers played their parts less professionally. Two had made elaborate pretrial "confessions" to the OGPU, but both withdrew them (one only temporarily) during the proceedings. Another defendant made the unprecedented claim in open court that the trial was "a frame-up . . . based on evidence of terrorized prisoners." All but one of the Russians were given prison sentences. So were two of the Metro-Vic engineers. The British government retaliated with a trade embargo, which was lifted in July 1933 when the engineers were released.[50]

As well as leading the campaign against industrial saboteurs, the OGPU also spearheaded the drive to collectivize agriculture during the First Five-Year Plan. The most spectacular achievement of the early months of forced collectivization was what Stalin described as "the liquidation of the kulaks as a class." Since kulaks were "the sworn enemies of the collective farm movement," their removal from their farms was a precondition of collectivization. The term "kulak" was applied not simply to the better-off peasants but to any peasants however poor—for example, devout churchgoers—suspected of opposing collectivization. The first mass arrests by the OGPU of heads of kulak families began late in 1929. All were shot. Then, early in 1930, whole kulak families were rounded up by the thousands, marched to railway stations, placed on cattle cars, transported to the Arctic or Siberian wilderness, and left to fend for themselves. The Politburo did not care if they lived or died.

　　This operation—eventually involving perhaps ten million peasants—was too large for the OGPU to run by itself; 25,000 young Party militants, hastily trained at two-week courses—the so-called "twenty-five thousanders"—were drafted into the countryside to help evacuate the kulaks and set up kolkhozes (collective farms). The young militants showed much the same ruthless fervor as the Red Guards in the Chinese Cultural Revolution a generation later, convinced that they were dealing with class enemies engaged in a counterrevolutionary conspiracy to prevent the victory of socialism. One of the "twenty-five thousanders," Lev Kopelev, later wrote: "I was convinced that we were soldiers on an invisible front, waging war on kulak saboteurs for the sake of bread that the country needed for the Five-Year Plan."[51] But for some veteran OGPU officers the suffering and the horror of forcing millions of peasants from their homes was too much to bear. Isaac Deutscher found one OGPU colonel broken by his recent experiences in the countryside:

> "I am an old Bolshevik," he said, almost sobbing. "I worked against the Tsar and then I fought in the civil war. Did I do all that in order that I should now surround villages with machine-guns and order my men to fire indiscriminately into crowds of peasants? Oh, no, no!"[52]

By the beginning of March 1930 the twenty-five thousanders had herded over half the peasants into kolkhozes and reduced the countryside to chaos. Stalin was forced to call a halt in order to allow the spring sowing to proceed. After the publication in *Pravda* on March 2 of his article "Dizzy with Success" hypocritically reproaching the militants for not observing the "voluntary principle," the population of the kolkhozes fell by over half. Once the harvest was safely gathered in, forced collectivization resumed.

The mayhem of collectivization, lower agricultural yields, sharply increased state procurements, drought and crop failure in 1932 combined to produce in 1932–33 the most terrible famine in the history of twentieth-century Europe, in which perhaps as many as seven million died. A Party activist in the Ukraine, the center of the famine, later recalled how:

> In the terrible spring of 1933 I saw people dying from hunger. I saw women and children with distended bellies, turning blue, still breathing but with vacant, lifeless eyes. And corpses—corpses in ragged sheepskin coats and cheap felt

boots; corpses in peasant-hunts, in the melting snow of the old Vologda, under the bridges of Kharkov.

But he did not lose his faith:

> I persuaded myself, explained to myself that I mustn't give in to debilitating pity. We were realizing historical necessity. We were performing our revolutionary duty. . . . For I was convinced that I was accomplishing the great and necessary transformation of the countryside, that their distress and suffering were a result of their ignorance or the machinations of the class enemy.[53]

Throughout the Ukrainian famine the OGPU continued to uncover cases of sabotage by "class enemies" and "counterrevolutionary conspirators": among them veterinarians accused of decimating livestock, the entire staff of the Meteorological Office charged with falsifying weather forecasts, civil servants alleged to have damaged tractors and infested seed corn with weeds, and collective farm chairmen who had failed to fulfill impossible quotas. Stanislas Kossior, the Ukrainian first secretary (himself later shot in the Great Terror), announced that "Whole counterrevolutionary nests were formed in the People's Commissariats of Education, of Agriculture, of Justice; in the Ukrainian Institute of Marxism-Leninism, the Agricultural Academy, the Shevchenko Institute, etc."[54]

The OGPU's continuing ability to discover imaginary rural saboteurs helped to sustain the gigantic conspiracy theory that increasingly dominated Stalin's world view. Lazar Kaganovich, one of Stalin's most trusted henchmen and one of the few Politburo members to survive the purges, claimed that kulaks who had survived the deportations, along with White Guards and other counterrevolutionaries, had succeeded in "sabotaging the collection of grain deliveries and sowing." When the novelist Mikhail Sholokhov wrote to Stalin in April 1933 to complain of "the mortal blow delivered to the collective farm economy" in the Don district, Stalin replied that "the esteemed grain-growers of your district (and not only of your district)" had tried to sabotage the bread supply to the towns and Red Army:

> That the sabotage was quiet and outwardly harmless (without bloodshed) does not change the fact that the esteemed

grain-growers waged what was virtually a "silent" war
against Soviet power. A war of starvation, dear Comrade
Sholokhov.[55]

Despite the preposterous nature of the allegations of sabotage by starving peasants, it is impossible to dismiss them simply as a cynical attempt
to provide scapegoats to divert attention from the crimes and blunders
of the Party leadership. Like the witch finders of an earlier age, Stalin
believed his own conspiracy theories, even if he felt free to embroider
them to suit his political purposes. Apart from finding nonexistent rural
saboteurs, the OGPU served two other main functions during the famine. The first was to seal off the starving Ukraine from the outside
world. No grain was allowed into the Ukraine. No Ukrainians without
special passes were allowed out. The last railway station between Kiev
and the Ukrainian-Russian border was occupied by an armed OGPU
detachment, which turned back all passengers without permits. Within
the Ukraine the OGPU also had to deal with some of the most horrific
consequences of the famine. Cannibalism became commonplace, but
since cannibals were not covered by the criminal code, they were
handed over to the jurisdiction of the OGPU.[56]

The OGPU also helped to prevent news of the famine from
crossing the borders it had sealed. One of the most successful Soviet
"active measures" of the 1930s was to persuade most of the outside
world, as well as gullible Western visitors and journalists actually in the
Soviet Union, that one of the worst famines in modern history was no
more than a piece of anti-Soviet propaganda. After five days in the
Ukraine, spent in official receptions, banquets, and carefully conducted
tours, Édouard Herriot, the French radical leader, twice prime minister
of his country, "categorically denied the lies of the bourgeois press
about a famine in the Soviet Union." After a tour of Potemkin villages,
Bernard Shaw announced: "I did not see a single under-nourished
person in Russia, young or old. Were they padded? Were their hollow
cheeks distended by pieces of india rubber inside?" The *New York
Times* correspondent in Moscow, Walter Duranty, awarded the Pulitzer Prize in 1932 for his "dispassionate, interpretive reporting of the
news from Russia," claimed in August 1933 that "any report of a
famine in Russia is today an exaggeration or malignant propaganda."
The gurus of British Fabian socialism, Beatrice and Sidney Webb,
reached the same conclusion after their tours of Russia in 1932 and
1933. They blamed the "partial failure of crops" in certain areas on "a

population manifestly guilty of sabotage," and castigated peasants who "out of spite" had taken to "rubbing the grain from the ear, or even cutting off the whole ear, and carrying it off for individual hoarding, this shameless theft of communal property."[57]

The inevitable consequence of the man-made famine in the countryside and the savage witch hunts against "class enemies," real or imagined, in both town and country was the brutalization of the Soviet Communist Party in general and of the OGPU in particular. "Terror," wrote Bukharin, "was henceforth a normal method of administration, and obedience to any order from above a high virtue."[58] But enough of the original idealism of the Bolshevik revolutionary dream remained for the depravities of the class war to provoke at least a muted protest. The most articulate protest was a letter drafted by a supporter of Bukharin, Mikhail Ryutin, signed by himself and seventeen others, which was circulated to members of the Central Committee on the eve of a meeting of its plenum in autumn 1932.

The text of the "Ryutin platform," made public only in 1989, contained such a forthright attack on Stalin and the brutality of the past few years that some Trotskyists who saw the letter wrongly concluded that it was an OGPU provocation.[59] It denounced Stalin as "the evil genius of the Russian Revolution who, activated by vindictiveness and lust for power, has brought the revolution to the edge of the abyss," and demanded his removal: "It is shameful for proletarian revolutionaries to tolerate any longer Stalin's yoke, his arbitrariness, his scorn for the Party and the laboring masses."[60]

The impact of the Ryutin platform on Stalin was heightened by simultaneous evidence of the stirring of the remnants of Trotsky's supporters. In October 1932 the Soviet official and former Trotskyist E. S. Goltsman met Trotsky's son, Sedov, in Berlin, and handed him a harshly critical document entitled "The Economic Situation of the Soviet Union," which was published anonymously in the following month's issue of the Trotskyist *Biulletin Oppozitsii*. Goltsman also brought a proposal for the formation of a united opposition bloc within the Soviet Union. All that remained by now of the Left Opposition was scattered, demoralized, and increasingly powerless remnants. But Trotsky, not for the last time, overestimated the strength of his own support in the Soviet Union. "The proposition of the bloc seems to me completely acceptable," he wrote to his son.[61] Stalin had an even more exaggerated view of the Trotskyite menace in the Soviet Union than

Trotsky himself. When in 1936 he accused his political police of being "four years behind" in "unmasking the Trotskyite-Zinovievite bloc," he had in mind what he saw as its feebleness in stamping down on both the Ryutin platform and Trotsky's supporters in 1932.[62]

Stalin was not yet ready to begin the manhunt for the exiled Trotsky. But he appears to have called for Ryutin's immediate execution. Despite OGPU support, he was voted down by a majority on the Politburo, apparently headed by the Leningrad Party boss, Sergei Kirov. The eighteen signatories of the Ryutin platform were, however, expelled from the Party on the nonsensical charge of having attempted to set up a bourgeois, kulak organization to reestablish capitalism and, in particular, the kulak system in the U.S.S.R. by means of underground activity under the fraudulent banner of "Marxism-Leninism." Zinoviev and Kamenev, now mere symbols rather than leaders of opposition, were also expelled for failing to inform on Ryutin's "counterrevolutionary group."[63]

At a joint session of the Central Committee and Central Control Commission in January 1933 Stalin argued the case for intensifying the "class struggle": "We must bear in mind that the growth in the power of the Soviet state will intensify the resistance of the last remnants of the dying classes." Characteristically, he blamed the famine and other economic problems on sabotage by these "dying classes," some of whom had "even managed to worm their way into the Party." Once again, however, Stalin encountered opposition. Central Committee secretary Postyshev argued that there was no longer any point in using the kulaks as scapegoats for the problems of running large collective farms: "By shouting that kulaks, wreckers, officers, Petlyurists [Ukrainian nationalists] and other such elements disrupt the harvest or sabotage grain-collection, we don't change the situation." So many speakers criticized the Party's agrarian policy that, for the last time in his life, Stalin virtually admitted he had made mistakes. "We are," he said, "to blame." A Party journal cited his speech as an example of "Bolshevik self-criticism."[64]

Two divergent trends were now apparent within the Party leadership. Stalin and his lieutenants were anxious to unleash the full force of the OGPU against the forces of counterrevolution. Others were anxious to restore "socialist legality." For a time Stalin thought it unwise to resist that trend openly. In May 1933 he accepted the circulation of a secret "instruction," condemning mass repression in the countryside. A month later the office of procurator of the U.S.S.R. was established, with the evident aim of limiting OGPU excesses. Yet at the same time the Stalin cult steadily expanded. At the May Day celebrations in 1933 the ceremonial address by Marshal Voroshilov referred for the first time to Stalin as "Leader" (Vozhd). On the anniversary of the October Revolution in Moscow Stalin's portraits outnumbered Lenin's by almost two to one.[65]

Opposition to Stalin resurfaced at the Seventeenth Party Congress early in 1934. It is nowadays stated as a fact in the Soviet Union that Stalin polled almost three hundred votes less than Kirov in the elections to the Central Committee. Stalin lost his title "general secretary" and was referred to simply as "secretary."[66] Party opposition to Stalin, however, was so muted that the vast majority of the Russian population were unaware of its existence. Even today it remains impossible to do much more than guess at its extent. Far more visible than opposition in 1934 was the growing extravagance of the Stalin cult. And though Stalin's domination of the Party was not absolute, his control of the means of repression continued to increase.

In May 1934 the invalid Menzhinsky died and was succeeded by his first deputy, Yagoda, who for some time had been acting head of the OGPU. In July the OGPU was transformed into the GUGB (Main Administration of State Security) and integrated into a reconstituted NKVD (People's Commissariat for Internal Affairs), headed by Yagoda. The political police, regular police, criminal investigation, border troops, internal troops, and, from October 1934, the entire penal system, were thus combined in one body. Though technically only a part of it, the political police was usually referred to as the NKVD. The whole immensely powerful force answered directly to Stalin himself.[67] Stalin's direct line to the NKVD ran through his own personal secretariat headed by A. Poskrebyshev.[68] According to the NKVD defector Aleksandr Orlov, Poskrebyshev and Georgi Malenkov headed a "Little Council," which evaluated all incoming intelligence for the Politburo.[69] Stalin's secretariat also provided the training ground for his protégé, Nikolai Yezhov, who in 1936 was to succeed Yagoda at the head of the NKVD and preside over the Great Terror.[70]

The assassination on December 1, 1934, of Kirov, Stalin's main potential rival, led to a further increase in NKVD powers. Kirov was shot in the back of the neck as he left his office in the Leningrad Party headquarters. His deranged assassin, Leonid Nikolayev, imagined himself the successor to the populist assassins of Tsar Alexander II. Remarkably, Nikolayev had twice previously been caught by Kirov's guards approaching him with a loaded revolver in his briefcase, but on each occasion had been released by the Leningrad NKVD. Fifty years later no one in the KGB with whom Gordievsky discussed the assassination doubted that the order for Kirov's murder derived from Stalin himself. But it was generally believed that Stalin had bypassed Yagoda, whom he did not fully trust, and had worked instead through the head of the Leningrad NKVD, Filipp Medved, and his deputy I. Zaporozhets.[71] Khrushchev later concluded, probably incorrectly, that Yagoda was also involved and had received verbal orders from Stalin.

On his arrival at Leningrad after Kirov's murder, Stalin gave one of the most brilliant acting performances of his career. He struck Medved, who had come to meet him at the railway station, with his gloved hand and then appeared overcome with grief on seeing Kirov's corpse. Officially Medved and Zaporozhets were sacked for criminal negligence, but both subsequently reemerged working for the NKVD in the Far East before being shot during the Great Terror in 1937, possibly, as Khrushchev later suggested, "to cover up all the traces of the organizers of Kirov's assassination."[72]

A directive on the evening of Kirov's assassination authorized summary action, including the death penalty, against suspected terrorists. According to Khrushchev, the directive was issued "without the approval of the Politburo" on the initiative of Stalin.[73] The NKVD thus acquired, and retained for twenty years, the power of life and death over those Soviet citizens it chose to label "terrorists." The first scapegoats found by the NKVD for Kirov's murder were an alleged conspiracy of White Guards who had infiltrated Russia across the Polish, Finnish, and Latvian frontiers. One hundred four of the imaginary conspirators were allegedly rounded up and shot.[74] Three weeks after Kirov's death another nonexistent conspiracy was uncovered. On December 22, 1934, it was announced that Nikolayev belong to an underground terrorist organization set up by the followers of Zinoviev. Stalin noted in his own hand the names of two groups of guilty Zinovievites, who were christened the "Moscow Center" and the "Leningrad Center." It was further disclosed that Nikolayev had received 5,000 rubles from the Latvian consul-general (subsequently expelled), who provided an alleged link between the Zinovievite conspirators and the exiled Trotsky. On December 30 it was announced that, after a brief trial without defense lawyers, the conspirators had been shot.

In January 1935 Zinoviev and Kamenev featured in the first

political trial of former opposition leaders. Both acknowledged only a vaguely worded political responsibility for Kirov's murder, which fell short of actual instigation, and were sentenced to, respectively, ten and five years' imprisonment. Bizarre though these proceedings were, the Soviet people had become so used to revelations of plots and conspiracies that they found them quite plausible.[75] After the trial Stalin summoned Yagoda and told him, "You're working badly, Genrikh Grigoryevich!" Zinoviev and Kamenev, he insisted, should have been tortured until they made a full confession. Yagoda was so shaken by the meeting that when he recounted it to his deputy Georgi Prokoviev he burst into tears.[76]

During 1935 Stalin laid the foundations for a much more massive onslaught on actual or potential opposition to his leadership. A purge of Party members, begun in 1933 and continued during 1934, had been aimed chiefly at rooting out corruption and inefficiency. In 1935 the purge became both more sinister and more political. "The evil murder of Comrade Kirov," said Stalin later, had revealed "many suspect elements within the Party." These could only be removed as the result of detailed inquisition, since, in the words of a Party spokesman, "lying, political jesuitry and double-dealing are the basic tactics of the Party's enemies."[77] Every local Party organization began a campaign of confession and self-criticism. "Big, packed halls," writes Evgenia Ginsburg, "were turned into confessionals":

> Every meeting had its soupe du jour. People repented for incorrect understanding of the theory of permanent revolution and for abstention in the vote on the opposition platform of 1932; for an "eruption" of great-power chauvinism and for undervaluation of the second Five-Year Plan; for acquaintance with certain "sinners" and for infatuation with Meyerhold's theatre.[78]

Stalin became increasingly obsessed with one great opponent beyond his reach, Leon Trotsky. One of the standard questions put by NKVD interrogators while taking political confessions was: "Do you agree or do you not that Trotsky is the chief of the vanguard of bourgeois counterrevolution?" Most of those expelled from the Party were branded as Trotskyites and Zinovievists. To Trotsky in his lonely exile this was vastly encouraging news. He wrote in January 1936:

Among the 10 to 20,000 "Trotskyites" expelled in the last months there are no more than a few tens, perhaps a few hundreds . . . of men of the older generation, oppositionists of the 1923–8 vintages. The mass is made up of new recruits. . . . It can be said with confidence that in spite of thirteen years of baiting, slander and persecution, unsurpassed in wickedness and savagery, in spite of capitulations and defections, more dangerous than persecution, the [Trotskyist] Fourth International possesses already today its strongest, most numerous, and most hardened branch in the U.S.S.R.[79]

Both Stalin and Trotsky now inhabited, at least intermittently, a world of make-believe in which each fed the other's fantasies. Stalin's belief in mostly nonexistent Russian Trotskyists infected Trotsky, whose pleasure at discovering these imaginary followers in turn persuaded Stalin that the Trotskyist menace was even worse than he had supposed.

The real reason why Trotskyists had disappeared from view within the Soviet Union was simply that, with very few exceptions, they had in fact disappeared. Stalin and most of the NKVD, however, believed that their apparent disappearance merely demonstrated that they had gone underground, often posing deceitfully as loyal party members. In the summer of 1936 a secret Central Committee resolution, passed on Stalin's initiative, gave the NKVD extraordinary powers to destroy all "enemies of the people."[80] In July a secret circular, sent in the name of the Politburo but possibly authorized by Stalin alone, warned all Party organizations:

Now that it has been demonstrated that Trotskyist-Zinovievite monsters are uniting in a struggle against Soviet power all the most embittered and sworn enemies of the toilers of our country—spies, provocateurs, saboteurs, White Guards, kulaks, etc.; now that all distinctions have been erased between these elements on the one hand and the Trotskyists and Zinovievites on the other—all our Party organizations, all members of the Party, must understand that the vigilance of Communists is required in any sector and in every situation. The inalienable quality of every Bolshevik in current conditions must be to know how to discover an enemy of the Party, however well he is disguised.

A press campaign over the next few weeks revealed that, "thanks to corrupt liberalism and a blunting of vigilance on the part of some Communists," there were still "Trotskyist-Zinovievite degenerates" in Party ranks.[81]

The trial of the main "degenerates" opened on August 19. Zinoviev, Kamenev, and their associates now confessed what they had been allowed to deny in January 1935: that they were the "direct organizers" of Kirov's assassination and had intended his murder as the prelude to the assassination of other Communist leaders, including Stalin himself, as a means of overthrowing the Soviet regime. Since 1932 they had acted on (nonexistent) instructions from Trotsky, conveyed through (equally nonexistent) secret agents. One of the accused described a meeting with Trotsky's son at a hotel in Copenhagen that turned out to have been pulled down twenty years earlier. For such imaginary crimes all the members of the "Trotskyite-Zinovievite Terrorist Center" were sentenced to death. Their public confessions marked an important stage in the elaboration of a vast conspiracy theory, which in its final form fused together all the opponents of Stalinism, both at home and abroad, into one stupendous plot.

The trial identified the remnants of the Left Opposition inside Russia not merely with the exiled Trotsky but also with the White Guards and fascism. The "Trotskyite-Zinovievite Terrorist Center," it was revealed, "sank definitively into the swamp of white-guardism," merged with it, and "became the organizing force of the last remnants of the exploiting classes which had been routed in the U.S.S.R." They had also collaborated with the Gestapo, with whom Trotsky had agreed on a joint terrorist campaign against the Soviet regime. In his final plea Zinoviev defined the relationship between his own supporters and the forces of Nazism and international fascism in an elegantly simple, if improbable, formula: "Trotskyism is a variety of fascism and Zinovievism is a variety of Trotskyism."[82]

To Stalin's satisfaction, the trial also implicated the remnants of the "Right Opposition": Bukharin, Rykov, and Tomsky. Tomsky took the hint and committed suicide. But while Stalin was on his annual holiday at Sochi in mid-September, he received the unwelcome news that Bukharin and Rykov had been cleared after an NKVD investigation. All Stalin's old suspicions about Yagoda welled to the surface.[83] Basking in his recent promotion to the rank of General Commissar of State Security (the equivalent of marshal) and the award of an apartment in the Kremlin, Yagoda overestimated the strength of his position, gave free rein to his growing vanity, and ordered public changing of the NKVD guard with neo-Tsarist music and ceremonial.[84]

On September 25 nemesis arrived in the form of a telegram to the Politburo from Stalin and his protégé Andrei Zhdanov demanding Yagoda's replacement by Nikolai Yezhov: "Yagoda has definitely proved himself to be incapable of unmasking the Trotskyite-Zinovievite bloc. The OGPU is four years behind in this matter": a clear reference to the allegedly weak response to the "counterrevolutionary" Ryutin platform and Trotskyite menace of 1932.[85]

Stalin probably already intended to launch a major purge of the NKVD but decided for the moment to lull its leadership into a false sense of security by removing only Yagoda and his deputy Georgi Prokoviev. For the time being, neither was executed or imprisoned. Instead, they became, respectively, commissar and deputy commissar of Communications. Yagoda's successor, the diminutive, boyish-looking Yezhov, was the first ethnic Russian to head the KGB. As secretary of the Central Committee and head of the Party Control Commission, Yezhov had been in effect supervising the NKVD on Stalin's behalf for some time. Within the Party apparatus he had created a security staff parallel to the NKVD itself; this staff had probably planned Kirov's assassination, also at Stalin's behest.

Yezhov had taken part in the preparations for the trial of the "Trotskyite-Zinovievite Terrorist Center," even setting up an office in the Lubyanka and taking part in the interrogations as Party representative in charge of security. He showed particular interest in the methods used to extract confessions from those prisoners who put up most resistance and would always ask the interrogators "what, in their opinion, was the last straw that broke the prisoner's back." Yezhov took personal pride in reducing one tough Old Bolshevik to tears by threatening his children. One of the NKVD interrogators who witnessed Yezhov's triumph said later: "In my whole life I have never seen such a villain as Yezhov. He does it with pleasure." Yagoda cannot have welcomed Yezhov's presence in the Lubyanka, but his suspicions were dulled by the honors heaped on him in 1936, his growing vanity, and the expectation of a place in the Politburo.[86]

Under Yezhov all the restraints that had hindered the liquidation of Stalin's imaginary enemies were removed. The next two years, usually known in the West as the Great Terror, are remembered in the Soviet Union as the Yezhovshchina. The next show trial, in January 1937, featured Pyatakov, Radek, and fifteen other imaginary traitors.

It purported to reveal that, in addition to the "Trotskyite-Zinovievite Terrorist Center" unmasked at the show trial in August 1936, Trotsky had also established a "reserve center," known as the "Anti-Soviet Trotskyite Center," in case the first center was discovered. The second "reserve center" was found guilty of conspiring with "enemy of the people L. Trotsky" and "certain representatives of Germany and Japan" "to overthrow the Soviet power in the U.S.S.R. and to restore capitalism and the power of the bourgeoisie by means of wrecking, diversion, espionage, and terrorist activities designed to undermine the economic and military power of the Soviet Union, to expedite the armed attack on the U.S.S.R., to assist foreign aggressors and to bring about the defeat of the U.S.S.R."

The Nazi regime and its intelligence service played, in absentia, a much greater part in the case against the "Anti-Soviet Trotskyite Center" than in the previous show trial. The Japanese government also appeared for the first time as a major conspirator. Trotsky, it was claimed, had promised the Ukraine to Germany and the Maritime Provinces and the Amur region to Japan as a reward for their assistance in overthrowing the Soviet regime. The "Anti-Soviet Trotskyite Center" had regularly supplied both the German and Japanese intelligence services with secret intelligence "of the utmost state importance," had organized widespread peacetime sabotage on their behalf, and made preparations for even more extensive wartime sabotage, including bacteriological warfare "with the object of contaminating troop trains, canteens and army centers with highly virulent bacilli."[87]

On March 18, 1937, Yezhov revealed an even more startling dimension of the imaginary counterrevolutionary conspiracy at a meeting in the NKVD officers' club. By the time his apprehensive audience assembled, some of Yagoda's leading department chiefs were already in prison, having been sent on train journeys ostensibly to carry out regional inspections, only to be arrested at the first railway station outside Moscow. The conspiracy, explained Yezhov, had penetrated the very heart of the NKVD. The chief traitor was Yagoda himself. After working for the Okhrana, Yagoda had been recruited by the German secret service and used by them to penetrate the Cheka. By the time of his dismissal, he had planted spies in every key position in the NKVD, some of whom were already under arrest.

Yezhov's audience applauded a speech that most of them knew to be rubbish. According to Walter Krivitsky, a senior INO officer who defected later in the year:

They applauded to demonstrate their devotion. Who knows?
A timely confession might yet save them from a bullet
through the base of the brain. Perhaps they might once more
buy the right to live by betraying their closest friends.

The first to take the floor was Artuzov, who saw an opportunity to
revenge himself on Abram Slutsky, who had replaced him as head of
INO in 1934. Artuzov began by confessing their collective "blindness"
in failing to discover Yagoda's treachery, and allowing him "to set the
OGPU against the Party." He gave as an example OGPU support for
Yagoda's attempts to freeze out Stalin's protégé Akulov in 1932: "I
must say frankly the entire Party organization in the OGPU was devoted to sabotaging Akulov." Then Artuzov moved to the offensive: "I
ask you who was head of the Party Organization in the OGPU at that
time?" He paused for dramatic effect, then shouted, "Slutsky!"[88]

Slutsky was caught off guard and stumbled at first as he tried
to defend himself. Then he discovered a promising line of counterattack:

I ask you, Artuzov, where did you live? Who lived opposite
you? Bulanov? And is he not now among the first batch
arrested? And who lived just above you, Artuzov? Os-
trovsky? He too is arrested. And who lived just beneath you,
Artuzov? Yagoda! And now I ask you, comrades, who,
under prevailing conditions, could have lived in the same
house with Yagoda without enjoying his absolute confidence?[89]

Artuzov was soon arrested and shot. So, within the next year, were
most of Yagoda's department heads.[90] The main exception was Slutsky,
who was spared for a time so that INO officers serving abroad who were
selected for liquidation could be lured back to Moscow in the mistaken
belief that their department was to be spared. By February 1938 he had
outlived his usefulness. He was invited to the office of Yezhov's deputy,
Mikhail Frinovsky, given tea and cakes, and expired on the spot, allegedly from a heart attack. Experienced NKVD officers who attended
Slutsky's lying-in-state are reported to have noticed on his face the
characteristic spots produced by hydrocyanic acid. An official obituary
signed by his "comrades in work," described Slutsky as a "fearless
fighter for the cause of the working class . . . Chekists knew his name

to the ends of our broad fatherland. Enemies feared that name."[91] Unlike his predecessors, Trilisser and Artuzov, however, Slutsky's portrait does not appear on the wall of the FCD Memory Room.[92]

The next great imaginary conspiracy to be uncovered by Yezhov involved the Red Army. On June 11 it was announced that Marshal Tukhachevsky, hero of the Civil War and the Soviet Union's leading military thinker, had been arrested with seven other generals, on a charge of treason. All were shot, probably the next day. Marshal Voroshilov reported that the traitors had "admitted their treacherousness, wrecking and espionage." They had, it was later revealed, been in league with both Trotsky and Nazi Germany. Preposterous though these allegations were, Stalin and Yezhov were possessed by such paranoid fears of counterrevolutionary conspiracy that they seem genuinely to have feared a military coup. Frinovsky, Yezhov's second-in-command, told Krivitsky: "We've just uncovered a gigantic conspiracy in the Army, such a conspiracy as history has never known. And we've just now learned of a plot to kill Nikolai Ivanovich [Yezhov] himself! But we've got them all. We've got everything under control."[93] The deputy head of INO, Mikhail Shpigelglas, gave much the same version of events to another future defector, Aleksandr Orlov:

> That was a real conspiracy! That could be seen from the panic which spread there on the top: all the passes to the Kremlin were suddenly declared invalid; our troops were held in a state of alarm. As Frinovsky said: "The whole Soviet Government hung by a thread. It was impossible to act as in normal times—first the trial and then the shooting. In this case we had to shoot first and try later."[94]

It later emerged that the Gestapo had tried to exploit Stalin's paranoia by planting forged documents in Czechoslovakia that appeared to show a plot by Tukhachevsky to carry out a coup d'état with German support. The Gestapo plot, however, was unnecessary. Stalin had decided to liquidate the imaginary military plot even before it was brought to his attention by President Beneš of Czechoslovakia. Unprompted by the Germans, Stalin and Yezhov decimated the Red Army high command with a thoroughness that must have exceeded the Gestapo's wildest hopes.[95]

The total number of victims of the Yezhovshchina may never be known with certainty. In response to a secret request from the

Politburo in 1956, the KGB produced a figure of about 19 million arrests for the period 1935 to 1940, of whom at least 7 million were shot or died in the *gulag*. The real death toll was probably higher still.[96] By a macabre irony, the most dangerous "enemies of the people" were discovered in the three institutions who shared responsibility for defending the Soviet state against them: the Party, the Red Army, and the NKVD. One hundred ten of the 139 members of the Central Committee elected at the 1934 Party Congress were shot or imprisoned. Only 59 of the 1,966 delegates reappeared at the next Congress in 1939. Seventy-five of the 80 members of the Supreme Military Council were shot. More than half the Red Army officer corps, probably well over 35,000 men, were executed or imprisoned. The NKVD hierarchy was purged twice. All 18 of Yagoda's commissars of state security, grades 1 and 2, were shot (save for Slutsky, who was probably poisoned) under Yezhov. Of Yezhov's top 122 officers in 1937–38, only 21 still held office under his successor in 1940.[97] The Yezhovshchina destroyed most of what remained of the idealism of the early Chekist leadership, convinced that their brutality was necessary to build a new society and defeat counterrevolution. One of those who witnessed at first hand the change in NKVD interrogators was the writer Nadezhda Mandelstam, wife of the persecuted poet Osip Mandelstam:

> The first generation of young Chekists, later to be removed and destroyed in 1937, was distinguished by its sophisticated tastes and weakness for literature—only the most fashionable, of course. In my presence Christophorovich said to [Osip] that it was useful for a poet to experience fear ("you yourself told me so") because it can inspire verse, and that he would "experience fear in full measure."

Mandelstam died in a labor camp. Christophorovich, the interrogator, was shot.[98] His successors were men of little culture and less idealism. Within the NKVD, as within the Party, the conditions of the Terror led to the survival of the morally unfittest, those most willing to save themselves by denouncing others. The teams of NKVD executioners stationed around the gulag commonly became alcoholics. Each morning when they collected their automatics from the guardroom they were each given a glass of vodka. Then they loaded the day's victims onto trucks, drove them to a pit dug by a team of criminal convicts, lined them up and started shooting:

Some were [silent], others started crying out that they were
good Communists, that they were dying innocent, and so on.
But the women only cried and huddled closer together.

In some places NKVD marksmen lined up the prisoners sideways
and tried to see how many they could kill with a single bullet. Then
the execution squads returned to camp, put their automatics back in
the guardroom, were given as much free vodka as they could drink,
and slept.[99]

The victims of the NKVD included foreign as well as Russian
Communists. A majority of the Comintern officials and foreign Communists resident in Moscow were unmasked as "enemy agents" or
"foreign spies" and shot. Those who were most vulnerable were the
members of illegal Communist parties and their families, who had lost
the protection of foreign nationality. Most had spent some time in
foreign jails, where, it was alleged, that capitalist secret services had
recruited them as agents. The two illegal foreign parties with the largest
number of imaginary spies among their exiled leadership were the Poles
and the Yugoslavs. The Polish Communists were most suspect of all:
their leaders were Jewish and had taken Trotsky's side at the time of
Lenin's death. All were shot. Manuilsky told the 1939 Soviet Party
Congress:

> In order to disrupt the Communist movement, the Fascist-
> Trotskyite spies attempted to form artificial "factions" and
> "groups" in some of the Communist parties and to stir up
> a factional struggle. Most contaminated by hostile elements
> was the Communist Party of Poland, where agents of Polish
> fascism managed to gain positions of leadership.

Stalin was almost as suspicious of the Yugoslav Communist Party,
whose first leader, Sima Marković, had challenged his views on the
nationality question in 1925. Ironically, the only leading Yugoslav
Communist whom Stalin trusted was the arch-heretic of the postwar
Soviet bloc, Josip Broz, alias Tito, who later recalled:

> In 1938, when I was in Moscow . . . we were discussing
> whether to dissolve the Yugoslav Communist Party. All the
> Yugoslav leaders at that time in the Soviet Union had been

arrested; I was alone, the party was weakened, without leadership; and I was there alone.[100]

The final revelation of the extent of the imaginary international counterrevolutionary conspiracy against Stalinist Russia came in February
1938 with the show trial of twenty-one members of the "Bloc of Rightists and Trotskyites," chief among them Bukharin, Rykov, and
Yagoda, accused of an expanded version of what had become the usual
catalogue of Trotskyite crimes: espionage, wrecking, terrorism, and
preparations for foreign invasion, the dismemberment of the U.S.S.R.,
the overthrow of the Soviet system, and the restoration of capitalism.
Previously the Trotskyites had been allegedly conspiring only with the
German and Japanese secret services; now they were accused of working for British and Polish intelligence as well. Trotsky himself was
revealed as a German agent since 1921 and a British agent since 1926.
Yagoda had for some time been "surrounded as with flies with German,
Japanese and Polish spies."

      The last show trial had disclosed that Trotsky and the assorted
counterrevolutionaries under his leadership had promised the Ukraine
to Germany and the Maritime Provinces and Amur region to Japan.
In February 1938 it was revealed that they had also promised Byelorussia to Poland and Uzbekistan to Britain. Trotskyite terrorism too
turned out to be even more devious and extensive than previously
supposed. Not content with assisting in Kirov's assassination, Yagoda
had pioneered "wrecking methods of medicine" and arranged the poisoning of his predecessor Menzhinsky, the great writer Maxim Gorky,
and the chairman of the State Planning Commission V. V. Kuybyshev.
He had also begun to poison Yezhov himself but had been caught in
the nick of time.[101]

      The most important novelty in the conspiracy theory unveiled
at the trial of the "Bloc of Rightists and Trotskyites" was the heightened emphasis given to the role of Western governments and their
intelligence services. The Trotskyites were no longer the mere auxiliar-
ies of foreign secret services but their "slaves," "bondmen of their
masters." The state procurator, Andrei Vyshinsky, declared during his
peroration:

      The "Block of Rightists and Trotskyites" is no political
      grouping; it is a gang of spies, of agents of foreign intelligence
      services. This has been proved fully and incontestably.

Herein lies the enormous social, political and historical significance of the present trial.

Ever since the Shakhty trial ten years before, the role of foreign intelligence services in plotting the overthrow of the Soviet system had loomed steadily larger in Stalinist and NKVD conspiracy theory. The final version of that conspiracy theory backdated the dominant role played by "the devilish work of the foreign intelligence services" in all counterrevolutionary activity to the origins of the Soviet state:

> The entire history of bourgeois counterrevolution in the U.S.S.R. is linked up with the active attempts of the most reactionary circles of the international bourgeoisie to overthrow the power of the Soviets. There has not been a single more or less serious plot against the Soviet power in the U.S.S.R. without the direct and most active participation of foreign capitalists and military cliques.[102]

Among those who attended the trial of the "Bloc of Rightists and Trotskyites" was Sir Fitzroy Maclean, then a young British diplomat at the Moscow embassy. At one point during the trial a clumsily maneuvered arc light illuminated a private box at the back of the courtroom and Maclean saw, to his astonishment, the drooping mustache and yellowish complexion of Stalin himself.[103] Though Stalin did not, of course, supervise every detail of the Terror or even know the names of most of its victims, his was nonetheless the directing hand. Gordievsky's father and other KGB veterans told him how from the death of Kirov onward Stalin used to receive late each evening first Yagoda, then Yezhov. The nightly meetings with Yezhov not uncommonly lasted from 10 P.M. to 2 A.M.[104] Stalin took an obsessional personal interest not merely in the persecution of the major figures in the Party, NKVD, and armed services, but also in the numbers of more humble "enemies of the people" being unmasked. His most trusted subordinates, such as Lazar Kaganovich, toured the provinces to make sure that local quotas for such "unmaskings" were being fulfilled or overfulfilled.

While the Great Terror was at its height Stalin was never satisfied with the numbers reported to him. The head of the militia in the Ivanovo region, Mikhail Shreider, later recalled one such visit of inspection by Kaganovich in 1937. Throughout his stay Kaganovich telephoned Stalin several times a day to report on the numbers of arrests. Though the local NKVD was already using what Shreider called "severe tortures" to extract confessions from imaginary enemies of the people, after each phone call Kaganovich insisted on speedier confessions. On one occasion Kaganovich phoned Stalin in Shreider's presence to report the latest number of arrests. Stalin, as usual, was dissatisfied, and Shreider heard Kaganovich repeating over and over again:

> "Will do, comrade Stalin. I'll press on the NKVD depart-ment heads not to be too liberal and to increase to the maxi-mum identification of enemies of the people."[105]

"Enemies of the people" with foreign connections were likely to have to confess that they were spies as well. Many years later Gordievsky still occasionally came across their files in the KGB archives. One fairly typical example that lodged in his memory early in his career was the file on a German Communist named Sturm, who had wandered half starved from the Ukraine to the Volga in 1937. The NKVD picked him up in Kuybyshev begging for bread. After a few interrogations, he wearily confessed to being a German spy and was shot.[106]

The Terror inevitably acquired a momentum of its own. The requirement that imaginary "enemies of the people" identify their equally imaginary collaborators, as well as the more general suspicion that surrounded their friends and relatives, built into the pattern of arrests in 1937–38 something approaching a geometrical progression. The prime mover of the Terror and the man most concerned to make it as pervasive as possible, however, was Stalin himself. Stalin never had any compunction in allowing the manufacture of whatever evidence was necessary to give the show trials the maximum dramatic effect. But both he and Yezhov undoubtedly believed in the vast conspiracy theory on which the trials were based. Underlying the preposterous claims of a combined assault by imperialist secret services and their Trotskyite hirelings was an impeccable Leninist logic. In an open letter published during the trial of the "Bloc of Rightists and Trotskyites," Stalin justi-fied his conspiracy theory in Lenin's own words:

> We are living not only in a State, but in a system of States, and the existence of the Soviet Republic side by side with imperialist States is in the long run unthinkable. In the end

either one or the other will triumph. But until that end comes, a series of the most terrible clashes between the Soviet Republic and bourgeois States is unavoidable. . . . We must remember that we are always within a hairsbreadth of invasion.

It was, claimed Stalin, "absurd and stupid" to suppose that the U.S.S.R.'s external enemies would not attack whenever they saw a favorable opportunity: "This could only be thought by blind braggarts or concealed enemies of the people."[107] Those who disagreed with Stalin's conspiratorial world view were thus identified as "enemies of the people." Starting from Leninist premises, it was impossible for the imperialists not to attempt the overthrow of the world's only worker-peasant state. And if they were plotting its overthrow, it was barely conceivable that their intelligence services were not hard at work trying to subvert it. To denounce the basis, if not the detail, of Stalin's conspiracy theory it was necessary to attack Leninism itself.

As Lenin's reaction to the "Lockhart plot" twenty years earlier had shown, his manichean vision of a world divided between bourgeois darkness and Bolshevik light rendered him continuously susceptible to attacks of conspiracy theory. A collection of documents published to mark "the glorious twentieth anniversary of the Cheka-OGPU-NKVD" in December 1937 quoted Lenin's own warnings against the counterrevolutionaries' "organized treachery in our rear," "sabotage of food production which threatens millions of people with starvation," and "extensive organization for espionage." Lenin called for "urgent measures" to uncover the "countless conspiracies" hatched by an unholy alliance of White Russian émigrés and foreign imperialists: "We have no answer other than the answer of an organization [the Cheka] which knows the conspirator's every step and which would not try to reason but would punish immediately."[108] But Lenin would never have succumbed to the wilder excesses of Stalinist wrecker mania and spy fever. He described it as "laughable to say that foreigners who will be assigned to administer certain trade concessions are dangerous or that we will not be able to keep an eye on them."[109] Almost all the charges at the Stalinist show trials would have been inconceivable in Lenin's lifetime.

Stalin's Russia was more susceptible to conspiracy theory than Lenin's for two reasons. First, twenty years of socialism in one country and capitalist encirclement had bred an acute sense of insecurity. The early hopes of exporting the Revolution abroad had given way to a preoccupation with the problems of defending the Revolution at home. "Help from the international proletariat," said Stalin in his open letter of February 1938, "must be combined with our work to strengthen the defenses of our country, to strengthen the Red Army and Navy, to mobilize the entire country for the fight against military attack and against attempts to restore bourgeois relations."[110]

The spy mania of the Stalin years also derived from what Khrushchev called Stalin's own "sickly suspicious" personality. "Everywhere and in everything he saw 'enemies,' 'two-facers' and 'spies.' "[111] The widow of Aleksandr ("Sasha") Kosarev, secretary of Komsomol, later recalled her husband's final meeting with Stalin at a Kremlin banquet:

> Stalin not only clinked his glass but embraced and kissed him. Returning to his seat, Sasha, pale and agitated, said to me "Let's go home." When we left, I asked him why he was so upset. He replied: "When Stalin kissed me, he said in my ear, 'If you're a traitor, I'll kill you.' "

Kosarev was shot a few months later.[112] The greatest Soviet psychologist of the interwar period, Vladimir Bechterev, concluded as early as 1929 that Stalin was a paranoid schizophrenic, and appears to have paid with his life for his diagnosis. A conference of leading Soviet psychiatrists in 1989, however, rejected that diagnosis as too simple.[113] Unlike truly paranoid personalities Stalin retained a capacity for cool, if devious, calculation and an instinctive sense of timing. But it is difficult not to detect at least a paranoid strain in Stalin's "sickly suspicious" personality.

Yezhov inhabited the same conspiratorial universe as Stalin himself. In private as well as in public he insisted that foreign intelligence services had mounted "a filthy network of intrigue in which enemies of all flags had combined as one."[114] He told a meeting of senior NKVD officers that there were bound to be "some innocent victims" in "the fight against fascist agents": "Better than ten innocent people should suffer than one spy get away."[115] Yezhov lived in continual fear of assassination from traitors within the NKVD. In order to reach his heavily guarded office in the Lubyanka, even NKVD officers had to take the elevator to the fifth floor, walk through a series of long corridors, go down a staircase to the first floor, walk along more corridors, and take another elevator to Yezhov's secretariat on the third floor. Their papers were checked at frequent intervals along the circuitous route.[116]

Yezhov may well have believed, as was alleged at the trial of the "Bloc of Rightists and Trotskyites," that Yagoda had tried to poison him. Stalin too took elaborate precautions against poison plots. He had a female servant whose sole function was to make tea from sealed packets kept in a locked cabinet opened only in the presence of an NKVD security guard. One day the guard discovered a broken seal and the tea maker was carted off to the Lubyanka.[117]

Most of the Soviet population accepted the official doctrine that they were threatened by a major conspiracy of spies and wreckers in the pay of foreign secret services. At every factory NKVD officers lectured workers on the danger from imperialist agents in their midst. Almost every film, comedies included, contained its obligatory quota of spies. Many of the imaginary spies and wreckers apprehended by the NKVD, particularly at the beginning of the Yezhovshchina, believed that though they themselves were the victim of some terrible mistake ("If only Stalin knew!"), other enemies of the people were guilty as charged. Old inhabitants of the gulag became so used to hearing this complaint from new arrivals that they accused them all of playing the same gramophone record.[118] Even those who grasped the bogus nature of the show-trial confessions commonly believed that the defendants were "objectively guilty." Party militants often took every word literally. Evgenia Ginsburg records that a woman she knew exclaimed when the NKVD came to arrest her husband in 1937:

> "So he lied to me? So he was really against the Party all the time."
>
> With an amused grin the agent said: "Better get his things together."
>
> But she refused to do this for an enemy of the Party, and when her husband went to his sleeping child's cot to kiss him good-bye she barred his way.
>
> "My child has no father."[119]

Such simple-minded fanaticism is less baffling than the credulity of many well-educated foreign observers. The American ambassador Joseph Davies reported to the State Department that the show trials had provided "proof . . . beyond reasonable doubt to justify the verdict of

guilty of treason." The award-winning *New York Times* correspondent
Walter Duranty concluded that "The future historian will probably
accept the Stalinist version." Sir Bernard Pares, then Britain's best-
known Russian historian, found the verbatim reports of the show trials
"impressive": "The plea that Stalin acted first to disrupt a potential fifth
column . . . is by no means unwarranted." The Webbs thought the
defendants were "behaving naturally and sensibly, as Englishmen
would were they not virtually compelled by their highly artificial legal
system to go through a routine which is useful to the accused only when
there is some doubt as to the facts or as to the guilt or innocence of the
conduct in question."[120] Such gullibility did not die with Stalin.

For many in the NKVD who survived the Terror or were
recruited to replace their liquidated predecessors, the primary aim was
simply to survive. Their minds numbed or brutalized by their work,
they preferred not to reflect deeply on the purpose of the horrors they
were perpetrating. Most, however, accepted the reality of the imaginary
conspiracy they were fighting. Mikhail Gorokhov, an engineer who
joined the NKVD in 1938, found most of the new recruits "Party
members, simple boys, who have been told that 'enemies of the Socialist
society' try to wreck our Soviet system and kill our leaders and that
these wreckers must be exterminated." Early in their training he and
his fellow recruits watched impassively the torture of a peasant, believing it essential to uncover his part in the conspiracy.[121] The future
defector Viktor Kravchenko was told by an old childhood friend in the
NKVD that the Terror had been "absolutely necessary . . . to free the
country from traitors and spies": "If you fell into our hands, it certainly
wouldn't be without reason."[122]

The old guard in the NKVD were less naïve. That, no doubt,
helps to explain why so many of them were liquidated. But even the
survivors of the Dzerzhinsky era became confused about the reality of
the "spies" and "wreckers" they were ordered to unmask. The widow
of the murdered NKVD defector Ignace Poretsky (alias Ignace Reiss)
remembered Abram Slutsky, head of INO from 1934 to 1938, as "a
likeable and mild-mannered man" who did his best to save some of the
victims of the Terror. But:

> Slutsky was a person of many contradictions. We knew of
> cases, after 1936, when he interceded courageously to save
> someone from arrest, and he would weep while telling of the
> interrogation of some of the defendants at the trials and

bemoan the fate of their families; yet in the same breath he could denounce them as "Trotskyite fascists."[123]

The Stalinist witch hunt against spies and wreckers faced Slutsky and most who thought like him in the NKVD with an insoluble dilemma. They knew that most of the victims of the Yezhovshchina were innocent. But as good Leninists they were bound to accept that Soviet Russia was menaced with a permanent conspiracy by world capitalism, whose secret services were necessarily seeking to subvert it. In reality the only dangerous anti-Soviet conspiracies organized by foreign intelligence services during the 1930s were the attempts by Germany and Japan to exploit the paranoia of Stalin and the NKVD by encouraging them to believe in yet more imaginary conspiracies. The intelligence service that did most damage in prewar Russia was the NKVD itself. Slutsky and the old guard in INO, though they grasped some of what was going on, could do little about it. They were intellectually as well as physically powerless: trapped by their ideology inside a conspiratorial universe from which, without renouncing Leninism, there was no escape.

5

"Enemies of the People" Abroad (1929–40)

The secret history of the KGB First Chief Directorate, prepared in 1980 to celebrate the sixtieth anniversary of the founding of INO, records that until the early 1930s the OGPU's main foreign target remained the White Guard movement centered on the headquarters of the ROVS (Russian Combined Services Union) in Paris.[1] The chief priority of the OGPU residency established in Paris at the beginning of 1925, following French diplomatic recognition of the Soviet Union, was the surveillance of, and the development of "active measures" against, the ROVS. The ROVS was an increasingly soft target. Its head, General Kutepov, calculated that though 90 percent of the White Russian diaspora of about two million remained "healthy patriots," the remaining 10 percent had become disillusioned. On Kutepov's own figures, 30,000 of the 300,000 White Russians in France, demoralized by homesickness, the privations of exile, and concern for relatives in the Soviet Union, had become possible targets for the OGPU.

But, despite the lesson of the Trust, Kutepov was curiously naïve about the danger of Soviet penetration of his entourage. There were OGPU agents even within the White Guard high command, among them Admiral Krylov, who seems to have hoped to resume his career in the Soviet navy; General Monkevitz, who staged a fake suicide

150

in November 1926 to conceal his flight to the Soviet Union; and Kutepov's own former chief of staff during the Civil War, General Steifon.[2]

OGPU penetration was used not merely for intelligence gathering but also for destabilizing the White Russian community. The revelation of the Trust deception was arranged so as to cause maximum damage to Kutepov's credibility. Grand Duke Nicholas, the Tsar's cousin, confessed to his intimates his "profound disappointment" with Kutepov. General Wrangel urged him to abandon all attempts to organize a secret anti-Bolshevik conspiracy within the Soviet Union. But Kutepov was not to be dissuaded. Despite his humiliation at the hands of the Trust, his naïveté continued to make him easy prey for OGPU agents provocateurs. He told the former White General Denikin in November 1929: "Great movements are spreading across Russia. Never have so many people come from over there to see me and ask me to collaborate with their clandestine organizations." At Kutepov's request, his former chief of staff Steifon made at least two secret trips to Russia to meet the imaginary conspirators, and returned full of OGPU-inspired optimism, which he transmitted to Kutepov.[3]

Kutepov was a tragicomic figure. Though known to his admirers as "the iron general," he more closely fits the description once applied to the last Tsarist commander-in-chief, General Kornilov: "a man with the heart of a lion and the brains of a sheep." The OGPU would have been well advised to allow him to remain in Paris, alternately deceiving and discrediting him to add to the demoralization of the White Russian diaspora. But neither the Cheka nor any of its successors has ever found it possible to take a sober and objective view of the real strength of counterrevolutionary forces. In the Stalin era the significance of all forms of counterrevolution was wildly exaggerated. Even Kutepov was perceived as such a potential menace at the head of the ROVS that he had to be liquidated. Since, unlike Savinkov and Reilly, he refused to be lured back to the Soviet Union, the OGPU arranged to kidnap him instead. The decision to do so was made on the orders of Stalin himself.[4]

The OGPU officer sent from Moscow to organize Kutepov's kidnap, Sergei Puzitsky, had taken part in both the Sindikat and Trust deceptions. The kidnap took place shortly before eleven o'clock on the morning of Sunday, January 26, 1930, in the middle of a Paris street in the seventh arrondissement. The trap seems to have been sprung by Kutepov's former chief of staff, General Steifon, who told him that two representatives from the Soviet Union of the anti-Bolshevik underground (in reality the OGPU resident in Paris, Nikolai Kuzmin, and a leading OGPU illegal, Andrei Fikhner) needed to see him urgently and were waiting in a taxi. The OGPU was also assisted by a Communist Paris policeman so that if any bystander saw Kutepov being bundled into a taxi (which one did), the kidnap would be mistaken for a police arrest (which it was).

Early in the afternoon of January 26 Steifon called at Kutepov's flat and asked to see the general. On being told by his wife that he had failed to return from a memorial service, Steifon successfully dissuaded her from calling the police for several hours by first offering various possible explanations for the general's absence and then suggesting inquiries within the White Russian community. Meanwhile the car containing Kutepov was speeding with an escort toward the Channel coast. Eyewitnesses, later interviewed by the Sûreté, saw him being bundled on board a Soviet steamer. The kidnap, however, went wrong. The combination of the anesthetic used to overpower Kutepov and the general's weak heart proved fatal. He died from a heart attack a hundred miles from the Soviet port of Novorossilsk. The OGPU interrogation of Kutepov, designed to lay bare the remaining secrets of White Guard conspiracies against the Soviet regime, thus never took place.[5]

Soon after Kutepov's abduction, the OGPU recruited another émigré general in Paris, Nikolai Skoblin, former commander of a White division in the Civil War.[6] Skoblin's wife, the homesick émigré singer Nadezhda Plevitskaya, popularly known as the "Kursk nightingale," had been in touch with the OGPU for some years. In the mid-1920s she had sought permission to return to the Soviet Union. Dzerzhinsky refused. She was, he believed, potentially too valuable among the émigrés.

In the weeks following the kidnap General Skoblin and Nadezhda Plevitskaya called almost daily on Kutepov's wife to offer sympathy and seek the latest news on the investigation into his disappearance. "Skoblin and his wife always used to tell me that my husband was still alive," Madame Kutepov later recalled. "When I expressed surprise at their certainty, Plevitskaya told me she had had a dream which confirmed it." Plevitskaya's skill in dissembling, combined with her ability to tug at émigré heart strings by her rendering of "Ah, Mother Russia, You Are Covered Deep in Snow" and other sentimental songs and ballads, gave both her and Skoblin the ability to penetrate White Russian communities all over Europe.[7]

For many years the OGPU and its successors indignantly disclaimed any part in Kutepov's kidnap. The truth was finally admitted almost casually in 1965 in a KGB obituary notice on the kidnap organizer:

Commissar of State Security Sergei Vasilyevich Puzitsky took part in the Civil War, was an ardent Bolshevik-Leninist and a pupil of F. E. Dzerzhinsky. Not only did he participate in the capture of the bandit Savinkov and in the destruction of . . . the "Trust," but he carried out a brilliant operation in the arrest of Kutepov and a number of White Guard organizers and inspirers of foreign military intervention in the Civil War. S. V. Puzitsky was twice awarded the Order of the Red Banner and received Chekist decorations.[8]

Kutepov's successor at the head of the ROVS, General Yevgeni Karlovich Miller, was no less naïve. Despite a beard and military mustache, his round reddish face, blue eyes, and cheerful expression gave him a genial rather than imposing appearance. One of his first acts as president was to place most of the ROVS funds in the hands of a confidence trickster named Ivar Kreuger. By the time Kreuger blew his brains out in March 1932, the funds had disappeared. The previous summer, even before the Kreuger scandal became known, Denikin had written morosely to a friend: "The ROVS has sunk into torpor. It no longer gives any sign of life other than constant internal intrigues. A real mess!" The most serious of these internal intrigues was led by General Shatilov, who, without prompting by the OGPU, engaged in a series of plots to undermine Miller's authority and challenged two other White generals to duels. Though both duels were called off, the French government threatened to withdraw his residence permit. In the end Shatilov was allowed to remain but only on condition he stayed strictly out of politics. He left the ROVS and—like a number of other Tsarist notables in reduced circumstances—took up work as a taxi driver.[9]

Thanks to Miller's inept leadership and Shatilov's intrigues, the ROVS succeeded in destabilizing itself without the need for OGPU assistance. The OGPU, however, accelerated its decline. The most influential OGPU mole within the ROVS remained General Skoblin. In 1933 Miller put him in charge of "secret work in Finland." A year later, with the help of Finnish intelligence, Skoblin smuggled two ROVS agents across the Finnish-Soviet border. Both were quickly intercepted by the NKVD but produced pistols from their pockets and made a remarkable escape back to Finland. The Finns refused all further cooperation in frontier crossings, strongly hinting that they possessed intelligence identifying Skoblin as an NKVD agent. Miller indignantly defended him as "a constant victim of intrigues and vicious slanderers," and appointed Skoblin "head of foreign counterespionage."[10]

In 1934 Miller's financial losses forced him to move the ROVS headquarters to less expensive premises. A Russian émigré businessman named Sergei Tretyakov offered him a ground-floor apartment at a modest rate. Unknown to Miller, Tretyakov was an NKVD agent code-named Ivanov. By the time Miller moved into the new ROVS headquarters, it had been fitted with an elaborate set of NKVD listening devices. For the next few years Tretyakov spent several hours a day in rooms immediately above the headquarters, transcribing conversations between Miller and his subordinates. His devotion to duty was commended in an exchange of NKVD telegrams late in 1934:

Paris to Center:

We consider it necessary to note Ivanov's conscientiousness and devotion to his work. On the night of November 23 he fell seriously ill, but in spite of his illness he spent all day taking down information, as you can see from the notes.

Center to Paris:

Give Ivanov a grant for medical treatment, in view of his conscientious and devoted work. Decide on the sum yourself, but it should not exceed one month's salary.[11]

The secret history of the First Chief Directorate concludes that by 1933 Leon Trotsky had replaced Miller and the ROVS as its chief overseas target.[12] Throughout his eleven and a half years of exile (in Turkey from the beginning of 1929 to the summer of 1933, in France from the summer of 1933 to the summer of 1935, in Norway from the summer of 1935 until the end of 1936, in Mexico from January 1937 until his assassination in August 1940) Trotsky's entourage, like Miller's, was successfully penetrated by the OGPU and NKVD. The most successful of the early OGPU penetration agents were the Sobolevicius brothers, sons of a rich Jewish merchant in Lithuania, later better known as Jack

Soble and Dr. Richard Soblen. For three years from the spring of 1929 both brothers were among Trotsky's closest confidants. They had access to the codes, secret inks, and cover addresses used by Trotsky to correspond secretly with his supporters in the Soviet Union, and Trotsky entrusted much of the correspondence to them—all of it betrayed, along with Trotsky's Soviet supporters, to the OGPU. The Sobolevicius brothers also spent much time, again for the benefit of the OGPU, visiting Trotsky's supporters in France and Germany. Both reemerged during the Second World War as Soviet agents in the United States.[13]

The only difficult moment in the penetration of Trotsky's entourage during his Turkish exile occurred in the summer of 1929. The OGPU learned, probably from one of its penetration agents, that Trotsky had received a secret visit from a sympathizer within OGPU ranks. The sympathizer was Yakov Blyumkin, who as a young LSR in the Cheka in 1918 had helped assassinate Count Mirbach, the German ambassador, in defiance of Dzerzhinsky's orders. He had subsequently been rehabilitated and had risen to become OGPU "illegal resident" in Istanbul. Blyumkin agreed to transmit a message from Trotsky to Radek and, according to the KGB version of events, "discussed methods for setting up illegal contact with the Trotskyite underground in Moscow."

Trilisser did not order Blyumkin's immediate arrest. Instead, probably in consultation with Yagoda, he ordered an attractive OGPU agent, Lisa Gorskaya, to "abandon bourgeois prejudices," seduce Blyumkin, discover the full extent of his conspiracy with Trotsky, and ensure that he returned to Moscow. At the Turkish end, the operation was handled by the "legal" OGPU resident, Nahum (Leonid) Aleksandrovich Eitingon (then using the alias Nahumov), later to achieve fame within the KGB as the organizer of Trotsky's assassination.[14] When Blyumkin was arrested in Moscow a few weeks later in Gorskaya's company, he realized, too late, that she had been used as an agent provocateur. "Lisa," he said, "you have betrayed me!" Blyumkin became the first Bolshevik to be shot for sympathizing with the opposition. According to Orlov, "He went courageously to his execution, and when the fatal shot was about to be fired, he shouted: 'Long live Trotsky!' " Soon afterward Gorskaya married the OGPU resident in Berlin (and later in Washington), Vasili Mikhailovich Zarubin.[15]

Trotsky's Russian supporters dwindled rapidly during his Turkish exile. Convinced that, as Trotsky himself had said in 1924,

"One cannot be right against the Party,"[16] most of the Left Opposition capitulated to the Stalinist line. One report reaching Trotsky (and doubtless the OGPU as well) at the end of 1929 put the number of his supporters in exile and in prison at no more than a thousand. Trotsky wrote defiantly to a group of Soviet disciples: "Let there remain in exile not 350 people faithful to their banner, but only 35. Let there remain even three—the banner will remain." Tourists and sympathizers in Western Communist parties traveling to the Soviet Union continued, mostly under OGPU surveillance, to act as couriers between Trotsky and the declining band of Russian faithful. Letters, often from the gulag, written on rough sheets of wrapping paper, sometimes on cigarette paper, hidden or disguised in a variety of ingenious ways, trickled through to him in Turkey for several years. On one occasion a matchbox arrived on his desk crammed with a complete political thesis penned in minuscule script. Then at the end of 1932, the trickle stopped.[17]

Trotsky's Western supporters were never numerous and always divided. Though Trotskyists have an incurable tendency to fragment ("Where there are two Trotskyists, there are three tendencies"), their fragmentation during the 1930s was cleverly accelerated and embittered by OGPU agents provocateurs. The Sobolevicius brothers succeeded in playing off the prominent Austrian Trotskyist Kurt Landau against Trotsky himself with such success that Landau was expelled from the movement. Another OGPU agent provocateur who won Trotsky's confidence, Henri Lacroix, suddenly came out with the demoralizing claim in March 1933 that in Spain "the [Trotskyist] Opposition gets no support and is neither known nor understood, while the support of the workers goes to the U.S.S.R. and to Communism in general, embodied in the Spanish Communist Party."[18]

On any objective assessment, Stalin should have found the evidence, regularly reported to him by the OGPU, of dwindling support and internal bickering within the penetrated Trotskyist movement deeply reassuring. But Stalin was incapable of objective assessment. Trotsky became an obsession that dominated many of his waking hours and interfered with sleep at night. Isaac Deutscher concludes:

> The frenzy with which [Stalin] pursued the feud, making it
> the paramount preoccupation of international communism
> as well as of the Soviet Union and subordinating to it all
> political, tactical, intellectual and other interests, beggars

description: there is in the whole of history hardly another case in which such immense resources of power and propaganda were employed against a single individual.[19]

Had Stalin been pursuing the real Trotsky, his obsession would be inexplicable. But the Trotsky with whom Stalin was obsessed was a mythical figure constructed by Stalin's "sickly suspicious" imagination, who bore increasingly little resemblance to the Trotsky whom he had sent into exile. As the menace of the mythical Trotsky loomed ever larger in Stalin's mind, so the power and influence of the real Trotsky steadily declined. Trotsky could not even find a secure European headquarters from which to rally Communist opposition. He left Turkey in search of a new base in November 1932 but was compelled to return four weeks later, having failed to find any government willing to allow him more than a transit visa. He was eventually allowed to move to France in the summer of 1933 but was not permitted to live in Paris, was subjected to a series of restrictions and finally expelled in the summer of 1935. From France Trotsky moved to Norway, where his political activity was once again restricted, before he was expelled, this time to Mexico, at the end of 1936.[20]

The chief organizer of the Trotskyite movement for most of the 1930s was not Trotsky himself but his son, Lev Sedov, who left Turkey for Berlin in 1931 and moved to Paris two years later after the rise to power of Adolf Hitler. It was Sedov who, until his death in 1938, organized publication of the *Bulletin of the Opposition (Biulletin Oppozitsii)* and maintained contact with Trotsky's scattered followers.[21] Sedov's entourage, like his father's, was penetrated by the OGPU and the NKVD. From 1934 until his death his closest confidant and collaborator was an NKVD agent, the Russian-born anthropologist Mark Zborowski (*alias* Étienne), who helped him publish the *Bulletin* and try to keep in contact with what opposition remained in Russia. Sedov trusted Zborowski so completely that he gave him the key to his letter box, allowed him to collect his mail, and kept Trotsky's most confidential files and archives in his house.[22]

Under Menzhinsky and Yagoda, OGPU and NKVD foreign operations against Trotsky and his followers were limited to surveillance, penetration, and destabilization. Under Yezhov the NKVD embarked on a policy of liquidation of the Trotskyite leadership. In December 1936 Yezhov set up an Administration of Special Tasks under his own personal direction, with "mobile groups" to carry out assassinations abroad ordered by Stalin.[23] Its main field of action during the next two years was Spain.

The Soviet government was slow to react to the outbreak of the Spanish Civil War in July 1936, wrongly believing that the Republican government would quickly defeat the rebellion by the Nationalist forces of General Francisco Franco. When the experienced diplomat Marcel Rosenberg eventually arrived as Soviet ambassador on August 27, however, he was accompanied by a large retinue, including as head of a Soviet military mission the former head of military intelligence, General Jan Berzin, a tall, gray-haired, taciturn man, ironically sometimes mistaken for an Englishman. Other Soviet military advisers included Generals Goriev and Kulik and the future Marshals Malinovsky, Rokossovsky, and Konev. Red Army officers fought in the Civil War under a variety of disguises: among them General Lazar Stern, *alias* General Emilio Kleber, provided by the NKVD with a Canadian passport and a "legend" to match, who won worldwide fame as the "Saviour of Madrid" at the end of 1936; General Mate Zalka, *alias* Lukacs, a former Hungarian novelist who had joined the Red Army and become probably the most popular commander in the International Brigades; General Janos Galicz, *alias* Gall, also of Hungarian origin and probably the least popular of the International Brigade commanders; General Dmitri Pavlov, *alias* Pablo, perhaps the ablest of the Republican tank commanders; and General Karol Swierczewski, *alias* Walter, a Red Army officer of Polish origin, later vice-minister of defense in the post–World War II Polish Communist government.[24]

There was an equally powerful, though far less visible, NKVD presence in Republican Spain, headed by the future defector Aleksandr Orlov, who arrived in September 1936 with the principal aim of securing the victory of Stalinism over the Marxist heresies that assailed it.[25] The ECCI informed the Spanish Communist Party in December:

> Whatever happens, the final destruction of the Trotskyists must be achieved, exposing them to the masses as a fascist secret service carrying out provocations in the service of Hitler and General Franco, attempting to split the Popular Front, conducting a slanderous campaign against the Soviet Union, a secret service actively aiding fascism in Spain.[26]

Such sectarian bigotry was far from the minds of most of the 35,000 foreign volunteers, a majority of them Communist, who set out for Spain to join the International Brigades in defense of the Republic. For them as for most of the European left, who mistakenly believed Franco's revolt to be a conspiracy orchestrated by Hitler and Mussolini, the war was a crusade against international fascism—for many, as for the poet, W. H. Auden, the greatest emotional experience of their lives:

> What's your proposal? To build the just city? I will.
> I agree. Or is it the suicide pact, the romantic
> Death? Very well, I accept, for
> I am your choice, your decision. Yes, I am Spain.

Stalin himself caught that mood in an open letter to the Spanish Communist leadership in October: "Liberation of Spain from the yoke of the Fascist reactionaries is not the private concern of Spaniards alone, but the common cause of all progressive humanity."[27]

Stalin's own main concern, however, was Trotskyite infiltration rather than the fascist menace. At the main recruiting center for the International Brigades in Paris, non-Party volunteers were usually questioned by NKVD officers, who concealed their identities. Most volunteers with passports were asked to surrender them on arrival in Spain; they were then forwarded to Moscow Center by diplomatic bag. The NKVD was particularly pleased with a haul of two thousand United States passports later used by its illegals.[28]

The International Brigades base in Albacete was controlled by a Comintern political directorate headed by the French representative on the ECCI, André Marty, who for some years had been working for Soviet military intelligence, and who collaborated enthusiastically in the NKVD's war on Trotskyism. No non-Russian Communist was more obsessed than Marty with rooting out anti-Stalinist heresy. With Marty came a high-powered contingent of Comintern functionaries. Some, like his Italian deputies, Luigi Longo (*alias* Gallo) and Giuseppe de Vittorio (*alias* Nicolette), loathed Marty's sectarian fanaticism. Others were doctrinaire Stalinists in the Marty mold, among them the future East German leader Walter Ulbricht, who ran an NKVD unit tracking down German, Austrian, and Swiss "Trotskyists" in the International Brigades.[29]

The support for the Republicans by the volunteers of the International Brigades could not equal the aid to the Nationalists from Nazi Germany and Fascist Italy. Though well aware that Franco was at heart a traditionalist rather than a fascist, Hitler looked on Spain as a suitable battleground on which to rehearse the techniques of Blitzkrieg later used to devastating effect in the early years of the Second World War. Hitler's prompt assistance in the summer of 1936 saved the military rebellion from early defeat and set Franco on the path to ultimate victory.[30]

The Republicans suffered from one further serious disadvantage. While the Nationalists were united, they were divided. Though the Russians did not cause the divisions, they turned them into a civil war within the Civil War. By the spring of 1937 Stalin's struggle against Trotskyism was in danger of overshadowing the war against Franco. Stalin feared that the Partido Obrero de Unificación Marxista (POUM), which had Trotskyite sympathies though it was sharply criticized by Trotsky himself, might give the great heretic a Spanish base. Its co-founder in 1935, Andreu Nin, who had once been Trotsky's private secretary in Moscow, was minister of justice in the Catalán government until ousted by the Communists in December 1936. In May 1937 the Spanish Communists, assisted by the NKVD, embarked on POUM's destruction. Slutsky, the head of INO, informed NKVD residents: "Our whole attention is focused on Catalonia and on our merciless fight against the Trotskyite bandits, the Fascists and the POUM."[31]

In June Nin was arrested, brutally tortured, then flayed alive when he refused to confess to imaginary crimes. The Communists tried unsuccessfully to conceal his death by pretending that Nin had been seized by a Nazi snatch squad.[32] Soon afterward, another of Trotsky's former secretaries, Irwin Wolf, who had worked for him during his Norwegian exile, was kidnapped in Barcelona and liquidated by the NKVD.[33] Among others of POUM's international sympathizers who died in suspicious circumstances were Trotsky's former supporter Kurt Landau; Marc Rhein, son of the old Menshevik leader Rafael Abramovich; José Robles, a former lecturer at Johns Hopkins University in the United States; and the journalist Bob Smilie, son of the English miners' leader. Many of the POUM rank and file were illegally shot after summary Communist court-martials. The remnants of the leadership were arrested in June 1937. Their lawyer Benito Pabón became so terrified of assassination that he fled to the Philippines.[34]

Dr. Juan Negrín, who became Republican prime minister in

May 1937, was aware of some of the horrors perpetrated by the NKVD.[35] But he was also astoundingly naïve. At the end of the war, when the Nationalists displayed the private prisons built by the NKVD-dominated Servicio de Investigación Militar (SIM), Negrín dismissed them as bogus fascist propaganda. Ten years later he admitted he had been deceived.[36]

While the NKVD and their SIM collaborators disposed of POUM supporters as discreetly as possible, Stalin's favorite Frenchman, André Marty, orchestrated a public witch hunt against Trotskyite treachery. "To Marty," wrote one of the French Communists who worked for him, "the enemy was more inside the International Brigades and Loyalist territory than on the other side of the lines." All breaches of military discipline were, in his view, part of a vast Trotskyite plot to "split and demoralize the International Brigades." His reputation as "the butcher of Albacete" led to his being summoned back to Paris to explain himself to the French Communist leadership. Marty freely admitted ordering the execution of five hundred members of the International Brigades. All, he declared, had committed "all sorts of crime" and "undertaken espionage in favor of Franco." Ernest Hemingway, for all his sympathy for the International Brigades, found Marty "crazy as a bedbug. He has a mania for shooting people. . . . He purifies more than Salvarsan."[37]

Though the NKVD "mobile groups" were most active in Spain, their operations also extended to leading Trotskyists and traitors as far afield as North America. On June 5, 1937, the disaffected American NKVD agent Juliette Stuart Poyntz left her room at the Women's Association clubhouse in Manhattan. She was never seen again. Evidence later emerged that she had been lured to her death by a former Russian lover in the NKVD, Schachno Epstein, and her body buried behind a brick wall in a Greenwich Village house.[38]

Most "wet affairs," however, were conducted on the other side of the Atlantic. In the summer of 1937, the NKVD discovered, probably from Mark Zborowski (*alias* Étienne), that one of its officers in Western Europe had made secret contact with the leading Dutch Trotskyist, Henryk Sneevliet. A "mobile group" commanded by the deputy head of INO, Mikhail Shpigelglas, a short, stout figure with fair hair and protruding eyes, was dispatched to Paris to track down and liquidate the culprit. On July 17 Walter Krivitsky, the NKVD resident in the Netherlands, was summoned to meet Shpigelglas in the Paris

Exposition grounds at Vincennes. Shpigelglas revealed that the traitor was a Soviet illegal of Polish origin in Paris named Ignace Poretsky (*alias* Ludwig, *alias* Reiss). Poretsky had just given a sealed dispatch to an NKVD officer in the Soviet trade mission for transmission to Russia, not expecting it to be opened until it arrived at Moscow Center. Shpigelglas opened it and showed Krivitsky the contents. They were ideally calculated to reinforce the paranoid fears of Stalin and Yezhov that a Trotskyist underground had penetrated the NKVD. The dispatch contained a letter to the Central Committee announcing Poretsky's defection, denouncing Stalin's crimes, and calling for "a fight without mercy against Stalinism." It concluded:

> I intend to devote my feeble forces to the cause of Lenin. I want to continue the fight, for only our victory—that of the proletarian revolution—will free humanity of capitalism and the U.S.S.R. of Stalinism. Forward to new struggles! For the [Trotskyist] Fourth International!

Six weeks later, on September 4, Poretsky's bullet-ridden body was found on a Swiss road near Lausanne. To lure him to his destruction, Shpigelglas used a friend of the Poretsky family named Gertrude Schildbach, a German Jewish Communist refugee who wrote to Poretsky to say that she urgently needed his advice. Schildbach met Poretsky and his wife at a Lausanne café. At the last moment she could not bring herself to follow NKVD instructions to hand Mrs. Poretsky a box of chocolates laced with strychnine (later recovered by the Swiss police). But Schildbach successfully lured Poretsky into a side road, where he was shot with a submachine gun at point-blank range by an NKVD assassin of Monegasque origin, Roland François Rossi (*alias* Abiate). At the last moment Poretsky realized that he was being led into a trap. When his body was found, he was clutching in his hand a clump of Schildbach's graying hair. The NKVD attempted to lay a false trail by sending an anonymous letter to the Swiss police identifying the body as that of an international arms smuggler. The plan failed. Though Rossi and Schildbach escaped, their part in the assassination was revealed to the Swiss police by Rossi's mistress. In Rossi's abandoned suitcase the police found a detailed plan of Trotsky's home in exile in Mexico.[39]

*   *   *

The next victim of the NKVD mobile groups was the head of the White Guard ROVS in Paris, General Miller. In December 1936 Slutsky, the head of INO, arrived in Paris to begin organizing Miller's kidnap. He sent a request to Krivitsky, the resident in the Netherlands, asking him to recommend two agents capable of impersonating German officers. It was only after Miller's kidnap eight months later that Krivitsky realized the purpose of the request.[40] On September 22, 1937, like Kutepov seven years earlier, Miller disappeared in broad daylight on a Paris street. Unlike Kutepov, however, he left a note with his secretary-general, General Kusonsky, to be opened if he failed to return. The note revealed that Miller had an appointment with General Skoblin at 12:30 P.M., and that they were due to meet two Germans: one the military attaché from a neighboring country, the other from the Paris embassy.

Skoblin's cover as an NKVD agent was blown. Late on the evening after the kidnap General Kedrov, vice-president of the ROVS, and General Kusonsky sent for Skoblin at ROVS headquarters and asked him where Miller had gone. Unaware of Miller's note, Skoblin replied that he had not seen him all day. When confronted with the note, Skoblin continued to deny that he had seen Miller. Kedrov and Kusonsky insisted that Skoblin accompany them to the police station. Skoblin pushed past them, ran down several flights of stairs, and escaped. His pursuers were hampered by burned-out lights on the staircase. By the time they reached the street, Skoblin had disappeared. From Paris he escaped to Spain, where he was probably liquidated by the NKVD. His wife Nadezhda Plevitskaya was brought to trial in December, found guilty of assisting in the kidnap, and sentenced to twenty years' hard labor. She died in prison in September 1940.[41]

The prosecution at Plevitskaya's trial claimed, on the basis of a Sûreté investigation, that Miller had been taken to a Soviet embassy building, killed, and his body placed in a large trunk, which was taken by Ford truck to be loaded onto a Russian freighter waiting at dockside in Le Havre. Several witnesses saw the trunk being loaded on board. Miller, however, was still alive inside the trunk, heavily drugged. Unlike Kutepov seven years earlier, he survived the voyage to Russia. Once in Moscow, he was brutally interrogated, given a secret trial and shot. Even Miller's interrogation and liquidation, however, failed to persuade the Center that the White Guards no longer posed any credible threat. When Sergei Tretyakov's transcriptions of discussions at the ROVS headquarters after Miller's abduction failed to reveal major new anti-Soviet plots, the Center concluded that Tretyakov (code-named

Ivanov) must have joined the plotters. It telegraphed to the Paris residency: "We believe that Ivanov is deceiving us, and instead of real conversations is sending us pure inventions."[42] In reality, it was the Center that was deceiving itself with further imaginary conspiracies.

Miller's kidnap had a devastating effect on the ROVS. Kusovsky was wrongly accused by some White Guards of having taken part in the plot. The ROVS moved its headquarters to Brussels, where, under its new head, General Arkhangelsky, it proved even more moribund than under Miller.[43] Belgium was also the site of the next NKVD assassination. At the beginning of 1938, after a long manhunt, the OGPU defector Georgi Agabekov, who had fled to the West nine years earlier, was murdered by a mobile group.[44] A manhunt also began for two more recent defectors: the NKVD Dutch resident Krivitsky and the great virtuoso of the Comintern front organizations, Willi Münzenberg, both of whom had refused orders to return to Moscow to certain liquidation in 1937. In July 1938 the manhunt was extended to cover the NKVD resident in Republican Spain, Aleksandr Orlov, who also refused a recall by Moscow Center.[45]

The chief "enemies of the people" hunted by the NKVD abroad, however, were the leading Trotskyists. The NKVD had three main targets: Trotsky's son and principal organizer, Lev Sedov; the secretary-designate of the Trotskyite Fourth International, which was to be founded formally in September 1938, Rudolf Klement; and finally the great heretic himself, Leon Trotsky, in exile in Mexico. Stalin's fears of Trotskyite infiltration of the NKVD were kept alive by the defection of Poretsky's friend Krivitsky in October 1937. The following month, Krivitsky obtained an introduction to Sedov in Paris through the lawyer of Poretsky's widow:

> When I saw Sedov I told him frankly that I did not come to join the Trotskyists, but rather for advice and comradeship. He received me cordially, and I saw him thereafter almost daily. I learned to admire this son of Leon Trotsky as a personality in his own right. I shall never forget the disinterested help and comfort he gave me in those days when the Stalin agents were after me. He was still very young but was exceptionally gifted—charming, well-informed, efficient. In the treason trials in Moscow it was said that he received vast sums of money from Hitler and the Mikado. I found him

living the life of a revolutionist, toiling all day in the cause of the opposition, in actual need of better food and clothing.[46]

Krivitsky, however, was unaware that Sedov's closest collaborator, Mark Zborowski (*alias* Étienne), was an NKVD agent. Stalin cannot have failed to see the most sinister significance in the "almost daily" meetings between Sedov and Krivitsky, dutifully reported by Étienne to Moscow Center. Those meetings must surely have played some part in the decision to proceed with Sedov's liquidation.

Trotsky was a demanding father with the unhappy knack of robbing all his children of their self-esteem. He did not share Krivitsky's admiration for his son's dedication and efficiency. While Sedov struggled in poverty and ill-health to publish the *Biulletin* and remain in touch with the feuding, disintegrating Trotskyite movement, his father wrote angrily from Mexico in January 1938: "I am utterly dissatisfied with the way the Biulletin is conducted, and I must pose anew the question of its transfer to New York."

Trying desperately to meet Trotsky's unreasonable demands, Sedov repeatedly postponed an operation for appendicitis, despite recurrent illness. After a severe attack on February 8, 1938, it was clear that he could delay no longer. Étienne helped to convince him that, to avoid NKVD surveillance, he must have the operation not at a French hospital but at a small private clinic run by Russian émigrés, which, though Sedov did not suspect it, was probably penetrated by NKVD agents. No sooner had Étienne ordered the ambulance than, as he later admitted, he alerted the NKVD.

Sedov was operated on the same evening. Over the next few days he seemed to make a normal recovery. For alleged security reasons, Étienne refused to reveal the address of the clinic (which he had instantly given to the NKVD) to French Trotskyites. Sedov was visited only by his wife, Jeanne, and Étienne. On February 13 he had a sudden, mysterious relapse and was found wandering, shouting deliriously, through the clinic corridors. The surgeon was so perplexed by Sedov's condition that he asked his wife whether he might have attempted to take his own life. Jeanne burst into tears and said he must have been poisoned by the NKVD.

Sedov's condition deteriorated rapidly despite repeated blood transfusions; he died in great pain on February 16 at the age of only thirty-two. A routine inquest attributed his death to postoperational complications, heart failure, and low powers of resistance. But there were serious discrepancies in the evidence. Though there is, unsurprisingly, no proof of NKVD involvement, the probability is that the NKVD was responsible.[47] The NKVD already had a sophisticated medical section, the Kamera (Chamber), probably established by Yagoda, who had trained as a pharmacist, which experimented in the use of drugs and poisons.[48] There can be no doubt that Sedov, like his father, was targeted by an NKVD mobile group, and once the NKVD lured him to a clinic which it had probably already penetrated, it is scarcely likely that it made no attempt to end his life.

Sedov's death gave the NKVD the leading place in the Trotskyist organization. Étienne took over responsibility for publishing the *Biulletin,* kept in touch with refugees from Stalinist Russia who tried to contact Trotsky, and became the main link with his European followers. He successfully embroiled Trotsky with Sneevliet, further embittered relations between Trotsky and Jeanne, and unobtrusively assisted the feuds between the Trotskyite sects. Étienne was so certain of Trotsky's confidence that he asked him how to respond to suspicions by Sneevliet and others that he was working for the NKVD. Trotsky advised him to challenge his accusers to substantiate their charges before an independent commission. Trotsky's own confidence in Étienne was unaffected.

The NKVD's next major Trotskyist target was the German Rudolf Klement, who was in charge of organization for the founding conference of Trotsky's Fourth International, due to be held later in the year. On July 13 Klement vanished mysteriously from his Paris home. About a fortnight later Trotsky received a letter ostensibly written by Klement and posted in New York, denouncing him for allying with Hitler and other imaginary crimes. Copies of the letter also reached a number of Trotsky's French supporters. Trotsky dismissed the letter, no doubt correctly, as either an NKVD forgery or a document written by Klement with an NKVD revolver held to his head. The NKVD's intention was probably for Klement simply to disappear after his fictitious denunciation. Soon after the letter's arrival, however, a headless corpse was found washed ashore on the banks of the Seine. Two French Trotskyists were able to recognize it as the body of Klement by identifying distinctive scars on the hands.[49]

The Fourth International was stillborn. Its founding "conference" opened at the home near Paris of the French Trotskyist, Alfred Rosmer, on September 3, 1938, attended by only twenty-one delegates, claiming to represent mostly minuscule Trotskyist groups in eleven countries. The "Russian section," whose authentic members had by now probably been entirely exterminated, was represented by the NKVD agent Étienne. Also on the fringes of the conference was Ramón Mercader (*alias* Jacques Mornard, *alias* Frank Jacson), lover of the American Trotskyist interpreter Sylvia Ageloff, and later to achieve fame as the assassin of Trotsky.[50]

Trotsky's biographer, Isaac Deutscher, fairly concludes that the newly founded International was "little more than a fiction," with almost negligible influence beyond the dwindling, faction-ridden ranks of Trotsky's supporters. Trotsky himself had become hopelessly out of touch in his Mexican exile. While recognizing "the disproportion between our strength today and our tasks tomorrow," he forecast confidently that "in the course of the coming ten years the program of the Fourth International will gain the adherence of millions, and these revolutionary millions will be able to storm heaven and earth."[51] Perhaps the only statesman who took Trotsky's prophecies seriously was Stalin himself. Messages from the NKVD to its residencies abroad and from the Comintern to its member parties constantly complained of the lack of energy with which Trotskyism was being rooted out. One angry telegram to Stockholm and Oslo that stuck in Gordievsky's memory was typical of many in the files. "The campaign against Trotskyist terrorist bandits," it declared, "is being pursued in your countries with intolerable passivity."[52] In Stalin's conspiratorial mental universe, Trotsky remained an even more dangerous opponent than Adolf Hitler. With Hitler Stalin foresaw, perhaps as early as the mid-1930s, the possibility of an accommodation. With Trotsky it was a struggle to the death.

After the last great prewar show trial in March 1938 the Great Terror in the Soviet Union began to wind down. In July Lavrenti Beria, head of the Transcaucasian NKVD, was made Yezhov's first deputy. By the time Yezhov was dismissed from the NKVD on December 8, effective power had already passed to Beria. Throughout the Great Terror, Stalin had avoided public responsibility. Yezhov's dismissal enabled Stalin to make him the scapegoat for such excesses of the Yezhovshchina as could be publicly admitted.[53] His successor, Beria, struck Stalin's daughter, Svetlana, as "a magnificent modern specimen of the artful courtier, the embodiment of oriental perfidy, flattery and hypocrisy."[54] He was also a man of awesome personal depravity, who used the NKVD to procure, in many cases to snatch from the Moscow streets, an endless supply of women—frequently schoolgirls—to be raped and sexually abused. Husbands or parents who complained were likely to end in the gulag.[55]

Under Beria, the Great Terror gave way to more selective terror. The manhunt for Trotsky, however, continued unabated. The real Trotsky in Mexico continued to bear little resemblance to the mythical Trotsky who haunted Stalin's diseased imagination. On May Day 1940, twenty thousand Mexican Communists marched through Mexico City with banners demanding, "Out with Trotsky!"[56] Even by the calculations of Trotsky's entourage, Mexico contained no more than thirty active Trotskyists, split into several feuding factions.[57] Despite their feuds, however, all took turns standing guard around Trotsky's home in Coyoacán.

The KGB remembers the assassination of Trotsky as one of its most important "special operations." The First Chief Directorate Memory Room, constructed in 1979, contains a portrait and eulogy of the organizer of the assassination, Nahum (Leonid) Aleksandrovich Eitingon, whose involvement in "wet affairs" went back to the liquidation of Blyumkin in 1929. Eitingon was one of the few Jews in the NKVD to survive the purges.[58] He was remembered by one of his officers as a heavily built man with a bald head, narrow forehead, and small, drilling eyes.[59] He took part in the Spanish Civil War under the alias General Kotov, advising the International Brigades on partisan warfare behind the Nationalist lines. While in Spain he became the lover of the Barcelona Communist Caridad Mercader del Río, and recruited both her and her son Ramón Mercader—the future assassin of Trotsky—as NKVD agents.[60]

As the plan of Trotsky's villa discovered by the Swiss police in Rossi's suitcase after the murder of Poretsky in 1937 showed, Trotsky was under close NKVD surveillance from the moment he arrived in Mexico.[61] The future defector Vladimir Petrov was able in 1948 to read one of the files, four or five inches thick, dealing with Trotsky's assassination. It included numerous photographs taken inside the villa, showing the guards, the fences, Trotsky with his wife, Trotsky having tea with friends, Trotsky's dog, and a variety of other subjects. Trotsky's entourage in Mexico was probably penetrated, in varying degrees and at various times, by several NKVD agents, each doubtless unaware of the others' identity. The first, according to Petrov's recollection of the file, was a woman secretary recruited during Trotsky's Norwegian exile.[62] The most influential mole within Trotsky's entourage, however, was Ramón Mercader.

Mercader had been well trained. Despite months of intensive questioning after his arrest, he revealed nothing about either his real identity (which was discovered only in 1953) or his work for the NKVD. He was highly intelligent, fluent in several languages, a trained athlete, a skilled dissembler and possessed of remarkable self-control. Sylvia Ageloff admitted that she never doubted his love for her until after Trotsky's assassination. Prolonged psychological testing showed that Mercader had an unusually rapid reaction time, an almost photographic memory, the ability to find his way in the dark, the capacity to learn quickly and remember complex instructions. He was able to take a Mauser rifle apart in the dark and reassemble it in three and three-quarter minutes.[63]

Mercader joined his Trotskyist mistress, Sylvia Ageloff, in New York in September 1939, traveling on a doctored Canadian passport obtained from a volunteer in the International Brigades, in the name of Frank Jacson (evidently an eccentric NKVD spelling of "Jackson"). In New York he made contact with the NKVD resident, Gaik Ovakimyan, through whom most instructions from Moscow Center on preparations for the assassination were forwarded.[64] Following NKVD instructions, Mercader moved to Mexico City in October, allegedly to work for an import-export agency. There he renewed contact with his mother and her lover, Nahum Eitingon. In January 1940, at Mercader's persuasion, Sylvia Ageloff followed him to Mexico City. As Eitingon had no doubt calculated, Ageloff made contact with her guru, Leon Trotsky, and spent two months doing secretarial work for him. Mercader drove her to Trotsky's villa and returned to collect her after each visit. While Ageloff was in Mexico, Mercader made no attempt to enter the villa compound but gradually became a well-known figure to the guards and won the confidence of Trotsky's French disciples Alfred and Marguerite Rosmer. Shortly after Ageloff's return to New York in March 1940, the Rosmers allowed Mercader into the villa compound for the first time.[65]

At this stage, Mercader's role was still that of penetration agent rather than assassin. The villa had been turned into a fortress defended by iron bars, electrified wires, an automatic alarm system, machine guns, a permanent ten-man police guard, and unofficial Trotskyist sentries. Mercader's main task was to provide the intelligence on the villa's defenses, inhabitants, and guards necessary to planning an armed attack. The attack itself was led by the celebrated Mexican Communist and painter, David Alfaro Siqueiros, a veteran of the International Brigades in the Spanish Civil War.

Just before four o'clock on the morning of May 23 a group of over twenty men, dressed in police and army uniforms, commanded by Siqueiros, surprised and overpowered the guard, and raked the villa bedrooms with machine-gun fire. Trotsky and his wife survived by throwing themselves beneath the bed. The police later counted seventy-three bullet holes in the bedroom wall. Siqueiros later claimed, improbably, that the object of the raid had been not to kill Trotsky but to stage a dramatic protest against his presence in Mexico. Released on bail, he escaped from Mexico with the help of the Chilean Communist poet Pablo Neruda.

Five days after the raid Mercader met Trotsky for the first time. Amiable as ever, he gave Trotsky's grandson a toy glider and showed him how to fly it. Over the next three months he paid ten visits to the villa, never overstaying his welcome, sometimes bringing small presents with him, and meeting Trotsky himself on only two or three occasions. He made perhaps two trips to see Ovakimyan in New York to complete preparations for the assassination. On August 20 Mercader arrived at the villa with an article he had written on which Trotsky agreed to give his comments. He also brought with him a dagger sewn into the lining of his raincoat, a revolver in one pocket and an ice pick in another. The murder weapon was to be the ice pick. The revolver was taken as a precaution, in case he had difficulty making his escape. The purpose of the dagger remains unclear; perhaps Mercader concealed it in his raincoat in case the other weapons were discovered.

The NKVD had used similar methods before. In the winter of 1938–39 an NKVD officer named Bokov had been summoned by Beria and asked if he was strong enough to kill a man with a single blow. "Yes, Comrade Commissar," replied Bokov. Beria explained that the NKVD had discovered that a Soviet ambassador in the Middle East was planning to defect. Bokov was sent with an assistant to ensure that the ambassador was "rendered harmless." On their arrival he was given a short iron bar by the NKVD resident, concealed it in his clothing, then went with his assistant and the resident to pay a courtesy call on the ambassador. Bokov maneuvered himself behind the ambassador, and killed him with a single blow to the skull. He and his assistant wrapped the body in a carpet to conceal the bloodstains, bundled it into a car, then drove out of the city and buried it. The ambassador's wife was told that her husband had been urgently recalled to Moscow and had made arrangements for her and the children to follow him by train. They were, almost certainly, stopped en route and transferred to a labor camp for "enemies of the people."[66]

Mercader too expected to kill with a single blow to the back of the head, and make his escape before the body was discovered. As Trotsky sat in his study, studying the article at his desk, Mercader took the ice pick from his pocket, closed his eyes, and brought it down with all the force he could muster on Trotsky's skull. But Trotsky did not die instantly. Instead he let out "a terrible, piercing cry" ("I shall hear that cry," said Mercader, "all my life"), turned, sank his teeth into the assassin's hand, and grasped the ice pick before his strength ebbed from him. He died in a hospital the next day, August 21, 1940.

The KGB file recounts the assassination in minute detail. It records, Petrov later recalled, that the fatal blow was struck with the broad, not the pointed, end of the ice pick.[67] Mercader was sentenced to twenty years in jail. His mother and Eitingon escaped to the Soviet Union by prearranged routes. In Moscow Señora Mercader was received by Beria, presented to Stalin in the Kremlin, and decorated with the Order of Lenin. Within a few years she was consumed by guilt. She told the Spanish Communist Party representative at Comintern headquarters:

> They [the NKVD] no longer have any use for me. . . . I am known abroad. And it is dangerous to use me. But they also know that I am no longer the woman I used to be. . . . Caridad Mercader is not simply Caridad Mercader, but the worst of assassins . . . Not only did I travel throughout Europe tracking down Chekists who have abandoned Paradise, so as to assassinate them pitilessly. I have done even more! . . . I made—and I did this for them—an assassin of my son, of Ramón, of this son whom I saw one day come out of Trotsky's house bound and bleeding and unable to come to me, and I had to flee in one direction and Leonid [Eitingon] in another.[68]

Ramón Mercader kept the Stalinist faith throughout his years in prison. History, he claimed, would see him as a soldier in the world revolution who had done the working class an immense service by ridding it of a leader who set out to betray it. He enjoyed singing the revolutionary song "The Young Guard," stressing the last line: "We work for a great cause!" Had Mercader been willing to reveal his true identity or his KGB connection, he could have won parole. He refused and served the full twenty-year term. In 1960 Mercader was freed from jail, left Mexico for Cuba, and traveled via Czechoslovakia to Russia. When he applied to join the Soviet Communist Party, his application was turned down.[69] Outside the KGB, Trotsky's assassin had become, in the post-Stalin era, an embarrassing reminder of a paranoid past.

6

Sigint, Agent Penetration, and the Magnificent Five from Cambridge (1930–39)

Of the score of portraits of Soviet intelligence heroes in the Memory Room of the First Chief Directorate, only one is of a non-KGB officer. The exception is General Yan Karlovich Berzin, commander of a Cheka detachment in the Civil War but best known as the head of Soviet military intelligence (then the Fourth Department of the General Staff, later the GRU, Glavnoye Razvedyvatelnoye Upravlenie) from 1924 to 1935.[1] Berzin was born in Latvia in 1890 and joined the revolutionary underground while still in his teens, spending several years in jail and hard labor in Siberia. In 1919 he served in the short-lived Latvian Soviet government. During his early years in military intelligence his closest collaborators, many of whom came from similar backgrounds, were known as the "Latvian fraction," just as Dzerzhinsky's chief lieutenants were known for a time as the "Polish fraction." In 1935 Berzin was sent on a Red Army mission to the Far East. He was recalled in August 1936 to become head of the Soviet military mission to the Spanish Republican government. A year later he was ordered back to Russia at the height of the Great Terror and liquidated.[2]

Berzin owes his place in the KGB hall of fame to his part in the expansion of foreign intelligence collection by both sigint and agent penetration. At the beginning of the 1930s he took part in setting up a combined OGPU/Fourth Department unit within the OGPU Special Department (Spets-Otdel), to handle both civilian and military sigint, headed by Gleb Boky of the OGPU with Colonel P. Kharkevich of the Fourth Department as his deputy. The unit was the most secret in the OGPU. Until 1935 it was housed not in the Lubyanka but in the building of the People's Commissariat for Foreign Affairs on Kuznetsky Bridge. According to Evdokia Kartseva (later Petrova), who joined the unit in 1933, the personnel were under strict orders not to reveal its address even to their parents.[3] Like most young women in the unit, Kartseva lived in fear of its head. Boky walked with a stoop and had the curious habit of wearing a raincoat all year round. Kartseva shuddered at his "cold, piercing blue eyes which gave people the feeling that he hated the sight of them." Though in his fifties, Boky still prided himself on his sexual athleticism and arranged regular group-sex weekends in his dacha. When Evdokia Kartseva asked a male colleague about Boky's orgies, he replied: "If you so much as open your mouth about this to anyone, he will make life unbearable for you. You are playing with fire." Kartseva lived in fear of being invited to Boky's dacha. On the night shift, when she felt most vulnerable, she wore her "plainest and dullest clothes for fear of attracting his unwelcome attention."[4]

Despite the personal depravity of its chief, the combined OGPU/Fourth Department was the world's largest and best-resourced sigint agency. In particular, it received far more assistance from espionage than any similar agency in the West. Most humint agencies acquired cipher materials from time to time, but during the 1930s only the OGPU and the Fourth Department, following a lead set by the Okhrana before the Revolution, made their acquisition a major priority. In the early years of the combined sigint unit, the foreign intercepts that had the greatest influence on Soviet policy were Japanese. Working in the Japanese subsection of the unit, Evdokia Petrova discovered that Japanese cipher materials "were being secured through agents."[5] Those agents included, at various times in the 1930s, officials in the Japanese embassies in Berlin and Prague.[6]

Berzin's second major claim to fame within both the KGB and the GRU is his part in adapting the techniques of agent penetration developed by the OGPU in the 1920s (principally for use against the White Guard emigration) to infiltrate foreign government bureaucracies and intelligence services during the 1930s. According to the classified history of INO prepared to commemorate its sixtieth anniversary in 1980, that strategy evolved in discussions between Berzin, Artuzov, the head of INO, and Pyatnitsky, the head of the Comintern's OMS. It seems likely that Berzin took the lead.[7] At the beginning of the 1930s, INO's chief targets for penetration remained the White Guards, soon followed by the Trotskyists. Berzin was more interested in using agent penetration as a means of foreign intelligence collection.[8] His lead, however, was swiftly followed by the OGPU and NKVD. The lines between Fourth Department and OGPU/NKVD responsibilities were frequently blurred during the 1930s. Fourth Department agents commonly collected political as well as military intelligence. The OGPU/NKVD less commonly collected military as well as political intelligence. Both increasingly took over OMS intelligence networks.

Berzin's most successful penetration agent was Richard Sorge. In 1964, twenty years after his death, Sorge was made a Hero of the Soviet Union, honored by a series of officially approved hagiographies and—most unusually for a foreign agent—a special issue of postage stamps. When Sorge joined the Fourth Department in 1929, he struck the Comintern agent, Hede Massing, as "startlingly good-looking," a "romantic, idealistic scholar" who exuded charm: "His cold blue eyes, slightly slanted and heavy-browed, had [the] quality of looking amused for no reason at all."[9]

Richard Sorge was born in the Caucasus in 1895, the son of a German oil driller, whom he later described as "unmistakably nationalist and imperialist," and a Russian mother. He went to school in Berlin, was wounded fighting in the First World War, became disillusioned by the "meaninglessness" of the devastation that it caused, and joined the revolutionary wing of the labor movement. The Bolshevik Revolution persuaded him "not only to support the movement theoretically and ideologically but to become an actual part of it." After the war Sorge gained a Ph.D. in political science from Hamburg University and worked as a Communist militant. Late in 1924 he moved to Moscow, beginning work for OMS early in 1925 and acquiring Soviet citizenship. From 1927 to 1929 OMS sent him on a series of intelligence missions in Germany and, he later claimed, to England and Scandinavia. In November 1929 he was personally recruited by General Berzin to the Fourth Department, though he also remained in touch with Pyatnitsky and OMS.

His first assignment was to run an espionage network in Shanghai under cover as a German journalist. There he recruited a Japanese journalist who later became his most important agent, Hotsumi Ozaki, a young Marxist idealist from a wealthy family having excellent connections with the Japanese government. In January 1933 Sorge returned to Moscow and was congratulated personally by Berzin on his achievements in Shanghai. His next, and by far his most important, assignment was Tokyo. En route he spent several months in Germany, strengthening his cover as a journalist and establishing himself as a convivial member of the Nazi Party. Dr. Goebbels himself attended his farewell dinner in Berlin.[10] On his arrival in Tokyo in September 1933 Sorge rapidly ingratiated himself with the German embassy. He boasted after his arrest eight years later:

> The fact that I successfully approached the German embassy in Japan and won absolute trust by people there was the foundation of my organization in Japan. . . . Even in Moscow the fact that I infiltrated into the center of the embassy and made use of it for my spying activity is evaluated as extremely amazing, having no equivalent in history.[11]

Sorge was unaware that there were by then several other penetrations that Moscow considered no less "amazing." It was Sorge's spy ring, nonetheless, that provided Moscow with its best intelligence from human sources on both German and Japanese policy.

During the greater part of Sorge's eight years in Tokyo the Kremlin considered Japan the main threat to the Soviet Union. The Great Depression of the early 1930s destroyed the shallow roots of Japanese democracy. For most Japanese soldiers the only answer to the problems created by the Depression was strong government at home and expansion abroad. The Depression created a climate of opinion in which the army was able to end its subjection to the politicians and win popular support for its territorial ambitions.

In September 1931 Japanese troops stationed near the Japanese-owned South Manchurian Railway blew up a section of the line. They then accused Chinese troops of responsibility for the explosion and used what became euphemistically known as the "Manchurian Incident" as a pretext to begin the occupation of Manchuria. The Japanese government accepted a League of Nations resolution calling for the withdrawal of its troops, but in the face of the nationalist fervor that swept Japan the politicians proved powerless to impose their will on the soldiers. Early in 1932 the army established the Manchurian puppet state of Manchukuo under the nominal rule of the last of the Manchu emperors. Japan now controlled a long land frontier with the Soviet Union.

Until the mid-1930s Moscow regarded Germany as a much less serious military threat than Japan. For several years it viewed the growth of Nazism with an equanimity bordering on complacency, regarding it as a sign of the death throes of German capitalism rather than the portent of a future German war of conquest in the East. Right up to the moment when Adolf Hitler became chancellor of Germany in January 1933, the Comintern urged German Communists to concentrate their fire on the socialist enemy on the left rather than the Nazi enemy on the right. Though Maxim Litvinov, commissar for foreign affairs, warned of the Nazi regime's "most extreme anti-Soviet ideas" in a general review of Soviet foreign policy at the end of 1933, he emphasized that the main threat continued to come from Japan. Over the next few years Soviet policy toward Japan and Germany, like that of the West, was based on appeasement. Its overriding priority was to avoid war with either.[12]

On his arrival in Tokyo in September 1933 Sorge was ordered "to give very careful study to the question of whether or not Japan was planning to attack the U.S.S.R." He wrote after his arrest eight years later:

> This was for many years the most important duty assigned to me and my group; it would not be far wrong to say that it was the sole object of my mission in Japan. . . . The U.S.S.R., as it viewed the prominent role and attitude taken by the Japanese military in foreign policy after the Manchurian incident, had come to harbor a deeply implanted suspicion that Japan was planning to attack the Soviet Union, a suspicion so strong that my frequently expressed opinions to the contrary were not always fully appreciated in Moscow.[13]

If Moscow's fears of Japanese attack were sometimes exaggerated, they were not without foundation. The Japanese army was split for several years into two warring factions: the Kodo-ha, which wanted war with Russia, and the less adventurous Tosei-ha, whose ambitions were centered on China. Not until 1936, after a failed coup d'état by the Kodo-ha, did the Tosei-ha gain a clear victory over their rivals. By then Western injunctions to Japan not to interfere in China were, said the

Japanese minister of war, "like telling a man not to get involved with a woman who was already pregnant by him." By the time Japan began open war in July 1937, it had already established indirect control over much of northeast China.[14]

When Hede Massing met Richard Sorge in 1935 for the first time since 1929, she found him visibly changed by his years in China and Japan. Though he was still "startlingly good-looking" and a dedicated Communist; "little of the charm of the romantic, idealistic scholar was left." A Japanese journalist described him as "a typical, swashbuckling, arrogant Nazi . . . quick-tempered, hard-drinking."[15] That image helped Sorge win the confidence of the German embassy. His closest contacts within the embassy were Colonel Eugen Ott, military attaché from March 1934, and Mrs. Ott, with whom Sorge had one of his numerous affairs. Sorge saw much of the information on the Japanese armed forces and military planning that Ott forwarded to Berlin, as well as many of the documents received by the embassy on German policy in the Far East. When Ott was promoted to ambassador in April 1938, Sorge had breakfast with him each day, briefing him on Japanese affairs and drafting some of his reports to Berlin. The most important member of Sorge's spy ring, Hotsumi Ozaki, had growing access to Japanese policy-making as a member of the brains trust of the leading statesman Prince Konoye. Late in 1935 he was able to photograph a planning document for the following year, which indicated that there was no immediate likelihood of a Japanese attack on Russia. Sorge correctly forecast the invasion of China in July 1937, once again providing reassurance that there were no plans for an invasion of Siberia.[16]

The officially authorized Soviet eulogies of Richard Sorge all contain at least one deliberate distortion, which has not so far been detected in the West. Sorge's intelligence reports are commonly used to conceal the successes of Soviet sigint, a form of intelligence that, even in the era of *glasnost,* remains officially unmentionable in the U.S.S.R. Sigint may well have been an even more important source of Japanese intelligence than Sorge himself. The single piece of intelligence that probably did most to arouse Soviet fears of a Japanese attack was a decrypted telegram from the Japanese military attaché in Moscow, Lieutenant Colonel Yukio Kasahara, a supporter of the Kodo-ha faction, to the General Staff in March 1931, six months before the "Manchurian Incident" and over two years before Sorge's arrival in Tokyo:

It will be [Japan's] unavoidable destiny to clash with the U.S.S.R. sooner or later. . . . The sooner the Soviet-Japanese war comes, the better for us. We must realize that with every day the situation develops more favorably for the U.S.S.R. In short, I hope the authorities will make up their minds for a speedy war with the Soviet Union and initiate policies accordingly.

Unsurprisingly, Moscow feared that the "Manchurian Incident" in September was the prelude to the attack on the Soviet Union advocated by Kasahara. It was further alarmed by remarks by Hirota, the Japanese ambassador in Moscow, to a visiting Japanese general, reported in another intercepted Japanese telegram:

Putting aside the question of whether or not Japan should make war against the Soviet Union, there is the need to take a strong policy vis-à-vis the Soviet Union, with the resolve to fight the U.S.S.R. at any time necessary. The objective, however, should not be defense against Communism but, rather, the occupation of Eastern Siberia.[17]

In the winter of 1931–32 Moscow experienced a major Japanese war scare. The Comintern secretariat harshly reprimanded foreign comrades for failing to grasp "the intimate connection between the Japanese attack on Manchuria and the preparation of a great anti-Soviet war." In February 1932 it demanded immediate action by member parties to sabotage arms production for, and shipment to, Japan:

Decisive mobilization of the masses is required, primarily against the transportation of weapons and military supplies, which travel to Japan along the tracks of every capitalist railway and from the ports of every capitalist country.[18]

So alarmed had Moscow become that in March 1932 it took the remarkable step of announcing: "We are in possession of documents which originate from officials of the most senior military circles in Japan, and contain plans for an attack on the U.S.S.R. and the seizure of its territory." Even more remarkably, *Izvestia* published decrypted extracts from intercepted Japanese telegrams revealing both Kasahara's appeal for "a speedy war" and Hirota's call for the occupation of Siberia.[19]

Moscow's willingness to publish this dramatic evidence of the Japanese menace derived, at least in part, from the knowledge that the Japanese were already aware that their diplomatic codes and ciphers had been broken. During 1931 the sacked American code breaker Herbert Yardley published a sensational volume of memoirs revealing that the United States "Black Chamber" had decrypted Japanese diplomatic traffic. There was an immediate diplomatic uproar, with the Japanese foreign minister publicly accusing the United States of a "breach of faith" by intercepting Japanese communications at the Washington conference ten years earlier.[20]

In the spring of 1932 Kasahara, whose call for "a speedy war" had so alarmed Moscow a year before, was appointed chief of the Russian section in the Second Department of the Japanese General Staff. His successor as military attaché in Moscow, also a supporter of the Kodo-ha faction, Torashiro Kawabe, reported to Tokyo that a Russo-Japanese war was "unavoidable." Kasahara replied that military preparations were complete: "War against Russia is necessary for Japan to consolidate Manchuria."[21] For the next few years the main priority of Soviet cryptanalysis, as of Sorge's espionage ring, was to monitor the danger of a Japanese attack that was never to materialize.

Perhaps the main sigint success of the mid-1930s was in monitoring the prolonged negotiations in Berlin between Baron Joachim von Ribbentrop and the Japanese military attaché (later ambassador), General Hiroshi Oshima, which culminated in the Anti-Comintern Pact between Germany and Japan, officially announced on November 25, 1936. The German embassy in Tokyo, which shared most of its secrets with Sorge, was in only distant touch with the progress of the negotiations. Thanks to sigint, Moscow was in closer touch. In the summer of 1936 an agent in Berlin run by Walter Krivitsky, the NKVD resident in the Netherlands, gained access to both the Japanese embassy's code book and its files on the German-Japanese negotiations. "From then on," boasted Krivitsky, "all correspondence between General Oshima and Tokyo flowed regularly through our hands."[22] Telegrams between Tokyo and the Japanese embassy in Moscow decrypted by the NKVD/ Fourth Department joint sigint unit were, no doubt, a supplementary source of intelligence on the progress of negotiations.

The published version of the Anti-Comintern Pact merely provided for an exchange of information on Comintern activities and cooperation in preventive measures. A secret protocol, however, added that if either of the signatories became the victim of "an unprovoked [Soviet] attack or threat of attack," both would immediately consult together on the action to take and neither would do anything to "ease the situation of the U.S.S.R.," a tortuous formula into which it was easy for the Kremlin to read more sinister intentions. Only three days after the publication of the Anti-Comintern Pact, Litvinov, the commissar for foreign affairs, announced to a Congress of Soviets:

> As for the published Japanese-German agreement . . . it is only a cover for another agreement which was simulta-neously discussed and initialed, probably also signed, and which was not published and is not intended for publication. I declare, with a full sense of responsibility for what I say, that it was precisely to the working out of this secret docu-ment, in which the word communism is not even mentioned, that the fifteen months of negotiations between the Japanese military attaché and the German super-diplomat were de-voted.[23]

Litvinov did not publicly identify the source of his knowledge of the secret protocol, but his speech contains a curious allusion to code breaking:

> It is not surprising that it is assumed by many that the German-Japanese agreement is written in a special code in which anti-communism means something entirely different from the dictionary meaning of this word, and that people decipher this code in different ways.[24]

For his assistance to Soviet sigint Krivitsky was recommended for the Order of Lenin, though he had yet to receive his award when he defected in the following autumn.[25]

The success of the joint OGPU/Fourth Department sigint unit in breaking British diplomatic codes and ciphers during the 1930s also owed much to assistance from espionage. The OGPU's first penetration of the Foreign Office resulted from what has become known in intelli-gence tradecraft as a "walk-in." In 1929 a cipher clerk in the Foreign Office Communications Department, Ernest Holloway Oldham, then accompanying a British trade delegation in Paris, walked into the Soviet Embassy, gave his name as Scott and asked to see the military attaché. He was seen instead by an OGPU officer, Vladimir Voynovich, who introduced himself as "Major Vladimir." Oldham announced that he worked for the Foreign Office and had with him a British diplomatic cipher, which he offered to sell for $2,000 U.S. Voynovich took the cipher and disappeared into an adjoining room, where he had it photographed. Possibly suspecting a provocation, he returned to the waiting Oldham, put on a show of indignation, threw the cipher into his lap, denounced him as a swindler, and ordered him to leave.[26]

The cryptanalysts in the OGPU/Fourth Department sigint unit quickly identified Oldham's cipher as genuine. Moscow Center reproved Voynovich for failing to give Scott money to establish a connection with him, ordered him to be given the $2,000 he had asked for, and insisted that contact be reestablished. To Voynovich's embarrassment, the OGPU officer who had followed Oldham back to his Paris lodging had noted the wrong address, and could not trace him. It took long, painstaking inquiries by Hans Galleni, a Dutch-based OGPU illegal known to his agents as Hans, before Oldham was tracked down in London in 1930.[27] Galleni met him one evening in Cromwell Road on his way back from work, addressed him by name, and made a short prepared speech: "I regret that we didn't meet in Paris. I know of the grave error made by Major Vladimir. He has since been removed and punished. I have come to give you what is rightfully yours." Then Galleni thrust an envelope into Oldham's hand, crossed the road, and disappeared into a crowd of office workers returning home. Bystanders, seeing Oldham clutch at his chest and his knees crumple, came to his assistance. Oldham stammered his embarrassed thanks, picked himself up, and went on his way.

When he opened the envelope at home he found that it contained $2,000 and details of a further rendezvous with Galleni. There is some evidence that Oldham went to the rendezvous intending to break off contact with the OGPU. But Galleni persuaded him to accept more money and provide further information on Foreign Office ciphers, security procedures, and his colleagues in the Communications Department. Though Galleni tried to encourage Oldham by taking him and his wife to expensive restaurants, the strain of the double life gradually proved too much. In September 1933 Oldham was found unconscious on the kitchen floor of his house in Pembroke Gardens, was rushed to a hospital, and pronounced dead on arrival. An inquest found that he had taken his life, while of "unsound mind," by "coal gas suffocation." Galleni returned to the Continent.

The OGPU used the information supplied by Oldham on the personnel of the Communications Department as the basis of a new recruiting drive. Two OGPU illegals were sent to Geneva, where several of Oldham's colleagues were working as cipher clerks with the British delegation to the League of Nations. One of the illegals, a former Russian sailor who had lived in the United States, proved so inept that the delegation accurately suspected him of being a Soviet spy. The other illegal, Henri Christian (Han) Pieck, a successful and convivial Dutch artist fired by enthusiasm for the Comintern, was run at different times by Hans Galleni (who had controlled Oldham), by the ill-fated Ignace Poretsky (liquidated in 1937), and by Teodor Maly (of whom more later). Under their direction Pieck used his considerable charm to such good effect in Geneva that he became a popular figure with a wide circle of British officials and journalists. He invited several of the cipher clerks to stay at his house in The Hague, lavished hospitality on them, and lent them money.[28]

The man whom he selected as most suitable for recruitment was Captain John Herbert King, who had joined the Communications Department as a "temporary clerk" in 1934 (a job without pension rights).[29] He was estranged from his wife, had an American mistress, and found it difficult to live within his modest income. Pieck cultivated King with great patience as well as skill. On one occasion Pieck and his wife took King and his mistress for an expensive touring holiday in Spain, staying in the best hotels. Mrs. Pieck later described the whole holiday as a "real ordeal," and King and his mistress "incredibly boring."[30] Han Pieck made no attempt to recruit King in Geneva, but waited till he returned to the Foreign Office Communications Department in 1935, then visited him in London. Even then Pieck concealed his connection with the NKVD. Instead he told King that a Dutch banker who was anxious for inside information on international relations could make them both a lot of money if King would supply it. King agreed.

To give himself a legitimate base in Britain, Pieck invited a British shop fitter named Conrad Parlanti, whom he had met through the cipher clerks, to join with him in setting up a decorating business for which he would provide the capital. Parlanti agreed and the two men took over a house in Buckingham Gate. Pieck kept a floor for his own use, which included a locked room where he photographed the documents supplied by King.[31] A file seen by Gordievsky indicates that some of the documents were considered so important that they were shown to Stalin himself. They included telegrams from the British embassy in Berlin reporting meetings with Hitler and other Nazi leaders.[32]

In October 1935 another and ultimately even more important Soviet agent, Donald Maclean, entered the Foreign Office. Maclean was the first of a group of British agents recruited at graduation from Cambridge University or soon after to succeed in penetrating Whitehall's corridors of power. The KGB still considers the five leading Cambridge moles the ablest group of foreign agents it has ever recruited. During the Second World War they became known as "the London Five" (by then all were run from the London residency) or simply as "the Five." After the release of the film *The Magnificent Seven,* they became known in the First Chief Directorate as "the Magnificent Five."[33] The first two of the Five to be identified publicly were Donald Maclean and Guy Burgess, who defected to Moscow in 1951. Kim Philby was christened the Third Man by the British media after his defection in 1963. The Fourth Man, Anthony Blunt, was unmasked in 1979. During the 1980s the media hunt for the Fifth Man followed a variety of false trails that ended in a series of blind alleys and mistaken identifications. His identity, discovered by Gordievsky while preparing the classified history of the FCD Third Department, is revealed in this chapter for the first time.

　　　　Unlike Oldham and King, who sold Foreign Office secrets for money, the motives of the Magnificent Five were ideological. The bait that drew them into work for the KGB was anti-fascism after the Nazi conquest of power in Germany. Anthony Blunt explained his own recruitment thus after his exposure in 1979:

> In the mid-1930s it seemed to me and to many of my contemporaries that the Communist Party and Russia constituted the only firm bulwark against fascism, since the Western democracies were taking an uncertain and compromising attitude towards Germany. I was persuaded by Guy Burgess that I could best serve the cause of anti-fascism by joining him in his work for the Russians.[34]

A majority of Cambridge undergraduates in the mid-thirties were apathetically Conservative. Though the Conservatives had the largest political clubs in Oxford and Cambridge, they appeared intellectually moribund with a general distaste for campaigning zeal. A writer in the *Cambridge Review* noted at the beginning of 1934:

> Political activity in the older universities during the last few years has been largely confined to the Socialists, and, to an increasing degree, to Communists. . . . The Russian experiment has aroused very great interest within the universities. It is felt to be bold and constructive, and youth, which is always impatient of the cautious delays and obstruction of its elders, is disposed to regard sympathetically (often irrespective of political opinion) this attempt to found a new social and political order.[35]

The growing sympathy among undergraduate idealists for "the Russian experiment" had as much to do with events in Britain as with events in Russia. What Kim Philby considered "the real turning point" in his own political development came, as for many young Soviet sympathizers, with "the demoralization and rout of the Labour Party in 1931." The great "betrayal" by the Labour leader Ramsay MacDonald in agreeing to head a Conservative-dominated National Government in August 1931 was followed by Labour's rout at the polls two months later. To Philby:

> It seemed incredible that the [Labour] party should be so helpless against the reserve strength which reaction could mobilise in time of crisis. More important still, the fact that a supposedly sophisticated electorate had been stampeded by the cynical propaganda of the day threw serious doubt on the validity of the assumptions underlying democracy as a whole.[36]

While Labour had lost its way in the depression, Russia was in the midst of the great economic transformation of the first Five Year Plan. The Magnificent Five were seduced not by the brutal reality of Stalin's Russia but by a myth image of the socialist millennium: a worker-peasant state courageously building a new society free from the social snobbery of the British class system. This myth image was so powerful that it proved capable of surviving even visits to Russia by those whom it seduced. Malcolm Muggeridge, perhaps the best of the British journalists in Moscow during the mid-thirties, wrote of the radical pilgrims who came from Britain to Stalin's Russia:

> Their delight in all they saw and were told, and the expression they gave to this delight, constitute unquestionably one of the wonders of our age. There were earnest advocates of the humane killing of cattle who looked up at the massive headquarters of the OGPU with tears of gratitude in their eyes, earnest advocates of proportional representation who eagerly assented when the necessity for a Dictatorship of the Proletariat was explained to them, earnest clergymen who reverently turned the pages of atheistic literature, earnest pacifists who watched delightedly tanks rattle across Red Square and bombing planes darken the sky, earnest town-planning specialists who stood outside overcrowded ram-shackle tenements and muttered: "If only we had something like this in England!" The almost unbelievable credulity of these mostly university-educated tourists astonished even Soviet officials used to handling foreign visitors.[37]

The American correspondent in Moscow William C. White noted the same naïveté among American visitors to Stalin's Russia:

> They are wildly enthusiastic over all they see but not always logical; they were enthusiastic before they came and their visit only doubly convinces them. A schoolteacher from Brooklyn was on a tour of one of the newspaper plants. She saw a machine which did wonders with the paper that was fed to it. "Really, that is remarkable," she commented. "Such an amazing invention could be produced only in a country like yours, where labor is free, unexploited and working for one end. I shall write a book about what I have seen." She was a trifle embarrassed when she walked to the rear and saw the sign "Made in Brooklyn, N.Y."[38]

For the Magnificent Five, however, the heady idealism of a secret war against fascism in the ranks of the Communist International was an even more powerful inducement than sympathy for the Soviet Union in drawing them into espionage for the NKVD. The anti-fascist crusade that led to the recruitment of the Cambridge moles was mounted by Willi Münzenberg, the great virtuoso of Comintern propaganda and originator in the 1920s of the "Innocents' Clubs" designed to "organize the intellectuals" in Communist-dominated front organizations.[39] During the Nazi anti-Communist witch hunt that followed the burning of the Reichstag, the German parliament building, on February 27, 1933, blamed by the Nazis on the Communists, Münzenberg was forced to move his headquarters from Berlin to Paris.[40] There in June 1933 he founded what proved to be the most influential of all the Innocents' Clubs, the World Committee for the Relief of the Victims of German Fascism.

The writer Arthur Koestler, who worked for it, noted that, as usual with the Innocents' Clubs, "great care was taken that no Communist—except a few internationally known names, such as Henri Barbusse and J. B. S. Haldane—should be connected with the Committee." The French section was led by a distinguished Hungarian émigré, Count Károlyi. The international chairman was a naïve British Labour peer, Lord Marley. The great physicist Albert Einstein also agreed to join the committee, and soon found himself described as "president." Their participation made the committee appear a nonparty philanthropic organization. In reality, wrote Koestler later, the Paris secretariat that ran it was "a purely Communist caucus, headed by Münzenberg and controlled by the Comintern. . . . Münzenberg himself worked in a large room in the World Committee's premises, but no outsider ever learned about this. It was as simple as that."[41]

From his Paris base Münzenberg organized the publication in August 1933 of the most effective piece of propaganda in Comintern history, the *Brown Book on the Hitler Terror and the Burning of the Reichstag.*[42] Quickly translated into over twenty languages ranging from Japanese to Yiddish, the *Brown Book* became, in Koestler's phrase, "the bible of the anti-fascist crusade." Koestler claimed, with some exaggeration, that it "probably had the strongest political impact of any pamphlet since Tom Paine's *Common Sense* demanded independence for the American colonies a century and a half earlier."[43]

According to the title page, the book was "prepared by the World Committee for the Victims of German Fascism (PRESIDENT: EINSTEIN) with an introduction by LORD MARLEY." "My name," wrote Einstein, "appeared in the English and French editions as if I had

written it. That is not true. I did not write a word of it." But since it
was all in a good cause, the great physicist decided not to complain.
"The fact that I did not write it," he said genially, "does not matter."[44]
Lord Marley's introduction, written from the "House of Lords, London
SW1" gave the fraudulent volume an air of establishment respectability
and scrupulous veracity. "We have not used the most . . . sensational . . . documents," the noble lord assured his readers. "Every statement
made in this book has been carefully verified and is typical of a number
of similar cases."[45] Lord Marley was naïve enough to have believed his
own introduction.

Like most successful deceptions, the *Brown Book* contained a
significant element of fact. But fact, as Koestler later acknowledged,
was mixed with forgeries and "brazen bluff" by "the Comintern's intelligence apparat." Most of the writing, according to Koestler, was done
by Münzenberg's chief assistant, Otto Katz (*alias* André Simone).[46]
Katz was a Czech Jew and, like Münzenberg, an unconventional, cosmopolitan Central European of great personal charm, who seemed far
removed from the doctrinaire Stalinism expected of Communist Party
apparatchiks. During the 1920s Katz had built up a remarkable range
of contacts in publishing, journalism, the theater and the film industry.
"In Hollywood," wrote Babette Gross, Münzenberg's "life partner,"
"he charmed German émigré actors, directors, and writers. Katz had
an extraordinary fascination for women, a quality which greatly helped
him in organizing committees and campaigns."[47] Koestler agreed that
Katz was "attractive to women, particularly to the middle-aged, well-
intentioned, politically active type, and used them adroitly to smooth
his path":

> One of Otto's tasks was . . . to spy on Willy for the apparat.
> Willy knew this and did not care. Willy needed Otto, but he
> hardly bothered to disguise his contempt for him. . . . In spite
> of all his seediness, Otto was, paradoxically, a very likeable
> human being. He had the generosity of the adventurer and
> he could be warmhearted, spontaneous and helpful—so long
> as it did not conflict with his interests.[48]

In writing the *Brown Book,* Katz was assisted by Alexander Abusch,
former editor of the German Communist Party (KPD) newspaper *Rote
Fahne* and later a minister in the postwar East German government,
and by a series of other Communist journalists.[49] Attempts by outsiders

to identify the exact composition of the World Committee for the Relief
of the Victims of German Fascism responsible for producing the *Brown
Book* were invariably frustrated. A curious American radical journalist
visiting Paris found his inquiries trapped inside an unhelpfully circular
explanation:

> I tried hard to find out who constituted the Committee and
> asked "Who is the Committee?" Answer: "We are." I made
> further enquiry: "Who are we?" Answer: "A group of people
> interested in defending these innocent men." "What group
> of people?" The answer came back: "Our Committee."[50]

The *Brown Book* countered the Nazi allegation that the Reichstag fire
was the result of a Communist conspiracy with the equally fraudulent
but more convincing claim that it was a Nazi plot. Forged documents
were used to demonstrate that Marinus van der Lubbe, the Dutch
arsonist responsible for the fire, was part of a plot devised by the Nazi
master propagandist Joseph Goebbels in which a group of storm troopers had entered the Reichstag through an underground passage that
connected it with the official residence of its Nazi president, Hermann
Goering, started the blaze, and made their escape by the same route.
The fictitious conspiracy was enlivened with sexual scandal based on
bogus evidence that van der Lubbe was involved with leading Nazi
homosexuals.[51]

The basic hypothesis of the *Brown Book,* instantly popular with
most anti-Nazis and subsequently embellished with further fabrications, was accepted until 1962, when the West German journalist Fritz
Tobias demolished both Nazi and Communist conspiracy theories and
demonstrated that in all probability van der Lubbe had set fire to the
Reichstag single-handedly in the vain hope of provoking a popular
rising.[52] Tobias's revelations proved unwelcome in the German Democratic Republic, which sponsored further forgeries to reestablish the
Brown Book version of events. During the 1970s the most skillful of
these forgeries, fabricated by a Croat émigré, Edouard Calic, successfully deceived an International Committee for Scientific Research on
the Causes and Consequences of the Second World War, subsidized by
the foreign ministry and press office of the Federal Republic and including some distinguished West German historians, until these documents
too were conclusively exposed as forgeries.[53]

Münzenberg used the *Brown Book* as the basis for one of his most ambitious stunts. In the summer of 1933 he visited Moscow and gained approval from the Comintern OMS for the creation of an International Committee of Jurists composed of sympathetic non-Communists who would pronounce with apparent judicial impartiality on the causes of the Reichstag fire and find the Nazis guilty.[54] On his return to Paris Münzenberg drew up plans with Katz for a Legal Inquiry into the Burning of the Reichstag, to be held in London shortly before the trial of van der Lubbe and his alleged Communist fellow conspirators opened in Leipzig.

The chairman of the "Legal Inquiry"—or "Counter-Trial" as it came to be called—was a leading British fellow traveler, D. N. Pritt, K.C., a prominent Labour M.P. and barrister who later defended Stalin's show trials against the "unscrupulous abuse" they received in England and was eventually expelled from the Labour Party for supporting the Soviet invasion of Finland.[55] Pritt's colleagues on the International Committee of Jurists were Arthur Garfield Hays, an American champion of civil liberties; Georg Branting, son of Sweden's first Socialist prime minister; Maîtres Moro-Giafferi and Gaston Bergery from France; Valdemar Huidt from Denmark; Dr. Betsy Bakker-Nort from the Netherlands; and Maître Pierre Vermeylen from Belgium.

Otto Katz traveled to London to organize the Counter-Trial. Foreign Office files reveal that though Katz was on the MI5 Black List as a "red-hot communist," he was allowed into Britain "as the result of intervention by Mr. Arthur Henderson [the former foreign secretary] and other members of the Labour Party" sympathetic to the Counter-Trial, who were probably unaware of Katz's links with Soviet intelligence. Despite MI5 opposition, the Home Office allowed Katz to make a second visit later in the year "rather than face Labour P[arliamentary] Q[uestion]s."[56] Once in London, Katz stayed hidden behind the scenes as, in Koestler's words, "the invisible organizer of the Committee." But he succeeded brilliantly in cloaking the Counter-Trial in an aura of establishment respectability.

On September 13 a reception was held for the international jurists by Lord Marley and Sidney Bernstein in the prestigious Mayfair surroundings of the Hotel Washington.[57] The Counter-Trial opened next day at Lincoln's Inn in the Law Society's Court Room, thus giving the proceedings the appearance of a British Crown Court. An opening address by the Labour lawyer Sir Stafford Cripps, K.C., later a wartime ambassador to Russia and postwar chancellor of the exchequer, emphasized that "none of the lawyers on the Commission belonged to the political party [i.e., the Communists] of the accused persons in Germany."[58]

Katz was understandably pleased with himself. The Counter-Trial, he later boasted, had become "an unofficial tribunal whose mandate was conferred by the conscience of the world."[59] Katz succeeded in combining respectability with melodrama. Witnesses came in disguise. The court doors were locked so that no one could leave while sensitive witnesses were giving evidence. Pritt, the chairman, claimed dramatically that Ramsay MacDonald's National Government was trying to obstruct the Counter-Trial.[60]

As the carefully staged proceedings dragged on, however, there was a slight air of anticlimax. Some prominent sympathizers like H. G. Wells became bored. And though the jurists do not seem to have suspected the dubious origins of some of the evidence presented to them, they were less emphatic in their conclusion than Münzenberg and Katz had hoped. Instead of ending in a ringing denunciation of the Nazi regime, the Counter-Trial concluded more cautiously that "grave grounds existed for suspecting that the Reichstag was set on fire by, or on behalf of, leading personalities of the National Socialist Party."[61]

Such mild disappointment as Münzenberg and Katz may have felt with the verdict of the Counter-Trial was quickly dispelled by the trial itself at Leipzig, which turned into a propaganda disaster for the Nazis. Despite the German judge's efforts to assist them, the evidence of some of the key Nazi witnesses fell to pieces. The leading Communist defendant, Georgi Dimitrov, the Bulgarian former head of the Comintern Western European Bureau in Berlin and a future Bulgarian Communist prime minister, made a brilliant defense. Goering became so irate at the collapse of the Nazi case that he lost his temper and shouted at Dimitrov, "You wait till I get you out of the power of this court!"[62] Van der Lubbe, who had insisted from the start that he was solely responsible, was found guilty and executed. All the Communist defendants were cleared. The public collapse of the Nazi conspiracy theory in open court served to reinforce the alternative Communist conspiracy theory of the *Brown Book*. A *Second Brown Book* was produced by Münzenberg, Katz, and their collaborators to exploit Nazi embarrassment at the Leipzig Trial, amend the less-convincing parts of the first edition, and include further fabrications.[63]

Like Münzenberg's earlier Innocents' Clubs, the Reichstag Fire campaign was designed to serve the purposes of the Comintern and Soviet intelligence *apparat* as well as to win a propaganda victory. Though his primary aim was to conquer public opinion, he also hoped to lure some British intellectuals into a secret war against fascism under Comintern direction. Preparations for a recruiting drive among young British intellectual "innocents" began at the same time as preparations for the Counter-Trial. One of Münzenberg's targets was Cambridge University. His emissary, Countess Károlyi, later recalled the naïve enthusiasm she found among Cambridge Communists when Münzenberg sent her to collect funds for the Counter-Trial and Dimitrov's defense in Leipzig:

> I remember my trip to Cambridge in the rickety car of a young communist undergraduate who, on the way, explained to me dolefully that it was imperative, though most regrettable, that the beautiful ancient universities of Oxford and Cambridge should be razed to the ground when the Proletarian Dictatorship was proclaimed. For centuries, he said, they had been the symbols of bourgeois privilege. He seemed suspicious of my genuine revolutionary spirit when I expressed my doubts as to the necessity for demolition. In Cambridge we drove to one of the colleges, where white-flannelled undergraduates were playing tennis on perfectly kept green courts. We were received most enthusiastically. It was odd to see students of such a famous university, obviously upper-class, with well-bred accents, speak about Soviet Russia as the land of promise.[64]

Münzenberg's main contact in Cambridge, who probably arranged Countess Károlyi's visit, was Maurice Dobb, an economics don at Pembroke College (and later at Trinity). There was nothing covert about Dobb's Communism. On the founding of the Communist Party of Great Britain in 1920 he became probably the first British academic to carry a Party card, and he made frequent speeches at the Cambridge Union extolling the achievements of Soviet society. In 1925 King George V demanded to know why such a well-known Communist was allowed to indoctrinate the young. But though Dobb attracted the attention of the Special Branch and MI5, it was as an open Communist propagandist and militant in front organizations such as Münzenberg's League Against Imperialism, rather than because of any suspected involvement with Soviet intelligence. In 1931, together with Roy Pas-

cal, a young modern-languages don at Pembroke, Dobb founded the
university's first Communist cell at Red House, his home in Chesterton
Lane.[65] But Dobb was naïve as well as militant. In proselytizing for
Communism and the Comintern's secret war against international fascism, it is quite possible that he failed to realize that he was also acting
as a talent spotter for the KGB.

The bait devised by Münzenberg to lure Cambridge innocents
and other young British intellectuals into working for Soviet intelligence was the heroic example allegedly being set by German workers
in forming secret *Fünfergruppen* ("groups [or "rings"] of five") to
launch a proletarian counterattack against Nazism. The phrase "group
(or "ring") of five" later became confused with "the Magnificent Five"
and other descriptions applied by the KGB to the five most successful
Cambridge moles during and after the Second World War. The origins
of the *Fünfergruppen,* however, went back to the revolutionary underground in Tsarist Russia. The first ring of five had been formed in 1869 by
the student revolutionary Sergei Nechayev, whom Dostoyevsky made
the model for Peter Verkhovensky in *The Devils.* Though Dostoyevsky
saw him as a psychopath, the conspirators of the People's Will and their
Bolshevik successors regarded Nechayev as a revolutionary visionary.[66]

During the tense final years of the Weimar Republic, which
preceded Hitler's rise to power, the German Communist Party (KPD)
revived the rings of five. In the summer of 1932 the KPD began replacing its existing semi-open cells of ten to thirty members with secret
Fünfergruppen, so called in honor of Nechayev. Not all the groups of
five had exactly five members. Only the leader of each group was
supposed to know the identity and addresses of the other members; and
he alone had the authority to make contact with the next level in the
Party hierarchy.

In the face of the challenge from Hitler the KPD behaved in
reality, as Koestler discovered, like "a castrated giant."[67] Before the
Nazi takeover it concentrated its fire not on the Nazi Party but on its
main rival on the left, the socialist SPD. After the Nazi takeover, many
Communists switched their support to Hitler. The bulk of what Communist resistance survived in the Nazi Third Reich was not an organized underground but an ill-organized opposition among the badly
paid construction workers of Hitler's labor army.[68] The Comintern,
however, disguised the reality of the KPD's ignominious failure to
counter the Nazi challenge by claiming that the Party had gone underground, and that the *Fünfergruppen* had created "a new subterranean

revolutionary Germany . . . dogging Hitler's every footstep."[69]

The chief propagandist of the groups of five was Semyon Nikolayevich Rostovsky, an OGPU illegal and associate of Münzenberg, who had established himself as a journalist in London under the alias Ernst Henri (later Henry or Ghenri). In August and September 1933 he wrote three articles entitled "The Revolutionary Movement in Nazi Germany" for the leading British left-wing weekly, the *New Statesman.* The first, subtitled "The Groups of Five ('Fünfergruppen')," revealed the existence of the groups publicly for the first time and made extravagant claims for their success:

> There is perhaps no other example in history of a secret revolutionary movement with a completely equipped organization and an effective influence extending over the whole country, being able to develop in so short a time. . . . These groups of five cover practically the whole of German industry; almost all the factories and the majority of the more important offices are honeycombed with them.

The groups allegedly contained many former socialists, republicans, liberals, and Catholics who, "under Communist leadership . . . have buried all previous differences and pursue only one policy—anti-Fascism." In addition to printing clandestine propaganda, coordinating demonstrations, and collecting intelligence on the "Hitler Terror," the groups of five had succeeded in infiltrating the Nazi labor movement and were preparing to paralyze the system from within. The example of the Fünfergruppen thus demonstrated the need for infiltration and intelligence gathering in the war against fascism. Nazism's secret networks, argued Henri, were already so powerful and widespread that they formed a covert "fascists' international." It followed that antifascists also must organize secretly as well as openly.[70] Wildly exaggerated though it was, Henri's romantic account of groups of five engaged in a proletarian crusade against Nazi tyranny struck so deep a chord in the *New Statesman* and many of its readers that they suspended their disbelief. The editor, Kingsley Martin, insisted that Henri's "facts" were "not open to question."[71]

In March 1934 Henri spelled out his arguments in greater detail in *Hitler over Europe?*,[72] a book twice reprinted over the next few months. It would, said *The Times,* "make the democrat's flesh positively creep."[73] Henri's message in this and later writings was that the choice confronting his readers was simple and stark—between Berlin and Moscow: "In the modern world, torn between [these] gigantic opposing forces and on the verge of its final transformation, there is no such thing as political and social impartiality, nor can there be." It was sheer liberal escapism to look for a middle way.[74] In private meetings with sympathizers, Henri put the same point more personally. "You English," he would say, "are such liberal do-gooders."[75]

The decent values of liberal democracy were thus plausibly portrayed simply as one facet of appeasement. The implication of Henri's message was that anti-fascist British intellectuals, if their anti-fascism amounted to more than mere words, should display "solidarity" (a key word in Münzenberg's lexicon for intellectual innocents) with the oppressed German workers by joining in their secret war against fascism. To Guy Burgess in particular, the most flamboyant of Cambridge's young Communists, this was an irresistibly heady message. According to one of those who knew him, Burgess set out to form his own "light blue ring of five."[76]

Hitler over Europe? was reviewed in the *New Statesman* in April 1934 by Brian Howard, one of Burgess's closest friends and, like him, a predatory Old Etonian Marxist homosexual. Though Evelyn Waugh, quoting Lady Caroline Lamb on Byron, called Howard "mad, bad and dangerous to know," he was rapidly becoming an influential literary figure. Howard eulogized *Hitler over Europe?* as "probably the best book on the Third Reich that has appeared in English": "Ernst Henri's book should be read at once by everyone who is seriously interested in understanding the real bases of Hitlerism. . . . It discloses, for the first time, the dynamics of the Nazi movement." Howard went on to endorse Henri's analysis of "the celebrated Revolutionary Groups of Five," and ended with a rallying cry to English anti-fascists to "band themselves together" without delay.[77]

Henri's career in Soviet intelligence spanned half a century, beginning as an OGPU illegal between the wars and ending in the Fifth Directorate of Andropov's KGB.[78] Having helped to recruit Burgess in 1933, Henri was instructed to keep a watchful eye on him a generation later during the final alcoholic years of Burgess's Moscow exile before his death in 1963. Unsurprisingly, Henri has always refused to discuss publicly the details of his intelligence career. But in 1988 he at last admitted to a Western writer that he had talent-spotted for the KGB at Cambridge in the 1930s and had kept in touch with both Burgess and Dobb.[79]

When Burgess met him for the first time, Henri was not yet thirty, short, slim, with a heavy mustache but already going bald. Like Münzenberg and Katz, he was an engaging, cosmopolitan extrovert quite unlike the doctrinaire, narrow-minded Stalinists who were steadily taking over much of the NKVD. Edith Cobbett, who worked for Henri a decade later when he was the editor of the *Soviet News* in London, found him "really a charismatic personality," who was always fun to be with: "I think I laughed during the period I worked with him as much as I've laughed at any time in my life." Henri preferred Picasso and Matisse to the officially favored artists of Socialist realism, dressed in well-made English suits, and enjoyed Westerns. He was also capable of an irreverence which, though it must have attracted Burgess, would have been unthinkable in the Soviet Union. After reading a typically tedious series of Stalinist speeches, Henri once said to Edith Cobbett: "Wouldn't it be fun if somebody said 'Sod Stalin!' for a change?"

But Henri was also an idealistic Communist and a Russian patriot with a tremendous pride in Soviet achievements and the economic transformation wrought by the Five Year Plans.[80] Throughout his long career in journalism and Soviet intelligence Henri preached the need to "stop underestimating the revolutionary moods and powers of the youth": "For nearly two centuries bourgeois society has really feared only the working class. It now finds it has to fear another force—young people who until recently were ordered to listen and do as they are told." Writing in 1982, Henri criticized "both Right and Left extremists" for playing on the emotions of "susceptible" students.[81] Half a century earlier he played with some success himself on the same emotions. He admitted in 1988 that he was "astonished" that his talent spotting in Cambridge for the KGB had not led to his arrest in the 1930s.[82]

Though four of the Magnificent Five and several less celebrated moles were recruited while still at Cambridge, the first and most famous of them entered the KGB by a slightly different route. Harold Adrian Russell ("Kim") Philby was born in India on New Year's Day 1912, the son of Harry St. John and Dora Philby. His father, then a civil servant of the British Raj, went on to become a celebrated Arabist. Like his son, who adored him, St. John Philby moved easily in two quite different worlds. He wrote for *The Times,* stood twice for Parliament, was a habitué of London clubland, and tried never to miss a test match. But he was equally at home dressed as an Arab, converted to Islam, and took a Saudi slave girl as his second wife.[83] Like Kim, though on a far more modest scale, St. John betrayed British secrets to a foreign power for which he felt a stronger loyalty. Having conceived an intense admiration for Ibn Saud, he passed to him classified documents on the Middle East.[84]

Kim went both to his father's old school, Westminster, where he was a King's Scholar, then in October 1929 to his father's Cambridge college, Trinity, which was also the college of Anthony Blunt and (from 1930) of Guy Burgess. One of Philby's first acts on going up to Trinity was to join the Cambridge University Socialist Society (CUSS), though for two years his involvement in it was limited to attending meetings. During those two years he read history, did little work, and gained only third-class honors in the examination for Part I of the Cambridge Historical Tripos.

In October 1931 he changed to economics for the second part of his degree course. His change coincided with a landslide election victory by Ramsay MacDonald's National Government, which reduced the Labour opposition to a rump of only fifty-two seats. "It was the Labour disaster of 1931," said Philby later, "which first set me seriously to thinking about possible alternatives to the Labour Party." He took a more active part in the now Communist-dominated CUSS, becoming its treasurer during his last year at Cambridge in 1932–33. But it was not until his last term at Trinity, in the early summer of 1933, that Philby threw off what he called his "last doubts." Two experiences were probably decisive in Kim's final conversion. The first was a visit to Berlin in March 1933 during his last Easter vacation, shortly after the burning of the Reichstag, when he witnessed at firsthand Hitler's persecution of the KPD and the setting-up of the Nazi police state. Philby returned to Cambridge for his final term burning to play his part in the fight against fascism.

In Cambridge the most importance influence on him was Maurice Dobb, one of the dons who set him economics essays and discussed each with him individually for an hour at a time, probably prolonging the discussion when the hour was up to talk about politics. To his disciples Dobb emphasized the role of the Comintern in the struggle against fascism. Another Trinity undergraduate who fell under Dobb's spell, V. G. Kiernan, wrote later: "We belonged to the era of the Third International, genuinely international at least in spirit, when the Cause stood high above any national or parochial claims."

Philby graduated in June 1933 with upper second-class honors in economics and "the conviction that my life must be devoted to Communism." He later revealed that on his last day in Cambridge he went to seek Dobb's advice on how best to work for the cause: "He gave me an introduction to a communist group in Paris, a perfectly legal and open group." The group, though Philby declined to identify it, was almost certainly Münzenberg's World Committee for the Relief of Victims of German Fascism. It is quite possible that in directing Philby to Münzenberg Dobb did not realize that he had begun Kim's recruitment as a Soviet agent. He was sufficiently naïve to have thought simply in terms of enlisting Philby in the Comintern's secret war against international fascism.

After making contact with Münzenberg's *apparat* in Paris, Philby was "passed . . . on to a communist underground organization in Vienna."[85] His contact address was the house of Israel and Gisella Kohlmann, Polish Jews who had arrived in Vienna shortly before the First World War. Israel was a minor civil servant who, together with his wife, spent most of his spare time in Jewish welfare work. Philby became their paying guest, nominally spending his time in Vienna learning German and working as a freelance journalist. The Kohlmanns' daughter, Litzi Friedmann, a short, vivacious divorcee, was already working as a Comintern agent. In the course of the winter, while out for a walk together in the snow, she and Philby became lovers. "I know it sounds impossible," Philby told a later mistress, "but it was actually quite warm once you got used to it." In February 1934 Litzi became Philby's first wife. By that time she had already introduced him to the Comintern underground.[86]

As Philby acknowledged half a century later in an interview a few months before his death, his work in Vienna "caught the attention" of the OGPU.[87]

The first to realize Philby's potential as a Soviet agent was the great illegal, Teodor Maly, whose portrait is among the score of KGB heroes that hang today on the walls of the First Chief Directorate Memory Room. The official eulogy beneath Maly's portrait cites as his greatest achievement his role in recruiting and running Philby and the Magnificent Five.[88]

Slutsky, then head of INO, ascribed Maly's success to his personal charm and instinctive tact. He was a large, handsome man nicknamed "der Lange," the tall fellow, within the Comintern underground of Central Europe. The NKVD defector Aleksandr Orlov, no admirer of most of his former colleagues, remembered affectionately Maly's "strong, manly face and large, almost childlike, blue eyes."[89] Beneath his strong exterior and passionate devotion to Comintern ideals, some of his agents sensed an inner vulnerability, which only strengthened their attachment to him.[90] Maly had little in common with the increasingly brutal *apparatchiks* who came to dominate the NKVD during the Great Terror. He was Hungarian by birth and had been ordained as a Catholic priest before the First World War. During the war he served as a chaplain in the Austro-Hungarian army before being taken prisoner by the Russians in the Carpathians. He later told one of his agents:

> I saw all the horrors, young men with frozen limbs dying in the trenches. I was moved from one [POW] camp to another and starved along with the other prisoners. We were all covered with vermin and many were dying from typhus. I lost my faith in God and when the revolution broke out I joined the Bolsheviks. I broke with my past completely. I was no longer a Hungarian, a priest, a Christian, even anyone's son. I was just a soldier "missing in action." I became a Communist and have always remained one.

Soon after he left POW camp, Maly's burning desire to defend the Revolution from counterrevolution earned him admission to the Cheka. The visionary faith in an earthly new Jerusalem free from the exploitation of man by man that replaced his religious faith during the First World War never left him. But it was shaken by the horrors of both the Civil War and collectivization. During the Civil War, he said later:

> Our Red detachments would "clean up" villages exactly the way the Whites did. What was left of the inhabitants, old men, women, children were machine-gunned for having given assistance to the enemy. I could not stand the wailing of the women. I simply could not.

When villages were being "cleaned up," Maly claimed that he would try to hide with his hands over his ears. Once counterrevolution had been defeated, he seems to have persuaded himself that the horrors of the Civil War were past. With collectivization they returned. "I knew what we were doing to the peasants," Maly admitted, "how many were deported, how many were shot. And still I stayed on. I still hoped the chance would come for me to atone for what I had done." He became personally involved in the case of a man who had been sentenced to death for stealing a small bag of potatoes to feed his starving children. Maly persuaded his chief to recommend that the sentence be commuted to imprisonment. He saw the man's wife and told her that her husband's life had been saved. "This case," he believed, "had become my atonement":

> Then I had to go away on a two-week assignment. When I got back the first thing I did was to look for "my case." I could not find the file. I ran to my chief. He did not know what had happened and both of us started to hunt for the file. We finally found it. Scribbled across it was one word: "Executed."

Next day Maly went to INO and asked for a foreign posting.[91] His first assignment, probably late in 1932, was as an OGPU illegal in Germany. A few months after the Nazi conquest of power, he moved to Vienna. His message to his Austrian agent Hede Massing—and no doubt to Kim Philby also—was rather different from that spread by Ernst Henri in England. Instead of stressing, like Henri, the success of the underground war waged by the German workers' Fünfergruppen, Maly argued that the struggle against Nazism had to be waged chiefly from beyond the German frontier: "The only way to fight fascism is from the outside. We did not succeed inside, now we must do it from the outside."[92] In the underground struggle against international fascism Maly rekindled his own early Bolshevik idealism, and inspired his agents with his own vision of the final victory of the Communist International.

Philby's first experience of illegal work for the Comintern in Vienna was as a courier between outlawed Austrian Communists and contacts in Hungary, Paris, and Prague. In February 1934 the struggle between left and right in Austria reached what Philby fairly described as "crisis point." The forces of the right-wing Dollfuss government and the even more extreme street fighters of the Heimwehr (whose founder, Prince Starhemberg, had taken part in Hitler's attempted Munich putsch of 1923) attacked trade-union headquarters, left-wing newspapers, Socialist offices, welfare offices, even housing complexes. Two of the largest Viennese housing complexes were demolished by artillery fire and nine Socialist leaders were strung up in the courtyard of the Supreme Court. If there was one episode that more than any other persuaded Maly of Philby's potential as an NKVD agent, it was probably his courage and ingenuity in smuggling Communists and Socialists out of the country. The *Daily Telegraph* correspondent Eric Gedye later recalled being visited by Philby in Vienna:

> I opened my wardrobe to select something. When Kim saw several suits there, he cried, "Good God, you have seven; I must have them. I've got six wounded friends in the sewers in danger of the gallows." The suits were stuffed in a suitcase and, according to Philby, used to smuggle his friends out of this hiding place in the sewers and across the border into Czechoslovakia.[93]

Philby later admitted to his children that during his time in Vienna he was "given the job of penetrating British intelligence, and told it did not matter how long it took to do the job."[94] It was Maly who gave him that assignment and in May 1934 sent him back to England to pursue it. To act as Philby's controller Maly sent to London an illegal who had worked for him in Vienna, Arnold Deutsch. Deutsch's portrait hangs today next to Maly's in the Memory Room of the First Chief Directorate. The citation beneath ranks his contribution to the recruitment and running of the Cambridge moles as virtually the equal of Maly's.[95]

Deutsch was a thirty-year-old Austrian Jew, an attractive, talented, cosmopolitan Central European in the Maly and Münzenberg mold. Born the son of a Jewish trader and brought up in an orthodox Jewish quarter of Vienna, he left his secondary school, a Vienna Realgymnasium, in June 1923, a month after his nineteenth birthday. The following autumn he entered the Philosophy Faculty at Vienna University. Despite the Faculty's name, many of its students, like Deutsch, were scientists. Though Deutsch took no first degree equivalent to the B.A. or B.S., his progress was more rapid than the regulations at any British or American university would allow. For four years he concentrated most of his studies in physics and chemistry, also taking courses in philosophy and psychology. He spent his fifth year writing up a Ph.D. thesis entitled "On Silver and Mercury Salts of Amidobenzothiazols and a New Method of Quantitative Silver Analysis."

On July 19, 1928, less than five years after entering Vienna University and two months after his twenty-fourth birthday, Deutsch was awarded the degree of doctor of philosophy with distinction. His dissertation, however, proved controversial. At the first oral examina-

tion, when he defended his thesis, one of the three examiners pronounced it "unsatisfactory"; Deutsch passed by a majority vote. At the
second oral examination, which covered a broader field of knowledge
and determined Deutsch's final grade, the two examiners also disagreed. Professor Schlick awarded him a distinction, Professor Reiniger
a pass. On the chairman's casting a vote, Deutsch received a distinction.[96]

The examiner chiefly responsible for Deutsch's distinction, Mo-
ritz Schlick, founder of the Vienna Circle of philosophers and scientists,
was distinguished as both a physicist and a philosopher. He was assassinated in 1936 by an aggrieved student, whose thesis on ethics he had
failed. A decade earlier he was probably an important influence on
Deutsch, who took his course on ethics in the summer semester of 1926.
Schlick equated moral values with feelings of pleasure, and human
fulfillment with ecstasy. But to achieve ecstasy in contemporary society
he argued that the individual must first endure torment; joy and sorrow
together produced a convulsion through which "the whole person is
affected to a depth which few impressions can reach." Schlick believed
that as civilization progressed it would gradually make it possible for
human beings to achieve pleasure without suffering.[97]

Throughout his time at Vienna University, Deutsch described
himself in university documents and his curriculum vitae as Jewish
both by religion *(mosaisch)* and by ethnic origin *(jüdisch)*.[98] His intellectual progression from orthodox Judaism to Marxist materialism
cannot be traced with certainty. But Deutsch's attraction to Schlick's
vision of a world in which joy would replace suffering seems to have
been accompanied, and in the end overtaken, by his growing commitment to the Communist International's vision of a new world order that
would free mankind from exploitation and alienation. In the late 1920s
he joined the "sex-pol" movement founded by the Viennese Jewish
psychologist, Wilhelm Reich, which opened clinics to counsel workers
on sexual problems. Deutsch ran the Münster-Verlag which published
Reich's work and other "sex-pol" literature.[99] At this stage of his career,
Reich was engaged in an ambitious attempt to integrate Freudianism
with Marxism. Political and sexual repression, he argued, went together
and paved the way for fascism. For a time he hoped that the Soviet
Union might be capable of ending both. In 1930 Reich left Vienna for
Berlin, where he joined the German Communist Party (KPD). After
Hitler's rise to power three years later, he was forced to flee from
Germany, returned briefly to Vienna, then left for Scandinavia where

he began a sometimes bizarre research program on human sexual behavior which earned him a reputation as "the prophet of the better orgasm." Deutsch's involvement in the "sex-pol" movement and his role in publishing some of Reich's work in Vienna brought him to the attention of the anti-pornography section of the Austrian police, which began an investigation of his activities in the spring of 1934, just as he was leaving for England.[100]

The citation beneath Deutsch's portrait in the First Chief Directorate Memory Room makes no mention of his association with Reich. Instead it records that he entered the OGPU after working for the Comintern OMS and that his first foreign mission was to Palestine, then under a British mandate.

In 1933 Deutsch and his wife, Josefine (née Rubel), whom he had married in 1929, visited Moscow. There Deutsch was trained as an OGPU illegal and his wife as a radio operator. While in Moscow Arnold Deutsch was given the cover name Stefan Lang, but in April 1934 he traveled to London under his real name, using his Austrian passport so that he could use his academic credentials to mix in university circles.[101] During his years in London, he posed as a "university lecturer" carrying out research. He lived at first at temporary addresses, but when his wife joined him in 1935 moved to a flat on Lawn Road, Hampstead. In May 1936 Josefine Deutsch gave birth to a daughter, Ninette Elizabeth.[102]

Kim Philby returned to England in May 1934, a month after Deutsch's arrival, living at first with his new bride Litzi in his mother's home in Hampstead. His first attempt to penetrate Whitehall was an application to join the civil service. But his two referees—his former Trinity director of studies in economics, Dennis Robertson, and a family friend, Donald Robertson (no relation)—had their doubts. Having consulted with his fellow referee about Kim's Communist sympathies at Cambridge, Dennis Robertson wrote to tell him that while they admired his energy and intelligence, they would feel bound to add that his "sense of political injustice might well unfit him for administrative work." Philby withdrew his application and settled instead for a long haul into the establishment. He took a job with the City-based liberal monthly, *Review of Reviews,* broke contact with his Cambridge Communist friends, and let it be known that his politics had changed. Arnold Deutsch, whom he knew only as Otto, was sympathetic, encouraging, and counseled patience:

He told me he appreciated my commitment; the question was
how best to use me. I should not go off and die on some
foreign battlefield or become a war correspondent for the
Daily Worker. There were more important battles for me to
fight but I would have to be patient. For the next two years
he gave me virtually nothing to do. He was testing my commitment. I would turn up for our meetings with nothing to
offer and would receive in return patient encouragement.[103]

Deutsch arrived in England with instructions to make contact with
Burgess as well as with Philby.[104] Already enthusiastic about the secret
war against fascism waged by the groups of five, Burgess had been
suggested for recruitment by both Philby and Henri. A more doctrinaire and less imaginative NKVD control than Deutsch might well
have concluded that the outrageous Burgess would be a liability rather
than an asset. Deutsch, however, shared Burgess's contempt for bourgeois sexual morality. His belief, derived from involvement in Wilhelm
Reich's "sex-pol" movement, that political and sexual repression went
together, commended him to all the Magnificent Five—but probably
most of all to Burgess. Despite Burgess's later embellishments, his
childhood seems to have been both privileged and fairly conventional.
He was the son of a naval commander who had married a rich wife.
     After a year at Eton, Guy had been sent to the Royal Naval
College at Dartmouth, where he shone both in the classroom and on
the playing field. Poor eyesight, however, disqualified him from pursuing a naval career, and at the age of sixteen he returned to Eton. In his
final year he won the Rosebery and Gladstone history prizes as well as
a scholarship in history to Trinity College, Cambridge. But despite an
increasingly flamboyant gregariousness, he failed to win election to
Pop, the exclusive Eton society, possibly because of his indiscreet homosexuality. Once at Cambridge in October 1930 Burgess threw what
remained of his discretion to the winds. At a time when homosexual
acts even between consenting adults in private were still illegal, Burgess
openly vaunted the pleasures of "rough trade" with young working-
class males.[105]
     But Burgess did not confine himself to Cambridge's gay com-
munity. His brilliant conversation, good looks, natural gregariousness,
and self-assurance made him one of the most socially successful undergraduates of his generation, moving with equal confidence in the exclusive Pitt Club and the more irreverent Footlights, the student society

devoted to satirical revue. Burgess also possessed formidable intellectual gifts, which displayed themselves, however, more in a talent for fluent generalization and well-chosen example than in a capacity for close textual analysis. Neither his diverse social life nor the bottle of 1921 Liebfraumilch that he consumed each day with lunch impeded his apparently effortless progress to first-class honors in Part I of the Historical Tripos in June 1932. Five months later he was elected to the Apostles, a secret intellectual discussion group of dons and undergraduates, which prided itself (not entirely accurately) on recruiting Cambridge's ablest students.[106]

When Goronwy Rees, then a young fellow of All Souls, first met Burgess, then on a visit to Oxford, in the summer of 1932, "he had the reputation of being the most brilliant undergraduate of his day":

> Indeed, he did not belie his reputation. He was then a scholar of Trinity, and it was thought that he had a brilliant academic future in front of him. That evening he talked a good deal about painting and to me it seemed that what he said was both original and sensitive, and, for one so young, to show an unusually wide knowledge of the subject. His conversation had the more charm because he was very good looking in a boyish, athletic, very English way; it seemed incongruous that almost everything he said made it quite clear that he was a homosexual and a communist. . . . It seemed to me that there was something deeply original, something which was, as it were, his very own in everything he had to say.[107]

By 1932, as Rees discovered at their first meeting, Burgess was a Marxist. By 1933 at the latest he had joined the Communist Party, probably recruited by Maurice Dobb. One of his favorite historical themes, in which he showed greater prescience than most of his lecturers, was the inevitable decline of the British Empire. At the society of Indian nationalists in Cambridge, the Majlis, he argued that revolution in the Empire would open the British road to socialism. Burgess's sense of living in the imperial twilight of British capitalism only seemed to heighten his sense of the pleasures it had to offer. Yet he also took increasingly to heart Marx's injunction that, whereas previous philosophers had tried to interpret the world, "the point, however, is to change it." In his final year as an undergraduate, Burgess became an activist.

He helped to organize a successful strike among Trinity College waiters against the casual-labor system, which laid most of them off during vacations. Enjoying to the full the decadent pleasures of a capitalist system to whose overthrow he was committed was characteristic of Burgess's youthful capacity to have his cake and eat it.[108]

Increasingly preoccupied by Party work as well as his flamboyant social life, Burgess did not cruise to a first in Part II of the Historical Tripos as easily as in Part I. During his final examinations in the summer of 1933 he suffered from (probably psychosomatic) illness and was awarded an aegrotat, an unclassed honors degree awarded to those judged to be of degree standard but unable to complete their papers. But he was still believed to have a brilliant academic future ahead of him and began work for a Ph.D. thesis on the "Bourgeois Revolution" in seventeenth-century England in the hope of winning a fellowship at Trinity.[109]

One of Burgess's most remarkable gifts even as an undergraduate was his ability to captivate dons as well as fellow students. Goronwy Rees, though a heterosexual who resisted Burgess's attempt to seduce him at their first meeting, immediately made great friends with him. From that moment on it was Burgess who dominated their relationship. Burgess's appeal to a number of homosexual dons was even greater. The distinguished Oxford classicist Maurice Bowra, then dean of Wadham College, with whom Burgess went to stay, was infatuated with him. Rees detected in Burgess "some conscious or unconscious will to dominate. . . . He saw himself sometimes as a kind of Figaro figure ever resourceful in the service of others in order to manipulate them to his own ends." Within what Bowra called the "homintern"—furtive, often frustrated homosexuals, sometimes guilt-ridden about their illegal sex lives—Burgess's power to manipulate was at least partly sexual:

> He was gross and even brutal in his treatment of his lovers, but his sexual behavior also had a generous aspect. . . . At one time or another he went to bed with most of these friends, as he did with anyone who was willing and was not positively repulsive, and in doing so he released them from many of their frustrations and inhibitions. . . . Such affairs did not last for long; but Guy had the faculty of retaining the affection of those he went to bed with, and also, in some curious way, of maintaining a kind of permanent domination over them. This was strengthened because, long after the

affair was over, he continued to assist his friends in their sexual lives, which were often troubled and unsatisfactory, to listen to their emotional difficulties and when necessary find suitable partners for them. To such people he was a combination of father confessor and pimp.[110]

The member of the "homintern" on whom Burgess had the most enduring influence was Anthony Blunt, from whom he derived some of the insights into painting that so impressed Goronwy Rees at their first meeting. Anthony Blunt, the most senior of Cambridge's Magnificent Five, was the son of a well-connected Anglican clergyman, the Reverend Arthur Vaughan Stanley Blunt, who died in Anthony's third year at Cambridge. Queen Mary, consort of King George V, wrote to his widow, Hilda: "What a loss he will be. Why should he have been taken, who was doing such good work on earth, when such useless, evil people are allowed to live?" Anthony had only a distant relationship with his saintly father but was deeply attached to his mother, described by his brother Wilfrid as a "woman of infinite goodness and almost puritanical simplicity, incapable of telling the whitest of white lies."[111]

When Blunt was four, his father had become chaplain at the British embassy in Paris. The next ten years, which the family spent almost entirely in France, gave Blunt what he described as "a very strong French leaning which has coloured my whole attitude to things ever since. I was brought up from a very early age, really almost unconsciously, to look at works of art and to regard them as of importance."[112] At school at Marlborough from the age of fourteen, Blunt acquired, according to his close friend and contemporary the poet Louis MacNeice, a reputation for "precocious knowledge of art and habitual contempt for conservative authority." Blunt himself told a later generation of Marlburians:

We went out of our way to be irritatingly provocative. We used to walk down the aisle of chapel flaunting our silk handkerchiefs—I used to wear mine from the strap of my wrist-watch and they could not stop me because there was no rule preventing it. And on Saturday evenings we used to go upfield to where other boys were playing rounders and infuriate them by playing catch with a large, brightly coloured ball right across their game.

At Marlborough Blunt's disdain for bourgeois convention expressed itself on an aesthetic rather than a political plane. According to Mac-Neice, "He told everyone who would listen that he . . . considered it very low to talk about politics."[113] Despite a number of crushes on other boys, Blunt may not yet have been a practicing homosexual by the time he left school; some of his closest schoolfriends, like MacNeice, were heterosexual.

The course that would have most interested Blunt at Cambridge, the History of Art Tripos, was not introduced until the early 1960s. When he arrived at Cambridge in 1926, no English university yet taught art history; the Courtauld Institute, of which Blunt later became director, was not founded until 1931. Blunt entered Trinity College with a scholarship in mathematics—a considerable achievement for a man whose main gifts were aesthetic and literary.[114] Math, however, did not suit him. After second-class honors in Part I of the Mathematical Tripos at the end of his first year in June 1927, he changed to modern languages, a subject less remote from his interests in continental art and culture. He took Part I of the Modern Languages Tripos in 1928, gaining first-class honors in French (in which he had been fluent since childhood) and an upper second in German. For the remainder of his degree course he was able to concentrate on French. He graduated in 1930 with first-class honors in Part II of the Modern Languages Tripos.[115]

In May 1928 Blunt was elected to the Apostles. It was probably his fellow Apostle, the King's mathematician Alister Watson (later senior scientific officer in the Admiralty and also a KGB agent, though not quite in the same class as the Magnificent Five), who first attracted Blunt to the serious study of Marxist theory.[116] But it was several years before Blunt's intellectual Marxism was translated into political activism. The impression formed of the undergraduate Blunt by the young Trinity history don Steven Runciman was shared by many who met him. "He was always, I think, rather pleased with himself. But he could be very good company." During his four years as an undergraduate Blunt also became an active, though discreet, homosexual.[117]

The most important influence in drawing Blunt into work for the KGB was Guy Burgess, who came up to Trinity as an undergraduate just as Blunt began postgraduate research in October 1930. It was Blunt who two years later introduced Burgess into the Apostles.[118] By then Blunt had been elected to a research fellowship at Trinity for his work on "The history of theories of painting with special reference to

Poussin." The new research fellow and the new Apostle were frequently in each other's company. Both were sufficiently well-known figures to be recognized together by an unruly Corpus Christi undergraduate, Valentine Lawford,

> as he stood in a window overlooking Trinity and threw a banana at the people emerging after luncheon through the Great Gate, not caring in the least which of three possible human targets it hit: the broad one who looked like a rowing blue, the short one whom I knew as Guy Burgess, or the long, thin one who was Anthony Blunt.[119]

Part of the bond between the two was sexual. Blunt felt a passionate physical attraction for the younger man. Burgess, much more casual in all his liaisons, probably released Blunt's remaining sexual inhibitions and introduced him to the proletarian pleasures of "rough trade." But, like Bowra and others in the homintern, Blunt was also enormously attracted by Burgess's intellectual flair, conversational brilliance, and breadth of vision. At their first meeting Goronwy Rees was enthralled by Burgess's ability to relate his interests in the arts to the Marxist interpretation of history and that in turn to a busmen's strike he was helping to organize in Cambridge.[120] In 1972, seven years before his own treachery was exposed, Blunt protested publicly against those who sought to belittle the remarkable gifts displayed in Burgess's Cambridge years:

> It is, I think, important to repeat that he was not only one of the most intellectually stimulating people I have ever known but also had great charm and tremendous vivacity; and those people who now write saying that they felt physically sick in his presence are not speaking the truth. They are throwing back to his early years things that may have been true about Guy in his later years in this country. He was a terrific intellectual stimulus. He had a far wider range of interests than either [John] Cornford or [James] Klugmann [the two most prominent student Party activists in Cambridge]. He was interested in everything and although he was perverse in many ways there was no subject which one could discuss with him without his expressing some interesting and worthwhile view.[121]

Burgess's most important influence on Blunt was to persuade him of his duty to translate his theoretical Marxism into an active commitment to work for the Comintern—and ultimately the KGB—in the international struggle against fascism. The core of Burgess's argument was probably accurately summarized in one of his favorite passages from a memoir by Claud Cockburn:

> A moment comes when your actions have to bear some kind
> of relation to your words. That is what is called the Moment
> of Truth.[122]

That moment came early in the academic year 1933–34, when Burgess, fired by Henri's vision of solidarity with the anti-Nazi Fünfergruppen of the German workers, set out to form a Cambridge group of five. Blunt himself made a veiled reference to this turning point in his career in an article published in 1973:

> Quite suddenly, in the autumn term of 1933, Marxism hit
> Cambridge. I can date it quite precisely because I had sabbat-
> ical leave for that term, and when I came back in January
> [1934], I found that almost all my younger friends had
> become Marxist and joined the Party; and Cambridge was
> literally transformed overnight.[123]

Blunt could not then reveal publicly how the "transformation" affected him. Burgess insisted that "the Moment of Truth" had come and that Blunt had now to commit himself to the Comintern's secret war against fascism. At the end of the Michaelmas (autumn) term 1933, Burgess visited Blunt in Rome, where he was spending part of his sabbatical staying with Ellis Waterhouse, then librarian at the British School in Rome. Waterhouse was not privy to all that passed between Burgess and Blunt. He noted, however, that until Burgess's arrival "We never talked politics at all. But that was all Guy wanted to discuss. He was exceedingly intelligent about politics and Anthony followed what he did." It was probably in Rome, the capital of Fascist Italy, that Burgess recruited Blunt to his secret ring of five to pursue the Comintern's secret war against international fascism.[124]

Apart from Blunt, the most important early recruit to Burgess's ring of five was probably the Trinity Hall undergraduate Donald Maclean, with whom eighteen years later he was to defect to Moscow. Maclean's father, Sir Donald Maclean, was a Presbyterian lawyer and Liberal politician of English birth but Scottish ancestry. At the time of his sudden death in 1932 he was president of the Board of Education in Ramsay MacDonald's National Government. Sir Donald's concern with high moral standards led him to send his son to Gresham's School, at Holt in Norfolk, whose headmaster, J. E. Eccles, emphasized to each new boy the importance "of truth, and frankness, and honour; of purity in thought, and word, and deed; of the value and importance of hard work and honest work." To encourage purity and limit adolescent sexual experimentation in daytime, each boy's trouser pockets were sewn up. One of Gresham's most famous pupils in the Eccles era, the poet W. H. Auden, claimed in 1934: "The best reason I have for opposing fascism is that at school I have lived in a fascist state."

Maclean reacted less strongly. There is no convincing evidence that he hated (even if he did not greatly love) either his father or his public school. He played for Gresham's at rugby, won an exhibition (slightly less prestigious than a scholarship) to Trinity Hall, Cambridge, and left school with no taint on his moral reputation. Unlike Philby and Burgess, however, he had his first serious contact with Communism at school. His school friend Norman John ("James") Klugmann, who went on to become a member of the political committee of the Communist Party of Great Britain, as well as the Party historian, later claimed that he became a Communist at Gresham's to annoy the school authorities.

Maclean had his first experience of leading a double life while still at school, concealing from his father both his loss of Christian faith and his increasingly left-wing political opinions. If he was not already a Communist by the time he arrived at Trinity Hall in 1931, he became one during his first year. It was probably his friend Kluggers, a modern-languages scholar at the neighboring Trinity College, who first introduced him to Burgess. And it was probably the predatory Burgess who became the bisexual Maclean's first lover.

Having liberated Maclean from his sexual inhibitions, Burgess moved on rapidly to other conquests. He later ridiculed the idea that Maclean's "large, flabby, white whale-like body" could have appealed to him. In reality Maclean's tall, dark, athletic good looks made him, like Burgess, attractive to both sexes.[125] Burgess also released some of Maclean's political inhibitions. It was probably in the autumn term, 1933, shortly before he traveled to Rome to see Blunt, that Burgess recruited him to his secret cell, to join the Comintern's secret war against international fascism.

In November 1933 Maclean gave an interview to the main Cambridge student magazine, *The Granta,* which contained a curious allusion to his double life on both the sexual and political planes. Maclean began the interview by stating that he had three different personalities. He then adopted each of them in turn: first the camp, homosexual aesthete Cecil, "Just slipping into my velvet trousers when I heard you call. . . . You must come to my next party. I am going to have real Passion flowers and everybody is going to dress up as a Poem of Today"; then the heterosexual sporting hearty Jack, "Just having a steak at the Pig and Whistle when I heard you shout. Some awfully good fellows there—and damn fine waitresses too (he winks)"; and, finally, the innermost Maclean, the deadly serious Marxist grind Fred, "Very busy just now trying to find out whether Middleton Murray [sic] is material or merely dialectic. . . . The point is this. Everybody ought to work. That's what I'm here for."[126]

Like some of the German Fünfergruppen on which it was modeled, Burgess's Ring of Five had a fluctuating membership that did not always total exactly five. Its earliest members probably also included Alister Watson and James Klugmann. Neither, however, was later regarded by the KGB as in the same class as Philby, Burgess, Blunt, Maclean—or the Fifth Man recruited in 1935.

In the spring of 1934 Burgess changed his research subject from the seventeenth-century "Bourgeois Revolution" to the "Indian Mutiny."[127] That project too ran out of steam as Burgess became preoccupied with the secret war against fascism. In May, soon after Philby returned to London, he visited Cambridge and gave Burgess a firsthand account of his adventures with the Comintern underground in Vienna.[128] Goronwy Rees found Burgess's admiration for Philby "so excessive that I found it difficult to understand on what objective grounds it was based."[129] It was probably also in May, and in an East End café, that Burgess had his first meeting with Arnold Deutsch, whom, like Philby, he knew simply as Otto.[130] Burgess wrote to tell Philby of his recruitment. Philby, by his own account, "replied congratulating him."[131] In the summer of 1934, with the encouragement of Deutsch, Burgess visited both Germany and Russia accompanied by the Oxford Communist Derek Blaikie (later killed in the Second World War). Their visit to Germany took place at a dramatic time. Shortly after they had discussed with a young German Communist how he might escape to Russia, they heard the sound of distant gunfire. It was June 30, 1934, the "Night of the Long Knives," when Hitler settled accounts with his opponents in the Nazi Party.[132]

During his visit to Moscow, according to one of his confidants, Burgess met both Pyatnitsky, the head of OMS, and Bukharin, the former Comintern leader.[133] The trip encouraged him in his conviction that he was working for the Comintern in a secret war against international fascism. But on his return Deutsch was able to persuade him that to pursue the secret war he, like Philby, must go underground and break all visible ties with the Communist Party. Burgess did so in a manner his friends found bizarre, comparing Stalin unfavorably with the fascist dictators, and pointing to fascism as "the wave of the future." Even at the secret meetings of the Apostles he hid his political convictions:

> In any discussion of ideas he was always ready with an apt quotation, an amusing anecdote, a suggestive analogy, a mocking riposte. If the question before the society was political, he spoke in metaphors that were distant and obscure. If he was challenged to state his own convictions, his bright blue eyes would widen. He would look at the challenger with a beguiling smile, and then speak of other things.[134]

As he coaxed Burgess into accepting at least some of the discipline of an NKVD agent, Deutsch also persuaded him to water down his original aim of a Comintern cell, conceived in imitation of the Fünfergruppen, working as a group. The Cambridge recruits were run individually by Deutsch and later by Maly.[135] But, in defiance of orthodox tradecraft, Burgess continued to look on intelligence as a semisocial activity carried on in collaboration with his friends. As Philby later acknowledged, "It was Burgess who insisted on maintaining the links with all of us."[136] It was that insistence which in 1951 almost led to Philby's downfall.[137]

At Deutsch's prompting, Donald Maclean cut his links with the Communist Party at the same time as Burgess. After graduating with first-class honors in modern languages in June 1934, he had intended either to go to teach English in the Soviet Union or to stay on in Cambridge to work for his Ph.D.; the subject he had in mind for his dissertation was a Marxist analysis of John Calvin and the rise of the bourgeoisie. Instead he announced to his mother in the course of the summer that he intended to try for the Foreign Office. Lady Maclean was pleased but asked whether Donald's intentions might not conflict with his Communist beliefs. "You must think I turn like a weather-cock," replied her son, "but the fact is I've rather gone off all that lately." He spent most of the next year at a crammer near the British Museum, preparing for the Foreign Office exams in August 1935.[138] He passed with flying colors. Maclean later described how at his final interview he was asked about his "Communist views" at Cambridge:

> I'm afraid I did an instant double-take: Shall I deny the truth, or shall I brazen it out? I decided to brazen it out. "Yes," I said, "I did have such views—and I haven't entirely shaken them off." I think they must have liked my honesty because they nodded, looked at each other and smiled. Then the chairman said: "Thank you, that will be all, Mr. Ma-clean."[139]

When Maclean mounted the steps of the Foreign Office in October 1935 as a new member of His Majesty's Diplomatic Service, he became the first of the Magnificent Five to penetrate the corridors of power.

It took Burgess longer than Maclean to gain access to official secrets. By the end of 1934 his research had ground to a halt and he decided to leave Trinity. His first job outside Cambridge, early in 1935, was as financial adviser to the mother of his Trinity friend and fellow Apostle, Victor (later Lord) Rothschild. But his long-term aim, agreed on with Deutsch at their regular meetings in East End cafés, was to penetrate the corridors of power—if possible the Secret Intelligence Service.[140] To that end, Burgess set out to exploit "cynically and con-sciously . . . the old boy network," deploying in the process all his considerable charm save that, as he later admitted, he "could never bother to keep his finger-nails clean."[141] He appears to have made an unsuccessful attempt to get a job in the Conservative Party Research Department, directed by Sir Joseph Ball, former head of MI5's Investi-gation Branch and a close adviser to the future prime minister Neville Chamberlain.[142]

By the end of 1935, however, Burgess had become personal assistant to the young homosexual Conservative M.P. Captain "Jack" Macnamara, whom Rees considered "so far to the right . . . that it was reasonable to call him a fascist." "Guy talked about his employer with a kind of genial contempt; he was once again playing his Figaro role of the servant who is really the master." Figaro and his employer went on a number of fact-finding missions to Nazi Germany, which, according to Burgess, consisted largely of homosexual escapades with sympathetic members of the Hitler Youth.[143] Burgess built up a remarkable range of contacts among the continental homintern. Chief among them was Édouard Pfeiffer, *chef de cabinet* to Édouard Daladier, French war minister from January 1936 to May 1940 and prime minister from April 1938 to March 1940. Burgess told friends lurid stories of how "He and Pfeiffer and two members of the French cabinet . . . had spent an evening together at a male brothel in Paris. Singing and laughing, they had danced around a table, lashing a naked boy, who was strapped to it, with leather whips."[144]

Unlike Philby, Burgess, and Maclean, Blunt did not need to adopt a new and bogus right-wing political identity. Having never been a Communist Party militant, he had no background as an activist to conceal. The Marxist-informed contextualism that underpinned his art criticism in the 1930s seemed remote both from the world of active politics and from the polemics of Stalinist theoreticians. Indeed, Blunt has been accused, probably unfairly, by one leading Marxist critic of de-politicizing art history and trying to render it "formalist and value-free." Blunt's basic premise, enunciated in the thirties, was to insist that art cannot be divorced from society:

> Works of art are produced by artists; artists are men; men live in society, and are in a large measure formed by the society in which they live. Therefore works of art cannot be considered historically except in human and ultimately in social terms.

After a trip to Russia in the summer of 1935 his Marxist sympathies became more explicit in his articles as art critic of *The Spectator*. "The intellectual," he declared, "is no longer afraid to own to an interest in the practical matters of the world, and Communism is allowed to be a subject as interesting as Cubism." He went on to call for artists' unions and the transformation of museums from pleasure palaces into classrooms.[145] It was probably after his visit to Russia that Blunt began regular meetings with Arnold Deutsch. Though a radical voice in the art world, he was persuaded by Deutsch to affect indifference to Party politics. Michael Straight, a young American economist at Trinity who joined the Apostles in March 1936, concluded from Blunt's part in the discussions that he was "totally unpolitical." He did not realize his mistake until early in 1937 when Blunt tried to recruit him as a Soviet agent.[146]

The most important agent talent-spotted by Blunt was the Fifth Man, the Trinity undergraduate John Cairncross. Together with Philby, Burgess, Blunt, and Maclean, he is remembered by the Center as one of the Magnificent Five, the ablest group of foreign agents in KGB history. But for the conspiracy theories surrounding the career of Sir Roger Hollis, and the other false trails that confused the media mole hunt in the 1980s, Cairncross might well have been unmasked as the Fifth Man even before Gordievsky provided the clinching evidence. Though Cairncross is the last of the Five to be publicly identified, he successfully penetrated a greater variety of the corridors of power and intelligence than any of the other four. In less than a decade after leaving Cambridge, he served successively in the Foreign Office, the Treasury, the private office of a government minister, the sigint agency GC & CS, and SIS. Gordievsky recalls Dmitri Svetanko, while head of the British desk in the First Chief Directorate, speaking of Cairncross "with awe, admiration and respect." "Cairncross's achievements," said Svetanko, "were the equal of any of the Five except Philby."[147] His student academic record was also as remarkable as that of any other member of the Five.

Cairncross was born in 1913 into a modest but intellectually gifted Glasgow family. His elder brother, Alec (who had no connection with the KGB), was a distinguished economist who became, successively, head of the Government Economic Service, Master of St. Peter's College, Oxford, and Chancellor of Glasgow University. Like Alec, John Cairncross won a scholarship to Hamilton Academy, near Glasgow. In 1930, at the age of seventeen, probably already influenced by the political traditions of Red Clydeside and the social injustices of the depression, he entered Glasgow University, where for two years he studied French, German, political economy and English.[148] He then moved to the Continent to improve his languages, spending the academic year 1933–34 in Paris at the Sorbonne. While there he gained the *licence ès lettres* in only a year, won a scholarship to Trinity College, Cambridge, and probably made contact with Münzenberg's World Committee for the Relief of the Victims of German Fascism.

By the time Cairncross arrived at Trinity to read French and German in October 1934, he was an open Communist. His *licence* from the Sorbonne allowed him to skip the first part of the modern-languages degree course and graduate with a Cambridge B.A. in only two years.[149] One of Cairncross's college supervisors in French literature was Anthony Blunt, who gave him a series of individual weekly tutorials (or "supervisions" as they are called at Cambridge). Blunt's patrician manner and Marxist intellectualism, apparently aloof from the harsh realities of the class struggle, jarred on the passionate young Scottish Communist. "I didn't like him," said Cairncross later, "and he didn't like me."

Blunt, however, talent-spotted him for Burgess, who met Cairncross during one of his visits to Cambridge and established an immediate rapport with him. Forty years later, in an interview in which he concealed most of his KGB career, Cairncross acknowledged that he had found Burgess "fascinating, charming and utterly ruthless."[150] During one of Burgess's visits to Cambridge in 1935, he recruited Cairncross as a Comintern agent in the secret war against international fascism and put him in touch with Arnold Deutsch.[151] By 1936 Cairncross had broken all overt contact with the Communist Party and applied to join the Foreign Office. In the summer of 1936 he graduated from Cambridge with first-class honors in modern languages, was elected by Trinity to a senior scholarship, and passed at the top of the Foreign Office entrance examinations, a hundred marks ahead of a brilliant fellow of All Souls, Con O'Neill (later a leading British diplomat). In the autumn he became, after John King and Donald Maclean, the third Soviet agent working in the Foreign Office.[152]

The growing potential of the Cambridge Five, the importance of the intelligence supplied to Pieck by Captain King from the Foreign Office, and the simultaneous development by Deutsch of an espionage ring in the Woolwich Arsenal, determined INO at the beginning of 1936 to send Maly to London to take overall charge of NKVD illegal operations. The NKVD "legal" resident at the London embassy, Aron Vaclavovich Shuster, took no part in any of these operations beyond providing a channel of communication to Moscow Center and other forms of illegal support.[153]

Slutsky, the head of INO, admired Maly's great gifts in recruiting, inspiring, and winning the loyalty of his agents, but remained concerned by his tendency to remorse about his past career. After bibulous evenings in restaurants with his agents, Maly was liable to reminisce about some of the horrors he had witnessed. Hede Massing later wrote of him: "A discreet man of the world when sober, he lapsed into terrible depression and fits of self-accusation when drunk. To learn of the nightmares under this polished exterior was frightening." Maly had a passionate love affair with one of Ignace Reiss's agents, named Gerda Frankfurter. "But Moscow," according to Hede Massing, "well aware of his alcoholic inclinations, forced him into marriage with a Russian girl whom he disliked. She was to act as a combination [of] nurse and police guard."[154]

Maly and his wife arrived in London early in 1936, using false Austrian passports in the name of Paul and Lydia Hardt. He introduced himself to Captain King as "Mr. Petersen," an executive of an imaginary Dutch bank, which King's NKVD controller, Pieck, had told him was purchasing inside information from the Foreign Office. Initially King delivered copies of Foreign Office documents on his way home from work to Pieck's office in Buckingham Gate. From Buckingham Gate copies or originals of the documents were taken to Maly by a British Communist electrical engineer, Brian Goold-Verschoyle (alias Friend), who for some years had acted as a Comintern courier.

Goold-Verschoyle, who had rebelled against a public-school education and been inspired by a romantic vision of the Soviet worker-peasant state, believed he was delivering political directives from the Communist International. He was shocked when one of King's packets came open and he discovered Foreign Office documents inside. Maly telegraphed the most important of King's material to Moscow from the Soviet embassy in Kensington, using the code name Mann. The remainder were taken by Goold-Verschoyle or another courier to be photographed at a studio run by Wolf Levit, a German NKVD photographer.[155]

Initially, Donald Maclean, who began his Foreign Office career in the League of Nations and Western Department (which dealt with Dutch, Iberian, Swiss, and League affairs), had access to a more limited range of Foreign Office material than the humbler but also more strategically placed King. The most useful intelligence he provided to the NKVD probably concerned the Spanish Civil War, of which Maclean wrote later: "We were all united in wishing the French and Soviet governments would intervene to save the Spanish government from Franco and the fascists." He probably conveyed to the NKVD the exaggerated view that British nonintervention was part of a broader policy of appeasement toward Germany designed to leave Stalin to face fascism alone.[156] But Maly saw Maclean chiefly as a long-term investment and urged him to concentrate during his early career in the Foreign Office less on obtaining intelligence than on advancing his own career as rapidly as possible.[157] In this Maclean was triumphantly successful. The personnel department provided the warmest of testimonials when it recommended him in March 1938 to the British ambassador in France for his first foreign posting as third secretary in the Paris embassy:

> Maclean, who is the son of the late Sir Donald Maclean, whom you may remember as a Liberal Member of Parliament, has done extremely well during his first two years here and is one of the mainstays of the Western Department. He is a very nice individual indeed and has plenty of brains and keenness. He is, too, nice-looking and ought, we think, to be a success in Paris from the social as well as the work point of view.[158]

By now Maclean's reputation had grown so rapidly that he was being tipped as a future permanent under-secretary.[159]

John Cairncross, who entered the Foreign Office a year after Maclean, in the autumn of 1936, did not fit in nearly as easily. Over the next two years he worked in the American, League of Nations, Western, and Central departments without finding a real niche for himself. For a time he worked with Maclean in the Western Department, gaining access to what he himself described as a "wealth of valuable information on the progress of the Civil War in Spain."[160] Cairncross lacked Maclean's easy charm and social graces; though he tried to cultivate a wide range of contacts within Whitehall, he did not make many friends. Sir John Colville, assistant private secretary to Neville Chamberlain and subsequently private secretary to Churchill, found him "a very intelligent, though sometimes incoherent, bore." He later recalled that "Cairncross was always asking people out to lunch . . . He ate very slowly, slower than anyone I've ever known." Cairncross did, however, make detailed notes of his lunchtime conversations in Whitehall, which he passed on to the NKVD.[161] After his first year in the Foreign Office, Maly suggested to him that he think of transferring to the Treasury, a department that, unlike the Foreign Office, the NKVD had yet to penetrate.[162] He finally did so in October 1938. The Foreign Office was probably glad to see him go, having concluded that his awkward manner made him unsuitable for a diplomatic career.

Burgess was doubtless frustrated by the ability of his recruit Cairncross to penetrate Whitehall more rapidly than he could. Late in 1936 he was taken on by the BBC as a producer. After a training course and producing, improbably, a series called *Keep Fit with Miss Quigley*, he moved to the Talks Department of the Home Service (now Radio 4) and began to seek out men with past or present intelligence connections to whom he made the tempting offer of giving a talk on the radio. His most important new contact was David Footman, deputy head (later head) of the Political Intelligence Department in SIS.[163] Footman would doubtless have been horrified to learn that the producer of his talk on Albania in the summer of 1937 was an NKVD agent. But no such suspicion crossed his mind, and a year later, much impressed by Burgess's obvious flair for international relations, he helped him to get a job in SIS.

Burgess continued for some years to return regularly to Cambridge to attend meetings of the Apostles and visit friends. Until Blunt left Trinity for the Warburg Institute in London in 1937, he consulted with Burgess on suitable recruits for Soviet intelligence. Michael Straight concluded after his own attempted recruitment by Blunt early in 1937 that Burgess was "the invisible man behind Anthony."[164] Blunt's most important recruit was Leonard Henry ("Leo") Long, who arrived at Trinity, already a Communist, in October 1935 with a brilliant academic reputation and a scholarship in modern languages. "I was a working-class boy," said Long later, "and had a deep sense of the inequity of society."[165] Blunt supervised his work in French and was probably chiefly responsible for his election to the Apostles in May 1937. At about the same time, Blunt also recruited him to work for the NKVD. Like Straight, Long found Blunt's recruiting technique so persuasive partly because he appeared compassionate rather than overbearing. "Blunt," Long later recalled, "never tried blackmailing or bullying me, because we shared a deep belief in the Communist cause."[166] During the Second World War Long was to be run personally by Blunt as a Soviet subagent.

Though Kim Philby ultimately became the most important of the Magnificent Five, his career took off more slowly than those of the other four. His unexciting work for the *Review of Reviews* after his return from Vienna left him intermittently despondent at how little he was achieving in the secret war against fascism and in need of encouragement from Deutsch. His first minor success was to gain acceptance by the pro-German Anglo-German Fellowship, whose "constant contact" with Goebbels and the Nazi Ministry of Propaganda and Enlightenment was denounced in a secret Foreign Office memorandum. Philby's enthusiastic part-time work for the fellowship opened up the prospect of a full-time job starting a new trade journal financed by German money. Though in the end the job failed to materialize, Philby had a number of meetings with the German ambassador in London, von Ribbentrop, and paid several visits to Goebbels's Propaganda Ministry in Berlin.[167]

Philby was in Berlin in July 1936 when he heard the news of the outbreak of the Spanish Civil War. It was that war which gave him his first major intelligence assignment, operating under journalistic cover. "My immediate assignment," he wrote in his memoirs, "was to get first-hand information on all aspects of the fascist war effort." As usual his memoirs fail to tell the whole truth. Gordievsky's information, however, makes it possible to solve the chief remaining mystery about Philby's time in Spain. Early in 1940 the NKVD defector Walter Krivitsky visited England, where he was debriefed by Jane Archer, whom Philby described as the second-ablest MI5 officer he ever encountered. From Krivitsky, writes Philby in his memoirs, Mrs. Archer "elicited a tantalizing scrap of information about a young English journalist whom Soviet intelligence had sent to Spain during the Civil War."[168] The "young English journalist" was Philby. The "tantalizing scrap of information" was about a plan to assassinate General Franco.

Early in 1937 Yezhov sent orders to Maly to use one of his British agents to travel to Spain under journalistic cover, penetrate General Franco's entourage, and help organize his assassination.[169] Philby persuaded a London news agency to give him a letter of accreditation as a free-lance war correspondent, and arrived in Spain in February 1937. Once there he bombarded *The Times* with unsolicited reports of the war written from areas controlled by Franco's forces.[170] His career as a Soviet agent in Spain was very nearly cut short before it began in earnest. By Philby's own reckoning, he escaped detection "almost literally by the skin of my teeth." Two months after he arrived in Spain he was wakened in the middle of the night by two Nationalist Civil Guards hammering on his bedroom door. As he dressed under the watchful eye of the guards he realized he had left his NKVD code written on a piece of ricepaper in the ticket pocket of his trousers. Unable to dispose of it on the way to the Civil Guards headquarters, he found himself ushered into an office lit by a single bright naked lightbulb to be interrogated by "an undersized major of the Civil Guard, elderly, bald and sour." Then he was told to turn out his pockets. The next few seconds were among the most critical in Philby's life:

> Taking first my wallet, I threw it down on [the] table, giving it at the last moment a flick of the wrist which sent it spinning towards the far end. As I had hoped, all three men made a dive at it, spreadeagling themselves across the table. Confronted by three pairs of buttocks, I scooped the scrap of paper out of my trousers, a crunch and a swallow, and it was gone.[171]

Thereafter Philby's fortunes rapidly improved. In May he was taken on officially by *The Times* as one of its two correspondents in Nationalist Spain. He traveled to London to settle the details of his work with both *The Times* and Maly. On his return to Spain Philby strengthened his cover by acquiring as a mistress Lady Frances ("Bunny") Lindsay-Hogg, the divorced wife of an English baronet and an ardent royalist. Philby dissembled brilliantly even in bed. Bunny later recalled: "He never breathed a word about socialism, communism or anything like that." At the end of the year Philby became a local hero. Three journalists sitting in a car in which he had been traveling were fatally injured by an artillery shell. Philby himself was slightly wounded. He reported modestly to the readers of *The Times:* "Your correspondent . . . was taken to a first aid station where light head injuries were speedily treated. Meanwhile Spanish officers worked gallantly in an attempt to rescue the occupants of the car regardless of falling shells." On March 2 General Franco himself pinned onto Philby's breast the Red Cross of Military Merit. Britain's only Communist M.P., Willie Gallacher, protested in the House of Commons. Philby later claimed, probably accurately:

> My wounding in Spain helped my work—both journalism and intelligence work—no end. Before then there had been a lot of criticism of British journalists from Franco officers who seemed to think that the British in general must be a lot of communists because so many were fighting with the International Brigade. After I had been wounded and decorated by Franco himself, I became known as "the English-decorated-by-Franco" and all sorts of doors opened for me.

In the opinion of one British diplomat "There was little that Philby did not know about the extent of the German and Italian military participation on the Franco side." Philby passed on the intelligence he gathered from within the Franco camp at meetings with NKVD officers across the French border at Hendaye or St. Jean de Luz.[172] But the mission for which Maly had sent Philby to Spain, to help organize the assassination of Franco, was abandoned in the summer of 1937 before Philby had won the confidence of Franco's entourage.[173]

In July 1937 Maly was recalled to Moscow. Most INO officers fell under suspicion during the paranoia of the purges; only a minority survived the Great Terror. Maly's religious background and revulsion at the use of terror made him an obvious suspect. The high praise he had received from Yezhov and the commendation from Stalin in the previous year left him with a faint hope that he might somehow be able to counter whatever charges were laid against him. But his main motive for returning was a curious sense of fatalism. He told Elizabeth Poretsky, the wife of Ignace Reiss: "They will kill me there and they will kill me here. Better to die there."[174] Aleksandr Orlov, who refused a similar order to return, records that Maly told him: "I know that as a former priest I haven't got a chance. But I have decided to go there so that nobody can say: 'That priest might have been a real spy after all.' "[175] The citation beneath Maly's portrait in the First Chief Directorate Memory Room records that he was shot late in 1937.[176]

Maly's liquidation left Kim Philby without a regular controller for over a year. At the time of Maly's recall final details of the plan, involving Philby, to assassinate General Franco, had yet to be approved by Moscow Center. Thereafter it was shelved. The assassination plan was at least partly compromised by the defection of Walter Krivitsky, who knew some of the details of it including the involvement of "a young English journalist." There had also been a change of NKVD priorities. For the remainder of the Civil War, the destruction of Trotskyists in Spain was a higher priority than the liquidation of Franco.[177]

But for his recall to Moscow, Maly might have been arrested in London. Though MI5 had no knowledge of either NKVD penetration of the Foreign Office or the recruitment of the Cambridge Five, one of its agents, Olga Grey, succeeded in winning the confidence of the head of a Soviet spy ring inside Woolwich Arsenal, Percy Glading, a veteran Comintern agent run successively by Deutsch and Maly. In February 1937 Miss Grey was asked by Glading to rent an apartment in Kensington to be used as a safe house. Two months later the apartment was visited by Maly, whom Glading introduced as Mr. Peters and described to Olga Grey as "an Austrian who had served during the war in the Russian cavalry." On August 16, a few weeks after Maly's recall to Moscow, Glading arrived at the apartment with Deutsch, whom he introduced as Mr. Stephens. Miss Grey agreed to help Mr. Stephens photograph documents brought to the apartment by Glading. She was no linguist and never discovered the Stephenses' nationality, let alone their true identity; in her presence Arnold and Josefine Deutsch spoke to each other in French.

Late in October Miss Grey noted the reference number of a document photographed by Josefine Deutsch, which enabled MI5 to identify it as the plan of a new fourteen-inch naval gun. Early in November Glading announced that the Stephenses were returning to Moscow because of the illness of their daughter; Mrs. Stephens was expected to remain in Moscow and her husband was unlikely to return to London until after Christmas. In the meantime Miss Grey was asked to practice using the photographic apparatus installed in the apartment by Mrs. Stephens so that she could take over from her.[178]

Unlike the recall of Maly, that of the Deutsch family seems to have been prompted less by the paranoia of the purges than by fear that their cover was in danger of being blown. In the summer of 1937 the Comintern agent Edith Tudor-Hart, used by the NKVD chiefly as a courier, lost a diary that contained compromising details about the Deutsches' intelligence operations. At about the same time Deutsch's application to found a private limited company, which would give him a permanent base in London, was turned down. With his residence permit about to expire, he was interviewed by the police and asked for details of his plans to leave the country.[179]

The arrest of Glading and the Woolwich Arsenal spy ring by the Special Branch in January 1938 ended any prospect that Deutsch might return to Britain. Had MI5 and the Special Branch moved earlier, they would probably have arrested either Maly or Deutsch—or, just possibly, both. They delayed in the hope of unraveling the spy ring as fully as possible before arresting Glading.[180] MI5 was not to know that by the beginning of 1938 the NKVD's entire London residency and illegal *apparat* would have been recalled to Moscow. Unlike Maly and most (if not all) of the London residency, Arnold and Josefine Deutsch were not liquidated on their return to Moscow. Arnold worked for several years in the Center as a handwriting and forgeries expert. The citation beneath his portrait in the First Chief Directorate Memory Room reveals that he was parachuted into his native Austria in 1942 to conduct intelligence operations behind enemy lines, but was quickly caught and executed by the Nazis.[181]

The departure of Deutsch and the entire NKVD residency from London at the end of 1937 left the Magnificent Five and the other Soviet agents in Britain without either direction or support. Though some of the abandoned agents managed to make intermittent contact with NKVD officers on the Continent, there was serious disruption during 1938 both in the flow of intelligence to Moscow Center and in its handling by the heavily purged INO.[182]

The significance of the first phase of Soviet penetration of Whitehall, brought to an end by the recall of Maly and Deutsch, has been generally misunderstood. Its main success was the recruitment of two cipher clerks—Oldham and King—and two young diplomats—Maclean and Cairncross—in the Foreign Office. Important though the contents of some of the documents they provided undoubtedly were, the documents were more important still in assisting the code breakers of the combined NKVD–Fourth Department sigint unit. The myth has developed that code-breaking coups are achieved simply by brilliant mathematicians, nowadays assisted by huge banks of computers. In reality, most major breaks of high-grade code and cipher systems on which evidence is available were achieved with the help of at least partial information on those systems provided by espionage. Soviet code breakers in the 1930s had vastly greater assistance from espionage than their Western counterparts. All four NKVD agents in the Foreign Office provided plain-text British diplomatic telegrams, which in some instances could be compared with the ciphered versions as an aid in breaking the ciphers. All four were also in a position to supply intelligence on the cipher systems themselves. It is safe to conclude, though Gordievsky has little direct information, that the successes of Soviet code breakers against the Japanese in the 1930s were paralleled by successes on a perhaps similar scale against the British.[183]

Like the rest of the NKVD and Fourth Department, however, Soviet sigint suffered some disruption at the climax of the Great Terror. Late in 1937 both Gleb Boky, the head of the combined NKVD–Fourth Department sigint unit, and his deputy, Colonel Kharkevich, were shot. After Boky's arrest, a secret cache of gold and silver coins was discovered in his suite. Boky's successor, Shapiro, lasted only a month before being arrested in his turn. At a lower level, however, the cryptanalysts were far less purged than INO. S. Tolstoy, the head of the Japanese section, perhaps the most productive in the unit, remained in office throughout both the Terror and the Second World War.[184]

Once the NKVD recovered from the disruption of the Great Terror, its penetration agents in Britain and elsewhere were to achieve greater successes than ever before. During the Second World War Soviet agents in Britain succeeded in penetrating not merely Whitehall but the British intelligence services themselves.

Though the United States represented a much lower priority than Britain for Soviet intelligence for most of the 1930s, it was even more vulnerable to Soviet penetration. As in Britain, the most important achievement of Soviet espionage targeted on the United States before the outbreak of war was the enormous assistance it provided to Soviet sigint. Before and during the Second World War, the American embassy in Moscow was probably even more comprehensively penetrated than that of any other major power. Diplomatic relations with the Soviet Union were established in November 1933 at a time when the United States had no civilian intelligence agency and American military intelligence was both small and disorganized. The first American ambassador in Moscow, William C. Bullitt, wrote to the State Department in 1936: "We should never send a spy to the Soviet Union. There is no weapon at once so disarming and effective in relations with the Communists as sheer honesty."[185] That honesty was taken to remarkable lengths. George Kennan, one of the original members of Bullitt's staff, later recalled that during its first winter of 1933–34 the embassy had no codes, no safes, no couriers, and virtually no security: "Communications with our government went through the regular telegraphic office and lay on the table for the Soviet government to see."

When a security system was installed, it was ineffective. At Bullitt's request, his embassy became the first to be guarded by marines. They were quickly provided with mistresses by the NKVD. Charles (Chip) Bohlen, like Kennan both a founder member of the embassy and a future ambassador in Moscow, was sitting one day in the lobby of the Savoy Hotel, where the marines were then lodged, when a heavily made-up Russian woman walked up to the reception desk and said she wished to go up to Marine Sergeant O'Dean's room. "I," she announced, "am his Russian teacher."[186] With the assistance of similar "Russian teachers," the NKVD recruited at least one of the first group of American cipher clerks sent to the Moscow embassy, Tyler G. Kent, who probably supplied cipher materials as well as classified documents.[187]

The ambassador's residence, Spaso House, was as porous as the embassy itself. Bohlen later recalled how its telephones "tinkled half-heartedly and indiscriminately, day and night; and when one answered them there was often no reaction at the other end, only labored breathing and a baffling verbal silence." Sergei, the caretaker, claimed ingeniously that the heavy breathing was that of the former people's commissar for foreign affairs, Chicherin, by now half crazed and living alone in a nearby apartment. Though his manner was genial and obliging, Sergei helped to organize the bugging of the embassy from his apartment, which he kept permanently locked. Not till Bohlen returned as ambassador in 1952 did the embassy demand a key to Sergei's locked apartment. By the time a key was grudgingly produced, after a delay of several weeks, all Sergei's apparatus had, predictably, been removed. Sergei himself retired shortly afterward.[188]

Most American diplomats in the 1930s had little grasp of the effectiveness of Soviet penetration and even less of Soviet sigint. Joseph E. Davies, who succeeded Bullitt as ambassador from 1936 to 1938, had less grasp than most. In Bohlen's view, "He had gone to the Soviet Union sublimely ignorant of even the most elementary realities of the Soviet system and of its ideology. . . . He never even faintly understood the purges, going far toward accepting the official Soviet version of the existence of a conspiracy against the state."

Colonel (later Brigadier General) Phillip R. Faymonville, military attaché from 1934 to 1939, though one of the embassy's few fluent Russian speakers, was even more naïve than Davies. Bohlen believed he had "a definite pro-Russian bias";[189] Major Ivan D. Yeaton, military attaché from 1939 to 1941, came to regard Faymonville as "a captive of the NKVD." When Yeaton left for Moscow in 1939, Faymonville, by then in Washington, gave him two classified French army manuals and asked him to give them to a friend in the Red Army. Faymonville also urged Yeaton to reemploy his Russian chauffeur, who, he said, would prove his "most valuable contact in Moscow." In the event Yeaton sacked the chauffeur and saw him a fortnight later dressed in the uniform of an NKVD captain.[190]

On his arrival in Moscow, initially as assistant military attaché, Yeaton was appalled by the state of embassy security. The embassy codes, he concluded, were compromised, and the consulate clerks gave frequent parties with girls "generously provided" by the NKVD. Yeaton also noted a number of homosexual liaisons.[191] Senior embassy officials were pursued, doubtless with NKVD encouragement, by ballerinas from the Moscow ballet. According to Bohlen: "There were usually two or three ballerinas running around the Embassy. They would go there for lunch and supper and would sit around talking and drinking until dawn. . . . Many temporary liaisons were formed." Attempts to seduce the ambassador, however, seem to have been unsuccessful. One of the ballerinas spent much of her time at the embassy professing "undying love" for Bullitt, whom she eloquently described as her "sun, moon and stars"—apparently without effect.[192]

Yeaton's criticisms of embassy security irritated rather than impressed most of his colleagues. When he reported that the French housekeeper of Laurence A. Steinhardt, ambassador from 1938 to 1942, was selling embassy supplies on the Moscow black market, Yeaton was "admonished" by Steinhardt, who refused to believe him. Shortly before the introduction of new State Department codes early in 1940, Yeaton decided on his own initiative to ask, via military intelligence in Washington, for an FBI agent to inspect the embassy to ensure that the new codes were not compromised like their predecessors.[193] The FBI agent, posing as a courier, visited the embassy's code room at night and discovered the safes open and code books lying with messages on the table. At one point the code clerk on duty left the code room unattended with the door open for forty-five minutes. It was clear that the Russian employees of the embassy, who were almost as numerous as the Americans, had many opportunities for access to both ciphers and classified documents. The agent also reported to the FBI: "Not being able to find normal female companionship, the men attached to the embassy turn to a group of Soviet prostitutes for companionship. . . . It is reported that all of these girls report constantly to the GPU." In addition, acts of homosexual "perversion" had taken place in the embassy code room.[194] Following the FBI report, "a small group of bachelors" was ordered back to Washington, and some improvements were made in embassy security.[195] But the FBI agent was not a technical expert. It did not occur to him to search the embassy for listening devices. When a search was finally ordered in 1944, a navy electrician discovered 120 hidden microphones on his first sweep of the building. Thereafter, according to a member of the embassy staff, "they kept turning up, in the legs of any new tables or chairs which were delivered, in the plaster of the walls, any and everywhere."[196]

Until the later 1930s intelligence gathering within the United

States was a comparatively low priority for Moscow Center. By the mid-thirties, however, several influential underground cells of the American Communist Party (CPUSA) were in varying degrees of contact with Comintern and Soviet intelligence officers. The main link between the Party underground and Soviet intelligence was Whittaker Chambers, a Communist journalist who was instructed in 1932 to break overt contact with the Party.[197] In 1933 Chambers was sent to Moscow for intelligence training. His main controller on his return was Sandor Goldberger, a former Comintern *apparatchik* bearing a striking resemblance to Groucho Marx. As well as working for the Fourth Department, Goldberger became, under the alias J. Peters, a grey eminence of the CPUSA for a quarter of a century.[198]

In 1934 Chambers began acting as courier between Goldberger and an underground cell in Washington founded by Harold Ware, a Communist official in the Department of Agriculture killed in a car crash in 1935. Its other leading members, according to Chambers's later testimony, included John J. Abt of the Department of Agriculture (later of the Works Progress Administration, the staff of the Senate Committee on Education and Labor, and the Justice Department); Nathan Witt of the Department of Agriculture (later of the National Labor Relations Board); Lee Pressman of the Department of Agriculture (later of the Works Progress Administration); Alger Hiss of the Department of Agriculture (later of the Special Senate Committee Investigation of the Munitions Industry, the Justice Department, and the State Department); his brother Donald Hiss of the State Department (later of the Labor Department); Henry H. Collins of the National Recovery Administration (later of the Department of Agriculture); Charles Kramer (Krevitsky) of the National Labor Relations Board (later of the Office of Price Administration and the Senate Subcommittee on War Mobilization); and Victor Perlo of the Office of Price Administration (later of the War Production Board and the Treasury Department).

In 1935 Alger Hiss, the ablest member of the Ware cell, was moved by Chambers to become the founder member of a "parallel apparatus."[199] Among other new agents who entered Chambers's net in 1935–36 were Harry Dexter White, a high flyer in the Treasury Department; George Silverman, a government statistician (later employed in the Pentagon), who probably recruited White; and Julian Wadleigh, an Oxford-educated economist who moved in 1936 from the Department of Agriculture to the Trade Agreements Division of the State Department. The motivation of the Washington moles was much the same as that of the Cambridge Five: the lure of the Comintern's secret war against fascism. Wadleigh wrote later: "When the Communist International represented the only world force effectively resisting Nazi Germany and the other aggressor powers, I had offered my services to the Soviet underground in Washington as one small contribution to help stem the fascist tide."[200]

In the autumn of 1936 a new Fourth Department resident, Boris Bykov, arrived to take control of Chambers's network from Goldberger. Chambers later described Bykov, whom he knew as Peter, as a middle-aged man, about five feet seven, tall with thinning, reddish hair, who wore expensive worsted suits, always with a hat, invariably carried his right hand inside his jacket ("Napoleon style"), had an "authoritative" manner and a "ferret-like way about him."[201] Bykov suggested that the members of the underground be offered money to "put them in a productive frame of mind." When Chambers objected, Bykov gave him a thousand dollars—then a considerable sum—to buy Bokhara rugs for his four most valuable agents: Hiss, White, Silverman, and Wadleigh. Each was told that the rugs were "gifts from the Russian people to their American comrades."[202]

In Britain by this time Soviet intelligence had so far succeeded in penetrating only one of the Whitehall ministries. In Washington, by contrast, Soviet agents were already installed in a steadily widening area of the Roosevelt administration. But the penetration of Washington was a much lower priority than the penetration of Whitehall. Moscow was still far more interested in the major European powers and Japan than in the United States. Bykov was not much concerned with the details of American policy making. Like Goldberger, his main aim was to collect intelligence on Germany and Japan, in particular "everything that bears on the preparations the Germans and Japanese are making for war against us." Bykov berated Wadleigh for failing to provide State Department documents on German and Japanese policy.[203]

He was more satisfied with Hiss, who in the autumn of 1936 became assistant to Francis B. Sayre, assistant secretary of State. Hiss had access to a wide variety of telegrams from both diplomats and military attachés. By early 1937 he was delivering packets of documents to Chambers at intervals of about a week or ten days. Perhaps the most valuable from Bykov's point of view were those that dealt with Japanese policy during the Sino-Japanese War. A cable of March 2, 1937, cited the view of unnamed "Japanese army chiefs . . . that they will be able to wage a successful war against Russia while holding the Chinese in check on their flank with little difficulty."[204] Within the State Department Hiss covered his tracks as successfully as Maclean in the Foreign Office. Even Wadleigh had no idea that Hiss was working for the Russians: "I regarded him as a very moderate New Dealer with strongly conservative instincts."[205] Sayre later concluded that the documents provided by Hiss would "presumably" have enabled the Russians to break U.S. diplomatic ciphers.[206] It did not occur to him that, thanks to the penetration of the American embassy in Moscow, they were broken already.

The comparatively low priority given to Soviet intelligence collection in the United States was reflected in both the personnel and the methods employed. Goldberger and Bykov did not begin to compare with Deutsch and Maly. During his intelligence training in Moscow in 1933 Chambers, no doubt against instructions, sent postcards to his friends at home—one to bestow "a Soviet blessing" on a newborn baby. Back in the United States he engaged in some intelligence mystification, adopting for example a slightly foreign accent, which persuaded Wadleigh and some of his other agents that he was not American.[207] But Goldberger and Bykov both allowed Chambers to get away with elementary breaches of intelligence tradecraft. Some of his friends knew that he was involved in "highly secretive work"; on one occasion he revealed that he was "engaged in counterespionage for the Soviets against the Japanese." Chambers treated his leading agent, Alger Hiss, as a family friend; he and his wife went to stay in the Hiss apartment. Others of Chambers's agents were to be found socializing at each other's homes, visiting art galleries, and playing table tennis together.[208]

The greatest security risk, however, was Chambers himself. In July 1937 he was summoned to Moscow. Increasingly disillusioned with Stalinism and rightly fearful of the fate that awaited him, Chambers temporized for the next nine months. Then in April 1938 he broke all contact with the NKVD. After spending the rest of the year largely in hiding, he began to tell his story to sympathetic listeners.[209] In a security-conscious state Chambers's extensive knowledge of Soviet penetration in Washington would have had catastrophic consequences for NKVD operations. But security in Washington was even feebler than in London. Over the next few years Chambers was to discover that the FBI and the administration from the president downward had no serious interest in his revelations.[210] The state that at the end of the Second World War was to be targeted by the NKVD as "the Main Adversary" was, until that point, the state most vulnerable to Soviet penetration.

Founders of the KGB

Stalin with Dzerzhinsky. *(David King Collection)*

OGPU medal with Dzerzhinsky's head framed in laurel wreath to commemorate the tenth anniversary (in 1927) of the founding of the Cheka. *(David King Collection)*

Oleg Gordievsky's identity card as colonel in the KGB, incorporating the shield from the original emblem of the Cheka.

Recruiters and Controllers of the Five

Teodor Maly, former Catholic priest and celebrated KGB illegal whose portrait hangs today in the Memory Room of the KGB First Chief Directorate (Foreign Intelligence).

Dr. Arnold Deutsch, protégé of Teodor Maly and first controller in England of the Magnificent Five, whose portrait hangs next to Maly's in the FCD Memory Room.

Memorial to Deutsch outside his Vienna flat that records his heroic role in the anti-Nazi resistance and execution by the SS in 1942, but makes no mention of his career in the KGB.

Anatoli Gorsky (*alias* Gromov), controller of the Magnificent Five while stationed at the KGB London residency from 1940 to 1944.

Gorsky under another alias as Professor Nikitin in the early 1970s, when conducting KGB operations against foreigners in Moscow.

Yuri Modin early in his career in the KGB. While stationed in the London residency from 1947 to 1953, he became the last KGB officer to control all the Magnificent Five, helping to arrange the flight of Burgess and Maclean in 1951. By the 1980s he was head of Political Intelligence in the FCD Andropov Institute. *(Channel 4)*

The Magnificent Five and Elli

Above Kim Philby in 1934.

Top right Guy Burgess in 1932. *(Peter Lofts)*

Right Anthony Blunt in 1933. *(Peter Lofts)*

Below Donald Maclean in 1932. *(Peter Lofts)*

Below right Leo Long (Elli) during the Second World War. *(Imperial War Museum)*

John Cairncross in 1979.
(Times Newspapers)

7

The Second World War
(1939–41)

Hitler's ultimate ambition was to turn most of Eastern Europe into a racist empire, where "subhuman" Slavs would provide slave labor for the German Herrenvolk and from which Jewish "poison" would be eradicated. The Führer never doubted that the crucial stage in the conquest of this empire would be a war against the Soviet Union. When he took power in 1933, however, few as yet took seriously the vision of an Eastern European empire depicted in the turgid pages of *Mein Kampf,* his rambling political testament composed almost a decade before. During the mid-1930s, Hitler himself concealed his megalomaniac ambitions in Eastern Europe from public view, and deceived the German people into believing that, by recovering "equal rights," the Third Reich would guarantee the peace of Europe.[1]

In 1922 revolutionary Russia and defeated Germany, the two great outcasts from the international system, had emerged from isolation, concluded the Rapallo Pact, and surprised the rest of Europe by reestablishing diplomatic relations, renouncing financial claims on one another, and pledging cooperation. For the next decade, despite a forlorn attempt to inspire a German revolution in 1923, Soviet Russia's diplomatic and trading relations with Weimar Germany were closer than with any other major power. By the close of 1933 the Nazi conquest of power had brought the Rapallo era to a close. Though Stalin did not grasp the full extent of the Nazi menace until the German invasion of 1941, Hitler's implacable hostility both to Marxism in all its forms and to the existing international order made Nazi Germany the most obvious European threat to Russian security. The Soviet sense of vulnerability was heightened by the simultaneous menace from Japan in the East. The result was a dramatic shift in Russian diplomacy. Official Soviet foreign policy was based henceforth on the search for collective security with the Western powers against the menace of Nazi and fascist aggression: a policy exemplified in 1934 by the Soviet entry into the League of Nations, which it had hitherto boycotted, and in 1935 by pacts with France and Czechoslovakia, the first defense agreements with capitalist powers. The chief apostle of collective security, Maxim Litvinov, foreign commissar from 1930 to 1939, had spent a decade in Britain before the Revolution, heading the émigré Bolshevik group and returning to Russia with an English wife. Litvinov showed greater flair than any other statesman of his generation for establishing friendly relations with Western statesmen and for appealing to Western radicals disillusioned by their governments' faint-heartedness in resisting first the threats, then the aggression, of Hitler and Mussolini.

As early as 1934, however, Stalin began secretly to consider an alternative way of meeting the German menace: to seek agreement with Hitler rather than collective security against him. At a Politburo meeting early in July 1934, shortly after the killing of the leader of the storm troopers, Ernst Röhm, and about 180 others in Hitler's "Night of the Long Knives," Stalin is said to have exclaimed: "Have you heard the news from Germany? About what happened, how Hitler got rid of Röhm? Good chap, that Hitler! He showed how to deal with political opponents!"[2] Stalin's decision to liquidate Kirov, his main potential rival, a few months later, may well have owed something to Hitler's example. Thereafter, Stalin's estimate of the "correlation of forces" in the West (a concept which, unlike the traditional calculus of the balance of power, took account of political will as well as military might[3]) increasingly favored Hitler.

He did not believe in the possibility of more than a temporary accommodation with any capitalist state. Stalin was convinced as an article of Marxist-Leninist faith that the natural tendency of all capitalists was to conspire against the Soviet state. For the moment, however, the capitalist world was divided within itself. Those divisions were Russia's opportunity. Given Hitler's hatred of Marxism, it would be more difficult to reach an accommodation with Nazi Germany than with the bourgeois democracies. But Stalin seems to have hoped that Hitler was a sufficiently skilled practitioner of Realpolitik to grasp the mutual advantages of a Nazi-Soviet division of Eastern Europe into spheres of influence.

In January 1937 the chief Soviet trade representative in Berlin, David Kandelaki, acting on instructions from Stalin and Molotov (Litvinov was never mentioned), made overtures for a Russo-German political agreement to be negotiated in secret. As yet Hitler showed no interest.[4] But when Kandelaki returned to Moscow, accompanied by the NKVD resident in Berlin, to report to Stalin, he gave, according to Krivitsky, an optimistic assessment of the future prospects for an accord with Germany—though his optimism may well have resulted from reluctance to admit the failure of his mission. Yezhov told Krivitsky: "Germany is strong. She is now the strongest power in the world. Hitler has made her so. Who can doubt it? How can anyone in his senses fail to reckon with it? For Soviet Russia there is but one course." And he claimed that Stalin had told him: "We must come to terms with a superior power like Nazi Germany."[5]

Stalin had less reliable intelligence from within Nazi Germany than from any other major power. Yet before Hitler came to power Soviet foreign intelligence had operated on a larger scale in Germany than anywhere else in Europe. The KPD, the largest Communist Party outside Russia, had organized a network of worker correspondents or *rabcors* (shortened from *rabochi cor*respondents) several thousand strong, whose ostensible purpose, as in France and other parts of Europe, was to report to the Communist press on working conditions. They also supplied, more covertly, technical information, which was used for industrial and military espionage.

In 1930 Hans Kippenberger, the KPD Politburo member responsible for liaison between the Party underground and the Soviet intelligence *apparat,* was elected a deputy to the Reichstag. For the next three years, until the Nazi conquest of power, he continued his intelligence work, assisted both by the protection of parliamentary immunity and by a seat on the Reichstag military commission.[6] Berlin was the main Western base for OMS operations and the capital of Münzenberg's front organizations and media empire. It also contained a large and highly professional Pass-Apparat, which assisted OGPU, Fourth Department, and OMS agents throughout Europe and beyond by providing passports and "legends" (false identities backed by elaborate biographical detail and bogus documents). Hans Reiners, one of the Pass-Apparat's passport experts, later gave the example of "Ivan Mueller" to illustrate its immense attention to detail:

> Mueller cannot simply emerge into the world supplied with only a passport; he must be armed with all the basic documents to enable him to confirm his identity, such as a birth certificate, employment record, social security book, etc. This set of personal identification papers is termed a collection, and to make a collection complete one must be a historian, geographer, and expert in knowledge of police habits. . . .
>
> Once the "collection" is ready, an additional precaution must be taken. When Ivan Mueller goes on his first trip across a frontier his passport must not look new. If a passport is shown on which a number of visas or frontier stamps confirm that the traveler has been checked, rechecked, and found in order, police will pay less attention than if a new document is presented. That is why the Pass-Apparat placed a number of false visas and frontier stamps on the passport. The route that the traveler had supposedly followed was carefully considered—everything must fit logically into the "legend" which he was to memorize.

According to Reiners, from 1927 to 1932 the Berlin Pass-Apparat produced about 450 "collections" of documents each year.[7]

The sheer scale of Soviet intelligence operations in Germany, the overlap between overt KPD activities and the Party underground, and the enthusiastic amateurism of the rabcors all combined to produce a number of public embarrassments for both OGPU (code-named Klara) and Fourth Department (code-named Grete) networks in the final years of the Weimar Republic. Between June 1931 and December 1932 more than three hundred cases of espionage, almost all involving Soviet intelligence, were tried in German courts.[8] Most of those convicted served only a few months in jail until April 1932 when a Decree on the Defense of the National Economy increased the maximum penalty for industrial espionage for a foreign power to five years' imprisonment. In November 1932 a police raid on an apartment used by the Pass-Apparat netted 600 blank passports (both forged and genuine), 35 partially completed passports, 800 passport photographs, 700 police forms, 2,000 official rubber stamps, and a great variety of other official documents used to construct legends.[9]

The greatest German embarrassment suffered by Soviet intelligence was the defection in 1931 of Georg Semmelmann, an OGPU agent who for the past eight years had operated from the Soviet trade delegation in Hamburg. After his defection Semmelmann wrote to a Viennese newspaper proposing a series of articles on Soviet espionage in Germany, Austria, and elsewhere, which would identify Kippenberger and other Soviet agents. Before the articles were written, however, Semmelmann was assassinated by Andrei Piklovich, a Serbian Communist working for the OGPU. At his trial in 1932 Piklovich admitted responsibility for the assassination but claimed that he had acted to prevent the betrayal and death of many "proletarian fighters." After a Communist-led press campaign in Piklovich's favor, the jury failed to agree and he was freed.[10]

Thanks largely to false documents provided by the Pass-Apparat, most leading KPD and Comintern officials were able to escape abroad after the Nazi conquest of power in 1933. But the establishment of a police state, the banning of the KPD, growing popular enthusiasm for Hitler's dictatorship, and a number of defections from the Communist underground shattered most of the Soviet intelligence network. An OGPU officer named Gruenfeld (code-named Bruno) was sent secretly to Germany to try to salvage the remnants of the Klara and Grete organizations. Moscow Center was dissatisfied with his reports and replaced him with a more senior officer, Dr. Gregor Rabinovich, a Jewish doctor who impressed one of his agents with "sadness but also . . . intelligence in his deep brown eyes. . . . His excellently tailored but conservative clothes enhanced his appearance of stability and solidity."[11] Rabinovich cut back the Fourth Department network to about twenty-five and seems to have wound up that of the OGPU altogether. The whole of the *rabcors* organization disappeared. The Pass-Apparat was transferred to the Saar in 1934, then to Moscow and Paris when the Saar voted to rejoin Germany the following year. Abram Slutsky, head of INO, told a KPD congress held near Moscow in 1935 that all mass intelligence networks in Germany had been terminated. Even the Grete network maintained by Rabinovich functioned more as an ineffective underground opposition to Nazi rule than as an intelligence-gathering network. In 1936 Rabinovich was moved to the United States to help direct the penetration of the Trotskyist movement.[12]

The liquidation of Soviet intelligence in Germany begun by

Hitler was almost completed by Stalin. Many of the Germans who had worked for Soviet intelligence perished with much of the exiled KPD leadership in Moscow during the Great Terror. One of the first to be shot was Hans Kippenberger, forced to confess in 1936 to the absurd charge of being "a spy for the German Reichswehr."[13]

The damage done by the near liquidation of the extensive German agent network was all the more serious because Germany was probably the one major power whose high-grade ciphers could not be broken by the combined NKVD–Fourth Department sigint unit in the NKVD Spets-Otdel (Special Department). When Beria became head of the NKVD in 1938, the combined unit was broken up. The NKVD sigint section of the Spets-Otdel moved into the former Hotel Select in Dzerzhinsky Street, where it concentrated on diplomatic traffic; most, but not all, military communications were the province of the GRU.

None of the variants of the complex Enigma machine ciphers used by the German armed forces were broken by either NKVD or GRU cryptanalysts before the invasion of June 1941; with few exceptions they were probably still unbroken at the end of the war.[14] The main German diplomatic ciphers—the "one-time pad" and a system known to British cryptanalysts as "Floradora"—were even more difficult to crack. Even the information on the construction of diplomatic ciphers and the documents obtained from the penetration of the German embassies in Tokyo and Warsaw did not enable Floradora to be broken. British cryptanalysts broke the Luftwaffe variant of Enigma in May 1940. But, despite obtaining a complete copy of the basic Floradora code book at about the same time, it was not until August 1942 that they made their first major break in that system.[15]

Soviet intelligence sought to compensate for its weakness inside Germany by operations targeted on Germany from outside, especially from the Low Countries, France, and Switzerland. In the later 1930s a number of gifted Fourth Department agents began to develop what became the Soviet Union's main wartime networks gathering intelligence from Nazi Germany. Two names stand out. The first is that of Leopold Trepper, a Polish Jew, who, after working for the Comintern's OMS, was recruited by Berzin for the Fourth Department in 1936. In 1938 he arrived in Belgium on a forged passport posing as Adam Mikler, a Canadian businessman with $10,000 to invest. With Leon Grossvogel, a Jewish friend who had also worked for OMS, Trepper founded the curiously named Foreign Excellent Raincoat Company to provide cover for his intelligence work. He became, he later claimed, "the very image of the well-to-do industrialist" as he built up an espionage network mainly composed of Jews outraged by Nazi anti-Semitism and willing to work against Hitler without pay. Though he ran a network, Trepper, like Sorge, was his own best agent. Before the war, however, he and his network gathered little intelligence of note. As Trepper himself wrote later, "Until the war broke out, we laid aside all intelligence work, properly speaking. Our objectives were to consolidate our commercial cover and to lay the necessary groundwork so we would be ready when the first shots were fired."[16]

Trepper's most outstanding contemporary was the Hungarian Alexander Rado, who, like Trepper, was Jewish, began his intelligence career in OMS, and was recruited by the Fourth Department. Also like Trepper, he set himself up in business, founding the cartographic firm Geopress in Geneva in 1936 to provide cover for his intelligence work. During the Second World War he was to run the Soviet Union's most important agent network targeted on Germany. But before the war his intelligence, like that of Trepper, was of marginal importance.[17]

The Soviet Union's most important prewar German intelligence came from the successful penetration of the German embassies in Tokyo and Warsaw. Sorge in Tokyo was in a class by himself. Once his friend Eugen Ott, previously military attaché, became German ambassador in April 1938, Sorge had, according to a senior member of Ott's staff, "free run of the embassy day and night." Sorge himself estimated that henceforth 60 percent of the intelligence sent by his spy ring to Moscow originated in the German embassy. On one occasion, at Ott's request, Sorge acted as embassy courier to Manila, Canton, and Hong Kong—a rare example of a Soviet agent operating under German diplomatic cover.[18]

According to his authorized Soviet hagiography, Sorge never knew that the director of the Fourth Department, General Berzin, was shot in 1938. There is thus an added poignancy to the letter he addressed to the director in October 1938:

> Dear Comrade! Don't worry about us. Although we are terribly tired and tense, nevertheless we are disciplined, obedient, decisive, and devoted fellows who are ready to carry out the tasks connected with our great mission. I send sincere greetings to you and your friends. I request you to forward

the attached letter and greetings to my wife. Please, take the
time to see to her welfare.[19]

Sorge's most important intelligence until and beyond the outbreak of
the Second World War, however, concerned Japanese rather than German policy. In the summer of 1938 he was able to assure Moscow, on
the basis of information supplied by his agent Ozaki, that the first
serious Russo-Japanese border clash at Lake Khasan on the frontier
with Japanese-occupied Manchuria was the responsibility of the local
Japanese commander and that the Tokyo government was anxious to
avoid war. Sorge sent the same reassuring message after Japanese violations of the Outer Mongolian frontier in May 1939.[20] On this occasion
Moscow did not believe him and concluded for a time that it was faced
with major aggression in the Soviet Far East.[21] By the summer of 1939
the Fourth Department had temporarily lost confidence in its ablest
officer. When Germany invaded Poland and began the Second World
War on September 1, 1939, Moscow sent Sorge a sharp rebuke:

> Japan must have commenced important movements (mili-
> tary and political) in preparation for war against Russia but
> you have not provided any appreciable information. Your
> activity seems to be getting slack.[22]

For two years before the outbreak of war Soviet intelligence had another agent inside a German embassy. In 1937 Rudolf Herrnstadt, a
German Jewish journalist (later editor of the East German *Neues
Deutschland*) working for the Fourth Department in Warsaw, recruited Rudolf von Scheliha, a forty-year-old counselor at the German
embassy. Von Scheliha came from a family of Silesian aristocracy and
had served as a cavalry officer in the Great War before entering the
diplomatic profession. By the mid-1930s, however, his salary and his
wife's income could no longer support both his gambling and his mistresses. Unlike Sorge, von Scheliha was a mercenary rather than an
ideological spy. In February 1938 the Fourth Department deposited
$6,500 U.S. in von Scheliha's account at a Zürich bank—one of the
largest payments to any Soviet agent between the wars.[23]

Von Scheliha was so highly regarded by the Fourth Department because of the unique insight that he provided into the development of German policy toward Poland, a subject of major concern to
Moscow. During Hitler's first five years in power he sought to disarm

Poland's well-founded fear of his territorial ambitions in Eastern Europe, signing a nonaggression treaty with her in January 1934. His aim was to placate the Poles until rearmament had made him strong enough to risk their hostility and in the meantime to secure Polish support against Russia. In October 1938 he proposed to Poland "joint policy towards Russia on the basis of the Anti-Comintern Pact." But in the aftermath of Munich it became increasingly clear that Hitler's demands for the port of Danzig (now Gdansk) were part of a policy ultimately designed to reduce Poland to a German satellite. By March 1939 Polish-German relations were at crisis point. Abandoning their previous policy of appeasement, Britain and France gave Poland a guarantee of "all support in their power" against German aggression.

Accurate intelligence on German policy from Sorge and von Scheliha was mixed with misinformation and conspiracy theories from other sources. The expansion of Nazi Germany into Austria in March 1938 and into the Czech Sudetenland after the Munich conference six months later coincided with the peak of the disruption caused by the Terror inside INO and NKVD residencies abroad. The result was a drastic decline in the flow of intelligence at the very moment when Hitler had begun to gear himself for war.

One of the dangers emphasized by, among others, Semyon Rostovsky (*alias* Ernst Henri), one of the leading NKVD illegals to survive the Terror, was the threat of "the military absorption of the whole of the Baltic by Germany." A key element in that threat was the danger of a German foothold in Finland to support its Baltic fleet and launch a land attack against Leningrad across the Karelian isthmus, a prospect that increasingly exercised the Leningrad party boss, Andrei Zhdanov.[24] The classified history of the KGB First (Foreign) Chief Directorate produced in 1980[25] concluded that the NKVD residency in Helsinki was modestly successful in the mid-1930s, with about half a dozen politicians and government officials working for it. After London, however, Helsinki was one of the residencies worst hit by the Terror. By the end of 1937 virtually all NKVD and Fourth Department officers had been recalled to Moscow to be shot or imprisoned, the Helsinki residency was left unmanned, and contact with the Finnish penetration agents was broken. The only NKVD officers to survive the inquisition in Moscow and return to Helsinki were Boris Nikolayevich Rybkin (*alias* Yartsev), who operated under diplomatic cover as second secretary, and his wife Zoya Nikolayevna Rybkina (*alias* Yartseva), who also worked as head of the Helsinki Intourist office.[26] Rybkin was promoted to resident and, with his wife, given the task of restarting NKVD operations in Finland in the spring of 1938.[27]

Though well aware that Rybkin worked for the NKVD, the future Finnish foreign minister Väinö Tanner found him "a lively individual, pleasant in a way. One could easily discuss with him even the most delicate matters, as though he were a man who did not have to be particularly careful of what he said, unlike many people in his position." Tall and blonde, Zoya Rybkina was also a social success in Helsinki—"a fine-looking woman past her first youth," in Tanner's opinion.[28] After the war she was to become head of the German and Austrian department in the reorganized INO.[29] Rybkin's open-minded, engaging manner with his Finnish contacts was deceptive. Within the NKVD he was a doctrinaire Stalinist, conscious that his Jewish origins made it all the more important for him to avoid any taint of unorthodoxy and follow the maxim *"Ugadat, ugodit, utselet"* ("Sniff out, suck up, survive").[30]

During 1938 Rybkin's instructions extended to secret diplomacy as well as intelligence collection. Hitler's unopposed invasion of Austria on March 12, immediately followed by its incorporation into the Third Reich, raised fears in the Kremlin that the Führer's next move would be to seek a foothold in Finland. These fears were strengthened by the celebration on April 12 of the twentieth anniversary of Helsinki's liberation, with German assistance, from Soviet rule. A delegation led by Count Rüdiger von der Goltz, who had commanded the German troops in 1918, took a prominent part in the ceremonies.[31]

Two days later Rybkin met the Finnish foreign minister, Rudolf Holsti. During his recent stay in Moscow he had, he said, received "exceptionally broad authority" to open discussions on Russo-Finnish relations, which must be kept secret even from the Soviet ambassador. The Kremlin, he told Holsti, was "wholly convinced" that Germany planned to land an army in Finland which would then invade Russia; it had also learned of a plot for a fascist coup in Finland if its government did not cooperate with the German aggressors. If the Germans intervened in Finland, so would the Red Army, leading to a war on Finnish soil. But if Finland was prepared to resist German intervention, Russia would provide arms and military assistance, and promise to withdraw her troops when the war was over. Over the next few months Rybkin made no progress toward an agreement. In June and July he had two meetings with the prime minister, A. K. Cajander. Once again

Rybkin insisted that he alone had authority to negotiate: the ambassador, he said scornfully, "did indeed talk a great deal to various individuals, but what he said was of no significance." Cajander proved no more willing than Holsti to abandon Finnish neutrality for a military alliance with the Soviet Union.

In December 1938 the talks shifted to Moscow. To the Finnish delegation's surprise they were received not by Litvinov, the foreign commissar, but by Anastas Mikoyan, commissar for foreign trade. Litvinov, they were told, knew nothing of the meeting (though he was later brought into the negotiations). The Finns continued to resist Soviet pressure for a military agreement. Nor would they agree to lease strategic islands in the Gulf of Finland to the Soviet Union. Talks petered out in March 1939, almost a year after Rybkin had made his first secret approach to Holsti.[32] By then, however, Soviet diplomacy was in the midst of a sea change.

The Munich conference in September 1938 had left the policy of collective security in ruins. Russia was not invited to the conference and Anglo-French pressure forced the Czechs to surrender the Sudetenland to Germany, thus depriving themselves of any effective defense when Hitler entered Prague six months later. Stalin, Beria, and, almost certainly, the Politburo as a whole increasingly interpreted Munich as part of a Western plot to encourage Hitler to turn east, leave Britain and France in peace, and focus his aggression on the Soviet Union. That conspiracy theory subsequently became Soviet historical orthodoxy. Even in the late 1980s Soviet historians were still asserting that "The leading Western powers not only indulged the fascist aggression but tried in a most obvious way to direct it against the Soviet Union."[33] In reality, though there was no shortage of Western statesmen who would have been quite content for the two dictators to come to blows, there was no Anglo-French plot to encourage a German attack on the Soviet Union.

Stalin was encouraged to believe in an Anglo-French plot not merely by his own natural predilection for conspiracy theory but also by the intelligence he received. The greater part of a generation of legal residents and illegals had been liquidated or, in a few cases like Orlov and Krivitsky, were on the run. Some NKVD residencies, like that in London, were still unstaffed. Those INO officers who avoided liquidation, and some who failed to do so, sought safety in the obsequious maxim *ugadat, ugodit, utselet.* More than at any previous moment in KGB history, INO was under pressure to provide intelligence that

supported the leadership's conspiracy theories. Those who failed to
provide evidence of Anglo-French attempts to provoke a Russo-German war risked arousing suspicion of colluding with the imperialists.
The new generation of *apparatchiks* who succeeded the cosmopolitan
officers purged from INO had, in most cases, little experience of the
outside world and had advanced their careers by demonstrating a
proven capacity for detecting and liquidating imaginary counterrevolutionary conspiracies.

　　　After the death of Abram Slutsky, probably by poisoning, in
February 1938, his deputy Mikhail Shpigelglas took over as acting head
of INO. Shpigelglas had run sabotage operations behind Nationalist
lines in Spain and organized the assassination of the defector Ignace
Reiss in Switzerland. A later defector, Vladimir Petrov, remembered
him as ruthless but also "correct, polite, business-like, and agile in
movements and mind." Like Slutsky, Shpigelglas was Jewish. After a
few months he too was liquidated.[34] When Beria arrived in Moscow in
July 1938 as successor-designate to Yezhov, he brought with him his
Georgian henchman, Vladimir Georgievich Dekanozov, as the new
head of INO.[35] Barely five feet tall, with a small beak nose and a few
strands of black hair plastered across a bald pate, Dekanozov was
insignificant in appearance. But the numerous death sentences he had
handed out in the Caucasus in the early 1920s had earned him a
reputation as "the hangman of Baku," later reinforced by his bloodthirsty behavior during the Terror as deputy chairman of the Georgia
Council of People's Commissars.[36] Dekanozov had no experience of
foreign affairs and was the first head of INO never to have traveled
outside the Soviet Union. Yet he was to have a greater role in Soviet
foreign policy than any of his far more experienced predecessors. Over
the next two years he was to become successively deputy foreign commissar and ambassador to Berlin.

　　　The thrust of the intelligence forwarded by Dekanozov to Beria
and Stalin after Munich can be gauged from the mythical version
believed in Moscow of talks by Neville Chamberlain, the British prime
minister, in Rome in January 1939. Litvinov told the Polish ambassador that he "had received information from a reliable source that in his
conversations at Rome Chamberlain had sought to raise the Ukrainian
question, allowing it to be understood that Britain would not view
German aspirations in this direction with disfavor." Moscow was so
confident of this further evidence of British attempts to encourage a
German attack on Russia that one of Litvinov's deputies was still

denouncing Chamberlain's mythical plot to the Italian ambassador three months later.[37]

At the very moment when the NKVD's foreign intelligence was at its least reliable, its influence on Soviet foreign policy was at its peak. The NKVD was used to open secret negotiations with both Finland in 1938 and Germany in 1939. An NKVD purge of diplomats tainted by alleged counterrevolutionary or Western sympathies continued throughout 1938 and extended into 1939. One of the diplomats who survived later recalled: "It often happened that you'd agree to meet a colleague to discuss some issue, and next day he was no longer at the Commissariat of Foreign Affairs—he'd been arrested." Those diplomats most suspect to Beria and Stalin were those with most experience and understanding of the West. The arrests went almost to the top of the Commissariat. The former deputy commissar N. N. Krestinsky was one of the "enemies of the people" sentenced to death at the trial of the Bloc of Rightists and Trotskyists, which opened in February 1938. Thereafter the tension under which his fellow deputy foreign commissar, Boris Spiridonovich Stomonyakov, worked became so great that colleagues would sometimes find him with his head wrapped in a wet towel to relieve his constant headaches. At the end of each day he took a cold bath to relieve the tension. Like Krestinsky, he was shot.[38]

With the discrediting after Munich of the policy of collective solidarity, Litvinov's own days as commissar were numbered. Molotov later complained that "there were some short-sighted people even in our country who, carried away by vulgar anti-fascist agitation, forgot about this provocative work of our [Western] enemies." His main target was clearly Litvinov, who, he implied, had by his pursuit of the chimera of collective security played into the hands of British and French "ruling circles" who were secretly trying to encourage Hitler to attack the Soviet Union.[39] In April 1939 Litvinov made his last attempt to turn collective security into reality, proposing talks with Britain and France on a pact for mutual assistance against "aggression in Europe." On the very same day, however, the Soviet ambassador in Berlin called at the foreign ministry and proposed talks on improving Russo-German relations.

The opening of the negotiations that led eventually to the Nazi-Soviet Pact appears to have been conducted through NKVD rather than diplomatic channels.[40] Litvinov, as both a Jew and the apostle of collective security, was clearly an obstacle to talks with Germany. On May 4 it was announced that Molotov had replaced him as commissar.

Soon afterward Dekanozov and Lozovsky, former head of the Red
International of Labor Unions, were appointed deputy commissars.
Though Litvinov, unlike his former deputies, survived, a star chamber
was established in the commissariat with Molotov, Beria, and Dekanozov as its leading members to root out remaining "Litvinovtsy." Molotov and Beria appeared in civilian suits; Dekanozov wore his NKVD
uniform. One by one commissariat officials appeared before them to
deny, sometimes unsuccessfully, any association with enemies of the
people.[41]

For several months Molotov conducted simultaneous negotiations for pacts with Britain and France in public and, after a hesitant
beginning, with Germany in secret. Anglo-Franco-Soviet talks began
without enthusiasm in either Britain or Russia. Chamberlain wrote
privately: "I have deep suspicions of Soviet aims and profound doubts
as to her military capacity even if she honestly desired and intended to
help."[42] Stalin, in all probability, saw the negotiations with Britain and
France mainly as a means of putting pressure on the Germans to sign
an accord—or, alternatively, as a second-best solution if a Nazi-Soviet
Pact proved unobtainable. Only the French showed any sense of urgency, correctly fearing that if the Anglo-French negotiations failed
Stalin would strike a deal with Hitler.[43] The NKVD devised the most
ingenious of "active measures" to try to bring pressure on the Germans
to conclude an agreement.

A few days after the approach by the Soviet ambassador to the
German foreign ministry on April 14 the German embassy in London
received and forwarded to Berlin the contents of the first of a series of
British diplomatic telegrams reporting the progress of negotiations with
the Soviet Union. The intercepted telegrams contained a number of
unexplained gaps and distortions, suggesting for example that the
Anglo-French negotiators were offering better terms and making more
rapid progress than was in fact the case. The source of the telegrams
is most unlikely to have been German intelligence. The Germans were
unable to decrypt British diplomatic traffic and almost certainly did not
possess an agent in the Foreign Office with access to the telegrams.[44]

As Professor Donald Cameron Watt has shown, the only plausible hypothesis capable of explaining the sudden and selective access
of the German embassy to British diplomatic traffic in April 1939, its
equally abrupt cessation a week before the conclusion of the Nazi-
Soviet Pact, and the omissions and distortions in the intercepted telegrams is that the source for them was the NKVD. On occasion von der

Schulenburg, the German ambassador in Moscow, was fed similar information, also designed to accelerate the negotiation of the Nazi-Soviet Pact.

The doctored telegrams planted by the NKVD on the German embassy in London came from one or both of two complementary sources. The first possibility was Captain J. H. King, the cipher clerk in the Foreign Office Communications Department controlled by Teodor Maly until his recall in 1937. King was probably, though not certainly, reactivated after the reestablishment of an NKVD presence in London during the winter of 1938–39. The second possible source of decrypted British diplomatic traffic was the NKVD sigint department, whose work was powerfully assisted by King, Maclean, and Cairncross. The intelligence from one or both of these sources planted by the NKVD in a doctored form on the German embassy in London has been fairly described as "a masterpiece of suppressio veri and suggestio falsi."[45] But it also proved unnecessary. The advantages for Hitler of a pact with Stalin as he prepared for the conquest of Poland were so substantial that he did not need covert persuasion by the NKVD. The Nazi-Soviet Non-Aggression Pact was signed on August 23. A secret protocol provided that, in the event of a "territorial and political rearrangement," Russia was to gain control of Eastern Poland, Estonia, Latvia, Finland, and Bessarabia (in Rumania). The pact took the Foreign Office and most of the outside world by surprise.

Both dictators were overjoyed by the pact. After its signature Stalin proposed a toast to Hitler. "I know," he said, "how much the German nation loves its Fuehrer. He is a fine fellow. I should therefore like to drink his health." Then Molotov toasted Ribbentrop, Ribbentrop toasted the Soviet government, and Molotov toasted Stalin as the man who in March had "introduced the reversal in political relations." Finally Stalin told Ribbentrop: "The Soviet government takes the new pact very seriously. I can guarantee, on my word of honor, that the Soviet Union will not betray its partner." Hitler was at dinner when he heard the news that the pact had been signed. He jumped up from the table, exclaiming, "We've won!" Poland was at his mercy.[46]

On September 1, exactly a week after the signing of the Nazi-Soviet Pact, a million and a half German troops crossed the Polish frontier. On September 17, with the Poles still putting up a brave but hopeless resistance to the Wehrmacht, the Red Army crossed into eastern Poland to claim its share of the territorial spoils. Where the two armies met, they fraternized, drank toasts together, even in some places held joint military parades.[47] In the final division of the spoils, Stalin swapped the Polish provinces of Lublin and Warsaw for Lithuania (which under the Nazi-Soviet Pact was to go to Germany). The Baltic States were allowed another nine months of limited independence. All, however, were bullied into accepting Soviet military bases. Stalin murmured to the Estonian delegation after it had given way to his demands: "I can tell you that the Estonian government did wisely. . . . What happened to Poland could have happened to you."[48]

Within Soviet-occupied Poland the NKVD rapidly organized rigged plebiscites on union with the U.S.S.R. Nikita Khrushchev, first secretary of the Communist Party of the Ukraine, which received southeastern Poland as "Western Ukraine," later recalled, apparently without intentional irony, the remarkable theatrical success achieved by the NKVD:

> Delegations were elected to an assembly at Lvov. . . . The assembly continued for a number of days amid great jubilation and political fervor. I didn't hear a single speech expressing the slightest doubt that Soviet power should be established. One by one, movingly and joyfully, the speakers all said that it was their fondest dream to be accepted into the Ukrainian Soviet Republic. It was gratifying for me to see that the working class, peasantry and labouring intelligentsia were beginning to understand Marxist-Leninist teachings.
>
> At the same time, we were still conducting arrests. It was our view that these arrests served to strengthen the Soviet state and clear the road for the building of Socialism on Marxist-Leninist principles.[49]

While the Gestapo organized the persecution of "racial enemies" in German-occupied Poland, the NKVD turned on "class enemies." NKVD decrees of 1940 listed fourteen categories of people to be deported. The first category, significantly, consisted of Trotskyists and other Marxist heretics. Also on the list were all those who had traveled abroad or had had "contact with representatives of foreign states"—a category so broad that it included even Esperantists and philatelists. Most of the deportees, however, were community leaders and their families: politicians, civil servants, army officers, policemen, lawyers, landowners, businessmen, hotel and restaurant owners, priests, and "persons active in parishes."

Like the SS and the Gestapo, the NKVD was engaged, as General Wladyslaw Anders later put it, in "beheading the community"—destroying any potential leadership that might organize resistance to Soviet rule. The NKVD, indeed, collaborated with the SS and the Gestapo, exchanging German Communists from the gulag for Russian émigrés and Ukrainians from Germany.[50] Margarete Buber-Neumann was one of the German Communists handed over to the SS at the bridge over the River Bug in Brest-Litovsk. After exchanging salutes, SS and NKVD officers greeted each other like old friends:

> When we were half-way across, I looked back. The NKVD officials still stood there in a group, watching us go. Behind them was Soviet Russia. Bitterly, I recalled the Communist litany: Fatherland of the Toilers; Bulwark of Freedom; Haven of the Persecuted.[51]

In all about 1½ million Polish class enemies were transported several thousand miles in huge railway convoys of cattle trucks to the wastes of Kazakhstan and Siberia. By the time an amnesty was declared after the German invasion in June 1941, almost half were dead. The 15,000 Polish officers died in killing fields closer to home.[52] The last entry in the journal of one of the officers, Major Solski, recounts his arrival under NKVD guard at the Katyn Woods near Smolensk on April 9, 1940:

> We arrived in a little wood which looked like a holiday camp. They took away our rings and watches, which showed the time was 6:30 A.M., as well as our belts and knives. What will happen to us?

Three years later Solski's body, with his journal still in his pocket, was discovered by German troops with the bodies of over four thousand others in mass graves in the Katyn Forest. Most had their hands tied behind their backs and a bullet in the base of the skull.[53] The NKVD's victims even included some of the Polish Communists who had survived the Moscow purges. In 1940 the future Party leader Wladyslaw Gomulka fled from the Soviet to the German zone.[54]

The Nazi-Soviet partition of Poland was swiftly followed by

renewed pressure on the Finns. Rybkin, the NKVD resident in Helsinki, told Stalin what he wanted to hear: that in the event of war the Finns would collapse as quickly as the Poles and the Finnish working class would support a new Communist regime.[55] In mid-October 1939 a Finnish delegation, unaware of the secret Nazi-Soviet protocol making Finland a Soviet sphere of influence, was summoned to the Kremlin to be informed by Stalin himself that the Soviet Union required them to concede island and coastal military bases and a strip of territory north of Leningrad in return for an unwanted slice of Soviet Karelia. "We civilians don't seem to be making progress," Molotov told the Finns after a fortnight's negotiations. "Now it is the soldiers' turn to speak."

During the summer two plans had been drawn up for an attack on Finland. General K. A. Meretskov, commander of the Leningrad Military District, forecast that the conquest of the Finns would take only three weeks. Marshal Shaposhnikov, the chief of the general staff, calculated that it would require several months. Stalin preferred Meretskov's plan.[56] Khrushchev later recalled a meeting with Stalin, Molotov, and Otto Kuusinen, the Comintern's Finnish secretary-general and one of Stalin's foreign policy advisers:

> When I arrived at the apartment, Stalin was saying "Let's get started today." . . . All we had to do was raise our voice a little bit, and the Finns would obey. If that didn't work, we could fire one shot and the Finns would put up their hands and surrender.[57]

The Soviet troops who crossed the Finnish border on November 30 and began the "Winter War" were told that the oppressed people of Finland were waiting to welcome them with open arms.[58] Red Air Force bombers dropped leaflets over Helsinki urging workers to join the Red Army in overthrowing their capitalist oppressors.[59] A puppet Democratic Government of Finland, headed by Kuusinen and, it declared, "deriving its support entirely from the people," was set up in Terijoki, the first Finnish town "liberated" by the Red Army. On December 2 it signed a treaty with the Soviet Union conceding all the territory previously demanded from the Cajander government and proclaiming that "through the heroic struggle of the Finnish people and the exertions of the Red Army of the Soviet Union there is to be liquidated that true focus of war infection which the former plutocratic government in

Finland had created on the frontiers of the Soviet Union for the benefit of the imperialist powers."[60]

The classified history of the First Chief Directorate accepts that some of the extraordinary false optimism with which the Winter War began reflected the aspirations of Rybkin's pro-Soviet agents, who represented a narrower spectrum of Finnish opinion than the broader range of sources exploited by the residency before its liquidation in 1937. Their wishful thinking, personally reported in Moscow by the obsequious Rybkin, reinforced that of Stalin himself.[61] In the early stages of the war Moscow was taken in by intelligence reports that the Finnish government had "left Helsinki for an unknown destination."[62]

The war, however, failed to go according to plan. A million Soviet troops with immensely powerful armor and air support were outfought by a Finnish army never more than 200,000 strong. Dressed in white, emerging on skis from the forests, the Finns split up long columns of Russian forces and destroyed them piecemeal. According to Khrushchev, Stalin screamed abuse at Marshal Voroshilov, the commissar for defense. Voroshilov shouted back: "You have yourself to blame for all this! You're the one who annihilated the Old Guard of the army; you had our best generals killed!" The row ended with the outraged marshal overturning a large dish of roast suckling pig.[63]

To stiffen the resolve of the Red Army NKVD units were drafted into the rear to shoot troops caught trying to retreat.[64] In the end Finnish resistance crumbled before the sheer weight of Soviet numbers and armaments. By a peace treaty negotiated in March 1940 Finland was forced to surrender the Karelian isthmus north of Leningrad, which contained one-tenth of her population, but Kuusinen's puppet government disappeared into the rubbish bin of history.

Soviet bungling in the Winter War was in striking contrast to the rapidity of the German conquest of Norway in April 1940 and the even more successful Blitzkrieg offensive in May and June, which defeated France and the Low Countries in only six weeks. Molotov summoned Schulenburg, the German ambassador, to the Kremlin to receive "the warmest congratulations of the Soviet government on the splendid success of the German Wehrmacht."[65] The Soviet Union had made a small but significant contribution to Hitler's victory: "Guderian's tanks operated largely on Soviet petrol as they dashed for the sea at Abbeville, the bombs that leveled Rotterdam contained Soviet guncotton, and the bullets that strafed British Tommies wading to the boats at Dunkirk were sheathed in Soviet cupro-nickel."[66]

As Hitler's forces overran the Low Countries, *Izvestia* told its readers: "The recent war events once more proved that the neutrality of small states, which do not have the power to support it, is a mere fantasy. Therefore, there are very few chances for small countries to survive and maintain their independence."[67] The days of the Baltic States were clearly numbered. During the night of June 15–16 Dekanozov summoned a number of officials, including his fellow deputy foreign commissar, Andrei Vyshinsky, the fearsome prosecutor in the show trials, to his office in the Lubyanka and told them they had been selected for "missions" to the Baltic States: "At the decision of the Politburo and at the request of Comrade Stalin, the security problem along our northwest frontier is now to be solved." Dekanozov claimed, and may even have believed, that the governments of the Baltic States had been plotting with "the stock exchanges of Paris and London." Molotov made a similar allegation to Schulenburg though he omitted the reference to stock exchanges. Dekanozov told the midnight conference that he would lead a mission to Lithuania, Vyshinsky was to go to Latvia, and Zhdanov to Estonia. If the workers in these states demanded the transformation of the bourgeois regimes into soviet socialist republics, "Comrade Stalin has said he will have no objection to such demands."[68] Some idea of the work of the three missions is given by the NKVD plan devised by Dekanozov for Lithuania, "preparatory to liquidation," dated July 7, 1940, later captured by the Germans. It provided for:

> Active abolition of the leading influence of parties hostile to the State: Nationalists, Voldemarists, Populists, Christian Democrats, Young Lithuanians, Trotskyists, Social Democrats, National Guardsmen and others. The action must be carried out simultaneously through all Lithuania on the night of 11/12 July 1940.

Elections in mid-July 1940 supervised by the NKVD produced low turnouts but satisfactory Communist majorities of 99.2 percent in Lithuania, 97.8 percent in Latvia, and 92.8 percent in Estonia. On July 21 the new assemblies requested union with the U.S.S.R. Their request was granted by the Supreme Soviet on August 3. Assisted by thousands of informers, the NKVD carried on arresting a steady stream of enemies of the people. On the night of June 14–15, 1941, alone, only a week before the German invasion of the Soviet Union, 60,000 Estonians, 34,000 Latvians, and 38,000 Lithuanians were loaded onto cattle trucks to begin several-thousand-mile journeys to Soviet prison camps. By the time the invasion began, about 4 percent of Estonians and 2 percent of Latvians and Lithuanians had been deported to distant gulags in Siberia and Uzbekhistan.[69]

On November 12, 1940, Molotov, Dekanozov, and Beria's deputy, Vsevolod Nikolayevich Merkulov, arrived in Berlin for talks on Russo-German spheres of interest. Though Dekanozov's experience of the outside world was limited to the subjugation of Lithuania, he was the best traveled of the three. For both Molotov and Merkulov it was their first trip abroad. While talks were proceeding on November 20, Stalin announced Dekanozov's appointment as ambassador to Germany.[70] On December 18 Hitler signed the now notorious secret directive number 21, Fall Barbarossa, ordering the completion by May 15, 1941, of preparations to crush Soviet Russia in a lightning offensive. Next day the Führer received Dekanozov for the first time.[71] His mood was cordial but the diminutive Dekanozov was flanked by two enormous guards specially chosen to emphasize his physical insignificance.[72] As the first former head of INO ever posted as ambassador abroad, Dekanozov was in theory the right man in the right place at a time when the Soviet Union had greater need of good intelligence from Germany than ever before in its history. But Dekanozov was not a Trilisser or Artuzov—or even a Slutsky. His sycophantic Stalinism, conspiratorial mindset, and ignorance of the outside world were to make him an accomplice in Russia's worst-ever intelligence disaster.

Throughout his period of almost seven months as ambassador in Berlin Dekanozov, like Stalin, was more concerned with imaginary British plots than with real German ones. Russo-German relations, though not without incident, caused him no serious anxiety. Soviet oil continued to flow westward to fuel the German war machine; German arms and machinery traveled east. In January 1941 the U.S.S.R. purchased the Polish district of Suwalki from Germany for $7.5 million in gold.[73] At the beginning of 1941 Hitler sent Stalin a personal letter telling him that since Central and Western Germany were "being subjected to heavy English bombing and were well observed by the English from the air," he was being forced to move large contingents of troops to the East (in preparation, he failed to add, for Operation Barbarossa).[74]

The main area of Russo-German tension was in the Balkans, where Germany's advance caused several official expressions of Soviet displeasure. On April 6 a vaguely worded Yugoslav-Soviet treaty was signed. Through not committing the Soviet Union to military support for Yugoslavia, it was greeted with a fanfare of publicity in the Russian press. On the following day Germany launched a Blitzkrieg offensive that forced the Yugoslavs to sue for peace after only eight days. Though Russia protested, Stalin went out of his way not to cause offense. During April 1941 Russian deliveries of raw materials to Germany reached their highest level since the signing of the Nazi-Soviet Pact: 208,000 tons of grain, 50,000 tons of fuel oil, 8,300 tons of cotton, 8,340 tons of metals. Russia also delivered 4,000 tons of rubber purchased in the Far East and shipped to Germany via the Trans-Siberian Railway. At the farewell ceremony for a Japanese delegation leaving Moscow in mid-April Stalin was at his most jovial with Schulenburg and the other Germans present, slapping a surprised assistant military attaché on the back and telling him, "We will be great friends with you!" At the May Day parade in Moscow Stalin put Dekanozov in the place of honor by his side on the reviewing platform above Lenin's mausoleum in Red Square.[75]

In his anxiety to avoid "provocations" that might antagonize Hitler and threaten the Nazi-Soviet Pact, Stalin imposed restrictions on intelligence work in Germany that existed nowhere else.[76] One of the priorities set by Stalin to both the NKVD and GRU residencies in Berlin was simply to discover the secret of Hitler's success: "What made the Nazi Party work, how it had trampled most of Europe underfoot." Ismail Akhmedov, a GRU officer sent to Berlin in the spring of 1941, was told by his chief that Stalin was "especially . . . interested in Hitler's source of strength," and that he should "give uncolored, unbiased reports" on this subject: a rare requirement in the era of ugadat, ugodit, utselet—and an indication of the strength of Stalin's interest.

Another priority of NKVD work in Berlin was to monitor the work of the GRU. The NKVD resident, Amyak Zakharovich Kobulov, enjoyed grilling GRU officers about their "legends" (cover stories) in front of their staffs. Akhmedov, who endured one such interrogation, concluded, probably correctly, that Kobulov "just wanted to see if I would make some mistake that could be used against me later."[77] The NKVD residency contained a room (found when the embassy was vacated after the German invasion) specially equipped for the interrogation, torture, and liquidation of "enemies of the people" discovered in the embassy and Soviet colony.[78] Dekanozov had overall charge of both NKVD and GRU operations, lording it over the embassy like a "little Tsar." At embassy meetings, recalled Akhmedov, "he enumerated tasks to be accomplished and matters to be aware of, then dismissed us almost peremptorily. . . . His performance was just to show who was boss."[79]

Espionage run from the Berlin embassy was kept on a tight rein. The NKVD seems to have had no agents of any significance. The GRU resident in the Soviet Trade Delegation, Aleksandr Erdberg (whose real name may have been Sergei Kudryavtsev, later to reappear in countries as far apart as Canada and Cambodia),[80] limited himself to recruiting a few carefully chosen members of the Communist underground, whom he encouraged to recruit their own rings of agents, and to maintaining contact, through a cut-out (intermediary), with Rudolf von Scheliha, the German diplomat recruited in Warsaw in 1937. His two key recruits from the Communist underground were Arvid Harnack and Harro Schulze-Boysen. Harnack was born in 1901, the son of a well-known historian and the nephew of an equally celebrated philosopher, and became a Marxist in the mid-1920s. During a visit to the Soviet Union in 1932 he met Kuusinen and Pyatnitsky and agreed to cooperate with the Comintern underground. In 1933 he joined the German Economics Ministry and progressed to the senior post of Oberregierungsrat. His contacts with Soviet intelligence were, however, intermittent until he was recruited by Erdberg late in 1940. A fellow member of the Communist underground, Reinhold Schönbrunn, later said of him:

> Fanatical, rigid, industrious, conspicuously energetic and efficient, Harnack was not precisely a likable person, not a jolly good fellow; always serious, he had little sense of humour, and we, his colleagues, did not feel at ease in his presence. There was something of the puritan in this man, something narrow and doctrinaire. But he was extremely devoted.[81]

Schulze-Boysen, Erdberg's other leading recruit, had a quite different personality. Leopold Trepper, "grand chef" of the wartime Rote Kapelle (Red Orchestra) espionage network, found him "as passionate and hot-headed as Arvid Harnack was calm and reflective."[82] Though born into a family of aristocrats, Schulze-Boysen became a Communist in 1933 at the age of twenty-four. He was briefly imprisoned by the Gestapo after the Nazi conquest of power, but his family used its influence to gain his release. Family influence also helped him make a career as

an intelligence officer in Goering's air ministry. A German counterintelligence report later dated his "proven treasonable activity" from
1936 when through an intermediary he provided the Soviet embassy in
Berlin with secret plans for military operations against the Spanish
Republican government. But it was not until Harnack introduced him
to Erdberg early in 1941 that Schulze-Boysen was finally recruited as
a GRU agent.[83]

Among the agents whom Schulze-Boysen recruited through his
air ministry contacts were Luftwaffe Colonel Erwin Gehrts, one of
those responsible for officer training; Johann Graudenz of the Mes-
serschmitt factories; Horst Heilmann, who in 1941 at the age of eighteen enlisted in the cipher section of the high command with access to
Abwehr communications; and Luftwaffe Lieutenant Herbert Gollnow,
who later became head of a section organizing parachute drops behind
Soviet lines. In May or June 1941 Erdberg supplied Harnack and
Schulze-Boysen with wireless transmitters for their groups of agents.
The sets failed to work. After the German attack on Russia, Harnack
and Schulze-Boysen were forced to send their intelligence by courier to
Belgium and Scandinavia for transmission to Moscow.[84]

Neither the Harnack nor the Schulze-Boysen group of agents
followed orthodox intelligence tradecraft. Many of the agents knew of
each other's activities and continued to work together in the Communist underground. Stalin's restrictions on intelligence work in Germany
made it impossible to give each agent an individual controller and to
set up relatively secure espionage networks entirely separate from the
political resistance to Nazi rule.

In addition to developing the Harnack and Schulze-Boysen
groups, Erdberg also maintained contact with the diplomat Rudolf von
Scheliha, who was transferred in August 1939 from the Warsaw embassy to the information section of the German foreign ministry. By
attending the daily meetings of the ministry's department chiefs, von
Scheliha was able to keep Moscow informed of the general development
of Nazi foreign policy. Ilse Stöbe, the mistress of Rudolf Herrnstadt,
who had recruited von Scheliha in Warsaw, succeeded in obtaining a
job in the ministry's press department, which gave her regular pretexts
to meet the Tass representative in Berlin. He in turn passed von
Scheliha's intelligence to the Soviet embassy, where, in all probability,
it was handled by Erdberg. Von Scheliha's motives remained purely
mercenary; in February 1941 Stöbe brought him 30,000 marks. The
strain on Stöbe was even greater than on von Scheliha; she contracted

a venereal disease and her health steadily deteriorated.[85]

After the fall of France and the Low Countries Trepper's network began for the first time to produce high-grade intelligence on German troop movements. Trepper moved his headquarters to German-occupied Paris and set up new businesses to provide commercial cover: Simexco in Brussels and Simex in Paris. Simex, with offices on the Champs Élysées, did extensive business with the nearby Paris headquarters of the Todt Organization, which supervised all construction and fortification work for the Wehrmacht. It was through an anti-Nazi engineer in the Todt Organization, Ludwig Kainz, that in the spring of 1941 Trepper obtained, and forwarded to GRU headquarters, his first warning of Operation Barbarossa. It was one of an increasing number of warnings of preparations for a German attack received by Moscow.[86]

The intelligence chief with whom Stalin most frequently discussed these warnings was Lieutenant General Filipp Ivanovich Golikov who, in July 1940, at the age of forty, became director of the GRU (the wartime successor of the Fourth Department). Golikov was the wrong man for the job. He had been chosen for his political reliability and military efficiency, most recently demonstrated when commanding the Sixth Army during the occupation of Poland, but had no previous posting in military intelligence. One of his officers, the future defector Ismail Akhmedov, later wrote of him:

> Although resplendent in the full uniform of a lieutenant-general of the Red Army, he did not cut much of a figure. He was short, no more than five feet two inches. He was stocky. He was completely bald. His face was rather unpleasantly flushed. The power of the man was quickly apparent, however, in his eyes. They were not remarkable for size, but they were steely blue and terribly penetrating when directed at another person.[87]

Golikov instructed his officers to develop "mutual understanding and cooperation" with the NKVD, a formula that GRU residencies interpreted as acceptance of their supervision by the more powerful NKVD. In September 1940 he told a meeting of his six operational division chiefs that he had instructions from Stalin and Malenkov to carry out a further purge of GRU residencies: "too many had been too long abroad, had too many foreign contacts, and were therefore security risks." Ismail Akhmedov, one of the divisional chiefs charged with carrying out the purge, went through the files looking for victims:

> Sometimes I was fortunate and found some luckless souls who had actual deficiencies or slip-ups against them and would have been ousted sooner or later. In the main, however, I had to rely on the formula of too much association with the West.[88]

After a lengthy meeting with Stalin in December 1940 Golikov summoned a conference of his entire top staff. His address to them reflected his dogmatic but committed Stalinism, and his crude grasp of international relations. Golikov described the Nazi-Soviet Pact as purely temporary, "a product of the dialectical genius of our Comrade Stalin." The prospects of a German attack were, however, slim. Britain, like France, would soon be defeated and her empire divided between Germany and Japan. The United States, "the heartland of classic capitalism," would then attack Germany in order to try to save the British Empire from total collapse. "Meanwhile the Soviet Union would wait patiently until the time came to fulfill its future role. Once the capitalists were bleeding and exhausted, we would liberate the world."[89]

Though most of the warnings of Operation Barbarossa generated by Soviet intelligence came from the GRU, copies also went to the NKVD or, from February 1941, to the newly founded NKGB. On February 3, 1941, the security and intelligence section of the NKVD, the former OGPU, was separated from it, to be reborn as the NKGB (Narodny Kommissariat Gosudarstvennoy Bezopasnosti, or People's Commissariat of State Security). Its head was another member of Beria's Georgian mafia, Vsevolod Nikolayevich Merkulov. After spending the decade from 1921 to 1931 in, successively, the Cheka, GPU, and OGPU, Merkulov had engaged in "party work" in Georgia for the next seven years before becoming Beria's first deputy in December 1938.[90]

Beneath Merkulov's dogmatic and brutal Stalinism lurked the decaying remnants of an idealistic Chekist, who had sacrificed most of his ideals as the price of survival during the Terror. Like Stalin, he was convinced that "sooner or later there will be a clash between the Communist bear and the Western bulldog. . . . Our healthy, socially strong, young idea, the idea of Lenin and Stalin, will be the victor!"[91] He once composed the scenario for a Stalinist morality film, in which the hero and heroine, victorious over the evils of capitalism, drove their new cooperative threshing machine into a crimson Soviet sunset. The Hungarian statesman Nicholas Nyaradi, who had to negotiate with Merkulov after the war, found him:

> A paradox: a man of great kindness and bestial cruelty, one who is in deadly earnest while being quite witty. He has the patience of Job and yet he chain-smokes 40 to 50 cigarettes during a business day. A man of such prominence that Russian ambassadors stand to attention in his presence, Merkulov is always diffident, a shy smile playing about his lips as he speaks. Merkulov was the man who [after the war] personally supervised the liquidation of nearly two million Estonians, Lithuanians and Latvians with heartless efficiency; but, like a gangster who bursts into tears at the strains of Brahms' "Lullaby," he has that typical Russian sentimentality about children, and, after I knew him better, he once showed me with welling eyes a photo of his soldier son.[92]

Despite what Nyaradi considered Merkulov's "gigantic intellect," in his relations with Stalin he did not deviate from the maxim *ugadat, ugodit, utselet.*

Within the newly established NKGB, INO was raised in status from a "department" to a "directorate," becoming the Inostrannoye Upravlenie or INU. The young head of INU, Pavel Mikhailovich Fitin, had succeeded Dekanozov as the last head of INO in 1940. Fitin was one of the ablest of a group of two hundred young Communists with university degrees chosen by the Central Committee at the end of 1938 to step into the shoes of liquidated NKVD officers.[93] Though prudent in the extreme, Fitin's instincts on the submission of intelligence analyses to Stalin were at least marginally less servile than those of Merkulov. Fitin's portrait, unlike those of his three predecessors as head of INO, Slutsky, Shpigelglas, and Dekanozov, hangs today, with an accompanying eulogy, on the wall of the First Chief Directorate Memory Room.[94]

Fitin received intelligence reports from GRU as well as NKGB residencies, but until the German invasion of June 22, 1941, was less influential than Golikov, the head of the GRU. Neither Fitin nor Golikov, however, was remotely as influential in assessing the German threat as Stalin himself. His Soviet biographer Dmitri Volkogonov concludes that "until the last moment Stalin relied on his own perspicacity and powers of prophecy."[95] His faith in his own perspicacity enabled him to dismiss most intelligence that failed to conform to his conspiracy theories.

A detailed study published in 1973 concluded that Moscow received eighty-four separate "warnings" of the plans for a German invasion. A similar study today would probably raise the total to over a hundred. Golikov claimed after the war that "Soviet military intelligence had trustworthy and tested sources for obtaining secret information on a whole series of countries, including Germany itself."[96] Before the German surprise attack on June 22, 1941, however, Golikov did not trust most of these sources. His intelligence assessments were always in two parts: the first dealt with intelligence "from reliable sources," the second with that from "doubtful sources." Golikov appears to have put most of the warnings of a German surprise attack in the second category.[97] Fitin seems to have been less skeptical. He later claimed that he had prepared a report on the reliability of the sources but that Merkulov had refused to sign it and submit it to Stalin. "Up there at the top," he is alleged to have told Fitin, "they [i.e., Stalin] know how to analyze it [intelligence] better than we do."[98]

On March 21, 1941, Golikov sent Stalin a report on the series of intelligence warnings of German plans for a surprise attack. But he concluded that such an attack was improbable until Germany had either defeated England or made peace with her: "Rumors and documents to the effect that war against the U.S.S.R. is inevitable this spring should be regarded as misinformation coming from the English or perhaps even the German intelligence service."[99] Marshal Zhukov, then chief of staff, later claimed that Golikov's reports went exclusively to Stalin: "[He] made no reports to anyone else, not even to the chief of staff or the commissar for defense, Marshal Timoshenko." Though this claim was probably exaggerated, neither Zhukov nor Timoshenko had access to much of the intelligence that pointed to a German attack. Golikov has been accused by Soviet historians such as Vyacheslav Dashichev of writing his reports "so as to please Stalin."[100] The probability is, however, that Golikov's reports were based on conviction as well as sycophancy. He had been chosen as director of the GRU in July 1940, despite his lack of intelligence experience, because he was a reliable Stalinist who shared Stalin's belief in a British plot to embroil him with Hitler.

Stalin's suspicions of a British plot were strengthened by

Churchill's attempts to warn him of Hitler's intentions. Of all Western statesmen Winston Churchill was probably the one Stalin mistrusted most. He remembered him as the evil genius who had preached an anti-Bolshevik crusade in the Civil War, sought to sabotage negotiations for the Anglo-Soviet trade agreement, and led the campaign within the British cabinet to break off diplomatic relations in 1927. Now that Churchill was back in power, Stalin believed that he was inevitably hatching some new anti-Soviet plot.

Probably the first serious warning of plans for a German attack on Russia was contained in a letter dated June 25, 1940, from Churchill to Stalin, personally delivered by the new British ambassador Sir Stafford Cripps on July 1. Churchill's warning was based not as yet on secret intelligence but on an accurate assessment of Hitler's future strategy. Stalin, however, saw the letter as evidence not of a German but of a British plot to provoke a Russo-German war. On Stalin's instructions Molotov handed Schulenburg, the German ambassador, a note informing him of the British warning. This was the first of a number of British and American warnings that Stalin passed on to the Germans, apparently fearing that if he failed to do so Hitler might suspect him of colluding with his enemies.[101]

In September 1940 the NKVD acquired a remarkable new insight into British government policy when John Cairncross became private secretary to Lord Hankey, then chancellor of the Duchy of Lancaster.[102] Hankey had longer experience of both the cabinet and Whitehall committees than anyone else in British public life. From 1912 to 1938 he had served as secretary of the Committee of Imperial Defence, and from 1916 to 1938 as secretary of the cabinet and many cabinet committees. On the outbreak of war in September 1939, Hankey became minister without portfolio in Chamberlain's war cabinet, numbering among his responsibilities the intelligence services, on which he wrote two long reports. When Churchill succeeded Chamberlain in May 1940, Hankey lost his place in the War Cabinet (initially only five strong) but retained his ministerial rank as chancellor of the Duchy of Lancaster, continuing to receive all cabinet papers, to chair many secret committees, and to oversee the intelligence services.[103]

Too many government papers passed through Cairncross's hands, as Hankey's private secretary, for him to pass more than a minority of them to the NKVD. But Dmitri Svetanko, head of the British desk in the Center in the late 1970s and early 1980s, told Gordievsky that Cairncross had provided "literally tons of documents.''[104] One of the first was probably the third of Hankey's six-monthly "War Appreciations," dated September 1940, which correctly forecast that German plans to invade Britain would fail and give way to a U-boat war against British shipping.

Among the committees chaired by Hankey which must have been of particular interest to the NKVD was the Scientific Advisory Committee, composed of some of Britain's most distinguished scientists, which met for the first time in October 1940 to coordinate the application of science to the war effort. Cairncross kept careful watch over Hankey's continued access to top-secret War Cabinet papers. When new War Cabinet regulations in June 1941 limited the circulation of diplomatic telegrams to Hankey, Cairncross as well as Hankey complained personally to the Foreign Office. The restrictions were quickly lifted.[105]

Information from War Cabinet papers and other intelligence provided by Cairncross and other Soviet agents did nothing to persuade Stalin that Churchill's warnings of a German invasion of Russia proceeded from genuine alarm rather than a Machiavellian plot to embroil him with Hitler.

On April 3, 1941, Churchill drafted an urgent warning to Stalin of preparations for a German invasion, based on "Ultra" intelligence from decrypted German communications, which he disguised as "sure information from a trusted agent." This message, wrote Churchill later, was intended to have "special significance and arrest Stalin's attention." Cripps, the ambassador in Moscow, accurately feared that Stalin would regard it as a provocation. To Churchill's fury he did not deliver it to Vyshinsky for forwarding to Stalin until April 19. Stalin's reaction then was exactly as Cripps had feared. Thereafter, he complained, "Not only Stalin but even Molotov avoided me like grim death. Stalin . . . did not *want* to have anything to do with Churchill, so alarmed was he lest the Germans find out."[106]

Stalin tended to see all warnings of a German attack, whatever their source, as further evidence of a British conspiracy. On April 17 the GRU resident in Prague sent a warning of an attack by Hitler during the second half of June, based on intelligence obtained from senior German officers in Czechoslovakia by the chief engineer of the Skoda works, a source who had already established his reliability. The report was sent to Stalin with a note on the source. He returned it with the comment scrawled across it in red ink: "English provocation. Investigate! Stalin."[107]

Stalin's belief in a deep-laid British plot to embroil him with Hitler was encouraged by the Germans. One of the deception methods used by the German high command to conceal preparations for Barbarossa was to claim that rumors of a German attack probably derived from a British attempt "to poison the wells."[108] This conspiracy theory was further reinforced by the mysterious flight to Scotland of Hitler's deranged deputy, Rudolf Hess, on May 10, 1941. Hess, it was believed, had been strongly influenced by a professor of geopolitics, Karl Haushofer, who had for many years advocated an Anglo-German alliance against the Soviet Union. Taken aback by Hess's unexpected and bizarre arrival, the British government maintained an embarrassed silence, which served only to strengthen Soviet suspicions that it was plotting with him. Stalin "was convinced that England was instigating Germany to attack the U.S.S.R. and that secret negotiations were in progress in London on the basis of Hess's proposals."[109] In reality Hess revealed nothing about plans for Operation Barbarossa. He insisted, on the contrary, that there was "no foundation for the rumors now being spread that Hitler is contemplating an early attack on Russia." The purpose of his mission, he claimed, was to make peace between Britain and Germany. Both sides correctly concluded that he was mentally disturbed.[110] Stalin did not.

Though the conspiracy theory uppermost in Stalin's mind until Operation Barbarossa began was that of a British plot, he increasingly suspected a German plot as well—though not one that aimed at a surprise attack. Stalin's suspicions of a bizarre German plot were strengthened by a remarkable secret warning from the German ambassador Count von der Schulenburg. Early in June Schulenburg invited Dekanozov, then on a brief visit to Moscow, to a private lunch at his residence. The only others present were Gustav Hilger, the embassy counselor, and V. N. Pavlov, the translator for Stalin and Molotov. Hilger's later claim that Schulenburg used the lunch to warn Dekanozov of the plan for a German surprise attack was dismissed by most of the Soviet historical establishment (though not by all Soviet historians) during the Brezhnev era as a "fantastic invention."[111] In 1988, however, a Soviet journal published an account of the lunch written over twenty years later by the retired KGB officer Ernst Henri, apparently based on an interview with Pavlov and confirming that Schulenburg had given a warning.[112] An article by the historian Georgi Kumanev published in *Pravda* in 1989 added further information obtained from Anastas Mikoyan. According to Mikoyan, Schulenburg told Dekanozov:

> It is possible that nothing like this has happened in the history of diplomacy, but I am going to reveal to you our state secret number one. . . . Hitler has taken the decision to begin war against the Soviet Union on June 22. You will ask me why I am doing this. I was raised in the spirit of Bismarck, who was always an opponent of war with Russia.

Dekanozov suspected a provocation but passed the message to Stalin, who told the Politburo: "Disinformation has now reached ambassadorial level!"[113] Ernst Henri was probably right to conclude that "Stalin considered the German ambassador's information was no more than a cunning move on Hitler's part aimed at forcing him to make new concessions to the Germans."[114] As it became increasingly difficult to hide German troop movements to the east, German intelligence deliberately spread rumors that Hitler was preparing to issue an ultimatum, backed by some display of military might, demanding new concessions from the Soviet Union. It was the illusory threat of that ultimatum rather than the real threat of a surprise attack that increasingly worried Stalin. He was not alone. A succession of foreign statesmen and newspaper correspondents were also taken in by the rumors of a German ultimatum in the offing.[115]

    The most important warnings of a German surprise attack that came through Soviet intelligence were those from Sorge and the networks inside Germany. After two messages forecasting a German attack at the end of May, Sorge reported on May 19: "Nine armies consisting of 150 divisions will be concentrated against the U.S.S.R."[116] The warning outraged Stalin. Sorge, he said angrily, was "a shit who has set himself up with some small factories and brothels in Japan." The GRU's reply to Sorge's warning was a curt "We doubt the veracity of your information." Sorge's radio operator, Max Clausen, was with him when the message arrived. "Those wretches!" Sorge shouted. "How can they ignore our message!" He strode around the room, clutching his head in his hands so ferociously that Clausen had the impression he might almost literally blow his top.

    The tension of the next month as Sorge sought vainly to persuade Moscow of a danger it refused to accept drove him to the edge of a nervous breakdown. Hitherto, his mistress, Hanako Miyake, had found him a considerate, sensitive lover. On one occasion during his *dialogue des sourds* with Moscow, he came home half drunk, seized her in his study, and made love so violently that she buried her face in her hands. On another occasion Hanako was astonished to find Sorge lying on a couch, tears streaming down his face. "I am lonely," he told her.

According to the authorized Soviet hagiography, *Comrade Sorge,* he reported on June 15: "The war will begin on June 22." After his arrest by the Japanese, however, Sorge never claimed to have pinpointed the exact date. The nearest he came seems to have been June 20. Unknown to Sorge, Clausen had become disillusioned with espionage and a grudging admirer of Hitler's achievements. For some time he had not been transmitting all Sorge's reports. "I received many manuscripts from Sorge saying that war would undoubtedly break out," Clausen claimed after his arrest. "But I sent out only a little from those manuscripts. I don't remember sending a message foretelling the time of the outbreak of war."[117]

According to a KGB-approved Soviet historian, the "most important" of the final warnings of a German attack was received in Moscow on the evening of June 16, 1941 from "two of our intelligence groups in Berlin"—probably those of Harnack and Schulze-Boysen.

> All Germany's military measures preparatory to an armed attack on the Soviet Union have been fully completed and the blow may be expected at any time. . . . Hungary will take an active part in the hostilities on the side of Germany. A wing of German aircraft consisting mainly of fighters has been deployed on Hungarian airfields.

At noon the following day Merkulov and Fitin were summoned to Stalin's presence. They found Stalin alone in his office. As soon as they entered, he addressed Fitin: "Chief of Intelligence, there's no need to repeat the special report, I have read it closely. Tell me what sort of sources are reporting this, where they work, how reliable they are, and how they are able to obtain such secret information." As Fitin replied, Stalin paced his office, occasionally firing further questions. After Fitin had finished his explanations, Stalin continued for some time walking up and down, drawing on his pipe. Finally he turned to Fitin. "Look here, Chief of Intelligence," he said, "there are no Germans who can be trusted, except for Wilhelm Pieck.* Is that clear?" "That's clear, Comrade Stalin," replied Fitin. What was clear to Fitin was that Stalin

---

*Wilhelm Pieck (1876–1960) was one of the few members of the KPD leadership in Moscow to survive the Terror. After the war he became joint president of the East German Communist Party (SED) and president of the German Democratic Republic.

suspected that the Berlin sources were Nazi Party members and Wehr-macht officers supplying deliberate disinformation. Stalin told him to recheck the intelligence and report back. Fitin dutifully prepared a detailed telegram to the NKVD residency in Berlin asking for "clarifi-cation of a number of questions." Before the residency had time to reply the German attack had begun.[118]

Last-minute warning of the German attack also came from Trepper in France. General Susloparov, the Russian military attaché to the French Vichy regime, who forwarded Trepper's reports to the GRU in Moscow, was usually skeptical of his intelligence. According to Trepper, "Every time I had handed him information on the prepara-tions for war against the Soviet Union, he had patted me on the shoul-der condescendingly and said, 'My poor fellow, I will send your dis-patches, but only to make you happy.' " Trepper later claimed that when he reported on June 21 that the attack would begin on the following day, Susloparov told him: "You're completely mistaken. Only today I met the Japanese military attaché, who had just arrived from Berlin. He assures me that Germany is not preparing for war. We can depend on him." Early next morning Trepper was wakened by the manager of his hotel, shouting in his ear, "It's happened! Germany is at war with the Soviet Union!"[119]

Though there was a peculiar perversity and intensity about the refusal of Stalin and his chief advisers to take warnings of a German surprise attack at their face value, many foreign statesmen and intelli-gence analysts also misread Hitler's intentions in varying degrees. As late as May 23, 1941, one day short of a month before the German invasion, the Joint Intelligence Committee (JIC) in London was still arguing that "The advantages to Germany of concluding an agreement with the U.S.S.R. are overwhelming."[120] One of the reasons for Stalin's persistent personal distrust of Churchill was intelligence from NKGB penetration agents revealing that Whitehall's assessment of the German threat to Russia differed markedly from that contained in Churchill's dramatic warnings of impending invasion.[121] Even when Whitehall as a whole came round to the view at the beginning of June that Germany was making preparations for an attack, it still expected Hitler to issue an ultimatum backed up by the threat of force rather than launch a surprise attack. Not until June 12, only ten days before the invasion began, did the JIC finally conclude that "Hitler has made up his mind to have done with Soviet obstructions and intends to attack her."[122]

The JIC, however, was more prescient than most foreign observers. The Japanese high command, foreign minister, and ambassador in Moscow all believed that reports of German preparations for an attack on Russia were simply designed to camouflage plans for an invasion of Britain. Ironically, the telegrams of Oshima, the Japanese ambassador in Berlin, which correctly predicted a German invasion, were read with more attention in Washington (which succeeded in decrypting them) than in Tokyo. But even in Washington some senior members of the administration were taken aback by the beginning of Operation Barbarossa on June 22.[123]

Stalin, curiously, trusted Hitler more than Hitler's generals, who, he feared, had become intoxicated by their astonishing run of Blitzkrieg victories. During the few days immediately before, and the hours after, the German attack, Stalin's judgment was affected by a third conspiracy theory. While still suspicious of a British plot to embroil him with Hitler and of a plot by Hitler to present an ultimatum demanding Soviet concessions, Stalin became preoccupied by the equally mistaken theory of a provocation being prepared by Hitler's intoxicated generals. According to Marshal N. N. Voronov, Stalin believed that "war between fascist Germany and the Soviet Union could occur only as a result of provocations on the part of the fascist militarists, and he feared these provocations most of all."[124] *Provokatsia* played a central role in the conspiratorial Stalinist world view. Like Stalin himself, Golikov, Beria, and most Soviet intelligence officers saw provocation as an inevitable tool of the unending conspiracy by capitalist powers against the Soviet state. If the U.S.S.R. allowed itself to be provoked on issues chosen by its capitalist opponents, it played into their hands and temporarily lost control of the march of history.

As reports of German troop movements multiplied on the eve of the invasion, Stalin visibly vacillated between the need, on the one hand, to bring Soviet forces to war readiness and, on the other hand, to avoid the (imaginary) provocations of German generals. On the evening of June 21-22 Stalin telephoned General I. V. Tyulenev, commander of the Moscow Military District, and ordered the combat readiness of the Moscow anti-aircraft defenses to be brought up to 75 percent. But soon afterward he told Marshal Timoshenko, the defense commissar: "We are starting a panic for nothing." When told that a German deserter had brought news that the attack was to begin the next day, Stalin ordered him to be shot for attempting to spread "disinformation."

Half an hour after midnight on June 22, three hours before

Barbarossa began, the Defense Commissariat finally issued a directive placing the armed forces on a state of combat readiness (though the directive failed to reach some military districts until after the attack began). But commanders who asked whether they should open fire if German troops crossed the border were told: "Don't give in to provocation, and don't open fire." Even after the invasion had started, Timoshenko telephoned General Boldin, deputy commander of the Western Special Military District, to inform him: "You must not take any actions against the Germans without our knowledge. . . . Comrade Stalin does not permit the opening of artillery fire on the Germans." Boldin shouted into the receiver: "How can that be? Our troops are being forced to retreat. Cities are burning, people are dying." Not till 7:15 A.M. did the Defense Commissariat order Soviet forces on to the offensive. Even then Stalin clung to the belief that what was happening was not the beginning of a war but a "provocation" by German generals.

Only at noon was the fiction of a provocation abandoned. In public Stalin stayed silent, but Molotov told the Soviet people in a radio broadcast that they were now at war. The eight hours since Barbarossa had begun had been spent by Stalin trying desperately to prevent the "provocation" from turning into war. He bombarded the German foreign ministry with radio messages; he sought the help of Japanese "mediation" to bring the "crisis" to an end. The German invaders meanwhile had secured all the railway and road bridges against which they attempted *coups de main,* struck at sixty-six Soviet airfields, destroying a thousand aircraft on the ground, and begun a rapid advance along a 930-mile front.[125]

With the largest foreign intelligence network in history, the Soviet Union suffered in the early hours of June 22, 1941, the greatest intelligence disaster of the Second World War. The disaster derived not from any shortage of intelligence but from the analysis and use made of it. The surprise achieved by the German invasion was made possible both by the nature of the Soviet intelligence system and by the personal failings of the dictator at the head of it. In Whitehall the patient examination of intelligence reports through the committee system eventually turned the belief that Germany saw the "overwhelming" advantages of reaching agreement with Russia into the recognition that Hitler had decided to attack. In Moscow the whole system of intelligence assessment was dominated by the fearful sycophancy encapsulated in the formula *ugadat, ugodit, utselet.*

But the failures of the system are not a sufficient explanation for the sheer perversity of Stalin's role as his own chief intelligence analyst. He was distracted from the immense threat posed by the German invasion by three nonexistent plots: by the British to embroil him with Hitler, by Hitler to present him with an ultimatum, and by German generals to provoke him into firing on their advancing armies. Imaginary conspiracies blinded him to the real conspiracy of Operation Barbarossa. As Cardinal de Retz had written in the seventeenth century, "The most distrustful persons are often the biggest dupes."

8

The Great Patriotic War
(1941–45)

Barbarossa was the mightiest invasion in military history. The Wehrmacht, boasted Hitler, would be victorious before winter set in: "We have only to kick in the door and the whole rotten edifice will come crashing down." At first it seemed that Hitler might be right. His forces advanced at fifty miles a day, sweeping all before them even more rapidly than in the Blitzkriegs in Western Europe. The Soviet Union also faced the terrifying prospect of a simultaneous Japanese attack in the East. Sorge reported from Tokyo that Ribbentrop was urging the German embassy to persuade the Japanese to break their treaty of neutrality with the Soviet Union concluded only three months before Barbarossa began. "Do everything," Ribbentrop instructed, "to rouse the Japanese to begin war against Russia. . . . The quicker this happens the better. Our goal remains to shake hands with the Japanese on the Trans-Siberian Railway before the beginning of winter."

Initially opinions were divided within the Japanese government and high command between the "northern solution" (war with the Soviet Union) and the "southern solution" (war with Britain and the United States). Sorge was able to keep Moscow informed, chiefly from intelligence obtained by Ozaki, as the supporters of the "southern solution" gained the upper hand. On August 15 he reported that war before the winter season had been ruled out because of the "excessive strain on the Japanese economy." But despite receiving belated thanks for his neglected warnings about Barbarossa, Sorge later claimed that his increasingly reassuring reports on Japan's intentions did not finally convince Moscow until the end of September. His radio message then that "The Soviet Far East can be considered safe from Japanese attack," prompted a special message of thanks from Moscow. In October Stalin set about moving half his Far Eastern Command to fight the Germans in the West. Sorge's final message to Moscow was a request to be recalled home or sent to Germany now that the threat of Japanese attack had disappeared. The message was never sent. On October 18 Sorge was arrested; so, within the space of a few days, were thirty-five members of his spy ring. According to the Japanese security police officer in charge of surveillance before his arrest, Sorge spent his last night at liberty sleeping with the wife of the German ambassador.[1]

All existing accounts of the intelligence on Japanese intentions supplied by Sorge's spy ring after the beginning of Barbarossa are based on one false assumption. Sorge's intelligence was not, as has been generally believed, unique. At least some of it came simultaneously in sigint derived from intercepted Japanese diplomatic telegrams. Indeed it was probably the corroboration provided by sigint that finally won Sorge the full confidence of Moscow only three weeks before his arrest by the Japanese security police. After Sorge's arrest, sigint continued to provide reassurance about Japan's intentions. A decrypted telegram of November 27, 1941, from Tokyo to the Berlin embassy (probably copied to the Moscow embassy), instructed the Japanese ambassador: "See Hitler and Ribbentrop, and explain to them in secret our relations with the United States. . . . Explain to Hitler that the main Japanese efforts will be concentrated in the south and that we propose to refrain from deliberate operations in the north."[2]

The greatest wartime successes of Soviet cryptanalysts were against Japanese codes and ciphers. In February 1941, the *Spets-Otdel* sigint unit had been integrated into a new NKGB (later NKVD) Fifth (Cipher) Directorate. At the heart of the directorate was a Research Section responsible for the main cryptanalytic attack on foreign code and cipher systems. The chief Japanese specialist in the Research Section, S. Tolstoy, became the most decorated Soviet cryptanalyst of the war, receiving two orders of Lenin. His principal assistants were Professor Shumski, a Japanese linguist, Colonel Gerasim Balasanov, Colonel Kotelnikov, and an Armenian called Kasparov. Tolstoy himself died

shortly after victory. The successes of his group allowed the Fifth
Directorate to take over from the GRU responsibility for decrypting at
least some Japanese military communications. One of the tasks of the
first section of the Fifth Directorate was to monitor the traffic of the
Japanese Kwantung Army to detect any preparations for an attack on
the Soviet Far East.[3]

The reassurance about Japanese intentions provided by Sorge
and the Fifth Directorate enabled Stalin to shift to the West half the
divisional strength of the Far Eastern command. During October and
November 1941 between eight and ten rifle divisions, together with a
thousand tanks and a thousand aircraft were flung into the fight against
Germany.[4] They arrived at the most critical moment of the war. On
October 2 Hitler began Operation Typhoon, the attack on Moscow,
which he described as "the last great decisive battle of the war." Two
days later he told an exultant crowd in the Berlin Sportpalast: "The
enemy has already been routed and will never regain his strength!" But
Moscow never fell. The defense of the Soviet state was transformed into
a Holy War for Mother Russia. Stalin became the symbol of national
unity against a brutal invader. Though government offices and diplomatic missions were evacuated in mid-October to Kuybyshev on the
Volga, Stalin stayed in the Kremlin. "Stalin is with us!" became the
rallying cry of the defenders of Moscow. Surkov's "A Soldier's Oath"
caught the mood of the people:

> Stalin has told me that the battle will be hard and bloody,
> but that victory will be mine. For my heart is burning with
> the tears of women and children. Hitler and his hordes will
> pay for those tears with their wolves' blood. I shoot without
> missing, for my bullet flies from my heart.[5]

The defenders of Moscow and Leningrad, however, never suspected
that Stalin's main aim in October 1941 was not to lead the Red Army
in heroic resistance but to use the NKVD to seek a negotiated peace
with Hitler.

On October 7 Georgi Zhukov, the ablest of the senior Red
Army commanders, was summoned to Stalin's office in the Kremlin,
where he found Stalin alone with Beria. Both were convinced that the
Red Army was facing defeat.[6] Beria by now had direct control once
again over the whole of the intelligence and security empire he had
inherited from Yezhov. In July 1941 the NKGB was reabsorbed into

the NKVD and did not reemerge as a separate agency until April 1943. War consolidated Beria's position as the most powerful security chief in Soviet history, with a seat on the five-man State Defense Committee (with Stalin, Molotov, Voroshilov, and Malenkov) formed after the German attack.[7]

Beria stayed silent as Stalin told Zhukov that the Red Army was not strong enough to resist the German attack on Moscow. It had become necessary to follow Lenin's example of March 1918, when, faced with no realistic alternative, he had signed the humiliating peace of Brest-Litovsk with Germany. Turning to Beria, Stalin instructed him to find ways of negotiating another "Brest peace" with Germany—even at the cost of losing the Baltic States, Byelorussia, Moldavia, and part of the Ukraine. NKVD agents chosen by Beria asked the Bulgarian ambassador in Moscow, Stotenov, to act as intermediary. Stotenov agreed but his overtures to the Germans were brushed aside.[8]

Even while the fate of Moscow hung in the balance, Beria was still continuing his purge of the high command. On the night of October 15–16 the central apparatus of the NKVD was evacuated to Kuybyshev, along with the most senior officers then being interrogated in the cellars of the Lubyanka. Three hundred others, for whom there was no transport, were shot. Interrogation of the survivors continued in Kuybyshev. After his arrest in 1953, Beria admitted: "Merciless beatings were administered; it was a real mincing machine." All save General A. D. Loktionov, who heroically resisted all tortures, confessed to the imaginary crimes of which the NKVD accused them. In the words of the Soviet military historian Lieutenant General Nikolai Pavlenko, "Hundreds of high-ranking military specialists awaited their death while at the same time regiments at the front were being commanded by lieutenants." Some of the commanders taken to Kuybyshev were shot on October 28. But then Stalin suddenly brought Beria's interrogations to an end. The two most senior imprisoned commanders, General K. A. Meretskov, former chief of the General Staff, and General B. L. Vannikov, former commissar for ammunition, were among those released and rehabilitated despite their admission of imaginary crimes.[9]

The suspension of the NKVD purge of the high command coincided with, even if it did not cause, a change in the fortunes of war. Moscow did not fall. Confident that the Red Army would be crushed before autumn ended, Hitler had boasted, "There will be no winter campaign." Without winter clothing, his forces froze. Even in field hospitals, wounded and frostbitten soldiers died from the cold. In December Zhukov launched a counterattack outside Moscow, which drove the enemy back and put the Wehrmacht on the defensive for the first time in the war. His victory made him a popular hero. Zhukov, however, was acutely aware that Stalin viewed his popularity with an evil eye. He said later: "I belong to that small number of military leaders who were never subjected to arrest, but the threat of it hung over my head for [the next] half a decade." Zhukov believed that the arrest in 1942 of his operations officer, Major General V. S. Golush-kevich, was Stalin's way of reminding him that he was not beyond the reach of the NKVD.[10]

Soviet accounts of the underground resistance groups in Germany led by Harro Schulze-Boysen and Arvid Harnack emphasize the contribution of the intelligence they supplied in helping to stem the German invasion:

> Starting in the autumn of 1941, the heroic members of the underground began to supply valuable information to the Soviet high command. Schulze-Boysen's work in the intelligence division of Luftwaffe headquarters and his wide contacts in military circles, including the Abwehr, made it possible for him to obtain extremely important information about the Hitlerites' plans.[11]

Schulze-Boysen and Harnack were arrested by the Gestapo on, respectively, August 30 and September 3, 1942. By December 22, when they were executed in Berlin, over eighty members of their networks had been rounded up. Though their most important penetrations were probably in the Luftwaffe, the Air Ministry, the War Ministry, and the high commands of the armed services, other contacts of varying importance were also established with the Propaganda Ministry, Foreign Office, Berlin City Government, Office for Racial Policy, and the German Office for the Protection of Labor. A Nazi Security Police and Security Service inquiry concluded, with Teutonic thoroughness, that the occupations of those arrested were:

29% academics and students
21% authors, journalists, and artists
20% professional soldiers, civil servants, and government
       officials

17% wartime recruits to the armed forces
13% artisans and laborers[12]

Soviet accounts have tended to exaggerate the value of the intelligence
supplied by the Schulze-Boysen and Harnack networks in order to
stress the significance of the Communist resistance inside Nazi Germany. Though valuable in assessing, in particular, Luftwaffe strength
and capabilities, and obtained at great personal risk, their intelligence
was not of major operational importance in helping to stem the German
invasion. The Nazi Security Police and Security Service listed nine
areas in which the Schulze-Boysen network had provided its most
valuable intelligence to the Soviet Union:

1. Report on the strength of the German Air Force at the
   beginning of the war with the Soviet Union
2. Information on the monthly production of the German
   aviation industry in the period June-July 1941
3. Information regarding the fuel situation in Germany
4. Information regarding the intended German attack on
   Maikop (Caucasus)
5. Reports on the location of German headquarters
6. Data on serial production of aircraft in the occupied areas
7. Reports on the production and storage of material for
   chemical warfare in Germany
8. Report on the capture of a Russian code near Petsamo
   [Probably the same as that obtained by the OSS from the
   Finns]
9. Reports on losses of German parachutists on Crete.[13]

By combining political resistance with espionage Schulze-Boysen and
Harnack made their eventual downfall inevitable. Schulze-Boysen and
his wife, Libertas, put their own safety in peril by holding evening
discussion groups for members and potential members of the anti-Nazi
underground. As small groups of young resisters pasted anti-Nazi posters on Berlin walls, Schulze-Boysen stood guard over them, wearing his
Luftwaffe uniform and holding his automatic pistol with the safety
catch off. During the running of the anti-Soviet exhibition "The Soviet
Paradise" in the Berlin Lustgarten in 1942, Schulze-Boysen organized
a rival poster campaign using the slogan:

Exhibition: The Nazi Paradise
War—Hunger—Lies—Gestapo
How much longer?

Both Schulze-Boysen and Harnack also wrote and distributed pamphlets, which a later Soviet eulogy described as "splendid examples of fighting anti-Hitlerite propaganda."[14]

The German diplomat Rudolf von Scheliha took far fewer risks. During the war, as before, he remained quite separate from the Schulze-Boysen and Harnack groups. But for the shortage of GRU radio operators in Berlin, he might have remained undetected for much longer. The capture of a radio operator in Brussels who had been used to transmit some of his intelligence eventually led to his downfall. After Barbarossa began, von Scheliha became reluctant to continue spying for the GRU. His contact Ilse Stöbe, now suffering from venereal disease, found it difficult to coax intelligence from him.

In October 1942 a GRU agent, Heinrich Koenen (son of a former KPD deputy), was landed in East Prussia by parachute and made his way to Berlin to establish contact with von Scheliha via Stöbe. With him he brought a radio set to transmit von Scheliha's intelligence to Moscow. Koenen also carried with him von Scheliha's receipt for $6,500 received from the GRU in 1938—almost certainly to use for blackmail if he proved unwilling to cooperate. A German Security Police and Security Service report reasonably concluded that Koenen's mission showed "how greatly interested Moscow was in the continuation of von Scheliha's work." The Gestapo, however, had arrested Ilse Stöbe in September. It was waiting for Koenen when he tried to contact her a month later.[15]

The Schulze-Boysen and Harnack groups were part of a loosely coordinated GRU network in Western and Central Europe collectively code-named the Rote Kapelle (Red Orchestra) by the German Central Security Office. The "musicians" were the radio operators who sent coded messages to Moscow; their "conductor" was Leopold Trepper, known within the organization as the "grand chef."[16] Trepper later claimed that on November 12, 1941, one of his "musicians" in Brussels radioed a message from a member of the Schulze-Boysen group, which gave Moscow its first warning of Hitler's Operation Blue, the strategic thrust that was to lead him to disaster at Stalingrad just over a year later:

Plan III, Objective Caucasus, originally scheduled for November, to be carried out spring 1942. Placement of troops to be completed by 1 May . . . Details follow.[17]

Trepper's account, however, is impossible to reconcile with the damage assessment by German intelligence of the most important information provided by the Schulze-Boysen group.[18] On May 12, 1942, again according to Trepper's later recollection, one of his couriers arrived in Moscow with "all the information on the major elements of the offensive."[19] Once again, Trepper's recollection does not square with the Soviet evidence. The first major intelligence on Operation Blue came from plans for the first phase of the offensive captured from a German aircraft that crashed inside Soviet lines on June 19, 1942. On June 26 Stalin announced that he did not believe a word of Operation Blue and denounced the intelligence staff for being taken in by such obvious disinformation.[20] Two days later Operation Blue began with a rapid German advance on a broad front from Kursk to the Northern Donets River, which renewed Hitler's confidence that the victory over Russia that had eluded him in 1941 would be complete before the end of 1942.

The Rote Kapelle in occupied Europe was gradually wound up during 1942 as German radio direction-finding tracked down the musicians. Trepper himself was captured while sitting in his dentist's chair in Paris on December 5, 1942. According to the Abwehr officer who arrested him, "For a second he was disturbed, then he said in perfect German, 'You did a fine job.' " After agreeing to cooperate with the Gestapo, Trepper became a double or possibly a triple agent, feeding misinformation, perhaps combined with warnings, back to Moscow. Remarkably, in September 1943 he escaped and remained in hiding for the remainder of the war.[21]

Ultimately, the most important wartime Soviet agent network with access to sources inside Germany was the Rote Drei (the Red Three) in Switzerland, so called from the presumed number of its radio transmitters, headed by Alexander Rado (code name Dora). By far the most important of the agents in Rado's network was Rudolf Roessler (Lucy), a Swiss intelligence officer of German extraction, whose intelligence reached Rado via a subgroup leader, Rachel Duebendorfer (Sissy), and a cut-out (intermediary), Christian Schneider (Taylor). Roessler had four important sources inside Germany to whom he gave the code names Werther, Teddy, Anna, and Olga. Though none has been identified with certainty, a CIA study later concluded that Roessler's four sources were probably Major General Hans Oster, the anti-Nazi chief of staff to the head of the Abwehr, Admiral Canaris, who was later hanged with Canaris for his part in the July 1944 bomb plot; Hans Bernd Gisevius, another Abwehr officer, who also served as German vice-consul in Zürich; Carl Goerdeler, civilian leader of the conservative opposition to Hitler, also executed after the bomb plot; and Colonel Fritz Boetzel, commanding officer of the intelligence evaluation office of the Southeast Army Group in Athens.[22]

The mystery surrounding the "Lucy ring" has given rise to numerous myths, among them the allegation that the ring was a cover through which British intelligence fed the Russians with Ultra sigint derived from breaking German ciphers while disguising its source.[23] Though British intelligence did not use Roessler as a conduit, the Swiss may well have done so. The sources that Roessler described as his own were probably those of Swiss intelligence, which used Roessler to pass it to the Russians. Some of the same intelligence seems to have reached the West through Colonel Karel Sedlaček, the representative in Switzerland of the Czechoslovak government-in-exile. Roessler's own motives were mainly mercenary. Rado reported to Moscow in November 1943: "Sissy states that the Lucy group no longer works when the salary stops."[24] Roessler is often alleged to have been sending intelligence to the Russians even before the German invasion. Rado's messages to Moscow show that, in reality, his first contact with Roessler did not occur until about September 1942.[25]

Brave and resourceful though the GRU agent networks were, the intelligence they provided did not begin to have a significant influence on Soviet military operations until after the battle of Stalingrad. In the initial shock of Operation Barbarossa, the Stavka (a wartime mixture of GHQ and high command) repeatedly lost track of the German invaders. Military intelligence failed to detect the sudden German turn south that led to the capture of Kiev in September 1941 and was taken aback by the intensity of the October assault on Moscow. It was taken by surprise again in the summer of 1942. Convinced that the main German threat would be a renewed attempt to take Moscow, Stalin and the Stavka misread the Wehrmacht's attack in the south.

Throughout the German advance to Stalingrad and the Caucasus, Soviet forces were constantly confused about where the next blow would fall.[26] When the Red Army encircled Axis forces in Stalingrad in November, it believed it had trapped 85,000 to 90,000 troops; in reality it had surrounded over three times as many.[27] The Stavka was equally misinformed about plans for the German relief expedition. The first the Red Army learned of the dispatch of six Panzer divisions from France was when Soviet cavalry ran into them.

The great victory at Stalingrad, sealed by the surrender of the German forces at the end of January and beginning of February 1943, bore witness to the quality of Red Army staff work, to its ability to improvise and change plans at short notice, and to the courage of Soviet soldiers. But it was a victory achieved in spite, rather than because, of the quality of Soviet operational intelligence.[28]

Throughout the Great Patriotic War, but particularly during its first two years, the NKVD/NKGB was better informed about Russia's allies than about Nazi Germany. Initially, the agent who provided the greatest insight into British policy was probably the Fifth Man, John Cairncross, who remained private secretary to Lord Hankey until March 1942. In July 1941 Hankey was moved from his position as chancellor of the Duchy of Lancaster to the less prestigious ministerial position of postmaster-general, but he retained full access to War Cabinet papers and the chairmanship of a series of important committees.[29] Cairncross continued to provide "tons of documents" to the NKVD during the first nine months of the Great Patriotic War.[30] Until October 1941 Hankey chaired the Allied Supplies Committee, which coordinated the dispatch of munitions and raw materials to Russia.

Cairncross probably gave the NKVD an exaggerated estimate of the level of opposition to Churchill. Hankey was Churchill's severest ministerial critic, and said privately that his "War Cabinet of 'Yes-Men' was hopeless." Early in 1942 he prepared an assessment of Churchill's strategic direction of the war, which he headed "The Indictment." Among Hankey's criticisms, doubtless reported by Cairncross to the NKVD, was "the priority given to supplies for Russia." When sacked from the government by Churchill in March 1942 Hankey replied: "For some time I have felt profoundly dissatisfied with the conduct of the war." Hankey's "profound dissatisfaction" was almost the last intelligence provided by Cairncross from Whitehall before he began the penetration of the wartime sigint agency at Bletchley Park.

Britain had been a high priority for Soviet foreign intelligence operations ever since the foundation of INO and the Fourth Department (the predecessor of the GRU). The United States, by contrast, was considered of only secondary importance until about a year before the Second World War. The Fourth Department, which ran most American operations in the 1930s, was chiefly interested in the United States not for its own sake but as a base for operations against the more important targets of Japan and Germany. In 1938 Fourth Department operations suffered a potentially serious setback after the defection of its main American courier, Whittaker Chambers.

For a time Chambers went underground, fearing assassination by the NKVD or Fourth Department and unwilling to invite prosecution by revealing his past career in espionage. In 1939 he reemerged in public as a writer (later editor) with *Time* magazine. Outraged, though not surprised, by the Nazi-Soviet Pact, Chambers agreed to tell his story on September 2, the day after the outbreak of war, to Adolf Berle, assistant secretary of State and Roosevelt's adviser on internal security. Berle assured Chambers that his information would go directly to the president and that he would not be penalized for agreeing to cooperate; but he stopped short of promising immunity from prosecution. After their meeting, Berle drew up a four-page memorandum entitled "Underground Espionage Agent," which listed Alger Hiss, Harry Dexter White, and the other leading Soviet agents for whom Chambers had acted as courier.

Roosevelt was not interested. He seems simply to have dismissed the whole idea of espionage rings within his administration as absurd. Equally remarkably, Berle simply pigeonholed his own report. He made no inquiries about Hiss until 1941, when he mentioned Chambers's charges to Hiss's former employer, Supreme Court Justice Feliks Frankfurter, and to the diplomat Dean Acheson. Both dismissed them out of hand. Berle took no further action; he did not send a report of his interview with Chambers to the FBI until the bureau requested it in 1943. Among others who brought Chambers's story to Roosevelt's attention were Ambassador William Bullitt, labor leader David Dubinsky, and journalist Walter Winchell. Once again, the president brushed the charges aside.

Chambers was eventually interviewed by the FBI in 1942 after an erstwhile associate in the Communist underground identified him as a former Soviet agent with "more material than you could ever hope to get by running around for a year." Perhaps fearing prosecution, Chambers was less forthcoming than he had been to Berle three years before, stressing his underground Communist activity rather than his involvement in espionage. FBI director J. Edgar Hoover airily dismissed an eight-page report on the interview as mostly "history, hypothesis or deduction." There was no follow-up interview with Chambers for the next three years. Of the individuals identified by Chambers, the FBI made cursory inquiries concerning only J. Peters, who was already in its files as a leading figure in the American Communist Party.[31]

After Chambers's defection in 1938, the main Fourth Department networks in Washington were taken over by the NKVD New York resident, Gaik Badalovich Ovakimyan, later christened "the wily Armenian" by the FBI.[32] Henceforth the United States became a major (by the end of the Second World War *the* major) target for Soviet espionage rather than, as previously, a base for intelligence operations directed elsewhere. In 1938 the NKVD had not yet grasped quite how light-heartedly the administration still treated the issue of Soviet espionage in the United States. Chambers's defection and the fears it inspired of an FBI inquiry thus caused some inevitable disruption to NKVD operations in Washington. Harry Dexter White in the Treasury was the most senior of several agents who abruptly ceased supplying information. His wife, who did not share his Communist sympathies, made him promise to give up espionage.

The man who did most to resuscitate the Washington network of Soviet informants was Nathan Gregory Silvermaster (not to be confused with his friend and fellow agent George Silverman), an official of Ukrainian Jewish origins in his early forties at the Farm Security Administration, later assigned to the Board of Economic Warfare. Emotionally incapable of accepting the brutal reality of Stalinist Russia, Silvermaster retained the untarnished idealism of the revolutionary dream. A chronic sufferer from bronchial asthma, which often left him gasping for breath, he believed: "My time is strictly limited, and when I die I want to feel that at least I have had some part in building a decent life for those who come after me." It was Silvermaster who coaxed Harry Dexter White back into supplying intelligence, probably soon after the outbreak of war. By Pearl Harbor he had gathered together a group of ten government officials working both for various parts of Roosevelt's wartime administration and for the NKVD. White did not join the group but provided intelligence individually to Silvermaster, who found him a timid man reluctant for "his right hand to know what the left is doing." To calm his nerves and allow him to reassure his wife that he had abandoned active espionage, Silvermaster told him his information was going only to one man on the Central Committee of the American Communist Party. Silvermaster had no doubt that White knew the truth but believed that he preferred not to think about it. He hid in his attic the valuable Bokhara rug given him by Bykov before the war. As the right-hand man of the secretary of the Treasury, Henry Morgenthau, White had access not merely to most of the Treasury's classified files, but also to secret information exchanged with other government departments.[33]

The courier for the Silvermaster group from 1941 was Elizabeth Bentley, a thirty-three-year-old Vassar graduate based in New York, who had become an ardent anti-fascist after spending a year in Mussolini's Italy and had joined the American Communist Party in 1935. In 1938 she was persuaded to break overt links with the Party, pose as a conservative, and work for the NKVD. Bentley's NKVD controller, Jacob Golos, another Ukrainian Jew, known to his agents as Timmy, broke NKVD rules by seducing her. Bentley later described the seduction during a New York snowstorm in clichés borrowed from a romance novel: "His hand touched mine, I looked at him, and then quite suddenly I found myself in his arms, his lips on mine." "Time and space seemed to stand still" until Bentley felt herself "float away into an ecstasy that seemed to have no beginning and no end." At the end of a long night they sat hand in hand in Golos's car watching "the most beautiful sunrise I had ever seen." Golos slightly spoiled the sunrise by explaining the NKVD rules he had just broken: "We are forbidden to form close friendships and, especially, to fall in love. You and I have no right, under Communist discipline, to feel the way we do about each other."[34]

Encouraged by Golos's bad example, Bentley mixed friendship and espionage in a way that would have horrified Moscow Center. Each Christmas she bought carefully chosen presents ranging from whiskey to lingerie from NKVD funds for the agents for whom she acted as courier. When a new controller tried to impose tighter security after Golos's death in 1943, she looked back nostalgically to "the good old days—the days when we worked together as good comrades."[35] The careless security of some of the agents in her net concerned even Bentley. J. Julius (Joe) Joseph, an agent in the wartime intelligence agency, the Office of Strategic Services (OSS), recruited in 1942, was one of several who "never seemed to learn the correct underground procedure":

He was continually getting into difficulties that had us alternately worried and amused. One famous time, having been told either to burn documents or flush them down the toilet, he crammed a mass of flaming papers into the toilet, with the result that the seat was set on fire. His puzzled landlord, surveying the damage, finally walked out of the apartment, muttering to himself, "I don't see how that could possibly have happened."[36]

Given the general indifference to Soviet espionage in wartime Washington, such lapses of security carried few risks. Elizabeth Bentley's intelligence haul from her fortnightly visits to the capital grew steadily. At first she brought back only a few typewritten summaries of classified information, with carbon copies of particularly important documents. Moscow Center soon demanded more. Thenceforth members of the Silvermaster group brought secret material to his home at 5515 35th Street, N.W., where Silvermaster and his wife microfilmed it at night. At first the output consisted of three or four rolls of microfilm averaging thirty-five exposures each, which the Silvermasters developed themselves. By the spring of 1943, however, Bentley was carrying back to New York in her knitting bag about forty undeveloped microfilms a fortnight to be developed in the laboratory of the NKVD residency. Each spool was accompanied by an itemized list of the documents on it in case any of the negatives proved unreadable. A number were.

The NKVD preferred to provide the Silvermasters with their microfilm direct in order for them to avoid attracting attention by a bulk purchase, which was difficult if not impossible for civilians to make in wartime. Handicapped by shortages, however, the NKVD sometimes supplied inferior slow-speed film, which made photographing documents extremely difficult. "How do they expect us to carry on when they can't furnish us with adequate films?" Silvermaster asked Bentley. ". . . Has something gone wrong with the United States government's Lend Lease program to the Soviet Union?"[37] Silvermaster's sarcastic suggestion that the NKVD should seek American government aid to assist its espionage in the United States was less fanciful than he may have supposed. At a meeting with the head of the U.S. Military Mission in Moscow in 1944 the head of INU, Pavel Fitin, and his assistant, Andrei Graur, requested "all information we could give them on the mechanics of taking and developing clandestine microfilm pictures with portable equipment, etc."[38]

Despite technical difficulties, Elizabeth Bentley collected in her knitting bag on her fortnightly trips to Washington what she immodestly described as "a fabulous amount" of intelligence from the Silvermaster group. In March 1944 she began acting as courier for a second group of eight government officials in Washington headed by Victor Perlo, then a statistician in the War Production Board. Bentley also later identified eleven other officials who did not belong to the Silvermaster or Perlo groups who supplied substantial amounts of classified material from government files. She considered the "most fruitful source" of the Silvermaster group's intelligence to be the Pentagon. To her inexperienced eye it seemed that the group supplied "every conceivable piece of data on aircraft-production figures, charts showing allocation of planes to combat areas and foreign countries, performance data, new and secret developments in numberless fields."[39]

The NKVD was doubtless particularly pleased by its penetration of the American intelligence community. Elizabeth Bentley later identified seven members of the headquarters staff of the Office of Strategic Services, the wartime predecessor of the CIA, who were also working for the NKVD.[40] Decrypted Soviet communications later revealed even more.[41] The most important may have been Duncan Chaplin Lee, a descendant of the Civil War General Robert E. Lee, Rhodes scholar at Oxford and brilliant young New York lawyer in the firm of William J. Donovan. Soon after Donovan became head of OSS in 1942, he took on Lee as his personal assistant. Golos, unsurprisingly, "attached great importance to Lee's intelligence."[42]

There was in general a staggering disproportion between what the OSS knew about the NKVD and what the NKVD knew about the OSS. Soviet penetration of OSS and the Roosevelt administration effectively torpedoed Donovan's one major coup against the NKVD. In November 1944 Donovan purchased from the Finns a partially charred fifteen hundred-page NKVD code book, which had been captured by them.[43] Alarm bells quickly began ringing among some of the Soviet agents in Washington who feared that they would be compromised by decrypted NKVD communications. According to later evidence by Elizabeth Bentley, Lauchlin Currie, administrative assistant to Roosevelt and a member of the Silvermaster group, came dashing into the house of another member of the group, George Silverman, "sort of out of breath, and told him that the Americans were on the verge of breaking the Soviet code." The news was quickly passed on to Bentley.[44]

Left to himself, Donovan would probably not have risked compromising his coup by bringing it to the attention of the secretary of State, Edward Stettinius. Others, quite possibly one or more of the NKVD agents in OSS, made sure that the secretary of State was informed. Stettinius urged on the president the view that gentlemen do not read their allies' mail. Roosevelt agreed. To his chagrin, Donovan was ordered to hand over the code book to the Russians.[45] In doing so, however, Donovan was careful to misrepresent his motives, assuring Fitin that he "took the only course open to a loyal ally in accepting this material as soon as he found it procurable":

> General Donovan would like General Fitin to know that we have made no study of this material and he, therefore, cannot positively state its value but has acted on the assumption that this is a matter of real importance to the Russian Government.[46]

And so it was. Fitin forwarded his "sincere thanks" for Donovan's action in "this very essential business." At his request the charred code book was handed over personally to the Soviet ambassador in Washington, Andrei Gromyko, and no other member of the embassy was told of its existence.[47] Fitin was not, of course, deceived by Donovan's high-minded display of loyal cooperation, though he must have been impressed by the naïveté of Roosevelt and Stettinius. The NKVD/NKGB changed its code book in May 1945. A copy of the charred 1944 code book, kept by Donovan when he handed over the original, was used from 1948 to help decrypt some NKVD/NKGB communications during the last year of the war, which were to be of great retrospective importance in identifying wartime Soviet agents.[48] Had the capture of the code book been concealed from the Russians in 1944, however, its value to American sigint would have been immeasurably greater.

Though most NKVD/NKGB agents in wartime Washington belonged to the Silvermaster and Perlo networks, a handful of the most important agents were run individually. Among them was Alger Hiss (code-named Ales), whose friendship with Whittaker Chambers seemed to have put him at particular risk after Chambers's defection in 1938.[49] From the summer of 1939 until May 1944 Hiss served as aide to Stanley K. Hornbeck, political adviser to the Far Eastern Division of the State Department. "Alger," said Hornbeck later, "had my full confidence and saw everything that I saw." There is no reason to doubt that he passed much of it on to the NKVD. The FBI briefly investigated one allegation against Hiss in 1942, but when assured by him that "There is only one government that I want to overthrow—and that is Hitler's," it took no further action.[50]

The NKVD would probably have preferred to run White, like Hiss, separately from the Silvermaster and Perlo nets. But after the shock of Chambers's defection, White was unwilling to deal with anyone but Silvermaster.[51] Hiss's wartime controller was the leading NKVD illegal in the United States, Iskhak Abdulovich Akhmerov, born in Baku in the closing years of the nineteenth century. In the United States he used the aliases Bill Greinke, Michael Green, and Michael Adamec.[52] When he first met the American Cambridge graduate Michael Straight, whom Blunt had tried to recruit to the NKVD, in a Washington restaurant in 1938, "He stood up, smiling a warm, friendly smile. . . . He stretched out his hand and held mine in a firm, friendly grip. . . . He was dark and stocky, with broad lips and a ready smile. His English was good, his manner was affable and easy. He seemed to be enjoying his life in America."[53] Akhmerov caused something of a stir in Directorate S, the illegals section of INU, by marrying Helen Lowry, the niece of the American Communist Party leader Earl Browder—a breach of NKVD rules, which he, like Golos, survived.[54] Akhmerov had no doubt that war would bring revolution in its wake. At a meeting with Straight late in 1939:

> Green's [Akhmerov's] dark eyes were bright. . . . The Soviet soldiers [in Finland] would be hailed as liberators—so he said. Revolution, starting in the East, would spread like wildfire across Germany and France. "Great days are approaching!" he said.[55]

Akhmerov also had a much tougher side. When Golos died in November 1943, Akhmerov (using the alias Bill) succeeded him as Elizabeth Bentley's controller. Before long he was putting heavy pressure on her to hand over to him direct control of the Silvermaster ring in Washington. "Night after night, after battling with him," wrote Bentley later, "I would crawl home to bed, sometimes too weary to undress." Bentley was both dismayed and impressed by the speed with which Akhmerov won Silvermaster's confidence at their first meeting:

> Bill [Akhmerov] was in his gayest mood and went out of his way to charm Greg [Silvermaster]. He insisted that he have the most expensive of meals, complete with wine; he flattered

him on the work he was doing, implying that he was one of
the pillars of the Soviet Union. I watched him cynically,
thinking of the real Bill that lay beneath all this veneer of
good fellowship. . . . If Bill continued to see Greg, he would
most certainly succeed in corrupting him.[56]

Early in his career in the KGB, while working in FCD Directorate S,
Gordievsky attended a lecture in the Lubyanka given by Akhmerov, by
then silver-haired and in his sixties. Akhmerov mentioned Hiss only
briefly. The main subject of his lecture was the man whom he identified
as the most important of all Soviet wartime agents in the United States:
Harry Hopkins, the closest and most trusted adviser of President
Roosevelt. Gordievsky later discussed the Hopkins case with a number
of officers in Directorate S and FCD American experts. All were agreed
that Hopkins had been an agent of major significance.[57] Gordievsky,
however, came gradually to the conclusion, as he discussed the Hopkins
case, that Hopkins had been an unconscious rather than a conscious
agent. That interpretation of Hopkins's connection with the KGB best
fits the evidence on his career available in the West.

So far as is known, Hopkins never discussed his occasional
meetings with Akhmerov with anyone. They remained unknown and
unsuspected in the West until revealed by Gordievsky. Hopkins kept
secrets easily; that was one of the reasons why Roosevelt chose him as
a confidant. His mother said of him: "I can't make Harry out. He never
tells me anything about what he's really thinking."[58] Hopkins's son
Robert found him reluctant to discuss even the plenary sessions of the
wartime conferences.[59] Akhmerov's technique in his contacts with Hopkins was to say that he brought personal and confidential messages from
Stalin.[60] He flattered Hopkins as successfully as he did Silvermaster,
making him believe he had a unique role to play at a critical period in
the development of Soviet-American relations. Hopkins's naïveté about
the NKVD (who in his view "looked neither more nor less obvious than
the American plainclothes man")[61] may well have led him to mistake
Akhmerov's significance. He probably regarded Akhmerov simply as
an unofficial intermediary chosen by Stalin because of his distrust
(shared by Hopkins) of the orthodox diplomatic establishment. What
is certain is that Hopkins came to feel an extraordinary admiration for,
and confidence in, Stalin, combined with apprehension for the future
"if anything should happen" to him.[62] Encouraged by Akhmerov, he
must have experienced a remarkable sense of secret pride that he en-

joyed the confidence of the two most powerful leaders in the world.

Gordievsky did not discover either from Akhmerov's lecture to Directorate S or from subsequent discussions in the KGB when and how he first established contact with Hopkins. They were already in contact, however, before Hopkins's first visit to the Soviet Union in the summer of 1941, just over a month after the German invasion.[63] On July 16, 1941, Hopkins arrived in Britain as Roosevelt's emissary for discussions with Churchill and the War Cabinet. On the 25th he telegraphed to the president: "I am wondering whether you think it important and useful for me to go to Moscow. . . . I have a feeling that everything possible should be done to make certain the Russians maintain a permanent front even though they may be defeated in the immediate battle."[64] Both the Soviet and American ambassadors in London, Ivan Maisky and John G. Winant, later claimed that their advice had helped to prompt Hopkins's visit.[65] So did Akhmerov.[66]

"The reception accorded Harry Hopkins by the Soviet Government . . ." wrote Laurence Steinhardt, the U.S. ambassador, "clearly indicated that extreme importance has been attached to this visit by this Government."[67] No previous Western envoy had received a reception like it. "In Russia," wrote Hopkins, "I shook hands as I have never shaken hands before. Several times I grinned at myself asking myself whether I was running for office. However, I kissed no babies." Hopkins was wined and dined even in his personal bomb shelter, which, to his amazement, he found fully equipped with champagne, caviar, chocolates, and cigarettes. (Steinhardt complained that he had never been offered a bomb shelter of any kind.) During their daily meetings Stalin instilled in Hopkins complete faith both in his own powers of leadership and in Russia's will to resist:

> Not once did he repeat himself. He talked as he knew his troops were shooting—straight and hard. He welcomed me with a few, swift Russian words. He shook my hand briefly, firmly, courteously. He smiled warmly. There was no waste of word, gesture, nor mannerism. . . . He curries no favor with you. He seems to have no doubts. He assures you that Russia will stand against the onslaughts of the German army. He takes it for granted that you have no doubts, either.[68]

Hopkins was no admirer of either the principle or practice of the Communist one-party state. But, wrote his first biographer, "through the years that followed, Hopkins was a sincere and even aggressive friend of Russia and an intense admirer of Russia's gigantic contribution to the winning of the war."[69]

The main purpose of Hopkins's July 1941 mission was to assess Russia's immediate and long-term needs in war material. He rapidly concluded, chiefly from his meetings with Stalin, that the State and War departments, like the British, had badly underestimated Soviet military potential. Hopkins's main importance to the Russians was his ability to convince Roosevelt that aid to Russia was worth the risk. As the president told his son Elliott: " 'I know how much faith the P.M. [Churchill] has in Russia's ability to stay in the war.' He snapped his fingers to indicate zero. . . . 'Harry Hopkins has more. He's able to convince me.' "[70] Hopkins also pleased the Russians by insisting on aid without strings. The American military attaché, Major Ivan Yeaton, tried to persuade Hopkins to demand the right to send military observers to the front as a quid pro quo. Ambassador Steinhardt later told an American journalist "of finding the two [Hopkins and Yeaton] pounding a breakfast table until the dishes danced in argument. The ambassador stuck his head in and hastily withdrew because he did not want to offend the President's personal envoy by supporting the military attaché's argument."[71] According to Yeaton, what most upset Hopkins was his comments on Stalin: "When I impugned the integrity and methods of Stalin he could stand it no longer and shut me up with an intense 'I don't care to discuss the subject further.' "[72]

As Stalin realized, Hopkins's unqualified support was of decisive importance in the development of American policy to the Soviet Union. Without his support, Roosevelt could scarcely have made an immediate promise of military aid. The promise of that aid in the summer of 1941 laid the foundation for Roosevelt's policy of wartime cooperation with the Soviet Union.[73] In backing Stalin and the Soviet war effort Hopkins acted from determination to prevent a Nazi victory rather than from a secret commitment to the Communist cause. But Akhmerov undoubtedly influenced Hopkins by delivering what he described as "personal messages from Comrade Stalin."[74] One of Comrade Stalin's desiderata was the replacement of "anti-Soviet" officials, who, he claimed, were hindering Soviet-American cooperation. Hopkins was instrumental in securing Yeaton's removal as military attaché in Moscow. He also arranged for a previous military attaché much appreciated by the Russians, Colonel Phillip R. Faymonville, who had served in Moscow from 1933 to 1938, to return to Russia to expedite American aid.

Faymonville was naïve as well as pro-Soviet. On his first tour of duty he had regarded as his "most valuable contact in Moscow" a man who subsequently turned out to be an NKVD captain; he passed classified documents on other European armies to the Russians, and failed to grasp the rudiments of embassy security.[75] When military intelligence objected to Faymonville's reappointment to Moscow, Hopkins retorted: "You might as well get his papers ready because he's going over."[76] Hopkins also pressed successfully for Steinhardt's replacement as ambassador on the grounds that he lacked Stalin's confidence. He was instrumental in persuading Roosevelt to move another of Stalin's critics, Loy W. Henderson, from his post as head of the Soviet desk in the State Department—despite the opposition of the secretary of State, Cordell Hull.[77]

When Stalin next encountered Hopkins at the Teheran conference in 1943, he went out of his way to greet him by walking over and warmly shaking his hand. Hopkins, said Stalin on another occasion, was the first American who had spoken to him *po dusham*—"from the soul."[78] But Hopkins did not depart from what he saw as American interests. His policy to the Soviet Union was based on a shrewd assessment of the ultimate potential of the Red Army, despite its early defeats, combined with a much more naïve belief, encouraged by his visit to Moscow in the summer of 1941 and by his contacts with Akhmerov, in the possibility of lasting friendship with Stalin. The President's Soviet Protocol Committee, chaired by Hopkins, reported in August 1943:

> Since Soviet Russia is the decisive factor in the war, she must be given every assistance and every effort must be made to obtain her friendship. Likewise, since without question she will dominate Europe on the defeat of the Nazis, it is even more essential to develop and maintain the most friendly relations with Russia.[79]

Though there was no British Hopkins in Churchill's entourage, Soviet wartime penetration in Britain was at least as remarkable as in the United States. Its most successful practitioners were the Magnificent

Five recruited at Cambridge, of whom four (Burgess, Blunt, Philby, and Cairncross) penetrated the British intelligence services. The first to do so was Guy Burgess. His opportunity came in 1938 with the creation by SIS of its first specialist dirty-tricks department, Section D (for "Destruction"). The tricks—delicately described as ways "of attacking potential enemies by means other than the operations of military force"—were not to be tried in peacetime. Until Britain went to war Section D was simply "to investigate every possibility."[80] One of the possibilities it investigated was broadcasting to Germany from illegal stations outside the United Kingdom.[81] Burgess's experience in the BBC, flair for international relations, and contacts in SIS made him an obvious candidate for the new section.

For more than a year Burgess had been using his considerable charm to cultivate the deputy head of political intelligence (Section I) in SIS, David Footman, whose first broadcast talk he had produced in 1937.[82] Burgess also made himself useful to Footman by relaying information from his disreputable friend Édouard Pfeiffer, a homosexual pederast who seemed to Goronwy Rees "to smell of every kind of corruption."[83] Pfeiffer was *chef de cabinet* to Édouard Daladier, French prime minister from April 1938 to May 1940. During 1938 Burgess made frequent trips to Paris, nominally as a courier for the Rothschilds, who had been his first employer after he left Cambridge. By his own later account, Burgess delivered confidential messages "on behalf of Pfeiffer" to the foreign secretary, Lord Halifax, and others in the Whitehall corridors of power.

After his defection in 1951 Burgess constructed a greatly exaggerated version of his prewar career, in which he had acted as, in effect, secret courier between the French and British prime ministers, bearing "the communications of a confused and panic-stricken patriot [Daladier] to an ignorant provincial ironmonger [Chamberlain]."[84] Though Burgess did not say so, he also acted as courier for the NKVD. With the NKVD residency in London temporarily out of action, he relayed to Paris some of the intelligence collected by its British agents.[85]

By January 1939 Burgess, with Footman's assistance, had found employment in Section D. Working in the outwardly respectable Joint Broadcasting Committee, whose notepaper bore a crest showing Big Ben flanked by armorial lions, he produced German-language records containing a mixture of propaganda, variety, and hit songs, ready to be broadcast in Germany as soon as (or even before) the balloon went up.[86] The head of Section D was the larger-than-life figure Major (later

Major-General) Laurence Grand, tall, thin, elegant, black-mustached, with a red carnation always in his buttonhole and identified by the secret symbol "D." Grand lacked the NKVD's experience both of "active measures" designed to influence foreign governments and public opinion, and of "special actions"—a euphemism for various forms of violence. According to Kim Philby, who later served briefly under him, he allowed his mind to range "free and handsome over the whole field of his awesome responsibilities, never shrinking from an idea, however big or wild."[87] The NKVD must certainly have followed with close attention the ample detail that Burgess provided on the birth of British active measures. But it must also have been baffled by some of the plans he reported. One of the official historians of British wartime intelligence has expressed some surprise, probably shared at the time by the NKVD, at a Section D sabotage scheme in Germany "to destroy the southern Siegfried line through the agency of two left-wing German expatriates, one stone deaf and the other going blind."[88]

In the long term Burgess's most important achievement during his two years in SIS was to smooth Kim Philby's entrance to it. Philby spent the first nine months of the Second World War as *The Times* correspondent to the British army headquarters at Arras. By June 1940, with the fall of France and the evacuation from Dunkirk, Philby was back in London, using his contacts to try to gain employment in one of the intelligence services. His first interview, "arranged by a mutual friend," was with Frank Birch, a former Cambridge history don who worked as a cryptanalyst in both world wars and was now recruiting for the Government Code and Cypher School, the British sigint agency, at its wartime headquarters at Bletchley Park. Birch finally turned him down, according to Philby "on the infuriating ground that he could not offer me enough money to make it worth my while."[89] Philby's explanation is unconvincing; the young dons and men from the professions recruited by Birch were paid £600 a year,[90] precisely the starting salary later received by Philby when he joined SIS. More probably, Birch simply thought Philby unsuited to sigint. Disconsolately, Philby went to take an army medical exam, expecting soon to be called up.[91]

At this crucial stage in his career, Guy Burgess came to Philby's rescue. Philby found himself summoned to an interview about "war work" (in fact for SIS) conducted by Marjorie Maxse, who struck him as "an intensely likeable elderly lady" who discussed with him "the possibilities of political work against the Germans in Europe." At a second interview a few days later Miss Maxse was accompanied by Burgess:

> Encouraged by Guy's presence, I began to show off, name-dropping shamelessly, as one does at interviews. From time to time, my interlocutors exchanged glances; Guy would nod gravely and approvingly. It turned out that I was wasting my time, since a decision had already been taken.

After a weekend drinking together, Philby presented himself formally in Burgess's office at the Caxton Street headquarters of Section D the following Monday morning. Burgess's secret symbol was DU; he gave Philby the symbol DUD. Philby's first major project was to draw up a detailed plan for Burgess's scheme for a training college for Section D agents. When the college was set up shortly afterward at Brickendon-bury Hall near Hertford, both Burgess and Philby became instructors.[92]

The NKVD/NKGB controller of Burgess, Philby, and the rest of the Magnificent Five from 1940 to 1944 was Anatoli Borisovich Gorsky, *alias* Anatoli Gromov, known to his agents simply as Henry. His early meetings with both Burgess and Philby took place on a park bench in Kensington Gardens, not far from the Soviet embassy. Gorsky was cast in a quite different mold from that of Maly, Deutsch, and the cosmopolitan illegals of the 1930s. Born in 1907, he was posted to London in 1936 originally as a minor technical employee of the Soviet embassy without diplomatic status. The purge of the entire NKVD London residency in 1937–38 allowed him to take over a number of minor intelligence duties and advance his career. In 1939 he was re-called to Moscow for intelligence training, promoted and returned to London as an NKVD officer working under diplomatic cover.[93] Gorsky, however, had one guilty secret that could have ruined his intelligence career at the outset. On NKVD forms and questionnaires he always described his father as a country schoolteacher in the Kras-noyarsk region. An investigation in 1953, when Gorsky was about to be appointed head of the American section in Moscow Center, revealed that his father had in reality been a Tsarist police officer, and he was instantly dismissed.[94]

One of his wartime agents described Gorsky as "a short, fattish man in his mid-thirties, with blond hair brushed straight back and glasses that failed to mask a pair of shrewd, cold eyes." He was tough, efficient, humorless, wore well-tailored clothes, and gave an impression of "well-fed flabbiness."[95] Blunt later claimed that he had found Henry "flat-footed" and unsympathetic.[96] When Gorsky discovered in August 1940 that, in defiance of orthodox NKVD tradecraft, Burgess and Blunt were sharing Victor Rothschild's London flat in Bentinck Street, he tried to persuade Blunt to move out. But he was flexible enough not to insist when Blunt refused.[97]

Neither Philby nor Burgess had much of interest to tell Gorsky during their time at Brickendonbury Hall. "We had little to do," wrote Philby later, "except talk to the Commander and help him draft memoranda for headquarters which seldom vouchsafed a reply." During the summer of 1940 Section D was merged into a new organization, the Special Operations Executive (SOE), which was instructed by Churchill to "set Europe ablaze" by imaginative use of subversive warfare. Though Burgess's imaginative powers were not in doubt, his irreverence did not appeal to his new masters. He was fired, "victim," he indignantly complained, "to a bureaucratic intrigue."

Philby, however, was kept on by SOE and appointed instructor at its training school at Beaulieu in Hampshire. SOE agents, Philby insisted, "required a certain amount of political indoctrination so that they would reach their fields of operation with at least one general idea of what the British Government had in mind for the future." This gave Philby frequent excuses to travel to London for briefings over pub lunches with the future leader of the Labour Party, Hugh Gaitskell, then principal private secretary to the Labour minister for economic warfare, Hugh Dalton, who was responsible for SOE. Philby found Dalton himself "always ready with a hospitable whisky and soda."[98]

Filtered through the distorting prism of Philby's own political convictions and conspiratorial interpretation of British policy, what he heard during his London briefings sounded suspiciously like a plot against the Soviet Union: "It often appeared that the British wanted a simple return to the status quo before Hitler, to a Europe comfortably dominated by Britain and France through the medium of reactionary governments just strong enough to keep their own people in order and uphold the cordon sanitaire against the Soviet Union."[99] On learning of Hess's flight to Britain on May 11, 1941, Philby jumped to the erroneous conclusion that his arrival was evidence of a deep-laid plot between appeasers in high places and the Nazi leadership. Even in 1990, the KGB was still quoting a report from Philby as evidence that Hess "brought the Führer's peace proposals with him and a plan for the invasion of the Soviet Union."[100] Forwarded to the Center by Gorsky,

Philby's distorted wartime assessments of Whitehall's postwar planning served to reinforce the prevailing Stalinist conspiracy theories about British policy. Contributing to Moscow's distrust of British intentions was to be one of Philby's main achievements as a wartime Soviet agent.

With the start of Operation Barbarossa on June 22, 1941, Philby—no doubt urged on by Gorsky—tried urgently "to get away from the rhododendrons of Beaulieu" and find a posting closer to the center of the British intelligence community. Before long he obtained the offer of a job in Section V (Counter-Intelligence) of SIS, whose Iberian subsection was attracted by the expertise that Philby had acquired as a newspaper correspondent in the Spanish Civil War.[101]

Philby's change of job did not mean the NKVD had no agent in SOE. Probably the most important SOE mole henceforth was Maclean's former schoolfriend and Cambridge contemporary James Klugmann, who progressed after the outbreak of war from the role of NKVD talent spotter and Party luminary to that of active Soviet agent. Klugmann joined the Yugoslav section of SOE-Cairo in February 1942, eventually rising to the rank of major. Throughout his time in Cairo, Klugmann's intellect, charm, and fluent Serbo-Croat gave him an influence entirely disproportionate to his rank. According to his superior Basil Davidson, "He could talk with brilliance on almost any subject, but what he really liked to talk about was politics." One of Klugmann's duties was to brief Allied officers about to be dropped into Yugoslavia. He unfailingly stressed the virtues of Tito's Communist Partisans and the vices of Mihailovich's Royalist Chetniks, telling one group of Canadian officers:

> You've got to see that this war has become more than a war against something, against fascism. It's become a war for something, for something much bigger. For national liberation, people's liberation, colonial liberation.[102]

From April to August 1945 Klugmann served in Yugoslavia with the military mission to Tito's forces. As a loyal Stalinist, he had later to eat many of his wartime words. When Tito fell afoul of Stalin in 1948, Klugmann wrote a book denouncing him.[103]

One other wartime Soviet agent in SOE deserves mention. In April 1943 MI5 discovered that Douglas Springhall, the national organizer of the Communist Party of Great Britain, who also did odd jobs for the NKVD, was obtaining classified information from Ormond

Uren, a Scottish junior staff officer in SOE's Hungarian section at its London headquarters. Springhall was sentenced to seven years' imprisonment on a quite different charge of receiving secrets from the Air Ministry. Uren also received a seven-year sentence. He later claimed facetiously that if he had been to Cambridge rather than Edinburgh University he might have got away with it.[104]

Following his move from SOE, Philby began work in Section V of SIS in September 1941. Though Section V was located in St. Albans and not, as he would have preferred, in Broadway Buildings, the SIS London headquarters, it had the advantage of being next door to the Registry, which housed SIS archives. Philby quickly succeeded in cultivating the archivist Bill Woodfield, with whom he shared a common appreciation of pink gins. In addition to consulting the files on Spain and Portugal, Philby also perused and passed on to Gorsky the contents of the two "source-books" giving details of SIS agents operating against Soviet targets.[105]

The most important intelligence received by the Iberian subsection of Section V was the intercepted, decrypted communications of the Abwehr, which by 1942 were giving "a very full picture" of German intelligence operations in Spain and Portugal.[106] Among the intercepts that most caught Philby's eye was one that reported a forthcoming visit to Spain by the head of the Abwehr, Admiral Wilhelm Canaris, and gave details of his route. Philby suggested that SOE try to assassinate him during Canaris's overnight stay in a small hotel between Madrid and Seville. Felix Cowgill, the head of Section V, approved the proposal and sent it to the chief of SIS, Sir Stuart Menzies. A few days later, Cowgill showed Philby the reply. According to Philby's later recollection, Menzies had written: "I want no action whatsoever taken against the Admiral." To Philby's suspicious mind this seemed further evidence of a plan for a secret deal with Nazi Germany rather than a reflection of Menzies's hope that Canaris, an opponent of Hitler executed for treason a month before V-E Day, might be turned round. As Menzies later told Philby: "I've always thought we could do something with the Admiral."

A few months before his death Philby admitted that what most interested Gorsky was intelligence on Britain's (nonexistent) plans for a separate peace with Nazi Germany and schemes to turn the war into one against the Soviet Union. Gorsky instructed Philby not merely to report such moves but to do his best to frustrate them. Philby interpreted that brief as applying to British contacts with anti-Nazis as well as with Nazis. Stalin feared that some anti-Nazis were plotting to overthrow Hitler, make peace with the Allies, and then join them in attacking Russia. Anti-Nazis willing to negotiate with the West had the further disadvantage that they might form a rival to the Moscow-sponsored Free Germany Committee, which Stalin wished to dominate postwar Germany. Retired MI5 officers have alleged that among the intelligence that Philby gave to Gorsky was a list of Catholic activists, provided by a Catholic defector from the Abwehr, who were marked down by the NKVD for liquidation after the war.[107]

While stationed in St. Albans Philby visited the SIS Broadway headquarters once a week, calling on as many senior officers as possible. He also volunteered for night duty at Broadway once or twice each month—"an instructive experience because, in the course of a single night, telegrams would come in from all parts of the world, throwing new light on the operations of the service." One file available to the night duty officer that Gorsky showed a particular interest in contained the correspondence between the War Office and the British Military Mission in Moscow sent through SIS channels.

During 1942–43 Cowgill enlarged Philby's field of responsibility to include North Africa and Italy, then made him his deputy "in all intelligence matters." Philby felt increasingly confident of his future SIS career. In 1943 Section V moved to Ryder Street in London, two minutes' walk from the MI5 wartime headquarters in St. James's Street—with which Philby found increasing opportunities for liaison—and fifteen minutes from Broadway.

Early in 1944, following the Springhall and Uren cases of Soviet espionage, SIS established a new Section IX "to study past records of Soviet and Communist activity." Initially it was run as a stop-gap measure by Jack Currie, an officer nearing retirement age transferred from MI5. "Towards the end of 1944," according to Philby, "the word around the office was that the Chief wanted to expand the section—more people, more resources. The job was rightfully Cowgill's but I had to make certain that I got it." Philby was informed by Moscow Center through his controller "that I must do everything, but *everything,* to ensure that I became head of Section IX. . . . They fully realized this meant that Cowgill must go." By a classic piece of bureaucratic back stabbing, in which Philby recruited the assistance of Cowgill's mortal enemy, Valentine Vivian, deputy chief of SIS, Philby got the job and Cowgill resigned. As one of his colleagues, Robert Cecil, later wrote: "Philby at one stroke had got rid of a staunch anti-Communist and ensured that the whole post-war effort to counter Communist espionage would become known in the Kremlin. The history of espionage records few, if any, comparable masterstrokes."[108]

This "masterstroke," extensively exploited after the war was over, made Philby, in the KGB's view, the most remarkable of the Magnificent Five. Philby apart, those whose wartime work was most highly rated were Blunt and Cairncross. The first of the eight thick brown operational files on Blunt in the KGB archives records that it took him almost two years of effort to penetrate MI5.[109] Late in 1938, overcoming the revulsion he had felt at Marlborough for the Officer Training Corps, Blunt had volunteered for military service. By his own later admission, he "used or rather abused" his brother Christopher's connections in the Territorial Army to try to persuade the War Office to offer him a commission in the Officers' Emergency Reserve. Blunt was unsuccessful. On the eve of the Second World War he tried again. Owing to confusion in the War Office, he received two replies by the same post: one letter of acceptance and one of rejection. Blunt tore up the rejection and in October 1939 began a five-week course at Minley Manor in Hampshire, designed to teach him the rudiments of military intelligence. A few days later he was removed from the course and summoned to the War Office after an MI5 report about some of his past Communist connections. At an interview with the deputy director of Military Intelligence, who disliked MI5, Blunt explained away his Communist record and returned to complete the course at Minley Manor. He graduated as a captain in the Field Security Police and was sent to France with the British Expeditionary Force in charge of a twelve-man platoon. According to one of those who served under him, "He had a great deal of languid charm. But he was a hopeless officer."[110]

While in France Blunt wrote to friends in London complaining about the pointless tedium of his work and angling for a post in SIS or MI5. His opportunity came with Dunkirk and the evacuation of the British Expeditionary Force in June 1940. Blunt's friend Victor Rothschild, then in MI5, put him up at his Bentinck Street flat off Oxford Street and introduced him to Guy Liddell, the director of MI5's B (Counter-Espionage) Division. Despite MI5's objections nine months earlier, Liddell recruited him. Within a few months Blunt was in charge of the surveillance of neutral embassies, especially those thought likely to be targets for enemy intelligence services. He proved adept at separating couriers from diplomatic bags for long enough to allow examination of their contents. Robert Cecil found Blunt "cool as a cucumber and obviously immensely enjoying the whole thing." Blunt was also highly successful at ingratiating himself with his superiors in MI5. Dick White, a future director-general of both MI5 and SIS, later recalled:

> He made a general assault on key people to see that they liked him. I was interested in art and he always used to sit down next to me in the canteen and chat. And he betrayed us all. He was a very nice and civilized man and I enjoyed talking to him. You cannot imagine how it feels to be betrayed by someone you have worked side by side with unless you have been through it yourself.[111]

Blunt's files in the KGB archives still give some sense of the excitement felt by Moscow Center at his penetration of MI5. During his first year in MI5 the volume of material handed over by Blunt to Gorsky at their meetings in London pubs and cafés increased steadily until he became one of the most productive agents in KGB history. Notes by Gorsky on Blunt's files frequently show concern that he is working too hard, tired from spending the night photographing MI5 documents, or nervous as the result of the accumulated tension of his double life.[112] Blunt's MI5 colleagues, however, rarely detected such signs of tiredness or tension. It seems likely that much of the stress noted by Gorsky derived from Blunt's nervousness at their meetings and lack of sympathy for Gorsky personally. The main initial concern shown by Pavel Fitin, the head of INU, was Blunt's refusal to accept money. Early in 1941 Fitin insisted that Blunt must do so, doubtless to give the INU a lever against him should he ever seek to break contact. In the spring of 1941 Blunt was persuaded by Gorsky to accept £200. Thereafter he was paid sums of £150–£200 three or four times a year. His files in the KGB archives contain thank-you notes and acknowledgments by Blunt for each payment, still in their original envelopes.[113]

Gordievsky was struck by the fact that, as he read through Blunt's files, he would find at about fifty-page intervals, for the period from the summer (or autumn) of 1941 until the end of the war, the note "The General Staff sends a highly complimentary assessment and asks for thanks to be conveyed to the agent."[114] Such notes on an agent's file were, in Gordievsky's experience, highly unusual. Though Blunt did not take to Gorsky, his sense of his own importance must surely have been sustained by the regular thanks and congratulations both of Moscow Center and of the General Staff. Blunt's KGB files show three major contributions to Soviet intelligence. First, he provided what seemed to Gordievsky "all possible details" on MI5, including its agents, and contrived access to files that went some way beyond the responsibilities of B Division. He spent many evenings photographing MI5 documents. Second, Blunt was able to provide the product of his own surveillance of neutral embassies. Third, he provided a wealth of intelligence on the German order of battle and operations. Blunt had increasing access to the details of the "double-cross system," by which false intelligence was fed to the Germans by "turned" Abwehr agents in Britain. His main source on the German order of battle was his former pupil Leo Long.[115]

When Long had graduated from Trinity College in 1938, the NKVD in Britain had been in serious disarray, with its London residency unmanned. Moscow issued no clear guidance on Long's future career.[116] Instead he spent the academic year 1938–39 teaching in Frankfurt in order to experience Nazi Germany at first hand. On the outbreak of war he enlisted in the Oxford and Bucks Light Infantry but was able to use his fluent German to gain a commission as second lieutenant in the Intelligence Corps. In December 1940 Long was posted to MI14 in the War Office, which collated and analyzed German battle order intelligence. There he had full access to the Ultra intelligence derived from the success of Bletchley Park in breaking the Luftwaffe variant of the Enigma machine cipher in May 1940. When the German army Enigma was broken in the summer of 1942, Long saw those decrypts also.

Early in 1941 Long resumed contact with Blunt. As Long later recalled, "Blunt took up where we left off" and asked him for "every piece of information that could be useful to the Russians." They had weekly meetings, usually at lunchtime, at a pub in Portman Square or at Rainer's snack bar in Jermyn Street, where Long passed beneath the table what he described as a "sort of boiled-down version of the weekly departmental appreciation." "Blunt never tried blackmailing or bullying me," Long said later, "because we shared a deep commitment to the Communist cause."[117]

Leo Long's file in the KGB archives resolves one mystery that has perplexed Western intelligence services and many writers on espionage ever since the defection of the Soviet cipher clerk Igor Guzenko, in Ottawa in September 1945. Guzenko's most important information, mostly limited to GRU operations, concerned a Soviet spy ring in Canada and atomic espionage. But he also revealed that there were two

GRU agents code-named Elli. The first was Kay Willsher, deputy registrar in the British High Commission, who was sentenced to three years' imprisonment in March 1946 for breaches of the Official Secrets Act. Guzenko did not know the identity of the second Elli, who, he said, worked in Great Britain. He provided, however, a series of incomplete, confusing, and sometimes garbled clues. According to Peter Wright's later recollection:

> [Guzenko] said he knew there was a spy in "five of MI." He had learned this from a friend, Liubimov, who had worked alongside him in the main GRU cipher room in Moscow in 1942. . . . There was something Russian about Elli, said Gouzenko, either in his background or because he had visited Russia, or could speak the language. Elli was an important spy because he could remove from MI5 the files which dealt with Russians in London. . . . Gouzenko said that when Elli's telegrams came in there was always a woman present in the cipher room who read the decrypts first and, if necessary, took them straight to Stalin.

In renewed questioning a few years later Guzenko varied some of the details. "Five of MI" became simply MI5. But by then Guzenko's alcoholism and increasingly confused memory made it difficult to clarify the incomplete and confused version of the second "Elli" story given at his first debriefing.[118]

The other Elli has been variously misidentified as, among others, Sir Roger Hollis and Kim Philby. In fact, Elli was Leo Long. That code name appears in large letters on the cover of Long's KGB operational file. The file is unusually thin. In accordance with standard KGB procedures, Blunt should have written a report on Long after each meeting but was usually too tired or too busy to do so. The contents of the file, however, resolve some of the main elements of confusion in Guzenko's account; the remainder derive from his (and possibly also Peter Wright's) faulty memory and incomplete knowledge of the case. Long's file records that though he was an NKVD/NKGB agent run by Blunt, the GRU made independent contact with him in 1943. Long was upset and asked Blunt to ask Moscow who he was working for. Gorsky passed the message on and the Center replied "For us." The GRU agreed to leave future contacts to Blunt.[119] Gorsky then had his only meeting with Long, to assure him that the GRU would not bother him again.

The fact that Long's intelligence arrived at the Center in reports from Blunt accounts for some further elements of confusion in Guzenko's story. It was Blunt, not Long, who "could remove from MI5 the files which dealt with Russians in London." The phrase "five of MI" could be simply a garbled version of MI5 and another reference to Blunt, Long's controller. But it could also be a confused combination of MI, where Long worked, and "the five" (as the leading Cambridge moles became known during the war) with whom he was linked. When Gordievsky first began reading the references in Long's file to detailed German battle order, he asked himself: "Did the British really have such fantastic human sources?" Then he saw the references to intercepts and realized that Long's main source was sigint.[120]

Moscow did not depend simply on its agents for access to Ultra. Within a few days of the German invasion, London began supplying officially some Ultra intelligence in a disguised form. Stuart Menzies, the chief of SIS, who also had overall control of GC & CS, advised Churchill against passing on intelligence from Enigma decrypts in any form because of the insecurity of the Russians' own cipher systems. In the opinion of Bletchley Park, "to tell the Russians that we were reading Enigma would be tantamount to telling the Germans too."[121] By July 1941 Ultra had revealed that the Germans were decrypting some Soviet naval traffic and signals from Russia's 17th Air Division, and that they understood the signaling system used by Russian aircraft in the Leningrad area.

As early as June 24, Churchill overrode Menzies's objections and instructed him to pass disguised Ultra intelligence to the Russians via the British Military Mission in Moscow, "provided no risks are run." Thereafter the prime minister commonly noted on important intercepts dealing with the Eastern Front minutes such as "Has any of this been passed to Joe?" The source for Ultra intelligence given to Stalin was disguised by formulas such as "a well-placed source in Berlin," "a most reliable source" or "an officer in the German War Office." Unit identifications and other details that might identify the true source as sigint were deliberately withheld. On July 11, 1942, for example, Bletchley Park decrypted the following intercept:

1. Increasing enemy pressure on the front of the Second Army is to be expected. The pinning-down of strong enemy forces on the Army's front is desirable taking into account the operations of the Eastern Army as a whole.
2. The task of the Army Group von Weichs is with the Second Hungarian Army to hold the Donets front between the mouth of the Potudan and the mouth of the Voronezh, and, together with the Second Army, to hold the bridgehead Voronezh, and the present position on the general line Olchowatka-Oserk-Bork-Kotysch railway station (east of Droskowo).

Two days later this was relayed by the British Military Mission in Moscow as:

For information of Russian General Staff. Our picture from various sources gives clear indication that Germans, including Hungarians, intend to hold Russians on front Livni-Voronezh-Svoboda, while armored forces push south-eastwards between rivers Don and Donets.

In the summer of 1941 a British air intelligence officer arrived in Moscow bearing details of Luftwaffe tactical codes, navigational aids, and call signs; he received some similar material in return. He was followed by a military intelligence officer, who provided captured documents on Wehrmacht wireless systems and explained how to break German police hand ciphers; the Russians replied with some captured documents but no sigint material. Thereafter, however, Whitehall became increasingly frustrated by the one-sided nature of the intelligence exchange. By the beginning of 1942 the Russians were usually unwilling to exchange even technical intelligence about captured enemy equipment.[122] It seemed to Bletchley Park that the Russians made little use of the intelligence that was given them. "In the case of the great tank battles of 1942," wrote one cryptanalyst later, "when they were warned that they were pouring men and materials into a huge German trap, it is difficult to suppose that they gave full credence to warnings, which, if heeded, would have saved them from terrible losses."[123]

From the summer of 1942 the amount of operational intelligence supplied to the Russians based on Enigma decrypts was drastically reduced. Exceptions continued to be made, however, on matters of particular importance. In December 1942, at a critical stage in the battle of Stalingrad, the Russians were given intelligence (probably already supplied by Philby and Blunt) on how to break Abwehr hand ciphers, in the hope of producing some Soviet response. None was forthcoming.[124]

At the very moment in the summer of 1942 when the amount of disguised Ultra forwarded to the Russians started to decline, John Cairncross began to provide it in unadulterated form. A few months after he ceased to be Lord Hankey's private secretary in March 1942, Cairncross succeeded where Philby had failed two years before in gaining entry to the sigint agency GC & CS at its wartime home in Bletchley Park.[125] His controller Anatoli Gorsky whom, like the rest of the Five, he knew as Henry, gave him the money to buy and run a cheap car to bring documents to London on days off.[126] Though Cairncross spent less than a year in GC & CS, his period at Bletchley Park coincided with both the turning of the tide on the Eastern Front and the point at which Stalin and the Stavka at last began to gear good intelligence to the conduct of operations. His main job was to analyze Ultra intercepts of Luftwaffe signals.

Cairncross himself believed that the finest hour of his fifteen years as a Soviet agent came before the battle of Kursk in the summer of 1943 when the Red Army faced Operation Citadel, the last great German offensive on the Eastern Front.[127] On April 30 the British sent Moscow a warning of an impending German attack on the Kursk salient, combined with German intelligence assessments of Soviet forces in the area derived from Enigma intercepts.[128] But Cairncross provided the text of intercepts themselves, together with the unit identifications, which were always omitted from the sanitized official version of Ultra intelligence sometimes supplied by Whitehall.[129]

The intercepts most appreciated by the NKVD were a series that identified the disposition of Luftwaffe squadrons before the battle. Fearing that a German offensive might begin as early as May 10 (though it did not in fact begin until July 5), Soviet bombers made a preemptive strike, prepared in the utmost secrecy, early on May 6 against seventeen German airfields, selected with the help of Cairncross's intelligence, in a zone twelve hundred kilometers long, stretching from Smolensk to the Sea of Azov. Many German aircraft were caught on the ground. Further attacks on German airfields took place on May 7 and 8, though inevitably without the degree of surprise achieved on the 6th. This series of three massive air raids was to be remembered as the greatest operation of the Red Air Force in the Great Patriotic War. Fourteen hundred missions were flown and over 500 German planes destroyed. Soviet losses totaled 122 aircraft.

Gorsky conveyed to Cairncross Moscow's special commendation for the intelligence he had supplied.[130] By now, however, the strain of transporting Ultra intelligence from Bletchley to London had become too much for Cairncross to bear. On the eve of the battle of Kursk, despite urging by Gorsky to remain in GC & CS, Cairncross accepted a job in SIS, working first on the German desk in Section V, then in Section I (Political Intelligence).[131]

The Red Army committed almost 40 percent of its combat troops and most of its armor to the defense of the Kursk salient. Smashing the Soviet forces there represented Hitler's last chance to recover from the disaster at Stalingrad. The Red Army had been victorious at Stalingrad despite the errors of military intelligence; at Kursk good intelligence made a major contribution to victory. On April 8, 1943, the deputy supreme commander, Marshal Zhukov, sent Stalin a report correctly predicting a German pincer movement against the Kursk salient from both north and south, coupled with an attack from the west designed to separate the two Red Army groups defending the salient. Both then and subsequently Stalin and the Stavka were less well informed about the date of the German attack. Hitler himself, however, kept changing his mind. May 3, the first date chosen by the Führer for the offensive, was subsequently postponed to June 12, then to July 3, and finally to July 5.[132] Important though the contribution of Ultra (via both the British Military Mission in Moscow and NKVD agents in Britain) was to victory at Kursk, there had also been since Stalingrad a major improvement in Soviet military intelligence collection and assessment.

It has been claimed that the most important intelligence available to Stalin and the Stavka before and during Kursk came from the Lucy ring in Switzerland.[133] There is no doubt that Lucy (Rudolf Roessler) did provide valuable strategic intelligence until his arrest in the spring of 1944. GRU headquarters radioed on February 22, 1943: "Convey to Lucy our appreciation for good work. Last information was important and valuable." The GRU was also anxious to reassure the mercenary Roessler (whose real identity it did not discover) that it would pay the money he demanded. It radioed in November: "Please tell Lucy in our name that . . . his group will be paid without fail in accordance with his demands. We are ready to reward him richly for his information."[134] But it is now clear that Lucy did not provide the key intelligence on Kursk. In late April the GRU was still preoccupied in trying to discover the identity of Lucy and his sources; on April 23 it bypassed Rado, the leader of the Rote Drei, and contacted one of his subordinates directly in a vain attempt to do so. Lucy's most important source, Werther, also made a number of errors; on June 23 he suggested that because of the heavy buildup of Soviet forces Operation Citadel would be called off.[135]

One of the keys to the transformation of Soviet military intelligence in the spring of 1943 was the improvement of sigint. Since the outbreak of war the Research Section of the INU Fifth Directorate and, no doubt, GRU cryptanalysts had been hard at work trying to break the Enigma machine ciphers. It was a task of enormous complexity. The German army, navy, air force and other organizations all used the Enigma machine to generate their own ciphers and employed different keys for different purposes in different theaters. From 1941 onward there were never fewer than fifty keys in use at the same time, all of them changed or reset daily. Even when the machine ciphers were broken, the keys had to be discovered promptly if the sigint thus obtained was to be of operational use.[136] The success of Bletchley, building on the earlier work of the Poles, in breaking all the main varieties of Enigma between 1940 and 1942, and in devising methods for mastering the daily key changes, was probably the greatest intelligence achievement of the war. The NKVD was informed of much of that achievement by Cairncross and, in less detail, by Long, Blunt, and Philby.

It was also assisted by the capture of a number of Enigma machines and German cipher material, probably beginning in December 1941 when the German Second Army lost several machines.[137] The biggest haul, however, almost certainly came at Stalingrad. The German forces surrounded at Stalingrad had among them at least twenty-six Enigma machines, and in the circumstances of the siege must have found it impossible to destroy many of them. In at least one instance, a German headquarters went on transmitting until Soviet troops were at the door. Further Enigma machines may also have been captured from the six German divisions annihilated outside the encirclement. Almost certainly a number of key settings also fell into the hands of the Red Army.[138] Perhaps equally important, the 91,000 prisoners who surrendered at Stalingrad included signals and cipher personnel, not all of whom can have resisted the pressing invitations of their captors to assist Soviet sigint.

On January 17, 1943, even before the Stalingrad surrender, the Signals Division of the Wehrmacht High Command concluded that in several specific cases it was a "certainty" that the Russians had decrypted Enigma messages, and introduced a number of improvements in cipher security.[139] The odds are, however, that Soviet cryptanalysts were unable to read Enigma traffic on any regular basis. Captured machines, keys, and signals personnel made possible the retrospective solution of a number of German intercepts. There was also a number of less complex Enigma machines, without the plug boards used in the high-grade versions, which were probably vulnerable, at least intermittently, to Soviet attack.[140]

But despite the individual brilliance of Russian cryptanalysts, the NKVD and the GRU lacked the state-of-the-art technology that was crucial to the Ultra intelligence produced by Bletchley Park. There seems to have been no Soviet equivalent of either the powerful electronic "bombes" first built at Bletchley Park in 1940 to break Enigma, or of Colossus, the world's first electronic computer, constructed in 1943 to decrypt Geheimschreiber messages (radio signals based on teleprinter impulses enciphered and deciphered automatically), which for the last two years of the war yielded more important operational intelligence than Enigma traffic.

The major advances in Soviet sigint on Germany during the spring of 1943 occurred among the foothills rather than the commanding heights of cryptanalysis: in direction finding, traffic analysis, and the breaking of low-grade hand ciphers, rather than in the attack on Enigma and Geheimschreiber. Military sigint in the field had suffered from the huge losses in trained signals personnel in the early stages of the war. At the end of 1942, however, the Stavka established special-purpose radio battalions, whose deployment led to what one Soviet military historian has called "a qualitative jump in the development of radio-electronic combat in the Soviet army." Soviet historians, influenced by the traditional taboo on discussion of sigint, have emphasized their role in radio jamming and disinformation operations. But each battalion was also equipped with eighteen to twenty radio intercept receivers and four direction-finding sets.[141]

Though the deployment of the special-purpose radio battalions began in the later stages of Stalingrad, they made a much larger contribution at Kursk. An intelligence report of the Soviet 1st Tank Army captured by the Wehrmacht revealed that sigint had identified the positions of the headquarters and units of II Panzer Corps, 6th Panzer, and 11th Panzer divisions before the offensive began. Other captured documents showed that 7th Panzer Division, XIII Corps, and Second Army HQ had suffered the same fate. Soviet battlefield sigint was by no means perfect. XLVI Panzer Corps to the north of the Kursk salient and XLVIII Panzer Corps to the south achieved tactical surprise in the initial German attack. But Wehrmacht signals officers had no doubt that sigint had played a significant part in the Soviet success and pointed to poor German radio discipline as one of the reasons for the failure of Operation Citadel. Soviet radio security, however, though it had improved over the past two years, was no better than the Wehrmacht's. Sigint was probably the most valuable source of operational intelligence for both sides during the battle of Kursk.[142]

Sigint on the Soviet side was accompanied by the other forms of intelligence gathering commonly used by modern armies. Air reconnaissance, which on the Western Front had already emerged as a method of wartime intelligence collection second in importance only to sigint, was more successfully carried out by the Red Air Force than ever before. About 6,000 sorties were flown prior to the battle. Units on the Central and Voronezh fronts carried out 105 reconnaissances-in-force, over 2,600 night raids, and 1,500 ambushes in the three months before the German attack. The 187 German soldiers captured in the course of these operations were also an important source of intelligence. Prisoners and deserters taken on the night of July 4 provided the final proof of the German offensive scheduled for the early hours of the following day.[143]

By Kursk a relatively flexible and devolved system for providing front commanders with intelligence had replaced the more centralized system in force until the spring of 1942. Henceforth front intelligence departments (razvedyvatenlyi otdel) provided commanders with tactical intelligence, while the GRU remained responsible for strategic intelligence.[144]

Kursk opened the way to a virtually continuous advance by the Red Army, which ended with Marshal Zhukov's accepting the surrender of Berlin in May 1945. With a four-to-one superiority in men over the Wehrmacht, large amounts of military equipment from the United States and Britain, and growing air superiority, the Red Army, though suffering enormous losses, proved unstoppable. The operational intelligence that assisted its victorious two-year advance was the primary responsibility of the Stavka, the GRU, and commanders at the front. The NKVD, however, also played its part. A recent Soviet estimate puts the total of NKVD troops at fifty-three divisions and twenty-eight brigades, "not counting numerous other independent units and border troops,"[145] probably at least three-quarters of a million men. Many were used as blocking detachments behind regular forces to prevent retreat, and to carry out punitive missions against "suspect" nationalities. A series of minority peoples—Chechens, Ingushi, Crimean Tartars, Karachai, Balkars, Kamlyks, Volga Germans—became the victims of mass murder and deportations carried out by the NKVD.[146] Stalin would have preferred to deport the Ukrainians too, but complained there were too many of them.

The NKVD's main contribution to the victorious advance of the Red Army was its leading role in partisan warfare. The head of the wartime NKVD Partisan Administration was Lieutenant-General Pavel Anatolyevich Sudoplatov, later head of the postwar Spetsburo, which carried out foreign assassinations. Despite his fearsome reputation, "his bearing, his polished manners, his quiet, confident speech," according to the defector Nikolai Khokhlov, "denoted an important and intelligent man. He also knew the value of that studied simplicity in which only those in power can indulge."[147] Sudoplatov's deputy, Major General Leonid Aleksandrovich Eitingon, had directed partisan operations behind Franco's lines in the Spanish Civil War under the pseudonym General Kotov, and won fame within the NKVD as well as a place in the Memory Room of today's First Chief Directorate as the organizer of Trotsky's assassination.[148]

The role of partisans in both intelligence collection and sabotage has been clouded by administrative confusion at the time and heroic myths spread since. One of the best-known partisan heroes behind German lines, Nikolai Kuznetsov (whose portrait also appears in the First Chief Directorate Memory Room), is said to have gained access to the office of the Reichskommissar for the Ukraine, Erich Koch, in April 1943, disguised as a German lieutenant. He was about to assassinate Koch, the story continues, when the Reichskommissar began to reveal details of Operation Citadel, the forthcoming German attack on the Kursk salient. Kuznetsov dropped his plan to kill Koch and instead passed the plans for Citadel promptly back to Moscow. The story may not be wholly apocryphal but, as Dr. Timothy Mulligan has observed, Koch could not have had detailed knowledge of the forthcoming offensive—and, in particular, could not have supplied the date since Hitler had yet to settle on it.[149]

A recent Soviet study of partisan intelligence collection lists a series of shortcomings prior to the battle of Kursk, among them inexperience and lack of training among the partisans in carrying out reconnaissance, poor cover documents, shortage of radio transmitters, and the lack of "proper coordination" between the partisans and intelligence activity at the front. An order of the supreme commander-in-chief of April 19, 1943, "On Improving Intelligence Work in Partisan Detachments," called both for better coordination and for better training of partisan leaders by NKVD and GRU specialists.[150]

The first full-scale partisan offensive behind German lines coordinated with Red Army front-line operations was the "war on the rail track" *(relsovaya voina)* designed to break Wehrmacht railway communications during the battle of Kursk with the aid of large quantities of explosive parachuted to the partisans. It was only partly successful. Though thousands of charges went off, the railway lines on which the Germans depended were not completely severed.[151] A recent Soviet assessment of partisan intelligence during the Great Patriotic War picks out as one of its greatest successes the work of the 11th Partisan Brigade before and during the offensive that ended the 880-day siege of Leningrad in January 1944. The brigade supplied comprehensive reports by radio of all German troop movements by road and rail:

> By the start of the offensive . . . the Brigade's scouts had established the numbers and location of units, and the names of their commanders; they had recorded the movement of the staffs and units of 21 enemy divisions and brigades, and had ascertained the location of the staffs of the XXXVIII Army Corps and the 18th Army as well as the position of four airfields. With the start of the Soviet troop offensive . . . the scouts frequently led the advancing units to the enemy flanks and rear.[152]

The Abwehr felt swamped by the sheer number of partisans operating behind German lines. By the summer of 1944 German counterintelligence had identified 20,000 Soviet agents, and estimated that they were increasing at the rate of 10,000 every three months.[153] Among the most difficult to detect were the Besprisorniki, teenage children who had been trained in reconnaissance and sabotage. Even the Wehrmacht admired their bravery. A report from one German unit described the case of "a half-grown boy" who had been caught making notes on troop movements. Under interrogation he steadfastly refused to say who had given him his orders and "kept telling clumsy lies." Finally, it was decided to frighten him into submission. First he was forced to witness the shooting of seven adult prisoners. Then he was told to prepare himself for execution. At the last moment, just as the firing squad was taking aim, the child was told that his life would be spared if he told the truth:

> The youth smiled cheekily and said he knew he would be killed even if he did speak up. When the interrogator assured him again that he could only save his life by naming his employer, the boy replied: "I know very well that I shall be shot even if I do tell you the truth. I'll tell you the truth now: I have lied to you six times and I'll do it a seventh!"[154]

The report does not mention the child's fate. He was almost certainly shot.

In the course of the Great Patriotic War, scientific, as well as political and military, intelligence began to have a major influence on Soviet policy. The most important scientific intelligence concerned the atomic bomb. The earliest intelligence on the Anglo-American decision to build an atomic bomb probably came from John Cairncross. In October 1940 the question was discussed at length by the British Scientific Advisory Committee, chaired by Lord Hankey, for whom Cairncross worked as private secretary. It was discussed again in the summer of 1941 after the secret "Maud" Committee report predicted—overoptimistically—that "a very powerful weapon of war," using Uranium-235, could be constructed by the end of 1943. The Scientific Advisory Committee recognized, like the "Maud" Committee, that production of the atomic bomb (code-named the "Tube Alloys" project) would require the greater resources of the United States, with whom secret cooperation had already begun. Hankey became a member of the Tube Alloys Consultative Committee formed in the autumn of 1941 to advise on policy.[155] Cairncross doubtless forwarded its early advice to the Center.

In April 1942, M. G. Pervukhin, deputy prime minister and commissar of the chemical industry, was given on Stalin's instructions a thick file of NKVD and GRU reports about foreign work on the atomic bomb. Pervukhin recommended that the reports be shown to physicists who could evaluate their importance.[156] In May the young Soviet physicist G. N. Flyorov, then a Red Air Force lieutenant, wrote to Stalin: "It is essential not to lose any time in building the uranium bomb." On looking through American and British scientific journals Flyorov had discovered that almost nothing on nuclear fission was any longer being published and that the leading physicists in the field had disappeared from print. He deduced correctly that nuclear research was now secret and that the United States was building an atomic bomb. Stalin was outraged that the nuclear danger to the Soviet Union had been detected not by the Academy of Sciences but by an air force lieutenant at the front.

At the end of 1942 the State Defense Committee under Stalin's chairmanship issued a decree setting up a laboratory within the Academy of Sciences to work on the development of an atomic bomb. The decision was made at a critical moment in the war, against the advice even of many Soviet physicists, who believed that the bomb would take ten to twenty years to develop. It was clear that the bomb could not be ready in time to use in the war with Germany and that research on it would divert desperately scarce resources from the war effort.

In deciding to build an atomic bomb in the middle of the battle of Stalingrad, Stalin was thinking not of the needs of the Great Patriotic War but of a postwar world in which, since the United States and Britain would have nuclear weapons, the Soviet Union must have them too. At the end of 1942 Stalin also seems to have envisaged that the war might end without the destruction of the Nazi state—in which case Russia might also face a postwar Germany armed with nuclear weapons. But it was, above all, intelligence reports on the progress of nuclear research by his allies that persuaded Stalin to embark on the construction of the Soviet atomic bomb.[157]

The first and probably the most important of the "atom spies" who provided scientific intelligence on the progress of Anglo-American nuclear research was Klaus Fuchs. His early reports were almost certainly among those which, on Stalin's orders, were shown in April 1942 to Pervukhin and subsequently to Soviet physicists. Fuchs was born into a family described by a German newspaper as "the red foxes of Kiel" (*Fuchs* is German for "fox") on account of the color of both their hair and their politics. His father was a prominent Quaker leader descended from a long line of Protestant pastors. Fuchs joined the KPD at the age of twenty-one in 1932 while at Kiel University and became leader of a group of Communist students. After Hitler's rise to power he was forced to flee from Germany, arriving in England as a refugee in September 1933. Soon afterward he joined the KPD underground in England, performing various minor tasks for it, mostly associated with propaganda.

In 1934 Fuchs began research at Bristol University for a Ph.D. in physics, which he completed in December 1936. While at Bristol he took an active part in meetings of a front organization, the Society for Cultural Relations with the Soviet Union. At the society's dramatized readings of transcripts of the show trials, Fuchs impressed his research supervisor, the future Nobel laureate Sir Nevill Mott, by the passion with which he played the role of Vyshinsky, "accusing the defendants with a cold venom that I would never have suspected from so quiet and retiring a young man." In 1937 Fuchs went to work in Max Born's laboratory at Edinburgh University, where he remained until May 1940, when he was interned, like many other "enemy aliens," in the "fifth column" scare that accompanied the fall of France. After seven months on the Isle of Man and in Canada he was released at the end of the year.

In May 1941 he was invited by another refugee German scientist, Rudolf Peierls (later knighted) to work under him on "war work" at Birmingham University. "I could not tell him what the project was until I had permission to do so," said Peierls later, "but I described the kind of theory necessary, and he agreed to join."[158]

After some delay caused by MI5's reluctance to give him security clearance, Fuchs found himself part of the top-secret Tube Alloys project, to design and build an atom bomb. Late in 1941, at a critical stage in Operation Barbarossa, when it still seemed possible that the Wehrmacht might enter Moscow, Fuchs decided to volunteer his services as a Soviet spy. He traveled from Birmingham to London, made contact with Juergen Kuczynski, leader of the KPD underground in Britain, and asked for his help in passing to the Russians what he had learned about plans to build an atomic bomb. Kuczynski arranged for him to meet the GRU officer Simon Davidovich Kremer (known to Fuchs as Alexander), whose cover job was secretary of the military attaché's staff at the London embassy. Apparently fearing a provocation, Kremer appears to have arranged their first meeting at the embassy. His attempts thereafter to persuade Fuchs to adopt orthodox Soviet intelligence tradecraft met with mixed success. According to Fuchs's later interrogation by the FBI:

Alexander suggested that he be careful to avoid being followed, that he should use taxicabs and double back in order
to throw anyone off the track who might be following him.
But [Fuchs] believed this to be too expensive and not so good
a method in his own judgment. He preferred to go to a large
place like some subway station in London where there was
both a lift and stairs, and to make contacts in such a place.[159]

In the summer of 1942 Fuchs was moved to another GRU controller,
Sonia, who he almost certainly never realized was the sister of Juergen
Kuczynski. They usually met in Banbury, almost midway between
Birmingham and Oxford, where Sonia lived as Mrs. Brewer, a Jewish
refugee from Nazi Germany.[160] Fuchs later said that he never knew
which branch of Soviet intelligence he was working for; indeed, he
claimed that he was unaware until after his arrest that more than one
branch existed.[161] His peculiar blend of scientific brilliance, narrow-
mindedness, doctrinaire idealism, and personal naïveté makes the claim
quite plausible.

The initial importance of Fuchs's intelligence lay less in its
technical detail than in what it revealed of the progress made by British
and American scientists.[162] By early 1942 Fuchs had access to classified
American reports on nuclear research. Together with Peierls, Fuchs
also prepared assessments of German progress in atomic research,
using both scientific journals and SIS reports. They concluded in February 1942 that German sources gave no "very new indications on work
or interest in the T.A. (Tube Alloys) field."[163] Fuchs's evidence of the
rapid progress of Anglo-American research was probably crucial to
Stalin's decision to enter the nuclear-arms race.

In December 1943 Fuchs sailed for the United States as a
member of a Tube Alloys mission to its American equivalent, the
Manhattan Project. Before he left Britain, Sonia had given him instructions on how to make contact with his American controller, Raymond.
Though Fuchs did not realize it, the GRU had been pressured into
surrendering him to the NKGB. Raymond was Harry Gold, a thirty-
three-year-old industrial chemist, who had been born in Switzerland of
Russian parents, entered the United States at the age of three, and from
1936 onward worked for the NKVD as an industrial spy and courier.[164]
Fuchs later recalled that his first meeting with Raymond was arranged
early in 1944 on New York's East Side. He was told to carry a tennis
ball in his hand and look for a man wearing gloves carrying a spare pair

in his hands.[165] When later questioned by the FBI, Gold remembered also having to carry a green-covered book.[166]

Fuchs claimed that during their meetings "the attitude of 'Raymond' at all times was that of an inferior."[167] Gold himself admitted that he was overawed by the terrifying potential of the nuclear intelligence Fuchs provided. Though he believed that the Soviet Union was entitled to it, Gold found handling information about the atomic bomb "so frightening that the only thing I could do was to shove it away as far back in my mind as I could and simply not think on the matter at all."[168]

In August 1944 Fuchs was posted to the top-secret atomic laboratory, containing twelve Nobel Prize winners, at Los Alamos near Santa Fe, where the atomic bomb was being assembled. British scientists, with access to different divisions of the compartmentalized project, often had a better overview of atomic research than their American colleagues. According to a Los Alamos security officer writing in September 1945, a month after the first bombs had been dropped on Hiroshima and Nagasaki, the scientists in the British mission had "substantially complete knowledge" of the gun assembly and implosion assembly of fissile material, the actual design of the bombs, and possible future developments, including the hydrogen bomb. But he believed that they knew only a "minimum of the engineering details." Everything of importance that Fuchs discovered was passed to the NKGB.[169] Not everything that Fuchs passed on, however, simplified the task of Soviet scientists. Some of Edward Teller's early work on thermonuclear fusion, stolen by Fuchs in 1944, contained serious errors, which must later have confused Soviet nuclear physicists when they began work on a hydrogen bomb.[170]

Fuchs had no idea that he was not the only Soviet spy at Los Alamos. David Greenglass, a twenty-two-year-old Communist GI, had arrived a few days before him to work as a machinist helping to make and maintain equipment used in the development of the atomic bomb. "I was young, stupid and immature," said Greenglass later, "but I was a good Communist." His letters to his wife, Ruth, described Stalin and the Soviet leadership as "really geniuses, everyone of them" who had only ever used force "with pain in their hearts": "More power to the Soviet Union and fruitful and abundant life for their peoples!" Greenglass later claimed that he hero-worshiped his older brother-in-law, Julius Rosenberg, who was part of an NKGB spy ring in New York, and was easily persuaded to supply Rosenberg with secret information from Los Alamos. "My darling," he wrote to his wife in November 1944, "I most certainly will be glad to be part of the community project that Julius and his friends [the Russians] have in mind."

While on leave in New York in January 1945 Greenglass gave Rosenberg a series of notes and sketches. In return Rosenberg handed him half of a fragment of a Jell-O box and told him that a courier would contact him later in the year in Los Alamos and identify himself by producing the missing fragment. When Harry Gold came to meet Fuchs in June he also called on Greenglass, received a series of notes from him, and handed over a sealed envelope containing $500. Anatoli Yakovlev, Gold's NKGB case officer, based at the Soviet consulate in New York, enthusiastically described Greenglass's intelligence as "extremely excellent and very valuable."

Greenglass provided a further installment to Rosenberg during his next leave in New York in September and received a further $200.[171] His information was important to the NKGB both because it provided some corroboration for Fuchs's more important scientific intelligence and because it filled in some of the engineering detail—precisely the area in which Fuchs was least informed.

By the spring of 1945 Soviet intelligence also had two important agents in the Anglo-Canadian nuclear-research team, headed by Professor John Cockcroft, director of the Atomic Energy Division at the Canadian National Research Council in Montreal. The first agent to be recruited was a British scientist, Allan Nunn May, a secret Communist who had been a contemporary of Donald Maclean at Trinity Hall, Cambridge, had begun work on the Tube Alloys project in 1942, and had made contact with the GRU soon afterward.[172] Unlike Philby, Blunt, and other leading Soviet agents, May experienced not the slightest frisson of pleasure at the danger and deception of the secret world. "The whole affair," he later claimed, "was extremely painful to me and I only embarked on it because I felt this was a contribution I could make to the safety of mankind." In retrospect, he shared Maclean's disillusioned view of espionage: "It's like being a lavatory attendant; it stinks but someone has to do it."[173]

May joined Cockcroft's research group in Montreal in January 1943. For reasons that remain obscure it took the local GRU some time to grasp his importance. It was not until late in 1944 that Lieutenant Pavel Angelov of the Ottawa GRU residency became his case officer. At some point during the first half of 1945, Angelov asked May to obtain samples of uranium, an assignment that a Canadian agent of the

GRU, Israel Halperin, had already described as "absolutely impossible." May, however, succeeded. On August 9, 1945, three days after Hiroshima, he gave Angelov a report on atomic research, details of the bomb dropped on Hiroshima, and two samples of uranium: an enriched specimen of U-235 in a glass tube and a thin deposit of U-233 on a piece of platinum foil.[174] Colonel Nikolai Zabotin, the GRU legal resident in Ottawa, considered these so important that he sent his deputy, Lieutenant-Colonel Motinov, to take them immediately to Moscow. Angelov pressed on May a bottle of whiskey and about $200 Canadian.

Soon afterward Zabotin was awarded both the Order of the Red Banner and the Order of the Red Star.[175] May was a member of a Canadian GRU espionage network that contained at least nineteen agents.[176] Among other military and scientific intelligence collected by the network was what a Canadian Royal Commission described as "information of the greatest importance" on radar ("next to the atomic bomb . . . perhaps the most vital work accomplished by the English-speaking Democracies in the technical field during the period in question"), asdic, explosives, propellants, and the V.T. fuse.[177] Zabotin's network included sources of political as well as scientific and military intelligence. Chief among them were Sam Carr (born Kogan in the Ukraine of Jewish parents), organizing secretary of the Canadian Communist Party since 1937, who recruited and handled agents for Zabotin; and Fred Rose (born Rosenberg in Poland of Russian Jewish parents), Party organizer for Quebec and a member of the Canadian Parliament, who supplied reports of secret parliamentary sessions.[178]

Most of the GRU network was wound up after the defection of Igor Guzenko from the Ottawa embassy in September 1945. The NKGB network of agents in Canada, however, remained largely intact. Among them was a second major atom spy in Montreal, Bruno Pontecorvo, a brilliant Italian émigré physicist. Unlike the retiring Allan Nunn May, Pontecorvo, usually known as Bruno or Ponte, was a popular extrovert whose film-star good looks gave him the further nickname Ramon Navarro. Born in 1913 of Jewish parents, Pontecorvo had left Italy during a fascist anti-Semitic campaign in 1936. Early in 1943 he joined the Anglo-Canadian nuclear research team in Montreal.

At some point over the next two years he wrote a letter to a Soviet embassy, probably in Ottawa, offering his services. The letter landed in the residency not of the GRU, as in the case of May, but of its "neighbor," the NKGB. Initially the resident paid no attention, presumably dismissing Pontecorvo as either a fraud or a provocateur.

Receiving no reply to a letter, Pontecorvo delivered a packet of classified documents and calculations to the embassy. The NKGB residency
failed to grasp their significance but forwarded them to the Center and
was surprised to receive a flash telegram ordering it to establish immediate operational contact with the scientist who had provided them.
Pontecorvo stayed in Canada, working as both a nuclear scientist and
a Soviet agent, until he transferred to the British atomic research establishment at Harwell early in 1949. KGB officers acquainted with the
case told Gordievsky that they rated Pontecorvo's work as an atom spy
almost as highly as that of Fuchs.[179]

By the summer of 1944 one of the Magnificent Five from Cambridge, Donald Maclean, was supplying both atomic and political intelligence. Though Maclean had been the most successful of the Five in
the 1930s his career in both the Foreign Office and the NKVD went
into partial eclipse in the early years of the war. In September 1938 he
had arrived at the British embassy in Paris as a third secretary with a
reputation as a sociable high flyer.[180] The strain of supplying intelligence
to the NKVD after the Nazi-Soviet Pact and especially after the beginning of the German Blitzkrieg against France in May 1940 gradually
tarnished his reputation, especially in the eyes of Sir Ronald Campbell,
who became ambassador in Paris soon after the outbreak of war. According to another senior British diplomat, after the fall of France
Campbell "commented unfavorably on Maclean's surprising dilatori-
ness and neglect of his duties during the last critical days. He thought
of him, perhaps a bit harshly, as something of a weakling."[181]

On his return from France, Maclean, though soon promoted to
second secretary, was posted to the unprestigious, newly created General Department of the Foreign Office, which dealt mainly with the
Ministries of Shipping, Supply, and Economic Warfare. Aubrey Wolton, one of his colleagues in the General Department, found him "a
rather withdrawn and lonely individual." His sense of isolation was
increased by the absence of his American wife, Melinda, whom he had
married in Paris, in the United States until the autumn of 1941 and by
the stillbirth of their first child shortly before Christmas 1940.

The German invasion of the Soviet Union in June 1941 gave
Maclean, as in varying degrees it gave all the Magnificent Five, a
renewed sense of purpose. Of the subjects dealt with by the General
Department over the next few years those that most interested his
controller, Anatoli Gorsky, and the NKVD included administrative
liaison with Allied troops stationed in Britain, of whom the most nu-

merous before the arrival of the Americans in force late in 1943 were the Poles and the French.

Though Stalin signed a military convention with General Sikorski's Polish government-in-exile in London after the German attack, he remained deeply suspicious of it. As Maclean was able to report, the suspicion was fully reciprocated. In April 1943, soon after German troops had uncovered the site of the NKVD massacre of Polish officers in the Katyn Forest, the Polish government in London called for an investigation by the International Red Cross. Moscow promptly broke off relations with Sikorski's government, denounced them as "Fascist collaborators," and blamed the massacre on the Germans. As the secret agent of the organization that had carried out the massacre, Maclean cannot have enjoyed briefing it on Polish reactions.[182]

In the spring of 1944 Maclean's career in both the Foreign Office and the NKGB/NKVD took a turn for the better with his posting to the Washington embassy, where he was soon promoted to first secretary. Soon after his arrival Maclean was appointed with his fellow first secretary Roddie Barclay to an Anglo-American committee working on the terms for a peace treaty with Italy. Barclay was impressed by Maclean's "skill at drafting and his ability to unravel complex issues." Robert Cecil, another of his contemporaries in Washington, recalls:

> No task was too hard for him; no hours were too long. He gained the reputation of one who would always take over a tangled skein from a colleague who was sick, or going on leave, or simply less zealous.

The most sensitive, and in the NKVD's view probably the most important, area of policy in which Maclean had become involved by early 1945 was collaboration between Tube Alloys and the Manhattan Project. His growing expertise in the atomic field was to lead to his appointment in February 1947 as joint secretary of the Combined Policy Committee, which coordinated Anglo-American-Canadian nuclear policy.[183] Throughout his time in Washington Maclean affected a reassuring concern for embassy security. While acting head of Chancery in the spring of 1946 he summoned the press secretary, William Clark, for a security briefing. Clark later recalled: "I had not been so excited since, a dozen years earlier, my housemaster had given me (similarly belatedly) my obligatory talk on sex." Maclean drew to Clark's attention the

fact that he had so far failed to sign a form acknowledging that the
terms of the Official Secrets Act had been brought to his attention. He
asked him to do so, then told him:

> "Of course you should talk to good journalists. It's not them
> we're after, it's people who might make use of the informa-
> tion. For instance"—and he carefully disconnected the
> phone by pulling out the jack on his desk—"I would always
> disconnect the phone when talking to businessmen, because
> of course our phones are tapped by the U.S. Government,
> and we don't want them to get all our trade plans. And one
> last thing, William, don't ever tell secrets to the French, they
> leak like sieves. Goodbye now, and be discreet."[184]

The importance attached by the NKGB to Maclean's position in Washington was demonstrated by the decision to send Anatoli Gorsky,
hitherto the London controller of all the Magnificent Five, to the
United States in July 1944 to maintain contact with him.[185] In October
1944 Gorsky also succeeded Akhmerov as Elizabeth Bentley's controller, and was given the task of overhauling the agent network run by
Jacob Golos with Bentley's help until his death late in 1943. Like
Akhmerov, Gorsky (known to Bentley as Al) quickly concluded that
Golos's methods were amateurish and insecure.[186] He told Bentley that
the existing setup was "full of holes and therefore too dangerous. I'm
afraid our friend Golos was not too cautious a man, and there is the
risk that you, because of your connection with him, may endanger the
apparatus." Bentley was therefore to hand over her agent network and
go "on ice" for six months until it was clear that she was not under
surveillance by the FBI. The NKGB would look closely into the background of her agents and decide which to keep. Gorsky also insisted
that she accept money and give him a receipt for it. "Let's have no more
nonsense about this. I have $2,000 right here in my pocket. It's part of
your salary. You're going to take it now! If you don't, I shall be forced
to the inescapable conclusion that you are a traitor!"[187] By the time
Bentley accepted the $2,000 she was indeed a "traitor." In November
1945, she became a double agent working for the FBI.[188] Though her
agent network was compromised, Maclean, who was run separately,
went undetected by the FBI investigation.

*   *   *

As well as penetrating the Anglo-American intelligence community during the Great Patriotic War, the NKVD/NKGB also had, ironically, for the only time in KGB history, official liaison arrangements with important sections of it. In August 1941, Colonel (later Brigadier) G. A. Hill (then code-named Dale) arrived in Moscow to head an SOE liaison team, which was given as cover name the "SAM Mission."[189] Hill was a somewhat eccentric choice. According to Kim Philby, briefly his colleague in SOE, "He was one of the few living Englishmen who had actually put sand in axle-boxes. Immensely paunchy, he looked rather like Soglow's King with a bald pate instead of a crown." Less than a decade previously Hill had published a grandiloquent account of his attempts first to assist, then to sabotage, the early Bolshevik regime. But he was ill-prepared for his wartime dealings with the NKVD. It was some time before he ordered a security check of the conference room in the SAM Mission. When the check took place, Philby gleefully relates, it "revealed a fearsome number of sources of leakage."[190]

Hill's opposite number in Moscow, Colonel (later General) A. P. Osipov, an NKVD subversive-warfare expert, seemed to Western eyes to bear an uncanny physical resemblance to Boris Karloff. After a slow start to SOE-NKVD collaboration, Osipov allowed Hill to accompany an NKVD unit behind German lines in February and March 1942 to study Soviet partisan tactics. Hill later claimed that on his return to Moscow he helped Osipov draw up the official Soviet handbook on guerrilla warfare.[191] His claim should be treated with caution. He had previously described how he had founded "a Bolshevik counter-espionage section" in 1918.[192] Hill's adventures behind German lines in the East, however, left him initially favorable to the idea of dropping NKVD agents behind enemy lines in the West and the Middle East. In the summer of 1942 he traveled to Istanbul and Cairo to discuss the idea of joint SOE-NKVD missions. Then he flew on to London accompanied by an NKVD agent, whom SOE parachuted into Belgium.

By now, however, Hill's initial enthusiasm for expanding NKVD operations westward had begun to cool. He wrote in his diary while arranging for the agent drop in Belgium: "Oh dear, I'm not at all pleased about this." SOE headquarters in London and Cairo vetoed the idea of joint operations from Turkey. According to SOE records, only "a small number" of NKVD agents were parachuted into Western Europe by the British, mostly in 1943.[193] Their drop was delayed by bad weather and operational difficulties. The NKVD protested, apparently suspecting a British plot. SOE provided data on explosive devices but got little in return.[194]

The head of the NKVD wartime mission in London, who arrived shortly after Hill had installed himself in Moscow, was Ivan Andreevich Chichayev, who also acted as Soviet counselor to Allied governments-in-exile. He was large, robust, capable, and sociable, but unusual in the NKVD for being almost teetotal. Initially, Chichayev combined his liaison post with that of NKVD resident in London.[195] The growing importance of the British agent network, however, led Moscow Center in 1943 to send a still more senior officer, Konstantin Mikhailovich Kukin, to take over from Chichayev as resident in London under diplomatic cover. Kukin basked in the reflected glory of the Magnificent Five. His portrait hangs today on the wall of the First Chief Directorate Memory Room together with a citation praising him as one of the most outstanding intelligence officers of the 1940s and 1950s. With Kukin taking over the running of the British agent network, Chichayev concentrated on the governments-in-exile.[196] As victory approached, his pressure on them mounted. General František Moravec, the intelligence chief of the Czech government-in-exile, at first found Chichayev friendly and accommodating.

> After Stalingrad the Soviet smiles faded. As the Russian military situation improved, Chichayev's attitude changed completely. Whereas before he had come to me every day and thanked me for whatever he received, he now became critical, imperious and even threatening.

Chichayev began demanding direct access to the Czechoslovak underground, criticizing the information it supplied and calling for intelligence that in Moravec's view it was impossible to obtain. He also started gathering information about Czechoslovak exiles and compiling lists of "undependables." Toward the end of the war Chichayev's demands for intelligence on the British intelligence services and on Edvard Beneš, head of the government-in-exile, led Moravec to break off contact with him.[197]

Despite the limited success of SOE liaison with the NKGB/NKVD, late in 1943 in the wake of the first meeting of the Big Three (Roosevelt, Stalin, and Churchill) at Teheran, General Donovan, the head of OSS, became enthusiastic about the idea of wide-ranging intelligence collaboration with the Russians. On Christmas Day 1943 in

Moscow, Donovan and Averell Harriman, the American ambassador, had talks with Molotov, the Foreign Commissar. Two days later Donovan met Fitin, the head of INU, and Osipov, the NKVD subversive warfare expert. According to the American account of the meeting, Fitin "listened with the closest attention" as Donovan briefed him on OSS organization and operations, then answered questions on "all available methods" of infiltrating agents into enemy territory and other technical matters. "General Osipov," the minutes record, "appeared particularly interested in the possibilities of plastic explosives. General Donovan promised to send to General Fitin . . . a standard type of small radio which was used by the OSS operatives."

Having thus sought to whet the appetite of his Soviet hosts, Donovan then proposed the establishment of an OSS mission in Moscow and an NKVD mission in Washington. The two missions would exchange intelligence (each side, Donovan believed, had information on the enemy "of great value" to the other), coordinate operations to prevent their agents from "working at cross purposes," and keep each other informed of preparations for sabotage missions. Donovan's proposal was accepted in principle with an alacrity rarely paralleled in American-Soviet relations. Fitin was avid for information on OSS operations in Eastern Europe and the Balkans, as well as for access to OSS weapons and technology. At a time when INU was considering the overhaul, after Jacob Golos's death, of Elizabeth Bentley's insecure Washington spy ring, he must also have welcomed the prospect of strengthening his residency in Washington by an officially accredited mission, which, as in London, could combine liaison work with espionage. Fitin told Donovan that he "heartily welcomed" his proposals. While some aspects would naturally have to be decided by higher authority, the presence in Moscow of an OSS liaison officer could be considered "as decided," and the exchange of some intelligence "should begin right away."[198] Harriman, the American ambassador, was as enthusiastic as Fitin. He wrote naïvely to Roosevelt:

> We have unsuccessfully attempted for the last two and a half years to penetrate sources of Soviet information and to get on a basis of mutual confidence and exchange. Here, for the first time, we have penetrated one intelligence branch of the Soviet Government and, if pursued, I am satisfied this will be the opening door to far greater intimacy in other branches.[199]

Washington, however, had cold feet. Anxious to avoid controversy in an election year, Roosevelt yielded to the determination of the FBI director, J. Edgar Hoover, not to allow an NKVD mission in Washington. In April 1944 Fitin and Osipov were told by the head of the U.S. Military Mission, General Deane, that the formal exchange of missions had been "postponed."[200] Though "disappointed," they were anxious to continue exchanging intelligence with OSS through Deane's office.

In August the OSS mission in London also began exchanging information with Chichayev.[201] Though the NKVD provided enough reports to establish the exchange and OSS was, to begin with, impressed with the sheer novelty of receiving Soviet intelligence, the exchange was increasingly one-sided, with OSS providing far more than it received.[202] From time to time, however, Fitin provided considerable detail when he had a clear interest in doing so. In September, for example, he provided details of eight enemy installations in Poland and East Germany, doubtless in the hope that they would be bombed by the USAF.[203]

Fitin also came to the rescue after the Soviet high command ordered all OSS and SOE officers out of Bulgaria on September 25. Two days later Fitin announced that he had made arrangements for them to be allowed back. But he made their return conditional on Donovan's giving him a list of all OSS personnel not merely in Bulgaria, but in Rumania, Czechoslovakia, Yugoslavia, and all areas occupied by the Red Army. Donovan agreed. Henceforth those partisans in Eastern Europe and the Balkans who made contact with OSS officers were likely to find their names on the NKVD black list. OSS officers watched helplessly as their NKVD colleagues suppressed opposition to Communist domination in the areas liberated by the Red Army.[204]

The establishment and initially high expectations of OSS-NKVD collaboration in 1944 stirred Brigadier Hill into unsuccessful attempts to revitalize SOE liaison with the Russians. In April 1944 SOE provided Major N. N. Krassovski of the NKVD with a wireless transmitter and small arms, and parachuted him into Yugoslavia to visit Tito's headquarters. SOE in Bari telegraphed London: "Krassovski completely unappreciative of efforts made on his behalf." In June Chichayev informed SOE that Krassovski had been recalled by Moscow "as efforts to establish liaison with SOE with a view to collaboration had failed." Brigadier Fitzroy Maclean, Churchill's liaison officer with Tito, commented that, on the contrary, the SOE mission's relations with Krassovski had been most cordial. Osipov told Hill: "Perhaps

Krassovski was the wrong type to send." Hill agreed, and invited Osipov to visit London to discuss future collaboration. Osipov failed to reply.[205]

As well as collecting vast amounts of intelligence on Russia's allies, the NKVD also carried out a series of active measures operations designed to influence Western opinion. While working on the classified official history of the First Chief Directorate, Gordievsky came to the conclusion that the NKVD's most remarkable active measures coup had been the success of one of its agents, Peter Smollett, in becoming head of the Ministry of Information's Anglo-Soviet liaison section. Born H. P. Smolka in Vienna in 1912, Smollett came from a family of Austrian Jews that made its fortune between the wars by manufacturing the first ski binding to snap open when twisted in a fall. He came to London in 1933,[206] probably at Maly's instigation, as an idealistic young NKVD illegal agent, working under journalistic cover for a Viennese newspaper. In 1934–35 he was briefly involved with Philby in an unsuccessful attempt to set up their own news agency.[207]

Smolka made his reputation in Britain with a series of vivid, well-written articles for *The Times* describing his travels in the Soviet Arctic regions in the summer of 1936. In 1937 the articles were turned into a book, *Forty Thousand Against the Arctic: Russia's Polar Empire,* which went through three printings in less than a year. By the standards of the day, Smolka's book was a sophisticated example of NKVD active measures, written from an apparently non-Communist perspective by a writer concerned simply to "give credit where it is due" and set aside old "grievances and reproaches." "Russia today," he told his readers, "is like a house in construction. They cannot hide the dirt, disorder and atmosphere of improvisation which astounds us in all building plots." But Smolka placed the emphasis on the impressive achievements of the Five Year Plans, of which the conquest of the Arctic wastes was a striking example. Proud of the achievements of socialist construction, preoccupied with "battles against nature" and the development of their resources, the Soviet people had lost interest in "the idea of carrying the torch of world revolution beyond their frontiers."

The most ingenious fabrication in Smolka's book was his portrayal of the hideous brutality of the gulag during the Great Terror as an idealistic experiment in social reform. He wrote of relations between guards and prisoners: "What I found new was the great and sincere belief of the young [NKVD] 'administrators' that they were really pioneers of the soul in the wilderness of these ruffians' [the prisoners'] minds." The reformed ruffians of the gulag were constructing convict colonies which, guided by the idealists of the NKVD, might one day become as free and prosperous as Australia, which had similar penal origins.[208]

Curiously, such fabrications did not dent the confidence in Smolka of either *The Times* or the Foreign Office Press Department, which was impressed by his "considerable reputation as a writer in international affairs." Soon after the Anschluss of Nazi Germany with Austria in March 1938, he became a naturalized British subject under the name H. Peter Smollett (initially Smolka-Smollett). A few months later he joined the Exchange Telegraph Company as head of its newly formed foreign department. In November 1938 he was given warm recommendations from the Foreign Office Press Department to the British embassies in Prague, Warsaw, Budapest, Bucharest, Belgrade, and Berne, where he had requested "an opportunity of discussing . . . the local press situation and particularly the question of how straight news from this country stands in relation to the tainted propaganda put out by other official and semi-official agencies." Smollett's own gift for skillfully "tainted" NKVD propaganda gives these discussions in British embassies a particular irony. He and his wife were in Prague during the German takeover in March 1939 and had to take refuge in the British embassy before returning to London.[209]

After the outbreak of war Smollett tried vainly to enter one of the intelligence services.[210] He found a job instead in the wartime Ministry of Information, where his career was helped by his acquaintance with the young and dynamic Brendan Bracken, who became Churchill's minister of information in June 1941.[211] In September Churchill asked Bracken "to consider what action was required to counter the present tendency of the British Public to forget the dangers of Communism in their enthusiasm over the resistance of Russia."[212] Soon afterward Smollett was appointed head of the recently founded Russian department.[213] He quickly and cleverly redefined the prime minister's brief by referring to Churchill's broadcast on June 22 promising to "give whatever help we can to Russia and the Russian people." The two priorities, reported Smollett, were to:

a. Combat such anti-Soviet feeling in Britain as might jeopardize execution of policy defined by the Prime Minister,

June 22. Counteract enemy attempt to split national unity over issue of Anglo-Soviet Alliance.

b. Attempt to curb exuberant pro-Soviet propaganda from the Left which might seriously embarrass H.M.G. Anticipate Communist-inspired criticism and prevent initiative from falling into the hands of C.P. [Communist Party].

The way to "curb exuberant pro-Soviet propaganda," argued Smollett, was "to 'steal the thunder' of radical left propaganda in this country by outdoing them in pro-Russian publicity while at the same time keeping this publicity on such lines as we think most desirable."[214] Stealing the thunder of the radical left turned out to involve celebrating the achievements of the Red Army in a way that identified the Russian people with the Soviet regime.

Smollett defined his own job as "directing the Branch in general" and liaison with the Foreign Office, the Soviet embassy and the Political Warfare Executive.[215] Ivan Maisky, the Soviet ambassador, wrote to assure Brendan Bracken in November 1941 that "everything possible will be done to assist Mr. Smollett to maintain close contact with the Embassy here."[216] Smollett's most important contact in the embassy was his NKVD controller, Anatoli Gorsky, who found meetings with him much simpler to arrange than with the Magnificent Five.[217] While never suspecting that Smollett was a Soviet agent, the Foreign Office grew mildly concerned at the extent of his dealings with the Soviet embassy. In 1942 it sought to "impress on Smollett the importance of exercising the utmost discretion in his use of information."[218]

Smollett successfully persuaded R. H. Parker, director of the Home Publicity Division, that the ministry should avoid using "both White Russians and Red Englishmen" to speak on Soviet affairs.[219] That apparently even-handed proposal suited NKVD policy perfectly. White Russians were, of course, anathema. But the NKVD also preferred to have the Soviet case put by apparently impartial British speakers rather than by open Communists. Smollett presented the Soviet embassy's willingness to distance itself from overtly pro-Communist groups as a major concession:

The Head of [the Embassy Press] Department asked me to state frankly whether I considered some of the pro-Russian organizations in this country to constitute an embarrassment to HMG. I replied equally frankly that as a Government body we should prefer to deal only with official Russian organizations and my partner immediately stated, with permission to be quoted, that the Embassy is prepared to disinterest themselves [sic] completely in the fate of such organizations as the Russia Today Society, the Friends of the Soviet Union and the newspaper *Russia Today.*

Smollett gained Parker's consent for his proposal to seek the embassy's help in "bringing from Russia some specially trained speakers who would adhere strictly to a brief agreed upon by both HMG and the Soviet Embassy."[220]

The Soviet propaganda effort organized by Smollett under the guise of stealing the thunder of the radical left was on a prodigious scale. A vast meeting at the Albert Hall in February 1943 to celebrate the twenty-fifth anniversary of the Red Army included songs of praise by a massed choir, readings by John Gielgud and Laurence Olivier, and was attended by leading politicians from all major parties. Official posters paid constant tribute to Russian civilians as well as soldiers. Numerous Soviet exhibitions toured the country. The film *U.S.S.R. at War* was shown to factory audiences of 1¼ million. In the month of September 1943 alone the Ministry of Information organized meetings on the Soviet Union for thirty-four public venues, thirty-five factories, one hundred voluntary societies, twenty-eight civil-defense groups, nine schools, and a prison; the BBC in the same month broadcast thirty programs with a substantial Soviet content.[221]

One of the Conservative whips in the Commons complained: "Films displayed by the Ministry of Information giving a colourful portrayal of life in Soviet Russia have served to change many people's ideas about Communism."[222] Smollett was also successful in suppressing a substantial amount of unfavorable comment on Stalinist persecution. The ministry even succeeded in persuading George Orwell's publishers not to bring out his satirical masterpiece *Animal Farm.*[223]

Smollett worked closely with the BBC, "vetting . . . scripts projecting Russia to be used on the home services."[224] With Guy Burgess as an influential talks producer from 1940 to 1944, the NKVD also had a powerful voice inside the BBC. In July 1941, a month after the German invasion, Burgess circulated a list of "Draft Suggestions for Talks on Russia" covering literature, science, culture, economic planning ("The Soviet Union were the pioneers"), the federal system of the

U.S.S.R. ("one in which the Soviet Union has done some interesting experiments"), and Soviet foreign policy ("Carefully handled there should be room for an objective talk"). Burgess's suggestions on Soviet culture had a particular irony, which the BBC management at the time failed to realize: "Dr. Klugender and Dr. Blunt are possible speakers on Art—neither are Communists. Christopher Hill (a fellow of All Souls) is a Communist but is also probably the best authority on Russian historical studies."[225]

Probably Burgess's most remarkable coup within the BBC on behalf of the NKVD was to arrange for a talk on the Eastern Front in January 1942 by the Soviet illegal Ernst Henri, who had first aroused his enthusiasm for the ring of five in 1933. Still working in London under journalistic cover, Henri told his listeners that the Red Army would be victorious because "they fight for the people, for their motherland and for the people's rule." Then Henri had a special message for the moles. The Soviet Union, he told them over the air, had "an intelligence service which is among the best in the world." The Gestapo (and, by implication, MI5) was powerless against it.[226] The Soviet agents who heard Henri's remarkable broadcast must have drawn heart from the NKVD's ability to advertise its success over the BBC.

The talks director of the Home Service (now Radio 4), George Barnes (later knighted), a friend of Burgess since Burgess had lodged in his Cambridge house, stoutly defended his staff against "the allegation that our broadcasts are biased towards the left"—though he acknowledged that his producers were mostly "young men and it is axiomatic that young men tend to mix in progressive circles." The NKVD, for its part, was annoyed that the more objective BBC home-news department failed to follow the lead of the talks department. In the spring of 1943 the Soviet embassy sent a savage protest at BBC news coverage of Soviet affairs to Brendan Bracken, who forwarded it to the director-general of the BBC. Bracken told the embassy that, while denying the charge, the BBC had been suitably chastened.[227]

While helping to run Soviet active measures in London in 1982–85 (and keeping British intelligence well informed about them), Gordievsky sometimes reflected on the precedent set by Smollett and Burgess during the Second World War. Brilliantly ingenious though the active measures orchestrated by Smollett and Burgess were, they were less influential than the KGB believed. For most of the British public the achievements of the Red Army spoke for themselves. The Soviet Union lost more soldiers at Stalingrad in the winter of 1942–43 than were lost by either Britain or the United States in all the battles of the war. The Home Intelligence Division of the Ministry of Information reported early in 1943:

> However successful or even sensational the news from other quarters may be, the eyes and hearts of the majority are turned towards "our great Allies." The victory at Stalingrad is said to have aroused more "intense admiration than any other Russian exploit," and it appears that the admiration and gratitude of the majority have never been higher.[228]

In the aftermath of Stalingrad, even the Foreign Office preferred to turn a blind eye to evidence of the NKVD massacre of Polish officers in the Katyn Forest. The active measures campaign orchestrated by Smollett at the Ministry of Information helped to blur the distinction between the heroism of the Russian people and the Stalinist regime, but by comparison with the victories and sacrifices of the Red Army its influence on British opinion was marginal.

Probably the most remarkable active measure designed to influence Western opinion was the sudden dissolution of the Comintern in May 1943. The primary purpose of this unexpected and dramatic gesture was to reinforce in the West the changing image of the Soviet Union as a power no longer concerned to export revolution through its domination of foreign Communist parties but intent instead on strengthening the wartime alliance and extending it into the postwar world. In an interview with Reuter's chief Moscow correspondent, Stalin gave as the first two reasons for the Comintern's abolition:

> a. It exposes the lie of the Hitlerites to the effect that "Moscow" allegedly intends to intervene in the life of other nations and to "Bolshevize" them. An end is now being put to this lie.
> b. It exposes the calumny of the adversaries of Communism within the Labour movement to the effect that Communist parties in various countries are allegedly acting not in the interests of their people but on orders from outside. An end is now being put to this calumny too.

Soviet policy, said Stalin, favored the union of all "progressive forces . . . regardless of party or religious faith" and "the future organization of a companionship of nations based upon their equality."[229] Smollett, meanwhile, was urging on the BBC and the rest of the media the argument that a "major change of direction . . . has taken place in Soviet policy under Stalin":

> While the Trotskyist policy was to bolster up the security of a weak U.S.S.R. by means of subversive movements in other countries controlled by the Comintern, Stalin's policy has been and continues to be one of maintaining a strong Russia maintaining friendly diplomatic relations with other governments. . . . Parallel with this development in Soviet policy there has been a change in the type of personnel in power in the U.S.S.R. The ideologues and doctrinaire international revolutionaries have increasingly been replaced by people of the managerial and technical type, both military and civil, who are interested in getting practical results.[230]

In reality, though foreign Communists were encouraged to turn themselves into nationalists in order to strengthen their prospects of postwar power, Stalin had no intention of releasing them from their traditional obligation to follow Moscow's lead. And at the very moment when Stalin was denouncing allegations of covert Soviet interference in foreign countries as "calumny," NKVD penetration in both London and Washington had reached record levels. The dissolution of the Comintern, however, was a propaganda success. Senator Tom Connally, chairman of the Senate Foreign Relations Committee, interpreted it as meaning that Russian Communism would no longer interfere in the affairs of other nations. The New York *Herald Tribune* argued that it marked the transformation of the U.S.S.R. into a national state run on Communist lines rather than the center of world communism.[231]

Part of Stalin's concern with the image of the U.S.S.R. in the West in 1943 derived from his desire to diminish the apprehensions of his allies at the spread of Soviet influence in Eastern and Central Europe before negotiations began on the shape of the postwar world. The NKVD/NKGB gave him a considerable bargaining advantage over his allies. Both British and American intelligence performed better against the enemy; Russia had no intelligence success against Germany that compared with Ultra. But Soviet intelligence devoted vastly more resources to penetrating its allies than its allies deployed against the U.S.S.R.—

contrary to the postwar myth encouraged by the KGB that Western intelligence had been actively waging the Cold War well before Germany had been defeated.

At the first meeting of the Big Three at Teheran in November 1943, there was an enormous disparity between the intelligence supplied to Stalin and that available to Churchill and Roosevelt. The NKGB was well provided with agents in both London and Washington. SIS and OSS had not a single agent between them in Moscow. Having successfully installed a comprehensive system of listening devices in the U.S. embassy in Moscow, the NKGB devised a simple but equally successful method of bugging Roosevelt and his entourage in Teheran. Molotov claimed, rather vaguely, to have information of a German assassination plot, and declared the American legation, situated a mile away from the adjoining British and Soviet embassies, to be insecure. Churchill suggested that Roosevelt stay in the British embassy. Not wishing to arouse Russian suspicions of an Anglo-American plot, the president refused. Instead he naïvely accepted Stalin's pressing invitation to stay with his delegation in a building in the Soviet embassy compound.

General Ismay, head of the military section of the War Cabinet secretariat, later mused in his memoirs: "I wonder if microphones had already been installed in anticipation!"[232] There is, of course, no doubt that they had. Housed in Soviet property, attended by NKVD servants, their conversations constantly monitored by their hosts, the United States delegation to the first summit meeting with a Soviet leader was condemned to practice something akin to open diplomacy.

Stalin's negotiating advantage did not stop there. Advising Roosevelt at Teheran was Harry Hopkins, whom the NKVD regarded as its agent. Hopkins's own view of his role was quite different. He was an American patriot with no desire to introduce the Soviet system in the United States. But he consented to receive secret communications "from Comrade Stalin" through Akhmerov and expressed in public as well as in private his conviction that "Since Russia is the decisive factor in the war she must be given every assistance and every effort must be made to obtain her friendship."[233] Unlike Roosevelt or the State Department, Hopkins had already concluded that the United States must come to terms with the fact that the Soviet Union would "without question. . . . dominate Europe on the defeat of the Nazis" and that Soviet-American friendship held the key to the postwar world. He encouraged Roosevelt's conviction that he could succeed where

Churchill had failed and establish a personal rapport with Stalin. According to Roosevelt's neglected secretary of State, Cordell Hull, who was not invited to Teheran, "the President hoped that, through a personal meeting with Stalin, he might iron out the problems that existed between Russia on the one hand and virtually all the United Nations on the other."[234]

Hopkins also believed that with American forces now in Europe and the United States providing most of the military equipment, it was time for her to assert her role as senior partner in the Anglo-American alliance. He said ominously to Churchill's doctor, Lord Moran, before the conference began, "Sure, we are preparing for a battle at Teheran. You will find us lining up with the Russians."[235] Charles Bohlen, who acted as American interpreter at Teheran, later described Hopkins's influence on the president as "paramount."[236] All other foreign policy advisers were kept at arm's length. The American diplomat Robert Murphy complained to Cordell Hull that the U.S. foreign service was not told what transpired in the secret conversations between Roosevelt and Stalin. Hull replied that he himself would have been grateful for any news from Teheran.[237]

It was at Teheran, Churchill later claimed, that he realized for the first time how small a nation Britain was: "There I sat with the great Russian bear on one side of me, with paws outstretched, and on the other side the great American buffalo, and between the two sat the poor little English donkey."[238] After the second session of the conference on November 29 Hopkins sought out Churchill at the British embassy, told him that Stalin and Roosevelt were adamant that Operation Overlord, the Anglo-American cross-Channel invasion of northern France, must take place in May 1944 and that British opposition must cease. Churchill duly gave way.[239] (In fact, Overlord was to begin on June 6.)

The most important political concession to Stalin was Anglo-American agreement to give postwar Russia her 1941 frontier, thus allowing her to recover the ill-gotten gains of the Nazi-Soviet Pact: eastern Poland, the Baltic States, and Bessarabia. Poland was to receive some territorial compensation in the west at the expense of Germany. The Polish government in London, headed since July by Stanislaw Mikolajczyk, was not consulted. When Stalin vilified Mikolajczyk's government ("The Polish Government and their friends in Poland were in contact with the Germans. They killed the partisans"), neither the president nor the prime minister thought it prudent to object.[240] Nor did Roosevelt or Churchill provoke disharmony by raising the question of the Katyn massacre. The sellout of the Poles derived not merely from illusions about Stalin's postwar behavior (much greater for Hopkins and Roosevelt than for Churchill) but also from a deep sense of the West's military debt to the Soviet Union at a time when the Red Army was still bearing the overwhelming brunt of the war with Germany.

Stalin returned from Teheran in high spirits. Soon afterward the U.S. embassy in Moscow reported an "almost revolutionary change" in the attitude of the Soviet press to Britain and the United States. The whole Soviet propaganda machine was geared to celebrating Allied unity and the "historic decisions" at Teheran.[241] In the Soviet view the Western Allies seemed to have recognized, as a Russian diplomat put it privately, Russia's "right to establish friendly governments in the neighboring countries." The Czechoslovak government-in-exile in London was quick to take the hint. On December 12, 1943, President Beneš signed in Moscow a treaty of friendship and alliance with the Soviet Union. Naïvely believing that he could keep the upper hand by staying on good terms with Stalin, Beneš told Czech Communist leaders in Moscow that he expected them to emerge after the war as the strongest party.[242]

The next conference of the Big Three, at Yalta on the Black Sea in February 1945 (the last attended by Roosevelt, who died in April), was another Soviet triumph. Once again Stalin held most of the military cards. The Red Army was close to controlling Poland, Czechoslovakia, and the Baltic States as well as a large slice of Germany, while the Western Allies, despite the success of Overlord, had yet to cross the Rhine. Stalin had an equally impressive advantage in intelligence. The NKVD had two able moles in the British foreign service: Donald Maclean at the Washington embassy, well placed to report on Anglo-American discussions before the conference, and Guy Burgess, who had left the BBC for the Foreign Office News Department in 1944. The NKGB's main source within the State Department, Alger Hiss, was actually a member of the American delegation at Yalta. As deputy director of the Office of Special Political Affairs since late in 1944, he had been actively engaged in preparations for the conference.[243] To the delight of the NKGB, Harry Hopkins, after losing some of his influence in the White House during 1944, reemerged, despite illness, to become, once again, chief adviser to the now visibly ailing Roosevelt.[244]

The Americans were put up in the former Tsarist summer palace at Livadia, the British twenty minutes away at what one of them described as "a sort of Gothic Balmoral," the Vorontsov Palace.[245] Both were comprehensively bugged. The Americans in particular seem to have taken few if any precautions. The NKGB sought with some success to distract attention from its surveillance by lavish and attentive hospitality, personally supervised by its first deputy commissar, General Sergei Nikiforovich Kruglov, who struck Joan Bright of the British War Cabinet secretariat as "the most powerful-looking man I had ever seen, with huge shoulders, face, hands and feet." On the eve of the conference Kruglov told Miss Bright that the British delegation was in the Russian bad books. He spread his enormous hands: "From the Americans we have received many requests and have done our best to fulfil them; from the British nothing, nothing. . . ." Miss Bright did her best to pacify him with a long list of requirements.[246]

Sarah Churchill, who accompanied her father to Yalta, wrote to her mother "Our paws are well buttered here. Wow." Over a thousand Russian soldiers had restored roads, rebuilt and decorated houses, and planted gardens. Walls were hung with masterpieces from Moscow art galleries, baronial fireplaces crackled with burning logs, Persian rugs carpeted the floors, starched and spotless linen adorned the table, the maîtres d'hôtel wore white tie and tails, the maids were dressed in black dresses with white aprons. Miss Bright found the food like "something out of a fairy tale." On one occasion she casually mentioned over lunch that she had never eaten Chicken Kiev. Within the hour she was served a dish of it by a butler who stood over her, "with a proud smile on his face," while she consumed it. When Sarah Churchill mentioned that lemon juice went well with caviar, a huge lemon tree weighed down with fruit appeared, as if by magic, in the Vorontsov orangerie. The Americans noted the same phenomenon at the Livadia Palace. General Kruglov, who presided over such minor miracles, was rewarded at the next Allied conference at Potsdam with a KBE, thus becoming the only KGB officer ever to receive an honorary knighthood.[247]

In the economic negotiations at Yalta, centered on the issue of reparations, Soviet negotiators were powerfully assisted by Harry Dexter White, the most important of several NKVD agents in the U.S. Treasury.[248] Since 1942, as the closest adviser of Morgenthau, secretary of the Treasury, White had taken the leading part in formulating American policy for the international financial order of the postwar world. Together with Lord Keynes, he was the dominating figure at the Bretton Woods Conference of July 1944, which drew up the blueprint for both the International Monetary Fund and the International Bank for

Reconstruction and Development. In January 1945 he became assistant secretary of the Treasury.[249]

Reparations negotiations at Yalta opened on February 5. Molotov asked for long-term American credits as well as massive German reparations. Maisky, then assistant foreign commissar, called for the deindustrialization of Germany, the physical removal of its arms industry and of 80 percent of the rest of its heavy industry. Confiscated industrial plant would contribute to a total reparations bill of $20 billion, of which half would go to the Soviet Union. Though not present at Yalta, White had already given strong backing to the Soviet case. In January 1945 he took the lead in drafting two memoranda sent by Morgenthau to the president. The first proposed a thirty-five-year loan to the U.S.S.R. of $10 billion at 2 percent interest, with optional repayment in strategic materials. The second memorandum declared it "essential" that German chemical, metallurgical, and electrical industries be removed in their entirety to prevent future German aggression:

> The real motive of most of those who oppose a weak Germany is . . . fear of Russia and of Communism. It is the twenty-year-old idea of a "Bulwark against Bolshevism,"— which was one of the factors that brought this present war down on us.
> . . . There is nothing I can think of that can do more at this moment to engender trust or distrust between the United States and Russia than the position this Government takes on the German problem.

White's advocacy failed to overcome State Department opposition to the $10 billion loan to Russia and to the dismantling of German industry. But Roosevelt, unlike Churchill, accepted the Soviet figure of $20 billion reparations, half going to the U.S.S.R., as "a basis for discussion" by a three-power Reparations Commission, which was to meet in Moscow.[250] White, however, had already facilitated a concealed American subsidy to the Soviet Union. In 1944 White provided the NKVD through Silvermaster with samples of the occupation currency printed by the Treasury for use in Germany. Thus prompted, the Russians decided to ask for the plates, ink, and paper samples in order to print notes of their own. The director of the Bureau of Printing and Engraving reasonably objected that "to permit the Russian government to print a currency identical to that being printed in this country would make accountability impossible." White protested that the Russians would interpret this as showing lack of confidence in their integrity; they "must be trusted to the same degree and to the same extent as the other allies." A week later they received the plates. In 1953 a Senate hearing was told that "there is no way of determining just to what extent the Russians did use these plates." The cost to the American taxpayer may well have run into millions of dollars.[251]

The main problems at Yalta were political. Most time was taken up with Poland. As Cadogan, the permanent under-secretary at the Foreign Office explained to his wife, "That will be the most important thing. . . . Because after all, if we couldn't get a decent-looking Polish settlement, none of our other high-falutin' plans for World Organization and suchlike would make much sense."[252] At Teheran Churchill and Roosevelt had effectively conceded both Russian dominance of Poland and Russia's choice of frontiers. Now, belatedly, they tried to reconcile that concession with the principles of the Atlantic Charter by demanding guarantees of Polish democracy incompatible with the principles of Stalinism. Poland, said Churchill poetically, must "be mistress in her own house and captain of her soul." This required a replacement for the puppet Lublin provisional government installed by the Russians and a guarantee of free elections. Stalin negotiated brilliantly, first playing for time, then making concessions on secondary issues after underlining their importance in order to retain his allies' consent to a Soviet-dominated Poland, the key to the establishment of a Stalinist order in Eastern Europe. Cadogan, usually a hard judge, wrote to his wife:

> I have never known the Russians so easy and accommodating. In particular Joe has been extremely good. He is a great man, and shows up very impressively against the background of the other two aging statesmen. The President in particular is very woolly and wobbly.[253]

Thus mollified by Stalin, Churchill and Roosevelt settled for a face-saving formula in Poland. The Lublin provisional government, instead of being replaced, was simply to be enlarged to include some "democratic leaders." Poland's postwar elections were to be overseen not by the Allies to ensure fair play but by the provisional government, which would rig the results with expert assistance from the NKVD.

At Yalta it was still uncertain (as Stalin knew from NKGB

reports) that the Manhattan Project would succeed in producing an
atomic bomb in time to force Japan to surrender without an enormously costly American invasion. Stalin allowed himself to be persuaded to declare war on Japan within three months of the defeat of
Germany in return for the acquisition of southern Sakhalin and the
Kurile islands from Japan and control of Manchuria and Outer Mongolia at the expense of China. Stalin also agreed, after initial opposition,
to allow France a zone of occupation in Germany (taken from the
Anglo-American zones) and a seat on the Allied Control Commission.
Again, after a show of reluctance, Stalin accepted the American voting
formula for the Security Council, thus ensuring the creation of the
United Nations. During the last session of the Yalta conference, Hopkins passed a note to Roosevelt, which began: "The Russians have given
in so much at this conference that I don't think we should let them
down."[254] The note was specifically concerned with reparations but
summarized Hopkins's view of the conference as a whole. Hopkins left
Yalta in a state of euphoric optimism and admiration for Stalin's genius:

> We really believed in our hearts that this was the dawn of the
> new day we had all been praying for and talking about for
> so many years. . . . The Russians had proved that they could
> be reasonable and farseeing and there wasn't any doubt in the
> minds of the President or any of us that we could live with
> them and get along with them peacefully for as far into the
> future as any of us could imagine. But I have to make one
> amendment to that—I think we all had in our minds the
> reservation that we could not foretell what the results would
> be if anything should happen to Stalin. We felt sure that we
> could count on him to be reasonable and sensible and under-
> standing—but we never could be sure who or what might be
> in back of him there in the Kremlin.[255]

Among those who shared Hopkins's euphoria was Alger Hiss. After the
conference he wrote to congratulate the secretary of State, Edward
Stettinius, in reality little more than a figurehead in the making of
American policy at Yalta, on the magnificent job he had done.[256] Hiss's
career appeared to offer the NKGB a remarkable opportunity within
the new United Nations. In April 1945 he became temporary secretary-

general of the UN "organizing conference" at San Francisco. Unsurprisingly, Gromyko expressed "a very high regard for Alger Hiss,
particularly for his fairness and impartiality." He told Stettinius that
he would be happy for Hiss to become temporary secretary-general of
the UN constituent assembly, a position that might well have led to his
appointment as first permanent secretary-general of the United Nations.[257]

Stalin ended the Yalta conference in great good humor. At the
final photo call he sought to entertain the Anglophones by jovially
repeating his only four phrases of English: "You said it!"; "So what?";
"What the hell goes on round here?"; and "The toilet is over there."[258]
The excellent intelligence available to Stalin from both penetration
agents and technical surveillance had been one of the keys to his negotiating success. He was probably better informed than either Churchill
or Stettinius on what territory Roosevelt was willing to offer him to
wage war on Japan. Roosevelt, by contrast, failed to grasp that Stalin
was eager rather than reluctant to take on Japan after the defeat of
Germany.

But, as always, Stalin's extreme suspiciousness, verging at
times on paranoia, limited his ability to derive maximum benefit from
the intelligence he received. He brooded long and hard on the reasons
for Churchill's and Roosevelt's resistance at Yalta to the Polish settlement agreed on in essence at Teheran over a year before. Since he
could not grasp that their objections, half-hearted though they were,
were based on genuine commitment to human rights, he inevitably
sought some more sinister explanation. In the process he became
preoccupied once again by conspiracy theories. In July 1952 he assured the Italian socialist Pietro Nenni that the American "Cardinal
Spellman had been at the Yalta conference in disguise: it was he,
Stalin said, who had hardened 'his friend' Roosevelt against him."

Nenni had no doubt about Stalin's sincerity; he interpreted
this bizarre theory as an indication of Stalin's recurrent obsession
with plots against him orchestrated by the Vatican.[259] The slender
basis for Stalin's theory of a Vatican conspiracy at Yalta was the
incongruous presence in the American delegation of Ed Flynn, the
Democratic boss of the Bronx, who stopped in Rome on his way
home from the Crimea[260] (and thereafter entered Stalin's conspiratorial imagination as Cardinal Spellman in disguise). Comment-

ing on the Spellman conspiracy theory, the British diplomat R. A. Sykes accurately described Stalin's world view as "a curious mixture of shrewdness and nonsense."[261] The mixture was to be as characteristic of Stalin's use of intelligence during the Cold War as it had been in the Great Patriotic War.

9

The Takeover of Eastern Europe (1944–48)

The wartime expansion of Beria's vast security empire had, in Stalin's view, made Beria himself too powerful. Early in 1946 he was made a full member of the Politburo and deputy chairman of the Council of Ministers. But at the same time he was replaced as head of the NKVD by his former first deputy, the huge bull-like Sergei Kruglov, holder of an honorary British knighthood in recognition of his security services at conferences of the Big Three. In March 1946 the NKVD and NKGB were raised in status from commissariats to ministries, becoming respectively Ministry of Internal Affairs (Ministerstvo Vnutrennikh Del or MVD) and Ministry of State Security (Ministerstvo Gosudarstvennoye Bezopasnosti or MGB). Soon afterward Beria's protégé Merkulov was replaced at the head of the MGB by Viktor Semyonovich Abakumov, who, like Kruglov, did not belong to Beria's Caucasian mafia. But if Stalin hoped that Abakumov would limit Beria's influence on state security, he had for once miscalculated. According to Khrushchev, Abakumov quickly became "Beria's man; he never reported to anyone, not even to Stalin, without checking first with Beria."[1]

Abakumov's management style in the MGB was brutal, corrupt, but, so far as his cronies were concerned, convivial. Anxious not to be overshadowed by symbols of the Chekist past, Abakumov was probably responsible for removing the MGB's most sacred relics, the death mask, effigy, and tunic of Dzerzhinsky, from their place of honor in the MGB officers' club. Abakumov was a regular nighttime visitor to the club, playing snooker with his cronies and having sex with his numerous mistresses in a private room, which he kept stocked with a great variety of imported liqueurs and French perfumes. MGB officers abroad were expected to curry favor with Abakumov by purchasing expensive hard-currency gifts in the West. The defector Pyotr Deryabin later recalled buying for his chief in Vienna a baby's pram and a dress worth 100,000 rubles. "Immorality" and corruption were to be among the official reasons given for Abakumov's arrest in 1951 and execution in 1954.[2]

Abakumov owed his position as minister for State Security to his wartime success as head of Smersh, which had originated in April 1943 from a reorganization of the NKVD "special departments" responsible for counterintelligence in the armed forces. Stalin himself chaired the meeting of senior intelligence officers at which Smersh was founded. According to an official Soviet account, the original name proposed was Smernesh: an abbreviation of the wartime slogan *Smert nemetskim shpionam!* ("Death to German Spies!"). Stalin, however, objected: "Why, as a matter of fact, should we be speaking only of German spies? Aren't other intelligence services working against our country? Let's call it *Smert Shpionam* ['Death to Spies']—Smersh for short."[3] Smersh's main priority, however, was less to detect foreign spies than to monitor disaffection and "cowardice" in the armed forces through a huge network of informers.[4] Stalin showed the importance he attached to Smersh by detaching it from the NKVD and placing it under his direct control as chairman of the State Defense Committee and wartime defense commissar.[5]

As the Red Army recovered Soviet territory from the Wehrmacht, Smersh hunted down all those suspected of collaboration with the enemy and suppressed nationalist opposition. At the end of the war Smersh was also responsible for screening well over five million Soviet citizens repatriated from enemy territory. In their anxiety to honor obligations to their ally, both the British and American governments collaborated in a sometimes barbarous repatriation.[6] Many of the two million Soviet citizens they returned home, often against their will, simply passed from Nazi to Stalinist persecution. As a Soviet official history euphemistically acknowledges, Smersh looked "with distrust" on the more than a million Russian POWs who had survived the horrors of German prison camps.[7] Almost all were treated as presumed deserters. In June 1945 the American ambassador in Moscow, Averell Harriman, reported to the State Department:

> The Embassy knows of only a single instance in which a repatriated prisoner has returned to his home and family in Moscow. . . . Train loads of repatriates are passing through Moscow and continuing east, the passengers being held incommunicado while trains stand in Moscow yards.

Some were shot after interrogation by Smersh. Most went to prison camps above the Arctic Circle, where many died. The most terrible fate of all awaited the members of General Andrei Vlasov's Russian Liberation Army, who were repatriated by the Americans. Vlasov, one of the heroes of the battle of Moscow, had been captured by the Germans in 1942 and subsequently denounced the Soviet regime as a tyrannical perversion of the October Revolution. His volunteer army, recruited from Russian POWs, fought briefly with the Germans on the Eastern Front in March 1945. The American soldiers who repatriated Vlasov's troops had to tear-gas them before handing them over; even so, eleven succeeded in hanging or stabbing themselves to death.[8] The Hungarian statesman Nicholas Nyaradi, who was in Moscow at the time of Vlasov's repatriation, wrote later:

> To make an example of his perfidy, the MVD tortured him to death in the most hideous possible way and allowed all of Russia to know just how Vlasov had finally managed to die and how long the actual process had taken. Vlasov's officers and troops were also just as painfully exterminated.[9]

In March 1946 Smersh was formally closed down and its work taken over by the Third Main Directorate of the MGB.[10] One of the tasks of Smersh as well as of the NKVD/NKGB at the end of the war was, in the words of an official history, to "help the people of liberated countries in establishing and strengthening a free domestic form of government": in other words to ensure the establishment of "people's democracies" along the U.S.S.R.'s Western borders.[11] Under Abakumov's leadership that was also one of the main priorities of the MGB. In conversation with the Yugoslav Communist Milovan Djilas in 1944

Stalin redefined the sixteenth-century maxim "cuius regio eius religio" which had allowed rulers to determine the religion of their countries:

> This war is not as in the past; whoever occupies a territory also imposes on it his own social system. Everyone imposes his own system as far as his army has power to do so. It cannot be otherwise.[12]

"People's democracies" were imposed on the countries of Eastern Europe by a combination of force and deception, in which the NKGB/MGB played a central role. Many of those who collaborated in turning their countries into "people's democracies" were careerists, time servers, or people who reluctantly accepted that Soviet power excluded other options. In every Eastern European state, however, there was also a (usually small) Communist or fellow-traveling minority possessed of the same visionary faith in socialist construction that had inspired the first generation of Bolshevik revolutionaries and young Soviet idealists during the first Five Year Plan. To the Hungarian Communist George Hodos, later one of the victims of a Stalinist show trial:

> It was a joy to be a communist, to serve the cause of humanity, to be present at the birth of a better future. After the horrors of the Second World War, at last the world seemed to be taking on a semblance of order. And what a beautiful order it promised to be. . . . We were building a socialist Hungary under the banner of the communist party.[13]

All over Eastern Europe faith in the future of socialist construction was inextricably intertwined with worship of Stalin. For the Communist faithful throughout the world the reality of the brutal, morbidly suspicious despot had been replaced by a heroic myth image, which personified their own vision of a better world. At the end of the war even Djilas and most Yugoslav Communists, soon to be condemned as arch-heretics, saw themselves as loyal Stalinists:

> Stalin was not only the undisputed leader of genius, he was the incarnation of the very idea and dream of the new society. This idolatry of Stalin's personality, as well as of more or less everything in the Soviet Union, acquired irrational forms and proportions. . . . Among us Communists there were men with

a developed aesthetic sense and a considerable acquaintance
with literature and philosophy and yet we waxed enthusiastic
not only over Stalin's views but also over the "perfection" of
the way he formulated them. I myself referred many times
in discussions to the crystal clarity of his style, the penetration of his logic, and the aptness of his commentaries, as
though they were expressions of the most exalted wisdom.[14]

In Poland, whose political transformation was the first to cause serious
dissension between Stalin and his allies, such enthusiasm was rare.
"Communism," said Stalin in 1944, "does not fit the Poles. They are
too individualistic, too nationalistic."[15] The interwar Polish Communist
Party was among the most unpopular in Europe—with Moscow as well
as with its own fellow citizens. Within Poland the Party was forced to
operate clandestinely, and many of its militants were jailed. Those who
fled to Moscow fared even worse: in the course of the Great Terror
nearly all were shot.[16] Almost the only militants to survive were those
who, like the future Party leader Wladyslaw Gomulka, were locked in
the comparative safety of Polish jails and a small number working for
the NKVD who had collaborated in the liquidation of their comrades.
The Polish Communist Party ceased to exist. In 1938 the Comintern
declared it formally dissolved. The main Polish wartime resistance
movement, the Home Army (Armia Krajowa or AK) was resolutely
anti-Communist, bitterly resentful of the Soviet part in the 1939 Polish
partition and of the Stalinist persecution that had followed.

After the German invasion of Russia, however, Stalin decided
that the time had come to resurrect Polish Communism. In December
1941 a group of Polish NKVD agents, led by Marceli Nowotko, Boleslaw Molojec, and Pawel Finder, landed by parachute to revive the
prewar Party under the new name Polish Workers Party (PPR). Finder
renewed contact with Wladyslaw Gomulka and made him secretary of
the Warsaw Party committee. Nowotko was also entrusted with a
secret mission to destabilize the Home Army. On instructions from the
NKVD he denounced a number of AK partisans to the Gestapo. Not
realizing that Nowotko's contacts with the Gestapo were part of an
NKVD plan, Molojec killed him as a traitor, and was himself sentenced
to death by a Party tribunal.

Finder's murder by the Gestapo then left the way clear for
Gomulka to become secretary-general of the PPR. He was not Stalin's
choice but became Party leader at a time when the radio link with

Moscow had been broken. Gomulka organized the People's Guard as an underground Communist militia, which was intended to rival the Home Army. The Party leadership, however, was well aware that its prospects of power depended on Soviet rather than Polish support.[17] Its leading ideologist, Alfred Lampe, wrote shortly before his death in 1943: "What kind of Poland would not be anti-Soviet?"[18]

On July 23, 1944, Stalin established a Polish National Committee of Liberation in Lublin as the nucleus of a future puppet government. As the Red Army approached Warsaw, a Soviet broadcast called its population to arms: "There is not a second to lose! . . . People of Warsaw to arms! Throw out the German invader and take your freedom!" On August 1 the Home Army in Warsaw launched an insurrection. For the next two months the people of Warsaw fought desperately while the Red Army looked on from the other side of the Vistula. While a quarter of a million Poles were killed, Stalin contemptuously dismissed their leaders as "a handful of power-seeking criminals," refusing for over a month even to allow Anglo-American aircraft flying supplies to the insurgents from Italy to refuel at Russian airfields and have their wounded air crews given medical attention. The suppression of the Warsaw Rising crushed the Home Army as an effective challenge to the Communists.[19]

In the wake of the Red Army as it advanced through the ruins of Poland came a powerful detachment of the NKVD to hunt down the remnants of the Home Army and establish Communist power. At its head was a future chief of both the KGB and the GRU: General Ivan Aleksandrovich Serov, short, tough, and brutal, an intense Russian nationalist who had supervised the mass deportations from the Caucasus.[20] Serov tracked down Home Army men by methods that ranged from infiltration by PPR members to intercepting and decrypting their radio communications.[21] In January 1945, when the Lublin Committee turned itself into a provisional government, the Home Army formally disbanded. Some of its members formed an anti-Communist underground; some joined the Communists; most gave up the struggle, grateful simply to have survived thus far.[22]

Besides liquidating opposition, the main priority of the NKVD was to found a Polish version of itself, eventually entitled the Urzad Bezpieczeństwa (UB). Its head, first as departmental director in the Lublin Committee, then as minister for public security until 1954, was Stanislaw Radkiewicz, a prewar Communist militant born in Byelorussia, who, like Gomulka, owed his survival to incarceration in a

Polish prison. Radkiewicz combined brutality with charm and persuasiveness. The first American ambassador in postwar Warsaw, Arthur Bliss Lane, wrote after calling on him in 1945:

> If his customary technique, as we had heard, was to instill terror in the hearts of his callers, to us he showed great cordiality and urbanity. He was a good-looking man, apparently of Russian Semitic origin, with carefully-combed oily black hair, and keen, mobile, aesthetic face. He opened our conversation by remarking, with understandable logic, that Poland had been so disorganized by the Nazis that the new government had been forced to call on one of her allies for assistance in the reconstruction of the country. The United States and England were far away; Russia was Poland's closest neighbor. . . . He frankly admitted that the Russians had lent him two hundred NKVD instructors, who would organize the Polish Security Police along Soviet lines.[23]

Immediately after the formation of the Lublin Committee, Radkiewicz had been summoned to Moscow to receive instructions from Beria. He returned to Poland with two senior NKVD/NKGB advisers, Generals Selivanowski and Melnikov, who supervised the setting up of the UB under the overall control of Serov.[24] The UB had a difficult birth. By December 1944 it had gathered 2,500 recruits, but Radkiewicz complained to the PPR Politburo that they were young and inexperienced, with "leaders of poor quality." His deputy, Roman Romkowski, a veteran NKVD agent, claimed, however, a series of successes against the Home Army: "We have hit the leadership in all provinces." The Politburo was also confidentially informed that conditions were "difficult" because "The Red Army was destroying and pillaging" (and, though the minutes are too squeamish to mention it, raping girls and women on a massive scale).[25] Nazi terror had been replaced by Soviet terror. General Zygmunt Berling, formerly commander of the Russian First Polish Army and a member of the Lublin Committee, later wrote to Gomulka:

> Beria's lackeys from the NKVD wreaked devastation over the whole country. Criminal elements from Radkiewicz's apparatus assisted them without hindrance. During legal and illegal searches the population had its property stolen and

entirely innocent people were deported or thrown into jail. People were shot like dogs. . . . Nobody knew what they were accused of, by whom they had been arrested or what it was intended to do with them.[26]

At the plenum of the PPR Central Committee in May 1945 Gomulka admitted that the UB, like the NKVD, had got out of control:

> Of course the security apparatus is never loved, but it seems to be developing into a state within a state. It has its own policy and nobody is allowed to interfere. . . . Our prisons treat their inmates like animals. Members of the security apparatus become demoralized and drop out. . . . The result will be that we will become the lowest NKVD front organization.

Radkiewicz was equally gloomy:

> There are signs of a crisis in Security which numbers 11,000 men but has only 25 percent of positions filled. . . . There is a large number of alien accretions and a considerable hostile element. . . . It is difficult to say whether the [Soviet] advisers have done more good than harm. In the first phase they helped us; in the second they did us harm. This has now been changed so that it is not necessary to get rid of them for the time being.[27]

Whether the NKVD advisers stayed, however, was determined not by the Poles but by Moscow, and Stalin had no intention of allowing them to leave. Throughout Eastern Europe Communist-run security services, supervised, save in Yugoslavia and Albania, by Soviet "advisers," played a crucial part in the transition to "people's democracies." Political development in most East European states followed the same basic pattern. More or less genuine coalitions, which gave significant representation to a number of non-fascist parties but left the security services and the other main levers of power in Communist hands, were established immediately after liberation. Following intervals of various lengths, these governments were replaced by Communist-run bogus coalitions, which paved the way in turn for one-party states taking their lead from Moscow.[28] In Poland, however, coalition government was bogus from the outset. The Lublin Committee, recognized by the U.S.S.R. as the Polish provisional government in January 1945, was rightly regarded by the Western Allies, who withheld recognition, as an unrepresentative puppet regime.

The destruction of Polish liberties, though its extent was only dimly grasped in Washington, was the main reason for the first serious clash between Roosevelt's successor, Harry S. Truman, and the Soviet Union. At his first meeting with Molotov on April 23, 1945, the new and inexperienced president declared bluntly that U.S.-Soviet relations could no longer be "on the basis of a one-way street": in future Russia would have to keep to its agreements. Molotov turned white and stuttered in reply: "I have never been talked to like this in my life." Truman, by his own account, retorted: "Carry out your agreements and you won't get talked to like that."[29]

Since Roosevelt's death Harry Hopkins had lived in near-bedridden seclusion at his Georgetown home.[30] He was to survive the late president by only nine months. Akhmerov, however, claiming to speak as usual on behalf of Stalin, helped to convince him that he had once again a crucial role to play at a critical moment in U.S.-Soviet relations.[31] In mid-May Averell Harriman, the American ambassador to Moscow, and Charles Bohlen jointly conceived the idea that Truman might send Hopkins on a mission to Moscow to thrash out current problems directly with Stalin. When they put the idea to him, "Hopkins' response was wonderful to behold. Although he appeared too ill even to get out of bed and walk across N Street, the mere intimation of a flight to Moscow converted him into the traditional old fire horse at the sound of the alarm."[32] The State Department and the new secretary of State, James F. Byrnes, thought Hopkins too inclined to take Soviet rhetoric at face value. Truman overrode their objections.[33] Moscow's reaction to the proposed visit was prompt and enthusiastic.[34]

At his first meeting with Stalin on May 26 Hopkins emphasized the importance of ensuring the survival of "the entire structure of world cooperation and relations with the Soviet Union which President Roosevelt and the Marshal had labored so hard to build." The main reason for Americans' current loss of faith in cooperation with the U.S.S.R. seemed to be "our inability to carry into effect the Yalta Agreement on Poland."[35] A number of historians, though unaware that the NKVD/NKGB regarded Hopkins as a Soviet agent, have nonetheless been struck by his pro-Soviet approach to the negotiations. Vojtech Mastny comments:

Hopkins deplored the recent unfavorable turn of American
public opinion about Russia but avoided linking the change
with any Soviet action. By commending Stalin for having
seconded Roosevelt's efforts at a new "structure of world
cooperation," he implied instead that the Russian leader
could not possibly be blamed. By elimination the absent
British were thus left the villains and Stalin lost no time in
blaming them.[36]

Stalin claimed that British Conservatives, Churchill included, opposed
the Soviet plan for a free Poland because they wished to recreate a
hostile *cordon sanitaire* on the frontiers of the U.S.S.R. Instead of
taking issue with this disingenuous interpretation of British policy,
Hopkins emphasized twice that American policy was quite different.
The United States wanted to see friendly states all along the Soviet
border. In that case, replied Stalin, they could easily reach agreement
on Poland. Hopkins said that he was glad to hear him say so.[37]

"We would," continued Hopkins next day, "accept any government in Poland which was desired by the Polish people and was at the
same time friendly to the Soviet government." Neither Hopkins nor, for
the moment, Truman grasped the embarrassing truth that no Polish
government could be both. Professor Mastny fairly concludes—again
without knowledge of the NKVD view of Hopkins—that "in the end,
Hopkins acceded to the Soviet formula. . . . The Polish question was
thus settled between Hopkins and Stalin without the British." The
Communist-dominated provisional government was enlarged by a
token representation of Polish exiles in London, with Stanislaw Mikolajczyk being given the prestigious but largely powerless position of
deputy prime minister. The insoluble problem of arranging free elections for a permanent government was put to one side.[38]

Though Hopkins had gone beyond his instructions, Truman
welcomed the agreement as a means of patching up the wartime alliance.[39] The NKGB believed that with Hopkins's help it had triumphed
over American imperialism.[40] The probability is, however, that though
Hopkins's influence on Roosevelt and, initially, on Truman served the
Soviet interest, he was never a conscious Soviet agent. The NKGB,
through Akhmerov, had once again exploited both his sense of a personal mission to secure the future of Soviet-American relations and his
naïveté in believing that Stalin shared his commitment to a new world
order.

The face-saving formula agreed on by Stalin and Hopkins survived the final meeting of the Big Three (from which Hopkins was absent) at Potsdam in July and August 1945. But, as the evidence of Soviet abuse of human rights in Eastern Europe became increasingly difficult to ignore, even Hopkins's faith in the future of U.S.-Soviet relations began to crumble. Scarcely had he left Moscow when a show trial began of sixteen Polish leaders for whom he had sought clemency.[41] He died in January 1946 an at least partly disillusioned man.

The American ambassador in Warsaw, Arthur Bliss Lane, gloomily concluded "that the NKVD and UB held the reins of power so tightly that no democracy in our sense of the word was possible for Poland for years to come."[42] Soviet control of the UB was tightest during the period 1944 to 1947, when there were Soviet advisers with the right of final decision in every UB office.[43] Instructors at the first UB schools had to submit drafts of their lectures to the advisers, who made what changes they pleased. Between 1947 and 1949 Soviet advisers were withdrawn from UB district offices. By Stalin's death in 1953 advisers outside Warsaw had been cut back to two in each provincial office.

In some operations, notably election rigging, the UB proved a backward pupil. At Yalta Molotov had declared that it would take only a month to organize Polish elections. In the event the UB was so unsure of its ability to deal with the challenge from the two leading opposition parties, the Peasant Party and the Christian Labor Party, that elections were postponed until January 1947, a month deliberately chosen because of its heavy snowfalls.[44] Even after two years to prepare for ballot rigging, the evidence of election fraud was so obvious that it embarrassed even the UB's Soviet advisers.

Within a year opposition parties had been effectively abolished. But to avoid further embarrassments at the next general election in 1952 and ensure a massive majority for the Communist-dominated Polish United Workers' Party (PZPR, formed after a "merger" with the Socialists in 1948), the UB's Soviet advisers organized a three-month training program run by Ms. Konopko, who gave detailed instruction in forgery and the methods necessary to prepare election results in advance. The power of the Polish Catholic Church, however, presented the UB with problems outside the immediate experience of its Soviet advisers. One of the UB's most cynical innovations was to train one of its officers, Lieutenant Colonel Jierek Labanowski, to pose, as required, as a Catholic priest, Protestant minister, or Jewish rabbi when those condemned to death exercised their legal right to ask for the presence of a cleric at their executions.[45]

In the spring of 1945, with the Communist takeover of Poland satisfactorily underway, the future chairman of the KGB, General Serov, moved to Germany to head the "internal" (NKVD/NKGB) section of the Soviet Military Administration (SMA), which installed itself under Marshal Zhukov in a huge compound in the Berlin suburb of Karlshorst, surrounded by an iron fence, barbed wire, sentries, police patrols, and dogs. Serov created an NKGB (later MGB) enclave within the SMA compound, with his headquarters in a former hospital, once-elegant family houses for his senior officers, and a large motor pool. Only NKGB/MGB personnel, eventually numbering about two thousand, were allowed to enter.[46] Serov organized a vast NKGB/MGB network in the Soviet zone, headed by Major General Melnikov, former adviser to the infant Polish UB. The zone was divided into regions (*Bezirke*), each with its own NKGB/MGB headquarters and further subdivided into districts (*Kreise*) controlled by "operation groups." This elaborate *apparat* monitored political parties, churches, and trade unions, and guided the process of sovietization. Karlshorst also became the largest base outside the U.S.S.R. for Soviet espionage directed against the West. There was a further NKGB/MGB base at Leipzig, which dealt with illegals.[47]

"Communism on a German," complained Stalin, "is like putting a saddle on a cow."[48] The KPD leadership returned from its Moscow exile on April 30, 1945, the day of Hitler's suicide in his Berlin bunker. Its two most prominent members, the sixty-nine-year-old Wilhelm Pieck (later first president of the German Democratic Republic) and the fifty-two-year-old Walter Ulbricht (later first secretary of the GDR's ruling party), were both veterans of the Comintern underground as well as long-standing NKVD protégés.[49] Serov and the KPD leadership trod warily at first, uncertain what the precise mechanics of a Communist takeover would be. Ulbricht announced to his inner circle on his return from Moscow: "It's got to look democratic but we must have everything under our control."[50]

His first tactic in the summer of 1945 was to bring the KPD and the three other parties authorized by the SMA into an informal anti-Nazi coalition. Free elections in the Soviet zone would probably have produced a Social Democrat (SPD) majority, but the orgy of rape and looting with which some units of the Red Army celebrated victory destroyed any prospect that the KPD could establish itself as the leading party without relying on the immense coercive power of the SMA and NKGB/MGB. Conscious of the much greater popularity of the Social Democrats, the Soviet viceroy Marshal Zhukov began putting pressure on the SPD leadership to agree to unification with the Communists. The British received complaints from two prominent Social Democrats who had been ordered by an NKGB officer "to agitate for unification on penalty of being arrested . . . if they did not. Some who refused had already been placed in Sachsenhausen prison"—previously a Nazi concentration camp.[51] Erich Ollenhauer, chairman of the West German SPD, later claimed that at least twenty thousand recalcitrant East German Social Democrats had been persecuted, imprisoned, or even killed between December 1945 and April 1946.

The result of the massive campaign of intimidation orchestrated by the NKGB was the fusion of the KPD and SPD as the Socialist Unity Party (Sozialistische Einheitspartei Deutschlands or SED) on April 22, 1946, the anniversary of Lenin's birth, and the effective suppression of social democracy in East Germany.[52] Despite intimidation, the first postwar municipal and regional elections in the autumn of 1946 gave the SED barely 50 percent of the vote but did nothing to halt progress toward a one-party state.[53]

In August 1947 Order Number 201 of the SMA created an East German security police, Kommissariat 5 (K-5), supervised by MGB advisers, which became the forerunner of the State Security Police (SSD) established after the founding of the German Democratic Republic (GDR) in October 1949.[54] The head of K-5, and later of the SSD, was Wilhelm Zaisser, a veteran German GRU agent, who, as General Gómez, had commanded the XIIIth International Brigade in the Spanish Civil War. Among his chief assistants was another long-standing GRU agent, Rudolf Herrnstadt, whose achievements had included the recruitment of the German diplomat Rudolf von Scheliha.[55] The expert instruction provided by the MGB in East Germany as in Poland included guidance in the techniques of ballot rigging.[56] The first GDR national elections in 1950 gave the SED a satisfying vote of 99.7 percent, twice its poll at the regional elections in 1946.

In interwar Germany, until the rise of Hitler, there had been a mass Communist Party. In Rumania, by contrast, the interwar Party had been almost as weak as in Poland, with a membership drawn largely from ethnic minorities. During the final year of the war the Party had to be reconstructed almost from scratch. In March 1944 the NKGB dispatched a three-man group headed by its Rumanian agent Emil Bodnaras to prepare the Party leadership for the arrival of the Red Army. Bodnaras succeeded in holding a secret meeting in a prison hospital with Gheorghe Gheorghiu-Dej and other jailed Communist leaders, at which Gheorghiu-Dej denounced the existing secretary of the underground Party, Stefan Foris, as a police informer. Gheorghiu-Dej became Party secretary in his stead, the first in a series of astute maneuvers that were eventually to give him victory in a power struggle with the Moscow Bureau of Rumanian Communist exiles, led by the NKGB agents Ana Pauker and Vasili Luca. After the Red Army occupied Rumania in August 1944 Gheorghiu-Dej was released and Foris thrown into jail. Two years later, on Gheorghiu-Dej's orders, Foris was hanged without trial.[57]

During the winter of 1944–45 Guards of Patriotic Defense, trained by Bodnaras and the NKGB, gradually took over key positions in the police and security forces. In March 1945, after seven months of broadly based coalition governments, King Michael of Rumania yielded to a Soviet ultimatum demanding a Communist-dominated "popular democratic" regime led by the fellow traveler Petru Groza. Rigged elections in November 1946 gave the Groza government a huge majority. In 1947 the main opposition parties were dissolved and a show trial was held of opposition leaders charged with plotting against state security. On December 31, 1947, King Michael was forced to abdicate and the Rumanian People's Republic was proclaimed. At its heart was the omnipresent People's Security (Directoratul General al Sigurantei Poporolui or DGSP) and its Soviet advisers.[58] Gheorghiu-Dej's even more megalomaniac successor, Nicolae Ceauşescu, later acknowledged that "in the past" (in other words, under Gheorghiu-Dej) internal Party matters "were sometimes referred to the security organs, thus creating conditions for interference in the life of the Party and seriously undermining its authority and leading role."[59] The DGSP was used not merely to enforce Stalinist orthodoxy but also to further Gheorghiu-Dej's personal ambitions. Since Gheorghiu-Dej repeatedly reaffirmed his loyalty to the Soviet Union and its great leader, however, his Soviet advisers allowed him to have his head.

Like Serov, who headed NKGB/MGB operations successively in Poland and East Germany, Dmitri Georgievich Fedichkin, chief Soviet adviser in Rumania from 1944 to 1947, was a tough, uncompromising high flier. Born in 1903, he had gained experience in the Balkans in the 1930s and acted like a viceroy in postwar Bucharest, giving frequent instructions to Gheorghiu-Dej.[60] His photograph, which shows a square-built man with round face and glasses, has a place of honor on the walls of the Memory Room in today's KGB First Chief Directorate. The citation beneath includes tributes to his work both as NKGB/MGB "adviser" in Bucharest and later in developing "active measures" against the West. Serov, who at the time was an even more prominent Soviet adviser and went on to become first head of the KGB, has no placc in the Memory Room, disqualified both by his closer involvement in Stalinist atrocities and by his suicide in 1962.[61]

The Communist takeover in Sofia, Bulgaria, was even more rapid than in Bucharest. Strengthened by Slavophil affinity with Soviet Russia, Communism, while far from the dominant force in Bulgarian society, had much stronger roots in Bulgaria than in Poland and Rumania. Though among the most backward of European states, interwar Bulgaria had the reputation of producing the Comintern's best Bolsheviks.[62] By his successful defense in Leipzig against the Nazi charge of responsibility for the Reichstag Fire in 1933, the charismatic Bulgarian Communist Georgi Dimitrov had made himself the hero of the anti-fascist movement. From 1935 to 1943 he was the Comintern's last secretary-general.

As the Red Army crossed the Bulgarian border in September 1944, the Communist-dominated Fatherland Front carried out a successful coup d'état. Within three months Communist Party membership had risen from 15,000 to 750,000. The Communist People's Militia, which replaced the old policc force, and an NKGB-supervised secret police began a reign of terror.[63] Even Dimitrov was well aware that his bodyguard and brother-in-law, Vulko Chervenkov, whom he had saved from liquidation during the Terror, had been recruited by the secret police to spy on him.[64] After four months of coalition government, a bogus coalition of Communists and fellow travelers took power in January 1945. Rigged elections in November 1945 gave the Fatherland Front an 88 percent majority. Despite a courageous rearguard action by the remnants of the opposition, Bulgaria became a people's republic in December 1947.[65] For the next generation it was the most loyal of Soviet satellites.

In Hungary and Czechoslovakia multiparty democracy proved more resistant to Communist takeover than elsewhere in Eastern Europe.

The Hungarian general election of November 1945 was won decisively by the Smallholders' Party, with 57 percent of the vote, the Socialists and Communists trailing behind with 17 percent each. In the new Hungarian Republic proclaimed on February 1, 1946, both the president, Dr. Zoltán Tildy, and the prime minister of the coalition government, Dr. Ferenc Nagy, came from the Smallholders' Party. The presence of Soviet occupation forces, however, ensured that the primacy of the Smallholders would be short-lived. The most powerful member of Ferenc Nagy's cabinet was the Communist deputy prime minister, Mátyás Rákosi (born Róth). The Smallholders' finance minister, Nicholas Nyaradi, considered him:

> . . . the most able Communist in Hungary, Moscow-trained in propaganda, sabotage, mob psychology and political warfare. Rákosi was one of the smartest men of *any* political persuasion I have ever met, and also a past master at that quality which makes actors, trapeze performers and politicians great—*timing*. His Russian training had told him exactly *what* to do; his own instinct for timing told him *when* to do it.[66]

The most formidable of the levers controlled by the Communists was the security police supervised by Soviet "advisers"; it was known initially as the AVO (Államvédelmi Osztály), later the AVH (Államvédelmi Hatóság). The AVO functioned from the first as a Communist private army. It was the one organization, Rákosi later admitted, "in which our Party demanded the leadership and tolerated neither division [of power] nor respect of the proportions in the coalition. . . . We held this agency in our hands from the day of its birth and saw to it that it remained a reliable, sharp weapon in the fight for a people's democracy."[67]

The head of AVO was a diminutive Jewish tailor with a Hitler mustache, Gábor Péter (born Benó Auspitz), who had previously worked for the NKVD. In the early stages of the postwar coalition Péter went out of his way to avoid alarming non-Communist ministers. Nyaradi found him "totally epicene":

> He flutters, he minces, lisps, his wrists are limp, his hands never still. When talking to him—in an unofficial capacity, that is to say—one always feels that he is about to whip out

his tape-measure, chalk one's suit here and there. . . . The other quality . . . is his love of flowers. The window-boxes of 60 Andrássy Út [AVO headquarters] burgeon ivy and pansies, while Péter's trim, sunny little office is like Titania's bower. Geraniums are everywhere—pink, red and white— their slightly sulphuric odor almost overpowering to the nostrils. To hold a conversation with Péter in his office is like talking to a fluttering maiden lady who has at last achieved a little garden plot of her own. He speaks with pruning-shears in hand, leaping from trellis to pot to vase to bowl. "Oh! Mr. Minister!" Snip at the *Pelargonium*. "Dear me, Dr. Nyaradi." Snip at the *Viola tricolor hortensis.* "Goodness, Mr. Minister!" Snip at the *Hedera helix.* It is almost laughable, unbelievable that such a man can be the most feared in Hungary.[68]

Most of Péter's visitors saw a different side to his character. "You had better realize that you can count on nobody's support, nobody's protection here," he told them. "You understand? The Party has delivered you into our hands." To make them more cooperative, Péter usually began by ordering a "soling," an expression borrowed from the shoe-making industry by the prewar Hungarian police to describe the beating of prisoners' bare soles with canes or rubber truncheons. More horrific tortures followed. Soviet advisers sometimes took part in interrogations but usually left torture to the AVO.[69]

By 1948 coalition government had gone and Hungary was transformed into a "people's democracy." Rákosi later boasted that he had "sliced off" the non-Communist parties in the coalition "like pieces of salami." The knife used to cut the political salami slices was wielded by the AVO. The first slice was the alleged "right wing" of the Smallholders Party. On the pretext of rooting out "fascist elements" from the Smallholders the AVO arrested those in the Party who had been most outspoken about Communist malpractice. The next slice was the "right wing" of the Social Democrats, again on the pretext of its alleged wartime collaboration with fascism. The largest salami slice, the main body of the Smallholders, was also the most difficult and required direct Soviet intervention. The AVO manufactured a conspiracy involving the Smallholders' secretary-general, Béla Kovács. When the National Assembly proved reluctant to suspend his parliamentary immunity, Kovács was arrested by Soviet military police on a charge of plotting against the occupation forces. In May 1947 the Smallholders' prime minister Ferenc Nagy was intimidated into not returning from a Swiss holiday by the threat of arrest if he did so.[70]

Even skillful salami tactics and electoral fraud, however, did not immediately produce a Communist majority. At the general election of August 1947 the Communists, though becoming the largest party for the first time, gained only 24 percent of the vote. According to an eyewitness, there was gloom at AVO headquarters at the comparative failure of its election rigging (subsequently remedied by MGB instruction).[71] The governing coalition, headed by the Communists, nonetheless gained twice as many votes as the opposition. The smallest of its three coalition partners, the National Peasant Party, which gained 9 percent of the vote, was already headed by a secret Communist, Ferenc Erdei. In the winter of 1947–48 Rákosi reduced the government to a bogus coalition, in which the presence of a few non-Communist figureheads inadequately disguised the reality of Communist rule. With the effective creation of a one-party state in 1948, sanctified by a new constitution in the following year, the anti-Semitic Beria derisively described Rákosi as "the Jewish King of Hungary."[72]

In Czechoslovakia, uniquely among the postwar Soviet satellites, the Communist Party, helped by memories of Western betrayal at Munich, emerged from the war as easily the most popular political party in the country. At free elections in 1946 it gained 38 percent of the vote, more than twice the share of any other party. The Communists also successfully infiltrated other parties in the ruling coalition. General Ludvik Svoboda, minister of defense from 1945 to 1950 (and later president of the Republic), was officially nonparty. But he later admitted that all the time he had been, in reality, "a faithful and well-disciplined" Communist, asked by the Party to conceal his membership in order to assist its eventual takeover.[73]

As in the rest of Eastern Europe, the Communists almost from the outset controlled the Ministry of the Interior and both the police and security service (Státní Bezpečnost or StB), which came under it. In the absence of a Soviet occupying force, their role was even more important in Czechoslovakia than in Hungary. At the insistence of President Beneš, Department Z in the Ministry of the Interior, which controlled the StB, was initially headed by a Social Democrat, Josef Bártík. Communists in the StB quickly used a former Gestapo collaborator to manufacture charges of wartime collaboration against Bártík and force his resignation. Bártík's successor and former deputy, Bedřich Pokorný, himself had to be replaced after he had used forged evidence to discredit the general secretary of the National Socialist Party (despite its name, not to be confused with the Nazis). The Communists then installed a nonparty front man, General František Janda, who left the running of Department Z to his Communist deputy Jindřich Veselý.[74]

The functioning of the StB was overseen by two NKGB/MGB advisers, who used the names Tikhonov and Khazyanov and ran numerous Czechoslovak agents. Tikhonov was the former NKVD/NKGB resident in wartime Britain, Ivan Chichayev. The Czech historian Karel Kaplan concluded from a close examination of Party and state archives in the late 1960s that the network of Soviet agents within the Communist Party was "in general very dense." Among them were Štěpán Plaček, successively head of the Provincial Security Department (1945–47) and commander of Domestic Intelligence (1947–48); Bedřich Reicin, commander of Defense Intelligence; and Karel Šváb, chief of the Registry Department of the Communist Party Central Committee, which gathered intelligence on other parties and the church. NKGB/MGB agents in other parties included Ján Ševčik of the Democrats and Vojtěch Erban of the Social Democrats.[75]

By the winter of 1947–48 both the StB and its Soviet advisers were seriously alarmed at the steady decline in support for the Communist Party. In January 1948 the Prague Institute of Public Opinion forecast that the Communist share of the vote in the spring elections would fall to 28 percent.[76] The exclusion from power during 1947 of the two strongest Western Communist parties, those of France and Italy, strengthened the foreboding of the Czechoslovak Party leadership. Chichayev and "Khazyanov" forwarded a stream of pessimistic assessments to Moscow Center. "Khazyanov" informed Plaček, the author of an alarmist report alleging preparations by non-Communist parties for a coup d'état, that his report had been praised by Stalin himself. Moscow Center ordered Plaček and its other agents to draw up a list of the Communists' leading opponents as part of a plan to "decapitate reaction." Simultaneously the StB began to accuse the Party leadership of "coddling reaction" and to demand that it hasten the emergence of a people's democracy.[77]

On the pretext of providing personal protection for members of the government, all ministers were given StB bodyguards, whose real job was to spy on them. A non-Communist minister complained in

January 1948 that StB officers were able to "come in at any moment to scan [ministers'] writing desks, to take an interest in where we keep the telephone in our apartments, with whom we speak on the telephone, who our other contacts are, and so on." Department F, an illegal StB unit directed by Karel Šváb, specialized in collecting compromising material on non-Communist politicians, and placed agents in the National Socialist and People's parties. A small group within the department, known as Commission RR, organized provocations, which ranged from shouting subversive slogans at non-Communist rallies, which were then broken up, to manufacturing an "anti-State conspiracy" in Slovakia. Karel Kaplan concludes, on the basis of his study of classified Czechoslovak archives, that the MGB advisers Chichayev and "Khazyanov" had "an increasingly predominant managing role" in running both Department F and Commission RR "behind the backs of the leading Communist politicians."[78]

Klement Gottwald, the Communist Party chairman (and, from July 1946, prime minister), did not believe alarmist StB reports of an imminent coup, involving the armed forces, engineered by other political parties. Nor did most of the Party leadership. But they were convinced that their opponents were seeking to maneuver them out of power, and that it was necessary to launch a preemptive strike. Early in 1948 Prokop Drtina, the National Socialist minister of justice, led an unsuccessful attempt by non-Communist ministers to establish a commission to investigate StB abuses. On February 19 the Soviet deputy foreign minister, V. A. Zorin, until recently ambassador in Prague, arrived to urge Gottwald to stage a final showdown with the Communists' opponents. Gottwald agreed to a showdown but rejected Zorin's pressing advice to request Soviet military assistance ("the one instance in his entire life," according to Kaplan, when he disobeyed Soviet instructions).[79]

In the event the opposition played into Gottwald's hands. On February 20 Catholic, Democrat, and National Socialist ministers resigned, believing they could force the government to dissolve and hold new elections. The Social Democrat ministers, however, remained. Instead of dissolving parliament, Gottwald on February 29 formed a new National Front government composed solely of Communists and fellow travelers. Self-appointed "action committees" of the National Front, under the benevolent eye of the police and StB, usurped the role of Parliament and approved wholesale nationalization. President Beneš gave in to Communist pressure. Rigged elections in May completed the

Communist conquest of power. In June Gottwald replaced Beneš as president. Gottwald died, appropriately, in 1953 from pneumonia contracted at Stalin's funeral.[80]

Yugoslavia was the only postwar East European state (until Albania in 1968) in which a Communist regime broke with Moscow. At the end of the war, however, there was no sign that the Yugoslav Party leader and prime minister, Marshal Tito, was destined to become one of the main targets of the MGB. Tito (born Josip Broz) had been one of the few leading Yugoslav Communists exiled in Moscow to survive the Terror, becoming secretary-general of the Yugoslav Party in 1937 as the protégé of the NKVD. At the time, as Tito's future critic Milovan Djilas later acknowledged, there seemed nothing demeaning about an NKVD connection:

> A link with Soviet Intelligence was necessary to the Party—
> especially given its illegal status—for organizational reasons,
> and a link between an individual Party member and Soviet
> Intelligence was regarded as a recognition, even an honor,
> and fortified one's prestige.

Tito dutifully denounced his purged comrades during the Terror in the Party organ *Proleter* with the usual Stalinist invective, as Trotskyists, traitors, factionalists, spies, and anti-Party elements.[81] When Tito became wartime leader of the Communist partisans, an NKVD agent, Josip Kopinić, code-named Vazduh (Air), acted as his radio link with Moscow. At the end of the war, writes Djilas, "Soviet Intelligence paid special attention to Tito."[82]

There was no hint at the end of the war of the violent confrontation between Stalin and Tito that was to erupt only three years later. Despite his own subsequent loathing for Stalinism, Djilas insisted even in retrospect:

> The fact is that not a single Party leader was anti-Soviet—not
> before the war, not during, not after. . . . Leaders and ordi-
> nary Party members could not have been as united or as
> imbued with ideology had they not been devoted to the
> "leading power of Socialism." Stalin and the Soviet Union
> were our cornerstone and point of spiritual origin.

Much of the Western press described Yugoslavia as the Soviet "Satellite Number One." Stalin too appeared to single Tito out for praise. When Tito's reception during his visit to Moscow for President Kalinin's funeral in 1946 was recounted by "leading comrades" after their return, "they were in ecstasy, with reason suspended, eyes shining, smiles gleaming. Even Tito would glow with pride in 'humble' silence and self-restraint."[83]

Stalin and the NKGB, however, were concerned by Tito's self-confidence and capacity for independent judgment. Unlike any of the people's democracies in the making, the Yugoslav partisans had won their victory against the Germans and Italians chiefly through their own efforts. Tito declared soon after V-E Day: "We will not be dependent on anyone ever again." At the end of the war, in order to avoid premature offense to his Western Allies, Stalin would have preferred a coalition government composed of representatives both of Tito's National Committee and of the London-based royal government-in-exile led by Ivan Subašic. But Tito made no serious attempt to abide by his own agreement with the government-in-exile concluded at the end of 1944. Though given the post of foreign minister, Subašic resigned in protest at Tito's breach of their agreement in October 1945. A month later Tito's government won a sweeping victory at rigged elections. Like a number of other foreign observers, the British and American representatives believed that in free elections the Communists would have been heavily defeated.[84]

The first, unpublicized Yugoslav-Soviet dispute concerned the interference of the NKGB in Yugoslav affairs. There were early clashes between the NKGB adviser in Belgrade, Lieutenant-Colonel Timofeev, and the head of Tito's security service, Aleksandar-Leka Ranković. Ranković was not easily intimidated. He had been imprisoned and brutally beaten in Yugoslav prisons in the 1930s, and captured and tortured by the Gestapo in 1941 before being rescued in a daring partisan raid. He ended the war as director of the Bureau of People's Protection (OZNA) in Tito's Ministry of Armed Forces. In February 1946 he became interior minister, retaining control of OZNA, which a month later was officially renamed the Administration of State Security (UDBA), though it continued to be unpopularly known by its former name. Djilas found that Timofeev, the Soviet adviser, "did not display those sudden onslaughts of friendliness so characteristic of Russians":

Timofeev would arrive at Ranković's office looking serious and anxious. He would leave either refreshed and invigorated or with his tail between his legs, depending on whether they had discussed mutual collaboration or Ranković had confronted him with indisputable facts about Soviet recruitment of Yugoslav citizens. They would always talk things out as if unimpeded by Ranković's scanty Russian and Timofeev's even scantier Serbian. Then some flagrant case of recruitment would be uncovered and Ranković would again press Timofeev, and the same excuses would be made: this was the work of individual agents; it was not official policy, and certainly not his own.[85]

The recruitment of Yugoslav agents was in reality the NKGB/MGB's major priority in postwar Yugoslavia. Two were in Tito's cabinet. The minister of industry, Andriya Hebrang, formerly partisan leader in Croatia, was successfully blackmailed by the NKGB, which discovered that under torture by the Gestapo he had betrayed some of his comrades. The finance minister, Streten Žujović, also acted as a Soviet informant. One case in 1945 that particularly angered Tito, then ignorant of the moles within his cabinet, was the NKGB's attempted seduction and recruitment of Dušica Perović, the woman who controlled Yugoslav cryptography. When informed of the case by Ranković, Tito exploded: "A spy network is something we will not tolerate! We've got to let them know right away." Tito complained in person to both the Soviet ambassador and the head of the military mission.[86]

　　Though Tito resisted NKGB interference, he had no hesitation in imitating its methods. In four years of warfare one in ten of Yugoslavia's fifteen million people had died. Tito and the Communists had emerged victorious not merely against the Germans and Italians but also in a civil war of unspeakable cruelty. After their victory OZNA began a reign of terror against Mihailovich's Chetniks and other former opponents. Dr. Milan Grol, a former member of the royal government-in-exile, declared while vice-premier in the summer of 1945: "This is not a state; it is a slaughterhouse." Mihailovich himself was captured in 1946 after one of his commanders, captured and recruited by OZNA, lured him from his hiding place; he was executed after a show trial.[87] "The effects of the control that the secret police exerted over all areas of life—seeping into all the pores, infiltrating family and private life," wrote Djilas later, "were poisonous as well for the ruling Party."[88] A British observer, Frank Waddams, wrote in 1946:

> OZNA has complete control over the life, liberty and property of all citizens, and if it chooses to arrest, to imprison without trial, to deport or "to liquidate" anybody, no-one may protest or ask the reason why. That is why the populace is in such a state of terror.

Show trials in 1947 unmasked numerous "spies in the service of foreign imperialists" among the ranks of former Chetniks, "capitalist scum," the Catholic Church, and other opponents of the regime.[89]

Within the Yugoslav Party leadership the sense of common purpose with the Soviet Union and the emerging, Stalinist people's democracies far outweighed resentment at MGB interference. Even at the beginning of 1948 there was no sense of the violent confrontation that was only months away. At the first meeting of Cominform, the postwar successor to the Comintern, in September 1947, the Yugoslav Party was held up as a model to other, less resolute parties. Belgrade was selected as the seat of the future Cominform secretariat. On the Yugoslav side, the main cause of conflict at the beginning of 1948 was the attempt by Soviet advisers in the Yugoslav army to subvert the loyalties of the high command. According to the future Yugoslav representative at the United Nations, Alex Bebler, "On Stalin's orders, Russians penetrated deeper and deeper into the organization of our army, and that is how the trouble started." The split was engineered from the Soviet side. Of all Tito's signs of independence, that which caused most alarm was probably his plan for a Balkan federation, which Stalin seems to have interpreted as a potential challenge to Soviet hegemony. In March 1948 the Soviet Union recalled its military and civilian advisers, and angrily denounced the Yugoslav Party as riddled with both ideological heresy and British spies. On June 28 the Cominform expelled the Yugoslavs and appealed to "healthy elements" in the Party to overthrow the leadership.[90]

Stalin greatly overestimated his own strength. He boasted, according to Khrushchev: "I shall shake my little finger and there will be no more Tito." When that failed, "he shook everything else he could shake," but Tito's hold over the Party, army and state machinery remained unequaled in any other people's democracy. The UDBA and MGB began a vicious intelligence war. Hebrang and Žujović, the two

Soviet moles in Tito's cabinet, were promptly arrested. Three senior Yugoslav officers recruited by Soviet intelligence were intercepted while trying to cross the Rumanian border. Other Soviet agents were discovered even in Tito's bodyguard. According to Djilas there was an MGB plot "to wipe out the Politburo with automatic rifles as they were relaxing over billiards in Tito's villa."

The UDBA's use of terror against Cominform "traitors" rivaled in horror, though not in scale, that of the NKVD in the 1930s. Djilas told Rankovic in the summer of 1948: "Now we are treating Stalin's followers as he treated his enemies." "Almost in despair, Rankovic retorted: 'Don't say that! Don't talk about it!' " Rankovic later admitted that twelve thousand supposed (and, in many cases, imaginary) supporters of Stalin and the Cominform were herded into a concentration camp on Goli Otok (Bare Island). The real figure was probably much greater. According to Djilas, "Evil and shame—evil beyond compare, undying shame—lay in store for the prisoners in the camp." On boarding the boat to Goli Otok, prisoners were thrown headfirst into the hold; on landing they were beaten by a double line of guards and inmates. In the camp they were systematically abused and degraded, their heads plunged into buckets of human excrement if they failed to recant their real or imagined heresies and crimes.[91]

The first major success of the MGB in its secret war with the UDBA was to engineer an anti-Tito coup in Albania. Until the break with Tito, Stalin had been content for Albania to remain a Yugoslav satellite. During the Second World War, Yugoslav "advisers" had reorganized the Albanian Communist Party under the leadership of Enver Hoxha as secretary-general and Koci Xoxe, who became minister of the interior in the Communist-controlled government. "Without the struggle of the peoples of Yugoslavia," said Hoxha after the war, "resistance by the small Albanian nation would have been unthinkable." Under OZNA pressure, the Albanian Party was purged of "deviators" and "Trotskyists," among them: Anastas Ludo, head of the Communist youth organization, shot for "Leftist deviation"; Lazar Fundo, one of the founders of the Albanian Communist Party, who returned disillusioned from Soviet exile in 1944 and was beaten to death before a horrified British military mission; and Mustafa Gjinishi, a Politburo member executed for forming a united anti-fascist front with "bourgeois" groups.

The Albanian Communist Party emerged from the war as virtually a branch of the Yugoslav Party. The Albanian security service, the Sigurimi, was as firmly under OZNA direction as most other East European security services were under NKGB control. Hoxha grew increasingly nervous at the threat to his position from his rival Xoxe, who as minister of the interior was responsible for the Sigurimi and enjoyed Tito's favor. In May 1947 Xoxe organized a show trial of nine anti-Yugoslav members of the People's Congress; all were given long prison sentences for "subversive activities." At the founding meeting of the Cominform in August 1947, the Albanians were represented by the Yugoslav Party. Four months later Stalin told Djilas: "You ought to swallow Albania—the sooner the better!"[92]

The Soviet-Yugoslav conflict in 1948 offered Hoxha the opportunity to win the struggle for power with Xoxe. While Soviet advisers were being withdrawn from Belgrade, MGB officers flooded into Tirana. After Tito's break with Moscow, Hoxha ordered the immediate expulsion of all Yugoslav personnel and turned on his rival. Xoxe tried in vain to save himself by affirming his loyalty to the Soviet Union. He was arrested with his supporters and replaced as minister of the interior by the pro-Soviet Mehmet Shehu, who brought in MGB advisers to purge and reorganize the Sigurimi. After five months of Sigurimi interrogation and torture, supervised by the MGB, Xoxe and his supporters made detailed confessions.

In March 1949 Hoxha visited Moscow to discuss preparations for the show trial of "Koci Xoxe and his gang," which opened two months later. Xoxe confessed that he had been recruited during the war by both British and American intelligence, that he had been personally informed by the head of the British military mission in 1943 that Tito was a British agent, and that he had taken part in a plot jointly devised by Tito and SIS to absorb Albania into Yugoslavia. He was shot for these imaginary crimes in July 1949.[93]

Xoxe's trial and execution were the prelude to a series of show trials of Tito's accomplices real or (more commonly) imagined, orchestrated by the MGB across most of Eastern Europe. Until Stalin's death in 1953 Tito wore the mantle inherited from Trotsky, the great heretic. Unlike Trotsky, Tito emerged unscathed and in the end victorious from a five-year war with the MGB. During the same period the MGB won a series of spectacular successes against Western intelligence services. But, as with the NKVD in the 1930s, much of its energy was simultaneously expended in a war with imaginary enemies.

10

The Cold War: The Stalinist Phase (1945–53)

From the end of the Second World War, the United States began to be referred to in NKGB/MGB communications as the "Main Adversary" *(Glavny Protivnik)*. Forty years later, when Gordievsky was KGB resident-designate in London, the same expression remained in daily use. Great Britain, the main prewar target of NKVD, slipped into second place after 1945, in keeping with its reduced role in the postwar world.[1]

During the Second World War, when British and American energies (despite later Soviet claims that both were already being geared to the Cold War) were overwhelmingly concentrated on the war in Europe and the Pacific, Russian intelligence operations in the West proceeded with fewer hindrances than they were ever to experience again. Peace brought new problems for Moscow Center. The first, paradoxically, was the demobilization of much of the American and British intelligence communities. President Truman's decision to wind up OSS in September 1945 instantly deprived the NKGB of a score of penetration agents in the secret service of the Main Adversary. When the Central Intelligence Agency was founded in 1947, Soviet intelligence had to start again from scratch; penetration of the CIA was never to compare with that of OSS.

In Britain, the postwar winding up of the Ministry of Information and SOE similarly removed Peter Smollett and James Klugmann from positions of influence. Smollett changed his name back to Smolka and returned to journalism in Vienna; Klugmann was demobilized and resumed his career as a Communist militant, eventually becoming the Party's official historian. Demobilization also deprived the Center of its only agent in MI5 and one of its two in SIS. Anthony Blunt left MI5 with the NKGB's blessing. Reports to the Center by his wartime case officers, Anatoli Gorsky and (from the summer of 1944) Boris Krotov, had regularly commented on his tiredness and the stress caused by providing sometimes thousands of documents a month. By the end of the war Moscow had concluded that Blunt's continuance in MI5 would carry serious operational risks. Fitin, the head of INU, wrote on his file in the autumn of 1945:

> This agent carried out such huge, titanic work for us during the war that he must be exhausted. We should leave him in peace for a period of five to ten years.[2]

Shortly before Blunt left MI5 in November 1945 to return to the art world as Surveyor of the King's Pictures and (from 1947) as director of the Courtauld Institute, the strain of his double life led to one extraordinary outburst, which helps to explain Fitin's belief that he was close to breaking point. Blunt told his colleague Colonel "Tar" Robertson, "Well, it's given me great pleasure to pass on the names of every MI5 officer to the Russians!"[3] Fitin seems to have hoped that Leo Long, whom Blunt had run as a subagent during the war, would succeed him in the security service. After the war, Long moved from MI14 in the War Office to the British Control Commission in Germany, where he eventually became deputy director of intelligence.

In 1946 Blunt recommended him for a senior post in MI5 but, allegedly by a narrow margin, the selection board chose another candidate.[4] Thereafter, Long rapidly cooled off, resisting attempts by the Center to put him in regular contact with a case officer. The Center attributed Long's recalcitrance both to the fact that Blunt was no longer available to act as his controller and to a change in his family circumstances. Long's first marriage, to a Communist, had broken up; he had remarried and was bringing up a family. Among the occasional errands that Blunt continued to run for the Center were two or three visits to Germany to seek intelligence from Long.[5]

Like most wartime intelligence recruits, John Cairncross was also demobilized at the end of the war. Unlike Philby, he had not got on well with his secret-service colleagues after leaving Bletchley Park for the SIS headquarters at the Broadway Buildings in 1943. His department chief during the last year of the war, David Footman, head of political intelligence in SIS, found him "an odd person with a chip on his shoulder."[6] Unlike Blunt, however, Cairncross did not take semiretirement from Soviet intelligence. After the war he returned to the Treasury, providing intelligence to his case officer, Boris Krotov, at monthly intervals. Two other members of the Magnificent Five, Guy Burgess and Donald Maclean, had influential positions within the other most prestigious Whitehall department of state. In 1946, Burgess became personal assistant to Hector McNeil, minister of state at the Foreign Office to Ernest Bevin in the postwar Labour government. Maclean, meanwhile, had reestablished his reputation as a high-flying young diplomat in the Washington embassy.[7] Soviet penetration of the Anglo-American intelligence communities had, however, been drastically cut back. The disbandment of OSS left the Center apparently without a single high-level intelligence source in Washington. The closure of SOE, combined with the departure of Blunt from MI5 and Cairncross from SIS, left only one major intelligence mole in London. He, however, was the most remarkable of all the Magnificent Five, perhaps the ablest penetration agent in KGB history. Kim Philby was the only wartime recruit to SIS decorated for his work at the end of the war. Some of his colleagues saw him as a future "C," chief of the secret service.

In addition to the loss of most of its leading wartime agents in the British and American intelligence communities, the NKGB also had to face the problem of two serious postwar defections in North America and an equally serious attempted defection in Turkey. In November 1945, Elizabeth Bentley began revealing to the FBI her extensive knowledge of NKGB operations in the United States. Her defection, in turn, led the FBI to investigate seriously for the first time Whittaker Chambers's evidence of prewar Soviet espionage. Though the usable, corroborated evidence necessary to secure conviction in a court of law was lacking for the great majority of Soviet agents identified by Bentley and Chambers, all ceased to be of significant use to the NKGB. Until Philby set its anxieties at rest after his arrival in Washington in 1949, Moscow continued to fear that the FBI would succeed in gathering enough evidence for a major spy trial of Bentley's former network. Of the four most important agents identified by Bentley and Chambers, only Alger Hiss was ever prosecuted. He left the State Department to become president of the Carnegie Endowment early in 1947, and was sentenced to five years' imprisonment for perjury in 1950. Harry Dexter White, who had left the U.S. Treasury to become first director of the International Monetary Fund in 1945, had a fatal heart attack soon after giving evidence to the House Committee on Un-American Activities in the summer of 1948; Duncan C. Lee, former personal assistant to General Donovan in OSS, and Lauchlin Currie, former assistant to President Roosevelt, both emigrated.[8]

The defection of the cipher clerk Igor Guzenko, in Ottawa in September 1945 was as big a blow to Soviet intelligence as that of Elizabeth Bentley two months later. Guzenko, however, very nearly failed to defect. When he first sought help on the evening of September 5 at the offices of the Ottawa *Journal* and the Ministry of Justice, he was told to come back in the morning. No help was forthcoming from either on the following day. Guzenko spent the evening with his wife and child hiding in a neighbor's flat while NKGB men broke down his door. It was almost midnight before the local police finally came to the rescue. Mackenzie King, Canada's prime minister since 1935, was even more naïve than Roosevelt had been about Soviet espionage in his own capital. At first, he disbelieved Guzenko's story. When finally persuaded by it, he told his diary how shocked he was at the thought that the Soviet Union had spied on a wartime ally:

> As I dictate this note I think of the Russian Embassy being only a few doors away and of them being a center of intrigue. During this period of war, while Canada has been helping Russia and doing all we can to foment Canadian-Russian friendship, there has been one branch of the Russian service that has been spying on [us]. . . . The amazing thing is how many contacts have been successfully made with people in key positions in government and industrial circles.[9]

As well as uncovering a major GRU spy ring in Canada itself, Guzenko also provided intelligence on Soviet cipher systems, further evidence of espionage by Alger Hiss and Harry Dexter White,[10] evidence that led to the conviction of the British atom spy Allan Nunn May in 1946, and clues to the identity of the Soviet spy code-named Elli in British intelligence, which remained unsolved until Gordievsky gained access to

Elli's KGB file in 1981 and discovered that he was Leo Long.[11]

An attempted Soviet defection in Istanbul very nearly did as much damage to NKGB operations in Britain as Elizabeth Bentley's defection caused in the United States. On August 27, 1945, the NKGB deputy resident in Turkey, Konstantin Volkov, working under diplomatic cover as vice-consul, wrote to the British vice-consul in Istanbul, C. H. Page, requesting an urgent appointment. When Page failed to reply, Volkov turned up in person on September 4 and asked for diplomatic asylum for himself and his wife. In return for asylum and the sum of £50,000 (around £1 million at 1990 values), he offered important files, documents, and information obtained while working on the INU British desk at the Center. Among the most important wartime Soviet agents, he claimed, were two in the Foreign Office and seven "inside the British intelligence system," one of whom was "fulfilling the function of head of a section of British counterespionage in London." Volkov insisted that London should be informed of his approach not by telegraph but by diplomatic bag; to his certain knowledge all diplomatic and intelligence cipher traffic between London and the Moscow embassy had been decrypted for the past two and a half years.[12]

On September 19 Philby was startled to receive a report of Volkov's attempted defection by diplomatic bag from the Istanbul embassy. The reference to the "head of a section of British counterespionage," though imprecise, pointed, he feared—probably correctly—to himself. "That evening," wrote Philby in his memoirs, "I worked late. The situation seemed to call for urgent action, of an extra-curricular nature."[13] The "urgent action" was, doubtless, an emergency meeting with his controller, Boris Krotov. It was one of the most dangerous moments in Philby's career. With slightly less luck in Ottawa a fortnight before, Guzenko would not have succeeded in defecting. With slightly more luck in Istanbul, Volkov might well have succeeded in unmasking Philby and dealing a body blow to the Magnificent Five. Volkov's most remarkable piece of ill-fortune was that the British ambassador in Istanbul was on leave and his chargé d'affaires had such a personal disdain for espionage that he declined to inform the SIS station commander, Cyril Machray, who would almost certainly have grasped the importance of the approach and successfully arranged Volkov's defection.[14]

Immediately after his emergency meeting with Philby on the evening of September 19, Krotov alerted the Center of Volkov's impending defection. On the 21st the Turkish consulate in Moscow issued visas for two NKGB hatchet men posing as diplomatic couriers. On the following day it was decided in London that Philby should fly out to Turkey to deal with the Volkov case. Because of various travel delays he did not arrive in Istanbul until September 26. According to the fictional version of Volkov's liquidation later concocted by Philby and the KGB for Western consumption, Volkov was not spirited out of Istanbul until "some weeks later."[15] In reality Volkov and his wife had left Istanbul aboard a Soviet aircraft sedated and on stretchers accompanied by the NKGB minders two days before Philby arrived.[16]

In his memoirs Philby describes how on his journey back to London he coolly drafted a report suggesting various explanations for Volkov's failure to defect: drink, indiscretion, NKGB bugging of his flat, or the possibility that he had changed his mind. "Another theory— that the Russians had been tipped off about Volkov's approach to the British—had no solid evidence to support it. It was not worth including in my report."[17] In reality, Philby wrote a quite different report and returned to London in much greater agitation than he would later admit. Coming so soon after Guzenko's defection, the whole episode left him seriously alarmed that he was about to be discovered, and too eager to discredit Volkov in his report. When a copy of his report reached the Center, it caused some anxiety.[18] Philby put down Volkov's desire to defect to the fact that he was "a traitor" whose "treachery" had been detected by the NKGB, an extraordinary way for an SIS officer to describe a defector.

In his anxiety to discredit Volkov's claims of Soviet penetration, which came uncomfortably close to pointing in his direction, Philby went to exaggerated lengths to discredit the intelligence that Volkov alleged he could provide. He described it as baffling, for example, that Volkov had failed to offer cryptographic information—and yet Volkov had laid great stress on Soviet success in breaking British ciphers over the past two years.[19] The crudity of Philby's attempt to discredit Volkov was in striking contrast to the much more sophisticated fictional version later fabricated for his memoirs during his Moscow exile. Faced with the threat of exposure for the first time since joining SIS, Philby had become badly rattled. For the moment he himself was so far above suspicion within SIS that the Volkov episode did not threaten him. But when suspicion fell on Philby after the flight of Burgess and Maclean in 1951, the file was reopened and his inept attempt to discredit Volkov became an important part of the case against him.

*   *   *

The greatest potential threat to Moscow Center's postwar operations in the West came from a breach of cipher security during the last year of the war. In 1944 OSS obtained fifteen hundred pages of an NKVD/NKGB code book captured by the Finns. Though the original was returned to Moscow on Roosevelt's orders, Donovan retained a copy.[20] By itself, the code book was of little help to Western cryptanalysts. The first stage in enciphering an NKVD/NKGB message was to replace each word (or, sometimes, letter) by a five-digit number group obtained from the code book. But the cipher clerk in an NKGB residency then added to each group another five-digit number obtained from a series of randomly generated numbers on a "one-time pad" of which the only other copy was in Moscow Center. If, as Center regulations insisted, the "one-time pad" was used once only, the ciphered message was virtually unbreakable. But in the last year of the war the sheer amount of intelligence being sent back by the residencies in the United States and Britain was so large that the Center sometimes sent out the same pad more than once. The cipher officer responsible is believed later to have been shot.[21] There were two further breaches of the usually rigorous Soviet cipher security at the end of the war. The FBI captured the plain-text version of some NKGB ciphered telegrams sent from New York to Moscow in 1944. After his defection in September 1945 Igor Guzenko was able to provide guidance on NKGB as well as GRU cipher procedures.[22]

The crucial breakthrough in exploiting these breaches of Soviet cipher security was made in 1948 by Meredith Gardner, a brilliant cryptanalyst in the U.S. Army Security Agency (ASA), which merged a year later into the Armed Forces Security Agency (AFSA), forerunner to the National Security Agency (NSA), founded in 1952. Gardner was a remarkable linguist as well as cryptanalyst, who was reputed to have learned Japanese in three months in order to work on Japanese code and cipher systems during the war. During 1948 he succeeded in decrypting fragments of NKGB messages to and from the Center sent during the last year of the war. At his first meeting with Gardner, Robert Lamphere of the FBI found him "tall, gangling, reserved, obviously intelligent, and extremely reluctant to discuss much about his work or whether it would progress any distance beyond the first fragments the FBI had already received."[23] Over the next few years, however, several thousand NKGB messages (code-named Venona) were decrypted in whole or part. The Venona secret and the technique used by Gardner were leaked to the Russians in 1948 by an ASA cipher clerk, William Weisband, who had been recruited by the MGB two years earlier. Weisband's treachery was discovered in 1950. Though he was sentenced to one year in jail for failing to answer a summons to appear before a grand jury, he was never prosecuted for espionage. ASA and its British counterpart GCHQ were agreed that Venona was too important a secret to be revealed in court even during proceedings in camera.[24]

It was immediately clear to the Center that Venona represented a series of time bombs of potentially enormous destructive force for its agent networks. Since there was no means of predicting which NKGB messages from the end of the war could be decrypted, there was no way of knowing when and where the bombs would go off. A partial solution to this dilemma was provided by Kim Philby when he became SIS liaison officer in Washington in October 1949. Meredith Gardner later recalled mournfully how Philby had stood smoking a pipe, looking over his shoulder and admiring the progress he was making with the Russian decrypts.[25] Until his recall in June 1951 Philby's access to the Venona material left him perfectly placed to warn Moscow when the net was closing in on one of its British or American agents.

As far afield as Australia, Venona did serious damage to Soviet intelligence operations. Until the establishment of the first Soviet diplomatic mission at Canberra in 1943, Australia had scarcely figured as a Soviet intelligence target. Thereafter, however, the NKGB residency under Semyon Makarov (1943–49) rapidly penetrated the Ministry of External Affairs, which was an important source for British as well as Australian classified documents (among them the reports of the British Chiefs of Staff Post-Hostilities Planning Staff). Makarov's two most important agents in External Affairs were both compromised by Venona.

Early in 1948 an MI5 team headed by the director-general, Sir Percy Sillitoe, and including the future director-general Roger Hollis, visited Australia to investigate Soviet penetration. In order to protect their source they deliberately gave the impression in Canberra that their information came not from intercepts but from a British mole in Soviet intelligence. The first Soviet agent to be identified in External Affairs was Jim Hill, code-named Tourist in the Venona traffic, the brother of a leading Communist lawyer. Venona made it possible to pinpoint the serial number of one of the diplomatic telegrams Hill had given to the Russians and so prove his guilt. Further clues from Soviet intercepts quickly identified another Soviet agent, with the code name Bur, as the

Communist diplomat Ian Milner, who had since left External Affairs for a post in the United Nations and was later to take refuge in Prague.

Soviet penetration of the Australian foreign and civil service during the Cold War seems never to have recovered. When the KGB resident Vladimir Petrov defected in 1954, he was able to provide reassurance that his residency had achieved only minor breaches of Australian security.[26]

The damage to postwar Soviet intelligence operations in the West caused by demobilization, defections, and the Venona decrypts caused the most anxiety at Moscow Center in two related areas of intelligence collection. The first was high-level penetration of the Main Adversary. The faith in the Soviet millennium that inspired thousands of talented young American idealists during the Depression and the Second World War had all but disappeared in the Cold War generation. So far as is known, despite some low- and occasionally middle-level Soviet penetrations in postwar Washington, there have been no successors to agents of the caliber of Alger Hiss in the State Department, of Harry Dexter White in the Treasury, of Duncan C. Lee in the intelligence community, or of Lauchlin Currie in the White House. Nor has there been any unconscious agent of the stature of Harry Hopkins.

By the time the Central Intelligence Agency (CIA) was created in July 1947, new screening methods were in force, which made impossible any repetition of the wholesale Soviet penetration of OSS. From William Weisband onward the most damaging Soviet penetrations of the United States intelligence community were to be in sigint rather than in humint. The problems of Soviet agent recruitment were compounded by the bungling of the first postwar residents in Washington. Grigori Grigoryevich Dolbin, who became resident in 1946, displayed conspicuous incompetence even before he began to show signs of insanity (due, it was believed at the Center, to the onset of hereditary syphilis). He was recalled in 1948. His successor, Georgi Aleksandrovich Sokolov, had been resident in Rio de Janeiro until a breach in Soviet-Brazilian relations late in 1947; on his departure he was pelted with eggs and other missiles by an angry crowd. During his time in Washington he, like Dolbin, was reprimanded for poor performance before being recalled in 1949.[27]

The second main anxiety at Moscow Center caused by the partial disruption of its wartime agent networks in the West was in the nuclear field. The use of the atomic bomb against Japan in August 1945, and the sense which it provoked of military inferiority to the Main Adversary, made atomic secrets the greatest immediate priority of Soviet foreign intelligence collection. After Hiroshima Stalin summoned the commissar of munitions, Boris Lvovich Vannikov, and his deputies to the Kremlin. They were joined by Igor Vasilyevich Kurchatov, the scientist in charge of the atomic program. "A single demand of you, comrades!" announced Stalin. "Provide us with atomic weapons in the shortest possible time! You know that Hiroshima has shaken the whole world. The balance [of power] has been destroyed!" So long as the Soviet Union lacked nuclear weapons, it would be in "great danger" from the West.[28]

Hitherto the atomic project had been under the overall control of Molotov. Some months earlier, however, Kurchatov had written to Beria criticizing Molotov's lack of urgency and appealing for Beria's help. The letter was handwritten; its contents were so sensitive that Kurchatov feared to have them typed, but they seem to have achieved their aim. After Hiroshima Stalin handed control of the project to Beria. The change of leadership had an immediate effect. According to Kurchatov's assistant, Professor Igor Golovin, "Beria's administrative abilities were obvious for all of us at that time. He was unusually energetic. Meetings did not drag on for hours; everything was decided quickly." Under Beria's direction, all the labor for the atomic project came from the gulag. According to Golovin, the scientists gave little thought to their use of slave labor:

> At that time we thought of just one thing: what we should do to complete the work as soon as possible—before the American atom bomb fell on us. The fear of a new atomic war outweighed all the rest—anyone who lived at that time will confirm this.[29]

Some scientists, however, were more critical of Beria's direction than Golovin. The great physicist Pyotr Kapitsa (later a Nobel Laureate) wrote to Stalin on November 25, 1945, asking to be relieved of his position in the atomic project:

> [Comrade Beria], it is true, has the conductor's baton in his hands. That's fine, but all the same a scientist should play first violin. For the violin sets the tone for the whole orchestra. Comrade Beria's basic weakness is that the conductor

ought not only to wave the baton, but also to understand the
score. In this respect Beria is weak.

Beria, wrote Kapitsa, was intent simply on imitating the American
construction of the bomb. Kapitsa argued, without success, that Soviet
scientists should try to devise a cheaper and quicker method of their
own.[30]

Beria, as Kapitsa complained, was obsessed with the attempt to
copy the Americans. By the autumn of 1945 many of the secrets of the
bombs that destroyed Hiroshima and Nagasaki were in Soviet hands.
But Beria was anxious for more and frustrated by the postwar decline
in nuclear intelligence from the West. Guzenko's defection in September 1945 led to the detection of Allan Nunn May and to tighter security
around nuclear research. The demobilization of David Greenglass in
February removed one of the two Soviet agents from Los Alamos. The
other, Klaus Fuchs, left Los Alamos in June 1946 for the new British
atomic energy establishment at Harwell. Though he continued to work
as a Soviet agent until 1949, his usefulness was much reduced. The
McMahon Act, which set up the U.S. Atomic Energy Commission
(AEC) in August 1946, effectively denied fresh nuclear information to
Britain. Cut off from American research, the British Labour government decided in January 1947 to build its own atomic bomb, but took
two years longer to construct it than the Soviet Union.

Despite the McMahon Act, Donald Maclean continued to have
limited access to atomic intelligence in Washington, since the prohibitions on the sharing of scientific information did not cover raw materials or the question of declassifying wartime atomic secrets. As the
official representative of the British embassy on political aspects of
atomic energy, he obtained a pass to visit AEC premises unescorted.[31]
It was later discovered that between the summer of 1947 and his
departure from Washington he visited the AEC twelve times, occasionally at night. According to an AEC damage assessment, he had access
to estimates of uranium ore supply and requirement forecasts for the
period 1948–52, though these later turned out to be inaccurate.[32]

Dissatisfied with the declining flow of high-grade nuclear intelligence, Beria instructed Kurchatov to send a letter via an MGB messenger to the Danish nuclear physicist Niels Bohr asking for details of
the latest atomic research that he had seen in the United States. Bohr
replied by the same courier that he himself had been refused access by
the Americans to the information Kurchatov requested.[33]

Both Stalin and Beria were constantly fearful until the first successful Soviet atomic explosion that some vital American nuclear secret remained undiscovered by their agents in the West and that without it the Soviet atomic program would fail. In an attempt to overcome Stalin's skepticism, Kurchatov brought the nuclear charge of the first Soviet atomic bomb—a nickel-plated plutonium ball about ten centimeters in diameter—to his study in the Kremlin.

"And how do we know that this is plutonium, not a sparkling piece of iron?" asked Stalin. "And why this glitter? Why this window-dressing?"

"The charge has been nickel-plated so that it would be safe to touch. Plutonium is very toxic, but nickel-plated it's safe," Kurchatov replied. "And to satisfy yourself that this is not merely a piece of iron, instruct anyone of your choice to touch the ball with his hand. It's warm, whereas iron would be cold."

Stalin handled the ball himself: "Yes, it's warm. And is it always warm?"

"It always is, Iosif Vissarionovich. The continuous nuclear reaction of alpha-disintegration is underway inside. It warms it up. But we shall excite a powerful fission reaction in it. This will be an explosion of great power."

At least partly convinced, Stalin authorized the testing of the first bomb. Until the last minute, however, Beria was haunted by the fear that, despite the success of Soviet scientists and the achievements of the atom spies, the inner secret of the atomic bomb had somehow eluded them. Ten minutes before the bomb was due to detonate at the test site in Kazakhstan on September 25, 1949, Beria said pessimistically to Kurchatov: "Nothing will come of it!"

When the explosion came, Beria hugged and kissed the relieved Kurchatov. But then he had second thoughts. Had the explosion really been a nuclear explosion? He telephoned a Russian observer of the American atomic test at Bikini Atoll and demanded to know if the mushroom cloud appeared the same. Reassured that it was, he telephoned Stalin. The phone was answered by Stalin's secretary Poskrebyshev, who told him that Stalin had gone to bed. Beria insisted that he be wakened. A few minutes later Stalin came to the phone. "Iosif, all's well," Beria told him. "The blast was the same as the Americans'!" "I already know," replied Stalin and put down the phone. Outraged that someone else had been the first to give Stalin the news, Beria shook his fist at those around him and exploded: "Even here you put spokes in my wheels, traitors! I'll grind you into powder!"[34]

At almost the same moment as the explosion of the first Soviet atomic bomb, Meredith Gardner successfully decrypted an NKGB message of 1944 that provided the first clue to the identity of the most important of the atom spies, Klaus Fuchs, by then deputy scientific officer at Harwell.[35] Fuchs confessed in January 1950 and was sentenced in April 1951 to fourteen years' imprisonment. He described his work for the Russians in words that aptly described the state of mind of some other Soviet agents in the West:

> I used my Marxist philosophy to establish in my mind two separate compartments: one compartment in which I allowed myself to make friendships, to have personal relations. . . . I could be free and easy and happy with other people without fear of disclosing myself because I knew that the other compartment would step in if I approached the danger point. . . . It appeared to me at the time that I had become a "free man" because I had succeeded in the other compartment in establishing myself completely independent of the surrounding forces of society. Looking back on it now the best way of expressing it seems to be to call it a controlled schizophrenia.[36]

At the time of Fuchs's arrest, another atom spy, Bruno Pontecorvo, was also working at Harwell. Security investigations that followed the discovery of Fuchs revealed that Pontecorvo had a number of Communist relatives but turned up no evidence of his involvement in espionage.[37] When arrests of atom spies began in the United States in the summer of 1950, however, the Center decided to take no further risks and evacuated Pontecorvo and his family to the Soviet Union along a well-tried escape route through Finland. Pontecorvo subsequently pursued a distinguished career in Soviet nuclear physics, receiving two Orders of Lenin and a string of lesser honors, while publicly denying any involvement in atomic espionage.[38]

As well as leading to the downfall of Fuchs, Venona also provided the first clues that led to the arrest of Julius and Ethel Rosenberg. In February 1950 a newly decrypted NKGB message of 1944 referred to an agent in a low-level job at Los Alamos. Other clues helped to identify the agent as Ethel Rosenberg's brother, David Greenglass, who admitted his own role in June 1950 and implicated Julius Rosenberg. Greenglass revealed in questioning (though it was never mentioned in public) that Rosenberg had boasted to him of running a Soviet espionage network that had provided not merely atomic secrets but a wide range of other scientific and technological intelligence, including preliminary studies for space satellites.[39]

Unlike the British atom spies Allan Nunn May and Fuchs, the Rosenbergs eloquently, even movingly, protested their innocence to the end. In April 1951 they became the only Soviet spies in the West to be sentenced to death. After over two years of unsuccessful appeals they died, one after the other, in the same electric chair at New York's Sing Sing prison on the evening of June 19, 1953. Ethel's last letter to her lawyer ended: "We are the first victims of American Fascism. Love you, Ethel." The courage with which both went to their deaths, their love for each other and their two sons, and the macabre squalor of their execution strengthened the suspicion of much of world opinion that there had been a miscarriage of justice. After each electrocution, the forty reporters, prison officials, and other witnesses were nauseated by the stench of burning flesh, urine, and defecation. Even after a current of 2,000 volts had passed through her body, Ethel still showed signs of life; and the current was repeated twice more, until a plume of smoke rose from her head.[40]

The Rosenbergs exemplify the idealist faith that Soviet Russia—or rather their own myth image of it—represented the hope of mankind, which still inspired naïve true believers in the West even after all the horrors of Stalinism. Both Julius and Ethel were dedicated, courageous Soviet agents, who believed that they could best serve the future of their cause by denying their own association with it.

Ever since their execution KGB active measures have encouraged the belief that the Rosenbergs were the innocent victims of an anti-Communist witch hunt. No KGB active measures campaign in the United States, however, has ever encouraged that belief as effectively as the leader of the witch hunt himself, Senator Joseph McCarthy. From the moment McCarthy announced on February 9, 1950, that he was in possession of a list of 205 (mostly imaginary) Communists in the State Department, his self-serving crusade against the Red Menace helped to make liberal opinion around the world skeptical of the reality of the Soviet intelligence offensive against the Main Adversary.

Skepticism about the guilt of the Rosenbergs was also encouraged by the continued refusal, on both sides of the Atlantic, to make any reference in court to Venona on security grounds. The secret was not to leak out publicly until the 1980s and even then was not officially acknowledged in either Britain or the United States. But in the early years of the Cold War it caused varying degrees of disruption to Soviet intelligence operations around the globe.

The early years of the Cold War and the problems of Venona coincided with a highly confused period in the organization of Soviet foreign intelligence operations. The confusion derived in part from power struggles within the Kremlin and in part from the founding in July 1947 of the Central Intelligence Agency. Reports on its founding of the agency from the MGB resident in Washington, Grigori Grigoryevich Dolbin, and from the Soviet ambassador, Aleksandr Semyonovich Panyushkin, were closely studied by Stalin and the Politburo.[41]

The original purpose of the CIA, as defined in the National Security Bill presented to Congress in February 1947, was to coordinate and evaluate foreign intelligence from all sources. Though that purpose was never fully achieved, Molotov argued persuasively that a unified civilian and military foreign intelligence system would give the United States a clear advantage over the fragmented Soviet system. The solution, he argued, was to combine the foreign intelligence directorates of the MGB and the GRU under a single roof. Molotov's proposal had the further advantage, from Stalin's viewpoint, of weakening the influence on security of Lavrenty Beria, whose protégé Abakumov headed the MGB.

In the autumn of 1947 the foreign intelligence directorates of the MGB and the GRU were combined to form a new foreign intelligence agency, the Committee of Information (Komitet Informatsii, or KI). Though the KI came formally under the control of the Council of Ministers, the appointment of Molotov as its first head gave the foreign ministry greater influence on foreign intelligence operations than ever before. Molotov sought to strengthen foreign ministry control by appointing Soviet ambassadors in major capitals as "chief legal residents" with authority over the civilian (ex-MGB) and military (ex-GRU) residents.[42] In the jaundiced view of the later defector, Ilya Dzhirkvelov, "This resulted in incredible confusion. The residents, the professional intelligence officers, resorted to incredible subterfuges to avoid informing their ambassadors about their work, since the diplomats had only amateurish knowledge of intelligence work and its methods. . . ."[43]

Some diplomats, however, took personal charge of intelligence operations. Chief among them was Aleksandr Panyushkin, Soviet ambassador in Washington from 1947 to 1951, who became actively involved in the secret war against the Main Adversary. After the confusion caused by the recall of Grigori Dolbin, Washington resident 1946–48, and his successor, Georgi Sokolov, resident 1948–49, for, respectively, insanity and incompetence, Panyushkin took direct operational control of the residency for a year. The next Washington resident, Nikolai Alekseevich Vladykin (1950–54), avoided major disputes with either Panyushkin or the Center. Panyushkin himself later became head of the KGB First (Foreign Intelligence) Chief Directorate.[44]

From 1947 to 1949 the deputy chairman of the KI under Molotov in charge of day-to-day operations was Pyotr Vasilyevich Fedotov, who had succeeded Fitin as head of INU soon after the Second World War. Like Fitin, Fedotov had a reputation within the Center as an intellectual. Dzhirkvelov recalls: "What really distinguished him from other highly placed KGB officials was that he did not disregard another person's opinion. If someone did not agree with him, he would not give orders but try to persuade him."[45] Another KGB defector, Yuri Nosenko, however, believes that Fedotov's apparent flexibility derived in part from indecisiveness; according to Nosenko, he had a habit of leaving files on his desk for two or three months while he made up his mind.[46]

The KI sought to unify sigint as well as humint. The foreign section of the MGB Fifth (Cipher) Directorate was combined with its military counterpart in the GRU to form the Seventh Department of the KI under its former MGB head, Colonel Aleksei Shchekoldin. The KI was, however, unstable from the moment of its birth. Almost all the departments were headed by former INU officers, and the general staff predictably complained that military intelligence had been reduced to a subordinate role. In the summer of 1948, after a prolonged dispute with Molotov, Marshal Nikolai Aleksandrovich Bulganin, the minister for the armed forces, succeeded in withdrawing all military intelligence personnel from the KI and returning them to the GRU. Probably with the support of Beria, Abakumov, the head of the MGB, then embarked on a long campaign to recover control of the remains of the KI. At the end of 1948 the Department of Counselors to the People's Democracies returned to the MGB. So did all KI officers working in the EM (Russian émigré) and SK (Soviet colonies abroad) lines. The KI, however, retained control of most nonmilitary humint and sigint collection and analysis until it was disbanded and reabsorbed by the MGB late in 1951.[47]

In 1949 Molotov, out of favor with Stalin, was succeeded as both foreign minister and chairman of the KI by Andrei Vyshinsky, the brutal prosecutor at the show trials, who had become Molotov's first deputy in 1943. Vyshinsky's managerial style was, he once explained, to "keep people on edge." According to Andrei Gromyko, one of his successors as foreign minister:

> When he summoned an assistant he would generally open on a high-pitched note of accusation, if not downright abuse. He spoke like this even to ambassadors and envoys. He took the view that he did this to emulate Beria.

Vyshinsky retained from the 1930s a sycophantic admiration for Beria, which, claimed Gromyko, was evident even on the telephone: "As soon as he heard Beria's voice Vyshinsky leapt respectfully out of his chair. The conversation itself also presented an unusual picture: Vyshinsky cringed like a servant before his master."[48] Under Vyshinsky, Beria's influence over the KI dramatically increased.

The contemplative, somewhat indecisive Fedotov, whom Molotov had put in day-to-day charge of KI operations, retained a position as one of the deputy chairmen. But he was succeeded as first deputy by the more brutal and decisive Sergei Romanovich Savchenko, a protégé of Beria who had been wartime head of the NKVD in the Ukraine and remained in the same post in the MGB from 1946 to 1949. Savchenko seems to have answered to Beria rather than to the foreign ministry. Vyshinsky took little part in KI affairs, handing over the chairmanship to two senior foreign ministry officials: first, Yakov Aleksandrovich Malik, then Valerian Zorin; there is no evidence that either played much more than a nominal role as KI chairman.[49]

Despite the partial postwar disruption of Soviet agent networks and intermittent administrative confusion at Moscow Center, the East-West intelligence conflict during the early years of the Cold War remained a one-sided contest. While Moscow retained important intelligence assets in the West, the West had none at all in Moscow. To build up their first postwar agent networks in the U.S.S.R., SIS and later the CIA concentrated on penetration along Soviet borders, using partisan groups resisting Stalinist rule. Almost all the attempted penetrations, from the Baltic States in the north to the Turkish frontier in the south, fell victim to a series of deception operations mounted by the Center in conscious imitation of the Trust deception that had ensnared Western intelligence services in the 1920s. When in 1953 Yuri Nosenko joined the MGB Second (Counterintelligence) Chief Directorate, which was responsible for running the deceptions, one of his first visits was to the Chekists' Study Room in the Lubyanka, where the main historical display beneath a portrait of Feliks Dzerzhinsky was devoted to the Trust. Nearby, displayed as a sacrificial offering to "Iron Feliks," were radios and other equipment used by SIS and CIA agents infiltrated into the Baltic States, Poland, the Ukraine, and other border regions.[50]

The postwar SIS controller for the Northern Area, Harry Carr, formerly station commander in prewar Helsinki and posted to Stockholm for most of the war, regarded the most promising area of the Soviet Union for SIS penetration as the Baltic States, then undergoing a resumption of the NKGB/MGB reign of terror suspended after the German invasion in 1941. Shortly before the end of the war with Germany, he provided radio sets for two agents being infiltrated into Latvia by an émigré organization to make contact with local partisans. It was agreed that the intelligence "take" would be shared with SIS. On the night of October 15, 1945, an SIS speedboat containing four more Latvian agents overturned just as it was approaching the Courland coast. The agents struggled ashore, but next day much of their equipment was found washed up on the beach by a border patrol. Within a few weeks they had been rounded up by the NKGB, though not until their radio operator had reported their arrival to SIS.

During the war the NKGB, like the British, had used captured German agents to transmit misleading intelligence by radio back to their headquarters. Major Janis Lukasevics, a thirty-five-year-old officer in the Second (Counterintelligence) Department of the Latvian NKGB, suggested using the captured emigré agents as the basis for a similar deception. By the time Lukasevics's proposal was considered, however, the Latvian agents had been too badly tortured by their NKGB interrogators to be of operational use. There was the further difficulty that the long radio silence after the agents' capture would inevitably have aroused SIS suspicions. Lukasevics eventually obtained permission for another partisan radio operator, Augusts Bergmanis, released from prison in return for his cooperation, to use the captured SIS radio transmitter and code book. Bergmanis began transmitting, with Lukasevics by his side, in March 1946, claiming to be a Latvian partisan who had been handed the radio and codes shortly before the agents' capture. Though it took some time for Bergmanis to win the confidence of SIS, his broadcasts marked the beginning of a deception that was ultimately to undermine all SIS operations in the Baltic States.[51]

Late in 1946, there was a second Latvian disaster. Rihards Zande, an SIS agent landed in August, had difficulty with his radio transmitter and was advised in November by the SIS station in Stockholm to make contact with Bergmanis. "The meeting was successful," Zande reported to Eriks Tomsons, who had landed with him. "I am satisfied that Bergmanis is not under MGB control." Lukasevics's superiors, still fearful that if Zande and Tomsons remained at liberty British espionage would escalate beyond their control, did not yet have the nerve to embark on a large-scale deception operation. In March 1947, Bergmanis radioed London at Lukasevics's dictation: "Great disaster. Zande and Tomsons arrested. I've escaped but fear Zande's interrogation. All activities have stopped. Will contact you when safe."[52]

A few months later Lukasevics revived the deception operation by recruiting a Latvian nationalist, Vidvuds Sveics, to penetrate the anti-Soviet partisans. In October 1948 Sveics "escaped" to the Swedish island of Gotland, posing as a Latvian partisan, and joined a group of refugees being trained by SIS and the Swedes for intelligence operations in the Baltic States. In May 1949 he landed by boat near the Lithuanian-Latvian border with five genuine SIS agents, whom he betrayed to the MGB; three were shot almost immediately. Sveics survived to continue the penetration of the Latvian resistance and to report to the MGB on its links with SIS. Six months later, two more SIS agents, Vitolds Berkis and Andrei Galdins, landed in Latvia. Though their landing on the night of October 31 went undetected, they compromised themselves almost immediately by contacting Bergmanis, who lodged them in an allegedly "safe house" provided by the MGB. Berkis and Galdins announced that they were the first in a new wave of agents whose mission was to contact partisan leaders. Henceforth agents were landed at six-month intervals from a former wartime German E-boat with a German captain and a maximum speed of forty-five knots, operating under cover of the British Control Commission Fishery Protection Service.

Lukasevics insisted that the time had come to create a fictional underground on the model of the Trust. This time his chiefs gave the assent they had refused two years before. During the winter of 1949–50, under Lukasevics's supervision, a bogus partisan group code-named Maxis, headed by Major Alberts Bundulis of the MGB, was trained in the Kurzeme Forest. In May 1950, Berkis and Galdins went to live in their encampment. At about the same time another SIS agent, Jonas Deksnys, was successfully turned by the MGB, and another of Lukasevics's agents, Jan Erglis, left for London to discuss plans for future operations. In the course of 1950 another fictitious partisan group, code-named Roberts, made contact with SIS. CIA operations in the Baltic States, though based on parachute drops rather than seaborne landings, fell victim to similar deceptions.[53]

The opportunity created by the Maxis and Roberts deceptions was never fully exploited. During the Second World War British intelligence had used the "Double Cross" system, based on turned Abwehr agents, to feed the Germans disinformation, which after the D-Day landings led Hitler and his high command to misdirect some of their forces at a crucial moment. Moscow Center, by contrast, refused to allow Lukasevics and his colleagues to feed SIS any information not already published in the press. Lukasevics was even denied permission to concoct bogus intelligence of any importance for fear that SIS would demand more and eventually become suspicious. The inevitable result was disappointment in London with the intelligence generated by Baltic operations and a downgrading of their importance. When reproached for not supplying more intelligence, the Maxis and Roberts groups replied—much as the Trust had before them—that they were freedom fighters rather than spies.[54]

Growing suspicions in London of the two partisan groups were brought to a head in 1954 when the SIS Scientific Section requested a sample of water from a Russian river where a nuclear power plant was believed to be located. The sample, when supplied, turned out to be so highly radioactive that it could only have come from the interior of a reactor. SIS's first reaction was to wonder whether a deliberate KGB deception could have committed so crass an error. Its second reaction was to realize that it had. A subsequent KGB investigation revealed a string of further errors—among them the fact that the route allegedly chosen by the agent who had collected the water sample passed next to a major military airfield, which he had failed to mention in his report. The investigation also disclosed that a number of KGB penetration agents among the partisans who visited London later revealed the deception to SIS.[55] In the end the KGB obtained a propaganda victory but not much more. The émigré agents landed in the Baltic republics (probably about twenty-five in number from 1949 to 1954) never stood any chance of disturbing Stalinist rule. The KGB devoted more resources to running a deception that it never properly exploited than SIS did to its unsuccessful Baltic operations.

The deception operation nonetheless launched Lukasevics (or Lukasevich as he came to be called after his move to Moscow Center) on a career that raised him to the rank of KGB general. According to a sanitized account of his career prepared for Western consumption in 1988, he was posted to Britain in the 1970s as head of "counterespionage operations" at the Soviet embassy.[56] In reality, he served from 1972 to 1980 under the alias Yakov Konstantinovich Bukashev as KGB resident in London. After a largely unsuccessful eight years in London he was sent back to Latvia to finish his career in a post of only major's rank with a cover job (and his general's salary) in the Latvian Ministry of Education. In November 1987 he appeared on Latvian television together with the aging Kim Philby to celebrate the seventieth anniversary of the Bolshevik Revolution and to publicize the claim, which both knew to be fraudulent, that nationalist demonstrations in the Baltic States were inspired by SIS.[57]

The deception operation in the Baltic States, begun in 1946 and expanded in 1949, became the inspiration for a series of similar operations along much of the Soviet frontier. One of the largest was in Poland. In 1947 the MGB, assisted by the Polish UB, succeeded in wiping out the last active remnant of the Home Army, which had taken the name Wolność i Niepodległość (WiN): Freedom and Independence. In 1948 the UB, acting on instructions from its Soviet advisers, resurrected a bogus version of WiN and in 1949 sent an equally bogus emissary to announce to WiN's former London supporters that it was still in being.

Beginning in 1950, the CIA, which was now committed to a policy of active support for anti-Soviet underground movements in Eastern Europe, began supplying the bogus WiN by parachute with arms, radio transmitters, and gold coins. As in the Baltic republics, however, the WiN deception was never fully exploited as a channel for bogus intelligence. Claims that WiN provided dramatic photographs of fictitious guerrilla attacks on police stations and Soviet tanks to sustain CIA support for it are probably mistaken. The UB officers in day-to-day charge of the operation later claimed, probably correctly, that the WiN reports they concocted "might just as well have been written in London or Paris on the basis of Warsaw newspapers. Gentlemen from the U.S. Secret Service did not get from us even such data concerning everyday life in our country as the prices of goods or the levels of supplies of consumer goods for particular centers, which they were so anxious to get." Frank Wisner, head of the Office of Policy Coordination, which ran CIA covert action, was, however, easily persuaded that WiN represented a serious threat to the Communist regime. He allegedly concluded that WiN needed only antitank weapons "to drive the Red Army out of Warsaw." WiN demands for American assistance grew steadily, culminating in the unsuccessful request for the airdrop of a U.S. general to help organize the Polish resistance.

Then in December 1952 the MGB decided to expose the deception. A mocking two-hour broadcast on Polish radio revealed that a million dollars sent by the CIA to WiN over the past few years had ended up with the Polish authorities. The alleged leaders of WiN (in reality UB officers) "confessed" that two years earlier they had realized that their support consisted solely of "people whose moral value was nil," while "The agents who were sent to us from abroad also were adventurers, cynical hirelings indifferent to the lot of the nation, interested above all in their own direct gains." Realizing that it was impossible to combat "the people's power . . . without acting at the same time against the interests of the Polish nation," they decided that they would no longer "recruit depraved young people for the U.S. Secret Service . . . The final stage of our activity consisted of efforts to paralyze the attempts of the Americans and their émigré hirelings to develop espionage and subversive work in Poland":

> There was no crime in Poland after the war . . . in which the U.S. intelligence did not have its fingers and its dollars, whether it was the part of the U.S. ambassador in the anti-Polish schemings between the Vatican and the reactionary section of the clergy, or systematic incitement by the dozens of radio yappers controlled by the U.S.A., and the recruitment of outcasts for mean and treacherous work. No chance of harming our country was neglected by the Wall Street monopolists.

As well as humiliating the CIA, the WiN deception had enabled the MGB and UB to flush out remaining opposition and demonstrate the futility of resistance to "the people's power."[58]

The main center of postwar resistance to Stalinist rule within the Soviet Union was the Ukraine. In 1947 the Organization of Ukrainian Nationalists (OUN) made the doubtless exaggerated claim that it had 100,000 partisans under arms.[59] By the time SIS and the CIA began Ukrainian operations in 1949, however, effective large-scale resistance had been crushed. Both the OUN and the rival National Labor Alliance (NTS), an émigré social-democratic organization favored by the CIA, had been penetrated by the MGB. The first SIS agents parachuted into the Ukraine to make contact with the OUN in 1949 were captured by the MGB; so were two further groups in the following year.[60] The MGB base at Karlshorst in the Berlin suburbs also succeeded in penetrating NTS bases in Germany. One of its most successful agents was a Soviet army officer who defected to the West in November 1949 in order to live with his German mistress. He was tracked down in West Germany by the MGB, which used threats to his family in the Soviet Union to recruit him as an agent. On MGB instructions, he joined the NTS, soon becoming both an instructor at the NTS school for agents infiltrated into the Ukraine and a consultant to U.S. military intelligence. He was eventually discovered after Moscow radio announced the execution in May 1953 of four NTS agents whom he had betrayed.[61] As in the Baltic republics and Poland, however, the MGB deception never became a full-fledged double-cross system. The Center refused, once again, to use the deception as a channel for feeding significant amounts of false intelligence to the West.[62]

The agent in the West who did most to assist MGB deception operations along Soviet borders was Kim Philby. While SIS station commander in Turkey from 1947 to 1949 he was able to betray agents who crossed the Russian border as well as their contacts and families inside the Soviet Union.[63] As SIS representative in Washington from 1949 to 1951 his liaison duties with the CIA allowed him to give his case officer many details of American as well as British operations. In Albania he alerted the MGB/KI to the first SIS-sponsored seaborne landings in October 1949, to plans for cross-border infiltration in the summer of 1950, and to the first CIA parachute drop in November 1950.[64] Among the many Anglo-American intelligence conferences attended by Philby was one in February 1951 when Harry Carr paid his first visit to the United States to coordinate SIS-CIA operations in the Baltic States. According to Philby's memoirs, "His visit ended disastrously with both Carr and his opposite numbers in CIA accusing each other, quite justifiably, of wholesale lying at the conference table."[65] Though often quoted, Philby's account is simple disinformation. In retirement Carr wrote to a CIA officer who had been present at the meeting to ask for his reaction to Philby's version of their meeting. Both agreed that the atmosphere around the conference table had in fact been remarkably cordial.[66]

Philby could not always resist gloating in his memoirs over the fate of the hundreds of agents he betrayed. In the spring of 1951, for example, not long before his recall from Washington, he gave his controller "precise information" about three groups of six agents who were shortly to be parachuted by SIS into the Ukraine. Philby comments with a macabre attempt at irony: "I do not know what happened to the parties concerned. But I can make an informed guess."[67]

As well as mounting a series of successful deception operations, Soviet intelligence, despite the postwar problems of its foreign agent networks, continued to receive an impressive flow of intelligence from the West. Four of the Magnificent Five (Philby, Maclean, Burgess, and Cairncross) remained active until 1951. From late 1944 to late 1947 all were controlled while in Britain by Boris Mikhailovich Krotov (born Krötenschild), a workaholic of enormous energy and great efficiency, whose Jewish origins were later to deny him the promotion his talents deserved. The London resident from 1943 to 1947, Konstantin Mikhailovich Kukin, basked in the reflected glory of Krotov's agent handling and in the Center's approval of his own imaginative running of the residency. At the founding of the Committee of Information in the autumn of 1947, Kukin was promoted to head of the First (Anglo-American) Directorate. His portrait is among the score that hang today on the walls of the KGB First Chief Directorate Memory Room. Beneath it is a citation praising Kukin as one of the outstanding intelligence officers of the 1940s and 1950s.[68]

The portrait of Kukin's successor, Nikolai Borisovich Rodin (alias Korovin), resident from 1947 to 1952 and from 1956 to 1961, does not appear in the Memory Room. Rodin was almost the stereotype of an arrogant *apparatchik,* treating his subordinates with contempt, secure in the knowledge that the agents run by his residency guaranteed his reputation in the Center. Krotov was succeeded as controller of the

Five and the residency's other leading agents by Yuri Ivanovich Modin, a PR (political intelligence) line officer stationed in London from 1947 to 1953 and from 1955 to 1958. Modin (known to the Five as Peter) was one of the ablest agent handlers in KGB history. As head of Faculty Number One (political intelligence) in the FCD Andropov Institute during the early 1980s he dismissed Rodin in his lectures as an arrogant, pretentious nonentity.[69]

For some years after the war Burgess, Maclean, and Philby were each at various times in a position to provide American as well as British intelligence. According to a damage assessment by the U.S. Joint Chiefs of Staff after the defection of Burgess and Maclean in 1951:

> In the fields of US/UK/Canadian planning on atomic energy, US/UK post-war planning and policy in Europe all information up to the date of defection undoubtedly reached Soviet hands. . . . All UK and possibly some US diplomatic codes and ciphers in existence prior to May 15, 1951 are in possession of the Soviets and of no further use.

This is clearly too alarmist; it takes no account, for example, of the use in cipher traffic of one-time pads, very few of which could have been betrayed by either Burgess or Maclean.[70] But there is no doubting the immense quantity of high-grade intelligence that both provided. The Petrovs, who defected from the KGB in 1954, were told by Filipp Vasilyevich Kislitsyn that while he was working as cipher clerk in the London residency from 1945 to 1948, Burgess handed over "briefcases full of Foreign Office documents which were photographed in the Soviet embassy and returned to him." Boris Krotov, his case officer until 1947, used to collect the bags from Burgess in the countryside near London, sometimes returning to the embassy with mud spattered on his clothes. Kislitsyn telegraphed the contents of the most important of Burgess's documents to Moscow and prepared the rest for dispatch by diplomatic bag. In 1949 he was put in charge of a new one-man section at Moscow Center that housed the files of documents supplied by Burgess and Maclean. The files were so numerous that many had not been translated. Kislitsyn used to select particular files or documents for high-ranking officials who visited his section to consult them.[71]

Both Burgess and Maclean, however, found the strain of their double life much greater in the Cold War than when Britain and the Soviet Union had been wartime allies. When George Carey-Foster,

head of the embryonic security branch in the Foreign Office, first encountered Burgess in 1947, he was struck by "his dishevelled and
unshaven appearance. He also smelt so strongly of drink that I enquired
who he was and what his job was." According to Goronwy Rees,
Burgess had also become addicted to drugs:

> He was now perpetually taking sedatives to calm his nerves
> and immediately followed them with stimulants in order to
> counteract their effect; and since he always did everything to
> excess, he munched whatever tablets he had on hand as a
> child will munch its way through a bag of dolly mixtures
> until the supply has given out.

Carey-Foster received increasing complaints of Burgess's "dissolute
behaviour." Fred Warner, who worked with him in the outer office of
Hector McNeil, minister of state at the Foreign Office, had to rescue
Burgess early one morning from a Soho nightclub; he found him lying
unconscious on the floor with congealed blood on his face and head.
Warner grew tired of McNeil's repeated rhetorical question: "What's
to be done with Guy?"[72]

Yet Burgess could still display fragments of the charm and
brilliance of his Cambridge years. Late in 1947, probably to get rid of
him, McNeil recommended Burgess to the parliamentary undersecretary in the Foreign Office, Christopher Mayhew, who was then organizing the Information Research Department (IRD), set up to counter
Soviet "psychological warfare." Mayhew made what he later described
as "an extraordinary mistake." "I interviewed Burgess. He certainly
showed a dazzling insight into Communist methods of subversion and
I readily took him on."[73] Burgess went the rounds of British embassies,
selling IRD's wares and simultaneously compromising the new department by reporting all its plans to his case officer, Yuri Modin, who
succeeded Krotov late in 1947. The chorus of protests at Burgess's
undiplomatic behavior from the embassies he visited led Mayhew to
sack him from IRD.[74]

Among those friends who still had confidence in him was David
Footman, head of political intelligence in SIS. Soon after Tito's break
with Moscow in 1948, an officer from Footman's department suggested
drafting a questionnaire on the working of the Cominform to be put to
Tito by the British ambassador in Belgrade. "Marvelous idea!" replied
Footman. "Go and talk to Guy." Together, Burgess and the SIS officer

prepared a list of questions to be sent to Belgrade. Tito's response intrigued Moscow Center and must also have delighted Footman.[75]

In the autumn of 1948 Burgess was transferred to the Far Eastern Department, where he remained until posted to the Washington embassy as second secretary in August 1950. There he was able to keep Moscow informed on the detailed formulation of British policy to the People's Republic of China, founded in 1949, and toward Korea in the period leading up to the outbreak of war in June 1950. Though only a grade 4 officer, Burgess had regular access to intelligence assessments from the Joint Intelligence Committee, the War Office, and General Douglas MacArthur's headquarters at Supreme Allied Command in Tokyo. Of particular interest to Moscow Center would have been a minutely detailed military intelligence analysis in April 1950 of "Russian assistance to the Chinese communist forces," which effectively revealed all that Western intelligence had gathered on that subject only two months before the outbreak of the Korean War. Burgess wrote a long minute on it in his customary bright blue ink and surprisingly neat handwriting.[76]

By then, however, his days in the Foreign Office were numbered. A trip to Gibraltar and Tangier in the autumn of 1949 had turned into what Goronwy Rees called a "wild odyssey of indiscretions," among them failing to pay his bills, publicly identifying MI5 and SIS officers, and drunkenly singing in local bars: "Little boys are cheap today, cheaper than yesterday." Burgess was surprised not to be sacked on his return.[77]

The Center concluded, probably correctly, that Burgess's breakdown in the autumn of 1949 was due to the shock of discovering that he was at risk from the Venona intercepts. Philby had been "indoctrinated" into Venona in September 1949 on the eve of his posting to Washington as SIS liaison officer and had passed on an urgent warning. In fact, the Venona decrypts were to reveal no clues to Burgess before his defection in 1951. But in the autumn of 1949 he seems to have feared that he might be discovered at any moment.

Donald Maclean reacted as badly as Burgess to news of the threat posed by Venona. In his case the danger seemed more immediate. Philby realized soon after his "indoctrination" that a so-far-unidentified Soviet agent code-named Homer, referred to in several Venona decrypts, must be Maclean.[78] Maclean's posting to Cairo in October 1948 as counselor and head of chancery at the age of only thirty-five had seemed to set him on a path that would lead him to the top of the diplomatic service, or a position close to it. He found the threat of exposure, a year later, too much to bear. Though his work remained highly professional, his drinking out of hours slipped out of control. His old friend and drinking companion Philip Toynbee saw him give way in Cairo to "berserk and murderous outbursts when, so to speak, the pot of suppressed anger has been filled."

In May 1950 the two men went on a drunken spree, broke into the flat of two girls working for the U.S. embassy, ransacked their bedroom, ripped apart their underclothes, then moved on to destroy the bathroom. There, Toynbee later recalled, "Donald raises a large mirror above his head and crashes it into the bath, when to my amazement and delight, alas, the bath breaks in two while the mirror remains intact." A few days later Maclean was sent back to London, where the Foreign Office gave him the summer off and paid for a course of treatment by a psychiatrist, who diagnosed overwork, marital problems, and repressed homosexuality. In the autumn, apparently back in control of himself, he was made head of the American desk in the Foreign Office. There, despite alcoholic evenings in the Gargoyle Club and a drunken description of himself as "the English Hiss," his work in office hours remained meticulously efficient.[79]

The impact in Moscow of Maclean's and Burgess's intelligence was probably at its peak after the outbreak of the Korean War in June 1950. Maclean's deputy on the American desk, Robert Cecil, concludes that the Kremlin would have found the documents provided by Maclean "of inestimable value in advising the Chinese and the North Koreans on strategy and negotiating positions."[80] In addition to supplying classified documents, Maclean and Burgess also provided their own anti-American gloss on them and thus heightened Soviet fears that the United States intended to escalate the Korean conflict into world war. Even within the Foreign Office Maclean denounced American policy at the end of 1950 as "scared, stubborn and dangerous." For perhaps the only time in his diplomatic career he showed open sympathy in an official minute with the crude Stalinist analysis of the inherently aggressive designs of American finance capital. There was, he said, "some point" to the argument that the American economy was now so geared to the military machine that all-out war might seem preferable to a recession produced by demobilization.[81]

Though such Stalinist nonsense found little favor in Whitehall, there was widespread concern at the end of 1950 about the direction of United States policy. In December President Truman gave an ill-judged reply to a question about the use of the atomic bomb in the Korean conflict: "Consideration of the use of any weapon is always implicit in the very possession of that weapon." Clement Attlee hurriedly arranged a trip to Washington to discuss with the President this and other policy issues of the war. Maclean was able to pass to Modin both the briefing papers for the visit and the cabinet paper reporting the outcome.[82] It was not in Stalin's morbidly suspicious nature ever to underestimate the aggressive designs of Western imperialists. By the end of 1950 he was convinced that there was an imminent danger of a Third World War.[83]

The Korean War had its origins in North Korean, rather than Soviet, territorial ambitions. But Western ignorance about the aims of Soviet policy and the continuing inability of the Anglo-American intelligence community to obtain any intelligence in Moscow that compared with that obtained by the KI in London and Washington led to mistaken fears that the war was part of a grand design for Soviet expansion. In the winter of 1950–51 there were widespread fears that aggression in Korea might be the prelude to a Soviet offensive in Germany. The War Office warned the British cabinet in February 1951: "War possible in 1951, probable in 1952."[84] Mistaken though genuine Western fears of a Soviet attack were, when reported to the Kremlin they were almost certainly interpreted by Stalin as a cover for the West's own aggressive designs. Intelligence from Maclean and Burgess helped to feed Soviet suspicions. Maclean must surely have expressed to Modin, probably in even stronger language, the fear recorded by him in a Foreign Office minute of March 1951 that American "fire-eating in the Far East and generally will land us unnecessarily in war."[85] Moscow, like Maclean, doubtless breathed a sigh of relief in April when Truman sacked the U.S. commander-in-chief in Korea, General Douglas MacArthur, the leading advocate of carrying the war into China. At the very moment when MacArthur was being relieved of his command, however, Maclean's career as a Soviet agent was suddenly put in jeopardy.

The downfall of Maclean, in the view of the KGB First Chief Directorate, remains the single most damaging consequence of the Venona decrypts. For the decrypts that identified Maclean began a chain of events that was to wreck the careers of the most prized group of penetration agents in its history, the Magnificent Five. Philby set sail for Washington as the newly appointed SIS representative late in October 1949. Because of his inside knowledge of Soviet operations, he had deduced well ahead of anyone else in the Venona circle that the Soviet agent code-named Homer was Maclean. In his memoirs he misleadingly attributes the fact that it took eighteen more months to track down Maclean solely to the Establishment's purblind inability to grasp that there could be a traitor in its ranks.[86] The first references to Homer discovered in the Venona decrypts, however, were remarkably unspecific. Not merely did they not identify Homer as a member of the British embassy; they did not even establish whether he was a British or American citizen. The initial field of suspects, which Harold Macmillan later claimed was several thousand strong, included almost anyone who might have gained access to secret transatlantic communications.[87] On his arrival in Washington, Philby was reassured to discover that "The FBI was still sending us reams about the Embassy charladies, and the enquiry into our menial personnel was spinning itself out endlessly."[88]

Though the Venona intercepts caused Philby, by his own admission, "deep anxiety," it was clear once he reached Washington that Maclean was not in immediate danger. His case officer told him that Moscow had decided that "Maclean should stay in his post as long as possible" and that plans would be made to rescue him "before the net closed on him."[89] The net did not begin to close until the winter of 1950–51. By the end of 1950 the list of suspects had been narrowed to thirty-five. By the beginning of April 1951 it had shrunk to nine.[90] Philby made a show of helping the hunt for Homer by drawing attention to a mildly misleading reference by the prewar defector, Krivitsky, at a 1940 debriefing to a Soviet agent in the Foreign Office of good family, educated at Eton and Oxford (rather than, as was actually the case, at another public school and Cambridge).

According to Philby, the embassy security officer, Bobby Mackenzie, offered him short odds that the mole was Paul Gore-Booth, a future permanent undersecretary at the Foreign Office who had been educated at Eton and Oxford. Since Gore-Booth was a distinguished classical scholar, the code name Homer seemed unusually appropriate—especially since its Russian form "Gomer" closely resembled "Gore."[91] In mid-April 1951, however, a further Venona decrypt cleared Gore-Booth and solved the mystery by revealing that for a period in 1944 Homer had met his NKGB controller twice a week in New York, traveling there from Washington on the pretext of visiting his pregnant wife—a pattern of activity that fitted Maclean and no other suspect.[92]

There still remained a breathing space of at least a few weeks in which to arrange Maclean's escape. The search for the evidence necessary to convict Maclean of espionage, complicated by the decision not to use Venona decrypts in court, made necessary a period of surveillance by MI5. After discussion with his case officer, Philby decided to use Burgess to convey a warning to Maclean. It was already clear, when Burgess arrived in Washington as second secretary in August 1950, that this posting was his last chance of making a diplomatic career. Within eight months it was also clear that the chance had gone. In April 1951 he was ordered home in disgrace after a series of escapades (almost certainly not preplanned) had aroused the collective ire of the Virginia state police, the State Department, and the British ambassador. On the eve of his departure from New York aboard the *Queen Mary,* he dined with Philby in a Chinese restaurant whose piped music inhibited eavesdropping, and discussed the escape plan for Maclean.[93]

By agreement with Philby, one of Burgess's first acts after landing in England on May 7 was to brief Yuri Modin, case officer for all the Magnificent Five during their periods in England. It was Modin who was responsible for implementing the escape plan. As head of the Number One (Political Intelligence) Department of the KGB Andropov Institute in the early 1980s, he was fond of explaining to new recruits how he had masterminded the escape. Gordievsky noticed that he invariably denied any credit to the arrogant and unpopular London resident at the time, Nikolai Rodin.[94]

Since mid-April Maclean had received no top-secret papers. Quickly realizing that he was under surveillance and assuming, correctly, that his phone was tapped, he dared not make contact with Modin. Out of the blue Burgess came to the rescue. Immediately after his return to Britain, during a visit to the Foreign Office at which Maclean was warned to expect a request for his resignation, Burgess managed to pass him a note giving the time and place of the rendezvous that would set his escape in motion.[95]

Soon after his return to London, Burgess received an urgent airmail letter from Philby, nominally about a car he had left in the embassy parking lot but ending with the thinly disguised warning: "It's getting *very* hot here." Burgess by now was at the end of his tether. As Philby later acknowledged:

He was close to a total nervous breakdown, closer than anyone realized. His career in Britain was finished, and this

would have made him little use to the KGB. We were all so
worried about Maclean that we didn't notice what had happened to Burgess.[96]

Modin, however, did. Burgess was now so afraid of being watched
himself that he asked Blunt to explain his fears to Modin rather than
make contact directly. Disturbed by Burgess's state of mind and doubtful of his ability to withstand interrogation, Modin put pressure on him
to defect with Maclean.[97]

The story of Burgess and Maclean's joint defection has been
confused by a number of bestselling conspiracy theories. It has frequently been alleged that on the morning of Friday, May 25, the foreign
secretary, Herbert Morrison, chaired a meeting at which it was decided
to begin Maclean's interrogation on Monday the 28th. It has been
widely assumed that Burgess was then almost immediately tipped off
in London by a so far unidentified mole (commonly misidentified as the
Fifth Man), and hurriedly arranged to flee with Maclean on the same
evening.

In reality there was no meeting on the 25th and no tip-off by
a fifth man. Morrison authorized the interrogation of Maclean on the
basis of a written submission by his officials but laid down no date for
it to begin. Owing to a mixture of staff shortages and misjudgments MI5
and the Special Branch failed to keep Maclean under surveillance at his
home in the village of Tatsfield on the Kent-Surrey border, thus making
possible his escape.[98] But even had MI5 prevented his escape, it might
well have failed to find the evidence for a successful prosecution. The
official policy of refusing to use Venona intercepts in court meant that
its only real hope of a conviction lay in securing a confession. This
technique had worked with Fuchs. But if Maclean's nerve had held, he,
like Philby later, could have brazened it out. That, however, was a
chance that at the time Modin and the Center dared not take.

The crucial tip-off to Maclean came from Philby via Modin and
Burgess. Philby reported to his case officer that the MI5 liaison officer
in Washington, Geoffrey Patterson, had been ordered to report to
London on the Homer investigations by Wednesday, May 23. He deduced that Maclean's interrogation was to begin on Monday the 28th.
Modin immediately put the escape plan into operation.[99] Boat tickets
to France were purchased on the 24th. On the evening of Friday the
25th, Burgess drew up in a rented car at Maclean's large Victorian
house just as he was sitting down to a dinner cooked by his wife Melinda

to celebrate his thirty-eighth birthday. Introducing himself to Mrs. Maclean as Roger Styles from the Foreign Office, Burgess insisted that he and her husband leave at once. Maclean hurried upstairs to say goodbye to his sons, gave a confused explanation to his outraged wife, and left in Burgess's car. Sharing the driving, they reached Southampton docks just in time to catch the midnight sailing of the *Falaise* to St. Malo. In France MGB/KI officers provided them with false papers, on which they traveled first to Vienna, then to Moscow.[100]

When lecturing on the Magnificent Five thirty years later at the Andropov Institute, Yuri Modin's main recollection of Burgess and Maclean in May 1951 was of the stress that both were under. His memory of Blunt was rather different. Krotov in 1945 had noticed in Blunt much the same level of stress that Modin observed in Burgess in 1951. But after six years of only occasional odd jobs for the MGB/KI, combined with academic distinction and royal patronage, Blunt's composure had returned. Though Modin noticed renewed signs of stress after Burgess's flight to Moscow, he also admired the cool professionalism that Blunt was able to summon up at a critical moment. He later told Gordievsky that it had been a "great honor" to run Blunt.[101] At the time of Burgess and Maclean's defection, Blunt still had the full confidence of his former friends in MI5. Since MI5 was reluctant to arouse premature publicity by pressing for a search warrant to Burgess's apartment immediately after his disappearance, Blunt agreed to ask Burgess's lover Jack Hewit to give him the key to the apartment. Before handing over the key to MI5, however, Blunt—doubtless with Modin's encouragement—spent a few hours removing compromising material from Burgess's chaotic collection of letters from lovers and other memorabilia stuffed into drawers and shoeboxes. Blunt successfully retrieved a number of embarrassing documents, including Philby's last-minute warning that things were getting *"very* hot."[102]

The fifth member of the Magnificent Five, John Cairncross, took no part in assisting the escape. Since the war he had worked in the Defence (Material) and Defence (Personnel) Divisions of the Treasury, out of contact with the rest of the Five. Cairncross continued to impress both Krotov and Modin with the sheer amount of material he provided at their monthly meetings.[103] He was probably able to inform Krotov of the decision to build a British atomic bomb. It is likely that he also had access to the accounts for the project as to much else concerning the defense budget. In 1947 Cairncross was closely concerned with the passing of the Radioactive Substances Act. Two years later he was actively involved in the financial problems of setting up NATO, chairing a subcommittee "to consider establishment problems."[104] His prickly personality, however, hindered his promotion prospects. Not till 1950, at the age of thirty-seven, was he confirmed in the rank of principal.

In May 1951 a lapse by Blunt brought Cairncross's career as an active Soviet agent to an end. While searching Burgess's flat, Blunt failed to notice a series of unsigned notes describing confidential discussions in Whitehall on the eve and at the beginning of the war. Sir John Colville, one of those mentioned in the notes, was able to identify the author as Cairncross. MI5 began surveillance of Cairncross and followed him to a hurriedly arranged meeting with his case officer. Modin, however, failed to turn up. At subsequent interrogation by MI5, Cairncross admitted passing confidential notes to the Russians but denied being a spy. He resigned from the Treasury and worked in North America for several years before joining the Food and Agriculture Organization of the United Nations in Rome. Cairncross finally confessed to MI5 after a further interrogation in 1964. But his career as an active Soviet agent had effectively come to an end when Blunt overlooked his notes in Burgess's flat in 1951.[105]

After his public unmasking in 1979, Blunt admitted that he had been "pressed" (by Modin, though he did not identify him) to follow Burgess and Maclean to Moscow in 1951.[106] Unwilling to exchange the prestigious scholarly surroundings of the Courtauld Institute for the bleak socialist realism of Stalin's Russia, Blunt refused. It was another thirteen years before MI5 finally obtained a confession from him in 1964. Even then, in the absence of the evidence needed for a conviction in a court of law, he was given immunity in return for his confession.

By contrast, suspicion fell on Philby immediately after the flight of Burgess and Maclean, though it was not shared by all his colleagues in either London or Washington. The immediate cause of the suspicion was his association with Burgess. During Burgess's year at the Washington embassy he had, at his own pressing insistence, lodged with Philby and his wife. Though dubious about the arrangement, Philby had concluded—incorrectly—that in view of their past association, turning Burgess away would do little to protect his own security. He also hoped that, while lodging with him, Burgess would be less likely to get into further "personal scrapes of a spectacular nature" than when living by himself. When just such a series of "personal scrapes" led to

Burgess's return to England in disgrace in May 1951, Philby did not suspect that Burgess would accompany Maclean to Moscow. Philby first heard the news from Geoffrey Patterson, the MI5 liaison officer in Washington:

> He looked gray. "Kim," he said in a half-whisper, "the bird has flown." I registered dawning horror (I hope). "What bird? Not Maclean?" "Yes," he answered. "But there's more than that . . . *Guy Burgess* has gone with him." At that, my consternation was no pretense.

Later that day Philby drove into the Virginia countryside and in a woods buried the photographic equipment with which he had copied documents for Moscow Center, an action he had mentally rehearsed many times since his arrival in Washington. The Center had worked out for him an emergency escape plan, but by the end of the day he had decided not to use it. Instead he would stay put and brazen it out.[107]

Philby was unable, however, to brazen it out in Washington. The head of the CIA, General Walter Bedell Smith, informed SIS that Philby was no longer acceptable as its liaison officer. But despite his recall to Britain, Philby still had influential supporters in Washington as well as in London. Among them, despite his later claims to have seen through Philby as quickly as Bedell Smith, was the future head of counterintelligence in the CIA, James Jesus Angleton. About a year after Philby's recall, Angleton told a colleague from the CIA, James MacCargar, who was visiting London, "I still think one day Kim will be Chief of SIS."[108] When Angleton eventually realized Philby's treachery, the shock of betrayal was all the greater. The most enduring damage done by Philby and the Magnificent Five to the Anglo-American intelligence community was to lead Angleton, Peter Wright, and a minority of intelligence officers on both sides of the Atlantic into a wilderness of mirrors, searching in vain for the chimera of a still vaster but imaginary Soviet deception.

On his return from Washington Philby was officially retired from SIS with a £4,000 golden handshake: £2,000 down and the rest paid in installments over three years. The decision not to pay the whole sum at once reflected, Philby correctly deduced, "the possibility of my being sent to jail within three years." In December 1951 he was summoned to a "judicial inquiry" at MI5 headquarters in Curzon Street, Mayfair, in effect an informal trial, of which Philby later gave a misleading account in his memoirs.[109] According to an MI5 officer of the time, "There was not a single officer who sat through the proceedings who came away not totally convinced of Philby's guilt."[110] Contrary to the impression Philby sought to create in Moscow after his defection, many of his own former colleagues in SIS also thought him guilty. But the judicial inquiry concluded that it would probably never be possible to gather the evidence for a successful prosecution. Philby, however, retained the support of a loyal group of friends within SIS to whom he cleverly presented himself as the innocent victim of a McCarthyist witch hunt.[111]

The rest of Philby's career as a Soviet mole, despite exaggerated claims made for his years in Beirut before his defection in 1963, was to be largely anticlimax. The great days of the Magnificent Five ended in 1951 with the flight of Burgess and Maclean, the discovery of Cairncross, and the dismissal of Philby from SIS. When the Five began their careers as Soviet agents in the 1930s, Moscow Center's most successful foreign recruiting ground had been in or on the fringes of Western Communist parties and the Communist International. The new generation of penetration agents that came to the fore during the Cold War was mostly recruited differently. After the postwar embarrassments caused by the public revelations by Igor Guzenko, Elizabeth Bentley, Whittaker Chambers, and others of the use of Western Communists as Soviet agents, the Center forbade its residencies abroad, save in exceptional circumstances, to recruit Party members for intelligence work.[112]

Just as the great days of the Magnificent Five were drawing to a close, however, one Cambridge recruit from the 1930s was reaching his prime. Alister Watson, one-time secretary of the Apostles, had played a major part in Blunt's conversion to Marxism and had probably become an early member of Burgess's ring of five. During his six years as a fellow of King's College (1933–39), however, his activities can scarcely have gone much beyond talent spotting. On the outbreak of war he joined the Admiralty as a temporary scientific officer, working on radar and engineering design. His most important work as a Soviet agent came after the war, particularly after he moved in 1953 to a post as senior principal scientific officer in the Admiralty Research Laboratories at Teddington, working on a top-secret project of great interest to the MGB, devising methods for the detection of submarines by low-frequency underwater sound.

At one stage Watson shared a house for two years with the

brother of the MI5 officer Peter Wright. Long before Watson was investigated by MI5, Wright took a dislike to him: "He was tall and thin, with a pinched, goatlike face and a strange affected tiptoed walk." Others, however, found Watson an engaging if eccentric conversationalist. Even in his seventies he was capable of greeting old friends with "in rapid succession, a proposition in four-dimensional geometry, a point about the structure of *Paradise Lost,* and a surmise about the languages of Egypt." As head of the Submarine Detection Section at the Admiralty Research Laboratory, he held, in Wright's view, "one of the most secret and important jobs in the entire defense establishment." The KGB took much the same view.

During the 1940s and early 1950s Watson had the same sequence of case officers as the Five: Gorsky, Krotov, and Modin. While Modin was back in Moscow from 1953 to 1955, Watson fell out with his successor, Sergei Aleksandrovich Kondrashev (later deputy head of the FCD). Watson told Peter Wright: "He was too bourgeois. . . . He wore flannel trousers and a blue blazer, and walked a poodle." Watson's later case officers included Rodin, probably Modin for a second time, and Nikolai Prokofyevich Karpekov, who from 1958 to 1963 was the London residency's expert in scientific and technical intelligence. After an MI5 investigation, Watson was eventually transferred to nonsecret work at the Institute of Oceanography in 1967.[113]

The classified history of the First Chief Directorate, prepared in 1980, lists, among major postwar successes, the increase of scientific and technical intelligence from the United Kingdom. Besides the intelligence on submarine detection systems provided by Watson, the London residency also claimed other successes in various aspects of nuclear power and military technology, and in navigational systems. One of those most active in scientific and technical (S&T) intelligence during the 1950s was Leonid Sergeevich Zaitsev, then a PR line officer. He was later to become head of a new Directorate T, which specialized in this work. S&T activity was to expand further during the 1960s.[114]

In the early 1950s the Center also achieved one major new penetration of the British intelligence community. Within a few months of Philby's dismissal from SIS in June 1951, the MGB had begun recruiting another SIS officer, twenty-nine-year-old George Blake, né Behar. Blake had been born in Rotterdam of a naturalized British father (by origin a Sephardic Jew from Cairo) and a Dutch mother, who called their son George in honor of King George V. During the Second World War Blake served successively in the Dutch resistance and the

Royal Navy, becoming a naval intelligence officer at the end of the war. After spending the academic year 1947–48 learning Russian at Downing College, Cambridge, Blake joined SIS. There was much, however, that SIS had failed to discover about its new recruit, notably the influence on him of his cousin Henri Curiel, a leading member of the Egyptian Communist Party, whom he had seen frequently in his teens. In 1949, Blake was posted by SIS to South Korea, working under diplomatic cover as vice-consul in Seoul. A year later, shortly after the outbreak of the Korean War, he was interned by the invading North Koreans.[115]

Moscow Center owed the opportunity to recruit Blake chiefly to the Chinese, whose "volunteer" forces intervened in support of the North Koreans. On the founding of the Chinese People's Republic in October 1949 the MGB had proposed sending a large group of advisers to China and invited the Chinese to send some of their own intelligence officers to Moscow for training. Mao Zedong accepted both suggestions. From the outset, however, the Chinese were determined that their intelligence services should not, like those of Eastern Europe, become controlled by the MGB. Though anxious to learn from Soviet tradecraft and technical expertise, they rejected MGB intelligence manuals as unsuited to Chinese conditions. MGB officers were also not allowed, as in Eastern Europe, to take part in Chinese intelligence operations. China did, however, provide much intelligence on U.S. military technology obtained during the Korean War, and gave the MGB a base on Chinese territory, where it could train ethnic Chinese illegals for work against the Main Adversary and other Western states. The MGB was also given unrestricted access to Western POWs held by the Chinese and North Koreans. Among them was George Blake.[116]

Blake's recruitment seems to have begun in the autumn of 1951. According to the first MGB officer to interrogate him, Grigori Kuzmich, Blake quickly expressed disillusion with Western policy in general and with Anglo-American intervention in Korea in particular but did not at first betray the secrets of SIS. By the time he and his fellow POWs were released in the spring of 1953, however, Blake was a fully recruited Soviet agent. For the remainder of the decade he was to betray SIS operations and agents as enthusiastically, though not quite as effectively, as Philby.[117]

During the early years of the Cold War Soviet intelligence achieved major penetrations in much of continental Europe. The penetrations to which the Center attached most importance were in France and West Germany. Penetration of the French official bureaucracy was facilitated by the record postwar support for the Communist Party, which won about a quarter of the vote for more than a decade, and by the presence of Communist ministers in coalition governments until 1947. Both Vladimir and Evdokia Petrova reported after their defection from Soviet intelligence in 1954 that the MGB and KI had "found intelligence work particularly easy in France. . . . The French operational section of the KI was littered with what looked like photostat copies of original official French documents."[118] The MGB/KI resident in Paris from 1947 to 1949 was Ivan Ivanovich Agayants (*alias* Avalov), an Armenian in his late thirties who spoke French, English, and Persian. Evdokia Petrova remembered him as the most likable of all her former colleagues: "charming, highly cultured, courteous, kind . . . an intelligent and able intelligence officer." Agayants's success in Paris led to his promotion in 1949 to head the Second Directorate of the KI, which was responsible for all Europe except the United Kingdom. His successor as Paris resident from 1950 to 1954, Aleksei Alekseevich Krokhin, also enjoyed his time in France. The Petrovs found him "always smiling, exuberant and pleased with life." Krokhin was later to return for a second spell in Paris from 1966 to 1972, a sure sign of the success of his first term as resident.[119]

The penetration agents who provided many, if not most, of the official French documents that the Petrovs saw in such profusion at the Center during Agayants's and Krokhin's terms as residents seem never to have been caught—or at least publicly identified.[120] The most important French Cold War mole ever to be convicted—though not until he had been working as a Soviet agent for twenty years—was Georgi Pâques. After a brilliant early academic career as *normalien* and *agrégé* in Italian, Pâques was recruited in 1943 at the age of twenty-nine by Aleksandr Guzovsky of the NKGB while working in Algiers as head of political affairs in the broadcasting service of General de Gaulle's provisional government. During the postwar Fourth Republic, controlled initially by Guzovsky, who moved with him to Paris, Pâques served as *chef de cabinet* and adviser to a series of ministers. Like a number of Cold War moles, Pâques's motives had more to do with self-esteem than with the ideological conviction that had inspired the Magnificent Five and an earlier generation of Soviet penetration agents. Determined to play a major role behind the scenes of international relations if he could not do so on the world stage itself, he set out to redress the balance of power between the Soviet Union and what he saw as an overmighty United States. His case officers were careful to pander to Pâques's vanity. He claimed to have been read a letter of congratulations from Stalin (and later from Khrushchev). The most productive period of Pâques's twenty years as a Soviet agent was to come after de Gaulle's return to power in 1958, when he gained access to major defense secrets.[121]

The division of Germany and the flood of refugees coming from the East made the Federal Republic, founded in 1949, an easier target for Soviet Bloc penetration than any other West European state. One of Moscow Center's first targets was the semiofficial foreign intelligence agency the Gehlen Org, which in 1946 was to be officially attached to the Federal Chancellery as the Bundesnachrichtendienst (BND). Penetration began in 1949 with the recruitment by the MGB's East German headquarters in Karlshorst of an unemployed former SS captain, Hans Clemens. In 1951 Clemens gained a job in the Gehlen Org, then successfully recommended a former SS comrade, Heinze Felfe, whom he had also recruited to the MGB. With the active assistance of Karlshorst, Felfe rapidly established himself as one of the most successful agents of the Cold War. In 1953 he astounded his colleagues by announcing that he had set up an agent network in Moscow headed by a Red Army colonel.

Much of the intelligence from the network—a blend of fact and fiction fabricated by the Center—was passed on to the West German chancellor, Konrad Adenauer, in Bonn. Karlshorst further promoted Felfe's career by giving him minutes of East German government meetings and leads that led to the capture of expendable East German agents. Felfe's career was to peak at almost the same time as Pâques's. By 1958 he had established himself as the German Philby, becoming, like Philby in 1944, head of Soviet counterintelligence. Felfe's motives, however, had more in common with Pâques's than with Philby's. He was, he told himself, the supreme intelligence professional, recognized as the rising star of the BND yet outwitting it at the same time. Karlshorst was careful to boost his ego, encouraging him to believe that his achievements were eclipsing even those of Richard Sorge. "I wanted," Felfe said later, "to rank as top class with the Russians."[122]

During the Cold War, as before, one of the distinguishing characteristics of Soviet intelligence operations was the extent to which they were targeted on imaginary enemies as well as real opponents. The hunt for real or, more commonly, imagined Trotskyists in the 1930s was paralleled at the height of the Cold War by search-and-destroy operations against mostly imaginary Titoist and Zionist conspirators. Like Stalin, Beria and Abakumov interpreted Tito's break with Moscow in 1948 as part of a wide-ranging imperialist conspiracy to undermine the Soviet Bloc. In July Stalin's protégé Zhdanov informed a meeting of the Cominform that the MGB had proof that Tito was in league with imperialist espionage agencies to subvert the people's democracies. Some of the allegations of Tito's involvement with Western secret services were part of a deliberate attempt to discredit him. Others were the product of Stalin's and the Center's paranoid tendencies. In the end the two strands became inextricably intertwined.

The main imaginary Western master spy orchestrating the imperialist-Titoist conspiracy uncovered by the MGB/KI in Eastern Europe was Noel Haviland Field, an eccentric, well-intentioned American former diplomat and relief worker, exposed in 1949 by Moscow Center as an "agent of the American espionage organization who smuggled his spies into the top ranks of the Communist parties in order to topple the socialist system in the service of the imperialists and Tito."[123]

Field was a romantic Communist dreamer, whose very naïveté was bound in the end to arouse the suspicions of the conspiracy theorists in the Center. While working at the State Department in 1934 he was recruited as an NKVD agent; he provided information but refused to provide documents. In 1936 he left Washington for the League of Nations disarmament secretariat in Geneva, believing, according to his biographer, Flora Lewis, "that as an international civil servant he would not have anyone to betray if he also worked on the side as a Soviet agent." Field's career with the NKVD was unusually accident prone. His first case officer in Geneva was Ignace Poretsky (*alias* Ludwig, *alias* Reiss), who promptly defected and was gunned down by the NKVD. Field's next contact, Walter Krivitsky, also defected in the following year, and, like Reiss, was branded by the NKVD as a Trotskyist. Late in 1937 Field and his wife journeyed to Moscow to try to reestablish relations with the NKVD. While there, however, their disillusioned former case officers in Washington, Paul and Hede Massing, came to their hotel room and called the NKVD to demand exit visas, saying that if they were refused they would go with the Fields to seek help from the U.S. embassy. The NKVD was understandably wary about using the Fields again.[124]

Despite these bizarre misadventures, Field kept his romantic, neo-Stalinist faith. "Stalin," he told friends, "knows what he's doing." During the war he organized relief work for the Unitarian Service Commission (USC), first in France, then from 1942 in Geneva, where he became the USC's European director. In Switzerland he offered assistance to many refugee German and Hungarian Communists. But he aroused NKVD suspicions by renewing contact with the OSS chief in Switzerland, Allen Dulles (later head of the CIA from 1953 to 1961), whom he had met while working at the State Department a decade earlier. Field won Dulles's support for a scheme for OSS to ally with German Communists in forming an anti-Nazi underground, which was, however, vetoed by OSS headquarters.[125]

In 1947 complaints about Field's Communist links and extramarital adventures led to his effective sacking by the USC. The Center, however, was even more wary of him than the Unitarians were. Field's visits to Eastern Europe in an attempt to establish a career as a freelance journalist or academic aroused suspicions that he was working under cover for Western intelligence. In the paranoid atmosphere that followed the breach with Yugoslavia, those suspicions became acute. During the war Field had been in close touch with Yugoslav Communists in Switzerland and had helped to convert Allen Dulles to support for Tito's partisans. In 1944-45 he had assisted Hungarian Communists and other émigrés in returning to Hungary by sending them, with OSS help, through Yugoslavia in Yugoslav uniform.[126] In 1948 the KI residency in Vienna obtained the copy of a letter written by Field to Dulles at the end of the war. Though it contained no reference to intelligence work, conspiracy theorists at the Center discovered in it nonexistent coded references to espionage.[127]

It remained only to discover Field's imaginary accomplices in Eastern Europe. In the summer of 1948 Mátyás Rákosi, the Hungarian Party first secretary, was summoned to Moscow to be told that the chief suspect was László Rajk, minister of the interior and by far the most popular of the Party leadership.[128] Even a Stalinist history of "the Rajk conspiracy" later regretfully acknowledged "his great physical charm": "He was very attractive to women and men responded to his compelling personality."[129] Though a loyal Stalinist, Rajk was the only member of the five-man inner circle of the Party leadership not to have passed the war years in Moscow as a protégé of the NKVD. He had fought in the Spanish Civil War and spent three years in French internment camps after the Republican defeat. In 1941 he managed to return to Hungary, became secretary of the underground Communist Central Committee and one of the leaders of the resistance. He was arrested by the Gestapo in November 1944 and spent the last six months of the war in a German concentration camp before returning to Budapest in May 1945.

Unhappily for Rajk, he owed a wartime debt of gratitude to Field. The two men had first met in Spain during the Civil War, and Field had been instrumental in gaining Rajk's release from a French internment camp in 1941 and assisting his return to Hungary.[130] To the conspiracy theorists at Moscow Center that was prima facie evidence of a plot to infiltrate Rajk as a penetration agent into the leadership of the Hungarian Communist Party. Rajk's fate was sealed by the evidence of a Yugoslav as well as a Field connection. Before Tito's break with Moscow, Rajk had, as Djilas later acknowledged, formed an "especially strong" bond with Ranković, his Yugoslav counterpart as interior minister.[131]

On Rákosi's return from his briefing session in Moscow in the summer of 1948, he summoned the rest of the inner circle of Party leaders, minus Rajk, to inform them of the Center's "evidence" that Rajk was working for U.S. intelligence. János Kádár (later Party first secretary from 1956 to 1988) was summoned to the meeting and told that in view of the serious suspicions against Rajk, "even if not proven beyond doubt," he could not remain as minister of the interior, responsible for the AVO. Kádár would therefore move to the interior ministry and, for the time being, Rajk would become foreign minister.[132] A top-secret section was set up within the AVO, run by its chief, Gábor Péter, and his two closest aides, Colonels Ernö Szücs and Gyula Décsi, to prepare the case against Rajk and other imaginary conspirators.

The initiative, however, remained with the MGB. General Fyodor Belkin, chief Soviet "adviser" for Southeast Europe, dispatched two MGB generals, Likhachev and Makarov, to Budapest to oversee preparations for the arrests and show trial. The team of MGB advisers eventually swelled to about forty. In May 1949, at the request of the AVO, Field was lured to Prague with the offer of a possible teaching post at a Czech university. But the head of the Czechoslovak StB, Jindřich Veselý, was skeptical of the MGB's Field conspiracy theory and initially resisted AVO pressure for his arrest. General Belkin then intervened personally. Veselý later claimed that he was told by President Gottwald: "If General Belkin . . . supports it, then do as they want." On May 11 Field was arrested in Prague. Next day he was taken to Budapest to be interrogated jointly by the MGB and AVO. On May 17 Péter called a conference of senior AVO officers and announced the discovery of a vast conspiracy linking Western intelligence services with "the chained dog of the imperialists," Josip Tito. An attempt was made to calm Rajk's suspicions for two weeks longer. On May 29 he and his wife were invited to Sunday lunch with the Rákosis.[133] Next day he was arrested. On June 11 Kádár, as the minister responsible for the AVO, briefed the Party Central Committee: "There were some, of course, who did not believe Rajk was guilty," he said later, "but most of them were paralyzed with fear." The briefing itself, he claimed, was prepared by Rákosi, the Party first secretary.[134]

Rajk's interrogation was overseen by Belkin and jointly conducted by the AVO and their Soviet advisers. Béla Szász, one of Rajk's alleged accomplices, noted how during interrogations, "The Hungarians smiled a flattering, servile smile when the Russians spoke to them; they reacted to the most witless jokes of the [MGB] officers with obsequious trumpetings of immoderate laughter." During interrogations Belkin chain-smoked American Old Gold cigarettes from a leather case. He was easily displeased. When Szász failed to incriminate Rajk,

> Belkin jumped up in a rage, flung down the sheaf of papers he was holding, snatched the leather case filled with Old Gold cigarettes from under my nose and shouted in Russian for a minute and a half. . . . "This is not a Trotskyist meeting, this is not the place for provocation!"

Though Belkin and the MGB advisers frequently ordered beatings and torture, they were always administered by the AVO.[135] One of the chief torturers, Vladimir Farkas, later claimed that he was simply carrying out orders from Moscow.[136]

Gábor Péter, the head of the AVO, complained that beating and torture had failed to make Rajk confess. Kádár, so he later claimed, then told him that "even Horthy's police had not been able to break Rajk. So they wouldn't get anywhere by beating him up. That's when they stopped using force."[137] Rajk was more affected by threats to his family than to himself. But he seems finally to have confessed chiefly out of a Stalinist sense of duty to the Party. Kádár visited Rajk in his cell and asked him to serve the Party by giving evidence at his trial that would expose Tito as the agent of imperialism. The entire Politburo, he assured Rajk, knew that he was innocent but asked him to make this sacrifice for the sake of the Party. His sentence, even if it was to execution, would be a mere charade. Kádár promised him and his family a new life under a new name after the trial, in the Soviet Union. The conversation between Kádár and Rajk was taped without Kádár's knowledge. To revenge himself on Kádár, Rákosi played the tape to the Central Committee shortly before he was ousted from power in 1956.[138]

The show trial of Rajk and seven of his imaginary accomplices before the People's Court in Budapest in September 1949 was devoted to the elaboration of a vast conspiracy theory linking Tito with the subversive schemes of Western intelligence services. The main supporting actors were Tibor Szönyi, head of the Party Cadre Department and the main alleged link between Rajk and the CIA; Lazar Brankov, former Yugoslav intelligence liaison officer in Budapest and the alleged link with Tito; and Lieutenant General György Pálffy, who confessed to preparing a military coup. The prosecutor told the court in his closing address:

> This trial is of international importance. . . . Not only Rajk and his associates are here in the dock, but with them sit their foreign masters, the imperialist instigators from Belgrade and Washington. . . . It is clear from the evidence heard at this trial, that even during the war against Hitler, the American intelligence services were preparing for the fight against the forces of socialism and democracy. Behind Ranković, there stand the shadows of Field and Dulles. . . . The plot in Hungary, planned by Tito and his clique to be put into action by Rajk's spy ring, cannot be understood out of context of the international plans of the American imperialists.

Rajk and four other defendants were condemned to death.[139] The MGB advisers, like the AVO, were well aware that most of the evidence used to mount the morality play in court was manufactured. Indeed the MGB instructed the AVO in the art of rehearsing the defendants beforehand to make their confessions word perfect.[140] But most MGB officers had no doubt that there was a huge conspiracy between the CIA and Tito, and regarded themselves as fully entitled to exploit the dramatic license allowed by a show trial in order to expose it. One of the MGB advisers at the trial, Valeri Aleksandrovich Krotov, who was also present at Rajk's execution, later worked with Gordievsky in Directorate S (Illegals) of the First Chief Directorate. The trial, he told Gordievsky, had been "a political necessity." His most vivid memory remained Rajk's last words before his execution: "Long live Communism!"[141]

Purges of other Hungarian agents of the imaginary Titoist-imperialist conspiracy continued in less spectacular fashion until the death of Stalin. Rajk's successor as interior minister, János Kádár, also came under suspicion. He was dismissed in 1950, imprisoned and tortured in 1951. Though he survived to be rehabilitated a year after Stalin's death, his successor as interior minister, Sándor Zöld, killed his wife, children, mother-in-law, and himself on learning that he was about to be purged. In 1952 the deputy head of the AVH (successor to the AVO), Ernö Szücs, visited Moscow Center and left a report for Stalin himself stating that the purge was out of control and threatened to destroy the party. Back in Budapest, he was arrested, interrogated by a combined MGB/AVH team, and hanged as a spy.[142]

The MGB-orchestrated search for subversive conspiracies by Tito and Western intelligence services spread throughout the Soviet Bloc and beyond into Communist parties in the West. The most dramatic of the show trials that followed Rajk's took place in Prague. At a meeting in Budapest on the eve of the Rajk trial, Belkin and Rákosi jointly pressed Karel Šváb, Czechoslovak deputy minister of the interior and head of security, to begin immediate arrests and interrogations. A week later President Gottwald and Rudolf Slánský, secretary-general of the Czechoslovak Communist Party, asked for MGB advisers with experience of the Rajk case to be sent to guide investigations. Soon afterward Generals Likhachov and Makarov arrived in Prague from Budapest.

There followed what a commission of inquiry appointed during the Prague Spring in 1968 called "a craze for hunting the 'Czechoslovak Rajk.' " Likhachov and Makarov denounced Czech security as weak, indecisive, and "soft" on the class enemy. Slánský responded by announcing the setting-up of a new security department independent of the interior ministry "to investigate Party and political offenses." At first it seemed that the leading candidate for the role of the "Czechoslovak Rajk" was the Slovak foreign minister, Vladimir Clementis, who was dismissed from his post in March 1950. During the spring a series of other "bourgeois nationalists" (including the future Party leader and state president, Gustáv Husák) were publicly vilified as class traitors, in preparation, it seemed, for a great show trial.[143] Then in the summer of 1950 Likhachov and Makarov were replaced by a new team of MGB advisers headed by Vladimir Boyarsky. There followed a rapid change of direction in the MGB-led witch hunt. The main emphasis henceforth was on Zionism rather than Titoism as the chief tool of the subversive plots of the Western intelligence services.[144]

The beginning of an anti-Semitic witch hunt, thinly disguised as a defensive campaign against Zionist subversion, reflected a dramatic change in Soviet policy to the new state of Israel. In the debates at the United Nations in 1947 the Soviet Union supported the partition plan for Palestine leading to the creation of a Jewish state. "This decision," Andrei Gromyko told the UN General Assembly, "meets the legitimate demands of the Jewish nation, hundreds of thousands of whose people are still without a land and without a home." The creation of the state of Israel was seen in Moscow as a blow to British imperialism in the Middle East, inflicted by progressive Jews of Russian and Polish origin. Arab attacks on the Zionists were regarded as the desperate response of reactionary feudal rulers to the emergence of a new progressive regime.

Both Soviet diplomatic support and the arms supplied to the Zionists from Czechoslovakia with Soviet blessing during their war with the Arabs were of crucial importance in the birth of Israel. In May 1948, the Soviet Union was the first to give the new state de jure recognition. Moscow counted on Zionist gratitude both for its early support and for the dominant role of the Red Army in defeating Hitler. Israel, the Kremlin believed, was destined to become the vanguard of the anti-imperialist revolution in the Middle East and to help the Soviet Union gain a foothold in the Mediterranean. Within the new state the left-wing Mapam Party described itself as "an inseparable part of the world revolutionary camp headed by the U.S.S.R."

Late in 1947 Colonel Andrei Mikhailovich Otrashchenko, head of the Middle and Far Eastern Department in the KI (and later in the KGB First Chief Directorate), called an operational conference at which he announced that Stalin personally had given the KI the task of ensuring Israel's alliance with the Soviet Union. The emigration of Russian Jews to Israel offered an ideal opportunity to send Soviet agents to work both within Israel and against the Main Adversary and other Western targets. The head of the Illegals Directorate in the KI (and later in the First Chief Directorate), the tall, athletic Colonel Aleksandr Mikhailovich ("Sasha") Korotkov, who had a Jewish wife, was put in charge of the selection and training of emigrants to Israel to work as Soviet illegals. His chief assistant, Lieutenant Colonel Vladimir Vertiporokh, better known as Dyadya Volodya, was appointed in 1948 as the first KI/MGB resident in Israel. He and Korotkov were both decorated and promoted to the rank of general for the success of the Jewish illegals operation.[145]

By 1950 there had been, for two reasons, a dramatic *volte-face* in Soviet policy to Israel. The first was the enthusiasm of Russian Jews for the new state. When Golda Meir and members of the new Israeli diplomatic mission visited a Moscow synagogue for Rosh Hashana on October 4, 1948, they were mobbed by thirty thousand Jews. The Jewish Anti-Fascist Committee, set up during the war to mobilize Jewish support in the struggle against Nazism, was first ordered to declare, "No! Never and under no circumstances will Soviet Jews exchange their Socialist homeland for another homeland"; then it was abruptly dissolved. According to Khrushchev, its former president, Solomon Mikhailovich Mikhoels, was thrown by the MGB beneath the wheels of a truck and killed. In the winter of 1948–49 the Jewish state theaters in Moscow and other cities were closed and virtually every major Yiddish writer and artist arrested. Even Molotov's Jewish wife, Zhemchuzhina, former head of the State Cosmetic Trust and responsible for products that included a perfume nicknamed "Stalin's Breath," was arrested and sent into internal exile in 1949. According to Khrushchev, Stalin "blew up" when Molotov abstained on a vote to remove his wife from the staff of the Central Committee. Molotov kept his place on the Politburo but lost his position as foreign minister.[146]

For about a year, despite the attack on Zionism at home, the Soviet Union continued to support Israel abroad. Then evidence of Israel's growing links with the West, above all the United States, persuaded the Kremlin to switch its support to Israel's Arab opponents. Thereafter, Zionism was officially interpreted as part of a gigantic imperialist plot to subvert the Soviet Bloc by manipulating its Jewish inhabitants. Belief in the Zionist menace brought to the fore in Stalin a latent anti-Semitism, which had never been far beneath the surface. Though he avoided anti-Semitism in his public speeches and writings, he entertained his sycophantic cronies in private with parodies of Jewish speech and mannerisms. Khrushchev later recalled Stalin telling him after the MGB and Party officials had reported unrest at an aviation factory: "The good workers at the factory should be given clubs so they can beat the hell out of those Jews at the end of the working day!"[147]

The announcement of the new anti-Zionist line caused some initial difficulty at the Center. When Colonel Otrashchenko told a meeting of the KI Middle and Far Eastern Department that Zionism was in league with imperialism, some of his officers were confused by the association of the two ideas. According to the KGB defector Ilya Dzhirkvelov, however, they soon collected themselves: "It was quite clear that this particularism did not fit with Marxism-Leninism. That meant it must be akin to Trotskyism, and we were all quite sure that it was bad."[148]

The first major MGB offensive outside Russia against the vast imaginary Zionist plot took place in Czechoslovakia. Vladimir Boyarsky, the chief MGB adviser in Prague from the summer of 1950, was given a free hand by the Czechoslovak Party leadership to expose the "Zionist conspiracy." "Our greatest enemy," he declared, "is international Zionism, which has at its disposal the most perfect espionage network."[149] The first major victim of Boyarsky's anti-Semitic witch hunt was the Jewish first secretary of the Brno regional Party Committee, Otto Šling, arrested in October 1950.[150] Large-scale arrests of Party members followed during the winter of 1950–51.

In February 1951, probably at Boyarsky's prompting, the notorious anti-Semite Andrej Keppert was appointed director of the StB's Department for the Search for Enemies of the State and immediately set up a special section on Zionism. Keppert used to tell his StB colleagues that whenever he saw a hooked nose he either opened a file on the owner or put him in jail.[151] Boyarsky increasingly insisted that the Zionist conspiracy must be headed by a more powerful figure than Šling. By the summer of 1951 he had identified the chief conspirator as the secretary-general of the Czechoslovak Party, Rudolf Slánský, in reality a loyal Stalinist.

According to Lieutenant Colonel Bohumil Doubek, head of the StB investigations branch, Boyarsky and the MGB advisers emphasized "the growing influence of Judaism in the international political arena; they pointed to Rockefeller, Rothschild, and others, and linked them all to Slánský's activities among us abetted by the Jews." In June 1951 Doubek and an assistant drafted a comprehensive report on espionage and subversion by "Jewish bourgeois nationalists," naming Slánský and Bedřich Geminder, Jewish head of the International Department of the Party Secretariat, as the chief culprits. After amendment by Boyarsky and the MGB advisers, the report was forwarded to President Gottwald and his minister for security, Ladislav Kopřiva.[152]

Stalin, however, regarded the report as too poorly constructed for a satisfactory anti-Zionist show trial. In a message to Gottwald on

July 20 Stalin told him that the evidence so far assembled was insufficient to bring charges against Slánský and Geminder, and announced that Boyarsky, whose handling of the case had been unsatisfactory, was to be recalled. Stalin added in a personal letter four days later that Boyarsky would be replaced by "a stronger, more experienced man," and that in the meantime reports from the MGB advisers made it clear that Slánský must be removed from his post as Party secretary-general.[153]

Stalin's decision to take personal charge of the Slánský case reflected both his growing obsession with the Zionist menace and his declining confidence in Abakumov as head of the MGB. In the autumn of 1951, Abakumov was jailed. Khrushchev, as Moscow Party secretary, came to the MGB officers' club to explain Abakumov's arrest. He gave two reasons. The first was Abakumov's corruption; he had become notorious within the MGB for keeping a string of private brothels and importing expensive luxuries from the West. The second reason given by Khrushchev was Abakumov's alleged slowness in detecting the "Leningrad plot," involving some of the leading protégés of the late Andrei Zhdanov, who were executed for "grave" but unspecified "state crimes."[154] (When Abakumov was eventually tried and executed in 1954, a year after Stalin's death, his alleged crimes included the opposite offense, of fabricating evidence against those convicted in the Leningrad case.) Stalin's main purpose in removing Abakumov, however, was almost certainly to curb Beria's influence, through Abakumov, on state security. The new head of the MGB, Semyon Denisovich Ignatyev, who now reclaimed the remnants of the KI, was a party *apparatchik* from the Central Committee, who, unlike Abakumov, owed no loyalty to Beria. Indeed, he launched a purge in Mingrelia, Beria's homeland in Georgia.[155]

Under Ignatyev's leadership and at Stalin's bidding, the MGB embarked on the most anti-Semitic phase in Soviet intelligence history. Early in November 1951 General Aleksei Dmitrievich Beshchastnov arrived in Prague as chief MGB adviser to replace the disgraced Boyarsky. On the 11th, apparently satisfied that there was now adequate material for a show trial to expose the Zionist conspiracy, Stalin sent the senior Politburo member, Anastas Mikoyan to deliver a personal message to President Gottwald, calling for Slánský's immediate arrest. When Gottwald hesitated, Mikoyan telephoned Moscow from the Soviet embassy and returned to say that Stalin insisted. Gottwald gave way and Slánský was arrested on November 24.[156]

Interrogation of Slánský and his imaginary accomplices was supervised by Beshchastnov and his two assistants, Yesikov and Galkin. The beatings and torture necessary to produce confessions were administered by the StB. Three further MGB advisers, G. Gromov, G. Morozov, and J. Chernov, were sent to supervise the year-long preparations for a show trial. The Trial of the Leadership of the Anti-State Conspiratorial Center led by Rudolf Slánský opened on November 20, 1952. After his opening speech, the prosecutor read out the names of the fourteen defendants, all high-ranking Party members. Eleven, including Slánský, were described as "of Jewish origin," two as Czech and one as Slovak. The MGB advisers had originally proposed the formula "Jewish nationality" or simply "Jew" but accepted a slightly vaguer description after objections by Gottwald and the Czechoslovak Politburo. Even so, the phrase "of Jewish origin" was unprecedented in Stalinist show trials. No reference had been made in the 1930s to the Jewish origins of Trotsky, or of Zinoviev, Kamenev, Radek, and other victims of the Terror. During the Rajk trial in Budapest there had been no reference to the Jewishness of three of the seven defendants. In the Slánský trial, by contrast, Jewish upbringing was used to account for treachery. As a well-rehearsed witness explained:

> What all those traitors had in common was their bourgeois-Jewish background. Even after they joined the Czechoslovak Communist Party and rose to high positions in the Party leadership, they always remained bourgeois nationalists and pushers. Their aim was to overthrow our Party's Bolshevik leadership and destroy the popular democratic regime. To achieve this, these elements contacted the Zionist organizations and representatives of the Israeli government, who are really agents of American imperialism.

Eleven of the defendants, including Slánský, were sentenced to death, and three to life imprisonment.[157]

The defeat of the imaginary Zionist conspiracy within the Czechoslovak Communist Party was followed by an intensified anti-Zionist campaign throughout the U.S.S.R. and the Soviet Bloc. Paranoia in the Center about Zionist plots reached such a level that some of its own most successful Jewish agents were believed to have been planted on it by Western intelligence services. Among them was Smolka-Smollett, wartime head of the Russian section in the British

Ministry of Information, who was, absurdly, publicly denounced during the Slánský trial as an "imperialist agent." There was even a plan in the Center (not in the end implemented) to kidnap him from Austria, where he was in the early stages of multiple sclerosis, and bring him to Moscow to answer allegations that during the war he had recruited another Jew, Ivan Maisky, then Soviet ambassador in London, to the British SIS.[158]

The purge of Jews from the Soviet *nomenklatura,* which reached its peak during 1952, was nowhere pursued more energetically than in the Center. By the spring of 1953 all Jews had been removed from the MGB save for a small number of so-called "hidden Jews," people of at least partly Jewish origin who were officially registered as members of other ethnic groups.[159] The climax of the MGB's onslaught on Zionism was the Jewish doctors' plot. Late in 1952 a junior Kremlin doctor, Lydia Timashuk, wrote to Stalin accusing her mostly Jewish superiors of a conspiracy to curtail the lives of Soviet leaders by sabotaging their medical treatment. As a reward for unmasking this nonexistent plot, she was later given the Order of Lenin.

On January 13, 1953, *Pravda* launched a public campaign against the "monsters and murderers [who] trampled the sacred banner of science, hiding behind the honored and noble calling of physicians and men of learning." The monsters, it revealed, were agents of British and American intelligence operating through a "corrupt Jewish bourgeois nationalist organization." *Pravda* berated the security services for not detecting the conspiracy at an earlier stage. According to Khrushchev, "Stalin was crazy with rage, yelling at Ignatyev and threatening him, demanding that he throw the doctors in chains, beat them to a pulp and grind them into powder. Stalin handed over interrogation of the doctors to Ignatyev's more brutal deputy, M. D. Ryumin. "It was no surprise," said Khrushchev, "when almost all the doctors confessed to their crimes."[160]

Among the other, equally improbable, Zionist conspirators uncovered by Ryumin was the MGB organizer of the Rajk trial, General Belkin. Stalin called Rákosi personally to tell him that Belkin had confessed to recruiting Gábor Péter, the Jewish head of the AVH, for the British and Zionist intelligence services. After Péter's arrest, the AVH quickly discovered an imaginary Jewish doctors' plot in Hungary, which exactly paralleled that in the Soviet Union.[161] The Cominform and the Communist press all over Europe described the Slánský trial and the doctors' plot as "links in the same chain, manifestations of the murderous activity of the Anglo-American imperialists and their lackeys, who are bent on launching another world war."[162]

At the end of his life Stalin seems to have been preparing for a new and terrible purge. At the Nineteenth Party Conference in October 1952, the first since 1939, the old ten-man Politburo was replaced by a new Presidium of thirty-six members. Khrushchev feared that this was part of a plan "for the future annihilation of the old Politburo members." Even Stalin seemed disturbed by his inability to trust anyone around him. "I'm finished," Khrushchev heard him mutter one day. "I trust no one, not even myself." In December 1952 he purged Aleksandr Poskrebyshev, the head of his secretariat for the past quarter of a century (once described by Churchill's interpreter as "About five feet tall, with broad shoulders, a bent back, large head, heavy jowl, long hooked nose and eyes like those of a bird of prey") on the preposterous grounds that he was leaking secret documents. Soon afterward he ordered the arrest of MGB General Nikolai Vlasik, the equally long-serving chief of his personal bodyguard. After his personal physician, Dr. Vinogradov, confessed involvement in the nonexistent doctors' plot, Stalin was afraid to allow any doctor to come near him. Even the success of Soviet intelligence in penetrating foreign corridors of power preyed on his mind. At the end of his life Stalin was haunted by the fear that Western intelligence services had achieved similar—or even greater—successes in Moscow. He suspected Marshal Voroshilov of being a British spy and Molotov of working for the CIA.[163]

The evidence suggests that Beria discovered in the winter of 1952–53 that Stalin was planning to remove him. "Hence," writes a recent Soviet historian, "the extent of his unconcealed hatred for Stalin, which revealed itself during Stalin's final illness."[164] On the night of March 1–2, 1953, Stalin suffered a stroke. Beria immediately began planning the succession. Khrushchev, who was still under Stalin's spell, found Beria's behavior "simply unbearable":

As soon as Stalin showed . . . signs of consciousness on his face and made us think he might recover, Beria threw himself on his knees, seized Stalin's hand and started kissing it. When Stalin lost consciousness again and closed his eyes, Beria stood up and spat.

When Stalin died on March 5, 1953, Beria was exultant. "To put it crudely," complained Khrushchev, "he had a housewarming over Stalin's corpse before it was in his coffin."[165] Within twenty-four hours Beria had amalgamated the MGB and MVD (Ministry of the Interior) into an enlarged MVD under his command. He sacked Ignatyev, arrested Ryumin, released Abakumov from jail, and placed his supporters in key positions in the new security apparatus.[166]

In agreement with the other two main contenders for Stalin's succession, Khrushchev and Malenkov, Beria brought the anti-Semitic witch hunt to an end. On April 4 *Pravda* denounced efforts by "provocateurs" in the former MGB "to ignite nationalist dissension and to undermine the unity of the Soviet people which had been welded together by internationalism." It was announced that all the doctors arrested in January were innocent and that those responsible for their persecution had been called to account. The former president of the Jewish Anti-Fascist Committee, Mikhoels, who had been pushed under a truck by the MGB, was posthumously rehabilitated and praised as a "prominent Soviet artist." Among the first of tens of thousands to return from internal exile and the gulag was Molotov's Jewish wife, Zhemchuzhina.[167]

But though the crude anti-Semitism of Stalin's final years ceased, belief in a Zionist conspiracy continued. The MVD, and later the KGB, took back none of the Jewish officers purged in the early 1950s and maintained a total ban on Jewish entrants. Throughout Gordievsky's career in the KGB, Zionism was regarded as one of the main vehicles, if not *the* main vehicle, for "ideological subversion" in the Soviet Union. Soon after his posting to London in July 1982, the KGB residency received a "Plan for Work against Zionism in the Period 1982 to 1986," which revealed Moscow Center's continuing obsession with what it believed was "all manner of subversive operations" mounted by international Zionism against the Soviet Bloc. Both the PR (political intelligence) and KR (counterintelligence) lines in London were required to report each year on operations against Zionist targets and plans for the following year.

Gordievsky knew of many KGB residencies in the West—including those in the United States, Canada, France, Italy, Greece, and Cyprus—where operations against Jewish organizations had an even higher priority than in Britain. Even some of the most intelligent and otherwise well-balanced of Gordievsky's colleagues still subscribed to vast conspiracy theories about Jewish control of Western capitalism.[168] The anti-Semitic paranoia of Stalin's final years had left a lasting mark on the KGB still clearly visible even in the early years of the Gorbachev era.

11

The Cold War After Stalin
(1953–63)

As the members of the Presidium stood grim-faced around Stalin's bier, most were already fearful that Beria would use his enormous power as head of state security to step into Stalin's shoes. Aware that Beria had them all under surveillance, however, they were wary of moving against him. Each member of the Presidium knew that Beria held a potentially embarrassing dossier on him.[1]

Beria was quick to strengthen his control over the foreign as well as the domestic side of his security empire. He installed as the new head of the Foreign Directorate[2] a loyal henchman from the MVD, Lieutenant General Vasili Stepanovich Ryasnoy, who had no previous experience of foreign intelligence and, according to the defector Pyotr Deryabin, "dared not take a decision without referring to Beria." At Beria's insistence, Ryasnoy recalled most residents abroad for discussions at the Center. Both Beria and Ryasnoy were later criticized for blowing residents' cover by summoning them simultaneously to Moscow.

Beria also ordered a massive overhaul of the huge MVD network in East Germany. Deryabin, then in the Austro-German section of the Foreign Directorate, estimates that about eight hundred MVD personnel were recalled from the German Democratic Republic

(GDR). On June 17, 1953, a spontaneous revolt by workers in East Berlin produced the first serious challenge to Communist rule in the Soviet Bloc. Two Russian armored divisions were called in and twenty-one demonstrators were killed before the rising was quelled. Within Moscow Center and probably the Presidium also, the failure to nip the rising in the bud was blamed on the chaos caused by Beria's reorganization of the MVD in East Germany. According to Deryabin, the Austro-German section in the Center regarded General Fadeykin, whom Beria had put in charge at Karlshorst, as completely out of his depth.[3]

As soon as news of the Berlin rising reached him, Beria flew out to investigate. Throughout his stay in Berlin, however, he kept a wary eye on his rivals in Moscow. When he learned that a meeting of the Presidium had been scheduled for an unusual hour, Beria immediately called the Presidium secretariat to demand an explanation. Despite being told that there was nothing on the agenda requiring his return, he flew back immediately.[4] Beria gave the Presidium a cynically accurate assessment of conditions in the German Democratic Republic. According to the future foreign minister Andrei Gromyko, who was present as an observer, Beria spoke "in a dismissive tone and with a sneer on his face":

> The GDR? What does it amount to, this GDR? It's not even
> a real state. It's only kept in being by Soviet troops, even if
> we do call it the "German Democratic Republic."

This was too much for the rest of the Presidium. "I strongly object," said Molotov indignantly, "to such an attitude to a friendly country." The other speakers virtuously agreed. According to Gromyko: "We were all shocked by such political crudeness."[5]

Nemesis, though Beria did not realize it, was only a few days away. The plot to bring him down was led by Nikita Khrushchev. Khrushchev's earliest allies were Nikolai Bulganin, the minister of defense, and his deputy Marshal Zhukov, who guaranteed the support of the armed forces. But it was not till May or June that Khrushchev won over Georgi Malenkov, Stalin's successor as first secretary and prime minister.[6] Also crucial was the support of one of Beria's deputies, Sergei Kruglov, holder of an honorary British knighthood for his services at the wartime conferences of the Big Three.[7] A special meeting of the Presidium was fixed for June 26. Khrushchev arrived with a gun in his pocket. By his own, less than modest, account:

Beria sat down, spread himself out and asked: "Well, what's on the agenda today? Why have we met so unexpectedly?" And I prodded Malenkov with my foot and whispered: "Open the session, give me the floor." Malenkov went white; I saw he was incapable of opening his mouth. So I jumped up and said: "There is one item on the agenda: the anti-Party, divisive activity of imperialist agent Beria. There is a proposal to drop him from the Presidium and from the Central Committee, expel him from the Party, and hand him over to the court-martial. Who is in favor?"[8]

Molotov, Bulganin, and others denounced Beria in turn. Before a formal vote on Khrushchev's motion had taken place, Malenkov pressed a secret button. Zhukov entered at the head of an armed group of army officers, arrested Beria, and took him away. In Beria's briefcase they found a sheet of paper on which he had written "Alarm" in red, hoping to summon help. Fearing an attempt by MVD troops to free their chief, Zhukov moved a tank division and a motor rifle division into Moscow, able if necessary to outgun the MVD units, who had only small arms.[9] It was some days before MVD officers learned officially that Beria had been arrested. For most, the first evidence of his downfall was the disappearance of his pictures. At the beginning of July the fourteen-year-old Gordievsky, on holiday in the Ukraine, received a letter from his father, then a colonel in the MVD Training Directorate, telling him, "There was a sensational event yesterday. Portraits of the boss were taken from the walls." A few days later a second letter arrived with the news, "The boss has been arrested and is being kept in a prison cell."[10]

Beria's arrest was publicly announced on July 10. Khrushchev, the leader of the coup, now emerged as the dominant figure in what was still officially described as a collective leadership. In September, he replaced Malenkov as Party first secretary. On December 24 it was announced that Beria and six co-conspirators (who included Merkulov, former head of the NKGB, and Dekanozov, former head of the INU) had been found guilty by the Supreme Court of a plot "to revive capitalism and to restore the rule of the bourgeoisie." Beria's most appalling crime—responsibility for mass murder—could not be mentioned for fear of bringing discredit on the regime. But the announcement of his execution referred briefly to "crimes which testify to his moral degradation." The Supreme Court was told at his secret trial that one of his guards was found in possession of a small piece of paper with

The Pursuit of Trotsky

Trotsky, his wife Natalya Sedova and Abraham Sobolevicius, early in his foreign exile in Turkey (1929–32). Sobolevicius was later unmasked as an OGPU agent sent to infiltrate Trotsky's household.
(David King Collection)

Mark Zborowski, alias Etienne *(inset)*, an NKVD agent who became the closest collaborator of Trotsky's son and chief European organizer, Lev Sedov (shown here with his father). Zborowski, almost certainly, helped to organize Sedov's assassination in 1938. *(David King Collection)*

The Assassination of Trotsky

Above Mexican police display the murder weapon. *(David King Collection)*

Left Mercader reenacts the assassination in Trotsky's study after his arrest, with a policeman sitting in Trotsky's chair. *(David King Collection)*

Below left The NKVD assassin, Ramón Mercader, in prison. *(Novosti)*

Below right Trotsky on his deathbed, August 1940. *(David King Collection)*

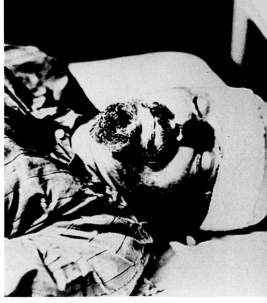

Stalinist Paranoia

МЕЧТЫ КРОВАВЫХ БАНДИТОВ

Ягода говорил: «Бухарин будет у меня не хуже Геббельса»
(Из показаний Буланова).

Рис. **Бор. Ефимова.**

A cartoon in *Izvestia* during the show trials shows Genrikh Yagoda, the disgraced head of the NKVD from 1934 to 1936, as a Nazi butcher with Hitlerian mustache, balancing on his ax the leading Old Bolshevik, Nikolai Bukharin, in the guise of Dr. Goebbels. *(David King Collection)*

Andrei Vyshinsky, chief prosecutor at the show trials (later Soviet ambassador to the United Nations), who unmasked numerous imaginary foreign spies and saboteurs. *(David King Collection)*

László Rajk, the former Hungarian Communist general secretary, unmasked as an imaginary Titoist and imperialist agent at his trial in 1949. His last words before execution were "Long Live Communism." *(David King Collection)*

"The Doctor's Plot" as portrayed in *Krokodil* in 1953: an imaginary plot by Zionists and imperialists to poison Stalin and the Soviet leadership. *(David King Collection)*

The KGB and the United States

Harry Hopkins, President Roosevelt's closest adviser, poses with Joseph Stalin. *(Photo by Margaret Bourke-White © Time Warner)*

Above right Harry Dexter White, the main Soviet agent within the wartime U.S. Treasury. *(Associated Press)*

The atom spies, Julius and Ethel Rosenberg, executed in the electric chair in 1953.

Alger Hiss, on the far right, sitting next to President Roosevelt during the Yalta conference in 1945. Stalin is on the far left.

Hiss, chief organizer of the founding conference of the United Nations at San Francisco in April 1945, shakes hands with President Truman.

President John F. Kennedy talks to KGB officer Georgi Bolshakov (second from right), whom he frequently used as a "back channel" to the Kremlin. *(UPI Bettmann Archive)*

Sigint

Above left William Weisband, an employee of the U.S. armed forces security agency, who revealed the Venona secret to the Russians in 1948.

Above right Geoffrey Prime, the KGB mole at GCHQ. *(Topham Picture Library)*

John A. Walker, Jr., the KGB's leading sigint agent in the United States, poses with hairpiece and electronic surveillance equipment after his arrest in 1983. *(Associated Press)*

Examples of the directions to dead-letter boxes given to Walker by his KGB controller in Washington.

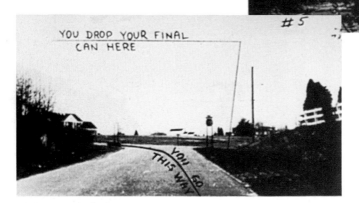

Below Aerial photograph of the largest Soviet sigint station outside the Warsaw pact at Lourdes in Cuba. *(U.S. Department of Defense)*

SOVIET COMMUNICATIONS INTELLIGENCE FACILITY LOURDES, CUBA

ANTENNA FIELDS

SATELLITE RECEIVERS

SOVIET HEADQUARTERS

the names and telephone numbers of four of the hundreds of women dragged to his house in Vspolny Pereulok to be raped by him; one was a sixteen-year-old girl.

The most remarkable charge on which Beria was convicted was that of working for British intelligence. The only evidence of a British intelligence connection produced at his trial was a file from his personal archives allegedly showing that he had worked for the counterintelligence service of the Mussavat (Transcaucasian nationalist) regime in Baku during the Civil War in 1919, at a time when the region was under British control. One of the investigators who prepared the case against Beria has since admitted that the file gave no indication "what tasks he had been given or how he carried them out." The official announcement of Beria's trial, however, reported that from 1919 onwards "Beria continued and widened his secret connections with foreign intelligence until the moment of his arrest." Beria thus became, following Yagoda and Yezhov in the 1930s, the third head of the KGB to be executed for crimes that included serving as an imaginary British secret agent.[11]

After Beria's arrest on June 26, he was succeeded as head of the MVD by one of his former deputies, Sergei Kruglov, who had sided with the plotters. For the time being the former MGB remained within the MVD. Ryasnoy, whom Beria had made head of the Foreign Directorate, was dismissed and disappeared into obscurity (though not, apparently, to the gulag). He was succeeded by the diplomat Aleksandr Semyonovich Panyushkin, probably at the suggestion of Molotov, restored since Stalin's death to his former post as foreign minister. Molotov wished to reassert the influence over foreign intelligence operations that he had possessed at the founding of the KI. Panyushkin had served as ambassador in Washington from 1947 to 1952 with spells both before and afterward in Beijing.[12] As well as becoming chief legal resident in Washington during the KI period, he had also taken direct charge of operations for a year after the recall of the legal resident Georgi Sokolov in 1949.[13]

A later defector remembered Panyushkin in 1953 as tall, lean, and stooped, with a gray suit and a gray complexion ("such as miners or workers in lead plants have"), but a simple, unpretentious manner.[14] He was introduced to Foreign Directorate staff in the conference room at the officers' club. Pyotr Deryabin, as one of the Party secretaries, met him at the club entrance and conducted him to a podium, where Kruglov, his deputy Ivan Serov, and other Party secretaries were already seated. Kruglov announced Panyushkin's appointment, then Panyushkin gave a brief description of his previous career and invited questions. Stunned by the comparative informality of the occasion, his audience remained silent and the meeting came to an end.[15]

Panyushkin's diplomatic background, however, did not imply any softening in MVD operational methods abroad. Indeed, one of the first foreign operations personally supervised by Panyushkin from the Center was Operation Rhine, the attempted assassination of a Ukrainian émigré leader in West Germany. A generation earlier the Trust deception had been followed by the kidnapping and assassination of the two main émigré White Guard leaders, Generals Kutepov and Miller, who declined to be lured back to the Soviet Union. Similarly, after the successful deception operations along Soviet frontiers during the early Cold War, the most influential émigrés—the leaders of the Ukrainian NTS in West Germany—were marked out for assassination.

The liquidation of the first intended victim, Georgi Sergeevich Okolovich, was approved, as in the case of all assassinations abroad, by the Presidium itself. The training of the chosen head of the MVD assassination team, Nikolai Khokhlov, was personally overseen by Panyushkin. Khokhlov's instructors included Mikhail Rubak, a Soviet judo champion, and Lieutenant Colonel Godlevsky, the winner of five national pistol tournaments. The execution weapon was an electrically operated gun, fitted with a silencer and concealed inside a cigarette packet, which fired cyanide-tipped bullets, developed in the MVD/MGB secret arms laboratory.

Khokhlov, however, proved to be more squeamish than the assassins of the Stalin era. He was at least half-persuaded by some of the NTS publications that he read while planning Okolovich's assassination. On February 18, 1954, Khokhlov called at Okolovich's flat in Frankfurt. His introduction was disconcerting. "Georgi Sergeevich," he told him, "I've come to you from Moscow. The Central Committee of the Communist Party of the Soviet Union has ordered your liquidation. The murder is entrusted to my group." He then informed the startled Okolovich that he had decided not to murder him. Instead Khokhlov defected to an initially skeptical CIA. On April 20, he gave a sensational press conference at which he revealed the murder plan and displayed the murder weapon.[16]

Since the beginning of the Cold War there had been no major Soviet intelligence defection. During the early months of 1954, however, Khokhlov's defection was one of five major embarrassments suffered by Moscow Center. In January, Yuri Rastvorov defected from the

Tokyo residency to the CIA; in February Pyotr Deryabin defected in Vienna, also to the CIA;[17] in April Vladimir and Evdokia Petrova defected in Canberra.

In March 1954, Soviet state security underwent its last major postwar reorganization. The MGB was once again removed from the MVD, but downgraded from a ministry to the Committee of State Security (Komitet Gosudarstvennoy Bezopasnosti or KGB) and formally attached to the Council of Ministers in an attempt to keep it under political control. The first chairman of the KGB was Kruglov's former deputy, the forty-nine-year-old General Ivan Aleksandrovich Serov, best known for the brutal efficiency with which he carried out wartime deportations from the Caucasus and crushed opposition to Communist rule in the Baltic States and Eastern Europe. Khrushchev, who was chiefly responsible for Serov's appointment, later said of him:

> I hardly knew Kruglov, but I knew Serov well, and I trusted him. . . . If there are a few dubious things about him, as there are about all Chekists, then let's just say he was a victim of Stalin's general policy.[18]

Serov's long experience of crushing dissent stood him in good stead during the most serious crisis of his five years at the head of the KGB: the Hungarian revolution of 1956. The suppression of the revolution also made the reputation of a new generation of KGB leaders. In 1954 the forty-year-old future KGB chairman, Yuri Vladimirovich Andropov, slim, sophisticated, and elegantly dressed in expensive, well-tailored suits, became Soviet ambassador in Budapest.[19] In 1955 another future KGB chairman, the thirty-one-year-old Vladimir Aleksandrovich Kryuchkov, arrived in Budapest as one of Andropov's third secretaries. Kryuchkov's role in helping to suppress the 1956 revolution was later to embarrass him. As late as 1984 his official biography as a deputy to the Supreme Soviet omitted all mention of his time in Budapest.[20] After becoming KGB chairman in 1988, however, Kryuchkov acknowledged that he had come "face to face" with "developments"—as he euphemistically described them—in Hungary in 1956. "However, looking back today I see many things in a different light, which is only natural."[21] Kryuchkov also nowadays claims an abiding love for Hungarian literature, while regretting that he lacks the time to read it.[22]

In the mid-1950s Andropov and, probably, Kryuchkov were quick to see that Rákosi's brand of neo-Stalinism was becoming a serious liability to Communist rule in Hungary.[23] It was even more seriously compromised after Khrushchev's "secret speech" to the Soviet Twentieth Party Congress in February 1956, published four months later in the West, denouncing Stalin's "cult of personality" and the "exceedingly serious and grave perversions of Party principles, of Party democracy, of revolutionary legality," which had flowed from it. On July 17, 1956, Mikoyan flew to Budapest and pressured Rákosi into resigning as first secretary, allegedly on health grounds, and retiring to the Soviet Union. His successor, however, was the hard-line Ernő Gerő rather than the popular and progressive Imre Nagy. Rákosi's downfall and the news of reforms in Poland whetted the public appetite for real political change—as did the ceremonial reburial of the posthumously rehabilitated László Rajk on October 6.[24]

As the Hungarian crisis worsened during October the chief KGB adviser, General Imelianov, was recalled to Moscow. General Serov himself flew to Budapest to take charge—the first time a KGB chairman had personally supervised a major operation outside Russia. On October 23 a student demonstration brought a quarter of a million people out onto the streets of Budapest calling for free elections, the return of Imre Nagy, and the withdrawal of Soviet troops. Soon after 9 P.M. AVH officers shot dead several members of an unarmed crowd demonstrating outside the Radio Building. When AVH reinforcements arrived concealed inside an ambulance, the crowd seized their guns. Over the next few hours freedom fighters obtained arms from sympathizers in the police and army, and from arms depots. Steelworkers brought a massive statue of Stalin crashing to the ground. The revolution had begun.[25]

At an emergency meeting that evening in the interior ministry, Serov was introduced as the new Soviet adviser, though he was not identified by name. Emphasizing every word, Serov told the meeting: "The fascists and imperialists are bringing out their shock troops into the streets of Budapest, and yet there are still comrades in your country's armed forces who hesitate to use arms!" Sándor Kopácsi, the Budapest chief of police, who was soon to side with the freedom fighters, replied scornfully: "Evidently the comrade adviser from Moscow has not had time to inform himself of the situation in our country. We need to tell him that these are not 'fascists' or other 'imperialists' who are organizing the demonstration; they come from the universities, the handpicked sons and daughters of peasants and workers, the fine flower of our country's intelligentsia, which is demanding its rights and wishes to show sympathy with the Poles." A quarter of a century later Kopácsi still vividly recalled the long withering glare in his direction from Serov's steel-blue eyes.[26]

On the same evening, October 23, Gerő, with Soviet approval, brought in Nagy as prime minister. Simultaneously, however, he sought the "fraternal assistance" of Soviet troops stationed in Hungary against the "counterrevolutionary" threat. Next morning, operating on the mistaken assumption that the workers would not support the students, the Red Army made its first attempt to suppress the revolution, assisted by the AVH. Several days of street fighting showed convincingly where the workers' sympathies really lay. On October 25 János Kádár replaced Gerő as Party first secretary. He and Nagy then announced that negotiations for the withdrawal of Soviet troops would start as soon as order was restored. For several days, Khrushchev later admitted, the Kremlin dithered, uncertain whether "to apply armed force" or to "get out of Hungary": "I don't know how many times we changed our minds back and forth."[27]

Suspecting an imperialist plot, Serov ordered about a score of KGB illegals living in the West under assumed identities and nationalities to travel to Hungary to report on the situation and, if necessary, stage provocations to help justify military intervention—a tactic repeated in Prague in 1968.[28] Meanwhile, the pace of change in Budapest quickened daily. On October 29 the hated AVH, which had killed hundreds of demonstrators and had several of its own officers lynched, was abolished. On October 30 the Kremlin emissaries Mikoyan and Suslov agreed to the removal of Soviet troops and to negotiations about Hungary's withdrawal from the Warsaw Pact.

Early that afternoon Nagy broadcast to the nation, announcing that he was forming a new multiparty government: "In the interest of the further democratization of the country's life, the cabinet abolishes the one-party system and places the country's government on the basis of democratic cooperation between the coalition parties as they existed in 1945." Until October 30 Moscow had regarded Nagy as its best Hungarian hope of containing counterrevolution. Thereafter it began secretly preparing his overthrow.[29]

The key role in deceiving the Nagy government fell to Yuri Andropov. An admiring junior Soviet diplomat in Budapest later claimed that Andropov had been the first to "see through" Nagy, and remained completely in control throughout the ensuing crisis: "He was so calm—even while bullets were flying, when everyone else at the embassy felt like we were in a besieged fortress."[30] On November 1 Nagy was awakened with the news that units of the Red Army were crossing into Hungary while other Soviet forces were withdrawing from Budapest. Andropov repeatedly assured Nagy that the withdrawal was proceeding as planned; the troops that had entered Hungary had done so only to safeguard the security of those who were leaving.[31]

Nagy announced Hungary's secession from the Warsaw Pact, proclaimed Hungarian neutrality, and asked the United Nations to put the Hungarian question on its agenda. Next day, November 2, the Hungarian government formally protested to the Soviet Union about the reentry of its troops and notified the UN.[32] While continuing to reassure Nagy that the troop withdrawal was continuing, Andropov secretly began to plot with Kádár the overthrow of the Nagy government. Kádár almost certainly was acting under duress, influenced both by memories of his own imprisonment and torture in 1951–54 and by Andropov's threat to bring back Rákosi if he refused to cooperate.[33]

On the evening of November 3, Nagy's minister of defense, Pál Maléter, was invited to Soviet military headquarters to discuss final details of the Red Army's withdrawal. At midnight, while toasts were being drunk, Serov burst into the room, brandishing a Mauser pistol, at the head of a group of KGB officers, arrested the entire Hungarian delegation and ordered each to be locked in a separate cell. A series of mock executions in the early hours of the morning left Maléter and each of his colleagues convinced that all the others had been shot.[34] Before dawn on November 4 the Red Army began its assault. To delay Hungarian resistance as long as possible, Andropov tried to maintain the deception until the last minute. When the Hungarian commander-in-chief phoned the prime minister to report the Soviet attack, Nagy replied: "Ambassador Andropov is with me and assures me there's been some mistake and the Soviet government did not order an attack on Hungary. The ambassador and I are trying to call Moscow."[35] Later that morning Nagy made his final broadcast:

> In the early hours of the morning, Soviet troops began an attack on the capital with the evident intention of overthrowing the legal and democratic government of Hungary. Our forces are fighting. The government is at its post. I bring this to the attention of the Hungarian people and the entire world.

Later that day Nagy and several of his ministers were given asylum in the Yugoslav embassy. Serov supervised the arrest of the most important "counterrevolutionaries" who failed to find asylum or refuge abroad. Among those he arrested personally was the Budapest police chief, Sándor Kopácsi. For the first time Serov identified himself to Kopácsi as chairman of the KGB; he reminded him of their encounter on October 23, then told him (inaccurately, as it turned out): "I'm going to have you hanged from the highest tree in Budapest." On November 21, the new Soviet-backed government headed by János Kádár gave Nagy and his ministers a guarantee of safe conduct from the Yugoslav embassy. As they left on the 22nd, they were dragged from the bus that had come to collect them, arrested by the KGB, and taken across the border into Rumania.[36]

The interrogation of Nagy and his associates was supervised by Boris Shumilin, chief KGB adviser "for counterrevolutionary affairs."[37] On November 26 Kádár declared over Radio Budapest: "We have promised not to make Imre Nagy and his friends stand trial for their past crimes, even if they later confess to them." In February 1957, the Hungarian foreign ministry reiterated that there was "no intention of bringing Imre Nagy to trial." When Nagy continued to resist the best attempts of the KGB and the AVH to persuade him to confess to his imaginary crimes, Moscow decided otherwise. Of the group of six arrested as they were leaving the Yugoslav embassy, one died at the hands of his torturers; a second was strangled when he went on hunger strike. Nagy and the three other survivors were put on secret trial in February 1958. The proceedings, having apparently failed to satisfy the KGB advisers, who had no experience of political trials in which defendants declined to plead guilty, were soon suspended. When the trial resumed in June 1958 three of the four principal accused persisted in proclaiming their innocence. All were found guilty, executed and buried in unmarked graves. Five others were given prison sentences.[38]

Shumilin and his AVH assistants found concocting the case against "Nagy and his gang of traitors" much more difficult than at any previous political trial in the Soviet Bloc. The posthumous rehabilitation of László Rajk and Khrushchev's speech to the Twentieth Party Congress had undermined the credibility of the enormously detailed conspiracy theories of the Stalinist show trials. By comparison with the confident, well-rehearsed courtroom dramas of the previous twenty years, the official account of "The Counter-Revolutionary Conspiracy of Imre Nagy and His Accomplices" has a curiously feeble, almost

defensive tone. Imperialism was duly denounced as the "principal organizer of the counterrevolution" and Nagy unmasked as its willing
accomplice. But the detail of the plot was thinner than in the past and
its rhetoric inhibited. Radio Free Europe was declared to have been
"the Foreign Military and Political Headquarters of the Counterrevolution" and Red Cross parcels the principal means by which imperialist
arms were smuggled across the Hungarian border. Within Hungary the
British military attaché, Colonel James Cowley, was said to have taken
"a direct part in the military direction of the uprising" and a West
German M.P., Prince Hubertus von Loewenstein, was identified as the
link with "big capitalist imperialists in West Germany." The Nagy
trial, even in its bowdlerized published version, was recognized in the
KGB well before the Gorbachev era as a public-relations disaster. It
was the last political trial in the Soviet Bloc to pass death sentences on
its victims.[39]

During his three years as head of the First Chief (Foreign) Directorate,
Aleksandr Semyonovich Panyushkin made little personal impression
on Moscow Center. His health, by now, was poor. One of his officers
was struck on a first meeting by "his stooped manner of walking, as
though he had no strength to carry himself straight." Panyushkin's
spacious office contained two large armchairs, one behind his desk, the
other by the window. Having selected the one in which to sit, he "sank
into it wearily, and, tall as he was, somehow curled himself up and
shrank."[40] Panyushkin's portrait does not appear today in the Memory
Room of the First Chief Directorate. In 1956 he was succeeded by his
former deputy, the much more dynamic Aleksandr Mikhailovich Sakharovsky, who was to remain head of the First Chief Directorate for
the record period of fifteen years. Sakharovsky also became the first
holder of this post since Fitin to earn a place in the Memory Room.
He is remembered in the FCD chiefly as an efficient, energetic administrator. Sakharovsky had, however, no firsthand experience of the West.
Having joined the NKVD in 1939 at the age of thirty, he had made his
postwar reputation as an MGB adviser in Eastern Europe, serving
mainly in Rumania.[41]

    Sakharovsky's appointment as head of the FCD coincided with
what the Center considered one of its greatest foreign coups. The KGB
regarded as its highest-ranking agent during and beyond the Cold War
the Finnish Agrarian Party politician Urho Kaleva Kekkonen, who
had regular meetings with a Soviet case officer. There was high excite-

ment in the Center in 1956 when Kekkonen became president of Finland, a post he was to hold for the next twenty-five years.[42] According to Anatoli Golitsyn, who defected from the Helsinki residency in 1961, the KGB also recruited another high-ranking Finnish politician, code-named Timo. By the end of the 1950s, there was something approaching open warfare over the handling of Timo between the resident, Zhenikhov, and the ambassador, Zakharov. Both Zhenikhov and Zakharov were summoned to Moscow to appear before the Central Committee, where they were reprimanded for their quarreling. It was agreed that the KGB resident should remain the main contact with Timo, but that the ambassador should have the right to be consulted.[43]

Twenty years later, there was a similar dispute over dealing with Kekkonen between the resident, Viktor Mikhailovich Vladimirov, and the ambassador, Vladimir Sobolev. Vladimirov struck Gordievsky as closer in appearance to the stereotype of a traditional English gentleman than any other KGB officer he ever met. He had a well-groomed mustache, wore English suits, ties, shoes, and overcoats, and looked to Gordievsky like a well-bred guards officer who had retired early to run his family's landed estate. In the mid-1970s, Vladimirov headed the RT Directorate of the FCD, which dealt with the recruitment of foreigners inside the Soviet Union and other operations against them. He was first posted to Helsinki in 1970–71, returning as resident in 1977. The prestige of handling Kekkonen helped to win him promotion to the rank of KGB general.[44]

The memoirs of Andrei Gromyko, Soviet foreign minister from 1957 to 1985, lavish greater praise on Kekkonen ("an inspiring figure not only in Finnish political life but also in the international arena") than on any other Western statesman: "Kekkonen . . . made his own contribution to many aspects of Soviet-Finnish friendship. . . . It was his foreign policy that earned Finland the world's admiration."[45] In private as well as in public Kekkonen was always careful to show himself a dependable friend of the Soviet Union. He sometimes agreed to include in his speeches "theses" prepared by the International Department of the Central Committee and handed to him by the resident. Whenever Kekkonen did so, the Helsinki residency telegraphed triumphantly to the FCD: "A high-level active measure has been carried out." On each occasion the Center proudly informed the Politburo.

For all its boasting about "active measures," however, the KGB never had a free hand in Finland. The Finnish Security Police, although outnumbered by Soviet intelligence officers, brought a series of KGB and GRU agents to book. President Kekkonen never intervened in any of these cases. Nevertheless, by the 1970s the KGB had more people they regarded as agents and "confidential contacts" in Finland than in all the other FCD Third Department countries combined (Britain, Ireland, Australasia, and the rest of Scandinavia). Helsinki also provided hospitality for the leading Soviet front organization. The World Peace Council, expelled from Paris and Vienna for "subversive activities," set up its headquarters in Helsinki in 1968.[46]

One of the main aims of Soviet policy in Finland was simply to keep Kekkonen in power. Moscow successfully put pressure on the strong Social Democratic candidate for the presidency, Honka, to withdraw from the presidential election of 1962, and Kekkonen was safely reelected. The Center, however, misunderstood, at times willfully, both Kekkonen's relationship with the Soviet Union and his long-term strategy. Kekkonen's overriding aim was simply to preserve Finnish independence. Finland's experience during and after the Second World War persuaded him that the only way to do so was by building bridges to Moscow. Finland was the only country defeated by the Soviet Union, apart from the Soviet zone in Austria, not to be incorporated into the Soviet Bloc.

It was clear to Juho Paasikivi, president from 1946 to 1956, that Finland could expect no serious assistance from the West to protect it against Soviet demands. As well as having to pay the U.S.S.R. enormous war reparations (five times those of Italy), Finland was also prevented by Soviet pressure from accepting Marshall Plan aid. Kekkonen came from the Finnish farming community, whose long historical experience of Tsarist rule had left it with the conviction that, though the Russians might be disagreeable to deal with, it was important to get on with them.

Collaboration, however, had its limits; in the words of an old Finnish proverb: "A Russian is a Russian, even when cooked in butter." Kekkonen was one of a number of Finnish politicians who looked on private Soviet contacts as a prudent adjunct to their careers. Such contacts became known as "Kotiryssä" (literally a "house Russian," by analogy with "Kotikissa," a pet cat). Though constantly anxious to reassure the Russians, and treating the KGB resident as his "Kotiryssä," Kekkonen was careful not to compromise Finnish independence. Any official or minister whom he suspected of doing so was quietly sidelined when a suitable opportunity arose. Having proudly announced to the Politburo that Kekkonen was a fully recruited agent, neither the FCD nor any of its Helsinki residents was ever willing to acknowledge that the president was, in reality, first and foremost a Finnish patriot.[47]

On becoming head of the FCD in 1956, Sakharovsky inherited a remarkable stable of penetration agents in Western Europe. The most famous of them, Kim Philby, was now only a shadow of his former self. For three years after his recall from Washington in 1951, his controller Yuri Modin considered it too dangerous to make direct contact with him because of MI5 surveillance. In 1954 Modin resumed contact through what Philby called "the most ingenious of routes."[48] The route was Anthony Blunt. One evening after a talk at the Courtauld Institute, Modin approached Blunt, probably for the first time since 1951, handed him a postcard reproduction of a painting, and asked him for his opinion of it. On the reverse was a message in Burgess's handwriting giving a rendezvous for the following evening at the Angel public house on the Caledonian Road. At the Angel, Modin asked Blunt to set up a meeting with Philby.[49] Thirty years later in lectures at the Andropov Institute Modin praised the professionalism with which Blunt had carried out the assignment.[50] The main message that Modin passed to Philby at their first meeting for several years was one of general reassurance, which, so Philby later claimed, left him "with refreshed spirit."[51]

Philby's need for spiritual refreshment derived from the defection of the KGB resident in Australia, Vladimir Petrov, and his wife Evdokia, who provided some intelligence on Burgess and Maclean, including the first solid (as opposed to circumstantial) evidence that both were in Moscow.[52] Modin was able to reassure Philby that the Petrovs knew nothing of his own career as a Soviet agent. Thus reassured, Philby bore with equanimity the claim made in the Commons in 1955 by Marcus Lipton, M.P., inspired by a leak from the FBI, that he was the Third Man. Philby later argued plausibly that Lipton's accusation actually did him a service. Though the government did not want to clear him, the fact that they lacked the evidence to bring a prosecution forced the foreign secretary, Harold Macmillan, to dismiss Lipton's charges. Philby gave a triumphant press conference in his mother's living room. He told the assembled journalists: "The last time I spoke to a Communist, knowing he was one, was in 1934."[53]

Philby's public vindication strengthened the hand of his friends in SIS, who believed he had been unfairly victimized. In 1956, they obtained a job for him in Beirut as a "stringer" (nonstaff correspondent) for the *Observer* and the *Economist*. After his defection to Moscow, Philby encouraged the belief that journalism had merely been a cover for his real job as "an SIS agent in Beirut."[54] Like all former SIS officers he was encouraged to remain in touch and pass on useful intelligence. But access to SIS intelligence was limited to off-the-record briefings by misguided friends. The chief of SIS throughout his time in Beirut was one of Philby's most determined opponents, Sir Dick White, previously director-general of MI5, who had been convinced of Philby's guilt since 1951.

Philby's file in London was reopened after the defection in December 1961 of the KGB officer Anatoli Golitsyn, who brought with him further intelligence on the Five.[55] Yuri Modin, who had left London in 1958, visited Beirut to warn Philby not to return to Britain because of the danger of arrest, and to make contingency plans for his escape to Moscow.[56] The clinching evidence against Philby was provided in 1962 by a prewar friend, Flora Solomon, who belatedly described how he had tried to recruit her. But SIS concluded that without a confession by Philby it still lacked the evidence for a successful prosecution. Since it believed that any attempt to lure Philby back to London would lead to his immediate defection, it was decided to confront him in Beirut.[57]

During his final two years in Lebanon Philby came close to the breaking point, constantly relapsing into drunken depressions. Friends became used to seeing him pass out at parties, then being carried to a taxi to take him home. His third wife, Eleanor, told friends that he suffered from terrible nightmares and would wake up shouting incoherently.

In January 1963, one of the closest of his former friends in SIS, Nicholas Elliott, ex-station commander in Lebanon, confronted Philby in Beirut. He found him with his head swathed in bandages, the result of falling on a radiator while drunk. According to his later recollection, Elliott told Philby: "You took me in for years. Now I'll get the truth out of you even if I have to drag it out. I once looked up to you. My God, how I despise you now! I hope you've got enough decency left to understand why." Philby confessed to being a Soviet agent, told part of the story, hesitated for some days over Elliott's offer of immunity from prosecution in return for a full confession, then defected. Once in Moscow he concocted the conspiracy theory, which has since seduced some Western journalists, that the purpose of Elliott's mission was less to gain a confession than to push him into defection as part of a bizarre embarrassment-control exercise in Whitehall.[58]

The twelve years between Philby's recall from Washington and his defection from Beirut were little more than an inconsequential, if long-drawn-out, epilogue to his remarkable earlier career as a Soviet penetration agent. The major achievements of the Magnificent Five ended in 1951 with the flight of Burgess and Maclean, the discovery of Cairncross, and the dismissal of Philby from SIS. For most of the 1950s, however, the KGB had another mole in SIS. In 1953, George Blake returned from prison camp in North Korea and resumed work at SIS, initially under the control of Yuri Modin. During Modin's absence from London in 1954, Blake was run instead by Sergei Aleksandrovich Kondrashev. Modin seems to have resumed as Blake's case officer in 1955.[59]

The first major operation that Blake compromised was Operation Gold, intended as a follow-up to Operation Silver, which had successfully tapped Soviet telephone lines in Vienna. Operation Gold was even more ambitious than Silver; it envisaged a five-hundred-meter tunnel under East Berlin to intercept land lines running from the Soviet military and intelligence compound in Karlshorst. The construction details were decided at a joint SIS/CIA meeting in London in the spring of 1954, chaired by George Young, deputy chief of SIS. The American team, headed by Bill Harvey, CIA station chief in Berlin, agreed to provide most of the technology and bear most of the cost; the British agreed to dig the tunnel. As the most junior SIS officer at the meeting, George Blake was left to lock the papers in the safe when it was over.[60] Blake was posted to Berlin in April 1955, two months after the tunnel became operational. By the time the KGB staged an accidental discovery of the Berlin tunnel in April 1956, the intelligence yield was so considerable that it took over two more years to process all the intercepts. One of the messages revealed the existence of a Soviet agent working for British intelligence in Berlin, but it was not until 1961 that evidence from a defector identified the agent as George Blake.[61]

During his four years in Berlin, Blake betrayed many British and American agents. Among them was Lieutenant General Robert Bialek of the GDR's State Security Service (SSD), who defected in 1953 and lived under an assumed name in West Berlin. One evening in February 1956, he was bundled into a car while taking his dog for a walk, taken back to SSD headquarters in East Berlin, and executed. Blake also betrayed Lieutenant Colonel Pyotr Popov of the GRU, who in 1953 had become the CIA's first important mole in Soviet intelligence. In 1959, a few months after Blake's return to London, Popov was caught by the KGB.[62] His secret trial in the main hall of the KGB officers club did not take place until 1963. All statements, including Popov's, were well rehearsed and the whole proceedings took less than two hours. Popov was executed by firing squad.[63]

When Nikolai Borisovich Rodin returned for a second term as KGB resident in London in the summer of 1956, once again under the alias Korovin, he took over the running of Blake himself, initially meeting him in Holland, where Blake was able to travel on the pretext of meeting relatives.[64] The London residency by now had a record total of sixty officers, working in unpleasantly cramped conditions. Rodin, who returned to London with the rank of KGB general, then rare in the FCD, was even more pompous and bombastic than on his first tour of duty and acquired a legendary unpopularity among his staff. Whereas the Soviet ambassador was at his desk punctually each day at 8:30 A.M., Rodin did not arrive until lunchtime, driven by the KGB operational driver, whom he had transformed into his personal chauffeur. At the embassy he inhabited a large air-conditioned office, served by a sycophantic personal staff, and treated his senior officers with imperious condescension. In 1958, he had a violent quarrel with the deputy resident and head of the PR (Political Intelligence) line, Yuri Modin, celebrated for his handling of the Magnificent Five, George Blake, and other British agents. Modin was recalled from London with a deep personal grudge against Rodin, which was still evident in his lectures at the KGB Andropov Institute in the early 1980s, when he used Rodin as a case study in how not to run a residency.[65]

Rodin, however, was a shrewd agent handler. For four years, he personally ran a spy in the Admiralty, John Vassall, a classic example of a vain, weak-willed, low-level employee with access to high-level intelligence.[66] In his memoirs Vassall himself expresses surprise that as "an obvious homosexual" he was not identified as a security risk when being posted to Moscow in 1954 as a clerk in the office of the British naval attaché. In 1955, he was blackmailed into working for the KGB after being photographed at a homosexual party organized by the Second Chief Directorate:

> At an appointed time I was shown a box of photographs of myself at the party. . . . After about three photographs I could not stomach any more. They made one feel ill. There I was, caught by the camera, enjoying every possible sexual

activity . . . having oral, anal or a complicated array of sexual activities with a number of different men.

Shortly before his return to Britain in 1957, Vassall was given a Minox camera small enough to fit inside a cigarette packet and trained in its use. Rodin flew to Moscow, introduced himself to Vassall as "Gregory," and arranged a rendezvous in London at the Finchley Road underground station. He struck Vassall as "an experienced man with an overpowering personality":

> One thing used to shock him, or so he led me to believe, and that was the idea that our activities came under the category of espionage. . . . He impressed upon me that any information I passed would be useful for the cause of peace and there was nothing wrong in what I was doing.

Back in London, Vassall was posted successively to the Naval Intelligence Division, the office of the Civil Lord of the Admiralty, and the Admiralty Military Branch. At meetings with Rodin during a period of almost four years, Vassall handed over thousands of highly classified documents on British and NATO naval policy and weapons development. Despite his contempt for Vassall, Rodin went out of his way to appear "genuinely sympathetic." According to the naïve Vassall, "He was a man of the world and understood and had respect for my feelings. We had quite a lot in common and used to talk about travel, painting, music and human nature." Rodin succeeded in persuading Vassall that he enjoyed their "many interesting conversations" at expensive restaurants. But he was also careful to make Vassal financially dependent on him by providing funds for him to live far beyond his means in a luxury flat in Dolphin Square.[67]

Rodin's second term as London resident came to an abrupt end as the result of intelligence on George Blake provided to SIS and MI5 by the Polish defector Michal Goleniewski. In April 1961, Blake was recalled by SIS from an Arab-language training course in Lebanon and arrested. Rodin left in haste for Moscow, never to return.[68] Blake was sentenced to the record prison sentence of forty-two years but was "sprung" after six by the combined efforts of an IRA bomber and two antinuclear campaigners. Vassall was caught in 1962 and sentenced to eighteen years in jail, of which he was to serve ten. In his flat MI5 found a miniature Praktina document-copying camera, a Minox, and photographs of 176 classified documents on 35-millimeter cassettes hidden in a secret drawer.[69]

Rodin's second term as legal resident in London coincided with the presence in Britain of one of the most gifted of all KGB illegal residents, Konon Trofimovich Molody, who operated entirely independently of the legal residency.[70] Molody was born in Moscow in 1922, the son of a prominent Russian scientist. At the age of seven he was sent by his mother to live with an aunt in Berkeley, California, and went to school in the United States. In 1938, instead of taking American citizenship, he opted to return to the Soviet Union and joined the NKVD during the war. In 1954, Molody entered Canada on a forged passport and obtained the birth certificate of a deceased Finnish-Canadian, Gordon Arnold Lonsdale, whose identity he adopted.

In 1955, under his new Canadian identity, Molody traveled to London, enrolled in a Chinese course at the School of Oriental and African Studies (SOAS), and set himself up with KGB funds as the director of several companies leasing jukeboxes, one-armed bandits, and vending machines.[71] As he explained to Gordievsky after his return to Moscow nine years later, the course at SOAS was undemanding since, though he concealed the fact from his lecturers and fellow students, he was fluent in Chinese already. Many of the other students were officers in Western intelligence services. Molody had joined the course deliberately to make contact with them. He was later fond of recalling in talks at the Center that a fellow student once told him: "Gordon, you and I must be the only people here who aren't spies!"

Molody was also proud of his business success. He showed Gordievsky the photograph of an electronic locking device produced by one of his firms that won a gold medal in 1960 at the International Inventors Exhibition in Brussels. Not merely did his espionage activities rapidly become self-financing; despite the large sums paid to his agents, he also produced a substantial profit for the KGB.[72] Molody later told a Soviet interviewer: "Let me remind you that all the working capital and profits from my four companies (millions of pounds sterling) which were increasing year by year without any help from me, were 'socialist property.' Strange but true!"[73]

Molody had a cynically professional attitude toward his British agents, which accurately reflected orthodox KGB tradecraft during the Cold War:

When the resident, who is known as the "chief," recruits an agent, or "assistant," he must make it look as though he is not recruiting him at all, but is simply buying information he requires. . . . Once he has his claws into the agent, there's no getting away. A good agent is one whose vital statistics are the following: he works, for example, in a military department and holds a middle-ranking but key position giving him access to information; he doesn't aspire to higher office, has a chip on his shoulder about being a failure (let's say that ill health prevented him finishing studies at the general staff college); he drinks (an expensive habit); he has a weakness for the fair sex (which is also not cheap); he is critical of his own government and loyal to the resident's government.

It was of course preferable, Molody conceded, for agents to have "a firm ideological base." Sadly, however, ideological agents like the Magnificent Five and George Blake had become "a very rare breed" in postwar Britain:

The average Englishman is apolitical and indifferent. He really couldn't care less who is governing him, where the country is going or whether the Common Market is a good or bad thing. All that interests him is his own wage packet, his job and keeping the wife happy.

Molody was equally cynical about the illegal's need to substitute casual sex for emotional involvement:

An intelligence officer cannot manage without a woman, but he'll find it impossible with one! One of my long-suffering colleagues noted with interest the arrival of au-pairs from France who had come to England to improve their English. . . . From my colleague's point of view, their main advantage lay in the fact that their stay in the country was for a limited period only. He used to turn up at all sorts of functions with these beautiful young ladies in tow, and then at the end of their three-month stay it was "Goodbye, my dear girl!" "Goodbye, kind sir!," and off they would go,

clutching a memento of his regard for them, such as a little
fur coat or a tiny ring.[74]

Molody's sexism was typical of KGB attitudes during—and after—the
Serov era. Serov was implacably opposed to the operational use of
women other than as sexual bait or—occasionally—to recruit other
women. He was also deeply prejudiced against the use of women as desk
officers, despite the high reputation of Rybkina and the handful of other
women with senior positions in the First Chief Directorate. Serov
placed an absolute ban on recruitment of female KGB officers for
operational work, which survived until the Gorbachev era.[75]

Like most of his colleagues in the KGB, Molody was prejudiced
against Jews as well as women. Soon after his return to Moscow in
1964, Gordievsky (who was then responsible for organizing cultural
events in the Illegals Directorate S) got him tickets for the Romany
gypsy folklore theater in Moscow. A few days later Molody accosted
Gordievsky in the corridors. "What have you done to me?" he said in
mock outrage. "You said it was a gypsy theater, but they're all Jews!"[76]

It was ironic that technical support for Molody during his six
years in London was provided by an American Jewish couple, Morris
and Lona Cohen, *alias* Peter and Helen Kroger, formerly part of the
Rosenberg spy ring in the United States, who had established themselves as successful antiquarian booksellers. When MI5 and the Special
Branch raided the Cohens' house at Ruislip in the London suburbs in
1961, they found a high-speed radio transmitter powerful enough to
reach Moscow and a short-wave radio for listening to Moscow on
high-frequency bands, both in a cavity beneath the kitchen floor, one-
time cipher pads hidden in flashlights and a cigarette lighter, a microdot
reader concealed in a box of face powder, equipment for microdot
construction, a canister containing magnetic iron oxide used for printing high-speed Morse messages onto tape, thousands of pounds, dollars
and travelers' checks, and seven passports.[77]

Only two of the British agents run by Molody with technical
support from the Cohens, Harry Houghton and his mistress, Ethel Gee,
were ever convicted. Houghton (code-named Shah) closely resembled
the cynical stereotype of the British spy described by Molody after his
return to Moscow. He worked as a clerk in the Underwater Weapons
Establishment at Portland, Dorset, where, helped by Ethel Gee who
was employed as a filing clerk, he had easy access to top secret information on antisubmarine warfare and nuclear submarines. It was a lead

to Houghton from a CIA mole in the Polish UB, Michal Goleniewski, that eventually led MI5 to Molody.[78] Houghton's memoirs, written over a decade later after he emerged from jail, are eloquent testimony to how successfully Molody deceived him. As Molody made clear in interviews in Moscow, he regarded agents like Houghton as mildly contemptible moral inadequates. Houghton, however, was pathetically convinced, like Vassall at his meetings with Rodin, that from his first encounter with Molody "a deep bond of friendship existed between us." Though Houghton claimed to regret his involvement in espionage, he confessed that what began under duress was turned by the apparent warmth of Molody's friendship into an activity he enjoyed: "There was a real camaraderie between us." Though an active sexual athlete with numerous mistresses, Molody even succeeded in persuading Houghton that "having intercourse with any of them was absolutely out."[79]

At their trial in 1961 Molody was sentenced to twenty-five years in prison, the Cohens to twenty, Houghton and Gee to fifteen each. Molody was freed in a spy exchange in 1964. The KGB made no serious attempt to rescue the others. Some of Molody's agents, however, were never caught. Molody's memoirs claim, probably correctly, that he obtained intelligence from inside the Microbiological Research Establishment at Porton Down—the "Germ Warfare Center," as he describes it. The doctored version of the memoirs prepared for publication, with Philby's assistance, by Service A, the FCD Active Measures Department, claims absurdly that Molody's main task was to thwart the plan by a crazed Nazi war criminal to spread a new strain of plague in the United Kingdom and then blame the KGB: "What can be more gratifying than the task to thwart criminal designs of maniacs developing lethal poisons and deadly germs for the destruction of human beings?"[80]

Some indication of Molody's importance is indicated by the fact that, during Gordievsky's career in the First Chief Directorate, he was the only postwar illegal chosen to appear in the pantheon of intelligence heroes in the FCD Memory Room. Molody died in 1970 at the age of only forty-eight after a prolonged drinking bout at a picnic on a hot summer's day. He lay in state on a funeral bier in the KGB officers' club. Colleagues displayed his large collection of medals on velvet cushions. The chairman of the KGB, Yuri Andropov, came to pay his respects. Molody's fame, however, caused some envy among other KGB illegals. One of his contemporaries, who had worked for fifteen years in West Germany, complained bitterly to Gordievsky: "Molody was a failure. He blew his operations, and it was expensive to get him out. I served for fifteen years without getting caught, and nobody has ever heard of me!"[81]

Though fewer KGB agents were caught in France than in Britain, Soviet penetration there was probably at least as successful. Until 1966 Paris had a particular priority for Moscow Center as the headquarters of NATO. Among the Soviet moles who penetrated NATO was George Pâques, first recruited in Algiers in 1944.[82] Pâques served as *chef de cabinet* and adviser to a series of ministers in the postwar Fourth Republic. Late in 1958, on the eve of the founding of the Fifth Republic, with General de Gaulle as its first president, he began to specialize in defense. Over the next four years, he had continuous access to classified defense documents at, successively, the French general staff, the Institut des Hautes Études de la Défense Nationale, and NATO headquarters. He met his last two case officers, successively Nikolai Lysenko and Vasili Vlasov, at fortnightly intervals to hand over documents in the forest of Meudon and other locations near Paris. Among the documents he handed over was the entire NATO defense plan for Western Europe. His controllers constantly assured him that he was having a direct influence on Soviet policy. Pâques's vanity was such that he was easily persuaded. He later claimed credit for ensuring that the Berlin crisis of 1961, which led to the building of the Wall, ended peacefully:

> The autobahns were blocked, air communication was threatened, Khrushchev was testing the military preparedness of the Allies. At this very moment I had a discussion with the embassy counselor [in fact the KGB case officer] whom I met periodically. He told me that his government was resolved to see its policy through to the end. I retorted that there was the same determination on the Allied side. He asked me if I could provide him with written proof. It was then that I handed over to him the documents [on the defense of West Berlin]. A fortnight later, he informed me that if Khrushchev had drawn back, it was because of the information I had provided. I did this to preserve the peace, and it is thanks to me that it was preserved.

A personal letter from Khrushchev, Pâques also claimed, had been shown to him.[83]

Convinced of his own unique role, Pâques failed to realize when he first gained access to NATO documents that the KGB already had another agent in place at NATO headquarters: Hugh Hambleton, a bilingual Canadian economist, whom the MGB had begun cultivating in 1951. From 1957 to 1961, Hambleton handed over so many NATO documents, ranging from military plans to economic forecasts, at fortnightly meetings with his Soviet controller, Aleksei Fyodorovich Trishin, that the KGB resident Mikhail Stepanovich Tsymbal (*alias* Rogov, in Paris from 1954 to 1959), established a special unit to deal with them, continued under his successor, Anatoli Ivanovich Lazarev. At some of Hambleton's meetings with Trishin, a large black van equipped with a KGB photographic laboratory parked nearby to copy NATO documents on the spot.[84]

As in the case of Pâques, Hambleton's extraordinary career as a KGB agent, which was to span over twenty years, seems to have derived more from self-importance and a craving for excitement than from ideological conviction. Trishin was careful to boost his ego by telling him at various times that the NATO documents were "pure gold," "extraordinarily valuable," and "read by Politburo members." Hambleton's delusions of grandeur were encouraged by an invitation to a private dinner and discussion of world affairs in Moscow with the KGB chairman, Yuri Andropov.[85]

The most successful KGB Cold War penetration in France was probably of the foreign intelligence agency, the Service de Documentation Extérieure et de Contre-Espionage (SDECE). On his defection in 1961, Anatoli Golitsyn alleged that the KGB had an agent network, code-named the "Sapphire Ring," operating within the SDECE. The head of the First Chief Directorate, Aleksandr Sakharovsky, had, he claimed, possessed in 1959 the entire reorganization plan for the SDECE drawn up by its director, General Paul Grossin, and received regular copies of SDECE reports. Golitsyn's allegations were given added credibility when he provided the clues that led to the arrest and conviction of Georgi Pâques in 1963. He also revealed that the KGB knew of SDECE plans to set up a section to collect scientific intelligence in the United States; just such a section became operational in the summer of 1962. But Golitsyn had only peripheral knowledge of KGB operations in France, and most of his information was unspecific. Even his clues that led to the arrest of Pâques only narrowed the field initially to seven suspects; surveillance of the seven then identified Pâques.

Knowledge of Golitsyn's allegations became too widespread

within the SDECE for it to be possible to mount prolonged secret surveillance of the kind that had led to Pâques's arrest. Investigation was further hampered by the spread, in the wake of Golitsyn's revelations, of conspiracy theories similar to those that in the United States led James Angleton to suspect the CIA's head of Soviet Bloc intelligence, David Murphy, and in Britain made Peter Wright and others equally suspicious of the director-general of MI5, Sir Roger Hollis. In France, as in Britain and the United States, the conspiracy theorists made a number of false identifications. SDECE sources claim that, though in the end part of the Sapphire network was discovered, "the biggest one got away." No cases came to court.[86]

The lack, during the Cold War, of public disclosures of Soviet moles in France as sensational as the revelations in Britain and the United States reflects the failure not of Soviet penetration but of French detection. Part of the failure of detection stemmed from the absence in France of the Venona intercepts, which had begun the downfall of the Magnificent Five and the atom spies. In the wake of the Pâques case, French material in the Venona traffic was reexamined during the mid-1960s in Britain and the United States, and the results were passed to the French security service, the Direction de la Surveillance du Territoire (DST). It revealed the existence of a group of Soviet agents in the prewar French Air Ministry recruited during the mid-thirties and run during the few years before the fall of France by the GRU illegal Henry Robinson.

One of the group, the scientist André Labarthe (code-named Jérome), who left the Air Ministry in 1938 to become head of a group of state research laboratories, was among the first of the small group of Free French to gather in London in June 1940 under the leadership of General de Gaulle.[87] For a few months Labarthe was de Gaulle's *directeur des armements* but quarreled with de Gaulle's entourage and left to found the monthly Free French journal, *La France Libre,* published from London; he later broadcast to occupied France over the BBC. In London, Labarthe passed on political and military intelligence to a Soviet controller whom he knew as Albert. In 1943, Labarthe became minister of information in the Free French provisional government in Algiers.[88] Among those who worked under him was Georgi Pâques, head of political affairs on the Free French broadcasting service.[89] After the war, Labarthe earned his living chiefly as a journalist, editing the magazines *Constellation* and *Science et Vie.*

The most important Soviet agent in the prewar Air Ministry

revealed by the Venona intercepts was Pierre Cot, six times minister of air and twice minister of commerce in the short-lived cabinets of the interwar Third French Republic.[90] As a radical politician in the 1930s, Cot was probably the most passionate advocate outside the Communist Party of a close military alliance with the Soviet Union. During the Spanish Civil War, he was accused in the press, probably correctly, of secretly passing to the Russians details of French aviation and weapons technology.[91] After his defection in 1937, Krivitsky also identified Cot as a Soviet agent, but his revelations, as in the United States, evoked little interest at the time.[92] Like many others on the French Left, Cot was stunned by the conclusion of the Nazi-Soviet Pact in August 1939, but, while condemning it, insisted that France and the Soviet Union must one day ally together.[93]

Rebuffed by de Gaulle after the fall of France in 1940, Cot spent the next few years in the United States, where he combined academic work with propaganda for the Allied cause. Venona intercepts later revealed that he was re-recruited in 1942 by the NKVD/NKGB resident in Washington, Vasili Zubilin (*alias* Zarubin), and remained in contact with him and another Soviet case officer for the next two years.[94] Late in 1943, Cot traveled to Algiers, where he joined the Free French Consultative Assembly. In March 1944, he was sent on a three-month mission to the Soviet Union on behalf of the provisional government. He returned full of praise for Stalin's commitment to the worth of the human individual—*"ce culte renouvelé de l'humanisme"*— which, even more than the military strength of the Red Army, had enabled Russia to emerge victorious. He concluded the report on his mission by declaring: "Liberty declines unceasingly under capitalism and rises unceasingly under socialism."[95] After the war Cot acquired a reputation both as one of the best orators in the postwar National Assembly and as "the ablest fellow traveler in Europe," taking a prominent part in Soviet front organizations and receiving the Stalin Prize in 1953.[96]

The Venona intelligence on Labarthe, Cot, and others, like that gathered in subsequent investigations, arrived too late to be of operational use. Labarthe confessed when interviewed by the DST. Because of the political sensitivity of the Cot case and his advanced age, Cot was left to die in peace.[97] A detailed history of Soviet agent penetration in France still remains to be written.

*   *   *

From its foundation in 1949 the West European state most vulnerable to Soviet Bloc penetration was the Federal Republic of Germany (FRG). One major episode in that penetration still remains controversial. In July 1954 Otto John, head of the FRG security service, the Bundesamt für Verfassungsschutz (BfV), disappeared from West Berlin and resurfaced at an East German press conference a few days later to denounce the alleged revival of Nazism in the Federal Republic. In December 1955, John reappeared in the West, claiming that he had been drugged by Wolfgang Wohlgemuth, a doctor working for the KGB. The West German Supreme Court was skeptical. According to other evidence, John was a heavy drinker, who had been persuaded to defect after Wohlgemuth had first plied him with whiskey, then played on his fears of a Nazi revival. In December 1956, he was sentenced to four years in jail.[98]

The KGB's most productive mole in FRG intelligence was Heinz Felfe, who in 1958 became head of the Soviet counterintelligence section of the foreign intelligence agency, the BND. With an imaginary agent network in Moscow created for him by the Center and other assistance from the KGB, Felfe built up a formidable reputation. The head of the BND, Reinhard Gehlen, proudly conducted distinguished visitors to Felfe's office, where they were able to admire a gigantic multicolored plan of the Karlshorst compound, which showed every detail of the KGB headquarters right down to the individual parking spaces and lavatories used by each KGB officer. The Karlshorst operation (code-named Diagramm) also generated five thick volumes full of layouts of individual offices, personality sketches, and internal telephone directories.

The BND headquarters at Pullach near Munich received constant requests from the CIA and other allied intelligence services for information on Karlshorst. These inquiries, boasted Felfe later, "revealed the specific interests of CIA stations all over Europe," and thus gave the Center a valuable insight into CIA operations. Felfe, meanwhile, was able to ensure that the BND and its allies had "a wholly distorted picture of Karlshorst." Service A in the FCD, which supervised the preparation of Felfe's memoirs, included a number of passages of self-congratulation. "In a very short time," it wrote, "the far-sightedness of the KGB's penetration plans had proved itself."

Felfe was simultaneously providing Karlshorst with copies of almost all the most important documents in BND files. Urgent reports were radioed to Karlshorst; the remainder went in the false bottoms of suitcases, on film concealed in cans of baby food, via dead-letter drops, or through a BND courier, Erwin Tiebel, who was also working for the KGB. In the two years before the building of the Berlin Wall in August 1961, at a time when, according to Felfe, the CIA and BND were plotting "to sabotage the political and economic development of the GDR," "heightening psychological warfare," and "luring away the workforce":

> I took many risks which could not always be calculated
> ... Rendezvous followed rendezvous, transmissions of intel-
> ligence succeeded one another in short order, everything was
> subordinated to giving the U.S.S.R. the basis for making
> their decisions. I had to assume that in those two years I was
> giving hostile counterespionage clues which they could work
> on. My arrest was to confirm this.

Like Pâques and Hambleton, Felfe's motives had more to do with vanity than ideology. His ego, like theirs, was massaged by personal congratulations from KGB generals and, on one occasion, from the chairman himself.[99] A CIA officer who served in Germany during the 1950s concluded after Felfe's arrest in 1961:

> The BND damage report must have run into tens of thou-
> sands of pages. Not only were agents and addresses compro-
> mised, but ten years of secret agent reports had to be re-
> evaluated: those fabricated by the other side, those subtly
> slanted, those from purely mythical sources.[100]

The KGB also profited from the vast campaign of penetration in West Germany organized by the foreign intelligence agency founded in 1952 within the East German Ministry of State Security: Main Department XV (Hauptverwaltung XV), renamed in 1956 the Main Department of Reconnaissance (Hauptverwaltung Aufklärung or HVA). The head of the department from its foundation and the mastermind of the penetration program for over a generation was Markus Johannes (Mischa) Wolf, the son of a well-known Communist writer forced to flee to Moscow after Hitler's rise to power. By his retirement in 1987, Wolf had established himself as among the ablest as well as easily the longest-serving of the Soviet Bloc's intelligence chiefs.[101] Wolf's most successful agent was Guenther Guillaume, the son of a retired doctor in East

Germany who had given shelter and medical treatment to the socialist politician Willy Brandt when he was being hunted by the Gestapo.

In 1955, at HVA direction, Dr. Guillaume wrote to Brandt, then mayor of West Berlin, asking him to help his son, who was suffering discrimination in the East. At their first meeting, Brandt was taken with Guenther and felt a responsibility to help him. In 1956 Guenther Guillaume and his wife, both HVA officers, gained acceptance as political refugees in the FRG. Within a few years both had obtained full-time jobs in the socialist SPD. The coming to power of an SPD-led coalition with Brandt as chancellor in 1969 gave Guillaume one of the most remarkable opportunities exploited by any penetration agent in modern times. He became the trusted secretary and personal companion of Willy Brandt in the chancellor's office in Bonn. Among the mass of high-level intelligence that Guillaume was able to supply to the HVA and, via the HVA, to the KGB was detailed briefing on the FRG's new Ostpolitik as it sought to establish the first formal ties with the GDR and the other states of Eastern Europe. The shock caused by Guillaume's exposure in 1974 was to be so great that it led to Brandt's resignation.[102]

Guillaume was merely the most remarkable of a massive incursion by East German moles into the Federal Republic. An HVA defector estimated in 1958 that there were already two to three thousand penetration agents in place, with far more waiting in the wings.[103] One of Markus Wolf's most successful strategies was the "secretaries offensive," based on the seduction of lonely, usually middle-aged female government employees with access to sensitive information. Among the victims of the Wolf offensive in the mid-fifties was Irmgard Roemer, a forty-four-year-old secretary in the Bonn Foreign Office, who handled communications with embassies abroad and gave carbon copies to her seducer Carl Helmers, an HVA illegal dubbed the "Red Casanova" by headline writers after his arrest in 1958. Over the next twenty years his place was taken by even more successful "Red Casanovas" dispatched by Markus Wolf.[104]

During the Cold War, as before, much of the Kremlin's best intelligence on the West came from sigint. In 1951 the Seventh (Cipher and Cryptanalytical) Department of the KI was reintegrated into the MGB Fifth Directorate, commanded by Lieutenant General Shevelyov. On the founding of the KGB in 1954, ciphers, communications, and cryptanalysis became the responsibility of the Eighth Chief Directorate, also headed by Shevelyov.[105] The cryptanalysts of both the KGB and the GRU lacked the advanced computer technology available to their American and British counterparts. At its birth in 1952 the National Security Agency had easily the largest bank of computers in the world.

Though Soviet sigint was technologically behind that in the West, it had two compensating advantages. First, it had unrestricted access to the best Soviet mathematicians and computer scientists, many of whom continue to spend periods of secondment with the KGB and GRU. Neither NSA nor GC HQ possesses the Soviet power of press-gang, at least in peacetime. Second, Soviet sigint had (and doubtless still has) far greater assistance from humint operations, which provide the kind of intelligence on foreign cipher systems that almost all the most important cryptanalytic successes depend on. Much of the assistance to Soviet cryptanalysts during the Cold War continued to come from embassy penetration.[106] The embassy of most interest to Moscow was, inevitably, that of the Main Adversary.

Though American diplomats in Moscow had grown less naïve about Soviet surveillance, their grasp of embassy security at the height of the Cold War remained rudimentary. When George Kennan arrived as U.S. ambassador in 1952 he discovered that his official residence "was really run by unseen hands, before whose authority I and all the rest of us were substantially helpless." The unseen hands were those of the Soviet employment agency for foreign missions, Burobin, which was in reality a wholly owned subsidiary of the MGB Second (Counterintelligence) Chief Directorate. Burobin staff appeared unpredictably at all hours of the day and night. One night a few months after their arrival, Kennan and his wife were awakened by a slight noise on the gallery next to their bedroom. On opening the bedroom door, Kennan later recalled:

I suddenly found myself face to face with an apparition which I was able to identify as the figure of a large woman— or so it seemed. I said, "Who are you?" The answer came back, "I'm the new night watchman."[107]

Since the discovery of several hundred listening devices in 1944,[108] periodic checks of the American embassy had revealed no new bugs. It occurred to Kennan that these negative findings probably had more to do with the increased sophistication of MGB electronic eavesdropping than with improvements in embassy security. In September 1952 two experts arrived from Washington to begin a thorough search of the embassy and ambassador's residence. At the experts' request, Kennan sat in his study dictating the text of an old diplomatic dispatch, hoping thus to activate any concealed listening device.

Suddenly one of the technicians began hacking away at the wall behind a wooden replica of the great seal of the United States. Finding nothing, he attacked the seal itself with a mason's hammer and triumphantly extracted from its shattered remains a pencil-shaped bug, which had been relaying Kennan's every word to an outside monitor. Next morning Kennan noted a "new grimness" in the MGB guards and Soviet embassy staff: "So dense was the atmosphere of anger and hostility that one could have cut it with a knife." Yet so remote were the precautions necessary to guard against MGB surveillance from the traditions of the State Department that Kennan wondered whether he had been right to take such drastic action to detect the listening devices. When writing his memoirs twenty years later, he was still uncertain:

> Was it proper for an ambassador to involve himself in this sort of comedy? Or would I have been remiss, in the eyes of my own government, if I had refused to do so?
>
> I am not sure, even today, of the answers to these questions.[109]

Largely because of State Department objections, the CIA was not allowed to station an officer in the Moscow embassy until 1953. The CIA's Moscow station got off to an unhappy start. Its first head, Edward Ellis Smith, was rapidly seduced by his MGB maid. He later confessed to Kennan's successor as ambassador, Charles Bohlen, and was sent home in disgrace. According to Peer de Silva, then chief of operations in the CIA Soviet Bloc division, "His work was not only worthless, but much had been fabricated."[110] The CIA station chief was one of no fewer than twelve of Bohlen's embassy personnel who admitted having been seduced by MGB/KGB "swallows" and then shown photographs taken during their seductions in an attempt to recruit them as MGB/KGB agents. According to Bohlen: "All of these people were out of the country in twenty-four hours."[111] It is unlikely, however, that all those who were compromised confessed.

In 1953 work began on a new U.S. embassy in Tchaikovsky Street. During construction work American security men were on guard all day to prevent the installation of listening devices on the two top floors. Their day-long vigil, however, was entirely pointless, since they were withdrawn at night. In his memoirs, Bohlen attributes their withdrawal to "carelessness" (presumably his own) and the desire "to save money."[112] In 1964, acting on intelligence from the KGB defector Yuri Nosenko, the embassy discovered over forty bugs concealed in bamboo tubes built into the walls behind the radiators in order to shield them from metal detectors.[113] Bohlen is at pains to diminish the significance of the security lapse. The bugging of the two floors which, he acknowledges, "were supposed to be the most secure in Moscow," and included the ambassador's office, the cipher rooms, and the CIA station, did not, he argues, "mean that the Soviets learned any real secrets."[114]

That retrospective judgment is an echo of the careless optimism that had earlier led Bohlen to withdraw the nighttime guard during the embassy's construction. It is true that embassy staff were more aware than before of the dangers of Soviet electronic surveillance and took a number of precautions. But the fact that twelve were sent home during Bohlen's four years as ambassador after admitting to being photographed engaging in various sexual acts with KGB partners scarcely suggests that all were models of discretion.

American embassy security, however, was probably no worse than average. Nor were American diplomats more easily compromised than most others. During Maurice Dejean's eight-year term as French ambassador in Moscow from 1956 to 1964 both he and his air attaché, Colonel Louis Guibaud, were seduced by KGB "swallows" after elaborate operations personally supervised by the head of the Second Chief (Counterintelligence) Directorate, General Oleg Mikhailovich Gribanov. Dejean was beaten up by a KGB officer posing as the enraged husband of the swallow who had seduced him; Guibaud was confronted with the usual compromising photographs of his sexual liaison. On this occasion, however, the seductions failed to achieve Gribanov's objectives. Guibaud committed suicide, and a KGB cooptee involved in arranging the seduction of Dejean defected to the West, revealing the operation before serious KGB blackmail had begun.[115]

At the height of the Cold War most diplomatic missions in Moscow were bugged. Among them was the West German embassy, where, Yuri Nosenko recalls, an ambassador in the late 1950s, probably with a future volume of memoirs in mind, each evening dictated an account of the day's events, including his correspondence with Bonn and his dealings with other NATO ambassadors, unknowingly into

KGB microphones. The more interesting excerpts from his draft memoirs were on Khrushchev's desk within two hours of their dictation. MGB/KGB embassy penetration was not limited to Moscow. Other Soviet Bloc capitals also offered opportunities for operations against the "Main" and lesser adversaries. With AVH assistance, the KGB succeeded in penetrating the U.S. embassy in Budapest.[116]

In a number of cases MGB/KGB officers gained physical access to foreign missions. According to Nosenko, each embassy raid had to be approved personally by Khrushchev, following a precedent established under Stalin. The most important break-in was probably at the Japanese embassy, where a cipher clerk gave the MGB access to both the embassy safes and Japanese diplomatic ciphers.[117] Of all major powers it is probably Japan whose ciphers have been most regularly broken by Soviet cryptanalysts since the 1920s.[118] In the 1970s the KGB was to recruit a cipher clerk in the Japanese foreign ministry who proved as cooperative as his counterpart in the Moscow embassy twenty years before.[119] The KGB similarly gained access to the Swedish embassy safes and ciphers by seducing the nightwatchman with one of its swallows and diverting the nightwatchman's dog with large chunks of meat.[120] The KGB defector Ilya Dzhirkvelov took part in other successful break-ins during the early 1950s at the Turkish, Egyptian, Syrian, Iranian, and other Middle Eastern embassies. "We were," he recalls, "rewarded with inscribed watches and the title of Honored Chekists."[121]

In the far distant day when the secrets of all archives are revealed, careful study of the millions of diplomatic intercepts decrypted by Soviet cryptanalysts, with the assistance of the massive humint support operations mounted by the KGB and GRU, is sure to cast new light on the making of Soviet foreign policy during and after the Cold War. In the meantime, precise estimation of the influence of the vast quantities of sigint supplied by the KGB and GRU remains impossible. Within the KGB it seems likely that only the chairman and the heads of the First Chief (Foreign) and Eighth Chief (Cipher) Directorates had unrestricted access to diplomatic sigint. In 1969 a newly established Sixteenth Directorate took over responsibility for sigint from the Eighth. None of the KGB defectors during the Cold War had more than fragmentary access to sigint. The files from the KGB archives seen by Gordievsky provided little further information. Many contained intelligence probably or certainly derived from sigint, but the intercepts themselves remain in the cryptanalytic archives, to which almost no officer in the First Chief Directorate had access. All but the most senior KGB officers saw only intercepts that were judged strictly necessary to their operational duties.

During the Cold War period intercepts were written on onion-skin paper and kept in large Red Books. Pyotr Deryabin, who defected from the First Chief Directorate in 1954, remembers being shown selected intercepts from the Red Book about twice a week in the office of his department head. Yuri Nosenko, who defected a decade later from the Second Chief Directorate, recalls that the Red Book was brought to him by a courier, who stood over him while he read the permitted pages; he was not allowed to take notes. Both Deryabin and Nosenko remember seeing intercepts from a number of Western countries, some resulting from KGB bugs in embassies.[122]

French communications security was generally regarded as particularly poor by both the British and Americans.[123] According to Peter Wright, in 1960 while posing as a telephone engineer, he personally planted bugs in the French embassy in London that allowed GCHQ to decrypt messages in the high-grade French diplomatic cipher.[124] The French embassy in Moscow was still being successfully bugged by the KGB at the end of the Brezhnev era.[125] Deryabin also remembers West German, Italian, and Belgian intercepts in the Red Book. Yuri Rastvorov, who defected in 1954, and Nosenko recall a plentiful supply of Japanese decrypts.[126] Decrypts from the Main Adversary were less plentiful or more highly classified—or, more probably, both. Nosenko remembers being shown only occasional American intercepts; Deryabin saw none at all. There were also, Nosenko recalls, "some successes" in decrypting British communications, but he can recall no specific examples.[127] It is clear, however, that the intercepts to which the KGB defectors of the Cold War period had access represent only the tip of a massive sigint iceberg.

During 1958, Serov's record as chairman of the KGB came under attack from two ambitious young Turks who had the ear of Khrushchev: Aleksandr Nikolayevich Shelepin, first secretary of the Komsomol Central Committee, who had mobilized several hundred thousand young people for Khrushchev's Virgin Lands Program, and Nikolai Romanovich Mironov, head of the Leningrad KGB. Both impressed Khrushchev with the case they presented for a more flexible, sophisticated role for the KGB and were rewarded with senior posts in the Central Committee apparatus. Serov's deserved reputation as a butcher had become something of a diplomatic embarrassment. When he visited London to oversee security preparations for the state visit by Khrushchev and Bulganin in the spring of 1956, the outcry in the press forced him to beat a hasty retreat. Rumors of his role in crushing the Hungarian Revolution later in the year confirmed his reputation in the West as a continuing symbol of neo-Stalinist repression.

For the KGB to acquire a cleaner image it was clear that it required a different head. In the autumn of 1958 the Presidium discussed criticisms by Shelepin of a recent report by Serov on the work of the KGB at home and abroad. Shelepin praised the KGB's effectiveness in unmasking and curbing "enemies of the people," and in penetrating the secrets of the imperialist powers. But its role had become too passive; it had done nothing to help the strategic and ideological struggle with the West. The Presidium sided with Shelepin. In December 1958 he was appointed chairman of the KGB. In recognition of his past services, Serov, instead of simply being dismissed, was moved to the less prestigious post of head of the GRU.[128]

Like Beria before him and Andropov after him, Shelepin's ambitions stretched far beyond the chairmanship of the KGB. As a twenty-year-old university student, he was once asked what he wanted to become. According to the Soviet historian Roy Medvedev, he instantly replied: "A chief!" Shelepin saw the KGB as a stepping-stone in a career that he intended to take him to the post of first secretary of the Party. In December 1961, he stepped down from the KGB chairmanship but continued to oversee its work as chairman of the powerful new Committee of Party and State Control. The new chairman was Shelepin's youthful protégé, the thirty-seven-year-old Vladimir Yefimovich Semichastny, who had worked under him in the Komsomol.[129]

The beginning of Shelepin's term as KGB chairman was marked by an immediate change in leadership style. One Scandinavian intelligence officer, responsible for analyzing KGB radio-telephone voice intercepts, noticed that the verb "demand" was invariably used to transmit the chairman's orders. Late in 1958 "demand" was suddenly changed to "request." Shortly afterward he discovered that Serov had been succeeded by Shelepin.[130] A new influx of university graduates, some of them his former protégés in Komsomol, began to replace the old guard. The change of personnel was particularly striking in the Second (Counterintelligence) Chief Directorate, which since the war had been poorly educated by comparison with the First. When Yuri

Nosenko served in the First (American) Department of the Second Chief Directorate from 1953 to 1955, only two of its sixty officers had university degrees; some had not even finished their schooling. Few spoke English. When Nosenko returned to the same department in January 1960, about 80 percent had university degrees and about 70 percent spoke English.[131]

Along with the new blood from Komsomol and the universities went an attempt to create a new public image. "Violations of socialist legality," claimed Shelepin in 1961, "have been completely eliminated. . . . The Chekists can look the Party and the Soviet people in the eye with a clear conscience." After twenty years in abeyance, the Dzerzhinsky cult was revived. Iron Feliks became once again the model of the cool-headed, warm-hearted Chekist selflessly protecting the Soviet people from the assaults of imperialist warmongers.[132]

In his initial review of KGB foreign intelligence operations during the winter of 1958–59, Shelepin was struck by the sigint successes of the cryptanalysts of the Eighth Chief Directorate made possible by embassy penetration in the Soviet Bloc and by the recruitment of foreign cipher personnel and diplomats in Moscow and abroad. Hitherto, however, he believed that the operations by the First and Second Chief Directorates in support of the Eighth had been inadequately coordinated. Shelepin set up a Special Section within the First Chief Directorate, under the direct control of its head, Aleksandr Sakharovsky, to coordinate the sigint support operations of the First and Second Chief Directorates and to liaise with the Eighth. The chief target of the new Special Section was, inevitably, the Main Adversary, the United States.

The head of the American section of the Eighth Directorate, Aleksandr Seleznyov, ordered the Special Section to collect intelligence on cipher systems of particular interest to the cryptanalysts.[133] The most ambitious project of the Special Section was to penetrate the United States National Security (sigint) Agency (NSA), the largest, best-funded of the American intelligence services, with its headquarters at Fort Meade near Washington. All Americans who watched television or read newspapers were aware of the existence of the CIA. Only a tiny fraction, however, were aware that the United States possessed a sigint service. Those in the know in Washington joked that NSA stood for "No Such Agency."

By 1960 Soviet intelligence had three agents in place at Fort Meade. This remarkable success, however, owed far less to careful planning by Sakharovsky's Special Section than to good fortune and poor NSA security. All three agents were walk-ins. In December 1959 two NSA cryptanalysts, thirty-year-old Bernon F. Mitchell and twenty-eight-year-old William H. Martin, flew undetected to Cuba, where in all probability they were debriefed by the KGB and given a shopping list of further sigint secrets. Somewhat surprisingly, Mitchell had been recruited by NSA despite admitting to six years of "sexual experimentations" up to the age of nineteen with dogs and chickens. During Martin's positive vetting, acquaintances variously described him as irresponsible and an insufferable egotist. During the selection procedure, however, their remarkable gifts as mathematicians were held to outweigh their personality defects and—in Mitchell's case—farmyard experiences.

Early in 1959 both broke NSA rules by complaining to Congressman Wayne Hays about airborne elint (electronic intelligence) missions that violated Soviet airspace. Mistakenly believing that the two had been sent by the CIA to test his ability to keep secrets, Hays took no action. Politically naïve and socially gauche, Martin and Mitchell were seduced by the myth image presented in Soviet propaganda magazines of the U.S.S.R. as a state so committed to the cause of peace that it would never engage in illegal overflights, and so progressive in its social system that it could offer them a sense of personal fulfillment they had failed to find in the United States. On June 25, 1960, at the beginning of their three-week annual leave, Mitchell and Martin flew to Mexico City. Next day they flew on to Havana, boarded a Soviet freighter, and delivered their response to the KGB's shopping lists to Moscow Center.

It was a week and a day after their three-week leave expired before NSA tried to track them down. Inside Mitchell's house NSA security officers found the key to a safe deposit box in a Maryland bank; the key had been deliberately left for them to find. Opening the box, the officers discovered a sealed envelope bearing a written request signed by Martin and Mitchell that its contents be made public. The envelope contained a long denunciation of the U.S. government for being "as unscrupulous as it has accused the Soviet government of being" and a bizarre eulogy of the U.S.S.R. as a society where "the talents of women are encouraged and utilized to a much greater extent . . . than in the United States," thus making Soviet women "more desirable as mates."

On September 6, 1960, in Moscow's House of Journalists, Martin and Mitchell gave perhaps the most embarrassing press conference in the history of the American intelligence community. The greatest embarrassment of all was their revelation that NSA decrypted the communications of some of the United States' own allies. Among them, said Martin, were "Italy, Turkey, France, Yugoslavia, the United Arab Republic, Indonesia, Uruguay—that's enough to give a general picture, I guess." Though they did not mention it at the press conference, they had also been well informed about the U-2 reconnaissance flights over the U.S.S.R. and had had advance knowledge, which they may have been able to pass on to the KGB, about the ill-fated flight of Gary Powers, which was shot down on May Day 1960 and led to a major Soviet propaganda triumph.[134]

Unknown to Martin and Mitchell, an even more important Soviet agent, thirty-two-year-old Staff Sergeant Jack E. Dunlap, remained in place at Fort Meade. Dunlap had won the Purple Heart and the Bronze Star for "coolness under fire and sincere devotion to duty" during the Korean War. But he was also a womanizer, the father of seven children, and short of money. In 1958 he became chauffeur to Major General Garrison B. Coverdale, chief of staff at Fort Meade, acting as courier for highly classified documents between different sections of the NSA. As driver of the chief of staff's car Dunlap had the rare privilege of leaving Fort Meade without being searched. At least six NSA staff members used Dunlap to smuggle typewriters and office furniture to their homes, thus increasing his access to NSA headquarters.[135]

Sometime in the spring or early summer of 1960, Dunlap is believed to have entered the Soviet embassy in Washington and offered NSA documents for money. A later inquiry concluded that thereafter he was probably controlled by a GRU rather than a KGB case officer.[136] The Dunlap case was so important that, almost certainly, his case officer thenceforth handled nothing else. Dunlap was able to provide instruction books, repair manuals, mathematical models, and design plans for the United States's most secret cipher machines. He also had access to CIA estimates on Soviet forces and missiles in Eastern Europe, especially East Germany.

In the summer of 1960 Dunlap suddenly became inexplicably prosperous. Despite earning only a hundred dollars a week, he supported a mistress as well as his large family and purchased a Jaguar, two Cadillacs, and a well-equipped thirty-foot cabin cruiser. Even when NSA sent an ambulance to collect him after an accident in a yacht-club regatta, his sudden affluence—for which he gave various improbable explanations—aroused no serious suspicion. But by the spring of 1963 the strain of Dunlap's double life had become too much. In March he admitted during polygraph tests to "petty thieving" and "immoral conduct"; in May he was transferred to a job in a Fort Meade orderly room. On July 22 he strung a length of radiator hose from the exhaust pipe of his car into the right front window, started the engine, and asphyxiated himself.

Three days afterward, like President Kennedy four months later, he was buried with full military honors at Arlington National Cemetery. His treachery might never have been uncovered but for his widow's discovery a month later of a cache of top secret documents he had failed to deliver to his controller. An NSA inquiry concluded that the importance of Dunlap's intelligence far exceeded even that jointly provided by Martin and Mitchell.[137]

On the day Dunlap's suicide was discovered, another former NSA officer, Victor Norris Hamilton, a naturalized U.S. citizen of Arab origins, revealed more of Fort Meade's secrets on the front page of *Izvestia.* Like Martin and Mitchell, Hamilton was a bizarre, inadequate personality who had somehow slipped through NSA's security net and joined the Near East section of its Production Office (PROD) in 1957 to work on Arabic material. In February 1959 NSA psychiatrists pronounced him "mentally ill," but PROD kept him on because of a shortage of Arab specialists. He was finally forced to resign in June when he was diagnosed as "approaching schizophrenic break." Four years later he resurfaced in Moscow and gave highly embarrassing public revelations of PROD's Near East successes:

> It is especially important to note that the American authorities take advantage of the fact that the UN headquarters is located on American soil. . . . The enciphered instructions of the United Arab Republic [Egypt and Syria], Iraq, Jordan, Lebanon, Turkey and Greece to their missions to the UN General Assembly fall into the hands of the State Department before arriving at their proper address.[138]

While Dunlap was smuggling documents out of Fort Meade to his GRU controller, the KGB simultaneously achieved at least one major penetration of American cryptographic secrets outside the United States. Its unlikely penetration agent was a disgruntled army sergeant and part-time pimp, Robert Lee Johnson, who while stationed in West

Berlin in 1953 crossed to the East and asked for political asylum for himself and his prostitute fiancée Hedy. The KGB, however, persuaded Johnson to stay in the West, pay off his scores against the U.S. Army, and earn a second salary by spying for the Soviet Union. Johnson soon recruited a homosexual fellow sergeant, James Allen Mintkenbaugh, who was assigned to identify other homosexuals in the American garrison who might work for the KGB. Despite this success, Johnson proved a difficult agent to handle and for several years provided only low-level intelligence. In 1956 he broke contact with the KGB, left the army, and traveled with Hedy to Las Vegas, where he planned to win a fortune in the casinos and make a career as a famous author. Failing to fulfill either fantasy, Johnson took to the bottle and forced Hedy to return to prostitution. By the end of 1956 Hedy was too ill to work and Johnson was broke.

Then in January 1957 Mintkenbaugh arrived at their trailer home with a $500 present from the KGB and an offer of renewed employment. The KGB wanted Johnson to enlist in the U.S. Air Force to gather intelligence about missile deployment. Unsurprisingly, Johnson was turned down by the air force. The army, however, apparently unaware of his involvement in prostitution, alcohol abuse, and gambling (not to mention espionage), accepted him back as a guard at missile sites in California and Texas. For two years Johnson supplied Mintkenbaugh with photographs, plans, and documents, and even, on one occasion, with a sample of rocket fuel siphoned off on KGB instructions. Mintkenbaugh then conveyed these to his KGB controller, Pyotr Nikolayevich Yeliseev, usually at rendezvous near Washington "burlesque" (striptease) theaters, for which, according to Mintkenbaugh, Yeliseev had a particular fondness.

Late in 1959 Johnson was transferred from Texas to a U.S. Army base in France. Soon afterward a new case officer, Vitali Sergeevich Urzhumov, whom he knew as Viktor, made contact with him in Paris, handing him $500 folded inside a pack of cigarettes. "It's a Christmas present!" Urzhumov said cheerfully. With Hedy now suffering from mental illness, Johnson was not an easy agent to control. But Urzhumov's patience, flattery, and dollar bills gradually paid off. Late in 1961 Johnson gained a job as a guard in the Armed Forces Courier Center at Orly Airport, which handled classified documents, cipher systems, and cryptographic equipment in transit between Washington, NATO, American commands in Europe, and the U.S. Sixth Fleet.

Over the next year, with patient coaxing from Viktor, Johnson gradually gained access to the triple-locked vault used to store classified material. At the second attempt he successfully took a wax impression of the key to the vault. Some time later he found a piece of paper in a wastepaper basket giving the combination to the second lock. Finally, with the help of a portable X-ray device supplied by the KGB, he discovered the combination to the third lock. In the early hours of December 15, 1961, Johnson entered the vault for the first time, stuffed an Air France flight bag with official pouches containing cryptographic material and highly classified documents, and took it to a rendezvous with a second case officer drafted in to assist Urzhumov, Feliks Aleksandrovich Ivanov, who transported it to the KGB residency in the Paris embassy. There a team of technicians was waiting to remove the seals on the pouches, photograph the documents, and reseal the pouches. In little more than an hour the flight bag was on its way back to Johnson. Well before the end of Johnson's shift, the bag's contents were back in the vault.

From the outset, according to Nosenko, the Orly operation was personally authorized by Khrushchev himself, and samples of the first haul from the vault were rushed to him and other Politburo members. Despite his famous satirical suggestion during his visit to the United States in 1959 that the U.S.A. and U.S.S.R. could save money by combining their intelligence services, Khrushchev had a continuing fascination with the imperialist secrets fed to him by his intelligence services. On December 26, 1962, Johnson was given the congratulations of Comrade Khrushchev and the Soviet Council of Ministers, told he had been awarded the rank of Red Army major, and presented with $2,000 to spend on a holiday in Monte Carlo.

By the end of April 1963 Johnson had provided seventeen flight bags full of documents, which included details of U.S. cipher systems, the locations of American nuclear warheads stored in Europe, and NATO and U.S. defense plans. But, because Johnson was becoming increasingly careless, the KGB then temporarily abandoned the operation for fear that it would be discovered. By the time the KGB was ready to resume, Johnson had been transferred. He was eventually caught in 1964 as a result of intelligence supplied by Nosenko after his defection.[139]

As well as giving greater impetus and coordination to the acquisition of cipher material, Shelepin also accorded increased priority and resources to "active measures" designed to influence Western governments and public opinion. In January 1959, he created a new disinformation section within the First Chief Directorate, Department D (later Service A), staffed initially by over fifty officers. Its head until his death in 1968 was General Ivan Ivanovich Agayants, a tall Armenian of grizzled appearance but considerable personal charm.[140] The defector Evdokia Petrova remembered him more warmly than almost any of her former colleagues as "charming, highly cultured, courteous, kind," and fluent in English, French, and Persian. He served as resident in Teheran from 1941 to 1943 and in Paris from 1947 to 1949 (under the pseudonym Avalov), then became head of the Western European Department in, successively, the KI, the MGB, and the KGB.[141]

Agayants owed his appointment as the first head of Department D to his success in sponsoring a series of bogus memoirs and other works: among them the "memoirs" of General Vlasov, *I Chose the Gallows;* the equally fraudulent *My Career in the Soviet High Command* by Ivan Krylov; and imaginary correspondence between Stalin and Tito published in the weekly *Carrefour,* in which Tito confessed his Trotskyist sympathies. The real author of most of these works was probably Grigori Bessedovsky, a former Soviet diplomat who had settled in Paris between the wars and later collaborated with the NKVD. Bessedovsky's forgeries, which later included two books about Stalin by a nonexistent nephew, were sophisticated enough to deceive even such a celebrated Soviet scholar as E. H. Carr, who in 1955 contributed a foreword to *Notes for a Journal,* fraudulently attributed to the former foreign commissar Maxim Litvinov.[142] Some of the forgeries and bogus news stories concocted by Service A that Gordievsky encountered in the 1970s and 1980s were crude by comparison.

One of Agayants's first targets as head of Department D in 1959 was West Germany, which the KGB sought to portray as riddled with neo-Nazis. To test one of his "active measures" before trying it in Germany, Agayants sent a group of his officers to a village about fifty miles from Moscow with instructions to daub swastikas, paint anti-Jewish slogans, and kick over tombstones under cover of darkness. KGB informers in the village reported that though the incident alarmed most inhabitants, a small anti-Semitic minority had been inspired to imitate the KGB provocation and commit anti-Jewish acts of their own.

During the winter of 1959–60 Agayants used the same technique with great success in West Germany. East German agents were dispatched to the West to deface Jewish memorials, synagogues, and shops, and to paint anti-Semitic slogans. Local hooligans and neo-Nazis then spontaneously continued the KGB campaign. Between Christmas Eve 1959 and mid-February 1960, 833 anti-Semitic acts were recorded by the West German authorities. The campaign then suddenly ceased, but not before the Federal Republic's international reputation had been gravely damaged. West German politicians and religious leaders publicly hung their heads in shame. The New York *Herald Tribune* summed up much foreign press reaction with the headline: "Bonn Unable to Eliminate Nazi Poison."[143]

In May 1959 Shelepin organized the largest intelligence conference in Moscow since the founding of the Cheka to review KGB priorities. Two thousand KGB officers attended, together with Aleksei Illarionovich Kirichenko representing the Presidium, members of the Central Committee, and the interior and defense ministers. Shelepin set out a far-ranging plan for mobilizing the intelligence services of the entire Soviet Bloc to promote the long-range objectives of Soviet policy and to neutralize the threat from the United States, its NATO allies, and Japan. Department D was to coordinate its active-measures program with the International Department of the Central Committee and the Party and government apparatus.[144]

Despite the comparative sophistication of Shelepin's active-measures program, he had no intention of abandoning more direct forms of "special action" abroad. Under Serov, Department Thirteen of the First Chief Directorate, which was responsible for "wet affairs," had suffered several public embarrassments. After the failure to liquidate the émigré National Labor Alliance (NTS) leader Georgi Okolovich in Frankfurt and the defection of the KGB assassin Nikolai Khokhlov in 1954,[145] a German contract killer, Wolfgang Wildprett, was hired by Department Thirteen to assassinate the NTS president, Vladimir Poremsky, in 1955. Like Khokhlov, however, Wildprett had second thoughts and told the West German police.[146] In September 1957 a Department Thirteen attempt to poison Khokhlov with radioactive thallium (chosen in the belief that it would leave no trace at autopsy) also failed. These failures, however, were followed by the successful assassination of two leading Ukrainian émigrés in West Germany: the main NTS ideologist, Lev Rebet, in October 1957 and the head of the Organization of Ukrainian Nationalists (OUN), Stepan Bandera, in October 1959.

These liquidations persuaded Khrushchev, who personally authorized both of them, and Shelepin that selective assassination remained a necessary part of KGB foreign operations. The Department

Thirteen assassin in each case, only twenty-five years of age when he killed Rebet, was Bogdan Stashinsky, who operated out of the KGB compound in Karlshorst. His murder weapon, devised by the KGB weapons laboratory at Khozyaistvo Zheleznovo, was a spray gun that fired a jet of poison gas from a crushed cyanide ampule, inducing cardiac arrest in the victim. Department Thirteen calculated correctly that an unsuspecting pathologist was likely to diagnose the cause of death as heart failure. Stashinsky tested the spray gun by taking a dog to a woods near Karlshorst, tying it to a tree, and firing at it. The dog had convulsions and died in a few moments. Confident of his weapon, Stashinsky killed both Rebet and Bandera by lying in wait for them in darkened stairways. In December 1959, Stashinsky was summoned to Moscow. At a ceremony in the Center Shelepin presented him with the Order of the Red Banner and read aloud a citation praising him "for carrying out an extremely important government assignment." Stashinsky was told that he would be sent to a course to perfect his German and learn English, following which he would spend three to five years in the West carrying out further assignments of the kind that had won him the Red Banner. What was expected of him, said Shelepin, was "difficult but honorable."[147]

Like Khokhlov and Wildprett, however, Stashinsky had second thoughts about assassination, encouraged by his anti-Communist East German girlfriend Inge Pohl, whom he married in 1960. In August 1961, one day before the Berlin Wall sealed off the escape route from the East, the couple defected to the West. Stashinsky confessed to the assassination of Rebet and Bandera, was put on trial at Karlsruhe in October 1962, and sentenced to eight years' imprisonment as accomplice to murder. The judge declared that the main culprit was the Soviet government, which had institutionalized political murder. Heads were quick to roll within the KGB. According to Anatoli Golitsyn, who defected four months after Stashinsky, at least seventeen KGB officers were sacked or demoted.[148] More important, the Khokhlov and Stashinsky defections led both the Politburo and the KGB leadership to reassess the risks of "wet affairs." After the worldwide publicity generated by Stashinsky's trial, the Politburo abandoned assassination by the KGB as a normal instrument of policy outside the Soviet Bloc, resorting to it only on rare occasions, such as the liquidation of President Hafizullah Amin of Afghanistan in December 1979.[149]

*   *   *

At the end of the Cold War, as at the beginning, the chief target of KGB foreign operations remained the Main Adversary. In the early 1960s the KGB succeeded for the first time in establishing a major operational base in Latin America, in the United States's backyard. Its opportunity came with Fidel Castro's overthrow of the Batista dictatorship in Cuba in January 1959. Hitherto the Kremlin had been profoundly pessimistic about the prospects for Latin American revolution, regarding American influence as too strong for a Communist takeover to succeed.[150] Castro himself had had a privileged upbringing even by the standards of affluent Cuban landowning families, and drew his early political inspiration from the Orthodox Party and the ideals of its anti-Marxist founder, Eduardo Chibás. Until the summer of 1958 the Cuban Communist Party, the PSP, continued to insist, with Moscow's backing, that Batista could be overthrown only by a popular uprising of Cuban workers led by the Communists.[151]

The Second (Latin American) Department of the First Chief Directorate saw Castro's potential ahead of either the Foreign Ministry or the International Department of the Central Committee. The first to do so was a young Spanish-speaking KGB officer stationed in the Mexico City residency during the mid-1950s, Nikolai Sergeevich Leonov. After release in 1955 from a Cuban jail, where he had been imprisoned for two years for organizing an attack on an army barracks, Castro spent a year in exile in Mexico and appealed to the Soviet embassy for arms to support a guerrilla campaign against Batista. Though the request for arms was turned down, Leonov was immediately impressed by Castro's potential as a charismatic guerrilla leader, began regular meetings with him, and offered him enthusiastic moral support.

Leonov regarded Castro's politics as immature and incoherent but noted his determination to retain complete personal control over his Twenty-sixth of July Movement and his willingness to give his own future regime some sort of socialist coloring. He noted also that both Castro's brother Raúl and his chief lieutenant, Che Guevara, already considered themselves Marxists. Initially, Leonov's optimistic assessments of the prospects of the guerrilla campaign, begun after Castro's return to Cuba in December 1956, found little favor in Moscow. But after Castro came to power, Leonov's far-sightedness and the early connection he had established with Castro launched him on a career that led to his appointment in 1983 as deputy head of the First Chief

Directorate, responsible for KGB operations throughout North and South America.[152]

Even when Castro took power in January 1959, Moscow still doubted his ability to resist American pressure. The PSP regarded its alliance with him as a tactical device akin to its support, at an earlier stage, for Batista. Castro, however, took the PSP by surprise, purged much of its old leadership, and used the party as a vehicle for attaining rapid control of Cuba. He then turned to Moscow for the arms and assistance required to consolidate the revolution and realize his personal dream of becoming the Bolívar of the Caribbean. In July 1959, Castro's intelligence chief, Major Ramiro Valdes, began secret meetings in Mexico City with the Soviet ambassador and KGB residency. The KGB dispatched over a hundred advisers to overhaul Castro's security and intelligence system, many drawn from the ranks of *los niños*, the children of Spanish Communist refugees who had settled in Russia after the Civil War. One Spanish Republican veteran, Enrique Lister Farjan, organized the Committees for the Defense of the Revolution, a Cuban neighborhood watch system to keep track of counterrevolutionary subversion. Another, General Alberto Bajar, set up a series of guerrilla training schools.[153]

But the Kremlin remained wary about giving open military support to Castro's unorthodox regime. Not for the last time, the Czechs were used as a stalking horse. In the autumn a Cuban delegation headed by Rául Castro arrived in Prague to discuss the possibility of Czechoslovak military assistance. Despite his habit of sleeping with his boots on and his obsession with blonde prostitutes, Raúl's Marxist fervor made a good impression on his hosts. The PSP, explained the chief of its propaganda department, Luis Mas Martin, was trying to use Raúl to influence Fidel: "Personally, I think Fidel is an anarchist, but his hostility to the United States will drive him into the Party's arms, especially if the Americans continue to react so stupidly." During his stay in Prague, Raúl received an invitation from Khrushchev to visit Moscow.[154]

In October 1959, while Raúl Castro was in Prague, a Soviet "cultural delegation," headed by the former KGB resident in Buenos Aires, Aleksandr Ivanovich Shitov (*alias* Alekseev), arrived in Havana to prepare for the opening of diplomatic relations. Shitov presented Fidel with a bottle of vodka, several jars of caviar, and a photograph album of Moscow, then told him of the Soviet people's "great admiration" both for himself and for the Cuban Revolution.

Castro opened the bottle and sent for crackers for the caviar. "What good vodka, what good caviar!" he exclaimed amiably. ". . . I think it's worth establishing trade relations with the Soviet Union." "Very well, Fidel," replied Shitov, "but what about the most important one, diplomatic relations?" When the Soviet Union at last gave Castro's regime full diplomatic recognition in May 1960, Shitov stayed in Havana, nominally as cultural counselor and Tass representative, in reality as KGB resident.[155]

After his initial hesitations, Khrushchev now gave the Cuban regime (though not yet Castro personally) enthusiastic public backing. He declared in a bellicose anti-American speech on July 9: "We shall do everything to support Cuba in her struggle. . . . Now the United States is not so unreachable as once she was." Next day Che Guevara boasted that Cuba was defended by "the greatest military power in history." Castro and his lieutenants began to claim in their speeches that the Cuban revolution was "only the first step in the liberation of Latin America."[156]

Despite lingering doubts about Castro's ideological reliability, his success in holding and maintaining power transformed both KGB and Kremlin strategy in Latin America. The traditional policy of concentrating on ideologically sound Communist parties was abandoned in favor of alliances of convenience with better-supported national liberation movements. The failure of the CIA-backed Bay of Pigs invasion to topple Castro in April 1961 further revised Soviet estimates of American strength. The United States was vulnerable even in its own backyard.[157]

Though Castro took an increasing dislike to the Soviet ambassador, Sergei Kudryavtsev, he formed a close personal friendship with the KGB resident, Aleksandr Shitov. In March 1962, Castro appeared on television to announce the dismantling of the old hard-line Cuban Communist Party with which Kudryavtsev had identified himself. He then told Kudryavtsev to leave, asked for and obtained Shitov (still using the alias Alekseev), as the new Soviet ambassador.[158] Within six months the growing Soviet foothold in Cuba was to produce the most dangerous international crisis since the Second World War. At the beginning of 1962, with new American Minuteman intercontinental missiles being installed and medium-range missiles already operational in Britain and Turkey, the United States had a clear lead in the nuclear arms race. Khrushchev calculated that he could gain an almost instant nuclear advantage by installing Soviet missiles in Cuba, only ninety miles from the United States.

This was a gambler's throw based less on intelligence assessment than on Khrushchev's own underestimate of American resolve in general and of the youthful President John F. Kennedy in particular. The Western democracies, Khrushchev told the American poet Robert Frost, were "too liberal to fight."[159] Kennedy's lack of confidence during the failed Bay of Pigs invasion convinced Khrushchev that the young President was "wish-washy": "I know for certain that Kennedy doesn't have a strong backbone, nor, generally speaking, does he have the courage to stand up to a serious challenge." By installing nuclear missiles secretly in Cuba, the Soviet Union could face Kennedy with a fait accompli, which he would reluctantly accept.[160] In the summer of 1962 Soviet engineers began constructing the Cuban launch pads for nuclear missiles with a range of over two thousand miles and the capacity to reach the major East Coast cities in a few minutes' flying time.

In all previous Cold War crises Soviet intelligence had been better, often vastly better, than that available to the West. During the missile crisis in October 1962 American intelligence was for the first time as good as, if not better than, that supplied to the Kremlin. Part of the explanation was the fact that the focus of the crisis was only ninety miles from the United States. But the Soviet intelligence lead had also been cut back by two major improvements in Western intelligence collection. The first was the growth of aerial reconnaissance. In 1955 President Eisenhower proposed to the Soviet Union an "open skies" policy allowing each side to monitor the other's military deployment from the air. When Russia refused, the United States went ahead unilaterally with overflights of Soviet territory by U-2 aircraft capable of cruising at seventy thousand feet. The shooting down and Moscow show trial of the U-2 pilot, Gary Powers, in 1960, proved only a temporary setback. Within a few months, the United States had launched its first spy satellite, though the early satellite photographs lacked the definition of those taken by the U-2s. By 1963, satellite surveillance, jointly engaged in by both sides and increasingly used for sigint as well as photographic reconnaissance, was tacitly accepted by the Kremlin.

From the mid-1950s there was also a significant, though less dramatic, improvement in Western humint from the Soviet Union. In the spring of 1961 SIS recruited the most important Western agent of the Cold War: Colonel Oleg Vladimirovich Penkovsky, a GRU officer attached to the State Committee for Science and Technology and a friend of both the head of the GRU, General Ivan Aleksandrovich Serov, and the commanding officer of Missile and Ground Artillery, Chief Marshal Sergei Sergeevich Varentsov. The intelligence supplied by Penkovsky—almost 5,500 exposures on a Minox camera over a period of eighteen months—was of the highest importance. It included up-to-date surveys of Soviet intercontinental ballistic missiles (several thousand fewer than U.S. estimates); the alert stages, checks, and firing sequence of the Soviet Strategic Rocket Forces; statistics on missile accuracy; and defects revealed in test firing. Penkovsky's revelations about increased Soviet reliance on missiles and a vast chemical warfare program led to a major rethink in NATO strategy. At peak periods, the intelligence provided by Penkovsky, who was run jointly by SIS and the CIA, kept busy twenty American and ten British analysts.[161]

Good intelligence in the West was crucial to the peaceful resolution of the Cuban missile crisis before the missiles themselves had been installed. On October 14, 1962, a U-2 over Cuba took the first photographs of a ballistic missile site under construction. CIA analysts were able to identify the nature of the site because of a top secret document detailing the stages in missile-site construction secretly photographed by Penkovsky at the headquarters of the Soviet Armed Forces Missile and Ground Artillery, to which his friendship with Chief Marshal Varentsov had gained him unauthorized access.[162] On October 16 the photographs were placed before the president. Kennedy reacted by creating a top secret crisis-management committee known as ExCom (Executive Committee of the National Security Council), which for the next thirteen days monitored developments minute by minute. By the 19th, U-2 flights had provided ExCom with evidence of nine ballistic sites under construction. On October 22, Kennedy announced the imposition of an American blockade to enforce "a strict quarantine on all offensive military equipment under shipment to Cuba." For almost a week the world lived in the shadow of a nuclear Armageddon.[163]

The KGB residency in Washington played an active part in both creating and helping to resolve the missile crisis. In addition to collecting intelligence, the residency had been charged with two other tasks: providing a private channel of communication with the White House, and spreading disinformation during the installation of Soviet missiles in Cuba. The main vehicle for both was Georgi Nikitovich

Bolshakov, a KGB officer in Washington working under journalistic cover.[164] For over a year before the missile crisis, Bolshakov acted as what he called the "hot-line" and "secret communication channel between John Kennedy and Nikita Khrushchev." After being introduced by an American journalist to the president's brother and close adviser, Robert Kennedy, in May 1961, the two men began fortnightly meetings.[165] Robert Kennedy seems never to have realized that Bolshakov, whose "honesty" impressed him, was a KGB officer. According to Kennedy:

> He was Khrushchev's representative. . . . Any time that he had some message to give to the President (or Khrushchev had) or when the President had some message to give to Khrushchev, we went through Georgi Bolshakov. . . . I met with him about all kinds of things.[166]

Bolshakov succeeded in persuading Robert Kennedy that he could short-circuit the ponderous protocol of official diplomacy, gain direct access to Khrushchev's thinking, and "speak straightly and frankly without resorting to the politickers' stock-in-trade propaganda stunts." According to Bolshakov, "both sides made the most" of the secret channel of communication he provided: "I must say that the Khrushchev-Kennedy dialogue gained in frankness and directness from message to message."[167]

During the run-up to the missile crisis, however, the main function of the KGB-run "hot line" was to help conceal the presence of intermediate-range Soviet missiles in Cuba until their installation was a fait accompli. On October 6, 1962, Bolshakov called on Robert Kennedy with another message from Khrushchev. Usually Bolshakov found Kennedy in his shirtsleeves with his top button undone and his necktie loosened. This time, however, the atmosphere was different:

> As distinct from our past meetings, my host wore a dark formal suit, and his unruly shock of hair was neatly combed and parted. His face bore an impassive expression. . . . Robert was dry and formal. Everything was meant to impart an official character to our meeting.

Bolshakov then delivered his message:

Premier Khrushchev is concerned about the situation being built up by the United States around Cuba, and we repeat that the Soviet Union is supplying to Cuba exclusively defensive weapons intended for protecting the interests of the Cuban revolution.

Robert Kennedy asked Bolshakov to repeat the message slowly, wrote it down, and gave it to a secretary to type. "All right," he said, "I shall pass Premier Khrushchev's message on to the president, and he will communicate his reply through me, if necessary." Next day Bolshakov was invited to lunch by the journalist Charles Bartlett, a close friend of the president. Bartlett told him that John Kennedy wanted Khrushchev's message "in detail in writing, not in his brother's wording of it." Bolshakov repeated word for word what he had told Robert Kennedy. Bartlett wrote the message down and passed it to the president.[168] Nine days later John Kennedy was shown the U-2 photographs of the Soviet missile sites under construction in Cuba. The presidential adviser Theodore Sorensen later recalled:

President Kennedy had come to rely on the Bolshakov channel for direct private information from Khrushchev, and he felt personally deceived. He *was* personally deceived.[169]

On October 24, Bartlett invited Bolshakov to the National Press Club in Washington, and showed him twenty U-2 photographs of the missile bases, still marked "For the President's Eyes Only" in the top right-hand corner. Bartlett asked Bolshakov: "What would you say to that, Georgi? I bet you know for certain that you have your missiles in Cuba." Bolshakov, by his own account, replied: "I have never seen such photographs, and have no idea of what they show. Baseball fields, perhaps?" Next day the photographs were made public. Bartlett phoned Bolshakov. According to Bolshakov's version of their conversation, he began:

"Well, Georgi, do you have missiles in Cuba or don't you?"
"We don't."
"O.K., Bobby asked me to tell you that you do. Khrushchev said it today. The President has just received a telegram from Moscow."

This, claims Bolshakov, "came as a bolt from the blue."[170]

With Bolshakov discredited, Moscow selected a new "secret communication channel" to the White House. Bolshakov's successor was the KGB resident in Washington, Aleksandr Semyonovich Feklisov, who had made his reputation in the Center as a successful PR line officer in London in the late 1940s. As resident in Washington from 1960 to 1964, Feklisov used the alias Fomin.[171] At 2:30 P.M. on October 26 he called ABC's State Department correspondent (later U.S. ambassador to the United Nations), John Scali, who he knew had access to the White House. Feklisov seemed agitated. He asked Scali to meet him at the Occidental Restaurant on Pennsylvania Avenue in ten minutes' time.

At the Occidental he said he had an important message to pass on. In exchange for the removal of Soviet missiles, would the United States be willing to issue a public pledge not to invade Cuba? "Would you," he asked Scali, "check with your high State Department sources?" Feklisov and Scali met again at 7:35 P.M. in the coffeeshop at the Statler Hilton. Scali said he had consulted the secretary of State, Dean Rusk, who was interested in Feklisov's suggestion.

By then a long, emotional message had been received from Khrushchev, putting much the same proposal.[172] Though no formal bargain was ever struck, the proposal first made by Feklisov in the Occidental Restaurant formed the basis for the resolution of the crisis. On October 28, Khrushchev announced that all missile bases in Cuba were to be dismantled. In return the United States gave an assurance that it would not invade Cuba, and that Jupiter missiles in Turkey, nearing the end of their operational life, would be withdrawn. Despite these concessions, Khrushchev's gamble had ended in spectacular failure.

Khrushchev's main immediate problem in the aftermath of the missile crisis was dealing with an infuriated Fidel Castro, outraged that Moscow had settled the crisis without consulting him. The chief responsibility for pacifying him fell to the KGB resident-in-Havana-turned-ambassador, Aleksandr Shitov, who had succeeded in retaining Castro's friendship. Shitov later boasted in Moscow Center that he had become Castro's personal adviser during the missile crisis. Castro treated the embassy as his second home; he and Shitov would sometimes cook meals together in the embassy kitchen.[173]

Oleg Penkovsky, whose intelligence played a major role in both the origins and resolution of the Cuban missile crisis, was arrested just as the crisis was reaching its peak. The trail that eventually led the Second (Counterintelligence) Chief Directorate to Penkovsky began as the result of an episode during surveillance of the British embassy early in 1962. Until 1959 the KGB had believed that the major Western intelligence services risked direct contact with their Russian agents only outside the U.S.S.R. and used dead-letter boxes (DLBs) for all communications inside Russia. In October 1959, however, they arrested a GRU officer, Lieutenant Colonel Pyotr Popov, who had been recruited by the CIA in Vienna six years before and had since passed on intelligence to his case officer in Moscow by "brush contact" (when, for example, brushing past each other in the street).

As a result of the Popov case the head of the Second Chief Directorate, General Oleg Mikhailovich Gribanov, decided in 1960 to begin blanket surveillance of both the United States and British embassies for periods of several weeks twice a year. These enormous operations, which extended to diplomats' families, newspaper correspondents, and resident businessmen as well as embassy staff, employed surveillance teams mostly supplied by the KGB Seventh (Surveillance) Directorate, acting under instructions from the Second Chief Directorate.

Early in 1962 a surveillance group followed the wife of Penkovsky's SIS case officer in Moscow, Janet Chisholm, as she left the embassy to receive the latest set of films from Penkovsky. In the Arbat area of Moscow the Seventh Directorate watchers observed a brush contact between Mrs. Chisholm and an unidentified Russian. Two of the watchers tailed Mrs. Chisholm back to the embassy but, because of instructions to remain unobserved, did not stop her and demand the packet she had received. Two others tailed Penkovsky but lost him about twenty minutes later. From this moment on the Second Chief Directorate knew that SIS had a Moscow agent, and suspected that it might even be dealing with a major British spy ring, but still had no clues that pointed to Penkovsky.

Soon afterward, however, Penkovsky's overconfidence began his downfall. All GRU and KGB officers who visited Western embassies were required to go through the routine of clearing their visits with the Second Chief Directorate beforehand. Penkovsky attended a British embassy reception without bothering to do so. When the Second Chief Directorate complained, the head of the GRU, General Serov, who was one of Penkovsky's drinking companions, wrote a placatory letter on his behalf. While appearing to accept Serov's excuse, General Gribanov took the personal decision to place Penkovsky under surveillance at both his apartment and office. A remote-controlled camera positioned in the windowbox of a neighboring apartment caught him tuning his radio carefully, listening, and making notes.

During a visit in July 1962 by the British businessman Greville Wynne, whom SIS used as a courier, Penkovsky committed another breach of security. He visited Wynne in his room at the Hotel Ukraine, an act which was in itself sufficient to arouse the suspicions of the Second Chief Directorate. In Wynne's room he aroused further suspicion by putting on the radio and turning on the taps in the bathroom to mask their conversation. In fact, Gribanov's technical experts managed to decipher snatches of the conversation, which provided prima facie evidence of espionage.

At this point the Second Chief Directorate sent the family in the apartment above Penkovsky on holiday to the Black Sea, drilled a small hole in his ceiling, and inserted a pinhead camera "eye," which showed him using a Minox camera, code books, and one-time cipher pads. In order to make a detailed search of his apartment the Second Chief Directorate devised a plan for him to spend a few days away from home. KGB toxicologists smeared a poisonous substance on Penkovsky's chair, which made him briefly but violently ill. GRU doctors, who had been suitably briefed, explained to Penkovsky that he would require a few days' hospital treatment. During those few days the Second Chief Directorate discovered the usual paraphernalia of espionage in Penkovsky's flat. It did not immediately arrest him, however, in the belief that if he remained at liberty he would lead them to a larger spy ring.[174]

Sigint, assisted by KGB penetration of NSA and the U.S. embassy in Moscow, was probably the main Soviet intelligence source during the missile crisis. Afterward Khrushchev reportedly "complimented the GRU for having provided him with information from phone intercepts in Washington clarifying the events and discussions in official circles that led to the final resolution of the crisis."[175] Given the speed with which the crisis developed, however, and the secrecy surrounding ExCom's meetings, sigint is likely to have provided only very limited insight into the crucial decisions being made by the president and his small group of advisers. Moscow Center's urgent appeals to Feklisov, the Washington resident, seem to have produced little hard intelligence. Feklisov's main source in Washington during the missile crisis bore some resemblance to Penkovsky. He was a U.S. military intelligence officer, code-named Sasha, recruited by Mikhail Aleksandrovich Shalyapin in 1959 while he was stationed with American forces in Germany. Sasha was a mercenary agent, whose affair with an expensive German mistress had run him into debt. In return for money from the KGB he initially provided what Yuri Nosenko later described as "trunkloads" of military intelligence documents. Sasha was stationed in Washington in 1962 but had no access to ExCom papers and was unable to supply more than low-level intelligence.[176]

Though Sasha survived the missile crisis, Penkovsky did not. Just as the crisis was reaching its climax, the pinhead camera in Penkovsky's ceiling showed him handling a forged passport. Fearing that an escape plan was about to be put into effect, Gribanov decided to make an immediate arrest. SIS and the CIA did not discover Penkovsky's arrest until November 2. On that date a mark left on a Moscow lamppost indicated to the CIA station that Penkovsky had left material for collection in a dead-letter box (DLB). The CIA officer who went to collect it, however, was promptly arrested by the KGB and claimed diplomatic immunity.

His arrest triggered a somewhat comic bureaucratic rivalry within the Second Chief Directorate. Until the CIA officer arrived at the DLB, the KGB had wrongly believed that Penkovsky was run solely by SIS rather than as part of a joint operation with the CIA. His case was thus handled by the Second (British, Canadian, and Australasian) Department of the Second Chief Directorate, which refused to take the First (American) Department into its confidence. The Second Department officer, who arrested the CIA officer, at first refused to believe that he was American and insisted that he must be British. When the bemused CIA officer established his identity, the Second Department was forced, to its immense chagrin, to share the winding-up of the Penkovsky case with the rival First.

Penkovsky was brutally tortured during a prolonged interrogation, sentenced to death at a show trial in May 1963, and shot.[177] His discovery led to the disgrace of his drinking companion General Serov, former chairman of the KGB. After Penkovsky's arrest Serov was dismissed as head of the GRU. Soon afterward, following a heavy drinking bout, he blew his brains out in a back alley in the Moscow Arbat. The only mention of his death was a brief press notice signed by an anonymous group of former comrades.[178]

12

The Brezhnev Era: The East, the Third World, and the West (1964–72/73)

By 1964, Khrushchev had alienated most members of the Presidium. The Cuban missile crisis was resented as a Soviet humiliation. After the poor harvest of 1963, Khrushchev was forced to use precious gold and hard-currency reserves to buy grain from the West, turning Russia into a net importer for almost the first time. Thenceforth, one of the tasks of the KGB was to monitor the international grain markets.[1] But the main source of discontent was Khrushchev's constant reorganization of the Party and state apparatus, which unsettled both his colleagues and thousands of *apparatchiks.* Among the most active plotters assisting his enemies on the Presidium were Shelepin and his protégé Semichastny, who arranged for the bugging of Khrushchev's private telephone lines. Khrushchev's son Sergei later complained: "Hitherto I had always assumed that the KGB and the other special services were there to help us. Suddenly . . . it was no longer the great protector but the great shadower, knowing our every move."

With the KGB's help, the plotters achieved a substantial element of surprise. When Khrushchev left for a holiday on the Black Sea in the autumn of 1964, he was seen off by smiling colleagues. On October 13, he was suddenly recalled to Moscow for an urgent meeting of the Presidium. Instead of being greeted by the usual welcoming party at the airport, he was met only by Semichastny and a senior security officer from the KGB. According to Khrushchev's son, Semichastny's expression was tense. He leaned toward Khrushchev and said in an undertone, "They've all gathered in the Kremlin and are waiting for you." "Let's go!" replied Khrushchev.[2]

Semichastny later claimed that several of Khrushchev's colleagues had suggested arresting him, but the Presidium had decided against it. Instead it was decided, if necessary, to confront him with evidence of his role in Stalin's purges in the Ukraine. Another of the plotters, Yuri Andropov, explained to a member of the Central Committee: "If Khrushchev is stubborn, we shall show him documents that bear his signature about arrests that took place between 1935 and 1937."[3] Khrushchev, however, quickly accepted the inevitable. In return for going quietly and contributing to the most orderly succession since the Revolution, he was allowed to keep his apartment on the Lenin Hills, his dacha, and his car, and given a pension of 500 rubles a month. Khrushchev's "resignation" was attributed in the Soviet press to "advanced age and poor health." Thereafter, he became officially almost an unperson, not mentioned again in the press until 1970 when *Pravda* published a brief note recording the death of N. S. Khrushchev, whom it described simply as a pensioner.[4]

For their part in Khrushchev's downfall Shelepin and Semichastny were both rewarded with immediate promotion. Shelepin became a full member of the Presidium without serving the usual apprenticeship as a candidate (nonvoting) member. Semichastny was coopted as a full member of the Central Committee. The real victor, however, was Khrushchev's successor as first secretary, Leonid Ilyich Brezhnev. Probably seen initially by most of the Presidium as an interim appointment, Brezhnev became the longest-serving of all Soviet leaders save Stalin. Although under Gorbachev the Brezhnev years were to be christened "the era of stagnation," in the mid-sixties the conservative majority in the Party *apparat* saw them as an era of stability after the unpredictable experiments and job insecurity of the Khrushchev decade. Between 1956 and 1961 Khrushchev had replaced more than two-thirds of provincial *(oblast)* Party secretaries and half the Central Committee. Brezhnev adopted the maxim "stability of cadres": in effect, job security for party functionaries. The era of stability in the 1960s became an era of gerontocracy in the 1970s. Between 1966, when the Presidium reverted to the old title Politburo, and Brezhnev's death in 1982, the average age of its members rose from fifty-six to sixty-eight.

Even those dismissed from leading positions in the Party could usually count on moving to less prestigious posts in the nomenklatura and keeping their dachas, cars, and other privileges.[5]

Though Stalin himself was at best partially rehabilitated after Khrushchev's fall, de-Stalinization came to an abrupt halt. Actively supported by Shelepin, Semichastny began an onslaught on Soviet dissidents, whom both saw as part of a Western-inspired plan for "ideological subversion." Among Russian intellectuals, Semichastny was already notorious for his denunciation of Boris Pasternak after the publication of *Doctor Zhivago* in the West in 1958: "Even a pig does not shit where it eats." In September 1965, Andrei Sinyavsky and Yuli Daniel, two writers who had been pallbearers at Pasternak's funeral in 1960 and, like him, had dared to publish "subversive" stories in the West, were arrested on Semichastny's orders. At a show trial in February 1966, whose transcript proved too embarrassing to be published officially, Sinyavsky was sentenced to seven years in labor camp and Daniel to five for "anti-Soviet propaganda." Semichastny allegedly declared that his aim was to arrest a thousand intellectuals *pour encourager les autres.*[6] The fears expressed by Aleksandr Solzhenitsyn, though perhaps exaggerated, accurately reflect the forebodings of the time. "We can say with near certainty," he wrote later, "that what was planned was an abrupt return to Stalin, with 'Iron Shurik' Shelepin in the lead."[7]

The days of both Shelepin and Semichastny, however, were numbered. Shelepin's unmistakable ambition, combined with his power as the Central Committee secretary responsible for the "organs of control," with his protégé Semichastny at the head of the KGB, aroused the anxiety of both Brezhnev and most of the Politburo. The improbable immediate cause of Semichastny's downfall was Stalin's daughter, Svetlana Alliluyeva, who was allowed to leave the country at the end of 1966 to attend the funeral of her third husband, an Indian Communist, and then defected. Blamed within the Soviet leadership for allowing Svetlana's defection, Semichastny then compounded his initial error of judgment by ordering an ill-advised kidnap attempt, which instead of bringing Svetlana back to Russia led to the exposure of a KGB strong-arm man, Vasili Fyodorovich Sanko, sent to New York to track her down. Thirteen years earlier he had tried unsuccessfully to bundle Evdokia Petrova onto a plane back to the Soviet Union after her husband defected in Australia.[8] When Semichastny's replacement was first proposed in March 1967, Shelepin managed to defend him. In

May, the issue came before the Politburo again while Shelepin was in a hospital for an emergency appendix operation. This time Brezhnev had successfully settled the matter beforehand. According to S. Sokolov, who was summoned to a meeting with senior Politburo members to be informed of the decision "to release Semichastny from his job" (the traditional formula for dismissal), "No discussion at all took place . . . All Brezhnev did was to appeal to the other members of the Politburo, saying, There's no need to discuss it, there's no need to discuss it." In accordance with Brezhnev's policy of offering consolation prizes when sacking senior members of the nomenklatura, Semichastny was shunted off to the Ukraine to become one of the deputy chairmen of the Council of Ministers with special responsibility for sports.

On his return from the hospital in June, Shelepin found himself demoted from his powerful position as Central Committee secretary responsible for the organs of control (including the KGB) to the chairmanship of the All-Union Central Council of Trade Unions.[9] On arriving at his spacious new office, Shelepin found that his predecessor, Viktor Grishin, had what Zhores Medvedev euphemistically describes as "a specially equipped massage parlor" in an adjoining room. Shelepin was outraged that, despite Grishin's libidinous behavior in office hours, he had been promoted to become first secretary of the Moscow Party Committee, and made it his business to circulate stories about him. "Brezhnev," writes Zhores Medvedev, "was tolerant in such matters as long as the offender was personally loyal to him."[10]

The main beneficiary of the sidelining of Shelepin and the removal of Semichastny was Yuri Andropov, who became the new chairman of the KGB. Two of Brezhnev's protégés, Semyon Konstantinovich Tsvigun and Viktor Mikhailovich Chebrikov (a future chairman), became deputy chairmen. The main purpose of Andropov's appointment, Brezhnev told Sokolov, was "to bring the KGB closer to the Central Committee." Since leaving Budapest in 1957, Andropov had been head of the Central Committee Department for Relations with Communist and Workers Parties of Socialist Countries. He was both the first senior Party official brought in to head the KGB and the first KGB chairman since Beria with a seat on the Politburo, initially as candidate (nonvoting) member, then from 1973 as full member.

Andropov's appointment, it has been said, "marked the completion of an evolution which had been going on since Stalin's death: the rapprochement of Party and KGB to the point where they functioned almost as two branches of the same organization." But though the Party leadership achieved Brezhnev's aim of establishing a secure dominance over the KGB, it did so "at the cost of absorbing much of its outlook on the world."[12] Andropov became the longest-serving and politically the most successful of all heads of the KGB, crowning his fifteen years as chairman by succeeding Brezhnev as general secretary in 1982.

Andropov's first major challenge as KGB chairman came in Czechoslovakia. Khrushchev's son-in-law, Aleksei Adzhubei, though an admirer of Andropov's handling of the Hungarian Revolution of 1956, noted that it "left a brutal mark on his outlook to eastern Europe."[13] Yet the experience of his years in Budapest and the role played by Rákosi's "goulash Stalinism" in provoking the revolution also persuaded him of the need for flexibility. Gordievsky was told that soon after his arrival at Moscow Center Andropov had told the First Chief Directorate: "Only by being flexible can we avoid a repetition of 1956." Khrushchev had drawn the same conclusion, ordering greater consideration for the national pride of the people's democracies. He banned the KGB from spying in Eastern Europe and ordered it to liaise with, rather than try to run, the local intelligence and security services.

In the mid-1960s, the more relaxed policy toward the Soviet Bloc seemed to be working. The Hungarian Party leader, János Kádár, installed after the 1956 Revolution, had built up a high reputation in the Center, constantly reassuring Moscow about the stability of his regime, and the unsubversive nature of his economic reforms. He was supported by the AVH and young careerists in the Hungarian Socialist Workers (Communist) Party, who believed in working within the system.

Such anxieties about Eastern Europe as existed in Moscow Center when Andropov became chairman centered on Rumania. Gheorghe Gheorghiu-Dej, secretary general of the Rumanian Communist Party from 1944 to 1965, had been trained as an NKVD agent in the 1930s. The MGB chief adviser in Bucharest from 1949 to 1953, Aleksandr Sakharovsky, approved his zeal in rooting out Titoist and Zionist agents. As head of the First Chief Directorate, however, Sakharovsky was much less content with the nationalist tendencies of Gheorghiu-Dej's successor, Nicolae Ceauşescu. Like a number of other Soviet officials concerned with Eastern Europe, he criticized Khrushchev's decision to withdraw Soviet troops from Rumania in 1958 as a serious error of judgment.

Ironically, there was far less concern about Czechoslovakia. Gordievsky was later told by a veteran Czechoslovak expert at the Center, Anatoli Aleksandrovich Rusakov, that in 1956 several analysts in the First Chief Directorate had predicted that within a few years Prague would follow the counterrevolutionary example set by Budapest. When it failed to do so and Czechoslovakia became fairly prosperous by the standards of the Soviet bloc, the Center was lulled into a false sense of security. The replacement of the aging neo-Stalinist first secretary of the Czechoslovak Party, Antonín Novotný, by the forty-six-year-old Alexander Dubček in January 1968 was initially welcomed in both the Center and the Kremlin. Dubček had spent most of his childhood in the Soviet Union, graduating with honors from the Moscow Higher Party School in 1958. He was known within the KGB as "our Sasha." When the Czechoslovakian reform program began, the Eleventh (East European) Department in the First Chief Directorate at first concluded that "our Sasha" was being cleverly manipulated by "bourgeois elements" in the Czechoslovak Party. When it became clear that Dubček was one of the moving forces behind the Prague Spring, there was a sense of personal betrayal in both the Kremlin and the Center.[14] According to an eyewitness account of the meeting between Brezhnev and Dubček after the Soviet invasion in August:

> ". . . From the very beginning, I wanted to help you in your struggle against Novotný," Brezhnev told Dubček. ". . . I believed you, I defended you," he reproached Dubček. "I said that our Sasha was a good comrade. And you let us down so horribly!" As he said this, Brezhnev's voice trembled with sorrow and broke; he seemed to be on the verge of bursting into tears.[15]

Unlike Nagy in 1956, Dubček made it clear that his government had no intention either of leaving the Warsaw Pact or of abandoning socialism. But Moscow calculated, no doubt correctly, that the "socialism with a human face" being propounded in Prague would, sooner or later, do irreparable damage to the leading role of the Communist Party.

The first major consequence of the Prague Spring at Moscow Center was the suspension of the rule forbidding KGB espionage in the people's democracies.[16] The chief KGB adviser in Prague, General

Kotov, obtained from the hardline head of the StB, Josef Houska, photograph copies of the personnel files of all his officers. Though the reforming minister of the interior, General Josef Pavel, was one of the KGB's bêtes noires, his deputy, Viliam Šalgovič, was recruited as a KGB agent. For a time during the Prague Spring, Šalgovič lodged at Houska's villa, thus enabling him to meet KGB officers regularly without attracting the attention of Dubček loyalists in the ministry. Jan Bokr, a senior Interior Ministry official also recruited by the KGB, enabled the KGB to monitor telephone conversations in the ministry. Listening devices were also installed in the homes of leading reformers. The intelligence thus obtained was used after the Warsaw Pact invasion to arrest StB officers and others loyal to the Dubček regime.[17]

Moscow Center also sent about thirty illegals living in the West to travel to Czechoslovakia posing as Western tourists. Among them was Gordievsky's brother, Vasilko Antonovich Gordievsky, traveling on a West German passport. Czechoslovak "counterrevolutionaries," the Center believed, would be much franker in revealing their subversive plans to those they believed came from the West than to their neighbors in Eastern Europe. The cryptanalysts of the Eighth Directorate provided, in addition, a continuous flow of sigint derived from decrypting Czechoslovak diplomatic traffic.[18]

Once again, the success of KGB intelligence collection was undermined by a failure of intelligence analysis. The Center's ideological blinkers rendered it incapable of interpreting opposition except in terms of plots and conspiracies. And behind all conspiracies in Eastern Europe, whether real or imagined, it saw the hand of the West in general and of its intelligence services in particular.[19] Western intelligence, it believed, was once again using Zionist agents. KGB agents within the Czechoslovak Interior Ministry were ordered to report on all officials of Jewish origin.[20] Though well aware that most of the evidence of Western conspiracy put on public display was fabricated, the KGB had no doubt about the reality of the plot.

As so frequently before, the Center discounted all intelligence that ran counter to its conspiracy theories. Some of the most important of that intelligence during the Prague Spring came from Washington, where the dynamic thirty-four-year-old head of the KR (counterintelligence) line, Oleg Danilovich Kalugin, gained access to what he claimed were "absolutely reliable documents" proving that neither the CIA, nor any other American agency, was prompting the political changes in Czechoslovakia. He reported that, on the contrary, the Prague Spring had taken Washington largely by surprise. His success in the United States launched him on a career that, six years later, was to make him the youngest general in the FCD. But in 1968 his reports were brushed aside. On returning to Moscow, Kalugin was "amazed" to discover that the Center had ordered that "my messages should not be shown to anyone, and destroyed." Instead, "The KGB whipped up the fear that Czechoslovakia could fall victim to NATO aggression or to a coup."[21] For all his sophistication, Andropov, like all his predecessors as KGB chairman, was a conspiracy theorist. He told KGB Komsomol members in October 1968, two months after the Soviet invasion, that "the shift of the correlation of forces in favor of socialism" inevitably led to Western attempts to undermine its successes:

> The enemy gives direct and indirect support to counterrevolutionary elements, engages in ideological sabotage, establishes all sorts of anti-Socialist, anti-Soviet and other hostile organizations and seeks to fan the flames of nationalism. Graphic confirmation of this is offered by the events in Czechoslovakia, where that country's working people, supported by the fraternal international assistance of the peoples of the nations of the Socialist community, resolutely nipped in the bud an attempt by counterrevolutionaries to turn Czechoslovakia off the Socialist path.[22]

Evidence of the monitoring by Western intelligence services of the reform process in Czechoslovakia was interpreted by Andropov as proof of their role in promoting the Prague Spring. On July 19, *Pravda* published extracts from an alleged CIA plan for the "ideological sabotage" of Czechoslovakia as a prelude to the "liberation of East Germany and Czechoslovakia," laying heavy emphasis on "penetration of Czechoslovakia's state security agencies, military intelligence, and her counter-intelligence services." Though the plan itself was fabricated by Department A (responsible for "active measures") of the First Chief Directorate, the Center's alarm at the effect of the Prague Spring on the StB and its alliance with the KGB was entirely genuine. In June, Pavel, the interior minister, began a purge of the StB and replaced Houska with a Dubček loyalist. Next month Pavel revealed publicly that six KGB liaison officers were attached to his office. If the Prague Spring continued, their days were clearly numbered.[23]

Simultaneously, a series of articles by Karel Kaplan, chief researcher for the official Piller Commission investigating the political trials of the 1950s, disclosed that KGB "advisers" during the trials had acted independently of the Czechoslovak authorities. Piller is said to have warned party leaders that his commission's report would contain such "shocking facts that its distribution could seriously shake the authority of the Party and some of its chief representatives." Though publication of the report was postponed, the Dubček leadership is believed to have accepted in principle the commission's recommendation to disband the political police. The Czechoslovak prime minister, Oldřich Černík, later claimed that Moscow's fears of declining Party influence in the security and armed forces, amplified by alarmist reports from Soviet advisers, were "the drop which made the cup brim over."[24]

Andropov was probably not a member of the inner circle of perhaps five Politburo members (Brezhnev, Kosygin, Podgorny, Suslov, and Shelest) who emerged as the main decision makers during the Czechoslovak crisis. The alarmist intelligence assessments provided by the KGB nonetheless played an important role. The inner circle of decision makers was initially divided and uncertain. Kosygin and Suslov urged caution; Shelest was probably the earliest advocate of armed intervention; Brezhnev tended to go along with the majority.[25] Andropov's warnings of the rapid progress of a large-scale imperialist plot to undermine Party control of Czechoslovak security had at least some influence on the final decision to opt for an invasion rather than less violent methods of coercion. Gromyko continued to insist until his death in 1989, the year in which the Warsaw Pact finally apologized for the invasion, that "Of course, outside help was also given to the enemies of the new [i.e., Communist] Czechoslovakia in much the same way as had happened in Hungary in 1956." He included in his memoirs bizarre details of alleged preparations for a coup d'état, which may well have derived from alarmist intelligence reports in 1968:

At fixed times, mostly at night, house numbers, and in some cases also street names, were changed. This was evidence that the enemies of the new Czechoslovakia were getting ready in good time and with care.[26]

Possibly even more important in influencing the decision to launch an invasion than alarmist reports of Western-supported plots were overoptimistic KGB intelligence assessments of the strength of Czechoslovak Party and working-class support for the replacement of the Dubček leadership. The KGB also fabricated most of the evidence of imperialist plots used to justify invasion. The thirty-odd KGB illegals posing as Western tourists were instructed to put up inflammatory posters and slogans calling for the overthrow of Communism and withdrawal from the Warsaw Pact. Gordievsky's brother also told him that the KGB had been behind the planting and discovery of arms caches, which *Pravda* instantly denounced as evidence of preparations for an armed insurrection by Sudeten revanchists. The East German Party newspaper *Neues Deutschland* went one better and published photographs of American troops and tanks inside Czechoslovakia. The origin of the photographs—never admitted in the East German press—was an American war film then being made in Bohemia with the assistance of Czech soldiers dressed in 1945 U.S. uniforms and tanks painted with U.S. markings provided by the Czechoslovak Army in return for payment in hard currency. According to the First Chief Directorate's veteran Czech expert, Anatoli Rusakov, who was in Prague in 1968, he and the KGB advisers had serious reservations about the provocation operations ordered by the Center, fearing that the risks of discovery were unacceptably high. Gordievsky's brother was equally nervous about the provocations he and the other KGB illegals were asked to undertake.[27]

The timing of the invasion by the Red Army, supported by contingents from other members of the Warsaw Pact, on the night of August 20–21, 1968, was dictated by the desire to preempt the meeting of the September Party Congress, which, in the Soviet view, was likely to democratize Czechoslovak Communism beyond repair. Just before the invasion, the Center discovered that the daughter of Vasili Bil'ak, one of the minority of hardliners in the Czechoslovak Presidium on whom it was counting to succeed Dubček, was studying in Britain. It sent an urgent message to the London resident, Yuri Nikolayevich Voronin, asking him to ensure that his residency tracked her down and persuaded her to return. By the time the invasion began, Miss Bil'ak was back in Czechoslovakia.[28]

The main military objectives of the invasion were achieved in less than twenty-four hours. Beginning at 11 P.M. on Tuesday, August 20, units of the Twenty-fourth Soviet Tactical Air Army took control of the main Czechoslovak airports and guided in hundreds of Antonov transport planes carrying troops and tanks. Simultaneously, Soviet and Warsaw Pact forces crossed the Czechoslovak borders in the north, east, and south, and sealed the border with West Germany. By the morning of Wednesday, August 21, the Czechoslovak army, which attempted no organized resistance, had been neutralized, and the country's road and communications networks were under Soviet control. Dubček and most of the leading reformers in the Czechoslovak Presidium were arrested by a group of StB and KGB officers headed by Lieutenant Colonel Bohumil Molnar, transported across the Soviet border, and interned in KGB barracks in the Carpathian Mountains. The KGB agent Josef Houska was swiftly reinstalled as head of the StB.[29]

During the invasion itself, the KGB performed less well than the Red Army. Its armed units, which accompanied Soviet regular forces, with instructions to carry out Smersh-style operations designed to identify and neutralize counterrevolutionary opposition, were poorly trained and performed badly.[30] Red Army soldiers, who had been told that the Czechoslovak people had requested their fraternal assistance, were bewildered when the same people swarmed around their tanks, told them they were not wanted, and appealed to them to go home. For several days underground radio stations continued to denounce the invasion. On August 22, there was a one-hour general strike accompanied by massive, and mostly peaceful, demonstrations throughout Czechoslovakia.

The most serious error of both the KGB and the Soviet ambassador in Prague, Stepan Vasilyevich Chervonenko, was to exaggerate wildly the potential support for intervention within both the Czechoslovak Party and the working class. Their mistakes derived partly from the traditional Bolshevik inability to grasp the reality of working-class opposition to a Bolshevik regime, and partly from appeals for help from Bil'ak and other hardliners who were aware that, without Soviet intervention, their own political careers would soon be finished. The Soviet Politburo decided on military intervention in the belief that it would be instantly legitimized by an urgent request from a majority of the Czechoslovak Presidium for "fraternal assistance" to put down counterrevolution, followed by the constitution of a new revolutionary workers' and peasants' government, which would purge the supporters of the Prague Spring. But the hardliners' attempt to gain Presidium support for such a request failed and no quisling government was formed.

Faced with the unexpected lack of a Czechoslovak Kádár, the Politburo was forced into a change of tack. Late on August 22, it concluded that there was no alternative to negotiating with the existing Party leadership.[31] After talks in Moscow, Dubček and the reformers were allowed to return to Prague, but saddled with an agreement that forced them to "normalize" the situation to the Kremlin's satisfaction. In October, Dubček was summoned back to Moscow to sign a treaty allowing the permanent stationing of Soviet troops in Czechoslovakia to guard against the imaginary "mounting revanchist ambitions of West German militarist forces."[32] With Dubček's replacement as first secretary by the devious careerist Gustáv Husák in April 1969, the Prague Spring gave way to a Soviet-imposed winter, which was to endure for twenty years.

One of the reasons for the KGB's alarm at the Prague Spring was the support for it by Andrei Sakharov and other Soviet intellectuals. There was a small but unprecedented demonstration in Red Square against the Soviet invasion, quickly crushed by the KGB. Aleksandr Solzhenitsyn later described the two days after the invasion as "of crucial importance to me":

> In those two days I was once again choosing a destiny for myself. My heart wanted one thing: to write something brief, a variation on Herzen's famous phrase: *I am ashamed to be Soviet!*[33]

In the weeks and months that followed the Soviet invasion Gordievsky was also "choosing a destiny for himself." The Soviet one-party state, he was now convinced, was by its very nature destructive of human liberties. He spent much of the next few years pondering how best to make his own contribution to the struggle for democracy. In the summer of 1968, few Soviet intellectuals sided publicly with the Prague Spring, but both the KGB and the Party apparatus were concerned by the level of sympathy for it. It took a full month for *Sovetskaya Kultura* to find seven national artists willing to sign a denunciation of one of the most celebrated radical manifestos of the Prague Spring, Ludvík Vaculík's "2,000 Words," published in June 1968. In July, the Propaganda Department of the Central Committee issued a directive emphasizing the urgent need to instill "ideological conviction among the Soviet intelligentisia."[34]

Andropov, noted Aleksei Adzhubei, "never gave himself over to a mood of panic, and still less to one of panic mongering. Yet . . . he thought that one could not be good humored when ideological mouths were blabbing. He spoke harshly about many writers, actors and producers."[35] Stories planted among foreign journalists by the

KGB gradually built up an image of Andropov for strictly Western consumption as, to quote *Time* and *Newsweek,* "a closet liberal" who "speaks English well," "collects big-band records and relaxes with American novels," and "sought friendly discussions with dissident protesters."[36] Andropov's distinguishing characteristic, however, was not sympathy with dissent but greater sophistication in suppressing it. In the wake of the Prague Spring he set up a new Fifth Directorate to study and crack down on dissent of all forms. Specialized departments within the Directorate were responsible for the surveillance of intellectuals, students, nationalists from ethnic minorities, religious believers, and Jews.[37]

Instead of being subjected to botched show trials like those of Sinyavsky and Daniel, dissidents were dispatched to mental hospitals, where the Fifth Directorate's tame psychiatrists, such as the infamous Dr. D. R. Lunts of Moscow's Serbsky Institute for Forensic Psychiatry, diagnosed "creeping schizophrenia" and "paranoid reformist delusions." Once certified insane, dissidents lost what remained of their civil rights and were abused with whatever drugs Lunts and his colleagues chose to prescribe. The abuse of psychiatry, however, was based on conviction rather than mere expediency: the belief generated by the one-party Soviet state that the only legitimate values were those of the Party and that dissenters from those values were—in the words of Andropov's successor as KGB chairman, Vitali Fedorchuk—"abnormal psyches" who needed to be "reeducated." To avoid the international opprobrium of certifying as insane men as well known in the West as Aleksandr Solzhenitsyn, some of the most prominent dissenters were gradually forced to emigrate.[38]

The shock of the Prague Spring influenced the policy of the Kremlin and the KGB to Eastern Europe for the next twenty years. For the first time, the restricted sovereignty of the people's democracies was formally spelled out in the "Brezhnev Doctrine" of September 1968, which insisted that while each had the right to take its "own separate road to socialism," the policies adopted by them "must damage neither socialism in their own country nor the fundamental interests of the other socialist countries, or the worldwide workers' movement which is waging a struggle for socialism." If such "damage" did occur in any people's democracy, the doctrine clearly implied that the other socialist states, led by the Soviet Union, had, as in Czechoslovakia, an "internationalist duty" to "act in resolute opposition to the antisocialist forces."

In the immediate aftermath of the invasion the StB showed

itself anxious to restore its reputation in Moscow by carrying out an energetic purge of Czechoslovak "antisocialist forces" in close collaboration with its KGB liaison officers. All the one and a half million Party members were questioned about their behavior during the Prague Spring: about a third were expelled or left the Party. Similar purges took place in the universities, the media, and other professions. The organizations most closely connected with the Prague Spring, such as the Writers' Union and the Academy of Sciences' Institute of Philosophy, were closed down or merged with more orthodox bodies. Yet a lingering unease remained in Moscow Center. A detailed study of the Prague Spring by the Eleventh (Soviet Bloc) Department of the First Chief Directorate concluded that speeches made during that period by both Gustáv Husák and President Ludvík Svoboda were "not consistent" with their later protestations of ideological orthodoxy. Lubomír Štrougal, who became prime minister in January 1970, was regarded as the most senior of a series of covert Dubčekists who had somehow hung on to their jobs. Moscow would have preferred either Vasili Bil'ak or his fellow hardliner Alois Indra to replace Husák as first secretary but concluded that both were so unpopular that their appointment would carry serious political risks.[39]

"Betrayal" by Dubček ("Our Sasha") in 1968, following the earlier "betrayals" by Tito, Nagy, Mao Zedong, Hoxha (who sided with Mao), and other foreign Communist leaders left a lingering sense of insecurity toward Eastern Europe in both the Kremlin and Moscow Center. By the 1970s, East European leaders were commonly divided by the Center into five categories: "nationalists," with an insufficient grasp of their internationalist duties; "revisionists," with latent pro-Western tendencies; the "unpredictable," who oscillated between Soviet loyalism and flirtation with the West; the "pro-Soviet but ineffective"; the "pro-Soviet and effective," but without much domestic support. Even during the Brezhnev era, Gordievsky heard a series of private outbursts in the Center and KGB residencies to the effect that "Underneath they'll always be anti-Soviet as well as unreliable and expensive allies. We'd do better to have done with the lot of them."[40] Under Brezhnev such a policy was never regarded as realistic even by those who uttered it in private, but the growing disillusion with Eastern Europe was one of the long-term causes of the abandonment by the Kremlin in 1989 of the Brezhnev Doctrine of 1968.

*   *   *

The Communist state that caused most consistent concern to the Kremlin and the KGB during the Brezhnev era was the People's Republic of China (PRC). When Khrushchev recalled the thousands of Soviet advisers from the PRC in 1960, most of the KGB left as well, leaving behind only a small residency in Beijing. Over the next few years most China specialists in both the Foreign Ministry and the KGB tried desperately to transfer to other work, believing a continuing reputation as Sinologists would blight their careers. The U.S.S.R. and the PRC initially attacked each other by proxy, Moscow denouncing Albanian hardliners, Beijing condemning Yugoslav revisionists. Then in 1964, just as China was testing its first atomic bomb, the conflict became public. Though most of the world's Communist Parties remained pro-Soviet, the majority of those in Asia sided with China.

By the mid-sixties China had become a major KGB concern. Sinologists who had earlier given up Chinese affairs returned to their former area of expertise. New China specialists were drafted into the KGB and a large residency was built up in Beijing.[41] The beginning in 1966 of the Cultural Revolution (officially "A Full-Scale Revolution to Establish a Working-Class Culture") increased further the priority accorded to Chinese intelligence. In an extraordinary attempt to refashion Chinese society on a utopian revolutionary model, Mao Zedong unleashed a general terror. Millions of young Red Guards were urged to root out bourgeois and revisionist tendencies wherever they found them. The Kremlin was denounced as "the biggest traitors and renegades in history."

As during the Soviet Great Terror thirty years before, most of the enemies of the people unmasked and persecuted by the Red Guards had committed only imaginary crimes. And as in Stalin's Russia the bloodletting was accompanied by a repellent form of Emperor worship. Mao was universally hailed as the "Great Helmsman," "the Reddest Red Sun in Our Hearts." Each day began with a "loyalty dance." "You put your hand to your head and then to your heart, and you danced a jig—to show that your heart and mind were filled with boundless love for Chairman Mao," one Party member later recalled.[42] Rival factions outdid one another in terrorizing the Great Helmsman's imaginary enemies, each claiming to be more Maoist than the others.

The KGB found intelligence collection in China during the Cultural Revolution more difficult and dangerous than anywhere else in the world. Diplomatic sigint seems to have provided little insight into the course of the Revolution. Recruiting Chinese officials as agents proved virtually impossible. Contact with them was minimal and closely supervised. The spy mania and xenophobia of the Red Guards made it difficult even for diplomats to walk around Beijing. Owners of foreign books were forced to crawl on their knees in shame; those caught listening to foreign broadcasts were sent to prison. As an official Chinese report later acknowledged: "The ability to speak a foreign language or a past visit to a foreign country became 'evidence' of being a 'secret agent' for that country."[43] The road leading to the beleaguered Soviet embassy was renamed "Anti-Revisionist Lane." The families of Soviet diplomats and KGB officers were manhandled as they left Beijing airport in 1967.

The best firsthand reporting to reach Moscow from Beijing came from KGB officers of Mongolian or Central Asian extraction, who, when suitably dressed, could pass as Chinese. They were smuggled out of the Soviet embassy compound after dark in the trunks of diplomatic cars and let out at some deserted location. Then they merged with the vast crowds roaming a city festooned with slogans, reading the day's wall posters, attending political rallies, purchasing "little newspapers," with news from Shanghai, Chungking, or Sinkiang. Larger numbers of KGB illegals, also mostly of Mongolian or Central Asian origin, were infiltrated across the Chinese border from bases in Alma Ata, Irkutsk, and Khabarovsk.

None had access to sources able to provide much insight into high-level policy making.[44] The intelligence KGB officers gathered at the grassroots during the Cultural Revolution gave a cumulative picture of a country sinking into chaos and terror. Elderly workers, sometimes shy of putting their writing on public display in a country where calligraphy is highly prized, would place their paper and ink on the ground, contemplate the blank sheet as a crowd assembled around them, and begin to set down some local grievance in a clumsy script.

Many of the wall poster campaigns, however, were concerted. Late in 1967, posters began attacking the head of state, Liu Shaoqi. After he was jailed in the following year, more than 22,000 people were arrested as his alleged sympathizers. Even a night-soil collector, who had been photographed being congratulated by Liu at a model workers' conference, was paraded through the streets with a placard around his neck, and maltreated until he lost his reason. Wall posters appeared calling for the prime minister, Zhou Enlai, to be burned alive (even though he had publicly denounced Liu as "renegade, traitor and scab"), but were then hurriedly covered over.

Acting on the principle that "Revolutionaries' children are heroes, reactionaries' children are lice," Red Guards killed one of Liu's sons by placing him across a railway track. Deng Xiaoping, Party general secretary and "the Number Two person in authority taking the capitalist road," was sent to do manual labor but—probably on Mao's personal instructions—allowed to survive. His eldest son, Deng Pufang, a physics student, was thrown from a second-floor window at Beijing University. No student dared to come to his aid; no doctor was willing to operate on him. He was paralyzed from the waist down.

The brutality of the Cultural Revolution shocked even KGB officers who had experienced the Second World War and seen the gulag at firsthand. The Red Guards in Inner Mongolia, probably no more brutal than most, employed seventy-five different tortures, each with its own special name. Dissidents who were thought likely to shout seditious slogans before their executions commonly had their windpipes cut and steel tubes inserted through the open wound into their throats to enable them to breathe but not to speak as they were led to the execution ground. Perhaps thirty million Chinese were persecuted during the Cultural Revolution; about a million (far fewer than the victims of Stalin's Great Terror) were killed.[45]

Moscow Center's main China expert, General Mikhail Markovich Turchak, who later became resident in Beijing from 1976 to 1981, told Gordievsky that during the Cultural Revolution the KGB had been a more productive and more influential supplier of Chinese news and intelligence to the Kremlin than the foreign ministry. But, fed with a relentless series of reports of chaos and atrocity from the KGB residency in Beijing and KGB illegals who had no access to high-level Party officials, the Center misread the situation. It interpreted the Cultural Revolution not as a convulsion in the life of a one-party Communist state, which, for all its horrendous brutality, was ultimately less homicidal than Stalin's Terror, but as a peculiarly Chinese descent into bloodthirsty oriental barbarism. Mao's heretical regime, predicted the First Chief Directorate, would degenerate into an aggressive Asian tyranny intent on reclaiming the large tracts of territory ceded to Tsarist Russia under the "unequal treaties" of the nineteenth century.

The border clashes in Central Asia and at Damansky Island between March and August 1969 seemed to prove KGB predictions right and presage a much more serious Sino-Soviet conflict. Particularly worrying was the fact that within a few years there would be a billion Chinese ruled by a regime with little apparent regard for human life and with nuclear missiles capable of destroying Moscow. Mao had told Nehru in the 1950s that nuclear war might be no bad thing. Even if half of mankind perished, the other half would survive and imperialism would vanish from the earth. In September 1969, two Chinese nuclear tests took place in Xianjiang. Moscow knew from satellite reconnaissance that the Chinese were developing their own satellite (successfully launched in 1970). As usual at moments of tension, the Center experienced a spate of black jokes. Remarque, it was said, was making a new film entitled *All Quiet on the Sino-Finnish Front.*[46]

A much more sinister development in the autumn of 1969 was the hints in articles for the Western press by the KGB-coopted journalist Victor Louis (born Vitali Yevgenyevich Lui) that the Soviet Union was considering a preemptive nuclear strike against China before it had the missiles to threaten the Soviet Union.[47] Simultaneously, KGB residencies in Europe and North America began spreading the same rumors. As Gordievsky discovered, even the KGB officers who spread the rumors were uncertain at the time whether they were engaged simply in an active measure, designed to unnerve the Chinese, or warning the West of proposals under serious consideration by the Soviet general staff.[48] In retrospect, the whole exercise looks more like an "active measures" campaign devised by Service A of the First Chief Directorate. In the short term the campaign helped to pressure Beijing, now emerging from the chaos of the Cultural Revolution, into reopening talks on the border dispute.

But the pressure ultimately backfired. Fear of a preemptive Soviet strike seems to have been one of the factors that led the Chinese to enter the secret talks with the United States that led eventually to President Nixon's visit to Beijing in 1972 and a Sino-American rapprochement.[49] There was prolonged discussion in Moscow Center at the beginning of the 1970s as to whether China now qualified for the title Main Adversary hitherto applied exclusively to the United States. In the end it was relegated in official KGB jargon to the status of Major Adversary, with the United States retaining its unique status as the Main Adversary. Because of uncertainty on how to interpret Chinese policy, KGB residencies abroad received more briefings on China than on any other state. This was still the case when Gordievsky left the KGB in 1985.[50]

*   *   *

The Kremlin's problems during the 1960s in preserving its primacy in the Communist world, notably in Beijing and Prague, were offset by its growing influence in the Third World. The most successful area for both Soviet diplomacy and KGB operations was the Middle East, where the postwar erosion of British and French power left a vacuum that the United States, because of its commitment to Israel, found it difficult to fill. The Soviet Union's opportunity to emerge as the champion of the Arab cause came in 1954 with the rise to power of Gamal Abdel Nasser, at only thirty-six years of age the first native ruler of an independent Egypt since Persian invaders had overthrown the last of the pharaohs in 525 B.C. "When I was a little child," wrote Nasser, "every time I saw aeroplanes flying overhead I used to shout:

'O God Almighty, may
A calamity overtake the English!' "[51]

Nasser's inspirational nationalism and his appeal to the masses throughout the Arab world were unequaled by those of any other Arab leader of modern times. In the 1960s, Nasser was to fall victim to his own inflated rhetoric and the heroic image he created of himself. But his early successes as Egyptian leader were the stuff of which heroes are made. In 1954, soon after coming to power, he survived an assassination attempt at a public meeting. Though the two men beside him were hit and others on the platform dived for safety, Nasser stood his ground: "Let them kill Nasser! He is one among many and whether he lives or dies the Revolution will go on!" In 1955, he shocked the West by announcing an agreement to purchase large quantities of Soviet arms via Czechoslovakia—an accord negotiated in such secrecy that even the Egyptian ambassador in Moscow was kept in ignorance. At a stroke the West's arms monopoly in the Middle East was broken.

In July 1956, Nasser nationalized the Suez Canal, hitherto a concession run by the Paris-based Suez Canal Company and, in Arab eyes, the supreme symbol of Western exploitation. The failure in November of the Anglo-French attempt, in collusion with Israel, to reassert control of the canal by armed force established Nasser as the hero of most of the Arab world, with the conspicuous exception of its traditional rulers. In 1958, Nasser was also given a hero's welcome during a three-week tour of the Soviet Union. The entire Soviet leadership turned out to welcome him at Moscow airport, and he was made guest of honor on the reviewing platform above the Lenin mausoleum in Red

Square at the annual May Day parade. On his return Nasser told a huge crowd in Cairo that the Soviet Union was "a friendly country with no ulterior motive," which held the Arabs in "great esteem."[52]

The courtship between Nasser and the Kremlin, however, had moments of tension. Nasser's persecution of Communists in Egypt and in Syria (during the period of its union with Egypt from 1958 to 1961) and his denunciation of Communists in Iraq caused serious friction. The KGB was almost certainly aware that after public criticism of Soviet policy in 1959 Nasser was contacted by the CIA and offered American aid.[53] By the early 1960s, however, Khrushchev and the Center, though not all of the Presidium, were convinced that a new "correlation of forces" existed in the Middle East, which had to be exploited in the struggle against the Main Adversary.

Syria and Iraq as well as Egypt had turned against the United States. In 1962, Ben Bella led Algeria to independence and brought some Communists into his government. The humiliation of the missile crisis reinforced Khrushchev's determination to defeat the United States in the struggle for influence in the Middle East. Castro's victory in Cuba also encouraged the new policy of alliance with anti-imperialist but ideologically unsound nationalists in the Third World instead of the traditional reliance on orthodox Communist parties prepared to toe the Moscow line.[54] Soviet ideologists devised the terms "noncapitalist path" and "revolutionary democracy" to define an intermediate stage between capitalism and socialism to which some Third World leaders had progressed. Nasser's decision to nationalize much of Egyptian industry in 1961 provided encouraging evidence of his own progress along the "noncapitalist path." Throughout the 1960s more Soviet hopes were pinned on him than on any other Afro-Asian leader. Egypt accounted for 43 percent of all Soviet aid to the Third World from 1954 to 1971. In 1965, the Egyptian Communist Party dissolved itself and its members applied for membership in the ruling Arab Socialist Union.[55]

Some of the enthusiasm with which the KGB supported the courtship of Nasser derived from its success in recruiting agents within his entourage. The most important was Sami Sharaf, a pot-bellied man with a drooping mustache and the improbable code name Asad ("Lion"), who in 1959, under the misleading title of Director of the President's Office of Information, became head of Egyptian intelligence and one of Nasser's closest advisers.[56] Sharaf's case officer, Vadim Vasilyevich Kirpichenko, later became KGB resident in Cairo from 1970 to 1974; his success in agent running led to his rapid promotion in the Center, where he eventually became first deputy head of the First Chief Directorate.[57] Sharaf was responsible for the security vetting of Egyptian government officials, and was able to tap any telephone of interest to himself or the KGB.[58] He further assisted the KGB and gave it additional opportunities for recruitment by sending Egyptian intelligence officers for training in Moscow.

Nasser was well aware of the pro-Soviet sympathies of some of his ministers—notably Ali Sabry, at various times prime minister, head of the Arab Socialist Union, and vice-president. But he seems to have regarded Sharaf as, like himself, a fervent Arab nationalist, anxious, as far as possible, to obtain Soviet support without compromising Egyptian sovereignty. Kirpichenko played on Sharaf's vanity by constantly assuring him of the importance attached to his intelligence, first by Khrushchev, then by Brezhnev. When Sharaf finally met Brezhnev a year after Nasser's death at the Twenty-Fourth Soviet Party Congress in 1971, he was profuse in his protestations of gratitude and friendship:

> I must thank Comrade Brezhnev for giving me this opportunity to see him in spite of all his preoccupations. I am sure
> . . . that this is a special favor for me personally. I trust relations between us will be everlasting and continuous, and that the coming days and the positions which we adopt will be taken as a sincere witness to the friendship which exists between the UAR [Egypt] and the Soviet Union, parties, peoples and governments. . . . I firmly believe . . . that, since Sami Sharaf is the son of the great leader, Gamal Abdel Nasser, he occupies a special position in relation to his Soviet friends.[59]

Despite the public praise lavished on Nasser by the Kremlin, his overblown reputation in the mid-1960s as the invincible hero of the Arab world was treated with some private ridicule both inside and outside Moscow Center. The award in 1964 of the U.S.S.R.'s highest decoration, Hero of the Soviet Union, never before given to a foreigner, to Nasser and his chief of staff was among the grievances leveled against Khrushchev at the Presidium meeting that sent him into retirement.[60] Nasser's award gave rise to a series of derisory jokes and songs that were popular within the Center.[61]

Despite the popularity of anti-Nasser jibes, there was a sense of overconfidence within the Center in the mid-1960s at the growth of

Soviet influence in the Middle East. The "correlation of forces" seemed to be moving steadily against the West. The two main pro-Western regimes, the monarchies of Jordan and Saudi Arabia, were reeling under the pressure of anti-Western Arab nationalism. The majority belief in the Kremlin, the Center, and the high command was that Egypt's military forces had been transformed by Soviet equipment and training. Egypt, backed by Syria and Jordan, was expected to make gains in a war with Israel. There was, however, one serious dissentient voice. In April 1967, Nikolai Grigoryevich Yegorychev visited Egypt and reported that both Egypt and Syria required much greater Soviet military assistance if they were to take on Israel successfully. His report was ignored. As tension between Egypt and Israel mounted during the spring of 1967, Sharaf's intelligence reports to Nasser reflected Moscow Center's optimistic assessment of the correlation of forces.[62]

The third Arab-Israeli War, which began with an Israeli surprise attack at 8:45 A.M. (Cairo time) on Monday June 5, 1967, lasted six days. It was virtually decided during the first three hours, when Israeli air raids destroyed 286 of 340 Egyptian combat aircraft on the ground, leaving the Egyptian army without air cover in the ensuing land battles in the Sinai desert. Not till 4 P.M. on June 5 did any of Nasser's generals dare to tell him that his air force had been destroyed. On being told the news, he insisted that American and British aircraft must be helping the Israelis. In the Sinai desert the Egyptians began with as many tanks as, and more troops than, the Israelis. In four days' fighting they lost 700 tanks and 17,000 troops were killed or captured. Nasser announced his resignation, but demonstrations by millions of Egyptians for whom he still remained the personification of Arab nationalism persuaded him to stay on as president.

Outside the Arab world, the military performance of Egypt and its Syrian ally was treated with widespread derision, skillfully encouraged by Israeli propaganda on alleged Arab cowardice in battle. Egyptian POWs stripped to their underwear were photographed next to undamaged Soviet tanks and in other unheroic poses.[63] In public, the Kremlin stood by the Arabs, denounced imperialist aggression, and (to its subsequent regret) broke off diplomatic relations with Israel. Privately, however, there was savage criticism of the incompetence of the Arab forces and outrage at the amount of Soviet military equipment captured by the Israelis. In Moscow Center, despite the continuing Zionist-conspiracy theories, Gordievsky noted widespread, if grudging, admiration for the Israelis' victory and frequent racist assertions that

Arabs could never match their military skill and bravery.[64]

The débacle of the Six Day War left the Kremlin with two options: either to cut its losses or to rebuild the Arab armies. It chose the second. Marshal Matvei Zakharov, chief of the Soviet general staff, visited Egypt with President Podgorny and stayed on to advise on the reorganization and reequipment of the Egyptian army. Soviet advisers in Egypt eventually numbered over twenty thousand. Desperate to resurrect his role as the hero of the Arab world, Nasser proved willing to make larger concessions in return for Soviet help than before the Six Day War. Moscow made one of its policy objectives the establishment of military bases in Egypt and, to a lesser extent, Syria, Iraq, and Algeria. The presence of the Soviet navy in the Mediterranean increased dramatically, thanks to repair and resupply facilities at the Egyptian ports of Alexandria, Port Said, Mersa Matruh and Sollum; at the Iraqi port of Um Kasr; and at Aden in the People's Democratic Republic of (South) Yemen. In 1970, at Nasser's request, Soviet airbases, equipped with SAM-3 missiles and planes with Russian crews, were established to strengthen Egyptian air defenses.[65]

The FCD Arabist Boris Bocharov, a Line N (Illegal Support) officer in Cairo, told Gordievsky that he had moved to the PR line in order to run "an extremely important agent in the Egyptian bureaucracy who prefers to speak Arabic." The successful recruitments achieved under the direction of Sergei Mikhailovich Golubev, Cairo resident from 1966 to 1970, led to his rapid promotion after his return to Moscow. Jokes were common within the Center about the "Soviet Egyptian Republic." KGB penetration of the Egyptian bureaucracy was now at its peak.[66]

The vast Soviet investment in Egypt, however, rested on a precarious base. The influx of Soviet advisers only served to underline the gulf between Soviet and Egyptian society. Hardly any Russians and Egyptians visited each other's homes. Of the fifteen thousand Arabs who studied in the United States during the late fifties and sixties, almost half married Americans. Marriages between Soviet advisers and Arabs were virtually unknown.[67]

With Nasser's sudden death in September 1970 the vast edifice of Soviet influence began to crumble. Almost two decades later the Soviet foreign minister Andrei Gromyko was still insisting that "had he lived a few years longer, the situation in the region might today be very different."[68] Aleksei Kosygin, the Soviet prime minister, told Nasser's successor, Anwar el-Sadat: "We never had any secrets from him, and he never had any secrets from us."[69] The first half of the statement, as Kosygin was well aware, was nonsense; the second half, thanks to Sharaf and others, came uncomfortably close to the truth. On his first day as president, Sadat had an immediate confrontation with Sharaf in his office. According to Sadat:

> He had a heap of papers to submit to me. "What is this?" I asked.
> "The text of tapped telephone conversations between certain people being watched."
> "Sorry," I said, "I don't like to read such rubbish . . . And, anyway, who gave you the right to have the telephones of these people tapped? Take this file away." I swept it off my desk.[70]

There were, however, occasions when Sadat took a greater interest in "such rubbish" than he cared to admit to Sharaf. One such occasion occurred on May 11, 1971, when, unknown to Sharaf, a young police officer, who Sadat claimed "was a stranger to me," brought a tape recording which allegedly proved that Ali Sabry, whom the KGB had optimistically expected to succeed Nasser, and other pro-Soviet politicians "were plotting to overthrow me and the regime." On May 16, Sadat ordered the arrest of Sharaf, Sabry, and the leaders of the pro-Soviet group within the Arab Socialist Union. Only eleven days later Sadat signed with President Podgorny in Cairo a Soviet-Egyptian Treaty of Friendship and Cooperation. His main motive, as he later acknowledged, was "to allay the fears of Soviet leaders," seeking to persuade them that he was engaged in an internal power struggle rather than a reorientation of Egyptian foreign policy. As he saw Podgorny off at the airport, Sadat appealed to him to tell the Politburo: "Please have confidence in us! Have confidence! Confidence!"[71] Confidence in Sadat was, however, already at a low ebb in Moscow Center. After the arrest of the Sabry group, a number of KGB agents began to distance themselves from their case officers.

The Center's main cause for optimism in the Arab world after Nasser's death centered on the prospects for a Communist takeover in the Sudan. The leaders of the Sudanese Communist Party were considered by the KGB to be the most loyal and dedicated in the Middle East.[72] In July 1971, an attempted coup by Sudanese army officers supported by the Communists was brutally suppressed with Sadat's assistance. Among those executed was the general secretary of the Sudanese Party, Abdel Mahgoub, and Lenin Prize winner Ahmed El-Sheikh. Simultaneously, Moscow Center discovered that a Soviet diplomat in the Middle East coopted by the KGB, Vladimir Nikolayevich Sakharov, was working for the CIA. Alerted by a prearranged signal—a bouquet in the back seat of a Volkswagen—he defected just in time. Among the secrets he betrayed to the Americans was Sharaf's role as a KGB agent.[73]

By the end of 1971, Sadat was commonly described within the Moscow Party *apparat* and the Center as a traitor. His director of intelligence, General Ahmed Ismail, was known to be in contact with the CIA. In 1972, Sadat ordered the Soviet advisers out of Egypt. Twenty-one thousand left by air in only seven days. For the time being, Moscow could not bring itself to sacrifice its hard-won position in the Middle East by an open breach with Sadat. Brezhnev concluded that the Soviet Union had no choice but to continue political and military support in case Sadat went over outright to the Americans.[74]

The Third World country on which the KGB eventually expended most effort was India. Under Stalin India had been regarded as an imperialist puppet. The *Great Soviet Encyclopedia* dismissed Mahatma Gandhi, who had led India to independence, as:

> A reactionary who . . . betrayed the people and helped the imperialists against them; aped the ascetics; pretended in a demagogic way to be a supporter of Indian independence and an enemy of the British, and widely exploited religious prejudice.

As under the British Raj, instructions from Moscow to the Indian Communist Party were frequently intercepted by the Intelligence Branch (IB) based in New Delhi. According to B. N. Mullik, head of the IB throughout Jawaharlal Nehru's seventeen years as the first prime minister of independent India (1947–64), until the early 1950s "every instruction that had issued from Moscow had expressed the necessity and importance of the Indian Communist Party to overthrow the 'reactionary' Nehru Government."[75] Early in 1951, Mullik gave Nehru a copy of the latest instructions from Moscow to the Indian Communists, which carried a warning that it must not fall into government hands.

Nehru "laughed out loud and remarked that Moscow apparently did not know how smart our Intelligence was."[76]

Khrushchev, however, saw the Non-Aligned Movement in the Third World, which began to take shape at the Bandung Conference in 1955, as a potential ally in the struggle with the West. With Nasser and Tito (with whom Khrushchev effected a partial reconciliation), Nehru emerged as one of the leaders of the Non-Aligned Movement. A triumphal tour of India by Khrushchev and Bulganin in 1955 began a new era in Indo-Soviet relations. United States reliance on Pakistan as a strategic counterweight to Soviet influence in Asia encouraged India to turn toward the U.S.S.R. During the 1960s, the two countries found common cause against Mao's China. Moscow valued Indian support at the United Nations as, with increasing frequency, the Third World tended to side with the Soviet Bloc rather than the West at votes in the General Assembly. In 1956, Nehru declared that he had never encountered a "grosser case of naked aggression" than the Anglo-French invasion of Egypt; but India simultaneously voted against a motion of the United Nations calling for the withdrawal of Soviet troops from Hungary and free elections under UN auspices.

Despite his experience of Stalinism Nehru clung to the conviction first formed in his late twenties that "the Soviet revolution had advanced human society by a great leap and had lit a bright flame which could not be smothered."[77] In later KGB-sponsored publications, Nehru was portrayed as a "political genius," "contemptuous of danger," whose "policies, humanist and moral principles . . . appealed to all humanity and became a phenomenon of worldwide significance." As late as 1989, a pamphlet put out by the Novosti Press Agency, which acts as one of the vehicles for Soviet "active measures" and provides cover posts for many KGB officers abroad, was still absurdly quoting Nehru's naïve assertion that "the [U.S.S.R.'s] problem of minorities has been largely solved" as evidence of the success of Soviet "nationalities policy."[78]

In the few years after Nehru's death and Khrushchev's fall from power in 1964, the Kremlin followed a more even-handed policy to India and Pakistan, hoping to wean Pakistan away from its ties with Washington and Beijing. Some policy makers in Moscow criticized Khrushchev for overcommitment to India in a conflict-prone region. Among the strongest supporters of a South Asian policy based on commitment to India was the KGB First Chief Directorate and its residents in New Delhi, Radomir Georgievich Bogdanov (1957–67), and his successor, Dmitri Aleksandrovich Yerokhin (1967–70).[79]

The KGB's enthusiasm for the India connection derived partly from the numerous intelligence opportunities that it offered as the world's biggest multiparty democracy with a large English-language press. In the early 1960s, acting in agreement with Department D, headed by Moscow Center's disinformation expert Ivan Agayants, Bogdanov helped to found an Indian newspaper, which has since been widely used in Soviet "active measures."[80] So, often unwittingly, have a number of other Indian papers. One of the KGB officers most active in planting forged documents in the Indian press before and during the election campaign of 1967 was Yuri Modin, the former case officer of the Cambridge Five. In an attempt to discredit the anti-Communist candidate S. K. Patil in Bombay, Modin circulated a forged letter in which the U.S. consul-general in Bombay, Milton C. Rewinkel, wrote to the ambassador, Chester Bowles:

> It would be reasonable for me to suggest tactfully that [Patil] should cease, at least for the period of the election campaign, his political intrigues with the Pakistanis, and that he should moderate his appetites, contenting himself meanwhile with our aid which is enough in all conscience. In this connection, we should keep in mind the fact that it is said in Bombay that he received more than half a million rupees from us for his election campaign.

Modin also circulated a telegram from the British High Commissioner, "Sir John Freeman," reporting to the Foreign Office that the Americans had donated vast sums to the election funds of right-wing parties and politicians. The real high commissioner, Mr. Freeman, had, however, still to receive a knighthood. Modin's failure to cover his disinformation tracks was probably responsible for his abrupt departure from India in April 1967, only nine months after he arrived.[81]

One of the most successful KGB "active measures" during Yerokhin's term as resident in the late 1960s was the circulation of a forged letter purporting to come from Gordon Goldstein of the U.S. Office of Naval Research and revealing the existence of (in reality nonexistent) American bacteriological warfare weapons in Vietnam and Thailand. Originally published in the Bombay *Free Press Journal,* the letter was reported in the London *Times* on March 7, 1968, and used by Moscow Radio in broadcasts beamed to Asia as proof that the

United States had spread epidemics in Vietnam. The Indian weekly
Blitz headlined a story based on the same forgery, "U.S. Admits Biological and Nuclear Warfare." Goldstein's signature and letterhead were
subsequently discovered to have been copied from an invitation to an
international scientific symposium circulated by him in the previous
year.[82] U.S. bacteriological warfare has been a recurrent theme in Soviet
"active measures" ever since the "germ warfare" campaign during the
Korean War deceived a number of Western scientists.[83]

The leading figure in Soviet front organizations during the
Brezhnev era was the Indian Communist Romesh Chandra, whose
enthusiasm for the Soviet Union dated back to his years as a student
at Cambridge University before the Second World War. In 1966,
Chandra became head of the World Peace Council (WPC), the most
important of the postwar Soviet front organizations, the successors to
Münzenberg's Innocents' Clubs. Originally based in Paris, the WPC
was expelled in 1951 for "fifth-column activities," moved to Prague,
then in 1954 to Vienna, where it was banned by the Austrian government in 1957 for "activities directed against the interests of the Austrian State." In fact, the WPC continued to operate in Vienna under
a cover organization, the International Institute for Peace, until it
established its headquarters in Helsinki in September 1968.[84] Chandra
gave the WPC a new lease on life, linking it to many Third World
issues. In his review of the 1960s at the WPC-sponsored World Peace
Congress in 1971, Chandra denounced "the U.S.-dominated NATO
alliance" as "the greatest threat to peace" not merely in Europe but
across the world:

> The fangs of NATO can be felt in Asia and Africa as well.
> . . . The forces of imperialism and exploitation, particularly
> NATO . . . bear the responsibility for the hunger and poverty
> of hundreds of millions all over the world.[85]

The WPC claimed to be funded by contributions from supporters in
national "peace committees" in almost every country. In reality, its
funds came overwhelmingly from the Soviet Union, which by the late
1970s was providing almost $50 million a year. The WPC followed
faithfully the line laid down by the International Department of the
Soviet Communist Party's Central Committee, which coordinated the
work of front organizations. It sought to establish itself as an independent movement by gaining accreditation at the United Nations, which

accepted WPC representatives in both New York and Geneva as well as at UNESCO in Paris, and by recruiting as vice-presidents peace militants such as the British Labour M.P. James Lamond, who, like the "innocents" seduced by Münzenberg, failed to grasp that they had joined a Soviet front organization. The KGB assisted the International Department by acting as secret postman for funds distributed to the front organizations controlled by the ID. The peace campaigns orchestrated by Chandra as general secretary and, from 1977, president of the WPC were directed uniquely against the West. There was, as he frequently explained, no Soviet threat to peace:

> The foreign policy goals of the U.S.S.R. . . . are to establish lasting peace and peaceful coexistence between States of different social systems. . . . The Soviet Union's military policy fully corresponds to these goals. It is of a purely defensive character.

Other front organizations commonly took their lead from the WPC.[86]

In the late 1960s and early 1970s, the main focus of both WPC public campaigns and of covert KGB "active measures" was on the Vietnam War. Moscow Center correctly saw United States involvement in the war as one of the U.S.S.R.'s greatest assets in extending Soviet influences in the Third World. The saturation bombing of a Third World country and the commitment of almost half a million U.S. troops both antagonized world opinion and divided the American people. Chandra and the WPC set out to encourage both processes, organizing the Stockholm Conference on Vietnam, which met annually from 1967 to 1972 to coordinate opposition to American policy. At its 1969 meeting, the conference agreed on "activity to isolate and subject to continuing protest and criticism representatives of the U.S. government"; assistance to "Americans abroad in refusing the draft, in defecting from the U.S. armed forces, [and] for carrying on propaganda within the army"; and "an extension of activity against United States products such as petrol, firms providing goods, arms or services for the war in Vietnam such as Pan-Am, and against other non-American firms supplying and feeding the war."[87]

Chiefly in recognition of its success in mobilizing world opinion against the Vietnam War, the active-measures section of the First Chief Directorate was raised in status in the early '70s from a department to Service A. As on a number of later occasions noted by Gordievsky, however, the Center claimed rather too much for its "active measures."[88] Despite the undoubted impact in the Third World of KGB-inspired allegations of American bacteriological warfare, no Soviet disinformation had as much impact on international opinion as the images of napalmed children and other horrors of war brought to the world's TV screens by American reporters. Similarly, President Lyndon B. Johnson's decision not to run for reelection in 1968 owed far less to campaigns against the Vietnam War orchestrated by Chandra and the WPC than to hearings by the Senate Foreign Relations Committee, which produced evidence that Johnson had deceived Congress about both the nature of the war and the scale of American involvement.

In 1969, the threat from China at last persuaded Brezhnev to make a special relationship with India the basis of his South Asian policy. Nehru's daughter, Indira Gandhi (prime minister from 1967 to 1977 and from 1980 to 1984), was ready to conclude an Indo-Soviet agreement, but as head of a minority government was not yet strong enough to resist opposition charges that such a treaty would compromise India's non-aligned status. After a landslide election victory in 1971, however, Mrs. Gandhi's government signed a Treaty of Peace, Friendship, and Cooperation with the Soviet Union.[89] According to the permanent secretary at the Indian Foreign Office, T. N. Kaul, "It was one of the few closely guarded secret negotiations that India has ever conducted. On one side, hardly half a dozen people were aware of it, including the prime minister and the foreign minister. The media got no scent of it."[90] Gromyko declared at the signing ceremony in August: "The significance of the Treaty cannot be overestimated." The Soviet Union was guaranteed the support of the leading state in the Non-Aligned Movement. The powers immediately issued a joint communiqué calling for the withdrawal of U.S. troops from Vietnam. India was able to rely on Soviet diplomatic support and arms supplies in the war against Pakistan, which was already in the offing.[91]

In a fourteen-day war in December, Pakistan, despite the diplomatic support of the United States and China, suffered a crushing defeat. East Pakistan gained independence as Bangladesh. Pakistan was reduced to a nation of 55 million people, no longer able to mount a credible challenge to India. For most Indians it was Mrs. Gandhi's finest hour. A Soviet diplomat at the United Nations exulted: "This is the first time in history that the United States and China have been defeated together!"[92]

In Moscow Center the Indo-Soviet rapprochement was also considered a triumph for the KGB. The resident in the late 1960s, Dmitri Yerokhin, returned to Moscow in 1970 as the KGB's youngest major general.[93] The KGB residency in New Delhi was rewarded by being upgraded to the status of "main residency" with Yerokhin's successor Yakov Prokofyevich Medyanik as main resident. Within the main residency, the heads of the PR (political), KR (Counterintelligence), and X (Scientific and Technological Intelligence) lines were given the rank of resident—not, as elsewhere, deputy resident. Medyanik had overall supervision of three other KGB residencies, located in the Soviet consulates at Bombay, Calcutta, and Madras. Each also had direct cipher communications with Moscow and, in Gordievsky's experience, tended to be controlled on a day-to-day basis by the Center rather than by New Delhi.

After the 1971 friendship treaty, the KGB presence in India rapidly became one of the largest in the world outside the Soviet Bloc. Of about 300 Soviet "diplomatic and operational staff" in India (excluding drivers, technicians, and secretarial staff), about 150 were, and are, KGB and GRU officers. The large scale of KGB operations in India was due partly to its priority in Soviet foreign policy, partly to the favorable operational environment that it provided. Gordievsky noted throughout his career in the First Chief Directorate a tendency to expand wherever, as in India, the local authorities failed to restrict the size of KGB residencies. Under both Indira Gandhi and her son Rajiv, India placed no ceiling on the number of Soviet diplomats and trade officials, thus allowing the KGB and GRU as many cover positions as they wished. Nor, like many other states, did India object to admitting Soviet intelligence officers already expelled by less hospitable governments.[94]

Colleagues of Gordievsky who served in India boasted to him that they had found no shortage of journalists or politicians willing to take money. According to S. Nihal Singh, successively editor of *The Statesman* and *The Indian Express*:

> The Indian élite takes a somewhat blasé attitude to Russian money coming in. Some members of the policy-making establishment suggested that Russian money, particularly to finance parties and individuals in elections, neutralized American money and money from other anti-Communist sources.[95]

In 1974, after a series of speeches by Mrs. Gandhi denouncing the ever-present menace of CIA subversion, the U.S. ambassador in New Delhi, Daniel Patrick Moynihan, ordered an investigation that uncovered two occasions during the Nehru era when the CIA had provided funds to help the Communists' opponents in state elections, once in Kerala and once in West Bengal. According to Moynihan:

> Both times the money was given to the Congress Party which had asked for it. Once it was given to Mrs. Gandhi herself, who was then a party official.
>
> Still, as we were no longer giving any money to *her*, it was understandable that she should wonder just to whom we *were* giving it. It is not a practice to be encouraged.[96]

Though KGB officers and operations in India comfortably exceeded those of any other foreign intelligence service, it was not the only service to exploit lax Indian security. In 1985, a major spy scandal erupted in New Delhi, which involved the French, the Poles, and the East Germans as well as the Russians. The French, whose ambassador and assistant military attaché were sent home, believed that they had been singled out for the sternest censure in order to minimize embarrassment to the Soviet Bloc.[97]

The KGB's main priority was less to influence Indian government policy, which under Indira and Rajiv Gandhi was regarded as reliably pro-Soviet, than to use India as a base for operations against the West and the Third World. By the 1970s New Delhi was the largest foreign base for KGB "active measures" anywhere in the world. The main resident, Medyanik, and his successors each had a "special assistant for active measures" with the rank of colonel or lieutenant colonel. With the expansion of scientific and technological espionage, India also became steadily more important as a channel through which to gain access to forbidden Western technology. Gordievsky recalls one occasion in the mid-seventies when the head of Directorate T, Leonid Sergeevich Zaitsev, outraged at the failure of Line X (scientific and technological intelligence) officers in the United States, Western Europe, and Japan to obtain a particular piece of equipment, swore violently and declared: "In that case, I'll have to get it through our Indian contacts! I know *they* won't let me down!"[98]

*   *   *

Besides India, the Soviet Union's main asset in the Third World after the death of Nasser was Castro's Cuba. When Castro arrived to a hero's welcome at the start of his first visit to the U.S.S.R. in the spring of 1963, the recriminations that had followed the missile crisis seemed to be forgotten. His interpreter throughout his trip, Nikolai Leonov, at thirty-five three years younger than Castro himself, was one of the rising stars of the First Chief Directorate. While stationed at the Mexico City residency in the mid-fifties he had been the first KGB officer to grasp Castro's potential as a revolutionary leader. For forty days, on secondment from his second tour of duty in Mexico, Leonov accompanied Castro on an unprecedented triumphal tour of the Soviet Union from Leningrad to Siberia. Wearing his olive-green battle fatigues when the temperature allowed, the charismatic guerrilla leader addressed curious, enthusiastic crowds at sports stadia, factories, town centers, and at a mass rally in Red Square; inspected a rocket base and the Northern Fleet; reviewed the May Day parade from the top of the Kremlin wall; was made a Hero of the Soviet Union; and received the Order of Lenin and a gold star. When the state visit was over, Leonov boasted in Moscow Center that he and Castro were now friends for life.[99]

In the wake of Castro's visit, the Center received the first group of officers from the Cuban foreign intelligence service, the Dirección General de Inteligencia (DGI), for training in Moscow. In Havana, Castro's closest Soviet contact remained the KGB resident-turned-ambassador, Aleksandr Shitov (*alias* Alekseev), who claimed that Fidel continued, as during the missile crisis, to treat the embassy as his second home, sometimes cooking meals with Shitov in the embassy kitchen. Shitov also worked with Che Guevara in selecting and training Latin American agents.[100]

Despite his friendships with Leonov and Shitov, however, Moscow found Castro a volatile and difficult ally. Proud of having descended on Havana to seize power straight from his guerrilla base in Sierra Maestra, Castro declared his own *via armada* rather than the *via pacifica* preferred by Moscow as the route to power for all Latin American Communist parties. By 1966 he was promulgating the heresy that Havana rather than Moscow held the key to national liberation and victory over imperialism. At the Twenty-third Soviet Party Congress in that year, the Cuban delegation even dared to criticize the Kremlin for not doing more to help the North Vietnamese. Castro simultaneously announced that, thanks to his war on "bureaucratism" and material incentives, Cuba was advancing more rapidly to Communism than the Soviet Union.

By the mid-sixties the real achievements of the Cuban revolution—the reforms in health and education, and the end of *gangsterismo* chief among them—had given way to an increasingly empty rhetoric, which bore little relation either to his regime's shambolic economic management or to its growing intolerance of dissent; even Castro admitted to holding twenty thousand political prisoners by 1965. Though unmoved by the political prisoners, the Kremlin watched aghast as its Cuban allies squandered its vast economic aid on such absurdities as the giant Coppelia ice-cream emporium.

Yet, thanks to his romantic image as a bearded David in battle fatigues blockaded on his island by the Goliath of American imperialism, Castro continued to have far more appeal than the bureaucratic Brezhnev in his stodgy suits to the young radicals of both the West and the Third World. The CIA did its bit to sustain Castro's heroic reputation by devising, originally with the blessing of the White House, a series of bizarre, never-implemented assassination attempts against him. Castro's image was also assisted by the heroic end in 1967 of Che Guevara, captured and executed while fighting with Bolivian guerrillas, and instantly immortalized on radical T-shirts around the world.[101]

The crisis in Soviet-Cuban relations reached a head in January 1968 with the trial of thirty-five members of a pro-Moscow "microfaction," sentenced to lengthy prison sentences for "clandestine propaganda against the line of the Party" and other ideological crimes. Rudolf Petrovich Shlyapnikov, the chief KGB adviser at the Cuban Ministry of the Interior, who was alleged to have conspired with the "microfaction," had been sent back to Moscow in the summer of 1967. "In Cuba," he claimed, "conditions are present for a new Hungary. . . . Internal dissension is great." The existing Cuban security apparatus, he believed, contained too many *petit bourgeois* to deal with a revolt.[102]

Shitov was accorded some of the blame by the Center for allowing his friend Castro to get out of control. In Moscow he was accused of going native, recalled allegedly for medical treatment, and replaced in 1968 by the tough career diplomat Aleksandr Soldatov, who had recently served as ambassador in London.[103] Unlike Castro's other KGB friend, Leonov, who went on to become deputy head of the First Chief Directorate, Shitov's career never fully recovered. He retired in 1980 after six years as ambassador in Madagascar. Shitov's son, Aleksei Aleksandrovich, who regarded his birth on Pearl Harbor Day as a good omen in the struggle against the Main Adversary, also became a Latin American specialist in the First Chief Directorate. When Gordievsky last heard of him in the mid-1980s, he was KGB resident in La Paz, using his father's old alias Alekseev.[104]

Castro's "rebellion" was ended by the threat of economic collapse, combined with warnings from his brother Raúl. Shlyapnikov had told the leader of the microfaction that three weeks' delay in sending oil from the Baku oilfields could strangle the Cuban economy. Early in 1968, with the Soviet Union putting pressure on Castro by cutting back its oil exports, Cuban sugar mills and factories were grinding to a halt. In August, Castro came close to selling his soul in public. For two days after the Soviet invasion of Czechoslovakia, Czech technical advisers and Cuban sympathizers paraded through Havana with banners proclaiming "Russians Go Home from Czechoslovakia."

Then, on the night of August 23, Castro addressed the Cuban people over radio and television. "Some of the things we are going to say here," he warned them, "will be in contradiction with the emotions of many. . . . Czechoslovakia was moving toward a counterrevolutionary situation, toward capitalism and into the arms of imperialism." The Czechoslovak leadership had been "in camaraderie with pro-Yankee spies," as well as "the agents of West Germany and all that fascist and reactionary rabble." Castro went on to endorse the Brezhnev doctrine: "The socialist camp has the right to prevent this [counterrevolution] in one way or another. . . . We look upon this fact as an essential one." By backing the Soviet invasion when scores of other Communist parties stood by the Czechoslovaks, Castro restored his credit in Moscow. In return for his loyalty the Soviet Union bailed out the Cuban economy. By the end of 1969, Cuba owed the Soviet Union $4 billion.[105]

The closer economic relationship was paralleled in intelligence. In 1970 the DGI (Dirección General de Inteligencia) was purged of officers considered anti-Soviet by the KGB, and a team of KGB advisers headed by General Viktor Semyonov was installed next to the office of the head of the DGI, Manuel Piñeiro Losado ("Redbeard"). With the assistance of KGB subsidies, the DGI began a rapid expansion of its foreign operations. By 1971, seven of the ten Cuban "diplomats" at the London embassy were DGI officers.

After the mass expulsion of Soviet intelligence officers from London in September of that year, they were given the task, along with other Soviet Bloc intelligence officers, of helping to plug the Center's intelligence gap. There was, however, no direct contact between KGB and DGI officers in London. Semyonov insisted that coordination of their activities be decided and controlled from Moscow and Havana. Piñeiro, a founder member of Castro's Twenty-sixth of July Movement, became increasingly resentful at growing KGB direction of DGI operations. In 1974, he left to become head of a new Departamento Americano (DA) to organize assistance to Latin American revolutionary movements and was succeeded as head of the DGI by the more pliant and pro-Soviet José Méndez Cominches.[106]

At home the Cuban Revolution was visibly aging. By the autumn of 1968, the bearded Castro was denouncing even long hair as evidence of the moral degeneracy that led to political and economic sabotage. Mass haircuts followed of some of the worst offenders. Public decency was further reinforced by dispatching miniskirted girls said to have made "passionate love in their school uniforms" to forced-labor camps in the countryside.[107] Abroad, however, the Revolution retained much of its vigor. With the election of the Marxist Salvador Allende as president of Chile in 1970, Castro gained his first Latin American ally. Allende gave his personal approval to the use of Chile by the DGI as a base from which to provide arms and training for Latin American revolutionary movements. Revolutionary leaders made their way to the Cuban embassy in Santiago, using false travel documents provided by the DGI. They received little money; the DGI expected them to finance themselves from bank robberies and kidnapping.[108]

Allende's international reputation, like Castro's, owed a good deal to overreaction in Washington. In the three years before Allende's overthrow and death in a military coup in 1973, the CIA, on White House instructions, spent $8 million seeking to destabilize him. Though not directly involved in the coup, the CIA seems to have had advance knowledge of it and was, surprisingly, blamed for it.[109] The KGB was less impressed by Allende than the CIA. By the end of 1972, with the Chilean economy in desperate straits, it was pessimistic about his prospects.[110] So was the Kremlin. At a time when the Cubans were given massive new credits, Allende was fobbed off with only token assistance and the award of the Lenin Peace Prize.[111] Allende's tragic death in the September 1973 military coup (whether by murder or suicide remains unclear) restored his reputation in Moscow.[112] It turned the head of a near-bankrupt regime into a martyr in the struggle against imperialism and left the CIA with a reputation for destabilizing and plotting the assassination of progressive leaders which, with some assistance from the Center, would seem likely to linger in the Third World for the remainder of the century.[113]

During the early 1970s, Castro began to set his sights on leadership of the Third World. In May 1972 he left Havana in his Ilyushin-62 airliner for a two-month tour of ten countries on two continents, ending with his first visit to the Soviet Union in eight years.[114] Castro was the star performer at the Fourth Conference of Non-Aligned Nations in Algiers in 1973, arguing the Soviet case more eloquently than any Soviet spokesman could have done. Algeria, which supported the traditional non-aligned policy of equidistance between East and West, supported the theory of "two imperialisms," one capitalist, the other Communist. Castro insisted that the socialist countries were the natural and necessary allies of the nonaligned:

> How can the Soviet Union be labeled imperialist? Where are its monopoly corporations? Where is its participation in multinational companies? What factories, what mines, what oilfields does it own in the under-developed world? What worker is exploited in any country of Asia, Africa or Latin America by Soviet capital?
>
> . . . Only the closest alliance among all the progressive forces of the world will provide us with the strength needed to overcome the still-powerful forces of imperialism, colonialism, neocolonialism and racism, and to wage a successful fight for the aspirations to peace and justice of all the peoples of the world.[115]

In the end, the Communist Bloc was not labeled as imperialist, and the "aggressive imperialism" of the West was denounced by the conference as "the greatest obstacle on the road toward emancipation and progress of the developing countries." Along with its role as the most eloquent advocate of the Soviet Union in the Third World, Cuba was also to play during the 1970s an increasingly important role in both Soviet intelligence and military operations.[116]

By the Brezhnev era high-level Soviet Bloc penetration of foreign civil services, intelligence communities, and armed forces was generally more successful in the Third World than in the West. The main exception, because of the unique opportunities presented by the division of Germany to the KGB and, especially, its East German ally, the HVA headed by Markus Wolf, was in the West German Federal Republic. On October 8, 1968, Rear Admiral Hermann Lüdke of the FRG, deputy head of NATO's logistics division and thus privy to, *inter alia,* the location of some thousands of tactical nuclear weapons, committed suicide after the discovery of photographs of top secret NATO documents taken by him with a Minox camera. Lüdke's friend Major General Horst Wendland, deputy chief of the BND, shot himself on the same day.[117] The official explanation for Wendland's suicide was "personal reasons"; a Czech defector, however, has since revealed that he was working for the StB.

Over the next fortnight there were a series of other suicides, among them Colonel Johann Henk, head of the Mobilization Department at the Bonn Ministry of Defense, and Hans Schenk, a senior official in the Ministry of Economics.[118] Simultaneously several high-ranking scientists and physicists, originally from the German Democratic Republic, who had been engaged in scientific and technological espionage, disappeared to the East. One who remained, Dr. Harold Gottfried of the Karlsruhe Atomic Center, was arrested in possession of more than 800 pages of classified documents.

Meanwhile, Markus Wolf's "secretaries offensive" continued unabated. In 1967 Leonore Sutterlein, a secretary at the Bonn Foreign Ministry, was convicted of passing 3,500 classified documents to the KGB via her husband Heinz. When she discovered that Heinz was a KGB agent who had married her simply to recruit her, she committed suicide in her cell.[119] Other convicted secretary spies working for the HVA included Irene Schultz (1970) of the Science Ministry and Gerda Schroeter (1973) of the West German embassy in Warsaw. Political penetration also occurred at a much higher level. More than one senior SPD politician had regular meetings with a KGB officer operating under diplomatic cover who persuaded him that he could smooth the course of *Ostpolitik.* The most important HVA agent in the Federal Republic was Guenther Guillaume, personal aide to Chancellor Willy Brandt from 1970 to 1974. Guillaume was able to keep Markus Wolf, and through him Moscow Center, fully informed about the development of Bonn's *Ostpolitik* and relations between Bonn and Washington, as well as providing much other information on NATO and the West German security service (BfV).[120]

In the Main Adversary, the United States, and its main ally, the United Kingdom, the KGB found it impossible during the Brezhnev era to recruit the American or British equivalents of Lüdke, Wendland, and Guillaume. KGB residencies in both countries depended on recruiting low- to middle-ranking penetration agents with access to high-grade secrets. In Britain during the 1960s, Moscow Center discovered a simple method of improving operational conditions. Under four successive residents—Nikolai Grigoryevich Bagrichev (1962–64), Mikhail Timofeyevich Chizhov (1964–66), Mikhail Ivanovich Lopatin (acting resident 1966–67), and Yuri Nikolayevich Voronin (1967–71)—the size of the residency steadily increased. Between 1960 and 1970, KGB and GRU personnel in London grew from about 50 to over 120—more than in the United States (excluding the UN) or any other Western country. Soviet Bloc intelligence services in Britain also expanded rapidly. The aim, quite simply, was to swamp the overstretched M15 with more intelligence officers than they could hope to keep under effective surveillance.[121] When the StB officer Josef Frolik was posted to London in 1964, he was told "that the British service was so short of funds and men that it would be relatively easy to throw off their tails."[122] Operational conditions improved further at the beginning of Voronin's term as resident in 1967, when one of his officers, Vladislav Savin, recruited a clerk in the Greater London Council motor-licensing department, Sirioj Husein Abdoolcader, who had access to the registration numbers of all M15 and Special Branch vehicles. A series of sophisticated M15 mobile surveillance operations was compromised by the ability of KGB officers to identify the vehicles used.[123]

The largest number of agents recruited and run by the London residency during the Brezhnev era was in scientific and technological intelligence—particularly the defense field. The residency's main expert in this area during the mid-1960s, Mikhail Ivanovich Lopatin, became one of the founders in 1967 of a new Directorate T in the First Chief Directorate, specializing in scientific and technological intelligence and serviced by Line X officers in residencies abroad. The head of Line X in London from the beginning of 1968 until his expulsion in the summer of 1971 was Lev Nikolayevich Sherstnev, a tough but amiable engineer who spoke almost flawless English with a Canadian accent and had a particular passion for Western hi-fi. In addition to using staff at the KGB and GRU residencies in London, both Directorate T and the GRU sent officers to Britain posing as members of Soviet trade delegations. They were also assisted by Soviet students studying at British universities. The classified history of Directorate T records substantial successes during the 1960s in a number of fields of industrial as well as defense technology: among them advanced electronics, computers, high-grade chemicals, and aerospace.[124]

MI5 was hampered in its response to the upsurge in scientific and technological espionage not merely by its own overstretched resources but also by the difficulty (which it was, understandably, not anxious to advertise) of bringing successful prosecutions. Unless it could obtain confessions or catch agents in the act of handing over material, it was usually impossible to secure convictions. Its difficulties were exemplified by the trial in 1963 of Dr. Giuseppe Martelli, a thirty-nine-year-old Italian physicist employed for the previous year at the Culham Laboratories of the Atomic Energy Authority. Arrested as the result of a lead provided by a KGB defector, Martelli was found in possession of a record of meetings with Nikolai Karpekov and other KGB officers, a set of partly used one-time pads for cipher communications hidden inside an ingeniously designed cigarette case, and instructions for photographing documents. But possession of espionage paraphernalia was not in itself a crime, and Martelli had no official access to classified information, though he was in contact with some who had. Martelli admitted meeting Karpekov but claimed that he was engaged in an ingenious scheme to turn the tables on a blackmail attempt by Soviet agents. He was acquitted.[125]

In 1965 another case involving scientific espionage also ended in acquittal. Alfred Roberts, an employee of the Kodak factory in Wealdstone, was accused with Geoffrey Conway, a fellow employee whom he was alleged to have recruited, of selling details of anti-static coatings and other film processes to the East German HVA. Since no official secrets were involved, both were charged only under the Prevention of Corruption Act. But the main witness at the trial, Dr. Jean-Paul Soupert, an industrial chemist and double (treble?) agent working for the HVA, KGB, and Belgian Sûreté de l'État, who claimed to have dealt with Roberts, was discredited by skillful cross-examination, and the case collapsed.[126]

It is reasonable to assume that the majority of scientific and technological espionage cases investigated by MI5 never came to court because of the difficulty in obtaining adequate evidence. In most cases evidence from defectors was inadmissible since, however convincing outside a courtroom, it usually counted as hearsay within it. Though the secret history of Directorate T rarely identifies agents by name, it makes clear that the cases that ended in conviction were only the tip of an iceberg.[127]

The three cases of convicted spies during the early years of the Brezhnev era all involved men with money problems working for mercenary motives and able to exploit lapses in security. In 1965 Frank Bossard, a fifty-two-year-old project officer at the Ministry of Aviation, was sentenced to twenty-one years in jail for passing secrets of guided-weapon development to the GRU. He had, he claimed, been recruited four years earlier by a case officer using the name Gordon, who struck up an acquaintance with him in the Red Lion public house in Duke Street, London W1, on the pretext of a shared interest in coin collecting, and paid Bossard £200 a few days after their first meeting.

It seems more likely that Bossard had volunteered his services some months earlier. He rarely met his case officer, Ivan Petrovich Glazkov. Every two months he left film of classified documents in one of ten dead letter boxes (DLBs) and collected variable sums of money in exchange—on one occasion £2,000 in bank notes. The choice of DLB was indicated by records such as the "Saber Dance" and "Moscow Nights" played on the Moscow Radio English-language broadcasts on the first Tuesday and Wednesday of each month; in an emergency, the playing of the "Volga Boat Song" indicated that operations were temporarily suspended. The investigation after Bossard's arrest revealed a criminal record that had never been properly investigated. In 1934 he had been sentenced to six months' hard labor for buying watches with bad checks, then selling them to pawnbrokers.[128]

In 1968 Douglas Britten, an RAF chief technician, was sentenced, like Bossard three years earlier, to twenty-one years' imprisonment. For the previous six years he had provided highly classified intelligence from top-secret RAF signal units in Cyprus and Lincolnshire. He was recruited in 1962 by a KGB officer using the name Yuri, who walked up to him in the Kensington Science Museum, identified himself as a fellow radio ham, and addressed Britten by his call sign "Golf Three Kilo Foxtrot Lima." Two months later Britten was posted to Cyprus and began to supply intelligence to a local case officer. When he tried to break off contact, the case officer produced a photograph of him receiving money and blackmailed him into continuing. In 1966 Britten was transferred to RAF Digby in Lincolnshire and handed over to a new KGB controller, Aleksandr Ivanovich Bondarenko.

A Security Commission inquiry after Britten's conviction in 1968 revealed a history of financial problems. He had been briefly investigated in Cyprus after he ran into debt with the NAAFI and his wife complained that he was having an affair with a cabaret dancer.

Once back at RAF Digby, he ran into more serious trouble after a series of bouncing checks in the sergeants' mess and at a local garage. The Security Commission concluded that Britten was "a good actor and an accomplished liar. When such a man decides to betray his country, he presents the security authorities with a formidable problem of detection."[129]

In 1972 Sub-Lieutenant David Bingham was sentenced, like Bossard and Britten, to twenty-one years' imprisonment. For the previous two years he had filmed secret documents for the GRU at the Portsmouth naval base. His money problems stemmed chiefly from his wife, who, in despair at her mounting debts in 1969, had briefly left home and put her children into foster care. After Mrs. Bingham visited the Soviet embassy early in 1970, Bingham was recruited as a spy by L. T. Kuzmin, who gave him £600 and told him part of it was for his wife. Having purchased a camera and light meter as instructed, he met his controller outside Guildford Cathedral and was instructed on the use of DLBs in the Guildford area and on the procedures for photographing documents. In 1972, unable to cope with mounting pressure both from the GRU and from his creditors, he confessed to his commanding officer.[130]

In London, as in other capitals, the KGB was assisted by other Soviet Bloc intelligence services. The most effective, at least until the defections that followed the Soviet suppression of the Prague Spring, was the Czechoslovak StB. The StB's most important recruit in the scientific and technological field was Nicholas Prager, son of a clerk in the British consulate in Prague. Both had become naturalized British citizens in 1948. The following year, falsely claiming to have spent all his life in England and to be British by birth, the twenty-one-year-old Prager joined the RAF. By 1956 he had established himself as an efficient radar technician, with access to top-secret defense material.

In 1959 Prager returned to Czechoslovakia for a visit. According to the later StB defector Josef Frolik, the StB was waiting for him. Exploiting both his Communist sympathies and his mercenary instincts, the StB recruited him as an agent with the code name Marconi. In 1961 Prager provided full technical details of the Blue Diver and Red Steer radar-jamming devices being fitted to the V bombers, Britain's nuclear strike force. Though usually sparing with its praise, Moscow Center described this as the best intelligence yet provided by the StB. For the next ten years, Prager was employed by English Electric, working on a number of secret defense contracts, which he reported to the StB. In 1971, as a result of information provided by the defectors Josef Frolik and František August, he was sentenced to twelve years' imprisonment. Prager's sentence would have been longer but for the fact that the only evidence usable in court related to offenses that by then were ten years old.[131]

In general, the KGB found that the StB's main value in London lay in approaching politicians and trade unionists who were less suspicious of Czechoslovaks than of Russians and sympathetic to a people betrayed by the West at Munich in 1938. The recommended technique within the StB for recruiting British M.P.s was for the recruiter, posing as an orthodox diplomat, to bemoan the mistrust between London and Prague, then add:

> I doubt if most of the powers-that-be in Prague have fully realized that the Cold War is long over as far as the British are concerned. If only we could find *someone* here who could convince our people—even in writing—that the British are only too eager to improve their relationships with their old wartime allies.

Any M.P. thus persuaded to write a report on the improvement of Anglo-Czechoslovak relations was paid for it on the pretext that "Of course, we couldn't allow you to write all this for nothing." If the recruiting strategy worked, other reports followed and the M.P. found himself trapped. During the 1960s the StB residency in London ran three Labour M.P.s. The most enthusiastic agent of the three was the Labour M.P. for Morpeth, Will Owen, recruited soon after his election in 1954 by Jan Paclik (alias Novak), an StB officer working under diplomatic cover as second secretary. Though his official StB code name was Lee, Owen was also known within the residency as Greedy Bastard. According to the defector Josef Frolik, who served at the London residency in the mid-sixties and saw some of Owen's product:

> "Lee" was interested solely in the five hundred pounds a month retainer which we gave him. . . . In spite of the obvious danger, he was always demanding free holidays in Czechoslovakia so that he might save the expense of having to pay for the vacation himself. He even went as far as pocketing as

many cigars as possible whenever he came to the Embassy
for a party.

For nearly fifteen years Owen met his case officer while taking his dog
for early-morning strolls in a London park. Though only a back
bencher, Owen became a member of the Commons Defense Estimates
Committee and provided what Frolik described as "top-secret material
of the highest value" on the British Army of the Rhine and the British
contribution to NATO.[132] Owen was eventually discovered after the
defection of Frolik and another StB officer acquainted with the Lee
case, František August. After an examination of Owen's bank account
revealed large sums on which he had never paid tax, he resigned his seat
in April 1970. At his trial at the Old Bailey the following month,
however, the prosecution failed to prove that Owen had betrayed classified information. Since neither Frolik nor August had been his case
officer, their evidence counted as hearsay and was therefore inadmissible. After Owen's acquittal, he confessed to MI5 in return for a guarantee of immunity from further prosecution. The Labour M.P. and lawyer
Leo Abse, who heard his confession, wrote afterward: "Owen certainly
did his best to rape his motherland."[133]

Frolik and August identified the most senior Labour M.P.
working for the StB as John Stonehouse, successively parliamentary
secretary at the Ministry of Aviation, parliamentary undersecretary of
state for the Colonies, minister of Aviation, minister of State for Technology, postmaster-general and minister of Posts and Telecommunica-
tions in the Wilson government of 1964–70. Stonehouse was, allegedly,
blackmailed by the StB after a sexual trap had been laid for him during
a visit to Czechoslovakia in the late 1950s. According to Frolik, he also
took money from the StB: "Although . . . not of Cabinet rank, [he] put
us in a position to know a great deal about certain British military and
counter-intelligence operations."[134] There is, however, no hard evidence
that Stonehouse had more than occasional dealings with the StB. A few
months before Wilson's fall from power in 1970, Stonehouse was confronted in the prime minister's presence with the allegations made by
Frolik and August. Stonehouse denied them vigorously. Since MI5 was
able to produce no evidence to support the defectors' information, the
matter was dropped.[135]

His later behavior does not encourage faith in his protestations
of total innocence. In 1974, faced with acute business problems, Stonehouse faked his own suicide, and disappeared with his mistress to

Australia. Having been successfully tracked down and brought back to England, he was sentenced in 1976 to seven years' imprisonment on eighteen charges of theft and fraud. Once out of jail he published a spy novel describing the entrapment of a senior civil servant in the European Commission named Ralph Edmonds by the seductive Lotte of East German intelligence. ("One of our best operators," Ralph's controller later tells him. "What she did was strictly in the line of duty.") Ralph spends an enjoyable evening with Lotte, who obligingly "sent sensations of joy to every crevice of his brain." Then, after one last "magnificent thrust," just before he went to sleep, "Ralph noticed their reflections in a huge, oval ceiling mirror." He is later handed souvenir photographs of the evening taken through the one-way mirror in the ceiling, and agrees to cooperate. Inept though Stonehouse's storytelling was, the account of Ralph's entrapment may well have drawn on his experience at the hands of the StB.[136]

The case of one other Czechoslovak contact in the Commons, code-named Crocodile, remains so confused as to defy straightforward analysis. Crocodile was Tom Driberg, M.P. for twenty-eight years, later a Labour peer, long-serving member of the Labour National Executive, and sometime chairman of the Labour Party: a man of great charm, political flair, and unresolved contradictions, with a compulsive addiction to homosexual activity in public restrooms, who died in 1976. In 1956, during a visit to Moscow to see his old friend Guy Burgess (about whom he wrote a highly misleading biography denying that he was a spy), Driberg was approached by the KGB and agreed to provide confidential information about the private lives and inner workings of the Labour leadership. He later told MI5 that the KGB gave him two identical briefcases. When he handed one containing his reports to his Soviet case officer, he received the other, containing his payment, in exchange. Driberg also admitted passing material to the Czechs. "All harmless stuff," he is alleged to have told MI5. According to Frolik, the StB was warned off by the KGB, which regarded Driberg as "their man." MI5 also seems to have made some use of him as a double (if not triple) agent. In the end even Driberg may not have been clear precisely who he was working for.[137]

A fourth alleged Czech agent in the Commons during the 1960s, code-named Gustav, has never been identified. According to Frolik, he was recruited by Václav Táborský in the mid-1950s and worked for money:

"Gustav" was not as important as "Lee," but he was in a
position to deliver interesting information about the domestic and foreign policies of the Labour Party while it was in
opposition, and, later, when the Wilson Government came
to power, about defense matters.[138]

The fact that Sir Barnett Stross, Labour M.P. for Stoke, was born in
Czechoslovakia, spoke fluent Czech, died in 1967, and was thereafter
unable to sue made it almost inevitable that he would be posthumously
identified as Gustav by some writers on espionage. The identification,
however, remains highly implausible.

Both the StB and the KGB believed that it was possible to
recruit Conservative as well as Labour M.P.s, but appear to have been
hopelessly inept in picking their targets. The StB residency in London
devised a bizarre plan to lure the Conservative leader Edward Heath
to indulge his passion for organ playing in a Prague church, compromise him, and then recruit him. The plan predictably failed: Heath
refused the invitation to Prague. Mikhail Petrovich Lyubimov, a brilliantly talented but overambitious PR line officer at the KGB residency
in the early 1960s, recruited an M.P.'s personal secretary but then, as
he later told Gordievsky, went on to target (without any prospect of
success) the Conservative journalist Peregrine Worsthorne and the rising young Conservative M.P. Nicholas Scott. He was expelled in 1965
after trying to recruit a cipher operator.

The steady increase in KGB and StB operations in Britain during the
1960s was compromised by three defections. Frolik and August, who
defected in the summer of 1969, had both spent periods working in
London and seem to have identified most of the StB's British agents.
The KGB suffered even greater damage as a result of the defection in
September 1971 of Oleg Adolfovich Lyalin from the London residency.
Lyalin, an expert in hand-to-hand combat as well as a highly proficient
marksman and parachutist, was a member of Department V[139] of the
First Chief Directorate, founded in 1969 to replace the old Thirteenth
("Wet Affairs") Department, which had been badly compromised by
the defections of Khokhlov and Stashinsky. Department V had a much
broader brief than its predecessor. Its function was to prepare contingency plans for the sabotage of foreign public services, transport, communications, and the nerve centers of government at the outbreak of
war and in some crises short of war.

In the spring of 1971, about six months before he defected, Lyalin was recruited by MI5 as an agent-in-place and provided details of sabotage plans in London, Washington, Paris, Bonn, Rome, and other Western capitals. He revealed that in each capital Department V officers had been ordered to select and monitor the movement of key figures for assassination in time of crisis. They were also to recruit local agents to assist them and provide support for Department V illegals. Sabotage plans in Britain included plans to flood the London Underground, blow up the missile early-warning station at Fylingdale, North Yorkshire, destroy V-bombers on the ground, and attack other military targets. Lyalin's main job was to identify vital installations, which undercover Soviet Spetsnaz (special forces) could immobilize at the outbreak of war.

Some of Department V's schemes were as bizarre as those devised by the CIA to eliminate Castro. One plan revealed by Lyalin was for Soviet agents posing as messengers and delivery men to scatter colorless poison capsules along the corridors of power, which would kill all those who crushed them underfoot. The British government released few details about Lyalin after his defection, but the attorney-general told the Commons that he was charged with "the organization of sabotage within the United Kingdom" and preparations for "the elimination of individuals judged to be enemies of the U.S.S.R." Lyalin's defection caused a major crisis in Moscow Center. Apparently on Politburo instructions, Department V was wound up and its officers recalled from foreign residencies.[140]

Soon after Lyalin's defection, MI5 persuaded the Heath government to order a mass expulsion of Soviet intelligence personnel. Ninety KGB and GRU officers in London were expelled. Fifteen others on leave in the Soviet Union were told they would not be allowed to return, making a grand total of 105. Moscow Center was stunned. The expulsions marked a major turning point in the history of KGB operations in the United Kingdom. Even in the mid-1980s, operations in Britain during the generation before the expulsions were still presented as a model for young intelligence officers at the FCD training school, the Andropov Institute. The three main faculty heads in the institute had all made their reputations in the London residency in the period before 1971. Yuri Modin, who was in charge of offensive intelligence training, was a former controller of the Magnificent Five. Ivan Shishkin, head of counterintelligence training, had run the KR (counterintelligence) line in London from 1966 to 1970 and was, in Gordievsky's view, the KGB's leading expert on the British intelligence community. Vladimir Barkovsky, who ran training in scientific and technological espionage, had specialized in that field in London from 1941 to 1946. In 1971 the golden age of KGB operations came to an end. The London residency never recovered from the 1971 expulsions. Contrary to the popular myths generated by media "revelations" about Soviet moles, during the next fourteen years, up to Gordievsky's defection, the KGB found it more difficult to collect high-grade intelligence in London than in almost any other Western capital.

The much-reduced number of KGB and GRU agents found themselves under much tighter surveillance. The London resident at the time of the expulsions, Yuri Voronin, was on leave in the Soviet Union and not allowed to return to Britain. Since the British government had embarked on what proved to be an effective policy of not allowing visas to identified intelligence officers, the Center was unable to install any of its favored candidates to succeed Voronin. Instead, a junior officer in the KR line, Yevgeni Ivanovich Lazebny, who worked as security officer at the trade delegation and had somehow escaped expulsion, was put in charge. During his fourteen months as acting resident, Lazebny tried to preserve his cover by keeping his office in the trade delegation and visiting the embassy each day to deal with residency matters. He proved totally out of his depth.

Lazebny was succeeded as resident at the end of 1972 by Yakov Konstantinovich Lukasevics (*alias* Bukashev), who owed his inflated reputation to his youthful success in the postwar deception operation in Latvia. Lukasevics lacked the flair of the previous generation of residents. He reminded Gordievsky of a small-town provincial policeman with little education and narrow political horizons. Moscow was impressed by the fact that there were no further expulsions during his eight years as resident. But when at the end of that period he had made little progress in rebuilding KGB operations in Britain, he was sidelined for the remainder of his career to a minor job in Latvia.[141]

In both Britain and the United States by far the most important KGB penetrations in the Brezhnev era and beyond were in sigint. By an astonishing coincidence, two of the KGB's most important agents were recruited within days of each other. Both were walk-ins. Early in January 1968 Corporal Geoffrey Arthur Prime was returning to the RAF sigint station at Gatow in West Berlin after his Christmas leave. As he passed through a Soviet checkpoint in Berlin, he handed a message to a Russian officer asking to be contacted by Soviet Intelligence.[142] A few days later, Chief Warrant Officer John Anthony Walker, a communications watch officer on the staff of the commander of submarine forces in the Atlantic (COMSUBLANT), drove from his base in Norfolk, Virginia, to Washington, D.C., parked his car downtown, looked up the address of the Soviet embassy in a telephone-booth directory, and hailed a taxi, which dropped him a block away from the embassy. Walker asked for "someone from security." He brought with him a month's key settings for the KL-47 cipher machine.[143]

Though Prime and Walker played similar roles within the KGB agent network, they had quite different personalities. Prime was a sexual and social misfit, a truant at school and a loner in the RAF. Unable to develop normal sexual relationships, he began making obscene telephone calls in 1962. By 1969, after a first marriage that was almost instantly unhappy, he was making indecent calls to little girls. Increasingly, Prime blamed his problems and the setbacks in his career on the capitalist system. He was attracted by the propaganda image of the Soviet Union and the people's democracies presented by *Soviet Weekly* and the Russian and East German broadcasts to which he listened. After his arrest in 1982, he claimed that he had begun work for the KGB "partly as a result of a misplaced idealistic view of Russian Communism which was compounded by basic psychological problems within himself."[144]

The note that Prime left at the Berlin checkpoint was passed to officers not from the First Chief Directorate but from the comparatively lowly Third Directorate. Though its main responsibility was the security and surveillance of the Soviet armed forces, the Third Directorate sometimes succeeded in making (usually low-level) recruits among the Western troops stationed in Germany. It was anxious to steal a march on the more prestigious FCD by gaining the credit for Prime's recruitment.[145] In his note Prime had asked an intelligence officer to meet him at a restaurant on the Leibnitzstrasse. Instead he found a message in a magnetic cylinder attached to the handle of his car door, giving him a rendezvous at the Friedrichstrasse S-Bahn station in East Berlin.

At a series of meetings with two Third Directorate case officers whom he knew only as Igor and Valya,[146] Prime was closely questioned both about himself and about his sigint work at Gatow. Though he claimed that his motives were ideological, he was given £30–40 at each meeting. His engagement with the RAF was due to end in August. In agreement with his controllers, he applied, successfully, for a job processing Russian intercepts at GCHQ. Before taking up his new job at the end of September, Prime spent a week at an apartment in the KGB compound at Karlshorst, being trained in radio transmission, cipher communication, microdots, photography with a Minox camera, and the use of dead-letter boxes. After each day's training, he was locked in the apartment for the night. Before flying back to Britain, changing planes at Hamburg, Prime was given the code name Rowlands and a briefcase containing a set of one-time pads, secret writing materials, and £400 in banknotes hidden in a secret compartment.

Prime's first six and a half years with GCHQ were spent at its London Processing Group (LPG), a specialist transcription service based in St. Dunstan's Hill. By the autumn of 1969 he had completed his training, passed the Linguist Specialist Open Competition, and begun work as a transcriber. He was informed by radio of a dead-letter box near Esher in Surrey. In it he found a letter of congratulations from Moscow Center and £400. Prime was unpopular at GCHQ and generally regarded as withdrawn and unsociable. For two reasons, however, he did not attract suspicion. "First," as a later Security Commission report disarmingly put it, "because of the nature of GCHQ's work and their need for staff with esoteric specialisms, they attracted many odd and eccentric characters." Second, his morose appearance was put down to his unhappy marriage and to his resentment at being passed over for promotion in favor of abler linguists than himself, who, he complained, were selected simply because they were graduates.[147]

While Prime was a loner, Walker was the life and soul of many parties. At bars in ports around the world, he liked to call out: "Bartender! I'll have a shot of the scotch that's named after me—Johnnie Walker."[148] His criminal career had begun early. He joined the navy as a teenage high school dropout to escape punishment after four serious burglaries. When he got into debt after the failure of business ventures, he tried to force his wife into prostitution to restore his finances. Walker drew his family into his work for the KGB. When his daughter's pregnancy threatened to interfere with his espionage, he tried to persuade her to have an abortion. Yet, despite an unprepossessing appearance (even with his expensive hairpiece), Walker had the power to manipulate and deceive family, friends, mistresses, colleagues, and superiors. A fitness report by his commanding officer concluded in 1972:

CWO-2 Walker is intensely loyal, taking great pride in himself and the naval service, fiercely supporting its principles and traditions. He possesses a fine sense of personal honor and integrity, coupled with a great sense of humor. He is friendly, intelligent and possesses the ability to work in close harmony with others.[149]

By the time this tribute was composed, Walker had been a KGB agent for four years. After walking into the Soviet embassy in Washington and displaying samples of his wares, he announced that he had total access at COMSUBLANT to cipher machines and keys and asked for a salary of $1,000 a week. He was given an advance of $2,000 or $3,000 (he could not later remember which) and arranged a further meeting a few weeks later at an Alexandria department store. Walker was then dressed in a large coat and hat, taken out a back door of the embassy, and driven out of the gates with his head down on the back seat, sheltered by a large Russian on either side. At the meeting in Alexandria in February Walker handed over a series of cipher key cards. In return he was given $5,000—an enormous sum by the KGB standards of the time and a clear indication of his exceptional importance. He was told that, for security reasons, there would be no more personal meetings except in an emergency. Communication would take place through DLBs. He was given detailed instructions, maps and photographs of sites, and a Minox camera. Walker found photographing Top Secret messages and cipher material with the Minox in the COMSUBLANT communications center so easy that he later claimed scornfully, "K Mart has better security than the navy." Walker's abused wife knew that her husband was a spy. Twice before their divorce in 1976, Mrs. Walker called the FBI before her courage failed her and she hung up. Instead, she took to drink.[150]

During the late 1960s the head of the KR line in Washington, whose responsibilities included penetration of the American intelligence community, was Oleg Kalugin. The development of Walker as the KGB's most important penetration agent in the United States was probably at the top of the list of successes that led to Kalugin's meteoric rise within the FCD; in 1974 he became its youngest general.[151] Some senior officers in Moscow Center argued that previous penetration agents inside British and American sigint agencies had not been fully exploited because they had been handled with insufficient care. Jack

Dunlap in NSA had committed suicide in 1963 when the pressure on him became too great. Douglas Britten, the KGB mole in RAF sigint, had been discovered through routine MI5 surveillance of the Soviet consulate in London, where he attempted to contact his controller.[152] Walker was handled quite differently.

The simultaneous recruitment of Prime and Walker helped to prompt a major reorganization of KGB sigint. Hitherto the Eighth Directorate had handled sigint as well as KGB ciphers and communications security. In 1969 a new Sixteenth Directorate was established under Nikolai Nikolayevich Andreyev to specialize exclusively in sigint. Andreyev was succeeded in 1973 by Major General Igor Vasilyevich Maslov. The new directorate worked closely with the Sixteenth Department of the First Chief Directorate, which thenceforth had exclusive control of all FCD operations to acquire foreign codes and ciphers, and to penetrate sigint agencies. Its officers in foreign residencies handled only one case each, which they kept entirely apart from the rest of the residencies' operations.[153] They maintained a remarkable level of secrecy even within the FCD. As KGB security officer in the Washington residency from 1975 to 1980, Vitali Sergeevich Yurchenko was entirely unaware of the existence of John Walker, the residency's most important agent.[154] It was also a strict Sixteenth Department rule never to meet its agents in the countries in which they worked. The Sixteenth Department's favorite meeting places were Vienna, Helsinki, and New Delhi, the three major capitals outside the Soviet Bloc where the KGB operated with the greatest freedom.[155]

Though Walker was taken over by an FCD Sixteenth Department case officer, Prime continued to be run by the Third Directorate, which refused to hand over its star agent to the rival FCD. He was given the choice of meeting his case officer in either Finland or Austria. Possibly because of his knowledge of German, he chose Austria. Prime probably also met his case officer during holidays in the Irish Republic in 1970, Rome in 1971, and Cyprus in 1972. Most of his contacts with the KGB, however, conducted via DLBs, were letters containing secret writing and broadcasts from Moscow.[156] Walker's communication with the FCD Sixteenth Department was even more secretive. After his rendezvous at an Alexandria department store in February 1968, he had no further direct personal contact with the KGB until August 1977, when he met his Sixteenth Department controller in Casablanca.

Thereafter, since Walker had retired from the navy in the previous year and was running a navy friend, Jerry Alfred Whitworth, as a subagent, his controller arranged to meet him about twice a year. Walker was given the choice of meeting in India or Austria. He chose Vienna. Though Walker sometimes ignored its advice, the Sixteenth Department continually urged caution on him: "If it's not safe, don't do it." The KGB's ideological message to both men, which Walker disregarded but which probably had some appeal to Prime, was simplistic: both were serving the cause of world peace. "We only want peace," they were told. "The imperialists want war."[157]

Though the Third Directorate's handling of Prime was less sophisticated than the Sixteenth Department's running of Walker, it preserved the same tight security. At no point either during Prime's seven and a half years with the London Processing Group (September 1968 to March 1976) or during his eighteen months at GCHQ Cheltenham (March 1976 to September 1977) did he come under suspicion. After leaving GCHQ he found employment as a taxi driver and wine salesman, and broke off contact with the KGB for three years. In 1980, however, the KGB renewed contact and persuaded him to meet his case officer in Vienna, where he handed over fifteen reels of film (most of which, he was told, did not develop properly) and some photocopies and notes that had been in his possession since he left GCHQ. The case officer did not criticize him either for leaving GCHQ or for breaking contact, but encouraged him unsuccessfully to rejoin GCHQ. He was given £600 on his departure.

In 1981 Prime traveled to Potsdam to answer questions about the documents he had handed over in the previous year. This time it was suggested, also unsuccessfully, that he become a Russian teacher at the Royal Army Education Corps, Beaconsfield, to act as a KGB talent spotter. He was given £4,000 as a leaving present.[158] Prime's espionage was not discovered by MI5 and GCHQ until he was arrested for sexually molesting little girls in the summer of 1982. Third Directorate operations remained so well insulated from the First Chief Directorate that Gordievsky, who had been working on the British desk at Moscow Center since 1981 and arrived at the London residency in June 1982, did not learn of the Prime case until after Prime's arrest.[159]

A Pentagon damage assessment on the Prime case put the cost to the U.K.–U.S. sigint alliance at a billion dollars. For a decade Prime had given the KGB comprehensive intelligence on GCHQ operating procedures, personnel, and bases at home and abroad; during his year at Cheltenham in 1976–77 he had access to high-grade intelligence about GCHQ's successes and failures in decrypting Soviet traffic and to details of two top secret American satellite intelligence systems, Big Bird and Rhyolite. The KGB owed its most important intelligence on U.S. satellites, however, to two American walk-ins. From April 1975 to late 1976 an American drug dealer, Andrew Daulton Lee, supplied the KGB residency in Mexico City with the operating manual for Rhyolite and detailed technical data on other satellite systems obtained from his friend Christopher Boyce, who worked for Rhyolite's manufacturer, TRW Corporation in California. Early in 1978 William Kampiles, who had been briefly employed by the Watch Center at CIA headquarters, traveled to Greece and walked into the KGB residency in Athens with the manual for KH-11 (Keyhole), the most advanced U.S. sigint satellite.[160]

Though Prime was the most important KGB mole in British sigint since Cairncross in 1942–43, the Lee/Boyce and Kampiles walk-ins suggest that the billion-dollar price tag put on his intelligence by the Pentagon may be exaggerated. After Prime's arrest criticisms of the Third Directorate's handling of the case began to circulate in the FCD. The Third Directorate had failed to maintain the continuous contact with Prime that the FCD Sixteenth Department established with Walker. At precisely the moment during his year in Cheltenham when he had the best access to GCHQ secrets, Third Directorate coded radio messages to him had become unreadable and contact with him had been broken. As a result much of what he learned at Cheltenham was only passed on to his case officer at their meeting in Vienna in 1980.[161]

No such problems arose in the Sixteenth Department's handling of the Walker case. John Walker worked for the KGB for seventeen years until his much-abused ex-wife finally summoned up the nerve to report him to the FBI in 1985. In addition to running Jerry Whitworth as a subagent for nine years, Walker recruited his son and elder brother in the early 1980s; he also tried, but failed, to recruit his daughter. He provided comprehensive information and technical manuals used not only by the navy but by the other armed services, the State Department, the CIA, and the FBI. The Sixteenth Directorate also required the daily keys used with the cipher machines in order to decrypt their cipher traffic. Walker's spy ring provided so many of these keys that a damage assessment after his arrest estimated that he had enabled Soviet cryptanalysts to decrypt a million U.S. messages. The most obvious Soviet gain from the decrypts was foreknowledge of U.S. operations. According to Theodore Shackley, CIA station chief in Saigon from 1968 to 1973 in the final phases of the Vietnam War:

They usually had forewarning of the B-52 strikes. Even when the B-52s diverted to secondary targets because of the weather, they knew in advance which targets would be hit. Naturally, the foreknowledge diminished the effectiveness of the strikes because they were ready. It was uncanny. We never figured it out.

Though doubtless an exaggerated estimate of Soviet and North Vietnamese foreknowledge, Shackley's assessment provides a powerful insight into the shattering psychological effect in warfare of the discovery that operational plans have leaked to the enemy. The U.S. Navy frequently discovered when they staged supposedly secret exercises that Soviet ships were close at hand. "It is as if they had a copy of the Op P plans," complained one admiral.[162] There were times when Moscow Center must have felt in exactly that position. During one of their meetings Walker's case officer solemnly informed him that, in recognition of his outstanding contribution to world peace, he had been awarded the rank of admiral in the Soviet navy. "Tell them thanks a lot," replied Walker.[163]

The Prime and Walker cases epitomize the problems and opportunities of KGB operations in Britain and the United States during the Brezhnev era. At the end of the Second World War the most important KGB penetration agents—the Magnificent Five in Britain; White, Hiss, Lee, and Currie in the United States—had been ideologically motivated high fliers with the apparent prospect of careers that would take them to the top of the government service. By the Brezhnev era the golden age of the brilliantly talented Anglo-American ideological mole was long past. The most important penetration agents in Britain and the United States during the 1970s were two cunning petty criminals, one with a record of burglary, the other with an undetected history of (as yet minor) sexual offenses, neither possessed of any exceptional talent, but both in low-level jobs that gave them access to some of the U.K.–U.S. alliance's most important sigint secrets.

13

The Decline and Fall of Détente
(1972–84)

On June 20, 1972, the First Chief Directorate moved into new head-quarters designed by a Finnish architect at Yasenevo, southeast of Moscow, half a mile beyond the outer ring road. The building had originally been intended for the International Department of the Central Committee. While it was under construction, however, the Central Committee decided that the site was too far from the center of Moscow and surrendered it to the KGB. The main Y-shaped office building was flanked on one side by an assembly hall and library, on the other by a clinic, sports complex, and swimming pool. Around the FCD compound was a double ring of fencing with guard dogs in between and armed sentries patrolling the perimeter. In the large grounds a massive head of Lenin on a granite block overlooked an ornamental lake. To celebrate the sixtieth anniversary of the KGB on December 20, 1977, a further monument was erected on the grounds to the "unknown intelligence officer." From the office windows there were fine views over hills covered with birch trees, green pastures, and, in summer, fields of wheat and rye.

Each day a massive fleet of buses brought staff from various Moscow locations, arriving at Yasenevo at intervals between 8:20 and 8:50 A.M. A fortunate minority (still only about 5 percent even in the mid-1980s) arrived by car; more private cars were—and are—parked at the FCD than anywhere else in Russia. The working day began officially at 9 A.M. On their arrival FCD staff passed through three checkpoints: at one of the outer gates, at the main entrance gate in the perimeter fence, and at the entrance to the building itself. Further checks followed between different sections of the building. The ordinary KGB identity card, with the name, rank, and photograph of the bearer, was not valid at Yasenevo. Each FCD officer was issued a new plastic pass that carried his (or occasionally her) photograph and identity number but no name. On the pass was a grid with holes punched to indicate parts of the building the bearer was not permitted to enter. Passes were never taken abroad. FCD officers working in foreign countries left them for safekeeping in their departments at the Center. Non-FCD visitors at Yasenevo were rare and almost always very senior. When FCD officers had discussions with those of other KGB directorates or with government or party officials, the meetings usually took place in central Moscow. The working day ended at 6 P.M. Buses left promptly at 6:15 P.M., removing the signs indicating their destinations once their passengers were on board. As they set off, police halted all other traffic on the outer Moscow ring road to speed them on their way.

Despite the elaborate security precautions, however, the FCD never, in Gordievsky's time, solved the problem of the canteen. Staggered by the quality and variety of the food they served, the canteen staff recruited in local villages stuffed as much as possible into their pockets. When they were strip-searched, however, they refused to come to work, and the searches were abandoned. The FCD probably continues today to improve the dreary diet of local villages via the pockets of its canteen staff.[1]

About a year before the move to Yasenevo, Aleksandr Sakharovsky had retired after a record fifteen years as head of the FCD. He was succeeded by his fifty-three-year-old former deputy, Fyodor Konstantinovich Mortin, a career KGB officer who had risen steadily through the ranks as a loyal protégé of Sakharovsky. Except for short trips as an occasional trouble-shooter to KGB residencies, he had no firsthand experience and little understanding of the West. In the new complex at Yasenevo, however, he presided in some style. Each day he and other senior figures in the FCD arrived at Yasenevo in their chauffeured black Zil or Volga limousines and entered the new headquarters by their own entrance and private elevator. Mortin had a large suite on the second floor with adjoining bedroom and bathroom. Though he had been a reliable, efficient second fiddle to Sakharovsky, rumors spread within the Center that Andropov found him too lightweight at a time when he was building up his own political power base. In 1974 Mortin was moved to a post as head of the Chief Directorate for Scientific and Industrial Cooperation in the U.S.S.R. State Committee for Science and Technology (GKNT), a key post in scientific and technological intelligence usually held by a KGB officer.[2]

Mortin's successor at Yasenevo was one of the toughest of Andropov's own personal protégés, the fifty-year-old Vladimir Aleksandrovich Kryuchkov, who was almost to equal Sakharovsky's record term as head of the FCD. After fourteen years at Yasenevo he was to become chairman of the KGB in 1988. Kryuchkov's official photographs, in which the corners of his mouth turn decisively downward, show a tough, unsmiling Tartar exterior thinly concealing a tough, unsmiling interior. Throughout his years in the FCD he displayed enormous energy, single-mindedness, and self-confidence, combined with administrative skill and political flair. He was also a humorless workaholic. In Gordievsky's experience he never strayed from his prepared texts at FCD meetings, never tried to coin a striking phrase, never showed any sign of a sense of humor.[3] In 1989, Kryuchkov was asked by an interviewer, "Do you know what 'spare time' means?" "I'm afraid not," he replied.[4]

Kryuchkov was fond of stressing his working-class credentials by recalling that he started out in life as a factory worker. He graduated from the U.S.S.R. Institute of Law by taking correspondence courses in the evening and served for some years as investigating officer and procurator. Then came what Kryuchkov called "a change in life": training at the Foreign Ministry's Higher Diplomatic School followed by five years (1954–59) at the Soviet embassy in Budapest, where he became a protégé of the ambassador Yuri Andropov. From 1959 to 1967 he worked, initially under Andropov, in the Central Committee's Department for Relations with Socialist Countries, dealing with the Warsaw Pact and other countries with ruling Communist parties. He said later of this period in his life:

Today it is "modish" to assail the Party apparatus. However, I would like to say that I learned a lot there and met some wonderful dedicated people, despite the unpleasant exceptions that are the case everywhere.[5]

He derived from these years a consummate mastery of Central Committee politics and personal intrigue. When Andropov became KGB chairman in 1967, Kryuchkov became head of his secretariat and custodian of the KGB's most sensitive secrets. In about 1971 he moved to the First Chief Directorate as deputy head, responsible for European intelligence, succeeding Mortin as head three years later.[6]

As well as being a workaholic, Kryuchkov was a fitness fanatic. He had the unnerving habit when talking to FCD officers of using hand exercisers or squeezing tennis balls to strengthen his grip. He had his own private gymnasium, complete with a massage table, constructed in the new FCD headquarters. Next to the gymnasium was Kryuchkov's personal sauna, where he sometimes had discussions with other KGB generals. Though only the most senior officers ever visited Kryuchkov in his sauna, Gordievsky was shown around it while on night duty one evening by a member of Kryuchkov's secretariat. It was the most luxurious sauna he has seen anywhere in the world, with the best that hard currency could buy: expensive wood specially imported from Finland instead of the usual Russian pine, elegant, specially designed Scandinavian fittings and lamps. There was a large array of imported fluffy towels and dressing gowns. Next to the sauna-gymnasium complex was a dining area, but no drinks cupboard. Kryuchkov was a teetotaler and caused dismay in the tradionally bibulous FCD by banning drinking parties for officers about to take up foreign postings.

Kryuchkov's main handicap on becoming head of the FCD was his complete lack of personal experience of intelligence operations and of life in the West. Gordievsky first met him in 1972 shortly before his posting as a PR line (political intelligence) officer in Copenhagen. Kryuchkov, who was then Mortin's deputy, immediately asked Gordievsky, "Tell me how you intend to acquire contacts when you get to Denmark." Having only just moved from Directorate S (Illegals), Gordievsky was about to give a reply that would later have struck him as naïve. As soon as he began to speak, however, Kryuchkov interrupted him with a monologue that continued for the remainder of the interview. To Gordievsky's amazement, Kryuchkov's views were even more naïve than his own, largely because of his ignorance of Western society. Those views derived from a series of ideologically based stereotypes and conspiracy theories, which began to soften only in the late 1980s. He did not take kindly to contrary opinions. The FCD's two most brilliant and level-headed analysts of British and American policy, Oleg Kalugin and Mikhail Lyubimov, were both removed from the Center in 1980 for disputing Kryuchkov's conspiracy theories. As head of the FCD, Kryuchkov relied increasingly on sycophants who exploited his growing weakness for personal flattery.[7]

The FCD's move to Yasenevo and Kryuchkov's emergence as its head coincided with the period of greatest Soviet-American détente between the onset of the Cold War and the Gorbachev era. In May 1972 Richard Nixon paid the first ever official visit to the U.S.S.R. by an American president. Brezhnev visited the United States in June 1973 and Nixon paid a second visit to Moscow a year later. More Soviet-American agreements were signed in these two years than in the entire previous period since the establishment of diplomatic relations. Chief among them were the Treaty on the Limitation of Anti-Ballistic Missile Systems and the first Strategic Arms Limitation Agreement (SALT 1), both signed during Nixon's first Moscow visit. "The historians of some future age," prophesied Nixon, "will write of Year 1972 . . . that this was the year when America helped to lead the world out of the lowlands of constant war to the high plateau of peace."[8] Though rivalry between the two superpowers continued, they seemed to have both the will and the capacity to join in preventing a nuclear Armageddon.

Gordievsky's main memory of the mood in Moscow Center was that at long last the United States was treating the Soviet Union as an equal. Nixon's resignation in August 1974, under threat of impeachment for his involvement in the Watergate scandal, gave rise to both dismay and suspicion. Dmitri Ivanovich Yakushkin arrived as KGB main resident in Washington early in 1975, already convinced that Nixon's fall was due less to public indignation over Watergate than to a conspiracy by the enemies of détente, in particular the Zionists, whose machinations via the Jewish lobby he saw all about him, and the "United States military-industrial complex," which he believed was trying to prevent lower arms expenditure.[9]

Underlying Yakushkin's misreading of the Watergate crisis was a much more basic misunderstanding of the American political system and way of life that was widespread in both the Center and the Kremlin. As so frequently before, their vision was constricted by ideological blinkers. Accustomed to strong central direction and a command economy, most KGB officers, like most Soviet diplomats, could not fathom how the United States could achieve such high levels of production, efficiency, and technological innovation with so little apparent regulation. The gap in Soviet understanding of what made the United States tick tended to be filled by conspiracy theory. The diplomat Arkadi Nikolayevich Shevchenko, who defected in 1978 while undersecretary general of the United Nations, noted of his Soviet colleagues:

> Many are inclined toward the fantastic notion that there must be a secret control center somewhere in the United States. They themselves, after all, are used to a system ruled by a small group working in secrecy in one place. Moreover, the Soviets continue to chew on Lenin's dogma that bourgeois governments are just the "servants" of monopoly capital. "Is that not the secret control center?" they reason.[10]

The period of U.S.-Soviet détente in the middle of the Brezhnev era was made possible partly by the presence in Washington of an unusually sophisticated Soviet diplomat, Anatoli Fyodorovich Dobrynin, ambassador from March 1963 to March 1986. Dobrynin's secret discussions with Henry Kissinger, Nixon's national security adviser (and later secretary of State), provided what the Center called a "back channel" between Moscow and Washington, and paved the way for détente. Kissinger was later to eulogize Dobrynin's "central contribution" to improved relations and the "consummate skill" of his diplomacy. But there were limits to Dobrynin's ability to challenge the conspiracy theories popular in Moscow. He was sometimes accused of becoming "Americanized" by opponents in the Central Committee and Foreign Ministry. Dobrynin felt forced to defend himself by pandering to at least some of Moscow's prejudices. According to Shevchenko:

> Although he understands the US governmental system, even Dobrynin dared not produce an accurate analysis of the division of power in America between the executive and legislative branches during the Watergate débacle.[11]

At least at a rhetorical level, détente survived the demise of Nixon. In August 1975 the Helsinki Final Act, the end product of the Conference on Security and Cooperation in Europe, pronounced all European frontiers "inviolable" and bound the major states of East and West to abide by enlightened standards of conduct in international relations and to respect human rights at home. "Helsinki Watch Groups," set up in the Soviet Union to monitor observance of the human rights thus guaranteed, were gradually closed down by the KGB, which arrested or banished into internal exile most of their members.

Nixon's successor and former vice-president, Gerald Ford, was viewed in the Center with mild contempt. Andrei Gromyko, who like Andropov became a voting member of the Politburo in 1973, wrote condescendingly of him:

> It sometimes happens that a man will occupy a high state position and yet will be written of and spoken of only in passing. Gerald Ford, president for barely two years, belongs in this category.[12]

Dismissive though Moscow was of Ford's ability, it was anxious for him to win the 1976 presidential election. The Kremlin's innate conservatism made it prefer a known lightweight like Ford to the unpredictable Democrat candidate, Jimmy Carter. Under Ford, it was believed, the "back channel" between Dobrynin and Kissinger could continue. As the election approached, both the Soviet embassy and the residency in Washington received increasingly urgent appeals for advance notification of the winner. "The Center," Dobrynin told Shevchenko, "has been bombarding Washington for months."[13] Both the embassy and the residency seem to have hedged their election bets.

Though one of the best-educated presidents since the Second World War, Jimmy Carter took office in 1977 as both an outsider in Washington and a novice in diplomacy. Gromyko was even more scornful of Carter than of Ford:

> Being a diligent man, Carter did his best, but when he tried to pronounce the names of towns and regions in the Soviet Union all that came out was a sequence of incomprehensible noises. More worryingly, we quickly discovered that he had difficulty in grasping even the most elementary basic features of the Soviet–United States relationship.[14]

After the carnage of Vietnam and the corruption of Watergate, Carter set out to rebuild American foreign policy on the high ground of moral principle and human rights. Soon after his inauguration, academician Andrei Sakharov, the dissident winner of the 1975 Nobel Peace Prize, wrote to Carter asking him to persevere in his campaign for human rights in the Soviet Union. To the outrage of the Kremlin and the KGB,

Carter publicly acknowledged and replied to his letter. Shortly afterward he received another Soviet dissenter, Vladimir Bukovsky, in the White House. Both Yakushkin and the Center mistakenly interpreted Carter's human-rights campaign chiefly as a ploy designed to strengthen the U.S. bargaining position for the next round of strategic arms talks after SALT 1 expired in October 1977.[15]

Service A (Active Measures) attached extreme importance to countering Carter's human-rights campaign by attacking the United States' own record. In 1977, it composed a number of letters to the president's wife, Rosalynn Carter, protesting against "the infringement of human rights" in the United States. While Gordievsky was stationed in Copenhagen, the residency succeeded in persuading a well-known liberal politician to send one of these letters to Mrs. Carter. The residency was so excited that it immediately sent a PR line officer to her hometown to obtain a copy of the letter and satisfy himself that it corresponded to the KGB draft. The two texts matched exactly, and a triumphant report was sent to the Center.[16]

The trials of Soviet human-rights activists in 1978 brought further official American condemnations. The KGB hit back with a crude attempt to link the Jewish dissident Anatoli Shcharansky with the CIA; he was sentenced to ten years in jail on a trumped-up charge by the KGB of passing secret information to an American journalist.[17] Though well aware that it had fabricated this particular plot, the KGB convinced itself that there was nonetheless a real conspiracy by the CIA and the White House to manipulate the human-rights campaign in the Soviet Union. Gromyko continued to insist even in the era of *glasnost* that the campaign was part and parcel of American "ideological subversion against the U.S.S.R. . . . Carter took a personal hand in the campaign of provocation."[18]

Détente in the 1970s was always fragile. Brezhnev was fond of repeating that détente did not alter "the laws of the class struggle." Even at its peak in 1972–74, the United States remained the Main Adversary. The FCD First (United States and Canada) Department was easily the largest geographical department at the Center and grew steadily in size. At the end of the 1960s it had only one deputy head; during the 1970s it acquired two more. It was also the only department that controlled two "main residencies" (a status accorded to the Washington and New York residencies in the early 1970s) run by KGB generals, as well as a third residency in San Francisco. The size of the KGB presence in both the United States and the UN delegation in New York increased more rapidly at the height of détente than at any other period: from about 120 officers in 1970 to 220 in 1975. At the very moment when the London residency was being sharply cut back, those in the United States were almost doubling in size.[19]

Washington was the chief center for political intelligence. Yakushkin, main resident from 1975 to 1982, was proud of his descent from one of the Decembrist conspirators of 1825. He also probably enjoyed the Washington *Post*'s assessment of him in 1982 as "the most powerful KGB officer outside the Soviet Union."[20] His period in Washington, however, was marred by one major embarrassment. A passer-by threw a packet into the grounds of the Soviet embassy on Sixteenth Street, not far from the White House. When opened, it contained what appeared to be classified documents, the sender's name and address, and the offer of more intelligence. Yakushkin dismissed the whole affair as a provocation and ordered the packet to be handed to the police. The documents, however, turned out to be genuine, and the sender was arrested.

Despite this contretemps, Yakushkin became head of the FCD First Department on his return to Moscow in 1982. Gordievsky found the atmosphere in the department more strained than anywhere else in the Center. Part of the explanation was Yakushkin's domineering behavior, which was in sharp contrast to the suave diplomatic manner for which he had become known at Washington cocktail parties. When roused, he bellowed into the phone at a higher rate of decibels than anyone else in Yasenevo. But the charged atmosphere in the First Department also resulted from its own prestige. The intense competition to gain entry to it and promotion within it gave rise to a higher level of intrigue than in any other department.[21]

On becoming head of the FCD, Kryuchkov rapidly introduced a series of organizational changes designed to take advantage of the new opportunities created by détente for work against the Main Adversary. A new Group North was set up within the First Department to coordinate intelligence operations against American targets in other parts of the world. Its first head was Vadim Kirpichenko, the former resident in Cairo who had recruited Nasser's intelligence chief Sami Sharaf. Residencies in most parts of the West and the Third World were instructed to set up "Main Adversary Groups" to organize operations against United states targets. Such groups usually contained one or two officers from Lines PR (political intelligence) and KR (counterintelligence), and one from Line X (scientific and technological intelligence), under a Line PR chairman. Officers from Group North occasionally visited residencies to inspect the work of Main Adversary Groups. Gordievsky's impression was that, because of bureaucratic rivalries, these attempts at coordination achieved at best only partial success.

The rapid expansion of contacts with the West at the height of détente initially persuaded Kryuchkov that new methods of intelligence collection should be employed against the Main Adversary. The hemorrhage of American official secrets as the Watergate scandal developed and the sensational revelations of investigative journalists convinced him that the traditional tradecraft of agent recruitment was becoming outmoded. Many secrets seemed to be there for the taking. On taking charge of the FCD in 1974, to the horror of Center veterans, he instructed residencies to concentrate on building up large numbers of overt contacts willing to talk openly about official secrets rather than engage in the much slower and more labor-intensive methods of cultivating and recruiting secret agents. A few disastrous experiences in Western restaurants, with KGB officers under diplomatic cover abandoning their traditional tradecraft and trying to imitate Bob Woodward and Carl Bernstein of the Washington *Post,* quickly persuaded Kryuchkov to abandon the experiment. He subsequently laid even greater emphasis than many of his department heads on the need to recruit a new generation of penetration agents in the West.[22]

The flowering of détente in the early 1970s also led to an attempt to exploit the neglected talents of Kim Philby, who began to dry out after his marriage to Rufa in 1971. The first to renew contact with Philby was the Center's leading British expert, Mikhail Petrovich Lyubimov, whom Gordievsky considered one of the most talented and likable FCD officers of his generation, with a deep knowledge of both English literature and Scottish single malts. Lyubimov had served at the London residency for four years before being expelled in 1964 at the age of thirty-one for trying to recruit a cipher operator. For two years after his return to Moscow he helped to debrief Philby. In the early 1970s Lyubimov began working on a thesis entitled "Special Traits of the British National Character and Their Use in Operational Work," which he discussed at length with Philby and presented with great success at the FCD's Andropov Institute in 1974. He subsequently used the thesis as the basis of the FCD's main classified textbook on the United Kingdom, which was still in use in the mid-1980s. Unable to become resident in London, where he was *persona non grata,*

Lyubimov was posted instead to Copenhagen in 1975.

Philby's other main patron was Oleg Danilovich Kalugin, the young and dynamic head of the FCD's Directorate K (responsible for counterintelligence, including the penetration of hostile intelligence services). During regular visits to Philby's apartment, Kalugin sought his advice on intelligence strategy in Britain. Philby argued plausibly that since the Foreign Office was increasingly seeking to recruit from provincial universities as well as from Oxbridge, SIS was probably doing the same. He suggested that the universities of Bradford, Bristol, Birmingham, Edinburgh, Essex, Hull, London (including the London School of Economics and the School of Oriental and African Studies), Salford, Surrey, and Sussex were worth detailed "study" by the KGB and that exchange visits to Russia by their students offered promising opportunities for recruitment.[23]

Philby was also consulted by the FCD's Service A (responsible for active measures designed to influence foreign governments and public opinion) on the production of forged documents allegedly emanating from the CIA, the State Department, and other imperialist agencies. Gordievsky was impressed by the quality of Philby's active measures work (though not by much of the rest of Service A's output)—all of it carried out in his apartment. During the winter months, from October to April, Philby ran seminars in a safe apartment on Gorky Street for young officers from the FCD Third Department (responsible for Britain, Ireland, Scandinavia, Malta, and Australasia) who were about to go on their first foreign postings. In the course of the seminars he set them problems and organized operational games in which he took the part of a politician, civil servant, intelligence officer, or businessman whom the student was trying to recruit.

At the end of each series of seminars Philby wrote reports on his students. Some were remarkably percipient. He described Valeri Aleksandrovich Kislov, who was due to be posted to the Copenhagen residency, as "unpredictable and liable to be carried away by his emotions." Once in Denmark Kislov fell in love with a married woman, followed her around in an embassy car, and was eventually sent home in disgrace by the KGB resident after he was found standing dejectedly outside her country home. One of Philby's lowest assessments was given to Viktor Ivanovich Muzalyov who, he said, had taken his course twice and learned nothing on either occasion. Muzalyov served in the London residency from 1983 to 1985 and Gordievsky fully endorsed Philby's judgment. He was expelled from London after Gordievsky's defection, though from the British point of view there was much to be said for allowing him to stay.

Philby was also sometimes consulted by the Third Department on operational problems, though the dossiers taken to his apartment invariably had the most sensitive material removed from them. Kryuchkov, however, remained suspicious of the sometimes unorthodox ideas both of Philby and of his two main patrons, Lyubimov and Kalugin, neither of whom concealed his scorn for some of the simplistic conspiracy theories about the West prevalent in the Center. In 1980 Kalugin was packed off to become deputy head of the Leningrad KGB after an argument with Kryuchkov. At about the same time, Lyubimov's divorce was used as a pretext to dismiss him from the Center on the grounds of "immoral" behavior. Philby fell into another deep depression.[24]

Throughout the Brezhnev era and beyond, the Center saw détente as leading not to the end of East-West rivalry but to a less tense form of competition. It saw the Soviet Bloc as still an island of socialism surrounded by Western imperialism in collusion with the Chinese. In order to end that encirclement the Soviet Union had to strengthen its influence in the Third World and its links with non-aligned movements. In Egypt, however, which Moscow had seen in the 1960s as the key to Soviet influence in the Middle East, it was by the early 1970s fighting a rearguard action. The Arab-Israeli Yom Kippur War of 1973 began well for Egypt but ended badly. The Center was well aware that Egypt and Syria had been saved from serious defeat less by Soviet arms than by American pressure on Israel to stop the war. Gordievsky found general agreement in the FCD that further Middle Eastern wars would be against the Soviet interest.

The Center was increasingly suspicious that Sadat was turning to the West rather than the East for the solution both of the Arab-Israeli conflict and of Egypt's economic problems. His unilateral denunciation of the Soviet-Egyptian friendship treaty in March 1976 caused less surprise in the Center than in the Kremlin.[25] Only three weeks earlier Brezhnev had praised the treaty in a major speech as "a long-term basis for relations in conformity with the interests not only of our two countries but also of the Arab world."[26] In November 1976 the Center produced a detailed memorandum *(zapiska)* accurately predicting that Sadat would continue to strengthen his ties with the West, especially the United States. It quoted the former Egyptian prime min-

ister, Aziz Sidiqi, as saying that Sadat's stated readiness for a reconciliation with the Soviet Union was simply "a maneuver." The KGB's assets
in Egypt were declining rapidly. Many of the agents recruited under
Nasser had broken contact. Because of increased surveillance by Egyptian security, meetings with those that remained usually took place in
Cyprus, Beirut, and other locations outside Egypt.[27]

On October 1, 1977, the Soviet Union and the United States
signed a joint statement on the need to resolve the Arab-Israeli conflict.
Brezhnev believed that he had at last secured U.S. recognition of the
Soviet role in Middle Eastern peace negotiations. Almost immediately,
according to the official history of Soviet foreign policy, "Under pressure from Israel, the Carter Administration treacherously violated the
agreement."[28] Only seven weeks after the agreement was signed, Sadat
traveled to Jerusalem to begin a dialogue with the Israelis. His visit was
one of the most stunning diplomatic *coups de théâtre* of modern times.
As Sadat stepped off the plane at Tel Aviv airport on the evening of
November 20, an Israeli radio reporter gasped over the air: "President
Sadat is now inspecting a guard of honor of the Israeli Defense Force.
I'm seeing it, but I don't believe it!" The former Israeli prime minister
Golda Meir said of Sadat and the Israeli prime minister, Menachem
Begin, at the end of the visit: "Never mind the Nobel Peace Prize. Give
them both Oscars!"

With its habitual tendency to conspiracy theory, never more
marked than in its attitude to Zionism and the Jewish lobby in the
United States, the Center saw the visit more as a plot than as a piece
of theater. Washington, it believed, had known about the trip when
signing the agreement with Moscow. Even when writing about Sadat
ten years later, Gromyko could still barely contain his sense of outrage:

> He has been called the "Egyptian darkness," after the big-
> gest dust cloud in human history which settled on Egypt
> 3,500 years ago when the volcanic island of Santorini
> erupted. . . . All his life he had suffered from megalomania,
> but this acquired pathological proportions when he became
> President.[29]

Within the Center Gordievsky heard a number of equally outraged
KGB officers say Sadat should be bumped off. Though there is no
evidence of a KGB assassination plot, he was one of the main targets
of the Center's active measures. Major residencies around the world

were sent a circular drafted by Service A, instructing them to promote stories that Sadat was a former Nazi; that Nasser's testament had described him as psychologically unbalanced and dominated by his wife; that he had a CIA bodyguard; that he was currently a CIA agent; and that, when finally forced to flee from Egypt, the CIA had promised him a villa in Montreux with round-the-clock protection.[30]

The active measures campaign was further intensified after the Camp David "Framework for Peace in the Middle East" was signed by Sadat, Begin, and Carter in September 1978—and instantly denounced by *Pravda* as "a sellout transacted behind the back of the Arab nation, one which serves the interests of Israel, America, imperialism, and the Arab reactionaries."[31] Gordievsky found the Center convinced that Carter and the CIA had lured Sadat into an American-Zionist plot intended to oust Soviet influence from the Middle East. An Israeli-Egyptian peace treaty was signed in March 1979, though plans at Camp David for a broader settlement of the Arab-Israeli dispute came to nothing. Sadat's assassination by Moslem fanatics in October 1981 was greeted in the Center with jubilation.[32]

One of the consequences of the Kremlin's estrangement from Sadat was growing support for the Palestine Liberation Organization (PLO). Its leader, Yasser Arafat, had for some time been cultivated by a KGB officer, Vasili Fyodorovich Samoylenko. Samoylenko served in Austria in the late 1940s and East Germany in the early and mid-1950s. There he became a lieutenant colonel in the KGB at the age of forty. When a PLO delegation visited the Soviet Union in the summer of 1974, Arafat was photographed with Samoylenko at a wreath-laying ceremony in Moscow. An official communiqué during the visit described the PLO as "the sole legitimate representative of the Arab people of Palestine."[33] Thenceforth the KGB trained PLO guerrillas at its Balashikha special-operations training school east of Moscow and provided most of the weapons used in its attacks on Israeli military targets. PLO intelligence officers also attended one-year courses at the FCD's Andropov Institute; while there some were recruited by the KGB.[34]

During the late 1960s Arafat had also been courted by the Cairo resident of the Rumanian foreign intelligence service (DIE), Constantin Munteanu, who brought him to Bucharest late in 1970 to meet Nicolae Ceaușescu. The two men became firm friends (it is fair to add that during the 1970s Ceaușescu was also well received at the White House and Buckingham Palace). Late in 1972 the DIE formed an intelligence alliance with the PLO, supplying it with blank passports, electronic surveillance equipment, and weapons for its operations. "Moscow is helping the PLO build muscles. I'm feeding its brain," Ceauşescu told the acting head of the DIE (and future defector), Ion Pacepa.

In 1975, Arafat and Ceauşescu jointly plotted an ingenious deception of King Hussein of Jordan. Ceauşescu took to Amman an intelligence file on the PLO, which, unknown to Hussein, had been prepared as bait by Arafat's intelligence chief, Hani Hassan, described by Arafat as his "clever fox." Hussein responded to this act of apparent generosity by giving Ceauşescu intelligence files that inadvertently revealed his own sources in the PLO. According to Pacepa, Hassan was "formally recruited" as a DIE agent code-named Annette in 1976, and was periodically paid amounts in hard currency of between $2,500 and $10,000.[35]

Moscow was much more concerned than Ceauşescu by PLO terrorism, some of it practiced by dissident groups opposed to Arafat, some of it secretly connived at by Arafat himself. During the Brezhnev era the Soviet Union was never the godfather of international terrorism depicted by some alarmist Western analysts. The Kremlin had an exaggerated fear that it might itself become a terrorist target. In 1969 a mentally ill army lieutenant succeeded in penetrating the Kremlin and shooting at a car in which he believed Brezhnev was traveling. A year later a group of Jewish refuseniks attempted to hijack an aircraft and divert it to Israel. Throughout the 1970s there were a series of mostly unpublicized—and mostly unsuccessful—hijackings. The case that most alarmed the KGB was the bombing of the Moscow subway by Armenian separatists in 1977. Three Armenians were later shot. It was rumored in the Center that, when the KGB and militia failed to track down those responsible, three other Armenian separatists had been selected as scapegoats in order to demonstrate that terrorists would always be caught and punished.[36]

But if the KGB was not the godfather of Middle Eastern terrorism, neither was it an innocent. Though it disapproved of attacks on civilian targets, the Center was well aware that some of the freedom fighters at Balashika were actual or potential terrorists. It also knew from its agents in the PLO that some terrorist operations were mounted with the help of PLO liaison officers and the Syrian, Libyan, and other embassies in Moscow and other Eastern European capitals.[37] Among those who attended Soviet and Cuban training camps was Ilich Ramírez Sánchez, *alias* Carlos the Jackal, son of a Venezuelan millionaire, who became the most notorious terrorist of the 1970s and early 1980s, working for both PLO splinter groups and Colonel Qaddafi of Libya. In 1975 he led a group of Palestinian and German terrorists who kidnapped the OPEC oil ministers in Vienna and extorted a huge ransom from Iran and Saudi Arabia.[38]

Carlos, however, was far from typical of the Third World guerrillas at Soviet training camps. A 1981 report on a training mission to the Soviet Union by 194 officers from ten different PLO factions suggests serious deficiencies in both the Soviet training and the standard of many PLO recruits. According to the PLO commander, Colonel Rashad Ahmed:

> The participants in the courses did not correctly understand the political aspects of sending military delegations abroad. As a result, the upper echelon of the delegation, namely the participants in the battalion officer courses, refused to study and asked to return, using all sorts of illogical excuses.

Ahmed reported that he had been forced to expel thirteen officers from the training course for offenses that included alcoholism, passing counterfeit money, and sexual "perversion." Had he enforced the code of conduct strictly he would, he claimed, have been forced to send home more than half the officers. He appealed for a higher standard of recruits for future courses in the Soviet Union.[39]

Though in private talks with the leadership Moscow sometimes voiced disquiet about PLO involvement in terrorism, it always maintained publicly that the PLO opposed terrorism. Moscow Radio declared in 1975:

> The PLO command recently took decisive measures to combat terrorism. . . . The PLO proceeds, in its just struggle, from a position of maturity and reality. It is well known that terrorist actions in no way belong to the means of revolutionary struggle; rather they greatly harm such a struggle.[40]

After the Syrian invasion of Lebanon in 1976, however, the Center feared that, as Syria's main arms supplier, the Soviet Union might itself become the target for terrorist attacks by PLO dissidents. On June 11, KGB residencies were warned that "bourgeois propaganda" had persuaded some Palestinians that Moscow supported the Syrian invasion.

There was therefore the possibility of assassination attempts against Soviet representatives abroad. Residencies were ordered to take special security precautions. An attempt was made to deflect Palestinian anger by hurriedly opening a PLO office in Moscow, agreed on in principle during Arafat's visit two years before. The Center also ordered an active measures campaign to distance Moscow from the Syrian intervention. The campaign had some success.[41] On July 15 Cairo Radio broadcast reports from "reliable Arab diplomatic sources" in Beirut of a nonexistent Soviet embargo on arms supplies to Syria. On July 22 in London the *Daily Telegraph* published a report of an equally imaginary Soviet ultimatum to Syria.

Moscow approved Arafat's increasing attempts to win international respectability. In 1979, he was invited to a meeting of the Socialist International in Vienna and began a successful European diplomatic offensive. By 1980 the countries of the European Community, but not the United States, had agreed that the PLO must be a party to peace negotiations in the Middle East. The British foreign secretary, Lord Carrington, declared: "The PLO as such is not a terrorist organization." Arafat's success in driving a wedge between the United States and its European allies considerably enhanced his standing in Moscow. In 1981, Brezhnev gave the PLO formal diplomatic recognition. When Israel attacked PLO bases in Lebanon in 1982, however, Moscow was reproached by the PLO for not coming to its aid.

Moscow Center, meanwhile, was increasingly disturbed by intelligence reports of secret meetings between PLO leaders and American officials. Arafat, it suspected, was giving way to Western efforts, greatly resented in Moscow, to exclude the Soviet Union from a Middle Eastern settlement. Gordievsky was struck by the fact that in official Soviet communications Arafat was no longer addressed as "Comrade"—a sure indication of his demotion in status from a socialist ally to a bourgeois nationalist. The head of the Middle Eastern department in the Foreign Ministry, Oleg Alekseevich Grinevsky, told Soviet diplomats and KGB officers at a meeting in the London embassy, attended by Gordievsky in 1983, that Moscow no longer trusted Arafat. In the long run it hoped that Marxist and "progressive" members of the PLO membership would take over from him. In the meantime, however, Arafat was the only man capable of holding the PLO together. The Soviet Union would continue to give him unenthusiastic public support.[42]

Soviet policy in the Middle East during the Brezhnev era aimed at constructing an "anti-imperialist" bloc against Israel and its American protector. For most of the 1970s Moscow's closest links were with Iraq, with which it signed a friendship treaty in 1972. Soon afterward the KGB concluded a liaison agreement with Iraqi intelligence. By 1977 liaison was so close that Iraq became the only country in the non-Communist world where Soviet espionage was discontinued. The Center took the unprecedented step of ordering all residencies to cease intelligence operations against Iraqi targets. Residencies with Iraqi agents were ordered to downgrade them to the status of "official contacts," who could be reactivated if Soviet-Iraqi relations deteriorated.

The special relationship with Iraqi intelligence suffered a serious blow in April 1979 when the Iraqi dictator General Saddam Hussein started imprisoning and executing large numbers of Iraqi Communists. KGB residencies were quickly ordered to reactivate their former Iraqi agents. Soviet-Iraqi relations were further complicated when Saddam Hussein attacked Iran in September 1980 and began the Gulf War. Moscow eventually decided to give secret backing to Iraq. Gordievsky was assured by Nikolai Vladimirovich Shishlin, a leading foreign-policy expert in the Central Committee secretariat (later an adviser to Gorbachev), that the route chosen to supply arms to Iraq had been so carefully selected as to make it virtually impossible to trace.[43]

Moscow also sought to include Iraq's neighbor and rival, Syria, in the anti-imperialist Middle Eastern bloc. Syria received even more Soviet arms than Iraq. Gromyko's memoirs eulogize the Syrian leader Hafez Assad, as

> a powerful and farsighted leader, respected in the Arab world and beyond, who has always understood the importance of Soviet-Arab friendship . . . Smartly dressed, a hint of a smile sometimes appearing on his face, he might look slightly ineffectual, but in fact he was highly self-contained with a spring-like inner tension.[44]

In private Gordievsky frequently heard Assad denounced both in the Center and in the Central Committee International Department as a petit-bourgeois chauvinist egomaniac. The Center had much greater confidence in Assad's intelligence chiefs, with whom it established what it considered a useful liaison during the 1970s.

In 1979 a new Twentieth Department was established in the FCD to supervise intelligence liaison with "progressive" countries outside the Soviet Bloc, such as Syria. In addition to the KGB resident in Damascus, whose identity was concealed from the Syrian government, an officer from the Twentieth Department was posted to the Soviet embassy to liaise with Syrian intelligence and arrange training in Moscow for Syrian intelligence officers. Though neither side shared its most sensitive material, on several occasions the Syrians passed on to the KGB promising cases involving Westerners. Assad also allowed the KGB Sixteenth Directorate to conduct operations from some of Syria's eleven sigint stations.[45]

The Soviet Union's closest ideological ally in the Arab world was the avowedly Marxist People's Democratic Republic of [South] Yemen (PDRY), set up after the British departure from Aden in 1968. In Gordievsky's experience, however, the PDRY was regarded by the Center as a constant headache. The main task of the massive KGB residency in Aden was to monitor the intrigues and power struggles that rent the ruling Yemeni Socialist Party. It could do little to control them. In 1985 President Ali Nasser Muhammad sent a bodyguard into the Cabinet Room to machine-gun his Politburo. The Center was constantly fearful also that Saudi Arabia might use its immense wealth to organize the overthrow of the Marxist regime. The main threat to the survival of the PDRY, however, was to come from the bloodthirsty incompetence of its rulers.[46]

It took Moscow several years to make up its mind about Colonel Muammar Qaddafi, who took power in Libya after a military coup in 1969. The Center found it difficult to assess his eccentric blend of Islam, socialism, and egomania, and was alarmed by his early attempts to purchase an atomic bomb from the Chinese. Though the KGB noted some signs of apparent mental instability, it tended to see him as a mixture of political naïveté, personal cunning, and childish vanity, the last exemplified by a flamboyant wardrobe that allowed him to change in the same day from naval uniform adorned with gold braid and medals to Arab dress with exotic Bedouin headgear to a gold cape over a red silk shirt. On the credit side, the Center noted Qaddafi's obsession with Zionist conspiracy and a sophistication in negotiating with Western oil companies that contrasted with his simplistic grasp of international relations.

Moscow was also impressed by the vast oil wealth that Qaddafi had available to spend on Soviet arms.[47] The breakthrough in Soviet-Libyan relations came during a visit to Moscow in 1974 by his right-hand man, Major Abdul Salam Jalloud, whom Moscow found (and finds) better balanced and more pragmatic than Qaddafi. A statement at the end of the visit declared "the identity and closeness of the positions of the Soviet Union and the Libyan Arab Republic on the most important international problems." There followed a series of major arms deals, which over the next decade earned the Soviet Union $20 billion in hard currency. Qaddafi, concludes a recent biography, "collected weapons as small boys collect stamps, until military expenditure became a burden even for Libya's oil-rich economy." Brand-new tanks lay unused in Tripoli warehouses; Soviet jet fighters remained mostly under wraps, lacking both pilots to fly them and technicians to service them.[48]

In about 1979 a secret Soviet-Libyan agreement was signed on intelligence and security, followed by the posting of a Twentieth Department liaison officer to the Tripoli embassy. The KGB supplied training for Libyan intelligence officers at the Andropov Institute, gave advice on security and surveillance methods in Libya itself, and provided reports on U.S. activities in the Eastern Mediterranean. In exchange Libya provided intelligence on Egypt, Israel, and North Africa, and assisted KGB operations targeted against Western diplomats in Tripoli. The level of Soviet-Libyan cooperation tended to decline in the early 1980s as Qaddafi himself became increasingly discredited. Qaddafi's first visit to Moscow, in 1981, left much Soviet resentment in its wake. In the Center he was described as an affected dandy *(khlyshch),* whose posturing and extravagant uniforms were deliberately designed to emphasize the contrast between his own virility and Brezhnev's growing decrepitude.

By the end of the Brezhnev era Soviet influence in the Middle East lacked any secure base. Saddam Hussein and Arafat were distrusted. Suspicions of Assad reached such a peak in 1983 that Oleg Grinevsky, head of the Foreign Ministry Middle Eastern Department, took seriously unconfirmed intelligence reports of a secret deal on Lebanon between Syria and Israel. The Kremlin was increasingly concerned by the intelligence reports of Qaddafi's role as the godfather of international terrorism, and began to distance itself from him while avoiding any open break. At a private briefing for Soviet diplomats and KGB officers in London in 1984, Aleksandr Bovin, chief political commentator of *Izvestia,* denounced Qaddafi as "a criminal and a fascist." The most enduring special relationships formed by the Soviet Union in the Arab world were those established by the KGB. Twentieth Department liaison officers from the FCD remained active in Syria, Iraq, Libya, and the PDRY.[49]

In the Far East, the main priority of Soviet policy during the 1970s remained the containment of the People's Republic of China (PRC). In addition to ordering a Soviet military buildup on China's long northern border and a major expansion of the Pacific Fleet, the Kremlin sought to ring China in the south with a chain of pro-Soviet states. The Center thus viewed with alarm the growing signs in the early 1970s of a rapprochement between Beijing and Kim Il Sung's neo-Stalinist regime in North Korea. In 1973 the Soviet Union suspended arms shipments, and the PRC became for the first time North Korea's main arms supplier. The GRU reported that markings on Soviet military equipment were being painted over with signs claiming that it had been manufactured in North Korea.

Within the KGB, Kim Il Sung's increasingly absurd pretensions were regarded with a mixture of outrage and contempt. The interminable platitudes of his Juche ("self-reliance") philosophy were quoted in the Center as comic texts. The carefully cultivated Second World War myth of "the ever-victorious, iron-willed, brilliant commander, Comrade Kim Il Sung" was treated with particular derision. According to Kim's authorized biographies, which exceed even the historiography of Stalinist Russia in sycophantic absurdity, he conceived a master plan for liberating Korea at the age of thirteen, founded Korea's "first revolutionary Communist organization" at fourteen, by the age of twenty was "a legendary young general" leading anti-Japanese guerrillas in prewar Manchuria, and finally conquered the Japanese in a campaign of unprecedented brilliance in August 1945:

> Tell, blizzards that rage on the wild Manchurian plains,
> Tell, you nights in forests deep where the silence reigns,
> Who is the partisan whose deeds are unsurpassed?
> Who is the patriot whose fame shall ever last?
> So dear to all our hearts is our general's glorious name,
> Our own beloved Kim Il Sung, of undying fame.

Much of the derision with which the "Song of General Kim Il Sung" was quoted within the Center derived from the KGB's knowledge that Kim had not even been in Korea in August 1945. While Korea was being liberated by Soviet troops, Kim had been serving in Russia both as a lieutenant in the Red Army and as an agent of the NKVD. And it was with MGB backing, based on his work for Soviet intelligence, that in 1946 he became chairman of the newly formed North Korean Provisional People's Committee, to which the Soviet occupying forces entrusted the government of North Korea.

During the 1970s, Kim Il Sung announced a grandiose campaign to "fan the revolutionary flame for anti-imperialist and anti-American struggle for all the peoples of the world." As well as sending military training missions to over thirty countries, Kim was also an ardent believer in the export of terrorism. The Center received numerous reports that North Korea was training guerrillas, from states as distant as Mexico and West Germany, to attack airports, aircraft, trains, and other targets, and recruiting terrorists for its own operations from the Korean community in Japan. The main mission of North Korean terrorism was to destabilize South Korea by a variety of methods that included attacks on its political leadership. Both Kim and his megalomaniac heir-apparent, "Great Leader" Kim Jong Il, sponsored attempts against the South Korean president. In 1968 North Korean intelligence organized an attack on the South Korean presidential palace; in 1974 a Japanese Korean failed in an attempt on the president's life but succeeded in killing his wife; in 1983 seventeen members of a South Korean government delegation to Rangoon were killed by remote-controlled bomb explosions, though the president once again survived.

Because of the tight security preserved in Kim Il Sung's police state, the KGB's Pyongyang residency found it difficult to collect intelligence. Most KGB operations against North Korea were thus conducted from foreign capitals where Kim's regime had diplomatic missions. In the West the main center for these operations was Scandinavia, all four of whose capitals contained North Korean embassies. (Elsewhere in Europe, North Korea had diplomatic relations only with Portugal and Austria.) The most successful of the Scandinavian residencies was the one in Copenhagen, which had good contacts both in the Danish–North Korean Friendship Society, founded in 1976, and in the Danish Socialist People's Party, a Communist splinter group that sent a delegation to Pyongyang in the same year. The Copenhagen residency discovered that North Korea's diplomatic missions in Scandinavia had been told that until further notice they would receive no more hard currency; they were ordered to pay their way by selling drugs and duty-free goods on the black market. In December 1977 the Center congratulated the resident, Mikhail Petrovich Lyubimov, on the quality of the seventeen reports on North Korea sent from Copenhagen over the previous year, and informed him that three had been submitted to the Politburo.

By the end of the 1970s, Soviet fears of a rapprochement between Kim Il Sung and the PRC had largely subsided. The Chinese invasion of Vietnam early in 1979 aroused fears in Pyongyang of PRC ambitions to dominate its Asian neighbors. Kim was quick to distance himself from Beijing and to improve his relations with Moscow. Soviet arms supplies to North Korea resumed. The Center also played its part in the improvement of relations with Pyongyang. Though still privately contemptuous of Kim Il Sung and Kim Jong Il, it agreed to a request in 1979 from North Korean intelligence for advanced surveillance equipment, special weapons and ammunition, and quick-action handcuffs. While the Chinese boycotted Soviet Army Day in February 1980, Pyongyang celebrated the "militant friendship" between the Soviet and North Korean armies.[50]

The principal new opportunities for the spread of Soviet influence in the Third World during the 1970s were in Africa. The break-up of the Portuguese Empire and the overthrow of Emperor Haile Selassie brought to power self-proclaimed Marxist-Leninist regimes in three major African states: Angola, Mozambique, and Ethiopia. In Angola, the richest of Portugal's colonies, the end of Portuguese rule was followed in 1975 by a full-scale civil war, in which the Marxist Popular Movement for the Liberation of Angola (MPLA) was opposed by the National Front for the Liberation of Angola (FNLA) and the Union for the Total Liberation of Angola (UNITA).

After talks between the MPLA leader, Agostinho Neto, and the KGB residency in Lusaka in August 1971, large-scale Soviet arms deliveries began via the port of Brazzaville.[51] The decisive factor in the struggle for power, however, was the arrival of Cuban troops in the summer of 1975. In February 1976 the MPLA regime was recognized by the Organization for African Unity (OAU) as the legitimate government of Angola. Though Cuban intervention was welcomed by Moscow, which provided both arms and transport planes, the initiative came from Havana. Castro looked on Angola as an opportunity both to establish himself as a great revolutionary leader on the world stage and to revive flagging revolutionary fervor at home.[52] Though the CIA provided covert funding for UNITA, in the aftermath of Vietnam

Washington had no stomach for a serious challenge to the Cuban presence.

MPLA intelligence officers were sent for one-year training courses at the FCD's Andropov Institute. A number were recruited by the KGB. Neto himself, who traveled several times to Moscow for medical treatment, was assessed by the Center as psychologically unstable and unable to cope with faction fighting in the MPLA, but no more-reliable heir apparent was identified. KGB residencies in Black Africa were instructed to monitor closely internal rivalries in the MPLA and threats to Neto's leadership.[53] The early idealism generated by the Angolan independence struggle was dissipated in faction fighting, economic mismanagement, and popular unrest. In 1977 Neto crushed an attempted coup. In 1978 he dismissed his prime minister and three deputy prime ministers. To help him control dissent, advisers from the East German SSD set up a security service, the Direção de Informação à Segurança de Angola (DISA) under the president's personal control.[54]

In 1979 the newly founded Twentieth Department at Moscow Center sent a liaison officer to the Soviet embassy in Luanda. At Angolan request, Vadim Ivanovich Cherny, a former colleague of Gordievsky in Copenhagen, was sent to advise the DISA on security. Cherny's tendency to drink and inexperience in the security field made him a dubious choice. His tour of duty was cut short when he fell and broke an arm after a bout of heavy drinking. He told Gordievsky that, despite this misfortune, the MPLA had given him a medal. In Gordievsky's experience, Cherny was typical of a number of KGB officers sent to advise "progressive" regimes in which Moscow had lost confidence.

After Neto's death from cancer in a Moscow hospital in 1979, the situation in Angola deteriorated further. With South African backing, UNITA established a solid base in the south of the country. KGB reports from Luanda in the early 1980s described the MPLA leadership as hopelessly divided and the economic situation as catastrophic. The International Department of the Central Committee was equally gloomy. One of its senior advisers, N. V. Shishlin, forecast privately that the MPLA's problems might eventually force it to come to terms with South Africa.[55]

Soviet policy in the former Portuguese East African colony of Mozambique followed a pattern quite similar to that in Angola, though without Cuban military intervention. Moscow sent arms to the Marxist

Front for the Liberation of Mozambique (FRELIMO), headed by President Samora Machel, who came to power in the summer of 1975. FRELIMO, like the MPLA, sent annual contingents of intelligence officers to Moscow for training at the Andropov Institute.[56] Within Mozambique as in Angola, advisers from the East German SSD helped to establish a security service, the Serviço Nacional de Segurança Popular (SNASP), which dispatched dissenters to labor camps officially known as "centers for mental decolonization."[57] As in Luanda, the FCD Twentieth Department posted a liaison officer at the Soviet embassy in Maputo.

Initially, the Center placed greater hopes in Machel than in Neto. During the struggle for independence he had shown himself a shrewd guerrilla chief and a charismatic political leader. By the early 1980s, however, KGB and diplomatic reporting from Mozambique was even gloomier than from Angola.[58] In 1981 Machel instituted a "legality campaign" aimed at curbing corruption and the use of torture by SNASP. A year later he announced the firing of 466 SNASP officers.[59] Moscow Center was unimpressed. The annual report for 1984 from the embassy in Maputo, widely circulated to other Soviet embassies and KGB residencies, was one of the most scathing attacks on a friendly Third World government that Gordievsky had ever seen. The FRELIMO leadership was denounced as disunited, incompetent, and corrupt. The Mozambique economy was said to be in ruins. Local government and the legal system had disintegrated. FRELIMO's commitment to socialism was dismissed as little more than a form of words. The rival, South African-backed Mozambique National Resistance (RENAMO), was gaining ground.

Despite its pessimism about the future, however, the Center was taken by surprise by the Nkomati nonaggression agreement between FRELIMO and South Africa signed in March 1984. The cost of saving Mozambique from drifting toward the West, it feared, might prove beyond Soviet means.[60] It is fair to add that self-styled Marxist-Leninist regimes in sub-Saharan Africa had no monopoly on economic mismanagement. In Angola's neighbor Zaire, the legendarily corrupt President Mobutu received hundreds of millions of dollars in American aid simply on the grounds of his committed anti-Communism. While Mobutu accumulated a personal fortune sometimes reckoned to be equivalent to the Zairean national debt, the inhabitants of a country with some of the finest natural resources in Africa became as impoverished as those of Angola and Mozambique.

In the main guerrilla war in Anglophone Africa during the 1970s, the Black independence struggle against the Ian Smith regime in Rhodesia, which had declared itself independent of Britain in 1965, Moscow backed the wrong faction. Robert Mugabe, the able Marxist leader of the Zimbabwe African National Union (ZANU), who was to become the first prime minister of independent Zimbabwe in 1980, had committed the unforgivable ideological sin of describing himself as a "Marxist-Leninist of Maoist Thought." The Kremlin therefore backed the "bourgeois nationalist" Joshua Nkomo and the Zimbabwe African People's Union (ZAPU).[61] At one stage during the long-drawn-out guerrilla war that preceded independence, the Soviet supply of heavy weapons to ZAPU forces in Zambia became so large that the Zambian president, Kenneth Kaunda, alarmed at the huge stockpile in his country, called a temporary halt.[62]

Nkomo conducted most of his arms negotiations in Lusaka through the Soviet ambassador, Vasili Grigoryevich Solodovnikov, who, as he acknowledges, was generally believed to be "associated with the KGB." Solodovnikov was one of the leading Soviet experts on Africa and the author of several books on African affairs, as well as an occasional coopted collaborator of the KGB.

> He was a very nice fellow, and we got on very well on the personal level. Moreover, he was entirely professional about his work, and if you discussed a request with him you could be sure that it would soon get onto the agenda of the right committee in Moscow, and the decision would come back without much delay.

Nkomo had what he described as "extensive correspondence," and at least one meeting in Moscow, with Andropov about "the training of security operatives."[63] The Cuban DGI also provided intelligence advisers to ZAPU. After independence, Moscow Center was fearful that the new prime minister, Robert Mugabe, would bear a grudge over the support given to his rival. It sent circular telegrams to residencies in Africa, London, and elsewhere calling for detailed intelligence on his policy to the Soviet Union.[64]

During the five-year period from January 1976 to December 1980 Soviet arms transfers to Black Africa totaled almost $4 billion, ten times the total of U.S. arms supplies.[65] By the late 1970s, disillusioned with the MPLA and FRELIMO, and having backed the wrong horse in

Zimbabwe, Moscow's main hopes in Black Africa centered on Ethiopia, where a vaguely Marxist military junta—the Derg—had taken power in 1974 under Lieutenant Colonel Mengistu Haile Mariam as head of state and commander-in-chief. At the height of Soviet arms deliveries to Ethiopia during the winter of 1977–78, at a critical point in its war with Somalia, Soviet military transport aircraft reportedly landed every twenty minutes over a period of three months. An estimated 225 planes were involved in an operation coordinated via a Soviet military reconnaissance satellite. Simultaneously, 17,000 Cubans were airlifted from Angola to join 1,000 Soviet military advisers and 400 East Germans, who were involved in training intelligence and internal-security units.[66] Because of the extent of the Soviet military presence in Ethiopia, the GRU played a greater intelligence role than the KGB. In 1979, however, the Twentieth Department sent an intelligence liaison officer to Addis Ababa. Groups of Ethiopian intelligence officers also went annually for training at the Andropov Institute.[67] Mengistu proved as big a disappointment as Neto and Machel. A decade after he came to power, the Ethiopian economy was close to collapse, millions were facing famine, and no end was yet in sight to the war with Somalia and Ethiopian separatists.

By the end of the Brezhnev era, the Center pinned its main hopes in Black Africa on the African National Congress (ANC), which led resistance to the racist apartheid regime ruling South Africa. Banned in South Africa and unable to acquire arms in the West, the ANC understandably turned to the Soviet Bloc. The Kremlin attributed the failure of the self-styled Marxist-Leninist regimes in Angola, Mozambique, and Ethiopia to their lack of a disciplined Communist Party.[68] The South African Communist Party (SACP), however, was both reliably pro-Soviet and played a key role within the exiled leadership of the ANC. Probably seven of the twenty-two members of the ANC National Executive Committee in the early 1980s belonged to the SACP, among them the ANC vice-president, Dr. Yusef Dadoo, chairman of the SACP, and the deputy chief of the ANC military wing, Joe Slovo, long-serving secretary-general of the SACP.[69]

Though encouraged to recruit agents in the ANC, the KGB was forbidden to do so in the SACP. Relations with the SACP were the responsibility of the International Department of the Party Central Committee, but the KGB was used to transmit funds to the SACP as well as the ANC. Between mid-1982 and January 1983, Gordievsky handed Yusef Dadoo a total of £54,000 for the SACP and

£118,000 for the ANC. When the money arrived at the London residency, Gordievsky put on gloves to remove the Moscow bank wrapper and count out the banknotes. Dadoo was welcomed at 18 Kensington Park Gardens by the Party representative, Aleksandr Fyodorovich Yekimenko, who was a KGB cooptee. On receiving the money from Gordievsky, Dadoo signed separate receipts on behalf of the ANC and the SACP. Instead of putting the money in a briefcase, he used to stuff it in all the pockets of his suit and overcoat. Gordievsky was struck by the way Dadoo's thin frame filled out with dollar bills before he set off home on foot, apparently unconcerned by the risk of theft en route.

Though Gordievsky found Dadoo's simplistic grasp of the Soviet system depressing, he never lost respect for Dadoo himself. None of the banknotes stuffed into Dadoo's pockets were ever spent on himself. He led an ascetic life totally devoted to the liberation struggle in southern Africa. After Dadoo's death in 1983, the London residency ceased to handle the transmission of funds to the ANC and SACP. The main official point of contact with the ANC was Lusaka, where the Soviet ambassador to Zambia spent at least half his time acting as ambassador to the exiled ANC leadership. Arms were supplied covertly to the ANC through Zambia, Angola, and Tanzania. The main West European capital where the KGB maintained contact with ANC agents was Stockholm, where the ANC had its largest office outside Africa, as well as public support and generous funding from the Swedish Social Democratic Party for its struggle against apartheid.[70]

Moscow Center saw little prospect that the SACP, despite its key role on the National Executive Committee, would ever take over the ANC as a whole. On the contrary, as the West gradually became less feeble in its opposition to apartheid, the Center was constantly afraid that the ANC would turn increasingly westward. By the early 1980s KGB residencies in Stockholm, London, New York, Paris, Rome, and African capitals where the ANC maintained offices were regularly bombarded with instructions to monitor threats to SACP influence and Western contacts with the ANC leadership. The Center was quick to show alarm at the slightest ideological shift. Soon after Gordievsky arrived in London in 1982, the London office of the ANC started showing resistance to the tedious articles supplied to it by a KGB officer working under cover as a Novosti correspondent for publication in African newspapers. Unwilling to accept that the probable explanation lay simply in the incompetence of the articles themselves, the Center reacted with consternation and instructed the London residency to redouble its efforts to track down the source of increasing Western influence in the ANC.[71]

Because of the absence of diplomatic relations between Moscow and Pretoria and the consequent lack of a KGB legal residency, the Center found it difficult to evaluate ANC activities within South Africa. But it was consistently skeptical of the ANC's claims about its military strength and its ability to mount an effective armed struggle. It was also well aware that SACP support within the predominantly Xhosa rank and file of the ANC inside South Africa was much weaker than in the exiled ANC executive. In Gordievsky's experience, though the ANC depended on the Soviet Union for most of its arms and part of its funding, Moscow had little influence on its policies.[72] Even the neo-Stalinist pro-Soviet loyalism of the SACP old guard was a wasting asset. (Not till January 1990 did a report by the veteran general secretary Joe Slovo finally come to terms with the reforms of the Gorbachev era and acknowledge that the SACP had hitherto followed a "distorted" path.) Paradoxically the key to Soviet influence in Black Africa during the 1980s remained the racist government in Pretoria and those in the West still prepared to offer it various forms of succor, rather than the crumbling Marxist-Leninist regimes in Angola, Mozambique, and Ethiopia. The KGB did less to advance the Soviet cause in Africa than President P. W. Botha and the Nationalist Government.

Moscow, however, had its own top-secret contacts with Pretoria over regulating the market in gold, diamonds, platinum, and precious minerals, in which the Soviet Union and South Africa between them had something approaching a world monopoly. Because of the extreme sensitivity of these contacts and the outrage that their public revelation would provoke in Black Africa, the KGB took a prominent part in arranging them. In 1984 the Kremlin decided to step up secret discussions with South Africa designed to regulate the international market. As a preliminary, KGB residencies in the United States, Britain, West Germany, France, and Switzerland were asked to supply intelligence on a whole series of South African financial institutions and businesses.[73]

The disappointments suffered by the KGB in Africa and the Middle and Far East during the 1970s led to a renewed concentration on Latin America in the early 1980s. A conference of senior officers at the Center in 1979, chaired by Kryuchkov, reviewed the recent past and assessed the KGB's worldwide priorities over the next few years. The key speech was given by Nikolai Leonov, head of the FCD Service 1 (Reports), who over twenty years before had been the first to grasp Castro's potential as a revolutionary leader and emphasized the new opportunities in the 1980s for expanding KGB operations and exploiting the weaknesses of the Main Adversary in Latin America. Leonov's assessment was vigorously supported by the resident from Venezuela. Both he and Leonov called for support for non-Communist liberation movements, which, like Castro's, could seize power in their countries and emerge as influential allies of the Soviet Union.[74]

There was, however, one unpublicized hitch in 1979 in the Center's relations with Castro. The DGI discovered the presence of a KGB agent in Cuba transmitting coded reports to Moscow by radio, in defiance of a formal Cuban-Soviet intelligence agreement that forbade espionage by either side against the other. To its profound embarrassment the Center was forced to apologize.[75] In public, however, Castro was a reliable and eloquent defender of Soviet foreign policy (even during the invasion of Afghanistan) and an increasingly dominant figure in the Third World. In September 1979 he hosted the Non-Aligned Movement's summit conference in Havana. Though ninety-two heads of state were present, Castro was never out of the spotlight. For the next three years he was chairman of the Non-Aligned Movement. In October 1979 he traveled to New York, bringing with him rum and lobsters for a huge reception at the twelve-story Cuban mission to the United Nations (the largest UN mission save for those of the U.S. and the U.S.S.R., and the main base for DGI operations in the U.S.). Then in a two-hour speech at the General Assembly he made an impassioned plea for "wealthy imperialists" to give the Third World $300 billion over the next decade.[76]

Meanwhile the tide of Central American politics seemed to be moving in Castro's direction. In March 1979 a pro-Cuban regime seized power in the tiny Caribbean island of Grenada, led by the Marxist-Leninist lawyer Maurice Bishop. Secret Party documents later captured during the U.S. invasion of 1983 made clear that Bishop's Marxism was of the variety once described by a French student revolutionary as "the Groucho tendency." In Bishop's words:

Just consider, Comrades, . . . how people get detained in this country. We don't go and call for no votes. You get detained when I sign an order after discussing it with the National

Security Committee of the Party or with a higher Party body. Once I sign it—like it or don't like it—it's up the hill for them.

After some initial hesitation, overcome partly by Cuban persuasion, Moscow poured in massive military aid. The Grenadan general Hudson Austin wrote to Andropov early in 1982 to thank him "once again for the tremendous assistance which our armed forces have received from your Party and Government," and to request training for four Grenadan intelligence officers.[77]

Of much greater significance than Bishop's seizure of power in March 1979 was the ousting of the brutal and corrupt Somoza dictatorship in Nicaragua by the Sandinista Liberation Front four months later. Despite Cuban backing and Leonov's advocacy, however, Moscow did not immediately rush to the Sandinistas' aid. Though welcoming Sandinista support for the Soviet invasion of Afghanistan and attracted by their national anthem, which branded *yanquis* as "enemies of mankind," the Kremlin continued for two years to nurture the hope that the small but orthodox Nicaraguan Communist Party might replace the unorthodox Sandinistas as the dominant force in the new regime. By the end of 1981, however, Castro and KGB reports had persuaded the Kremlin that the Sandinistas were genuine revolutionaries, who would follow the Cuban path to Soviet loyalism.

With Cuban and Soviet assistance, the Sandinistas increased the Nicaraguan army in six years from 5,000 to 119,000, making it the most powerful military force in Central American history. (Despite American backing, the inept Contra guerrillas fighting the Sandinistas never exceeded 20,000 on the most optimistic estimate.) Moscow Center was quick to conclude an intelligence agreement with Managua and to send a Twentieth Department officer to establish liaison with "our Nicaraguan friends" (KGB jargon for friendly intelligence services).[78] According to Miguel Bolaños Hunter, a defector from the Nicaraguan intelligence service, the director of the service was a Cuban DGI officer using the alias Renán Montero. The Center provided seventy advisers and built a Nicaraguan school for state security.[79] Among the Nicaraguan facilities provided in exchange were the sites for four Soviet sigint bases.[80]

The counterproductive fury of the Reagan administration's response to the Sandinista revolution played into the hands of both the Sandinistas and of Moscow Center. United States help to the Contras, and the revelation in 1984 of CIA involvement in the mining of Nicaragua's harbors and the destruction of the Corinto oil-storage tanks, overshadowed the Sandinistas' abuse of human rights and economic mismanagement, unleashed a wave of anti-Americanism in Latin America and beyond, and won international support for the Sandinista struggle against American imperialism. Despite his own personal popularity, Reagan's appeals for further funding for the Contras failed to convince either Congress or the American public.[81] Aid to the Contras ended officially in 1984. Attempts to continue it unofficially embroiled the White House, to the delight of Moscow Center, in the long-drawn-out black comedy of the Iran-Contra scandal.

Nikolai Leonov, meanwhile, basked at the Center in reflected glory from Central America. His achievement in 1979 in identifying the region as the most promising area for the expansion of KGB operations, following his success in spotting Castro a quarter of a century earlier, led to his promotion in 1983 to the position of deputy head of the FCD, responsible for all KGB operations throughout North and South America.[82]

Cuban-Soviet intelligence cooperation continued to expand in sigint as well as humint. The joint KGB-GRU sigint base at Lourdes in Cuba, less than a hundred miles from the U.S. coast, greatly enlarged in the mid-1970s, was described by President Reagan in 1983 as "the largest of its kind in the world" with "acres and acres of antennae fields and intelligence monitors." According to a joint report by the State and Defense departments two years later, Lourdes contained about 2,100 Soviet technicians:

> From this key listening post, the Soviets monitor US commercial satellites, US military and merchant shipping communications, and NASA space program activities at Cape Canaveral. Lourdes also enables the Soviets to eavesdrop on telephone conversations in the United States.[83]

Within Western Europe two major new sources of KGB concern emerged in the mid-1970s. The first was the European Community (EC). Until 1976 KGB residents in Western Europe were instructed that the EC, unlike most of its member states, was of little interest to the Center; they were to collect intelligence on matters of major political significance only. The report to the Community by the Belgian prime minister Leo Tindemans in December 1975 caused a major reassessment by the FCD. Tindemans urged the EC Council of Ministers to end the "schizophrenic" contradiction between the Community's economic integration and its political fragmentation. In particular, he argued, the EC required common defense and foreign policies. The impact of the Tindemans report at the Center was heightened by signs of growing Chinese interest in Community affairs. In September 1975 the first Chinese ambassador was accredited to the EC, and promptly opened trade negotiations.[84]

By the summer of 1976 Kryuchkov had concluded that the Tindemans report and the Chinese presence in Brussels were both evidence of a dangerous anti-Soviet conspiracy. In July 1976 a circular bearing his signature (a certain indication of its importance) instructed residents to "activate all operational possibilities" as a matter of urgency to obtain the fullest intelligence on EC policy. There was, he claimed, a real danger that the European Community would become "a military-political bloc which may be led by aggressive and revanchist forces." The Community and China were already drawing together in an anti-Soviet alliance. A month later the Center circulated a much more detailed assessment of the growing threat from the EC, which greatly exaggerated both the pace of political integration and the prospects for military integration. The FCD continued to attach a deeply sinister significance to the Tindemans report, laying heavy emphasis on its conclusion that "European Union will be unstable until it has a common defense policy." The August 1976 circular claimed that the main aim of the Community was now "to undermine the foreign policies of the Socialist states." "Leading EC circles" were also looking for ways to subvert the socialist system from within.

American support for European integration was further evidence that the whole process was part of an anti-Soviet conspiracy. Over the next few years Moscow Center regularly reiterated the same conspiracy theory. A circular in the spring of 1977 interpreted even plans for direct elections to the European Parliament in the following year as a threat to the U.S.S.R. because they were likely to hasten political integration. The Community, it declared, had turned itself into "a coordinated center for collective economic, political and ideological actions aimed at undermining the international prestige of the Soviet Union and other countries of the Socialist Community."

In order to discover the precise nature of the EC's anti-Soviet master plan, there was an urgent need to gain access to its secret documents. This could only be achieved by building up a "solid agent base" in the main organs of the Community. Residents in all EC countries were instructed to appoint a senior KGB officer, normally the deputy resident in charge of the PR (Political Intelligence) line, to coordinate operations against the Community. The Center recommended as particularly promising locations for agent recruitment the European College at Bruges, the European University in Florence, and the European Institute in Amsterdam. Successful students from these institutions, the FCD believed, were well placed to become penetration agents in Brussels.

The coordinating officer for EC operations in each residency, however, had many more-humdrum tasks. He was instructed to send the Center at regular intervals EC telephone directories, lists of diplomats and journalists accredited to the EC, and full details of all EC officials traveling to the Soviet Union. The Center also emphasized the need for active measures to hold back European integration, including direct elections to the European Parliament. Residencies were instructed to plant stories in the media emphasizing disagreements both between individual member states and between the Community, the United States, and Japan. Other circulars continued to emphasize the danger of the Community and China's forming an anti-Soviet bloc.

Despite recurrent disputes between EC countries and the failure of Tindemans's vision of a common defense policy to materialize, there was no letup in the Center's anxiety about European integration. The same themes remained constant in its circulars right up to, and doubtless beyond, Gordievsky's departure from the KGB. A circular in the spring of 1984 from Viktor Grushko, first deputy head of the FCD with responsibility for Western Europe, rehearsed the conspiracy theories first elaborated in 1976 with, if anything, added emphasis. Growing cooperation between China and the Community was, he reported, causing "alarm" at the Center; the EC was pursuing far-reaching plans to undermine the international prestige and political unity of the Soviet Bloc; plans by "reactionary groups" for European military integration presented "a special danger." In all its aspects, concluded Grushko, "The integration of Western Europe runs counter to the interests of the Soviet Union." The Politburo (the Instantsiya in KGB jargon) had named the EC as one of the "main targets for intelligence penetration."[85]

It was an ironic tribute to the progress achieved in European integration since the signature of the Treaty of Rome in 1957 that the Community found itself elevated by the early 1980s to virtually the same target status as the United States (the traditional Main Adversary), NATO, and China. Despite the wealth of information available in the Center on the European Community (which had, in any case, fewer high-level secrets to protect than virtually any of its member states), the Center remained deeply dissatisfied with the quality of intelligence obtained from it. It complained to London and doubtless to other West European residencies that the quality of its operations against the EC was "poor." All residencies were ordered, "in accordance with the instructions of Comrade Kryuchkov," to step up agent penetration and all forms of intelligence collection on the Community. The Center's complaints, however, reflected not any real shortage of EC intelligence but rather the lack of evidence for its own conspiracy theories. When the Center failed to receive detailed accounts of plots in Brussels to subvert the states of Eastern Europe, it drew the conclusion not that the plots did not exist but that its residencies were falling down on the job. Kryuchkov repeatedly demanded "more initiative" in active measures to stall progress in European integration.[86]

The second major new concern of the Center in Europe in the mid-1970s concerned its Arctic fringe, the archipelago of Svalbard (which includes Spitzbergen) and the Barents Sea. Though Svalbard comes under Norwegian sovereignty, the thirty-nine signatories of the 1920 Svalbard treaty have the right to exploit its economic resources. Growing Western interest in Svalbard's oil and natural-gas resources after the oil crisis of 1973–74 seemed to the Center to pose a major strategic threat. Fears that Western oil rigs in Svalbard and the Barents Sea could be equipped to monitor the surface ships and submarines of the Soviet Northern Fleet, allied to the problems posed by the pending delimitation with Norway of the Barents Sea, led to the creation in the winter of 1975–76 of a Soviet interministerial commission on the Arctic chaired by N. A. Tikhonov, first deputy prime minister, with Kryuchkov as one of its key members. Intelligence collection on Norway and the Arctic was considered of such vital importance that it was personally supervised by Andropov himself.[87]

　　　　When the interministerial commission was formed, the Center had two major assets in Norway, one nearing the end of her long career as an agent, the other rapidly approaching his prime. The first of the agents, Gunvor Galtung Haavik, was an elderly secretary at the Norwegian Foreign Ministry who over thirty years before had fallen in love with a Russian prisoner of war named Vladimir Kozlov, whom she had nursed in a hospital when Norway was under Nazi occupation and had helped to escape to Sweden. In 1947 Haavik was posted to the Norwegian embassy in Moscow and resumed her affair with Kozlov, who had since married and was used as bait by the MGB. Following a now well-established routine, she was blackmailed in 1950 into becoming a Soviet agent, and code-named Vika. In 1956 she returned to Norway with the new code name Greta and continued to receive messages from Kozlov as well as money from her controllers.

During her twenty-seven years as a Soviet agent she had more than 250 meetings with eight different case officers, to whom she handed thousands of classified documents.[88] Gordievsky first discovered her existence while stationed in Copenhagen in the mid-1970s and he warned SIS.[89] Haavik was arrested by Norwegian security on the evening of January 27, 1977, as she handed documents to her current controller, Aleksandr Kirillovich Printsipalov, in a dark side street of an Oslo suburb.

Printsipalov put up a violent struggle before he claimed diplomatic immunity and was released. In his pocket was an envelope containing 2,000 kroner in 100-kroner notes, which had been intended for Haavik. For a few hours after her arrest, Haavik admitted only her love affair with Kozlov, which, she claimed, accounted for her meetings with Soviet diplomats who brought her his letters. Then she fell silent, thought for a while, looked up, and announced: "I shall now tell it as it is. I have been a Russian spy for nearly thirty years." Six months later she died in prison of a heart attack before she had been brought to trial.[90]

In 1978 the Third Department at the Center gave Philby a sanitized file on the Haavik case, from which even her name and nationality had been removed, and asked for his comments. Philby concluded that the only plausible explanation for the agent's arrest was a mole within the KGB. After reading Philby's report, the Third Department head, Viktor Fyodorovich Grushko, told a meeting of his staff: "So, if Philby is right, there's a traitor right here in the Department!" Happily Grushko did not pursue the subject. Among those at the meeting was Oleg Gordievsky. For the first time since adolescence he felt a tremendous fear of blushing. It required a major effort of self-control to prevent the flush around his neck from rising to his cheeks. Philby had come uncomfortably close to ending his career.[91]

During Haavik's interrogation Norwegian security got the impression that in the months leading up to her arrest she had not been fully exploited by the KGB. The suspicion arose, not confirmed for several years, that there was an even more important agent in the Foreign Ministry. Norwegian security had another tantalizing clue. The wife of a young KGB officer in Oslo, Vladimir Ivanovich Zhizhin, was overheard asking him, immediately after Haavik's arrest, whether anything serious had happened. He replied cheerfully: "It could have been worse!"[92]

The Center's most important Norwegian agent, Arne Treholt, was cast in the same mold as Georgi Pâques and Hugh Hambleton: a victim of his own vanity as well as of the KGB. Aged almost thirty-five at the time of Haavik's arrest, blond, good-looking, narcissistic, married to a glamorous television personality (his second wife), Treholt was widely regarded as one of the young high fliers of the Norwegian Labor Party. As a political-science student at his university, his main motivation seemed to be anti-Americanism. In the late 1960s he helped organize campaigns in Norway against the military junta that had seized power in Greece with, he believed, American support. Treholt became assistant to the distinguished international lawyer Jens Evensen, who argued the case against the junta in the European Court. The Oslo residency noticed Treholt and began to cultivate him. Treholt enjoyed every moment of his seduction. "We had glorious lunches," he later recalled, "where we discussed Norwegian and international politics."

Treholt's first case officer, Yevgeni Belyayev, who controlled him from 1968 to 1971, gradually succeeded in persuading him to accept money, initially for information of little importance. Just before Belyayev left Oslo in 1971 he introduced Treholt at a farewell lunch in the Coq d'Or restaurant to his next controller, Gennadi Fyodorovich Titov, who was to serve from 1972 to 1977 as KGB resident in Norway. Nicknamed "The Crocodile," Titov was deeply unpopular among his KGB colleagues (though not his superiors), and—save for a small group of protégés—feared by his subordinates. Gordievsky remembers him as the most unpleasant and unprincipled KGB officer he ever met.

Titov was a Soviet Karelian, born in 1932. When he was five or six his father was shot by the NKVD at the height of the Great Terror. Titov was brought up in a semi-criminal milieu, becoming expert in the Soviet form of street wisdom required to prosper in the final years of Stalinist rule. To his surprise, despite his family history, he was accepted for training in 1955 by the Leningrad Military Institute of the KGB. Thereafter, he sought to compensate for his background by showing conspicuous devotion to duty as a KGB officer. His most remarkable talent in dealing with both his superiors and his agents was a prodigious gift for flattery, which seduced both Treholt and Kryuchkov. Treholt found him "a very fascinating and exciting type," well informed, entertaining, and full of jokes and anecdotes about Soviet leaders. Titov was also a good listener. As Treholt expounded his views about Vietnam, Greece, NATO, the United States, and the peace movement, Titov seemed greatly impressed by his insights. He had, Titov told him, a unique contribution to make in building bridges between East and West in a way that was beyond the capacity of routine, bureaucratic diplomacy.

Treholt acted partly as a Soviet agent of influence, helping to organize the successful campaign run in 1972 by the left wing of the Labor Party against Norwegian membership in the EEC. But his main role was as a supplier of classified information on Norwegian and NATO policy. That role became of major importance when Treholt's former mentor, Jens Evensen, was put in charge of the Law of the Sea negotiations. At his suggestion Treholt was appointed undersecretary in charge of the issue. Thenceforth he was by far the most important intelligence source for the interministerial commission in Moscow on Svalbard and the Barents Sea. During Norwegian-Soviet negotiations in 1977 on the delimitation of the Barents Sea, Treholt not only kept the KGB fully informed of the Norwegian negotiating position but also acted as a Soviet agent of influence in the Norwegian negotiating team. The Barents Sea agreement signed by Norway and the Soviet Union on July 1, 1977, was heavily criticized in Norway for being tilted in the Soviet interest.[93]

Titov was expelled from Norway in 1977 as a result of the Haavik case. For the next two years he worked at the Center as Kryuchkov's special assistant, flattering him as ingeniously as he flattered Treholt. From 1979 to 1984 he was head of the FCD Third Department, responsible for Britain, Ireland, Scandinavia, and Australasia. Well aware that Treholt was his main career asset, Titov persuaded Kryuchkov to allow him to go on handling the case.[94] He continued to meet Treholt at intervals in Helsinki and Vienna, the KGB's favorite European meeting places for important agents, and delegated much of his routine handling to two other case officers who had worked at the Oslo residency, Vladimir Zhizhin and Aleksandr Lopatin.

Late in 1978 Treholt was appointed to the Norwegian mission

in the UN. His appointment came at a fortunate time for the KGB since for part of his time in New York Norway was a member of the Security Council. Shortly before Treholt left for the UN, Titov introduced him in Helsinki to Zhizhin, who was to control him in New York. They agreed to meet in restaurants and leave notes for each other inside newspapers in the UN delegates' lounge. Save for some initial complaints by Treholt about the quality of the restaurants chosen by Zhizhin, the arrangements worked smoothly.

After enjoying the good life in the Big Apple, Treholt became careless. He speculated in gold and silver, and bought a horse, which he entered in trotting races. From 1982–83 he was at the Norwegian Defense College, cleared for NATO Cosmic Top Secret material. The prosecutor at his trial likened Treholt's activities in the college to those of a fox let loose in a chicken farm.[95] In NATO strategy Norway is "the key to the North":

> The Kola peninsula, where Norway borders the Soviet Union, has been described by one American Navy Secretary as "the most valuable piece of real estate on earth." On the Russian side there are the immense naval facilities centered around Murmansk. It is a NATO truism that "the battle of the Atlantic must be fought in the Norwegian Sea," and that the Soviets would try to seize Norway and operate their submarines out of Norwegian fjords.[96]

Partly as a result of leads supplied by Gordievsky, Treholt had been put under surveillance by the FBI during his time in New York at the request of Norwegian security. Though there was, in the opinion of Norwegian security, insufficient evidence to bar his entry to the Defense College, his meetings thereafter with Titov in Helsinki and Vienna were closely monitored. In Vienna, Treholt and Titov were photographed walking together, by a camera hidden in a baby's pram. Titov, short and stout, waves his arms expansively; Treholt, taller, trimmer, and already in training for the New York marathon, grins amiably.[97]

At the beginning of 1984 Titov achieved his main career ambition, with his promotion to the rank of KGB general, a success due more to Treholt than to himself.[98] Simultaneously the Norwegian Foreign Ministry appointed Treholt as its press spokesman during the visit to Oslo of the American secretary of State, George Shultz. On the morning of Friday, January 20, shortly after Shultz's departure, Treholt arrived at Oslo airport to catch the 12:45 flight to Vienna for another rendezvous with Titov. In his hand was a briefcase containing sixty-six classified Foreign Ministry documents. He waited in the departure lounge for the final call. Then, as he was about to board the plane, he was arrested by Ørnulf Tofte, deputy head of Norwegian security. Contrary to later press reports, the arrest was undramatic. According to Tofte: "Treholt was calm and did not say a word. We did not need handcuffs or any form of restraint. He was taken through a sidedoor straight into a waiting car, and driven to police headquarters."[99]

At his trial in 1985 Treholt was to claim that he had simply been building bridges between East and West. The court concluded that this showed "such an exaggerated sense of his own position as to be scarcely credible." Treholt's conceit, sedulously cultivated by Titov, however, had become so grotesque that he may well have deluded himself into believing his fantasy role as a unique bridge between East and West. Titov had also encouraged Treholt's greed. The court later confiscated over a million Norwegian kroner, which it calculated he had earned from espionage. It was probably an underestimate; in addition to his earnings from the KGB, Treholt also received $50,000 from Iraqi intelligence.

Had Treholt's arrest occurred only a few weeks earlier, Gordievsky is convinced that Titov's promotion to general would never have occurred. Soon after the arrest was announced, Kryuchkov sent Titov to East Berlin to become deputy head of the KGB compound at Karlshorst. With him went Treholt's two other case officers, Vladimir Zhizhin and Aleksandr Lopatin.[100] A year later Treholt was sentenced to twenty years in jail.

In 1981 the Center had also lost the man it considered its other most important Scandinavian agent, when President Urho Kekkonen of Finland stepped down because of ill-health.[101] By then the KGB in Finland was running about 160 fully recruited agents and "confidential contacts"—more than in all the rest of the FCD Third Department countries (the remainder of Scandinavia, Britain, Ireland, and Australasia) combined. The Helsinki resident Viktor Vladimirov and his rival, Ambassador Vladimir Sobolev, both confidently predicted that Kekkonen's Center (formerly Agrarian) Party colleague Ahti Karjalainen would succeed him. The residency had not made the mistake, as in the case of Kekkonen, of claiming to the Center that Karjalainen was a fully recruited agent, classifying him instead as a "confidential contact," but was rashly confident of its future influence over him as president, referring to "Our Man Karjalainen" or "The Man in Our Pocket."

The main Finnish expert in the FCD, Albert Petrovich Akulov, in Gordievsky's view probably its most brilliant analyst, forecast that Karjalainen's reputation as a heavy drinker would lose him his party's nomination. Vladimirov brushed this prediction aside and called on the Center Party chairman and foreign minister, Paavo Väyrynen, to assure him secretly of Soviet support for Karjalainen and its opposition to his Social Democratic rival, the prime minister Mauno Koivisto.[102] According to Karjalainen:

> Vladimirov told Väyrynen that he was going to use his in-
> fluence with the Communists and also with other parties to
> support my position. He asked Väyrynen frankly what the
> Soviet Union could do to further my election. . . . Vladimi-
> rov developed the idea of stage-managing economic cooper-
> ation in such a way as to produce a situation which would
> benefit me.[103]

But, as Akulov had predicted, despite Vladimirov's active measures in his favor, Karjalainen failed to get the Center Party nomination. The Social Democrat Koivisto, opposed by Vladimirov, won an easy victory in the 1982 presidential election.[104]

The Swedish statesman on whom the KGB pinned most of its hopes during the 1970s was the Social Democrat, Olof Palme. Before Palme became Prime Minister in 1969, the Center had paid little attention to him. Thereafter, however, his outspoken opposition to the Vietnam War, calls for the West to spend less on arms, and support for progressive causes in the Third World quickly aroused Soviet interest. The Center devised a plan to recruit Palme as an agent of influence by posting a Swedish-speaking KGB agent of Latvian origin, N. V. Neyland, to head the Novosti bureau at Stockholm in 1972. Neyland came from the same part of Latvia as Palme's mother, struck up a friendship with him by playing on his affection for his Latvian roots, and even arranged for Palme to pay a short sentimental visit to Latvia. He also succeeded in arranging regular meetings with one of Palme's leading advisers in the Social Democratic Party. The Center went to enormous pains to provide Neyland with formulations of Soviet policy that it hoped Palme would find attractive. Especially after he lost power in

1976 and went into opposition, Palme appeared to have a clear preference for Soviet rather than American policy on peace and disarmament. The Palme Commission, set up in 1980 to consider disarmament issues, was greatly valued in Moscow for its criticisms of American positions.

In his reports to the Center, Neyland tried to take the credit for much of Palme's sympathy with Soviet policy. Kryuchkov, in turn, reported to both Andropov and the Politburo that Palme, though not a fully recruited agent, was subject to KGB influence. Once again, however, the FCD exaggerated its own success. While Palme's regular contacts with Neyland (whose job with Novosti should, in itself, have been sufficient to arouse his suspicions of a KGB connection) showed a surprising political naïveté, there is no hard evidence that Neyland had a major influence on his policy. That influence, such as it was, in any case ceased when Neyland left Stockholm in 1980. Neyland's successor failed to win Palme's confidence and the KGB lost direct access to him. Though the Center welcomed Palme's return to power in 1982 and his qualified support for Soviet policy on disarmament during his second term as prime minister (which was to be cut short by his assassination in 1986), it now regarded him as an essentially Western political leader who championed Western values.[105]

What remained of East-West détente at the end of the 1970s was destroyed during the final week of the decade by the Soviet invasion of Afghanistan. In April 1978 a Communist coup had overthrown the republican regime of Mohammed Daoud, slaughtering him and his entire family in the process. The choice for Daoud's successor lay between Babrak Karmal, who headed the Parcham faction in the Afghan Communist Party, and Noor Mohammed Taraki, the leader of the rival Khalq faction. Moscow Center backed Karmal, who had been a KGB agent for many years. But Taraki had the upper hand and the backing of Brezhnev, who was impressed by him at a brief meeting, and won the succession struggle. Karmal took refuge in Czechoslovakia.[106] In September 1979 Taraki was murdered by his deputy prime minister Hafizullah Amin. Moscow turned a blind eye to the murder, congratulated Amin on his "election," and expressed "the conviction that in the future too the fraternal relations between the Soviet Union and revolutionary Afghanistan will continue to develop on the basis of [their] treaty of friendship, good-neighborliness and cooperation."[107] The Center, however, predicted disaster. Reports from the Kabul residency reported bitter opposition to Amin from Islamic leaders, the threat of mutiny from the Afghan army, and imminent economic collapse.[108]

The removal of Amin was discussed and agreed on, like all KGB operations against foreign political leaders, by the Politburo. Since the reorganization that followed the defection of Oleg Lyalin in 1971 and the public exposure in the West of the FCD's Department V, "wet affairs" and other "special actions" had become the responsibility of a newly constituted Department Eight in Directorate S, which handled illegals. Department Eight selected as Amin's assassin Lieutenant Colonel Mikhail Talebov, an Azerbaijani who had spent several years in Kabul and was able to pass as an Afghan. In the late autumn of 1979 Talebov arrived in Kabul equipped with poison provided by Department Eight. Posing as an Afghan chef, he obtained a job in the kitchens at the presidential palace. But, according to Vladimir Kuzichkin, who defected from Directorate S a few years later, "Amin was as careful as any of the Borgias. He kept switching his food and drink as if he expected to be poisoned."[109]

While Amin was successfully evading poisoning by Talebov, the situation in Afghanistan deteriorated still further. Reports to the Center from the Kabul residency, which had a network of well-placed agents in the Afghan official establishment, forecast that, unless Amin was removed, the Communist regime would be replaced by an anti-Soviet Islamic republic. The prime mover in calling for military intervention was the International Department of the Central Committee, which insisted that the Soviet Union could not permit the overthrow of socialism in a bordering country. Majority opinion in both the Center and the Foreign Ministry, better informed than the International Department about opinion in the West and the Third World, opposed invasion for fear of its international consequences. Andropov, like the FCD, originally opposed sending in the Red Army but, as the situation deteriorated after Amin's coup, Andropov's opposition weakened.[110] According to a Soviet study published in 1989, he began to see a parallel with his own experience in Hungary in 1956, when Soviet tanks had crushed "counterrevolution" and reestablished a stable Communist government.[111]

It was believed in the Center that the final decision in favor of military intervention caused no serious split within the Politburo.[112] The decisive argument, according to Kuzichkin, was the prospect that, without intervention, Islamic fundamentalism, following its victory over the Shah of Iran a year before, might triumph over socialism in

Afghanistan: "The repercussions of such a blow to our prestige would be unpredictable. The Soviet Union could not run such a risk."[113] Nonvoting candidate members of the Politburo were not consulted by the inner circle who made the decision to intervene. Eduard Shevardnadze has since claimed that he and Mikhail Gorbachev, who became candidate members in November 1979, first heard of the invasion from radio and newspaper reports.[114]

At nightfall on Christmas Day 1979 Soviet military transport aircraft began a massive airlift to Kabul International Airport, landing and taking off at three-minute intervals. More Soviet forces entered Afghanistan by road. On the evening of December 27 a Soviet armored column moved out of the airport in the direction of the presidential palace. At its head was an assault group of specially trained KGB commandos led by Colonel Boyarinov, commandant of the Department Eight special operations training school at Balashika. All were dressed in Afghan uniforms and traveled in military vehicles with Afghan markings. On the way to the palace the column was stopped at an Afghan checkpoint. As Afghan troops gathered round, the flaps of the front vehicle went up and KGB troops machine-gunned the Afghans. Colonel Boyarinov led the assault on the presidential palace himself. The president and his mistress were shot in a bar on the top floor. Boyarinov ordered that no witnesses in the palace were to survive to tell the tale. In the course of the operation, while still in Afghan uniform, he was mistaken for a member of the palace guard and shot by his own troops.[115] About a dozen other KGB commandos and Soviet troops were also killed in the course of the operation.[116]

Immediately after the storming of the palace, the exiled Afghan Communist and veteran KGB agent Babrak Karmal, who had been chosen by Moscow to succeed Amin, broadcast a statement claiming that he had taken over the government and appealed for Soviet military assistance. Though his broadcast purported to come from Kabul, it was actually transmitted from inside the Soviet Union; Kabul Radio was still broadcasting normally at the time of Amin's assassination. In the early hours of December 28, Kabul Radio, now in Soviet hands, broadcast the news that Amin had been "executed" on the orders of a revolutionary tribunal.[117] In Moscow Amin was posthumously demoted from "Comrade Amin" to "a bloodthirsty agent of American imperialism."[118]

Babrak Karmal denounced his predecessor as a CIA agent and demanded, absurdly, that the American government hand over all documents on its dealings with him.[119] The Center also seized on the theory of a CIA conspiracy, spreading the story that Amin had been recruited by American intelligence while a student at Columbia University.[120] There were some at Moscow Center who more than half believed their own propaganda. A Soviet historian wrote ten years after the invasion: "The fact that Amin had studied at Columbia University in New York in his youth whipped up our bestial spy mania."[121] Even Kim Philby, in an interview a few months before his death in 1988, was still insisting that "there was more than a suspicion that Amin was dickering with the Americans."[122]

Though the Center had, by and large, opposed military intervention, the consequences were even worse than it had expected. According to Kuzichkin, "We made two major errors of judgment: we overestimated the willingness of the Afghan army to fight, and we underestimated the upsurge of Afghan resistance." By the spring of 1980, 80,000 Soviet troops (whose numbers later grew to well over 100,000) were needed simply to hold the major towns and shore up the crumbling Afghan army against rebel attacks. By the mid-1980s, according to UNICEF estimates, Afghanistan's population had fallen by half; Afghans accounted for one-quarter of the world's refugees. In the small hours of one morning in the early 1980s a KGB general told Kuzichkin what many at the Center thought privately but dared not say openly:

> Afghanistan is our Vietnam . . . We are bogged down in a war we cannot win and cannot abandon. It's ridiculous. A mess. And but for Brezhnev and company we would never have got into it in the first place![123]

In addition to the residency in Kabul, upgraded to a main residency after the invasion, there were eight KGB branch offices in the other main towns. Total KGB officer strength was about three hundred with one hundred support staff. Those stationed in Afghanistan slept with pistols and machine guns by their beds. A young cipher clerk who spent seven months at a provincial residency played Gordievsky recordings he had made of the rebels' nighttime attacks, to which he had added his own vivid taped commentary on the alternate brutality and tedium of the war.

The KGB main resident in Kabul, General Boris Semyonovich Ivanov, appointed shortly after the Soviet invasion, was withdrawn in about 1982, suffering from battle fatigue. Surprisingly, however, KGB applicants for Afghan postings exceeded the jobs available. Young and ambitious officers from the Center looked on the war as an opportunity to make their reputations and advance their careers. In all, the Center received about one hundred detailed reports a month on conditions in Afghanistan. In Gordievsky's experience they pulled no punches and were clearly superior to those from the Kabul embassy because of the KGB's extensive agent network. GRU reports concentrated, as usual, on military assessments.[124]

Soon after the assassination of Amin, the KGB installed the brutal, energetic thirty-two-year-old Mohammed Najibullah as head of the new Security Service, Khedamat-e Etela'at-e Dawlati (KHAD), set up in January 1980 to replace Amin's bloodthirsty secret police.[125] Embarrassed by the reference to Allah in his surname, Najibullah asked to be known as "Comrade Najib." President Karmal announced that KHAD, unlike its predecessor, would not "strangle, pressure, or torture the people":

> On the contrary there will be established within the government framework an intelligence service to protect democratic freedoms, national independence and sovereignty, the interests of the revolution, the people and the state, as well as to neutralize under PDPA [Communist] leadership the plots hatched by external enemies of Afghanistan.[126]

KHAD was trained and organized by KGB officers. In the brutal conditions of an unwinnable counterinsurgency war, the KGB revived on Afghan soil some of the horrors of its Stalinist past. Amnesty International assembled evidence of "widespread and systematic torture of men, women and children" at KHAD interrogation centers. A common theme in its reports was the presence of Soviet advisers directing the interrogations, much as during the Stalinist purges in Eastern Europe a generation earlier. A woman teacher in Kabul, who later escaped to Pakistan, dared to protest to KHAD that her Soviet interrogator "did not have any right to question an Afghan in Afghanistan. This angered them and they tied my hands and burned my lips with a cigarette." On instructions from the Soviet interrogator, KHAD officers then beat her unconscious. When the teacher revived, she was buried up to her neck in the snow. In the days that followed, electrified needles were pressed into her body and she was subjected to other horrific forms of electrical torture, usually in the presence of a Soviet adviser. Remarkably, the teacher survived her ordeal. Many did not.[127]

As a retired KGB general publicly acknowledged in 1989, even in the era of glasnost, the KGB's role in the Afghan War "has still to be told honestly."[128] Najibullah crowned his career at the head of KHAD by succeeding the less resolute Babrak Karmal first as general secretary in 1986, then as president in 1987. Paradoxically, the withdrawal of the Red Army in 1988 was to give a new lease on life to Najibullah's discredited regime. Once Soviet forces had left, the fragmented forces of the Mujahedeen found it even more difficult than before to overcome their own deep internal divisions.

As well as Afghan resistance to the Soviet invasion, the international reaction was also even worse than the Center had anticipated. The KGB had calculated that, as after the Soviet invasion of Hungary in 1956 and Czechoslovakia in 1968, business would return to normal after a brief period of protest.[129] But much of the Third World as well as the West drew a clear distinction between Soviet intervention in Eastern Europe and in Afghanistan. For the first time the Red Army had invaded a country in the Third World.

Events in Poland worsened still further the East-West tension caused by the Soviet invasion of Afghanistan at the end of 1979. A number of celebrated revolutions (among them those in Paris in 1789 and Petrograd in February 1917) have been sparked by bread riots. In Poland rises in meat prices in the summer of 1980 began the strike wave that gave birth to the independent trade-union movement Solidarity, under the charismatic leadership of the hitherto unknown Lech Walesa, a thirty-seven-year-old unemployed electrician who began each day at mass. At the end of August 1980 the deputy prime minister, Mieczyslaw Jagielski, traveled to the Lenin shipyard in Gdansk to negotiate with Walesa and the strike leaders. The Gdansk agreement that ended the strike wave made an unprecedented series of political concessions, ranging from recognition of the right to strike to agreement to broadcast mass each Sunday over the State Radio.

Moscow Center was appalled at the damage done to the "leading role" of the PZPR, the discredited Polish Communist Party. All available Polish-speaking KGB officers were dispatched to the Warsaw residency and liaison office, and to the Soviet consulates in Gdansk, Krakow, Poznań, and Szczecin. As during the Hungarian Revolution in 1956 and the Prague Spring in 1968, many KGB illegals living in the

West were ordered to visit Poland posing as tourists in the belief that counterrevolutionaries would speak more freely to Westerners than to Russians. Though the Center was still formally forbidden to recruit Polish citizens as agents, hardliners in the Polish security service (SB) and PZPR flooded the KGB with alarmist, sometimes almost hysterical, reports of counterrevolutionary subversion. The sheer volume of KGB reporting on the Polish crisis was far greater than that through either Party channels or the Warsaw embassy. A long and pessimistic assessment in the autumn of 1980 by the head of the FCD Polish desk, Ninel Andreevich Tarnavskiy, predicted a bloodbath as the probable outcome.[130]

Solidarity's influence continued to grow during 1981. With, at its peak, nearly ten million members, it represented almost every family in Poland. KGB reports claimed that it had penetrated even the SB and the police, and that Party loyalists were being intimidated by Solidarity activists. Gordievsky was struck by the ill-concealed anti-Semitism of the Center's Polish assessments, which pointed to the prominent role in Solidarity of Jewish "internationalists," such as Jacek Kuron, Adam Michnik, and Mojzesz Finkelsztein (all former members of the Workers' Defense Committee, KOR), as evidence of a Zionist conspiracy.[131] The theme was taken up in public by several of Poland's neighbors. Prague television, reporting a meeting in Warsaw of the anti-Semitic Grunwald Patriotic Association, noted approvingly that speakers had denounced "the treacherous activity of the Zionists" and revealed that Michnik's "real name" was Szechter.[132]

The Center reported that the Ninth Congress of the PZPR, due to meet in July 1981, was likely to consolidate the influence of Solidarity within the Party. It urged that maximum pressure be brought on Stanislaw Kania, who had become PZPR first secretary in the wake of the Gdansk agreement, to postpone the Congress. The ailing Brezhnev, who now had less than eighteen months to live, plainly did not wish to be troubled by bad news. Andropov, for his part, did not wish to damage his chances of the succession by introducing a new element of controversy into the Politburo.

To the Center's considerable annoyance, no pressure was put on Kania, and the Ninth PZPR Congress went ahead in July. It fulfilled the KGB's worst forebodings, voting by secret ballot to sack seven-eighths of the old Central Committee. The Center estimated that 20 percent of the new Central Committee were open supporters of Solidarity and another 50 percent were secret sympathizers. After the Congress was over, Kryuchkov and General Vadim Pavlov, head of the KGB in Warsaw, were summoned to brief the Politburo. Supported by Andropov, both argued that Kania had lost control. Unless a more reliable PZPR Central Committee replaced that elected at the Ninth Party Congress, the socialist system in Poland was threatened with collapse. The Center, however, had lost faith in virtually the entire PZPR leadership. No civilian alternative to Kania attracted serious support.[133]

Within the Politburo, as within the Center, it was accepted that in the last resort the Red Army would have to intervene. But Moscow was more reluctant to send in troops than the West realized. Gordievsky's contacts in the Central Committee told him there was general agreement that intervention in Poland, following that in Afghanistan, would destroy all prospect of détente and arms control for years to come. The Center also predicted serious problems for Soviet occupying forces. It believed that Western intelligence services were conspiring with Solidarity to organize a well-armed and well-equipped underground resistance to wage guerrilla warfare against the Red Army. The only solution, the Center concluded, was for the Polish army to mount a coup d'état. The KGB had much greater confidence in the leadership of the army than in that of the Party. Most Polish officers had trained at Soviet military academies, and many senior officers were veterans of the wartime Polish army based in the Soviet Union. Once the army had restored order and crushed Solidarity, the Center calculated, it would be possible to purge the Party and elect a reliable Central Committee.[134]

The KGB's candidate to lead the coup was General Wojciech Jaruzelski, member of the PZPR Politburo and long-serving defense minister. In February 1981 Jaruzelski had become prime minister. Slim, erect, habitually wearing dark glasses and an inscrutable expression, Jaruzelski was an enigmatic figure for most Poles. Initially, however, he had made a good impression, appointing a reputed "liberal," Mieczyslaw Rakowski, as deputy prime minister responsible for trade-union affairs. Rakowski committed himself to creating with Solidarity "a system of partnership." In October 1981, after much Soviet lobbying, Jaruzelski replaced the discredited Kania as Party first secretary and called for a new "national accord" and a "unity front" with Solidarity and the church. Early in November he met Walesa and Archbishop Glemp for talks in Warsaw.[135]

Jaruzelski, however, was playing a double game. It was believed in the Center that by the time he became first secretary he had already agreed with Moscow to carry out a military coup and had begun detailed planning. The final details of the coup were settled during two sessions of secret talks in Warsaw with General Kryuchkov and Marshal Viktor Kulikov, commander-in-chief of the Warsaw Pact forces. The Central Committee apparatus, however, had less confidence than the FCD in Jaruzelski. A senior Party official, Valentin Mikhailovich Falin, then first deputy head of the International Information Department, told a meeting of KGB officers that it was still not clear whether Jaruzelski could bring the situation under control. Secret talks, Falin told them, were under way to persuade Jaruzelski to delay the next intake of army conscripts for fear that the many Solidarity supporters among them would weaken military discipline. In the event, the call-up proceeded without serious problems. Gordievsky was told by colleagues in both Kryuchkov's secretariat and the FCD Polish section that Jaruzelski had twice asked Moscow for the go-ahead before launching the coup. Brezhnev, in failing health with only a year to live, was now reluctant to make major decisions. Andropov and his Politburo colleagues finally succeeded in persuading him that decisive action could not be further delayed.[136]

The declaration of martial law in Poland on December 13, 1981, was brilliantly planned and executed. There was widespread praise, as well as relief, in the Center for the skill shown by Jaruzelski, the Polish high command, and the SB.[137] For some days before, dense cloud cover had prevented American spy satellites from observing preparations for the coup by the army and militia.[138] The Polish people too were taken by surprise. Most Solidarity leaders were arrested in their beds. Poles awoke on the morning of December 13 to find an army checkpoint at every crossroad and proclamations of martial law posted at every street corner. Jaruzelski himself probably believed that he had saved Poland from a Soviet invasion. Most protest strikes and popular resistance were swiftly crushed by mobile squads of paramilitary ZOMO police. By the year's end the army was visibly in control. Graffiti on the walls of Polish cities proclaimed optimistically: "Winter Is Yours. Spring Will Be Ours!" But spring did not return until 1989, with the formation of a Solidarity-led government under Tadeusz Mazowiecki and the disintegration of the Communist one-party state.

The early 1980s saw the most dangerous period of East-West tension since the Cuban missile crisis twenty years before. During the American presidential election campaign in 1980, Moscow had expected the anti-Soviet rhetoric of the victorious Republican candidate Ronald Reagan to mellow once he had been elected, much as Nixon's had done a decade earlier. Not till Reagan entered the White House did the Kremlin fully grasp that his hostility to the Soviet Union derived not from campaign tactics but from deep conviction.[139] At his first news conference Reagan denounced the Soviet leadership for its continuing commitment to "world revolution and a one-world socialist or communist state."

> They reserve unto themselves the right to commit any crime, to lie, to cheat in order to attain that. . . . So far, détente's been a one-way street that the Soviet Union has used to pursue its own aims.

Reagan's first secretary of state, Alexander Haig (succeeded in June 1982 by George Shultz), was determined to signal the dawn of a new era in Soviet-American relations:

> In the morning of an Administration, the air is fresh and still relatively quiet, and friends and adversaries are alert and watchful. It is the best time to send signals. Our signal to the Soviets had to be a plain warning that their time of unrestricted adventuring in the Third World was over, and that America's capacity to tolerate the mischief of Moscow's proxies, Cuba and Libya, had been exceeded.

"Every official of the State Department, in every exchange with a Soviet official" was instructed to repeat the same message.[140]

The Reagan administration was convinced that as the result of the growth of Soviet military might over the past decade "the American deterrent had been placed in doubt." The defense budget was increased in real terms by 10 percent—double Reagan's campaign promise. Reagan took a much tougher line than Carter on arms control, publicly condemned the SALT treaties, and showed himself in no hurry to return to the negotiating table until the U.S. nuclear strike force had been strengthened. Carter had suspended work on the MX missile and B-1 bomber. Reagan reinstated both.[141] In his sometimes simplistic denunciations of the Soviet Union as the "evil empire," Reagan overlooked one dangerous Soviet vice: its tendency to paranoia in interpreting the West. Andropov saw the policy of the Reagan administration as based on an attempt to give the United States the power to deliver a successful nuclear first strike. During the early 1980s Reagan's evil-empire rhetoric combined with Moscow's paranoia about Western conspiracies to produce a potentially lethal mixture.

In May 1981 Brezhnev denounced Reagan's policies in a secret address to a major KGB conference in Moscow. The most dramatic speech, however, was given by Andropov. The new American administration, he declared, was actively preparing for nuclear war. There was now the possibility of a nuclear first strike by the United States. The Politburo had accordingly decided that the overriding priority of Soviet foreign intelligence operations must thenceforth be to collect military-strategic intelligence on the nuclear threat from the United States and NATO. To the astonishment of most of his audience, Andropov then announced that the KGB and the GRU were for the first time to cooperate in a worldwide intelligence operation code-named RYAN: a newly devised acronym for Raketno Yadernoye Napadenie—Nuclear Missile Attack.

Though endorsed by Kryuchkov (the head of the FCD), Andropov's apocalyptic vision of the nuclear threat from the West was regarded by the main American experts in the Center as seriously alarmist. While they did not doubt his genuine alarm at Reagan's policies, they believed that pressure for Operation RYAN originated with the high command. Its leading advocate within the Politburo was probably the veteran defense minister, Marshal Dmitri Fyodorovich Ustinov, who had been Stalin's armaments commissar as far back as 1941. He would also prove to be one of Andropov's key supporters in the struggle to succeed Brezhnev.[142]

Kryuchkov entrusted the planning of Operation RYAN to the FCD Institute for Intelligence Problems, established in 1978–79 to work on "the development of new intelligence concepts." In November 1981 individual instructions were sent to the residents in all Western countries, Japan, and some states in the Third World. In some cases instructions were brief. The Helsinki residency, for example, was simply told to look out for the evacuation of the U.S. embassy, the closure of American businesses, and other obvious signs of impending crisis. Much more detailed instructions were sent to residencies in NATO countries, calling for close observation of all political, military, and intelligence activities that might indicate preparations for mobilization. Residencies were expected to make Operation RYAN the first priority of their "Work Plans for 1982," submitted to the Center in December

1981. The FCD sent out further guidance in January 1982. Gordievsky was struck by the comparatively low priority accorded to intelligence on new developments in Western missile technology. Much the most important intelligence task remained the detection of preparations for a surprise nuclear attack. In March 1982 Vasili Iosifovich Krivokhizha, a First (North American) Department officer hitherto responsible for coordinating Operation RYAN at the Center, was sent to the Washington main residency to take personal charge of RYAN intelligence collection in the United States.[143]

In May 1982 Andropov left the KGB for the Central Committee Secretariat in order to consolidate his position as heir apparent to the increasingly moribund Brezhnev. It soon became clear that he had displaced his main rival for the succession, Konstantin Chernenko, as effectively second party secretary to Brezhnev. But Andropov was not yet strong enough to place his own man at the head of the KGB. His successor as chairman was a sixty-four-year-old Brezhnev loyalist, Vitali Vasilyevich Fedorchuk, who since 1970 had been chairman of the KGB in the Ukraine. His appointment was unpopular in the Center, where he was generally regarded as a second-rate figure, likely (as turned out to be the case) to be replaced as soon as Andropov became general secretary. Fedorchuk, however, was reassuring for Ustinov and the military. Until 1970 his career had been spent in military counterintelligence; in the late 1960s he had been head of the KGB Third (military counterintelligence) Directorate. He was easily persuaded of the priority of Operation RYAN.[144]

Before leaving to take up a post as a PR line (political intelligence) officer at the London residency in June 1982, Gordievsky was briefed about RYAN requirements in Britain by one of the FCD's leading experts on NATO political and military affairs. The best way to collect intelligence on preparations for a nuclear-missile attack, he told Gordievsky, was through well-placed agents. But it was also important to monitor other telltale indications of impending crisis, such as the number of lights on at night in government offices and military installations, the movements of key personnel, and meetings of committees.

On his arrival at the London residency in June 1982, Gordievsky discovered that all his colleagues in the PR line viewed Operation RYAN with some skepticism. They were, and remained, less alarmist than the Center about the risks of nuclear war. None, however, was willing to put his career at risk by challenging the FCD's assessment. RYAN created a vicious circle of intelligence collection and assessment. Residencies were, in effect, required to report alarming information even if they themselves were skeptical of it. The Center was duly alarmed by what they reported and demanded more. The problems of accurate reporting from the London residency were compounded by the bizarre personality of Arkadi Vasilyevich Guk, who had succeeded Lukasevics as resident in 1980. Guk was the least able KGB resident in Britain since before the Second World War, and owed his posting largely to the British policy since 1971 of refusing visas to known KGB officers. Like Lukasevics, Guk had made his reputation liquidating nationalist opposition in the postwar Baltic republics. Thereafter he transferred to the Second Chief Directorate in Moscow, and served in the KR (Counterintelligence) line at the New York main residency before moving to London.

Guk looked back nostalgically to his years in the Baltic republics and complained that both the Center and the Kremlin had since gone soft on traitors. While stationed in New York he had discovered the whereabouts of the KGB defector Nikolai Khokhlov (the target of an unsuccessful assassination attempt in 1957) and proposed his liquidation. The Center had refused permission, saying that its two main targets were the more senior defectors Golitsyn and Nosenko, and that no other "wet affairs" could be approved in the United States until these two cases had been disposed of. He had also proposed liquidating Stalin's daughter Svetlana and the chairman of the Jewish Defense League—again without success. Guk was a conspiracy theorist as well as a frustrated assassin, convinced that the West was plotting the destruction of the Soviet system. Though careless about the details of Operation RYAN, Guk did not challenge its basic assumptions.[145]

By the time Gordievsky arrived in London Guk's wife was doing her best to ration her husband's formidable alcohol consumption. Guk gained a head start each evening by swallowing a tumbler of vodka before leaving for home. Drink brought out his natural tendency to boast about his own achievements. In July 1982 he briefed the newly arrived embassy counselor Lev Parshin about a mass demonstration in London against the deployment of Cruise missiles. Though a few KGB agents and contacts joined the march, the demonstration had been wholly organized by the Campaign for Nuclear Disarmament (CND) without any assistance from the residency. Guk, however, assured Parshin: "It was us, the KGB residency, who brought a quarter of a million people out onto the streets!" Parshin nodded politely and appeared impressed. As soon as Guk had left the room, he turned to Gordievsky and exclaimed "Whoever heard such nonsense?"

Guk would frequently berate Soviet diplomats for giving away secrets by discussing embassy business in their apartments, which, he assured them, were bugged by MI5. After a few drinks in the same apartments, however, he would regularly boast of his operational successes in London. "That's Guk for you," a Soviet diplomat told Gordievsky one morning. "Last night in our apartment he gave away all your secrets to us and to the British!"[146]

For all his boasting about his successes in London, Guk incurred the displeasure of the Center for failing to foresee that the British were prepared to go to war with Argentina over the Falklands. Guk's first telegram to the Center on the Falklands (or Malvinas as he preferred to call them) was not sent until April 4, 1982, two days after the Argentinian invasion. Thereafter he tried to compensate for his lapse by sending two telegrams a day, mostly based on British media reports, while the embassy sent only one or two a week.

Guk expected the arrogant British to be "taught a lesson." When, to his and the Center's surprise, the British won, Guk opted for a characteristically conspiratorial explanation of "the British colonial war against the Falklands." Mrs. Thatcher and the Conservative government had seized the opportunity to restore their declining popularity by a quick victory against a weak opponent, and NATO had welcomed the opportunity to test new tactics and equipment. The embassy's post-mortem on the war followed the general lines of the residency's analysis. Guk also devised a conspiracy theory to explain the main new development in British politics during the early 1980s, the founding and initial success of the Social Democratic Party (SDP). It had been created, Guk argued, with the help of the CIA and the U.S. embassy in order to split the Labour Party and keep the Conservatives in power.[147]

On September 30, 1982, the FCD sent to its residencies in the United States and elsewhere a circular telegram containing a general review of American policy. By forcing the Warsaw Pact to increase its arms budget in line with Washington's, the Center argued, the Reagan administration was seeking to sow discord between socialist countries, to retard their development and to weaken their links with progressive Third World countries such as Nicaragua and Mozambique. The Center insisted on the need to counterattack with active measures designed to discredit U.S. policy.

In late October the Washington main residency implemented Operation Golf, designed to plant fabricated material discrediting the U.S. ambassador to the United Nations, Jeane Kirkpatrick, on the unsuspecting American correspondent of the London *New Statesman*. On November 5 the *New Statesman* duly carried an article entitled "A Girl's Best Friend," exploring "the often secret relationship" between Jeane Kirkpatrick and South Africa. The article included a photograph of a forged letter to Ms Kirkpatrick from a counselor at the South African embassy conveying "best regards and gratitude" from the head of South African military intelligence and allegedly enclosing a birthday present "as a token of appreciation from my government." The use of the word "priviously" [*sic*] indicated that, as sometimes happens with its forgeries, Service A had forgotten to check its English spelling.

Operation Golf was accompanied by Operation Sirena II, which used another document forged by Service A, this time purporting to provide evidence of American interference in Polish affairs. Like a number of similar active measures, however, Sirena II proved insufficiently sophisticated for a Western market. In general Service A had far greater success in the Third World. The main purpose of active measures in Western Europe was to prevent the deployment of Cruise and Pershing missiles scheduled for late 1983. Since European peace movements scarcely required Soviet encouragement to mount protest campaigns, it is reasonable to conclude that the vast expenditure of time and effort by the Center in this field achieved little of real importance. Guk was not, however, the only resident to claim credit for antinuclear demonstrations on which he had only a marginal influence.[148]

Leonid Brezhnev's last speech, delivered in the Kremlin on October 27, 1982, to a meeting of senior officers and Defense Ministry officials, gave a deeply pessimistic assessment of East-West relations. He denounced the policies of the Reagan administration, and declared that the preservation of peace would demand "the doubling, tripling of our efforts."[149] By the time Brezhnev died two weeks later on November 10, the succession was a foregone conclusion. Andropov was "unanimously" elected general secretary. Though the Party leadership was unwilling to contemplate major reforms, it was eager to have done with the stagnation and corruption of the Brezhnev era.

At this juncture in the Party's history Andropov seemed both a reassuring and an encouraging figure. His treatment of dissidents as chairman of the KGB made it clear that he would have no truck with "ideological subversion." But his record in leading a KGB anticorruption drive, which had reached as far as the Brezhnev dynasty itself, held out the promise of a war on economic inefficiency. Andropov himself seemed to believe that better work discipline and the elimination of corruption were sufficient to revive the Soviet economy. He told Moscow machine-tool workers in January 1983: "Introducing good order doesn't require any capital investment, but it can produce good results." Andropov's new broom produced a brief flurry but no lasting reforms. In little more than a year he sacked about one regional *(oblast)* party secretary in five, often as part of his anticorruption drive. Their average age, however, slightly increased.[150]

Almost as soon as Andropov became general secretary, he received a delegation from the Collegium (senior governing body) of the KGB, headed by one of its deputy chairmen, Filipp Denisovich Bobkov, and including the heads of the main directorates and provincial KGBs. All complained that Fedorchuk's bumbling arrogance had made him impossible to work with, and threatened to resign unless he was removed. Fedorchuk was swiftly kicked upstairs from the KGB to become minister of Internal Affairs, with the rank of army general. Fedorchuk's successor as chairman of the KGB was one of his deputies, fifty-nine-year-old Viktor Mikhailovich Chebrikov, who, unlike Fedorchuk, was respected in the Center as an efficient administrator. Chebrikov had begun his career in the Party apparatus, moving to the KGB in 1967 as head of the Personnel Directorate and, from 1968, one of the deputy chairmen.[151]

Andropov's election as general secretary gave added impetus to RYAN. At the beginning of 1983 some Soviet Bloc intelligence services joined the operation. In London the main support came from the Czechoslovak StB, whose resident told a KGB colleague that this was the first time his service had dealt with military questions. In February residents in NATO capitals received "strictly personal" directives, which they were told to retain in their personal files, giving further guidance on the Western nuclear threat and the steps required to monitor it. The deployment of Pershing II missiles in West Germany at the end of the year would, the Center claimed inaccurately, put Russian targets within four to six minutes' flying time—leaving Soviet leaders without time even to reach their bunkers. (At no time were the Soviet SS20s already targeted on Western Europe mentioned in KGB telegrams.)

The February directive sent to Guk contained unintentional

passages of deep black comedy, which revealed terrifying gaps in the Center's understanding of Western society in general and of Britain in particular. Guk was told that an "important sign" of British preparations for nuclear war would probably be "increased purchases of blood and a rise in the price paid for it" at blood-donor centers. He was ordered to report any change in blood prices immediately. (The FCD had failed to grasp that British blood donors are unpaid.) The Center's bizarre, conspiratorial image of the clerical and capitalist elements in the establishment, which, it believed, dominated British society, also led it to instruct Guk to explore the possibility of obtaining advance warning of a holocaust from church leaders and major bankers. Other sections of Guk's directive were less eccentric. He was given probably accurate details of the alert stages used by U.S. and NATO forces as guides to their mobilization procedures.[152]

The RYAN workload laid on NATO residencies by the Center was staggering. The London residency, probably like others in Western Europe and North America, was instructed to carry out a regular census of the number of cars and lighted windows both in and out of normal working hours at all government buildings and military installations involved in preparations for nuclear warfare, and to report immediately any deviations from the norm. It also had to identify the routes, destinations, and methods of evacuation of government officials and their families, and devise plans to monitor preparations for their departure. All this was too much for Guk. While paying lip-service to the Center's unrealistic demands, Guk delegated the tiresome detailed observations required of the residency to the junior officer who ran the registry. The officer concerned did not even have the use of a car. (Even had he done so, he would have been unable to travel outside London without Foreign Office permission—an important detail that the Center's instructions had unaccountably overlooked.) Under Guk's sometimes alcoholic direction, there were moments when the British end of Operation RYAN more closely resembled the Marx Brothers than Dr. Strangelove.[153]

On February 25, 1983, the Center instructed its three residencies in the United States to begin planning active measures to thwart Reagan's reelection in the presidential election due in November 1984. The Center was convinced that the president considered a nuclear first strike as a serious policy option. Though arms-control negotiations still continued at Geneva, there was, it claimed, no prospect of agreement. Any other presidential candidate, whether Republican or Democrat, would thus be preferable to Reagan. American residencies were instructed to acquire contacts in the staffs of all possible presidential candidates and in both party headquarters. Residents outside the United States were ordered to report on the possibility of sending agents to take part in this operation. The main purpose of these contacts was to gather as much information as possible to discredit Reagan during the campaign and to open up new channels for its dissemination. Simultaneously all residencies in NATO countries and many in other parts of the world were ordered to popularize the slogan "Reagan means War!" ("Reagan: eto voina!").

The Center announced five active measures "theses" that were to be used to discredit Reagan's foreign policy: his militarist adventurism, his personal responsibility for accelerating the arms race, his support for repressive regimes around the world, his administration's attempts to crush national liberation movements, and his responsibility for tension with his NATO allies. Active measures theses in domestic policy included Reagan's alleged discrimination against ethnic minorities, corruption in his administration, and his subservience to the military-industrial complex.[154]

Residents around the globe found it easy to claim the credit, frequently undeserved, for the many anti-Reagan articles that flooded the world's press. But the limitations of their achievements in the West were shown by the failure of any residency in a NATO country to popularize the slogan "Reagan means War!," to which the Center attached such importance. While the FCD was secretly—and ineffectually—plotting Reagan's downfall, the president himself was publicly calling on all Americans to "pray for the salvation of all those who live in that totalitarian darkness [the U.S.S.R.]." The Soviet leadership, he explained to the National Association of Evangelicals at their annual convention in Orlando, Florida, on March 8 was the "focus of evil in the modern world."[155] It was clear that he spoke from the heart.

Two weeks later the nuclear threat from the United States took on a new dimension when Reagan announced the Strategic Defense Initiative (SDI), popularly known as "Star Wars," a defensive shield in space that would use laser technology to destroy Soviet missiles in flight before they reached American targets. To help extract the vast budget for SDI from a tight-fisted Congress, the administration mounted a TV advertising campaign that showed American (but not Western European) children sleeping peacefully beneath an astrodome defense, which seemed to owe more to science-fiction comics than to scientific research.

Initially Star Wars appeared too impracticable to pose a serious threat (though the Center later changed its mind on SDI's potential). But the rhetoric of SDI seemed to demonstrate Reagan's growing belief that the United States could win a nuclear war.[156]

The Center was also anxious to do what it could to damage the electoral prospects of Ronald Reagan's main ally, Margaret Thatcher. The KGB had been conducting active measures campaigns against her outside as well as inside the United Kingdom ever since she became prime minister in 1979. Many of the active measures, however, were too crude to be effective. Gordievsky was personally involved in the case of one of the journalists used by the KGB, Arne Herlov Petersen, a Danish agent of influence, recruited in 1973 by Leonid Makarov, later KGB resident in Oslo. Petersen was a naïve left-wing intellectual carried away by enthusiasm at various times for such improbable anti-imperialist heroes as Kim Il Sung, Pol Pot, and Muammar Qaddafi. From 1973 to 1981, when he was run successively by Makarov, Stanislav Chebotok, Vadim Cherny, and Vladimir Merkulov, Petersen agreed not merely to write articles along lines suggested to him by his case officers, but also to publish under his own name occasional articles and pamphlets written for him in the English language by Service A. Their literary merit was as slight as their political sophistication.

The first of the KGB-Petersen co-productions attacking Mrs. Thatcher was a pamphlet entitled *Cold Warriors,* published in 1979, which gave her pride of place as Europe's leading anti-Soviet crusader. Though the Center was unaccountably proud of its composition, the pamphlet contained such obvious errors as the description of the former Conservative cabinet minister Reginald Maudling as a "rightist Labour politician." Mrs. Thatcher herself, the pamphlet alleged, was out to appeal to "racist sentiments," to promote "capitalist influence," and to wage "war against the British working class." The other "cold warriors" denounced by Service A were its *bêtes noires,* Lord Chalfont (repeatedly described as "Minister for Disarmant" [sic]), Senator Henry ("Scoop") Jackson, Senator Barry Goldwater, Joseph Luns, Axel Springer, and Franz-Josef Strauss.

The next pamphlet, published in 1980, *True Blues,* was devoted solely to attacking Mrs. Thatcher. It made the mistake of attempting satire—always a weak area of KGB active measures—and carried the feeble subtitle "The Thatcher That Can't Mend Her Own Roof." Satire, however, soon gave way to frontal assault. Handicapped by her notorious "lack of appropriate competence in doing Government business," but sustained by "personal ties with big business" and "big monopolies interests," "Tahtcher [*sic*] ha[d] chosen the war path." On this high point the KGB-Petersen co-productions ended. Petersen was arrested in November 1981 and charged with collaborating with the KGB. In 1982, however, the Danish minister of justice, noting that the main guilty parties, the KGB officers concerned, had left the country, granted Petersen *tiltalefrafald* (a waiver of charges). To the obvious dismay of the Danish security service, he was released.[157]

On May 16, 1983, the Soviet ambassador in London, Viktor Ivanovich Popov, called a meeting of senior diplomats and KGB and GRU officers to discuss the June general election in Britain. There was general agreement that Mrs. Thatcher and the Conservatives were bound to win, and that neither the embassy nor the KGB residency could influence the result. Moscow, however, thought differently. On May 23 or 24 the Soviet embassy received the text of a Soviet reply to an earlier letter from the Labour Party about disarmament, which Moscow believed would help the Labour election campaign. When the text was presented to Labour headquarters, however, it declined to receive it until after the election. On May 23 the KGB residency received a telegram announcing that an important document would shortly be telegraphed indicating "themes" that should be introduced into Labour campaign speeches. The text of the telegram, couched in a curious mixture of English and Russian, took some time to decipher and was not ready until May 27. The residency regarded the suggestion that it be used to influence the Labour campaign as impracticable. It took no action.[158] On June 9 Mrs. Thatcher won a landslide election victory.

Shortly after the British general election, the London residency received a telegram from the Center stating that the Reagan administration was continuing its preparations for nuclear war and emphasizing, once again, the priority of Operation RYAN. None of the PR line officers in the residency believed there was any prospect of a Western nuclear attack except as the result of a major East-West crisis. Gordievsky and a colleague tried to persuade Guk that the Center's instructions to collect intelligence on preparations for nuclear attack, followed by the sending of intelligence to Moscow listing possible preparations, which then prompted further instructions from the Center, had created a vicious spiral which was steadily and dangerously raising tension in Moscow. The Center had, for example, praised a report from the London residency on a government campaign to recruit more blood donors. In this instance as in others, it clearly attached a deeply sinister significance to a campaign that was in reality a normal feature of British life.[159]

On August 12, 1983, the Center sent out further RYAN instructions signed personally by Kryuchkov to residencies in NATO countries, listing activities by Western intelligence services that might indicate preparations for a surprise nuclear attack. The checklist of suspicious activities provided by the Center was largely a mirror image of the KGB's and GRU's own contingency plans for war with the West. They included "an increase in disinformation operations" directed against the U.S.S.R. and its allies; "secret infiltration of sabotage teams with nuclear, bacteriological and chemical weapons" into the Warsaw Pact; "expanding the network of subversion-training schools," making particular use of émigrés from Eastern Europe; and an increase in "repressive measures by the punitive authorities" against progressive organizations and individuals.[160]

The most serious moment of East-West tension since Reagan's election followed the shooting down in the Sea of Japan during the early hours of September 1, 1983, of a Korean airliner, KAL 007, en route from Anchorage, Alaska, to Seoul, which had blundered badly off course over Soviet air space. A Japanese sigint station at Misawa, 360 miles north of Tokyo, listened as the pilot of a Soviet interceptor aircraft fired two missiles, then announced at 3:26 A.M. Tokyo time: "The target is destroyed." At first Misawa wondered if it had been eavesdropping on a Soviet exercise in which the missile firing had been simulated. Several hours later, however, it realized that it had heard the last moments in the flight of KAL 007. All 269 of the passengers and crew were killed.[161]

The KAL 007 tragedy derived from the incompetence of both the Red Air Force and Korean Air Lines, combined, in the Soviet case, with disregard for human life. Five years earlier, when another Boeing 747 of Korean Air Lines, KAL 902, badly off course on a flight from Paris to Seoul, had crossed the Soviet frontier near Murmansk, Soviet air defense had lost track of it over the heavily fortified Kola Peninsula. It was finally intercepted and forced to land on a frozen lake three hundred miles south of Murmansk, after being hit, but not destroyed, by a heat-seeking missile, which killed two of its passengers and wounded thirteen others.

Soviet air defenses have been described, with some justice, as "the agricultural sector of the Soviet armed forces."[162] In 1987 they were to become an international laughingstock when a young West German, Mathias Rust, succeeded in landing his Cessna in Red Square in the heart of Moscow. On the night of August 31–September 1, 1983, according to the London resident Arkadi Guk, who was on leave in Russia at the time, eight of the eleven tracking stations on the Kamchatka Peninsula and Sakhalin Island, overflown by KAL 007, were not functioning properly. Recent administrative changes, which had disbanded the previously independent "military districts for air defense" and brought them under the normal military command structure, added to the chaos. The regional command lacked experience in dealing with serious violations of Soviet air space, and responded with a mixture of confusion and brutality.[163]

When KAL 007 was finally reported over Soviet air space, Khabarovsk air force command made several attempts to seek instructions from Moscow. After a confused exchange of messages (monitored by U.S. and Japanese sigint) Khabarovsk reminded the command center on Sakhalin Island of the rules of engagement requiring visual identification of the intruder before shooting it down. Sakhalin ignored these rules. KAL 007 was destroyed by two missiles fired by a Soviet fighter pilot who failed to identify what he was shooting at. At various stages in the crisis some of those in the confused chain of command that dealt with the intruder believed they were dealing not with a civilian 747 but with a U.S. RC 135 intelligence-gathering aircraft.[164] Guk, however, was adamant that by the time the plane was shot down Khabarovsk realized that it was a civilian aircraft.[165]

The official Soviet reaction to the shootdown was initially to deny that it had happened. Soviet fighters, explained Tass, had merely "tried to give assistance in diverting the aircraft to the nearest airfield." Confusion in Moscow over the handling of the tragedy was so great that for three days neither the Soviet embassy nor the KGB residency in London (as, no doubt, in other capitals) received any guidance on what explanation to offer. Then on September 4 three "flash" *(molniya)* telegrams from the Center arrived in quick succession at the residency; the embassy simultaneously received similar communications from the foreign ministry.

The first telegram claimed that KAL 007 was being used by the Reagan administration to whip up worldwide anti-Soviet hysteria. This campaign had become so virulent that the residency was instructed to coordinate measures with the ambassador, the GRU, and the party representative to protect Soviet nationals, buildings, ships, and aircraft against attack. The second and third telegrams contained active measures "theses," which were intended to pin the blame on the Americans and Koreans. The Center insisted that there was close military and intelligence cooperation between the United States and Korean Air Lines. It had therefore to be assumed that KAL 007 had been performing an intelligence role when overflying Soviet territory.[166] This story was later embroidered with bogus reports that the Korean captain, Chun Byung-In, had boasted of previous intelligence missions and shown his friends the espionage equipment on his aircraft.[167] None of the telegrams dispatched by the Center on September 4 acknowledged directly that a Soviet interceptor had shot down KAL 007, though they implied as much. More significant was the fact that they did not explain whether or not the Soviet air force had known that it was attacking a civilian airliner.

Two or three days later the Center sent out two further telegrams with active measures theses claiming that the Americans and Japanese were in full radio contact with KAL 007 during its intrusion into Soviet air space and knew its exact position throughout. At one point, it was falsely claimed, the pilot had radioed: "We're going over Kamchatka." To help elaborate its conspiracy theories, the Center also asked residencies to collect information about those on board; it was particularly anxious to discover links between passengers and Western intelligence services, which could be used to support the Soviet version of events. At a two-hour press conference in Moscow on September 9, the chief of staff of the Soviet armed forces, Marshal Nikolai Ogarkov, announced that a Soviet state commission had "irrefutably proved that the intrusion of the plane of the South Korean Air Lines into Soviet airspace was a deliberate, thoroughly planned intelligence operation. It was directed from certain centers in the territory of the United States and Japan."

All the Soviet diplomats and KGB officers with whom Gordievsky discussed the case were dismayed by the damage done to the Soviet Union's international reputation. Few had any confidence in the official Soviet explanation. Many regarded it as laughable.[168]

The Center was outraged by an interview given to the BBC on September 18 during a visit to London by the editor-in-chief of *Pravda,* V. G. Afanasyev, which cast doubt on the official version of the shootdown. "I wouldn't say that I was very pleased with our first reports . . ." Afanasyev told the interviewer. "I think that in this respect, our military people are guilty. Probably they let some inaccuracy slip by, perhaps they were not certain what had happened."[169] The London residency received a flash telegram from the Center requesting the full text of Afanasyev's interview. A KGB typist began transcribing a recording made by the embassy duty officer, but failed to finish it by the time she stopped work for the day. Next morning a second flash telegram arrived from the Center demanding the transcript immediately. The typist hurriedly finished her work.[170]

    In the immediate aftermath of the shootdown the Reagan administration experienced what Henry E. Catto, Jr., assistant secretary of Defense, later called "the joy of total self-righteousness." The "evil empire" had shown itself to be just that. Visibly angry and waving a secret intelligence report in his hand, Secretary of State George Shultz insisted on the morning of September 1 that there was no possible doubt that the Soviet pilot had identified KAL 007 as a civilian airliner and shot it down in cold blood. President Reagan took the unprecedented step of playing sigint excerpts from the Soviet pilot's exchanges with his ground control in a dramatic television broadcast designed to demonstrate that "There is no way a pilot could mistake this for anything other than a civilian airliner."

    Ambassador Jeane Kirkpatrick played a further set of recorded sigint excerpts in an audiovisual presentation at the United Nations. The presentation was curiously prudish as well as highly dramatic. Soviet expletives were deleted in the translation prepared for the General Assembly. The Soviet pilot's exclamation just before he fired his missiles *"Yolki palki!"* (roughly "Holy shit!") was absurdly toned down to "Fiddlesticks!"

    The main point of the theatrical exercise was to demonstrate, in Jeane Kirkpatrick's words: "The fact is that violence and lies are regular instruments of Soviet policy." Not for the last time, the Reagan administration damaged a powerful case by overstating it. A closed hearing of the Senate Foreign Relations Committee was told that NSA analysts believed the Soviet pilot did not know that his target was a civilian airliner. The issue gradually shifted from Soviet responsibility for the deaths of 269 passengers and crew to the credibility of the American indictment. As the administration struggled to defend its original charge of deliberate, cold-blooded murder, the language of official spokesmen became increasingly tortured.[171]

    One of the main priorities of KGB residencies during the final months of 1983 was to promote the conspiracy theory of a CIA intelligence-gathering mission by KAL 007 devised in Moscow. In its annual review for 1983 the PR line in the London residency claimed considerable success: "We succeeded in inspiring a number of speeches and publications on this question which were favorable to us. Thanks to the Residency's efforts a special program was shown on television exposing the lying intention of the American administration." The Center congratulated the London residency on the results it had achieved: "The efforts of PR line staff to counteract the anti-Soviet campaign over the South Korean airliner deserve special and particular attention."[172]

As frequently happened, however, the KGB overstated the success, at least in the West, of its own active measures. Within the West doubts about the Reagan administration's original version of events did as much to encourage the CIA conspiracy theory as Soviet propaganda. In Britain the most influential version of that conspiracy theory, by the Oxford political scientist R. W. Johnson, owed nothing to Soviet inspiration. "At an early stage," wrote Johnson later, "I became acutely dissatisfied with the official explanation of the event offered by the Reagan Administration, which seemed to beg too many questions."[173] When the Soviet *Literaturnaya Gazeta* published an edited version of a *Guardian* article by him, Johnson made an "angry protest." Some Soviet active measures were simply counterproductive. A visit to Moscow at Soviet invitation by the Pulitzer prize-winning journalist Seymour Hersh helped to undermine his belief in the CIA conspiracy theory. Deputy foreign minister Georgi Kornienko told Hersh bluntly: "Your mission is to find that [the plane] was an intruder."[174]

The most dangerous consequence of the KAL 007 tragedy was its repercussions in Moscow, where it strengthened the belief at both the Center and the Kremlin in a far-reaching anti-Soviet plot by the Reagan administration. Though well aware of the grotesque errors by Soviet air defenses, much of the Soviet leadership—Andropov, Ogarkov, and Kryuchkov almost certainly among them—convinced itself that KAL 007 had been on an American intelligence mission. Gromyko continued to insist, even in the Gorbachev era, that it was clear "to anyone with a grain of intelligence . . . that Washington was in fact defending a plane of its own, that the airliner had simply been carrying a South Korean label." Even those who were skeptical about the CIA conspiracy theory regarded Washington's handling of the crisis as provocative in the extreme and a deliberate escalation of East-West tension. Soviet students were withdrawn from the United States on the grounds that anti-Soviet hysteria was putting them in physical danger.

They were welcomed on their return home as if they were refugees from a war zone.

The Soviet-American dispute over the shootdown quickly torpedoed the meeting of foreign ministers to discuss European security, which opened at Madrid on September 8. "The world situation," said Gromyko, "is now slipping toward a very dangerous precipice. . . . Problem number one for the world is to avoid nuclear war." Gromyko said later of his talk with Shultz at the meeting: "It was probably the sharpest exchange I ever had with an American secretary of state, and I have had talks with fourteen of them."[175]

Shortly before the shootdown, Andropov, now seriously ill, had disappeared from public view, never to reemerge. From his sickbed, however, he issued on September 28 a denunciation of American policy couched in apocalyptic language unprecedented since the depths of the Cold War. The United States, he said, was a "country where outrageous militarist psychosis is being imposed." Reagan was guilty of "extreme adventurism. . . . If anyone had any illusions about the possibility of an evolution for the better in the policy of the present American administration, recent events have dispelled them once and for all." Andropov not merely wrote off any possibility of doing business with Reagan; he also suggested ominously that a major international crisis might be approaching. "The Reagan administration," he said, "in its imperial ambitions, goes so far that one begins to doubt whether Washington has any brakes at all preventing it from crossing the mark before which any sober-minded person must stop."[176] The consequence of the KAL 007 tragedy was thus to add still further to the priority accorded by the Center to Operation RYAN. Andropov spent the last five months of his life after the shootdown as a morbidly suspicious invalid, brooding over the possible approach of a nuclear Armageddon.

At the height of the KAL 007 crisis, though for reasons unrelated to it, the London resident Arkadi Guk suddenly became the laughingstock of Moscow Center. On Easter Sunday five months previously, Michael Bettaney, a disaffected alcoholic working for MI5's counterespionage directorate, had stuffed an envelope through the mail slot in Guk's door in Holland Park. Guk found inside an account of the case put by MI5 for expelling three Soviet intelligence officers in the previous month together with details of their detection. Bettaney offered further information and gave instructions on how he could be contacted. Guk was presented with the first opportunity to recruit an MI5 or SIS officer for a quarter of a century. His addiction to conspiracy theory, however, encouraged him to look the gift horse in the mouth. The whole affair was, he suspected, a provocation. The head of the KR line, Leonid Yefremovich Nikitenko, who was reluctant to argue with the irascible Guk, agreed. Gordievsky said little but secretly informed MI5.

In June and July, Bettaney stuffed two further packets of classified information through Guk's door, providing what Guk believed was clinching evidence of an MI5 provocation. Having despaired of Guk, Bettaney decided to try his luck with the KGB in Vienna. He was arrested on September 16, a few days before he planned to fly out. Guk's reputation never recovered. Shortly after Bettaney was sentenced to twenty-three years' imprisonment the following spring, Guk himself was declared persona non grata. The farcical end to his time in London made a fitting conclusion to his four years as resident.[177]

Guk stayed in London long enough, however, to preside over the most dangerous phase of Operation RYAN in Britain. Tension continued to mount for two months after the KAL 007 shootdown. On October 6 Lech Walesa, whom the Center saw as part of a Western-Zionist plot to destabilize Eastern Europe, was awarded the Nobel Peace Prize. On October 25 the White House spokesman Larry Speakes informed the media that the suggestion that the United States might invade the island of Grenada was "preposterous."[178] The following day U.S. troops did just that, overthrowing the self-styled Marxist-Leninist regime of Maurice Bishop. The Sandinistas in Nicaragua feared that they were next. So too did the Center.

Paranoia in the Center reached its peak during the NATO command-post exercise Able Archer 83, held from November 2 to 11 to practice nuclear release procedures. Soviet contingency plans for a surprise attack against the West envisaged using training exercises as cover for a real offensive. The Center was haunted by the fear that Western plans for a surprise attack on the Soviet Union might be the mirror image of its own. Two features of Able Archer 83 caused particular alarm in Moscow. First, the procedures and message formats employed in the transition from conventional to nuclear warfare were quite different from those on previous NATO exercises. Second, on this occasion imaginary NATO forces were moved through all the alert phases from normal readiness to general alert. Though there was no real alert involving any NATO troops, alarmist KGB reporting persuaded the Center that there was. Surveillance teams around American bases in Europe reported changed patterns of officer movement and the observation by some bases of one hour's radio silence between 1800 and 1900 hours, Moscow time. In the tense atmosphere generated by the crises and rhetoric of the past few months, the KGB concluded that American forces had been placed on alert—and might even have begun the countdown to nuclear war.[179]

On November 6 the Center sent the London residency a detailed checklist of possible indicators of preparations for a surprise nuclear attack. For the first time the Center revealed the time scale of the nonexistent Western plan for a first strike: "It can be assumed that the period of time from the moment when the preliminary decision for RYAN is taken, up to the order to deliver the strike, will be of very short duration, possibly seven to ten days." During that brief interval before Armageddon, "preparations for the surprise attack would necessarily be reflected in the work pattern of those involved." The Center supplied lists of individuals in Britain likely to be involved in negotiations with the Americans before the first strike, key installations of the Ministry of Defense, underground command-post bunkers for central and local government, NATO offices in Britain, British and American nuclear airbases, nuclear submarine bases, repair bases, and ammunition depots, and communications and technical intelligence centers. In addition to "unusual activity" at these bases combined with the cancellation of leave, the Center also expected the approach to the holocaust to be signaled by "unusual activity" at 10 Downing Street, the appearance on the streets of large numbers of soldiers and armed police, the clearing of some news channels for future military purposes, and the evacuation of the families of the "political, economic and military élite" of the United States resident in Britain. U.S. embassy and CIA staff were expected to stay behind in embassy bunkers.[180]

On November 8 or 9, 1983 (Gordievsky cannot recall which), flash telegrams were sent to both KGB and GRU residencies in Western Europe reporting a nonexistent alert at U.S. bases. The Center gave two possible reasons for the alert: concern for the security of U.S. bases following the death of over 240 American marines in a Beirut bombing, and forthcoming army maneuvers at the end of the year. But the Center's telegrams clearly implied that there was another possible explanation for the (imaginary) American alert: that it marked the beginning of preparations for a nuclear first strike. Residencies were instructed to report as a matter of urgency on the reasons for the alert and on other RYAN indicators.[181]

With the end of Able Archer 83 the alarm at Moscow Center

eased slightly. It is reasonable to assume some connection between Gordievsky's warnings to SIS of the Center's reaction to the exercise and various attempts at indirect Western reassurance that followed. But there was no immediately visible easing of East-West tensions. On November 23, 1983, just as Cruise and Pershing II missiles began arriving in Britain and West Germany, the Soviet delegation walked out of the stalled Geneva negotiations on Intermediate Nuclear Forces. Nor did the Center yet show any willingness to lower the priority of Operation RYAN.

In his annual review of the work of the London residency at the end of 1983 Guk was forced to admit "shortcomings" in obtaining intelligence on "specific American and NATO plans for the preparation of surprise nuclear missile attack against the U.S.S.R." The Center did not hide its displeasure.[182] What neither Guk nor the Center could grasp was that the failure to discover "specific American and NATO plans" was due simply to the fact that there were no plans to discover. Had such plans existed Treholt would surely have discovered them during, if not before, his period at the Norwegian Defense College in 1982–83 when he was cleared for NATO Cosmic Top Secret material. But, as so frequently in the past, the Center's conspiracy theories about the West were so deeply entrenched that, at least in the short term, neither lack of evidence nor their inherent improbability did much to undermine them.

Early in 1984 the Center instructed the London residency to monitor four additional RYAN indicators: attempts to build up "anti-Soviet feeling," especially in the civil service and armed forces; the movement of the ninety-four cruise missiles that the Center claimed were based at Greenham Common, surrounded by peace protesters, and of others due to be deployed at Molesworth; the deployment of noncombat units (such as U.S. army transport) and civilian agencies likely to be placed on a war footing as the crisis developed; and the activities of banks, post offices, and slaughterhouses. The last category of indicators revealed some of the bizarre conspiracy theories that continued to distort the KGB's understanding of the threat from the West. The Center's ideological blinkers persuaded it that in the aftermath of a nuclear attack capitalist states would regard the preservation of the banking system as one of their main priorities: "Banking personnel at any level may in these circumstances have at their disposal information of interest to us about the action being taken." Similarly, the Center believed that the food industry had contingency plans for the mass slaughter of cattle, whose carcasses would then be put into cold storage.[183]

In January 1984 the Center held a high-level conference to review "the results of work in 1982–1983." Kryuchkov's opening address reaffirmed that Operation RYAN remained the FCD's overriding priority and provided dramatic evidence of his own personal paranoia about the threat from the West. The risk of nuclear war had, he said, reached "dangerous proportions." That threat derived from the contradictions inherent in the capitalist system: "American monopolies would like to recover the positions they have lost in recent decades and conquer fresh ones." The Pentagon's plans for nuclear war were based on "the fantastic idea of world domination." The White House was engaged in "the psychological preparation of the population for nuclear war." The deepening economic and social crisis in the capitalist world, marked by industrial recession and mass unemployment, had led American imperialists in particular to see war as an escape from their difficulties. The capitalist decision to abandon détente and prepare for a nuclear war was a "class reaction to the consolidation of the socialist position," demonstrated by the worldwide advance of national liberation movements and progressive forces. Obtaining copies of the secret war plans of the United States and NATO was thus the single most important task facing the FCD. Associated with the external imperialist threat was a marked increase in "the subversive activity of émigré, nationalist, and Zionist organizations," and of Western intelligence services. Copies of Kryuchkov's speech were circulated to residencies abroad.[184]

London cannot have been the only residency in which some KGB officers were now more concerned by the alarmism of the Center leadership than by the threat of surprise nuclear attack from the West. Over the next few months they were encouraged to note the emergence in Moscow of a less paranoid interpretation of American and NATO policy. The change seemed to be assisted by Andropov's death on February 9, 1984. Like Andropov, his successor and former rival Konstantin Chernenko was already in failing health when he became general secretary and had only just over a year to live. But he was less morbidly suspicious of Western conspiracies than Andropov had become at the end of his life. Gordievsky learned from Kryuchkov's secretariat that he viewed Chernenko's election with consternation and feared that, as a former Andropov protégé, he might be demoted.[185]

A marginal lessening of East-West tension was apparent even

at Andropov's funeral, which was attended by Mrs. Thatcher, Vice-President Bush, and other Western leaders. The Soviet ambassador in London, Viktor Popov, told a combined meeting of embassy and KGB staff that Mrs. Thatcher had gone out of her way to charm her hosts. She had looked suitably solemn at the lying-in-state in the Palace of Congresses and, unlike other Western leaders, had not chattered inattentively during the funeral ceremony, which had ended with some lack of dignity due to the accidental dropping of Andropov's coffin. Chernenko had had a forty-minute meeting with Mrs. Thatcher, as compared with the twenty-five minutes he had spent with Bush. The prime minister's sensitivity to the occasion and formidable political brain had, concluded Popov, made a deep impression. Though he stressed Moscow's caution on prospects for improved East-West relations, it was clear that the ambassador did not take seriously the idea of a nuclear surprise attack. In March N. V. Shishlin, a senior foreign-affairs specialist in the Central Committee secretariat, visited London and spoke at length on international relations to embassy and KGB staff. He made no mention of a nuclear surprise attack.[186]

The Center, however, continued to insist that NATO residencies send fortnightly reports on preparations for nuclear attack, with flash telegrams for urgent intelligence. The main immediate priority for the London residency was field exercises involving Cruise missiles based at Greenham Common. The first such exercise took place on March 9, 1984, a Soviet holiday. Guk heard the news on the BBC, summoned to the embassy the junior officer responsible for collating RYAN intelligence, who was taking the day off, and said: "What's going on? The enemy are preparing for atomic war, and we have no one in the residency!" The resident is unlikely to have believed that World War Three was really about to begin. He was, however, annoyed that Moscow would have heard the news about the Cruise-missile exercise from Tass before hearing it from his residency. The junior officer quickly drafted a flash telegram based on British press reports, beginning:

In connection with our task to watch for signs of enemy preparations for a sudden nuclear missile attack against the Soviet Union, we report that on March 9 the U.S. and British armed forces conducted the first field exercises of the Cruise missiles based at Greenham Common.

On March 29 the same officer heard a report on the BBC morning news that another exercise had taken place at Greenham Common during the previous night. Since the report had come too late for the morning newspapers, he wondered whether to wait for the *Evening Standard.* In order not to be beaten by Tass, however, he decided to send a flash telegram based solely on the BBC news. On this as on other occasions, the Center was probably unaware that an urgent report from the London residency was based not on an intelligence source but on the British media.[187]

Intelligence from NATO during the spring of 1984 added to the Center's suspicions. On April 25 it sent out a circular telegram inaccurately reporting that Instruction MC 225 from the NATO Military Committee had raised the state of preparedness of NATO communication systems to virtually a war footing. The Center urgently requested further intelligence on the subject. Following the conviction of Michael Bettaney and Guk's return to Moscow in May, his successor as acting resident, Leonid Nikitenko, found it difficult to take Operation RYAN seriously any longer. On July 4 he received a reprimand from the Center reminding him of the residency's obligation to send fortnightly reports even if it had a nil return: "You are not fulfilling this instruction and you are not sending reports once every two weeks. We ask you strictly to fulfill the Directive on this question." Probably never before in the history of the KGB had an operation been considered so vital as to require regular nil returns when there was no intelligence to report. The London residency tried to take credit, without much justification, for the well-publicized protests by CND and the women at Greenham Common against Cruise missiles. Initially, the Center had been skeptical that, with three hundred Soviet medium-range missiles, each with three nuclear weapons, already deployed against European targets, the Cruise missiles at Greenham Common would arouse mass protests. When, against KGB expectations, large demonstrations by the peace movement occurred, the Center wrongly assumed that its own active measures were largely responsible.[188]

By the summer of 1984 KGB officers returning from leave in Moscow had the sense that the priority of Operation RYAN was steadily declining and that the obsession of Kryuchkov and the Center leadership with the threat of nuclear surprise attack was no longer shared either by the International Department of the Central Committee or by the Foreign Ministry. Anxiety in the Center too, was visibly declining.[189] RYAN was further undermined during the second half of

1984 by the disappearance of the two leading military alarmists. In September Marshal Ogarkov, chief of staff and deputy minister of defense, was posted out of Moscow, allegedly for "unparty-like behavior." Three months later the minister of defense himself, Marshal Ustinov, died. His successor, Marshal Sergei Sokolov, was not given full membership in the Politburo.

The world did not quite reach the edge of the nuclear abyss during Operation RYAN. But during Able Archer 83 it had, without realizing it, come frighteningly close—certainly closer than at any time since the Cuban missile crisis of 1962. Among the members of the Politburo who followed the crisis generated by Soviet paranoia and American rhetoric was its rising star Mikhail Gorbachev. He cannot have failed to draw the conclusion that East-West détente was an urgent priority. By October 1984 Western correspondents were reporting that Gorbachev favored "urgent measures to get back to the negotiating table."

14

The Gorbachev Era
1985–

By the closing months of 1984 it was clear to Gordievsky and the London residency that the KGB was backing Mikhail Gorbachev for the succession to the increasingly moribund Chernenko. Before Gorbachev's visit to Britain as head of a Soviet parliamentary delegation in December 1984, during which he had his first talks with Margaret Thatcher, the Center bombarded the London residency with requests for briefing papers for Gorbachev. Unusually, supplementary inquiries continued to arrive after the reports had been supplied. It was clear that some of the questions had been put by Gorbachev himself to those in the KGB who were briefing him. What was the likely outcome of the miners' strike, now eight months old? What were the miners living on? What funds was their strike pay coming from? How much were they getting a week? Was it enough to live on? During Gorbachev's visit, the Center continued to be on edge, insisting that Gordievsky brief him daily. The visit was an obvious success. If Mrs. Thatcher decided that she could "do business" with Gorbachev, it was clear he had concluded he could do business with her. Operation RYAN was effectively dead.[1]

The Center continued to fear, however, that the United States and NATO were seeking some major strategic advantage over the Soviet Union. In February 1985 the London residency was sent a brief from the Center entitled "American Policy on the Militarization of Space," the first it had received on this subject. A covering letter from the Third Department head, Nikolai Petrovich Gribin, cited American plans in space as further evidence of the "American administration's persistence in striving to gain military superiority over the Soviet Union." The United States was said to be planning to equip the shuttle with "a weapon for putting the transmitters of Soviet satellite orientation systems out of action or to use this craft as a bombing agent." SDI ("Star Wars") was also seen as a more serious potential threat than when first officially unveiled two years before. In April 1985 Colonel A. I. Sazhin, head of the London embassy's military attaché section, told a meeting of diplomats and intelligence officers that Moscow thought that SDI systems might sooner or later be able to intercept 90 percent of Soviet strategic missiles. He saw little chance of Soviet SDI research keeping pace with that in the United States.[2]

At the root of the Soviet Union's increasing difficulty in competing with the West was the sorry state of its economy. As the organization best informed about the West, the FCD was more conscious than any other section of Soviet bureaucracy of the West's huge and growing economic advantage and of its increasing view of the Soviet Union as an "Upper Volta with missiles," rather than a genuine superpower. Paranoia about Western plans for a nuclear first strike had given way to paranoia about a Western conspiracy to exploit the weakness of the Soviet economy. The Center was particularly alarmed by a CIA document it had obtained listing priorities for economic intelligence gathering in the Soviet Union: among them, Soviet requirements for imports of grain and other agricultural produce, Soviet foreign currency reserves, the U.S.S.R.'s need for foreign credits, and import and handling procedures for foreign foodstuffs.

Early in 1985 the FCD circulated an urgent warning to Western residencies about the danger of "subversive operations" to "inflict serious economic damage" on the Soviet Bloc. The main immediate danger arose from Soviet grain imports:

By exploiting certain difficulties which we are having in the field of agricultural production, the U.S.A. is attempting to pursue a line which would make the U.S.S.R. dependent on grain imports, the aim being to make use of the food weapon in future to exert pressure on the Soviet Union.

Whereas the West believed that the Soviet Union was obtaining grain and other food imports at bargain prices, the Center believed that it was being exploited. It quoted the president of one grain-trading firm as saying: "The Russians are easy to work with. They don't haggle, they overpay by eight dollars a ton." The FCD recommended "active use" of informers within Soviet trade organizations to discover whether any of their representatives were being bribed to sign unfavorable contracts. It also raised the "unsolved problem" of deterioration of food imports during transit, which had caused "considerable financial loss": "It cannot be excluded that the adversary's special [intelligence] services may use grain delivery firms for deliberately infecting grain imported by the Soviet Union, even in the transshipment ports."[3]

Without a change in Soviet leadership, the KGB saw no end to the problems of the Soviet economy and no end, either, to Western attempts to exploit them. Unable to grasp that the problem lay with the Soviet system itself, it looked to Gorbachev to provide the dynamism and discipline necessary to break out of the Soviet Union's economic stagnation and establish a stable "correlation of forces" with the West. In the months before Chernenko's long-expected death in March 1985, the KGB put great care into briefing Gorbachev in a way that would allow him to impress the rest of the Politburo with his grasp of both Soviet and world affairs. And the reports that it provided to the Politburo as a whole were deliberately designed to support Gorbachev's arguments. Gorbachev's election as general secretary in March 1985 was not, of course, due wholly or even mainly to support from the KGB. But the Center saw the election nonetheless as a major victory.[4] In April KGB chairman Chebrikov, who had been a candidate member of the Politburo since December 1983, was elected a voting member while the minister of defense remained only a candidate member.

Gorbachev quickly demonstrated his support for the KGB outside as well as inside the Soviet Union. In the past, when Soviet intelligence personnel had been expelled from Western countries, Moscow had usually responded with a smaller number of expulsions of Western personnel, which took account of the lower level of Western representation in Moscow. When the Norwegians expelled six Soviet intelligence officers after the Haavik case in 1977, the U.S.S.R. had expelled only three Norwegians. In 1985–86, however, Gorbachev adopted a strict tit-for-tat policy on expulsions. When Britain expelled thirty-one Soviet intelligence personnel in September 1985, Moscow expelled a similar number. When the United States expelled about eighty Soviet intelli-

gence officers from Washington, New York, and San Francisco in
September and October 1986, it was almost impossible to find the same
number of Americans in equivalent positions to expel from the Soviet
Union. But at the suggestion of the KGB, the Kremlin forbade the
numerous locally employed Soviet personnel to continue working in the
American embassy, thus temporarily disrupting embassy routine. In his
early support for the KGB, Gorbachev lived up to Gromyko's celebrated description of him as a man with "a nice smile and teeth of
steel."

Soviet foreign intelligence at the beginning of the Gorbachev era was
coming to the end of an unbroken period of expansion that stretched
back over twenty years. The most dramatic expansion was in its worldwide sigint network. Because the greater part of this network monitored
military and naval targets, the main beneficiary of the expansion had
been the GRU rather than the KGB. By the mid-1980s the Soviet army
had 40 sigint regiments, 170 sigint battalions, and over 700 sigint
companies. The GRU organized sigint collection by over 20 different
types of Soviet aircraft and over 60 surface vessels. In the twenty years
after the launch of Kosmos 189 in 1967, the Soviet Union put over 130
sigint satellites into orbit to fulfill requirements laid down by the GRU
Space Intelligence Directorate based at Vatutinki, fifty kilometers
southwest of Moscow.

The KGB Sixteenth (Sigint) Directorate, though smaller than
the vast Sixth (Sigint) Directorate of the GRU, also expanded rapidly.
Today, in addition to its headquarters in the main KGB building in
Dzerzhinsky Square, it has its own computer complex in central Moscow and a large research laboratory at Kuntsevo, fifteen kilometers
northwest of Yasenevo, off the outer Moscow ring road. The Sixteenth
Directorate, like the GRU, has stations in Soviet diplomatic and trade
missions in over sixty countries; most engage almost solely in sigint
collection, leaving processing and decryption to Moscow. The KGB
and GRU also share in running a series of sigint stations in other Soviet
Bloc or pro-Soviet countries, the largest of which are at Lourdes in
Cuba, near Aden in South Yemen and at Cam Ranh Bay in Vietnam.
Though the GRU is in principle concerned with military communications and electronic intelligence, while the Sixteenth Directorate con-
centrates on diplomatic and economic sigint, there appears to be enormous duplication of effort between the two agencies.[5]

The Sixteenth Directorate continues to depend on the FCD

Sixteenth Department to obtain cipher material from foreign agents. The Sixteenth Department officer in the London residency told Gordievsky in 1985 that there was currently no British source providing high-grade cipher material. There were, however, numerous successes in the Third World, many of whose communications remained an open book for the cryptanalysts of the Sixteenth Directorate, and in a number of other NATO countries. The London residency was informed by the Center in 1984 that a cipher clerk in the foreign ministry of another NATO power, who had been working for the KGB for the past decade, was about to be posted to a London embassy. The agent, however, died suddenly on the eve of his London posting.[6]

The continuing vulnerability of the U.S. embassy in Moscow was shown once again in 1986 when two U.S. marine guards admitted giving KGB agents access to the embassy. In 1987 one of the guards, Sergeant Clayton J. Lonetree, who had been seduced by a KGB cooptee named Violetta Seina, was sentenced to thirty years in prison. But improved security devices meant that Lonetree probably did less damage than other seduced embassy personnel a generation earlier. It now seems unlikely that the KGB succeeded either in gaining access to the cipher room or in planting bugs in other sensitive areas of the embassy.[7]

The most important sigint penetration in the United States in the early 1980s was probably the case of Ronald William Pelton, who had worked for NSA from 1964 to 1979 and volunteered his services to the KGB main residency in Washington in January 1980. For almost six years, until he was arrested in November 1985, Pelton provided detailed intelligence in long debriefings of NSA successes and security procedures in the 1970s which, though not fully up to date, was treated by the Sixteenth Department as of the highest importance. He drafted a sixty-page document which he entitled the "Signal Parameters File," detailing which Soviet communications were given top priority by NSA, how they were analyzed, and with what success. Pelton also compromised five sigint collection systems, among them Operation Ivy Bells, which tapped an underwater Soviet cable in the Sea of Okhotsk. The KGB defector (and redefector) Vitali Yurchenko, who identified Pelton in 1985, appears to have known of no more recent NSA penetration by the KGB.[8]

The KGB, when Gorbachev became general secretary, was a huge security and intelligence empire with about 400,000 officers inside the Soviet Union, 200,000 border troops, and a vast network of informers. Despite the importance of the sigint it supplied, the Sixteenth

Directorate had not yet been accorded the status of a "chief directorate." The most prestigious section of the KGB remained its foreign
intelligence arm, the First Chief Directorate, which, though comparatively small by internal KGB standards, had undergone a major expansion in the previous twenty years. In 1985 a new eleven-story building
was opened at Yasenevo, together with a twenty-two-story annex to the
original Finnish-designed headquarters. The FCD had grown from
about 3,000 strong in the mid-1960s to 12,000 in the mid-1980s. Its
sphere of operations was expanding, too. Japan and the Pacific were
rising rapidly up the Center's list of priority targets.

Aleksandr Aleksandrovich Shaposhnikov, who became Resident in Tokyo in 1983, had a reputation as one of the FCD's high fliers.
The KGB agent network in Japan, which during the 1970s had included some prominent politicians, journalists, businessmen, and civil
servants, had been partially disrupted by the defection in 1979 of an
officer from the Tokyo residency, Stanislav Levchenko. Under Shaposhnikov it seemed to be on the rise again. In the FCD "Plan for
Work" for the period 1982–85, the Pacific Ocean was for the first time
made a major priority, though Japan still ranked behind the United
States, China, India, the Federal Republic of Germany, Britain, and
France as a target. Australasia was given little attention until the mid-
1980s, with only three Third Department officers in the Center assigned
to it. (They also had to look after Ireland and Malta.)

At a meeting of the FCD Party Committee in the autumn of
1984 attended by most of its senior officers, the head of the Third
Department, Nikolai Gribin, was asked why his staff was getting so
little intelligence on China from Australia, given the large Chinese
émigré community. Gribin replied by asking his questioner if he knew
the size of the KGB residency in Australia. He admitted he did not. Nor
did the other senior officers present. Gribin told them that there were
only seven legal KGB officers in Australia and hardly any illegals. It
was agreed that the KGB presence must be strengthened. KGB activity
in Australasia was also increased as the result of the election of David
Lange's Labour government in New Zealand on an antinuclear program in 1984. Hitherto the KGB presence in New Zealand had been
so small that in late 1979, with the KGB Resident, Nikolai Aleksandrovich Shatskikh, on leave and another KGB officer recently expelled,
the ambassador, V. N. Sofinsky, was instructed to pass funds secretly
to the Socialist Unity Party, a task normally entrusted to the KGB. He
was caught and declared persona non grata. The Center, however, was

jubilant at Lange's election and told the London residency that it attached "huge importance" to organizing European support for his decision to ban U.S. ships carrying nuclear weapons from New Zealand ports and for his antinuclear policies in general.[9]

With the exception of a modest increase in its representation in the Pacific and a few new consulates elsewhere, the KGB was no longer expanding abroad at the beginning of the Gorbachev era. It had plans, when diplomatic relations were established or restored with Israel, South Korea, Chile, and South Africa, to open residencies there. In general, however, the fall in oil prices and the growing economic crisis in the Soviet Union denied it the further hard currency it needed to continue its unbroken expansion of the past quarter of a century.

Jobs in the FCD remained, nonetheless, some of the most sought after in the vast Soviet bureaucracy, with enormous competition for the three hundred places each year at its training school, the Andropov Institute. Traditionally, the commonest route into the FCD was through a number of prestigious Moscow institutes, especially MGIMO (Moscow State Institute for International Relations), from which Gordievsky had graduated in 1962. Lebedev, the MGIMO rector, took advantage of the fact that he was frequently lobbied by KGB officers seeking places for their sons. He asked one KGB resident who called on his son's behalf for a West German hunting catalogue. Lebedev then selected from it a hunting rifle with telescopic sights. The resident supplied the rifle and his son got into MGIMO. Despite influential Central Committee connections, Lebedev survived only eighteen months of the Gorbachev era. He was sacked in late 1986.

By the mid-1980s there were increasing complaints in the FCD that too many candidates from the prestigious Moscow institutes were the spoiled children of privileged parents pulling strings on their behalf. As a result, an increasing proportion of recruits to the Andropov Institute came from the provinces. The Center regularly invited provincial KGBs to nominate some of their best young officers as candidates for the First and Second Chief Directorates. Some of those accepted for training by the FCD had never visited Moscow until they arrived at the Andropov Institute.

Entry was racially selective. No Jews were allowed in the KGB. The only exceptions were a handful of recruits with non-Jewish fathers and Jewish mothers who had registered themselves under non-Jewish nationalities. Also banned from the KGB were the national minorities

deported to Siberia in the Second World War (Crimean Tartars, Kara-
chay, Kalmyks, Chechens, Ingushi), as well as ethnic Greeks, Germans, Koreans, and Finns. Most remarkable of all in an institution that
laid fresh flowers each day at the Yasenevo shrine of Feliks Dzerzhinsky, no Poles were allowed into the FCD. Lithuanians, Latvians,
and Estonians, all of whom had played a prominent part in Dzerzhinsky's Cheka, were regarded with suspicion at Yasenevo but not
automatically excluded. Armenians were also suspect because many
had relatives abroad. The sole KGB officer in Malta during the 1970s
was an Armenian named Mkrtchyan, working under cover as a Tass
correspondent. When Mkrtchyan tried to obtain a posting in the United
States, it was discovered that he had American relatives. He was sacked
by the FCD. Most other minority groups experienced no discrimination
by the Center. Internal KGB statistics showed that Georgians, Azer-
baijanis, Uzbeks, and other Central Asian nationalities were more reliable than Russians and Ukrainians. The Andropov Institute also dis-
criminated on the grounds of sex and religion. All the entrants were
male (save for some FCD wives on special wives' courses). Religious
practice was forbidden.[10]

In 1990 the FCD made its first ever public statement about the
qualities it looked for in the graduate entry to the Andropov Institute:

> What is, of course, desirable is robust health and an ability
> to learn foreign languages. Each employee of [the FCD]
> speaks two languages; many speak three or more. . . . How-
> ever, the main requirement for all the future intelligence-
> gathering operatives, without exception, is to be absolutely
> reliable and devoted to the cause.

It was also announced in 1990 that applicants to the FCD are expected
to make parachute jumps from aircraft: "Those who are too afraid are
not suitable candidates."[11]

The Andropov Institute has probably changed little since the
mid-1980s. Then it ran one-, two-, and three-year courses, chosen
according to the entrants' previous education and experience. On arrival, new students were given false identities and "legends" (cover
stories), which they kept throughout their training. They usually kept
their first names and patronymics and adopted aliases beginning with
the first letters of their real surnames. Letters sent to students by their
families were handed to them personally by the staff to protect their

identities from other students. Though given military rank, students wore civilian clothing. Those on a three-year course worked a six-day week with forty-four hours of lessons: fourteen hours of language tuition, twelve hours studying operational intelligence, eight hours of current affairs and area studies, four hours of "scientific socialism," four hours of sports and physical exercise, two hours of military training. Students had access to two libraries: a lending library that contained works by many foreign authors still banned in the Soviet Union, and a nonlending operational library, which contained classified KGB material and theses such as Mikhail Lyubimov's study of "Special Traits of the British National Character and Their Use in Operational Work."[12]

In the mid-1980s, the heads of the three main faculties at the Andropov Institute were all men who had made their reputations working at the London residency before the mass expulsions of 1971: Yuri Modin, head of political intelligence; Ivan Shishkin, head of counterintelligence; and Vladimir Barkovsky, head of scientific and technological intelligence. Some of the most popular lectures were given by retired illegals who described their own experiences working in the West. (Konon Molody, *alias* Gordon Lonsdale, had been a regular lecturer until his death.) Kim Philby, who might well have proved the most popular of all, was not allowed to lecture. Like other defectors from the West, even when his talents were exploited by the FCD, he was kept at arm's length.

Every six months students spent a week in Moscow at "The Villa," an operational training center headed by a commandant with the rank of general, going through a range of exercises, both individually and in small groups: agent recruitment, rendezvous with agents, surveillance, brush contacts, filling and emptying of dead-letter boxes, and other tradecraft. Some of the most difficult information to absorb was local knowledge about the West. To many students, the concept even of such basic features of everyday life as mortgages could be difficult to grasp. Training also included driving lessons. The lack of driving practice and experience among young KGB officers was believed to account for the high accident rate during their first foreign postings.[13]

Graduates of the Andropov Institute in the mid-1980s did not (and doubtless still do not) visit the FCD headquarters at Yasenevo until arriving to begin work after their graduation. For their first week or so, they shadowed the KGB officer whose job they were to take over, listening in to telephone conversations, learning how to fill out forms, open new files, requisition documents from the archives. On taking over from his predecessor, a new officer completed a special form making him responsible for the files relevant to his desk. Telegrams from residencies abroad went in the first instance to the department head, who would then decide which to pass to his subordinates for action or comment.

Before his first foreign posting, a young FCD officer had to go through a number of hoops. If still only a candidate member of the Party, he would have to become a full member. He would also have to marry; the FCD refused to post single officers abroad, believing that their sexual liaisons would make them security risks. Officers selected for foreign postings also had to accustom themselves to their cover jobs, usually as diplomat, journalist, member of a trade delegation, or transport official. Each officer had become thoroughly immersed in his legend; a "devil's advocate" grilled him intensively to try to pick holes in it. Then came a final lengthy positive vetting. Until Stanislav Levchenko's defection in 1979, officers being considered for foreign postings required personal recommendations from three of their colleagues. Afterward five were demanded.[14]

Following his vetting, each officer had to prepare his own "preposting training plan" and get it approved. Gordievsky recalls the case of a young PR (political intelligence) line officer from the Third Department (Britain, Ireland, Scandinavia, Australasia) destined for Copenhagen. Because of the expected opportunities for operations against non-Danish targets, he spent over a week going around the First (North America) Department, the NATO Section of the Fifth (NATO and Southern Europe) Department, and the Sixth (China) Department. Then came over a month in the Directorate of Intelligence Information, a few weeks in Directorate K (Counterintelligence), up to two weeks in Service A (Active Measures) and a week in Directorate OT (Operational Technical Support). Next were a short field refresher course in operational techniques and more driving lessons. Finally came training in his cover job: three to four months in the foreign ministry for a KGB officer under deep cover, perhaps six months at the Novosti Press Agency for those posing as journalists.

Throughout this preposting period the KGB officer would be working hard on the language of the country to which he was posted, and reading novels and reference books. Officers being posted to London would be assumed to have read Dickens already. Their recommended reading list of novels ranged from Fielding's *Tom Jones* to the latest le Carré. Among reference books, the latest edition of Anthony Sampson's *Anatomy of Britain* was virtually required reading. So was Mikhail Lyubimov's classified thesis and a book on Britain by the former *Pravda* correspondent Ovchinnikov.[15]

The officer's wife was expected to attend a three-month course held one evening a week and occasionally during the day, run at a special training center at Zubovskaya Square in Central Moscow, founded in 1980. There she heard lectures on the work of the KGB and the country in which she would be living, combined with exhortations not to complain when her husband had to spend the evening working. In August 1983, the Andropov Center began one-year training courses for specially selected wives who were to work, usually under their husbands' direction, in husband-and-wife teams.

Remarkably, the FCD had fewer women in responsible jobs during the early years of Gorbachev than during the last years of Stalin—and that in a country in which 90 percent of the teachers, 80 percent of the doctors, and 30 percent of the engineers (but no Politburo member or senior diplomat) are women. Of the labor force at Yasenevo, about 10 percent were women, almost all of them secretaries, typists, computer programmers, canteen workers, and cleaners. To meet a woman in a corridor of the main departments was an event. One of the few women with a job of officer rank, in the French section of Service A (Active Measures), was the butt of endless sexist jokes, and was popularly known as "the lady who sits on France."[16]

Since the KGB began its public relations campaign in 1988, its lack of female personnel has become something of an embarrassment, but there are as yet few signs of change. During a televised Moscow phone-in late in 1989, the interviewer asked five senior (and inevitably all male) KGB officers: "Are there women in the KGB? And if there are, what percentages do they make up and in what jobs do they work?" Major General Anatoli Petrovich Bondarev gave the embarrassed reply: "There are women in the KGB. In some sectors they are simply irreplaceable. But as far as the percentage is concerned, it is difficult for me to say now. I simply did not expect this question and did not get those statistics." None of Bondarev's colleagues seemed inclined to recall either the statistics or the "irreplaceable sectors" (canteens and typing pools chief among them) of women workers in the KGB. The interviewer moved on to a less embarrassing topic.[17]

*   *   *

Gordon Lonsdale

Gordon Lonsdale, one of the leading postwar illegals, whose portrait appears in the FCD Memory Room, photographed here with one of his many girlfriends in London.

Men's room at the Classic Cinema, Baker Street, London, used by Lonsdale as a dead-letter box. Notes and radio spare parts were hidden inside a condom in the cistern.

Lonsdale as a director of the Master Switch Co. Ltd., which won a gold medal at the International Inventors Exhibition in Brussels in 1960. He was proud of this portrait of himself beneath two union jacks and showed it to Gordievsky.

Philby

Above Kim Philby explains his innocence to Alan Whicker and others at a 1955 press conference in his mother's flat. *(Topham Picture Library)*

Below Donald Maclean and his soon-to-be-estranged wife at Burgess's cremation in Moscow in 1963. Burgess's ashes, like those of Maclean later, were interred in Britain. Philby is buried in Moscow. *(Associated Press)*

Oleg Kalugin, the youngest FCD general and head of the FCD Directorate K in the mid 1970s, who became Philby's main protector within the KGB but was sacked from the FCD in 1980 for holding views similar to Philby's. *(Novosti)*

Below Philby with KGB General Lukasevics (*alias* Bukashev), former KGB resident in London 1972–80, appearing on Estonian television in 1987 to advance the theory that nationalism in the Baltic States was being whipped up by Western intelligence.

Philby's funeral in 1988. *Right* His grave in Moscow. To his chagrin, Philby was denied officer rank within the KGB and died with the code name "Agent Tom." *(both, Associated Press)*

The 1980s

Arkadi Guk, heavy-drinking KGB resident in London 1980–84, whose expulsion paved the way for Oleg Gordievsky's appointment as resident, pictured here with his wife. *(Solo Syndication)*

Michael Bettaney, in an early photo, who in 1983 became the first MI5 officer for many years to offer himself for recruitment as a KGB agent. Guk, suspecting a provocation, declined the offer. *(S&G Press Agency)*

The Norwegian Arne Treholt *(left)*, one of the KGB's most important Scandinavian agents, secretly photographed at a meeting with his main Soviet controller, Gennadi Titov *(center)* and Aleksandr Lopatin, also of the KGB, at a meeting in Vienna in 1983. Titov's running of Treholt earned him promotion to the rank of KGB general. *(Associated Press)*

Terrorism

Above KGB assassin Nikolai Khokhlov shaking hands with his intended victim Georgi Okolovich in 1954. After his defection Khokhlov himself became the victim of an almost-successful KGB assassination attempt. *(Associated Press)*

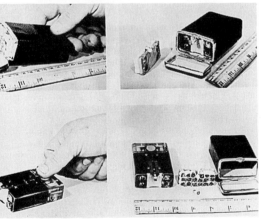

One of the murder weapons supplied to Khokhlov: a gun concealed inside a cigarette packet. *(Associated Press)*

Georgi Markov, the Bulgarian dissident murdered in London in 1978, and the poisoned pellet, fired from an umbrella, that killed him. The poison used was supplied by KGB General Golubev of the FCD. *(both, Press Association)*

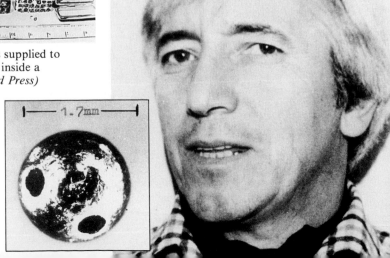

PLO leader Yasser Arafat laying a wreath in Moscow in
1974. Immediately behind him is a KGB officer, Vasali
Samoylenko, chosen by the Center to cultivate Arafat.
(Associated Press)

By the early 1980s Colonel Qaddafi's recurrent obsession
with terrorism was causing some alarm in the KGB. The
Center had evidence that the shooting from the Libyan
embassy in London that killed WPC Fletcher *(inset)* in
1984 was on Qaddafi's personal instructions.
(Syndication International; Metropolitan Police)

KGB Publications

Left *Imperialism: The Tragedy of Ulster* by Nikolai Gribin—a denunciation of British policy in Northern Ireland published in 1980. As head of the FCD's 3rd Department in 1985, Gribin visited Dublin to try to improve the performance of the KGB residency.

Below left Two children's books by Zoya Rybkina (*alias* Yartseva, *alias* Voskresenskaya). Rybkina became one of the very few women to achieve the rank of colonel as an operational KGB officer in the early 1950s; no other woman in the FCD has since achieved this rank.

Below right An example of KGB active measures: a forged letter from the South African embassy to the U.S. ambassador to the United Nations, manufactured by FCD Service A and foisted on the unsuspecting *New Statesman. (New Statesman)*

FOREIGN NEWS: DIPLOMACY

A girl's best friend

Claudia Wright explores the often secret relationship between US Ambassador to the UN, Jeane Kirkpatrick, and South Africa

THE UNITED STATES Ambassador to the United Nations, Jeane Kirkpatrick, celebrates her birthday on 19 November. Last year the South African government sent a special courier to the Ambassador's New York office to deliver a birthday greeting. It was signed by Pieter Swanepoel, the Information Counsellor at the South African Embassy in Washington, that just arrived from Pretoria. There were also 'best regards and gratitude' from Lieutenant-General P. W. van der Westhuizen, head of South Africa's military intelligence. With the letter (see illustration) came a birthday gift, a 'token of appreciation', honouring Kirkpatrick's 'activity for freedom and democracy'.

New birthday presents are normal enough among friends and Kirkpatrick has been a friend, if not of freedom and democracy, at least of the parody version practised in South Africa. According to United States law, Mrs Kirkpatrick is obliged to report any gift to the Protocol Office of the Department of State. If it is of more than nominal value, she may not keep it for herself.

Kirkpatrick has not reported her gift from the South African government. In the annual list of gifts to US officials – published in the Federal Register on 26 March 1982 – Kirkpatrick remembered to record a small rust and green rug, worth $300, given to her on 30 August 1981, by General Mohammed Zia of Pakistan – but that was all. When I asked the Ambassador's office about a gift from South Africa in 1981, the response was there had been none. Swanepoel and the South African ambassador, Brand Fourie, also say that they 'know nothing about such a gift'.

Forgetfulness in reporting gifts has caused trouble for exalted officials in the Reagan Administration, among them the President's first Assistant for National Security Affairs, Richard Allen, who lost his job because of a Japanese watch and honorarium. More important, however, in the case of Mrs Kirkpatrick are the reasons General van der Westhuizen and the Pretoria government felt so grateful to the ambassador.

DURING 1981, General van der Westhuizen had several reasons for being personally grateful to Kirkpatrick. She was, for example, the most senior US official to meet him and four other South African military intelligence men on 15 March (see *NS* April 3, 1981). Until that meeting, the US had barred official visits by South African officers of brigadier rank or above. Early reports about Kirkpatrick's meeting were denied. She then admitted there had been a meeting, but lied about her knowledge of van der

Westhuizen's identity. The then Secretary of State, General Alexander Haig, intervened to tell the press that Kirkpatrick's meeting with van der Westhuizen had his personal authorisation.

The South African general returned to the US again, on 23-24 November, to attend a negotiating session on Namibia which was held near Washington. The State Department admits that Assistant Secretary of State for Africa, Chester Crocker, was at this meeting van der Westhuizen at that time. He returned for another visit (his third at least), this time to the State Department in Washington, on 22-23 February, this year. In Kirkpatrick's absence, the meetings were monitored by an official from her office.

Each of van der Westhuizen's visits have preceded major shifts in US policy, and large, usually secret, concessions to South African demands. Kirkpatrick's role on each occasion has been that of a 'go-between', according to officials at the UN, relaying South African requests to Washington, and helping to coordinate joint American-South African positions and negotiating tactics. According to a State Department official, she is one of several members of 'President Reagan's entourage (whose) furtive association . . . with some foreign governments, the South African regime in particular . . . will inflict serious damage to the long-term interests of my country'.

After the March 1981 meeting with van der Westhuizen, the administration sent Assistant Secretary Crocker to Pretoria. Summaries of his talks there were leaked and

published by the *Covert Action Information Bulletin*. The documents reveal that Crocker told the South Africans that 'top US priority is to stop Soviet encroachment in Africa. US wants to work with SAG (South African Government) but ability to deal with Soviet presence severely impeded by Namibia . . . USG (US Government) assumes Soviet/Cuban presence is one of (SA's) concerns and we are exploring ways to remove in the context of Namibia settlement.' This was the beginning of a US-South African shift on the terms of the settlement for Namibia, undermining the current UN resolution on Namibia and ending the effective negotiating role carried out so far by the Namibia 'contact group' – the US, UK, Canada, France and Germany. It was also the beginning of the 'linkage' in US and South African policy between the withdrawal of South African forces and the independence of Namibia on the one side, with a simultaneous withdrawal of Cuban forces from Angola to the north. According to South African officials, the idea of this 'linkage' was 'something the Americans initiated, wanted, and pursued'.

The Kirkpatrick and Crocker meetings in early 1981 were also the green light for general van der Westhuizen and his fellow generals to widen their military operations in Namibia and Angola and to escalate covert operations against Mozambique and Zimbabwe. As South African troops advanced into southern Angola in August 1981, Kirkpatrick played the role of public defender at the UN. The draft resolution requested by Angola condemning the South African invasion had overwhelming support in the Security Council on 31 August. But Britain abstained and Kirkpatrick cast the American veto. The justification she gave was that South Africa's attack was a legitimate reprisal for SWAPO raids from Angolan bases into Namibia – the same view Crocker had privately offered in Pretoria on 15 April.

Kirkpatrick was to play the same role protecting South Africa from UN votes on sanctions through the autumn of 1981, and

Kryuchkov and the FCD

Vladimir Kryuchkov, head of the FCD 1974–88, the first foreign intelligence chief to become chairman of the KGB. *(Associated Press)*

Prezydent Wojciech Jaruzelski przyjął Wladimira Kriuczkowa

26 bm. prezydent Wojciech Jaruzelski przyjął przebywającego z roboczą wizytą w Polsce przewodniczącego Komitetu Bezpieczeństwa Państwowego ZSRR Wladimira Kriuczkowa.

Wizyta u premiera Mazowieckiego

Tego samego dnia prezes Rady Ministrów Tadeusz Mazowiecki przyjął Wladimira Kriuczkowa. W spotkaniu uczestniczył gen. broni Czesław Kiszczak.

The beginning of the end of the Communist order in Eastern Europe. Kryuchkov visits Warsaw in 1989 for talks with Poland's first Solidarity prime minister, Tadeusz Mazowiecki. Eight years earlier, though Kryuchkov has never admitted it, he had visited Poland to discuss the crushing of Solidarity with General Jaruzelski.

The FCD's Finnish-designed headquarters at Yasenevo. The layout appears in Appendix C.

Abroad, as at Yasenevo, the working routine of FCD officers seems to have changed little since the beginning of the Gorbachev era. Most officers in foreign residencies work in one of three "lines": PR (Political Intelligence), KR (Counterintelligence and Security), or X (Scientific and Technological). The head of each line has the status of deputy resident. The ratio of officers in many residencies is roughly PR 40 to KR 30 to X 30. Before their arrival new officers would have attended a series of alarmist briefings on the ever-present danger of "provocations" by Western intelligence services. In Gordievsky's experience, they began by suspecting their neighbors, local shopkeepers, even the gardeners in the London parks they crossed, and imagined themselves under constant surveillance. Most gradually got over it.

The working day in the residency begins at 8:30 A.M. PR line officers begin the day by looking over the day's newspapers. In London, they are expected to read all the main daily and Sunday newspapers, together with periodicals, of which the *Economist* and *Private Eye* are probably read with greatest attention. At the start of each day residency officials collect their working satchels *(papka)* from the safe. These are larger than most briefcases, have two compartments, and open with a zipper. The most important of their contents is the officer's working notebook *(rabochaya tetrad),* which contains notes on all his operational contacts and the main items from correspondence with the Center. Another notebook is used to draft telegrams and reports to Moscow. Each officer has an individual seal with a distinctive emblem and number, which is usually kept on his key ring. At the end of each working day he closes his working satchel, applies a piece of Plasticine to the end of the zipper and presses his seal on it.[18]

Though Soviet embassies send their reports to Moscow on ordinary paper, KGB residents use 35-mm film negative. Residents' communications are first enciphered by a KGB cipher clerk, then filmed by an OT (operational and technical support) operative. Incoming correspondence from the Center arrives on developed film, which is read on a microfilm reader. By the beginning of the Gorbachev era there was an increasing tendency to print out paper copies of important communications from the microfilm. Report telegrams to the Center began with a standard formula, as in the following example.

Comrade IVANOV
I–77-81090-91-111-126

This decodes as follows:

"IVANOV" is the code name for the department in the Center to which the telegram is addressed, in this case the First (North American) Department.

"I" indicates that the telegram is reporting intelligence, rather than, say, active measures or operational details concerning agent running.

Number sequences beginning with 7 tell how the text was drafted: 77 indicates drafting by the residency, 78 by the source, 79 the translation of an official text.

The number 8 prefaces the month and year of the report, in this case October 1990.

The number 9 indicates the type of source: 91 is an agent (as in this instance), 92 a confidential contact, 93 a target for close study *(razrabotka),* 94 an official contact.

The number 11 prefaces assessments of reliability: 111 is reliable (as in this case), 112 untested, 113 unreliable.

The number 12 refers to the occupation of the source; for example, 121 indicates a source in government, 126 in the foreign ministry, 1213 in the press.[19]

In Gordievsky's experiences, however, much KGB reporting was far less precise. Residencies would rarely fabricate details about, or intelligence from, individual agents. But in reports on particular topics they would commonly attribute to unnamed agents information obtained from the media or even invent details they thought would please the Center. Such practices were still common at the beginning of the Gorbachev era. On March 25, 1985, the London residency was asked for urgent information on British reactions to Gorbachev's meetings with the Consultative Committee of the Socialist International. Unable to contact residency sources in the time available, the PR line simply invented a series of responses flattering to Gorbachev; it gave as its sources a range of fictional contacts. Next day the residency was asked for another urgent report, this time on negotiations on Spanish and Portuguese entry to the European Community. This time the PR line reports officer V. K. Zamorin simply went through the British press and concocted a report attributed once again to secret or confidential sources. Soon afterward the residency found an article that impressed it in the *Economist Foreign Report,* identifying areas in which the Soviet Union had succeeded in acquiring advanced Western technology and others where it had failed. Knowing that the article would be rejected by the Center as disinformation, the residency did not send it to Moscow. Instead it sent a report based on the article to the Center, claiming that it derived from residency contacts. As most officers in the Center had been guilty of similar abuses themselves when stationed abroad, they rarely voiced their suspicions about the source of some of the reports they received.[20]

Making contact with fully recruited agents, which all residencies see as their most important form of intelligence collection, is an enormously labor-intensive business because of the elaborate counter-surveillance procedures laid down by KGB tradecraft. For a rendez-vous with an agent at 4 P.M., a case officer would usually leave the residency at 1 P.M., drive by an elaborate route worked out beforehand to an inconspicuous parking place, preferably near a large block of apartments. He would avoid parking either outside a private house where his diplomatic license plate might attract attention or in a parking lot where the police might carry out checks. After parking his own car the case officer would be picked up by another officer, who would drive around for an hour checking that they were not under surveillance. Meanwhile the KR (counterintelligence) line in the embassy would be trying to monitor radio communications from surveillance teams of the local security service to detect any sign that the case officer or the agent was being followed: an activity code-named "Impulse." The car radios of the case officer and his colleague were tuned to the wavelength of the embassy transmitter, which broadcast a coded warning consisting simply of the repetition in Morse of one letter of the alphabet (the letter chosen indicating the KGB officer to whom the warning was directed). At about 3 P.M., if no surveillance had been detected, the officer would leave his colleague's car and make his way on foot and by public transport to the 4 P.M. rendezvous with the agent.[21]

Despite all the changes in the KGB over the last half century, the main operational priority of its foreign intelligence arm has scarcely altered since the recruitment of the Magnificent Five. In the operational section of the 1984 work plan circulated to foreign residencies, Kryuchkov repeated the traditional formula: "The main effort must be concentrated on acquiring valuable agents." He went on to exhort residencies to explore new possibilities of agent recruitment "especially among young people with prospects for penetrating targets of interest to us."[22] There is no indication that Kryuchkov has changed his mind since becoming chairman of the KGB in 1988.

*   *   *

From the moment that he came to power in March 1985, Mikhail Gorbachev saw two main priorities for KGB foreign operations. First, he was convinced that a dynamic foreign policy required a dynamic intelligence service. The unprecedented range of initiatives on which he embarked abroad made it vital to have the fullest possible political intelligence on Western responses to them.

The increased demands on the PR line were already apparent before Gordievsky's escape from Russia in the summer of 1985 and have no doubt expanded since. The main priority of the FCD as it entered the 1990s was clearly exemplified by the choice of Leonid Vladimirovich Shebarshin to succeed Kryuchkov as its head in September 1988.[23] Like Aleksandr Semyonovich Panyushkin, head of the FCD from 1953 to 1956, Shebarshin began his career as a straight diplomat, serving in Pakistan from 1958 to 1962 and again from 1966 to 1968, where he began cooperating with the KGB residency. Following his second term in Pakistan, he transferred to the KGB and after training at the Andropov Institute began work at Yasenevo. In 1971 he was posted to India, where he headed the PR line before becoming main resident in New Delhi from 1975 to 1977. After the fall of the Shah in 1979 he became resident in Teheran, remaining there until his expulsion in 1983. When Gordievsky left the FCD in the summer of 1985, Shebarshin had been working for about a year as deputy head of Directorate RI, which prepares FCD reports for the top Soviet leadership.[24] For Shebarshin to have leapfrogged several more senior candidates to succeed Kryuchkov in 1988 is a certain indication that his reports in the previous few years had greatly impressed the Politburo. And for them to have impressed the Politburo, they must have dealt with such major issues as the West's response to the "new thinking" of the Gorbachev era. Just as Gordievsky's appointment as London resident was helped by his briefings to Gorbachev in December 1984, so Shebarshin's promotion to head of the FCD probably also reflects Gorbachev's confidence in his intelligence assessments.

During the 1990s the KGB will continue to exploit the traditional fascination of the Soviet leadership with highly classified reports. As in the past, the KGB doubtless continues to present some of the material it obtains from open sources as coming from secret agents. Shebarshin defines the main function of the FCD as "the task of ensuring that the Soviet leadership has reliable and accurate information about the real plans and designs of the leading Western countries with regard to our country and about the most important international problems."[25] The FCD will continue for as long as possible to foster the myth that only it truly understands the West. Its influence will only be increased by the Soviet Union's military, ideological, and economic problems. As the Warsaw Pact gradually disintegrates, the Kremlin is withdrawing hundreds of thousands of troops from Eastern Europe. And as the ideological foundations of the Soviet state begin to crumble, Moscow's prestige as the pilgrim center of the Communist faith is crumbling, too. The crisis in the Soviet economy is simultaneously compelling a decline in Soviet aid to developing countries. Intelligence thus takes on an enhanced importance as a means of preserving the Soviet Union's declining influence in the outside world.

Gorbachev's second main interest in Soviet foreign intelligence operations lies in the field of scientific and technological espionage (S&T). When he addressed the staff of the London embassy at a private meeting attended by Gordievsky on December 15, 1984, he singled out for praise the achievements of the FCD Directorate T and its Line X officers abroad. It was already clear that Gorbachev regarded covert acquisition of Western technology as an important part of economic *perestroika.*

For some years Directorate T had been one of the most successful in the FCD. Its dynamic and ambitious head, Leonid Sergeevich Zaitsev, who had begun specializing in S&T while at the London residency in the 1960s, campaigned unsuccessfully for his directorate to leave the FCD and become an independent directorate within the KGB. Kryuchkov, however, was determined not to allow such a prestigious part of his intelligence empire to escape from his control. Zaitsev claimed not merely that his directorate was self-supporting but that the value of the S&T it obtained covered the entire foreign operating costs of the KGB. Despite failing to win its independence, Directorate T functioned increasingly independently of the rest of the FCD. Its officers trained separately in the Andropov Institute from those of other departments and had their own curriculum. Almost all came from scientific and engineering backgrounds. In foreign residencies Line X officers mixed relatively little with their colleagues in other lines. Directorate T, however, was only part—though a crucial part—of a much larger machinery of S&T collection.[26]

S&T intelligence gathering in the defense field—the chief priority—was coordinated in the early 1980s by the Military Industrial

Commission (VPK), upgraded under Gorbachev to the State Commission for the Military-Industrial Complex, which oversees all weapons production. The VPK is chaired by a deputy prime minister and tasks five collection agencies: the GRU, FCD Directorate T of the KGB, the State Committee for Science and Technology (GKNT), a secret unit in the Academy of Sciences, and the State Committee for External Economic Relations (GKES). Documents provided during the early 1980s by a French penetration agent in Directorate T, code-named Farewell, show that in 1980 the VPK gave instructions for 3,617 S&T "acquisition tasks," of which 1,085 were completed within the year, benefiting 3,396 Soviet research and development projects.[27] Ninety percent of the intelligence judged most useful by the VPK in the early 1980s came from the GRU and the KGB. Though much S&T came from unclassified sources in the West such as scientific conferences and technical brochures, secret intelligence was judged to be of crucial importance. In 1980, 61.5 percent of the VPK's information came from American sources (not all in the United States), 10.5 percent from West Germany, 8 percent from France, 7.5 percent from Britain, and 3 percent from Japan.

Though no statistics are available for the Gorbachev era, all the evidence suggests that the scale of Soviet S&T has tended to increase rather than to decrease. Among the VPK's major successes have been a Soviet clone of the U.S. airborne radar system, AWACS; the Russian Blackjack bomber, copied from the American B1-B; the RYAD series of computers plagiarized from IBM originals; and integrated circuits purloined from Texas Instruments.[28] The Soviet armed forces have come to rely on S&T successes like these. Currently about 150 Soviet weapons systems are believed to depend on technology stolen from the West.

Less than half the work of Directorate T, however, follows VPK requirements. Of the 5,456 "samples" (machinery, components, microcircuits) acquired by it in 1980, 44 percent went to defense industries, 28 percent to civilian industry via the GKNT, and 28 percent to the KGB and other agencies. In the same, possibly exceptional, year, just over half the intelligence obtained by Directorate T came from allied intelligence services, the East Germans and Czechoslovaks chief among them. Soviet bloc S&T continued to expand until 1989.[29] Even at the beginning of 1990 some East European foreign intelligence services were trying to impress their new political masters by concentrating on the sort of Western technology required to modernize their outdated industries. The director of the CIA, William Webster, claimed in February 1990 that the KGB was still expanding its work, "particularly in the United States, where recruiting of people with technical knowledge or access to technical knowledge has increased."

Directorate T's successes in Western Europe included intelligence from Italy on the Catrin Electronic Battlefield Communications System being developed for introduction by NATO in the early 1990s; and the use of a team of West German computer hackers to gain access to the Pentagon data bank and a variety of other military business and research computer systems. The main expansion of Line X work at the start of the 1990s, however, appeared to be taking place in Japan and South Korea.[30] The application of S&T to Soviet industry is an increasingly complex business. The imitation of the new generation of American and Japanese microcircuits involves tracking hundreds of thousands of connections and mastering a whole series of complex production procedures. The most plentiful S&T in intelligence history has failed to prevent the growing gap between Soviet and Western technology, particularly outside the defense field. That growing gap, in turn, makes the imitation of some of the most advanced Western inventions progressively more difficult.

As well as providing large amounts of political, scientific, and technological intelligence, the KGB also made a broader contribution to the "new thinking" of the Gorbachev era. The disintegration of the one-party Soviet system, as Ernest Gellner has persuasively argued, was due partly to a two-stage process of internal decay. Under Stalin it had been sustained by both the fear of its subjects and an officially prescribed faith, which few of them dared to question. Under Khrushchev fear largely disappeared. Those who believed and those who conformed were relatively safe from the often random terror of the Stalinist era. For most Soviet citizens, repression gave way to stagnation. By the end of the Brezhnev era, after the brief false dawn of the Andropov succession, faith in the system had vanished, along with much of the fear it had once inspired. What remained was what the Soviet historian Batkin has termed serocracy, "the rule of the gray": a faceless, dreary, stagnant, and corrupt bureaucracy.[31]

The transformation of the decaying Soviet system and the adoption of a more enlightened foreign policy were also due, however, to a change in its leadership's perception of the outside world, particularly of the West. No Politburo member between the beginning of Stalin's dictatorship and the dawn of the Gorbachev era ever really understood the West. Their ability to make sense of the political intelligence provided by the KGB was impaired by their own ideological blinders and incurable addiction to conspiracy theory. In their dealings with the West they compensated for their lack of understanding with tactical shrewdness, ruthlessness, relentless striving to gain the upper hand, and knowledge of some of the West's weak points provided by their diplomats and intelligence officers. In its efforts to become and remain a global superpower, however, the Soviet Union steadily built up a huge army of diplomats, intelligence officers, journalists, and academics who gradually assembled a critical mass of information on the West, which eventually undermined some of the certainties of a system already decaying from within.

In Mikhail Gorbachev the Soviet Union at last found a leader who, though imbued with many traditional dogmas and misconceptions of the outside world, was well aware that the Communist system was losing its way, and was ready to listen to fresh ideas. Gorbachev's most influential adviser when he took power was an academic who knew the West from personal experience, Aleksandr Nikolayevich Yakovlev, ambassador in Canada from 1973 to 1983, a man whose vision was only slightly dimmed by the mists of Marxism-Leninism. But Gorbachev's new thinking was also powerfully influenced by his many briefings by the KGB, which grew dramatically less alarmist as Operation RYAN became discredited.

By 1987, however, the extent and the pace of Gorbachev's new thinking had become too much for Viktor Chebrikov. He used the 110th anniversary of Feliks Dzerzhinsky's birth to revive the old conspiracy theory of a gigantic plot by Western intelligence services to spread ideological subversion, Trotskyism included:

> One of the main targets of the subversive activity of the imperialist states' special services is still our society's moral and political potential and the Soviet philosophy. . . . That is why the subversive centers spare no effort to carry out acts of ideological subversion, step up their attempts to discredit Marxist-Leninist theory and Communist Party policy, and seek in every way to discredit the Soviet state's historical path and the practice of socialist construction. To this end bourgeois ideologists are reworking their threadbare bag-

gage, and they not infrequently draw arguments for their insinuations from the arsenal of Trotskyism and other opportunist currents.

Chebrikov attacked, in particular, two forms of "ideological subversion" currently being practiced by imperialist intelligence agencies. The first was their attempt to "split the monolithic unity of Party and people, and install political and ideological pluralism." The second was their spreading of "the virus of nationalism," which had produced "recent provocative sorties by nationalists in the Baltic republics."[32] It is quite likely that Chebrikov actually believed much of this nonsense. Gorbachev, however, was at least mildly embarrassed by it. By 1987, he was far closer to the more adaptable Kryuchkov, who had grasped that the traditional conspiracy theories had to be somewhat toned down to meet the needs of the new thinking. Gorbachev took the unprecedented step of taking Kryuchkov, traveling incognito, with him on his first trip to Washington in December 1987 to sign a treaty on the elimination of intermediate- and shorter-range missiles, the first treaty reducing the nuclear arsenals of the superpowers. Never before had a Soviet leader been accompanied on a visit to the West by the head of the FCD.[33]

In the summer of 1988 Gorbachev paid a warm tribute to the "purposeful work" of the leadership of the KGB and GRU, "aimed at improving their activities in the conditions created by the present stage of the development of our society and of the unfolding of democratic processes."[34] By then, however, Chebrikov's days as chairman of the KGB were already numbered. He was succeeded by Kryuchkov in October 1988, though he remained in the Politburo for another eleven months before surrendering his place to Kryuchkov. The appointment for the first time ever of the head of the KGB's foreign intelligence arm as its chairman was evidence both of the prestige of the FCD in the Gorbachev era and the importance Gorbachev himself attached to briefing by it.

Kryuchkov gave his valedictory address as head of the FCD, entitled "An Objective View of the World," at a conference in the Soviet Foreign Ministry. It was a remarkable mixture of the old and new thinking, which bore witness to the extent of the changes in the FCD's assessment of the West since the most alarmist phase of Operation RYAN only five years earlier. In general he took an optimistic view. Progress toward disarmament, in particular "the removal of the threat of major military conflict," had become a "fully realizable" goal. The international image of the Soviet Union had been transformed by *perestroika:*

> The "enemy image," the image of the Soviet state as a "total-
> itarian" "half-civilized" society, is being eroded and our ide-
> ological and political opponents are recognizing the pro-
> found nature of our reforms and their beneficial effect on
> foreign policy.

Kryuchkov also added a note of self-criticism about the KGB's—and his—traditional view of the West. In interpreting the business world in capitalist countries, he confessed, "we have always been submerged in clichés and stereotypes." More generally:

> We were not good at distinguishing between the social and
> political strata of contemporary capitalist society and the
> many shades and currents in the dispositions of political
> forces in a region or individual country. Unless we have an
> objective view of the world, seeing it unadorned and free of
> clichés and stereotyped ideas, all claims about the effective-
> ness of our foreign policy operations will be nothing but
> empty words.

Kryuchkov's address made clear, however, that the old suspicions and conspiracy theories still lurked at the back of his mind. Without men-tioning Operation RYAN by name, he attempted a retrospective justi-fication of it:

> Many of [the FCD's] former responsibilities have not been
> removed from the agenda. The principal one of these is not
> to overlook the immediate danger of nuclear conflict being
> unleashed.

Kryuchkov also made a traditional attack on Western "and above all American" intelligence services:

> These have retained in full measure their role of a shock
> detachment of right-wing forces, one of the sharp instru-
> ments of the imperialist "brake mechanism" on the road to

improvement of the international position. It is no chance
occurrence that in the West the wide-ranging campaign of
spy mania and brutal provocation employed against Soviet
institutions abroad has not lost its impetus.

In the first half of 1988 alone, he claimed, there had been over nine
hundred "provocation operations" against Soviet missions and nationals.[35]

Once chairman of the KGB, Kryuchkov's attitude, at least in
public, mellowed somewhat as he embarked on an unprecedented public relations campaign. "The KGB," he declared, "should have an
image not only in our country but worldwide that is consistent with the
noble goals which I believe we are pursuing in our work."[36] At the
beginning of 1989 Kryuchkov became the first chairman in KGB history to receive the United States ambassador in his office. Over the next
few months he and other senior KGB officers gave interviews and press
conferences to Western correspondents and starred in a film *The KGB
Today,* which was offered for sale to foreign television companies.
Kryuchkov also gave a series of press and television interviews for
Soviet audiences and appeared at confirmation hearings before the
Supreme Soviet to answer ninety-six questions put to him by deputies.
Though he was confirmed as chairman by a large majority there were
twenty-six abstentions and six votes against.

Throughout the public relations campaign Kryuchkov's basic
message never varied. The KGB followed "strict observance of Soviet
legality," was under "very strict Party control," gladly accepted—and
indeed had suggested—supervision of its work by a new Supreme Soviet
Committee on Defense and State Security, had distanced itself totally
from the horrors of its Stalinist past, and proposed "an entire system
of guarantees" to ensure that they did not return.[37] Professional and
remarkably novel though Kryuchkov's public relations were, he over-
sold his product. His claim that "The KGB has no secret informers,
only assistants" flew in the face of the experience of millions of Russians—as Boris Yeltsin told him to his face:

In the first place, most of the major organizations have no
assistants but a proper network of agents from the State
Security bodies, and this causes great moral damage to our
society. . . . This is quite intolerable for us in this period of
democratization.

Despite a KGB active measures campaign designed to discredit him, Yeltsin was elected chairman of the Russian Supreme Soviet in May 1990. After his election, he took the unprecedented step of refusing to accept a KGB guard. His security was entrusted instead to a new unit in the Supreme Soviet secretariat.[38]

The biggest change in KGB foreign operations during the late 1980s was at the level of rhetoric and public relations. In 1990 Leonid Shebarshin became the first head of the FCD to be publicly identified. A *Pravda* correspondent was, for the first time, allowed into FCD headquarters at Yasenevo. He found Shebarshin's office somewhat less forbidding than when it was occupied by Kryuchkov. A photograph of Shebarshin's small grandson stands on a shelf. The bookcase contains books on the KGB published in the West, as well as works by Solzhenitsyn and other authors formerly condemned as anti-Soviet. "Nowadays," Shebarshin told *Pravda,* "we are striving to bring out everything positive in world politics, to take every opportunity to improve further international relations, and to arrive at mutually acceptable solutions." Shebarshin does not take kindly, however, to revisionist interpretations of FCD history: "I am quite categorically unable to agree with those who are now trying to place the blame for the Cold War on the Soviet Union." Nor, he insists, has the threat from the West disappeared: "We must in no case fail to look into everything for intrigues and machinations of hostile forces."[39]

　　Though most changes in the FCD during the first five years of the Gorbachev era were cosmetic, there were at least two changes of note at the operational level. The first was in active measures. When Gorbachev became general secretary it was business as usual in this area, and he showed no sign of seeking to interfere with it. Between 1975 and 1985 Service A (Active Measures) had grown from about fifty to eighty officers at Yasenevo, with a further thirty to forty in the Novosti Press Agency offices at Pushkin Square. Kryuchkov himself was an enthusiastic supporter of active measures, with, in Gordievsky's view, an exaggerated faith in their effectiveness. He would frequently discuss major active measures campaigns with the International Department of the Central Committee, which tended to share his enthusiasm. Early in 1985 L. F. Sotskov, the first deputy head of Service A, told Gordievsky that the service was concentrating on three key themes: material calculated to discredit all aspects of American policy; a campaign to promote conflict between the United States and its

NATO allies; and support for Western peace movements. One of the proudest boasts of Service A at the beginning of the Gorbachev era was that it had organized the heckling of President Reagan's address to the European Parliament in May 1985. A senior FCD officer dealing with active measures assured Gordievsky that the KGB had even influenced the slogans used by the hecklers.

In principle, about 25 percent of the time of PR officers in residencies was supposed to be spent on active measures, though in practice it was often less. Gordievsky noted a wide variation in the quality of forgeries and other material produced by Service A, which reflected the distinctly uneven quality of its personnel. About 50 percent of its officers were specialists in active measures; the rest were rejects from other departments. Few of the ablest and most ambitious FCD recruits wanted jobs in Service A; it rarely offered the opportunity of overseas postings and was widely regarded as a career dead end. Several active measures had to be aborted as a result of Gordievsky's defection, among them schemes to discredit Keston College in Britain, which monitors religious activity in the Soviet Union, and to fabricate a statement by Mrs. Thatcher on defense policy to the chairman of the U.S. Joint Chiefs of Staff.[40]

During the late 1980s active measures operations in the West, though not the Third World, became less aggressive. The articles, pamphlets, and speeches attacking Reagan and Thatcher that Service A had prepared in the early 1980s for use by Western agents of influence, such as Arne Petersen, were gradually phased out. There were signs too of growing Soviet disenchantment with the increasingly discredited front organizations. In 1986 Romesh Chandra, the long-serving president of the World Peace Council, was obliged to indulge in self-criticism. "The criticisms made of the president's work," he acknowledged, "require to be heeded and necessary corrections made." The main "correction" made was the appointment of a new Finnish general secretary, Johannes Pakaslahti, who was intended to displace Chandra as the leading figure in the WPC. Changes of personnel, however, were insufficient to revive the WPC's fading influence. In 1988 the chairman of the Soviet Peace Committee, Genrikh Borovik, Kryuchkov's brother-in-law, called for the WPC to become "a more pluralistic organization." The WPC lost most of its remaining credibility in 1989 when it admitted that 90 percent of its income came from the Soviet Union.[41] Though there has been some change in methods and priorities during the Gorbachev era, there is no sign that active measures themselves are likely to be discontinued. The International Department of the Central Committee continues to supervise "gray" or semicovert active measures through front organizations and other channels with a partly visible Soviet presence. In cooperation with the International Department, Service A conducts "black" or covert active measures, whose Soviet origin is kept concealed.

The chief area of current active measures operations by both the International Department and Service A is the Third World. During the late 1980s Service A produced about ten to fifteen forgeries of U.S. official documents a year. Some were "silent forgeries," shown in confidence to influential figures in the Third World to alert them to allegedly hostile operations by the CIA or other American agencies. Others were used to promote media campaigns: among them, in 1987 a forged letter from the CIA director William Casey on plans to destabilize the Indian prime minister Rajiv Gandhi; in 1988 a forged document from the National Security Council containing instructions from President Reagan to destabilize Panama; and in 1989 a forged letter from the South African foreign minister "Pik" Botha to the State Department referring to a secret agreement for military, intelligence, and economic cooperation with the United States.[42]

Probably the most successful active measure in the Third World during the early years of the Gorbachev era, promoted by a mixture of overt propaganda and covert action by Service A, was the attempt to blame AIDS on American biological warfare. The story originated in the summer of 1983 in an article published in the pro-Soviet Indian newspaper *Patriot,* alleging that the AIDS virus had been "manufactured" during genetic engineering experiments at Fort Detrick, Maryland. Initially, the story had little impact, but it was revived with great effect by the Russian *Literaturnaya Gazeta* in October 1985. In its resurrected form, the AIDS story was bolstered by a report from a retired East German, Russian-born biophysicist, Professor Jacob Segal, which sought to demonstrate through "circumstantial evidence" (since thoroughly discredited) that the virus had been artificially synthesized at Fort Detrick from two natural, existing viruses, VISNA and HTLV-1. Thus assisted by quasi-scientific jargon, the AIDS fabrication not merely swept through the Third World but also took in some of the Western media. In October 1986 the conservative British *Sunday Express* made an interview with Professor Segal the basis of its main front-page story. In the first six months of 1987 alone the story received major coverage in over forty Third World countries.[43]

At the very height of its success, however, the AIDS active measure was compromised by the "new thinking" in Soviet foreign policy. Gorbachev told a Soviet media conference in July 1987: "We tell the truth and nothing but the truth." He and his advisers were clearly concerned that Western exposure of Soviet disinformation threatened to take a little of the gloss off the new Soviet image in the West. Faced with official American protests and the repudiation of the AIDS story by the international scientific community, including the leading Soviet AIDS expert, Viktor M. Zhdanov, the Kremlin for the first time showed signs of public embarrassment at a successful active measures campaign. In August 1987, U.S. officials were told in Moscow that the AIDS story was officially disowned. Soviet press coverage of the story came to an almost complete halt; it has not been mentioned at all by Soviet media since September 1988.[44] In 1990, however, the story was still circulating not merely in the Third World but also in the more gullible parts of the Western media. A further interview with Professor Segal, along with film of Fort Detrick, the alleged home of the AIDS virus, was featured prominently in a documentary on AIDS produced by a West German television company in January 1990 for Britain's Channel Four and Deutsche Rundfunk WDR, Cologne.[45]

The official abandonment of the AIDS story in August 1987 was followed by other equally scurrilous anti-American active measures in the Third World, some of which also had an impact on the West. One of the most successful was the "baby parts" story, alleging that Americans were butchering Latin American children and using their bodies for organ transplants. In the summer of 1988, the story was taken up by a Brussels-based Soviet front organization, the International Association of Democratic Lawyers (IADL), and publicized extensively in the press of over fifty countries. In September 1988, a French Communist member of the European Parliament, Danielle de March, proposed a motion condemning alleged trafficking in "baby parts" and cited an IADL report as evidence for her charges. The motion passed on a show of hands in a poorly attended session. Among those taken in by the baby parts fabrication were groups as remote from the KGB as the Jehovah's Witnesses, who published the story in 1989 in their magazine *Awake,* which had a circulation of eleven million copies printed in fifty-four languages. A Greek newspaper reported that human hearts were on sale in the United States for between $100,000 and $1 million each.[46] Among other active measures fabrications still circulating in the Third World in 1990 was the claim that the United

States was developing, or had actually developed, an "ethnic weapon" that would kill only nonwhites. By 1990, the "new thinking" of the Gorbachev era had dramatically reduced the level of anti-Western disinformation in the Soviet press, but still had little effect on Service A operations in the Third World.

The early years of the Gorbachev era also saw some change in the KGB's attitude to terrorism. Moscow's growing distaste for some of its terrorist associates in the Third World was particularly evident in the case of Colonel Qaddafi. The turning point in Soviet attitudes to Qaddafi was the demonstration by anti-Qaddafi Libyans on April 17, 1984, outside the Libyan embassy, renamed the People's Bureau, in St. James's Square, London. In the course of the demonstration a Libyan intelligence officer opened fire with a Sterling submachine gun from a first-floor window, killing police constable Yvonne Fletcher. Britain broke off diplomatic relations and expelled more than sixty Libyan officials and other Qaddafi supporters. *Pravda* reported the killing with what at the time was unusual frankness:

> Shooting suddenly started . . . and a British policewoman died and several other people were wounded as a result. . . . What is more, Washington spread the news that one of its reconnaissance satellites supposedly picked up a coded message from Tripoli to London in which People's Bureau staff were allegedly given the order to shoot at demonstrators. This news was followed the very next day by the British authorities' decision to break off diplomatic relations with Libya.

Though the official Libyan denial of involvement in the problem was duly reported, *Pravda* readers were left in little doubt that the shot had been fired from the People's Bureau.

The KGB, however, knew far more about the killing of WPC Fletcher than *Pravda* told its readers. On April 18, 1984, the London residency was informed by telegram that the Center had received reliable information that the shooting had been personally ordered by Qaddafi. The telegram revealed that an experienced hit man from the Libyan intelligence station in East Berlin had been flown in to London to supervise the operation. Thereafter the Center tended to show some sympathy for President Reagan's description of Qaddafi as a "flaky barbarian." Qaddafi's three-hour speech to a People's Congress in March 1985, calling for the hunting down of "stray dogs," was widely assessed in the Center as providing further evidence that he was becoming unhinged.[47] "We have the right to take a legitimate and sacred action—an entire people liquidating its opponents at home and abroad in broad daylight," declared Qaddafi. He announced the formation of a new Mutarabbisoun ("Always Ready") force of 150 highly trained terrorists ready to carry out liquidations around the globe.[48]

The Center also looked askance at Qaddafi's willingness to supply money and Soviet Bloc arms and explosives to the Provisional IRA. In the late 1970s, after the British press reported that the PIRA had received Soviet arms, an urgent inquiry by a senior KGB officer established that the arms had come from Libya. At that point Moscow took the formalistic view that it was not responsible for what Qaddafi did with his vast Soviet arms purchases. By the mid-1980s, however, it took a much less relaxed view and became concerned by the adverse publicity caused by terrorists' use of Soviet weapons.

On a number of occasions during the 1970s and 1980s, the PIRA made approaches to KGB officers in Dublin and to officers from the London residency visiting Belfast under journalistic cover. The approaches were reported to the Center, which refused permission for them to be followed up. The residency in Dublin was usually reluctant to make contact with any illegal group because of what it regarded as the near-impossibility of keeping secrets in the Irish Republic. KGB officers claimed that merely by listening to conversations in a number of public houses frequented by Sinn Fein supporters they were able to learn a surprising amount. The Center was less pleased with the Irish intelligence it received. In February 1985, the head of the Third Department, Nikolai Gribin, who had published a book on Northern Ireland a few years earlier, visited Dublin to inspect the KGB residency and try to improve its performance. The Center by then was making increasing use of Ireland as a training ground for young illegals to familiarize themselves with Irish and British life by stays of six months or more before moving on to work against what the KGB considered more important targets.[49]

Part of the Center's growing reluctance during the mid-1980s to involve itself with terrorist groups derived from an increasing, though exaggerated, fear that the Soviet Union was becoming a terrorist target. In April 1985, a circular telegram from the Center signed by Kryuchkov himself referred to a series of explosions in Bulgaria during the previous August and September. Though the culprits had yet to be tracked down, Kryuchkov claimed that the sophisticated nature of the devices used pointed to the possible involvement of one of the Western "special services." Kryuchkov's natural tendency to conspiracy theory led him to suspect a Western plot to use terrorism to destabilize the Soviet Bloc. The use of Bulgarian émigrés to carry out terrorist acts might, he feared, become a precedent for similar operations in other socialist countries. Kryuchkov suggested that residencies consult local police forces to emphasize the need for international cooperation against the terrorist menace. Such consultation in fact had already begun. During his four years as London resident, from 1980 to 1984, Guk had approached the police on about a dozen occasions with information about terrorists, usually from the Middle East. Guk's primary concern was to alert the police to threats to Soviet targets, but he occasionally passed on intelligence about possible attacks on non-Soviet citizens also.[50]

At about the time that Gordievsky received Kryuchkov's circular telegram on the Bulgarian explosions, he also received a personal request from the head of Directorate S (Illegals and Special Operations), Yuri Ivanovich Drozdov (formerly resident in New York), for a bizarre collection of items related to terrorism and special operations. Perhaps the oddest request was for a copy of the feature film *Who Dares Wins,* which Drozdov seemed to believe might reveal some of the operational methods of the British SAS. Other material requested included intelligence on left-wing terrorist groups, British "special military units," arms-dealing operations, and murders in strange or mysterious circumstances. Directorate S also wanted details of bulletproof vests weighing less than two kilos, which it believed were being manufactured in Britain. Drozdov was a devoted fan of the writer Frederick Forsyth; he told Gordievsky that his novel *The Fourth Protocol* was "essential reading." The book described what Drozdov regarded as the ultimate fantasy of a KGB special operations expert: the explosion by Soviet agents of a small nuclear device near a U.S. airbase in Britain just before a general election, with the aim of bringing to power a left-wing neutralist government.

Drozdov's shopping list reflected in part a desire to be informed on special operations and terrorist activity. But it was also clear to Gordievsky that he was engaged in at least contingency planning for KGB special operations in Britain. Drozdov asked the London residency to obtain information on the leasing of empty warehouses and gave Gordievsky the impression that he was looking for storage space for weapons and equipment. Some of the other information he requested was to help devise cover for a KGB operation.[51]

There is little doubt, however, that for Kryuchkov fear of the spread of terrorism to the Soviet Union outweighed the attraction of Drozdov's schemes for a new wave of potentially risky special operations in the West. Once Kryuchkov succeeded Chebrikov as chairman of the KGB in October 1988, the need for East-West collaboration against international terrorism became a major theme in the unprecedented round of speeches and interviews on which he embarked.

The hijacking of an Ilyushin transport plane from the Caucasus to Israel in December 1988 "ushered in," according to Kryuchkov, "a whole new era in our work."[52] Over the previous fifteen years there had been fifty mostly unpublicized attempted hijackings in the Soviet Union, which had been stopped with considerable loss of life.[53] When the Armenian hijackers demanded to fly to Israel in December 1988, however, the KGB, according to Kryuchkov, actually "encouraged them, as we were sure we would reach understanding [with the Israelis]." As a result, instead of another bloodbath, "Not a single child, nor a single rescue operative and not even a single terrorist suffered."[54] The Soviet foreign minister, Eduard Shevardnadze, publicly thanked the Israelis for their help in ending the hijacking peacefully and returning the hijackers. So too did the KGB. General Vitali Ponomaryov, one of Kryuchkov's deputy chairmen, held an unprecedented press conference to give an account of the hijacking to Western correspondents. It was, he declared, "the first example of such cooperation between the Soviet Union and other countries." Another of Kryuchkov's deputies, General Geni Ageev, gave further details to Tass, including the fact that the drug addict leading the hijacking, Pavel Yakshyants, had been given drugs by the KGB "because we thought it might calm him down."[55]

During 1989, Kryuchkov made a series of speeches calling for cooperation between the KGB and the CIA and other Western intelligence services in fighting terrorism:

> One wing of terrorism is directed against the USA, and the other against the Soviet Union. We all have an interest in overcoming this most dreadful phenomenon of this century. If we take most decisive measures, we shall do away with this evil rather quickly. Some remains of terrorism may be left over but they will be remains and not terrorism itself.[56]

In a speech to the Supreme Soviet in July and later in a newspaper interview, Kryuchkov underlined the coming danger of nuclear terrorism as a pressing reason for East-West intelligence cooperation:

> At the Supreme Soviet hearings I was guilty of an inaccuracy when I said that several tons of enriched uranium had disappeared in the world. Not several tons, but several hundred tons and where they went we do not know, although we can guess. There is so much knowledge and technological potential around the world today that it is easy enough to put together a nuclear device and use it to blackmail an entire nation, not just one city. Nor can I rule out the desire by somebody to put nuclear weapons to use. There are such criminals. In short, we are prepared to cooperate in the drive against terrorism and drug trafficking.[57]

In October 1989, Kryuchkov announced the abolition of the Fifth Directorate, which had hitherto monitored dissident intellectuals (and whose responsibilities in a watered-down form were reabsorbed by the Second Chief Directorate) and the creation of a new Directorate for the Defense of the Soviet Constitutional System to coordinate the struggle against "the orgy of terrorism which has swept the world since the early 1970s." He revealed that during the 1970s the KGB had identified in the Soviet Union "more than 1,500 individuals with terrorist designs."[58] Simultaneously, Kryuchkov dispatched two recently retired senior KGB officers, Lieutenant General Fyodor Shcherbak, former deputy head of the Second Chief Directorate, and Major General Valentin Zvezdenkov, a former counterterrorist expert from the same directorate, to take part with former senior CIA officers in a private conference in California to discuss methods of combating terrorism.[59]

Kryuchkov set clear limits to the unprecedented peacetime intelligence collaboration he was proposing:

> Intelligence is a game without rules. There are certain specific features, which I regret to say, prevent us from reaching agreement with anyone on how and according to which rules we should conduct intelligence operations against one another. But I think we should always have decency, even in our business.[60]

One of the consequences of the limited collaboration proposed by Kryuchkov was some decline in the traditional demonization of Western intelligence services. As recently as the final years of the Brezhnev era, the Soviet press, when denouncing the CIA, commonly excoriated "the repulsive bared teeth of the monster fed on the money of unsuspecting taxpayers, a monster which trampled underfoot all norms of morality and insulted the dignity of an entire nation."[61] Among those who have taken the lead in attacking the neo-Stalinist tradition of spy mania have been the two brightest radical critics of Kryuchkov within the FCD during the 1970s, the British expert Mikhail Lyubimov, dismissed in 1980, and the American expert Oleg Kalugin, formerly the FCD's youngest general, banished by Kryuchkov to Leningrad, also in 1980.[62]

Though careful to apportion blame to the intelligence services of both East and West, Lyubimov pours scorn on the KGB's traditional version of its own history:

> Even the minutest successes used to become cast in solemn bronze. The secret services could be compared to Lewis Carroll's beasts and birds running in a circle and answering the question "Who is the winner?" with the chorus cry: "We are!"

Like its counterparts in the West, the KGB had propagated spy mania, "undermined constructive diplomatic efforts," and "contributed to the deterioration of the international situation." Lyubimov believes that satellite intelligence has "a stabilizing effect" by reassuring both sides about the possibility of surprise attack. But in 1989 he became the first former KGB resident to call, in the Soviet press, for a reduction in the size of the FCD as well as of the KGB's huge domestic security apparatus.[63] In 1990 Lyubimov published *Legend About a Legend,* a farce lampooning the enormously expensive secret war between the KGB and the CIA. *Moscow News* suggested that it would make "a good musical comedy."[64]

Oleg Kalugin began public criticism of the KGB after he was sacked as deputy head of the Leningrad KGB in 1987, following his attempts to investigate a number of politically embarrassing bribery cases.[65] In 1988 he made a thinly disguised attack on the paranoid strain in the FCD during Kryuchkov's fourteen years at its head:

Just a few years ago those at the august rostrum would have us believe that the reasons for the different distortions in our life lay not in the defects of the system but in hostile encirclement, in the intensifying pressure being brought to bear on socialism by the forces of imperialism, and that the antisocial activity of individuals and the crimes against the state they committed were a consequence of hostile propaganda and CIA provocations.

It was for expressing similarly unorthodox opinions in 1980 that Kalugin had been sacked by Kryuchkov from the FCD. Though criticizing American covert operations, Kalugin also attacked the KGB's traditional demonization of the CIA. While head of the KR line in Washington during the late 1960s and early 1970s, Kalugin had been impressed by intelligence which indicated that the CIA took a much more realistic view than the Pentagon of the outcome of the Vietnam War:

On quite a few occasions I have had a chance to meet with CIA staff members, although they did not introduce themselves as such. They were highly refined and educated interlocutors who avoided extremes in their judgments. Although I did not delude myself over their friendly smiles, I was nevertheless inclined to perceive them as individuals who were not necessarily burdened by class hatred for everything Soviet.

Kalugin praises the current director of the CIA, William Webster, as a man "not even ashamed to sour relations with the White House when he felt he was defending a just cause."[66] He plainly does not feel as warmly about Kryuchkov. In 1990 Kalugin dismissed Kryuchkov's reforms as little more than a cosmetic exercise. "The KGB's arm or shadow is in absolutely every sphere of life. All the talk about the KGB's new image is no more than camouflage."[67]

Like the rest of the world, the KGB failed to foresee either the speed or the timing of the disintegration of Communist rule in Eastern Europe that began in 1989. But it may nonetheless have been the first intelligence agency to sense that the Soviet Bloc created at the end of the Second World War was doomed. During the early and mid-1980s there was already a growing exasperation combined with fatalism in the

Center about the future of Eastern Europe, and it gathered momentum at the end of the decade. By the beginning of the Gorbachev era Gordievsky was hearing increasing numbers of complaints about the unreliability of the Communist regimes and outbursts such as: "We'd do better to adopt a policy of 'Fortress Soviet Union'—and have done with the lot of them!" Though not yet intended seriously, such outbursts were straws in the wind of change that in 1989 was to replace the Brezhnev Doctrine with the satirically entitled "Sinatra Doctrine," allowing the states of Eastern Europe to "do it their way."

Three states in Eastern Europe were, for somewhat different reasons, already giving the Center serious cause for anxiety by the time Gorbachev succeeded Chernenko as general secretary in March 1985. The first was Poland. The FCD had been severely shaken by the mushroom growth of Solidarity in 1980–81. Though it had admired the skill with which Jaruzelski, the Polish army, and the SB had carried out a military coup and crushed Solidarity in December 1981, it was better aware than most Western observers that it had achieved only a temporary respite.

The Center's main source of anxiety was the visible fact that the moral authority in Poland of a Polish Pope eclipsed that of the Polish government. The days were long past when any Soviet leader was tempted to repeat Stalin's scornful question at the end of the Second World War: "How many divisions has the Pope?" In retrospect, the Polish experts in the Center were inclined to trace the origins of the Polish crisis to the election in October 1978 of the Polish Cardinal Karol Wojtyla as Pope John Paul II.[68] When he had visited Poland seven months later, almost a quarter of the Polish people had come to see and hear him; almost all the rest witnessed his triumphal nine-day tour on television. At the end of his progress through Poland, as the Pope bade farewell to his former home city of Krakow, where, he said, "every stone and every brick is dear to me," men and women wept uncontrollably in the streets. The contrast between the political bankruptcy of the regime and the moral authority of the church was plain for all to see.[69]

Opinions were divided within the Center on the likelihood of KGB involvement in the assassination attempt against the Pope in 1981. About half of those to whom Gordievsky spoke were convinced that the KGB would no longer contemplate a "wet affair" of this kind even indirectly through the Bulgarians. The other half, however, suspected that Department 8 of Directorate S, which was responsible for special operations, had been involved; some told Gordievsky they only regretted that the attempt had failed.

The lack of authority of the Communist government in Poland was laid bare once again when John Paul II returned in 1983, urging those who opposed the regime to turn to the protection of the church. In October 1984, the Polish church gained a new martyr when the SB religious-affairs department abducted and murdered the pro-Solidarity priest Father Jerzy Popieluszko. Half a million attended his funeral. Walesa declared at the graveside: "Solidarity is alive because you have given your life for it." Desperate to distance himself from the crime, Jaruzelski ordered a public trial of the murderers, thus causing a new wave of alarm in the FCD. At the end of 1984 a circular from the Center ordered a series of active measures during 1985 designed to discredit the "reactionary" John Paul II.[70]

The Center's concerns about East Germany were quite different from those about Poland. Though the KGB had no illusions about the unpopularity of the Communist regime, at the beginning of the Gorbachev era it did not yet believe that it was in danger of losing control. Its anxieties centered instead on what it regarded as the growing reluctance of the East German leader Erich Honecker to follow Moscow's lead. When the seventy-eight-year-old Walter Ulbricht retired as SED general secretary in 1971, Moscow had wanted Willi Stoph to succeed him. When Honecker had been chosen instead, the embittered Stoph had warned Moscow that Honecker's nationalism threatened the future of Soviet-GDR relations. And so it proved.

The domineering behavior of Soviet diplomats and KGB officers that had been tolerated by Ulbricht gave rise under Honecker to a series of incidents. In the mid-1970s, following the arrest for drunken driving of a KGB officer from its Karlshorst headquarters, the KGB chief General Anatoli Ivanovich Lazarev had complained about "the use of Nazi methods against a fraternal power." Honecker then complained even more forcibly about Lazarev. At his insistence Lazarev was recalled to Moscow. The Soviet ambassador, Petr Andreevich Abrasimov, was recalled after similar complaints by Honecker about his viceregal attitude in 1983; once back in Moscow he was put in charge of tourism. Both Erich Mielke, the East German minister of state security, and Markus Wolf, the veteran head of the HVA, complained to the Center that Honecker was restricting the intimacy of Soviet-GDR intelligence collaboration. The situation was further complicated by the fact that Mielke and Wolf were themselves scarcely on speaking terms. There were endless discussions in the Center, some of them witnessed by Gordievsky in Grushko's office, on how to strengthen Mielke's and Wolf's hands against Honecker, and how to prevent Mielke and Wolf themselves from coming to blows. In 1985, however, the Center did not yet foresee that *perestroika* in the Soviet Union would add a further element of tension to relations with the German Democratic Republic.[71]

The East European state that the Center believed to be in greatest danger of collapse at the beginning of the Gorbachev era was Nicolae Ceauşescu's corrupt and megalomaniac neo-Stalinist dictatorship in Rumania, already semidetached from the Warsaw Pact. A long assessment by FCD Department Eleven (Eastern Europe Liaison) in 1983 forecast that, with Rumania already on the verge of bankruptcy, there was a serious danger of economic collapse within the next few years. In that event, it predicted, loss of control by the regime might well lead Rumania to turn toward the West. By the time Gorbachev succeeded Chernenko, that prospect was being taken very seriously. During his last two years in London as deputy resident and resident, Gordievsky received several requests from the Center for intelligence on Western attitudes to Rumania.[72] In the end, Ceauşescu's dictatorship was almost the last of the East European Communist regimes to succumb to the tide of democratic revolution in 1989, though the end, when it arrived, came with even greater speed, and brutality, than in the other countries of the Warsaw Pact.

By the time the Communist order in Eastern Europe began to collapse, the Center was probably already reconciled to the disintegration of what its internal documents commonly called the "Socialist Commonwealth." That disintegration, however, threatened to disrupt the elaborate network of Soviet Bloc intelligence collaboration, which went back to the early years of the Cold War. In every country of Eastern Europe, the local security service, modeled on the KGB, was seen by its inhabitants as one of the main instruments of oppression and instantly became one of the chief targets of the democratic reformers. By early 1990 most had been emasculated. In most parts of Eastern Europe the foreign intelligence services, which had hitherto been an integral part of the security services on the model of the KGB's FCD, turned themselves into independent agencies in order to try to survive.

By the beginning of 1990 the KGB could no longer count automatically, as in the past, on the help of the East German HVA in its operations against NATO and West Germany; on the Czechoslovak

StB and the Polish SB in its work against France; or on the Bulgarian DS against Yugoslavia, Turkey, and Greece. The intelligence alliance with East Germany was already doomed. In a reunited Germany the external HVA, like the internal SSD, will cease to exist. Dismantling the KGB apparatus in Karlshorst will be an enormous task; at a stroke the Soviet Union will lose its largest foreign intelligence base. The end of the Soviet-GDR intelligence alliance threatens to compromise some of the KGB's own intelligence operations. The central name-trace system in the Center, known as SOUD (System for Operational and Institutional Data), uses an East German computer. Hitherto the Cuban as well as the Warsaw Pact intelligence services have had access to it.[73]

The KGB's alliances in Latin America were also threatened by the crumbling of the Soviet bloc. Though Castro has lasted longer than Honecker, he showed himself even more ill-disposed to Gorbachev's "new thinking." By 1987, the KGB liaison mission in Havana was already complaining that the Cuban DGI was holding it at arm's length. The situation was judged to be so serious in the Center that Chebrikov himself visited Cuba to try to restore the intelligence alliance.[74] It is unlikely that he secured a lasting improvement. The defeat of the Sandinistas, probably against KGB expectations, in the Nicaraguan elections of February 1990 placed the future of the four Soviet sigint stations in Nicaragua at risk. Castro's increasingly uncertain prospects of survival as his huge Soviet subsidies were scaled down raised doubts about the future of the much larger sigint station at Lourdes in Cuba.

The greatest threat to the future of the KGB is its own past. From its headquarters in Dzerzhinsky Square it directed during the Stalinist era the greatest peacetime persecution and the largest concentration camps in European history. The people's deputy and Soviet sporting hero Yuri Vlasov told the Congress of People's Deputies in 1989: "The KGB is not a service but a real underground empire which has not yet yielded its secrets, except for opening up the graves."[75] The Center's acute nervousness about revealing the contents of its archives demonstrates its awareness of the threat they pose. Its preparations for Lithuanian independence in 1990 had as a major priority the disposal of hundreds of thousands of embarrassing files. Radio Vilnius reported that the chairman of the Lithuanian KGB, Eduardas Eismontas, had virtually admitted that much of his archives had been shredded or removed to Moscow. Soon afterward Eismontas resigned.[76]

Those files that cause the greatest embarrassment to the KGB concern its foreign operations. During the late 1980s it fought a long though hopeless rearguard action to avoid accepting responsibility for the wartime massacre of Polish officers by the NKVD in the Katyn Forest. In March 1989 Poland's last Communist government finally nerved itself to pin the blame for the massacre on the KGB. The Polish press published documents found in the pockets of the murdered officers proving that they had been prisoners of the NKVD at the time of their execution. For another year, however, the KGB press bureau continued to blame the killings on the Germans and refused to "anticipate" the long-delayed findings of a Soviet-Polish commission.[77] When *Moscow News* challenged the KGB to "confirm or deny" the Polish evidence, threats were made against its editor-in-chief. NKVD veterans with information on the Katyn massacre told *Moscow News* the KGB had ordered them not to reveal the truth.[78] Not until April 1990, when President Gorbachev handed President Jaruzelski a portfolio of documents proving the NKVD's role in the massacre, did the KGB finally bow to the inevitable and accept responsibility. Over the next few months several more mass graves of Polish officers were uncovered.

The Center's apprehensions at the potential embarrassments even in the file of a single foreigner are well illustrated by the case of the Swedish diplomat Raoul Wallenberg. While stationed in Budapest in 1944–45, Wallenberg saved the lives of many thousands of Jews by giving them Swedish diplomatic protection. Soon after the Red Army occupied Hungary, however, he mysteriously disappeared. Ever since his disappearance the Swedish government, the Wallenberg family and the Raoul Wallenberg Society have repeatedly pressed Moscow to reveal the truth about his fate. The KGB's refusal to release his file led to repeated rumors—all, sadly, unfounded—that Wallenberg was still alive somewhere in the gulag. In 1957 Andrei Gromyko, then deputy foreign minister, handed the Swedish ambassador in Moscow a memorandum claiming that Wallenberg died of a heart attack in a Soviet prison in 1947. That falsehood is still described by the Soviet authorities as "irrefutable fact." In October 1989, however, an attempt was made to defuse international pressure for the release of the KGB file on the Wallenberg case by inviting representatives of the Raoul Wallenberg Society, including his half sister, Nina Lagergren, and his half brother, Guy von Dardel, to talks in Moscow. There they were received by Vadim Petrovich Pirozhkov, a deputy chairman of the KGB, and Valentin Mikhailovich Nikoforov, a deputy foreign minister, who handed over Wallenberg's passport, some of his personal belongings, and a bogus death certificate dated July 17, 1947, signed by the chief doctor of the Lubyanka Prison. Pirozhkov and Nikoforov expressed "deep regret" that, despite "painstaking" searches in the KGB archives, no further documents could be discovered.[79] Andrei Sakharov, among others, was publicly skeptical that such an important KGB file on a foreign diplomat was missing. In reality the file has never gone astray. It is simply considered too embarrassing to make public.

What the KGB's file on Wallenberg reveals is that, shortly after the arrival of the Red Army in Budapest, the NKVD tried to recruit him as an agent. When Wallenberg refused point-blank, the NKVD became worried that he might reveal its approach to him, arrested him, and deported him to the Soviet Union. Further attempts in Moscow to persuade Wallenberg to become a Soviet agent also failed. He was shot not later than 1947.[80] To muddy the waters of the Wallenberg case during 1989, the KGB brought in one of its leading active measures veterans, Radomir Bogdanov, then deputy director of the Academy of Sciences Institute for the Study of the United States and Canada, as well as vice-chairman of the Soviet Peace Committee. As resident in New Delhi from 1957 to 1967 Bogdanov had played a leading part in establishing India as one of the main centers of Soviet active measures.[81] During the spring of 1989, Bogdanov began informing foreign visitors and journalists in Moscow that Wallenberg had acted as intermediary in secret negotiations during 1944 between Lavrenti Beria and the head of the SS, Heinrich Himmler.[82] The Moscow *New Times,* formerly used as a vehicle for active measures, continued the smear campaign by portraying Wallenberg as a playboy, womanizer and friend of Adolf Eichmann, chief administrator of the Final Solution.[83]

The KGB, however, is no longer master of all its own secrets. The democratic revolution in Eastern Europe confronts it with the embarrassing possibility that, as during the Prague Spring in 1968, some of its secrets may escape from the files of its former Soviet Bloc allies. One of those that must surely worry Kryuchkov personally is the Bulgarian DS file on the murder of the Bulgarian émigré writer Georgi Markov in October 1978. Some months earlier the Bulgarian general secretary Todor Zhivkov had sought KGB assistance in silencing émigrés like his former protégé Markov who were attacking him in the Western media. The Center made available to Zhivkov and the Bulgarian Durzharna Sigurnost (DS) the resources of a highly secret KGB laboratory, the successor to the Kamera of the Stalinist era, attached to Directorate OTU (Operational-Technical) and under the direct control of the KGB chairman. Kryuchkov personally approved the secondment of General Sergei Mikhailovich Golubev of FCD Directorate K to liaise with the DS in using against Bulgarian émigrés poisons developed by the KGB laboratory. (Seven years later Golubev was to supervise the drugging of Gordievsky with drugs from the same laboratory in an unsuccessful attempt to get him to confess.[84]) Golubev visited Sofia three or four times during 1978 to help plan operations against the émigrés.

The first target was a Bulgarian émigré living in England. While he was on holiday on the Continent, the DS smeared surfaces in the room where he was staying with a poison that, once absorbed through the skin, would, according to the KGB laboratory, prove fatal and leave no trace. Though the target became seriously ill, however, he survived. With Kryuchkov's approval, Golubev returned to Sofia to work out a new plan of attack. At Golubev's request, the KGB main residency in Washington purchased several umbrellas and sent them to the Center. Directorate OTU adapted the tip to enable it to inject the victim with a tiny metal pellet containing ricin, a highly toxic poison made from castor-oil seeds. Golubev then took the umbrellas to Sofia to instruct a DS assassin in their use. The first victim was Georgi Markov, then working for the Bulgarian section of the BBC World Service. Before he died in a hospital Markov was able to tell doctors that he had been bumped into by a stranger on Westminster Bridge, who apologized for accidentally prodding him with his umbrella. A tiny stab wound and the remains of a pellet scarcely larger than a pinhead were found in Markov's right thigh, but by the time of the autopsy the ricin had decomposed.

A second assassination attempt a week later in Paris against another Bulgarian émigré, Vladimir Kostov, failed. This time the steel pellet failed to distintegrate and it was removed from Kostov's body before the ricin had escaped. The arrest of Todor Zhivkov late in 1989 was followed by the visit to Sofia of Markov's widow in an attempt to discover those responsible for her husband's death. Even if the DS files on the Markov case have been shredded or sent to Moscow, there are undoubtedly DS officers who know the truth about his assassination. As Bulgaria progresses toward democracy they may well be tempted to reveal it.[85]

*   *   *

Despite its unprecedented public relations campaign, the KGB is almost the only unrestructured institution in Gorbachev's Russia. For all his attempts to change his image, Kryuchkov is a relic from a discredited past. His main deputies, Vladimir Petrovich Pirozhkov, Filipp Denisovich Bobkov, Geni Yevgenyevich Ageev, and Vladimir Yakovlevich Lezhepyokov, all held senior KGB posts in the Brezhnev era. Today's KGB does its best to distance itself from both the Stalinist Terror and the lesser crimes of the "years of stagnation." As the enormity of its horrific history emerges, however, Soviet citizens are bound to ask themselves if such an organization can ever really be reformed. The peoples of Eastern Europe have already condemned their own security services created in the image of the KGB. Sooner or later the KGB too will be disowned by its own citizens. The 1989 candlelit vigil that encircled the KGB headquarters to commemorate its millions of victims marked the beginning of that disavowal.

Like every major modern state, Russia needs both a domestic security service and a foreign intelligence agency. For it to possess an intelligence community worthy of its citizens' respect, however, it will have to close down the KGB and start afresh.

Appendix A
KGB Chairmen

Feliks Edmundovich Dzerzhinsky   1917–26
(Cheka/GPU/OGPU)

Vyacheslav Rudolfovich Menzhinsky   1926–34
(OGPU)

Genrikh Grigoryevich Yagoda   1934–36
(NKVD)

Nikolai Ivanovich Yezhov   1936–38
(NKVD)

Lavrenti Pavlovich Beria   1938–41
(NKVD)

Vsevolod Nikolayevich Merkulov   1941(Feb.)–41(July)
(NKGB)

Lavrenti Pavlovich Beria   1941–43
(NKVD)

Vsevolod Nikolayevich Merkulov   1943–46
(NKGB/MGB)

Viktor Semyonovich Abakumov   1946–51
(MGB)

Sergei Ivanovich Ogoltsov (Acting; MGB)	1951(Aug.)–51(Dec.)
Semyon Denisovich Ignatyev (MGB)	1951–53
Lavrenti Pavlovich Beria (MVD)	1953(Mar.)–53(June)
Sergei Nikiforovich Kruglov (MVD)	1953–54
Ivan Aleksandrovich Serov (KGB)	1954–58
Aleksandr Nikolayevich Shelepin (KGB)	1958–61
Vladimir Yefimovich Semichastny (KGB)	1961–67
Yuri Vladimirovich Andropov (KGB)	1967–82
Vitali Vasilyevich Fyodorchuk (KGB)	1982(May)–82(Dec.)
Viktor Mikhailovich Chebrikov (KGB)	1982–88
Vladimir Aleksandrovich Kryuchkov	1988–

Appendix B
Heads of the First Chief Directorate
(Foreign Intelligence)

Mikhail Abramovich Trilisser	1921–29
Artur Khristyanovich Artuzov	1929–34
Abram Aronovich Slutsky	1934–38
Mikhail Shpigelglas (acting head)	1938(Feb.)–38(July)
Vladimir Georgievich Dekanozov	1938–40
Pavel Mikhailovich Fitin	1940–46
Pyotr Vasilyevich Fedotov (deputy chairman KI 1947–49)	1946–49
Sergei Romanovich Savchenko (deputy chairman KI 1949–51)	1949–53
Vasili Stepanovich Ryasnoy	1953(Mar.)–53(June)
Aleksandr Semyonovich Panyushkin	1953–56
Aleksandr Mikhailovich Sakharovsky	1956–71
Fyodor Konstantinovich Mortin	1971–74
Vladimir Aleksandrovich Kryuchkov	1974–78
Leonid Vladimirovich Shebarshin	1988–

Appendix C

THE ORGANIZATION OF THE KGB

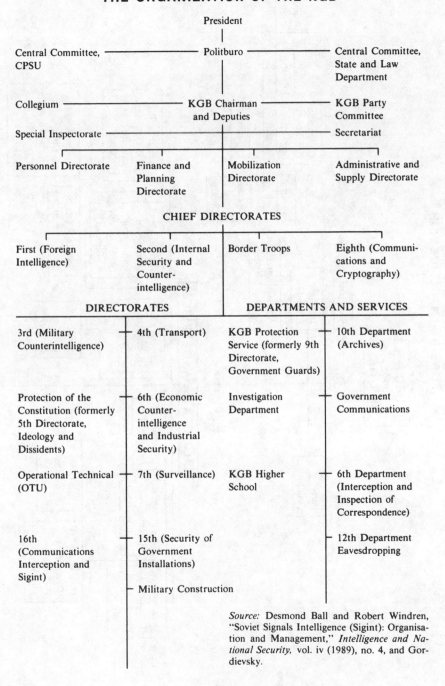

President

Central Committee, ———————— Politburo ———————— Central Committee,
CPSU   State and Law
                                                            Department

Collegium ———————————— KGB Chairman ———————— KGB Party
                              and Deputies   Committee

Special Inspectorate ——————————————————————— Secretariat

Personnel Directorate   Finance and   Mobilization   Administrative and
                         Planning   Directorate   Supply Directorate
                         Directorate

CHIEF DIRECTORATES

First (Foreign   Second (Internal   Border Troops   Eighth (Communi-
Intelligence)   Security and   cations and
                        Counter-   Cryptography)
                        intelligence)

DIRECTORATES   DEPARTMENTS AND SERVICES

3rd (Military   4th (Transport)   KGB Protection   10th Department
Counterintelligence)   Service (formerly 9th   (Archives)
                                            Directorate,
                                            Government Guards)

Protection of the   6th (Economic   Investigation   Government
Constitution (formerly Counter-   Department   Communications
5th Directorate,   intelligence
Ideology and   and Industrial
Dissidents)   Security)

Operational Technical   7th (Surveillance) KGB Higher   6th Department
(OTU)   School   (Interception and
                                                                Inspection of
                                                                Correspondence)

16th   15th (Security of   12th Department
(Communications   Government   Eavesdropping
Interception and   Installations)
Sigint)

                        Military Construction

Source: Desmond Ball and Robert Windren,
"Soviet Signals Intelligence (Sigint): Organisation and Management," *Intelligence and National Security,* vol. iv (1989), no. 4, and Gordievsky.

THE ORGANIZATION OF THE KGB FIRST CHIEF DIRECTORATE (FOREIGN INTELLIGENCE)

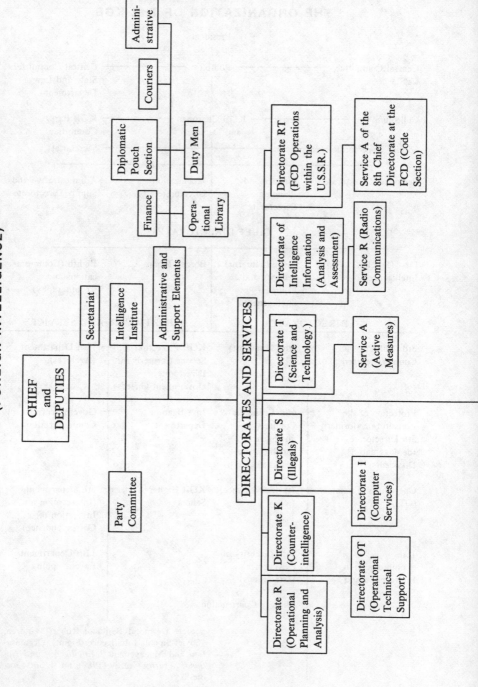

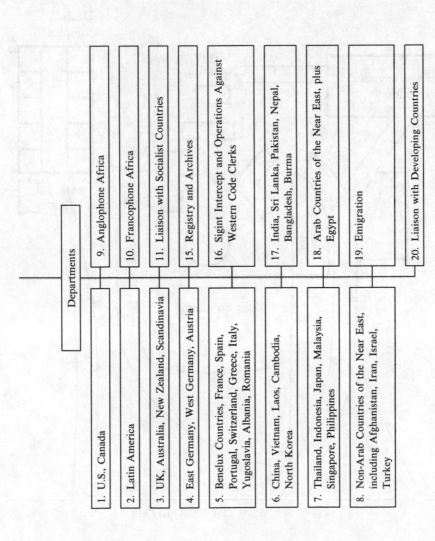

Departments

1. U.S., Canada

2. Latin America

3. UK, Australia, New Zealand, Scandinavia

4. East Germany, West Germany, Austria

5. Benelux Countries, France, Spain, Portugal, Switzerland, Greece, Italy, Yugoslavia, Albania, Romania

6. China, Vietnam, Laos, Cambodia, North Korea

7. Thailand, Indonesia, Japan, Malaysia, Singapore, Philippines

8. Non-Arab Countries of the Near East, including Afghanistan, Iran, Israel, Turkey

9. Anglophone Africa

10. Francophone Africa

11. Liaison with Socialist Countries

15. Registry and Archives

16. Sigint Intercept and Operations Against Western Code Clerks

17. India, Sri Lanka, Pakistan, Nepal, Bangladesh, Burma

18. Arab Countries of the Near East, plus Egypt

19. Emigration

20. Liaison with Developing Countries

Source: Desmond Ball and Robert Windren, "Soviet Signals Intelligence (Sigint): Organisation and Management," *Intelligence and National Security*, vol. iv (1989), no. 4, and Gordievsky.

KGB FIRST CHIEF DIRECTORATE (FOREIGN INTELLIGENCE) HEADQUARTERS, YASENEVO

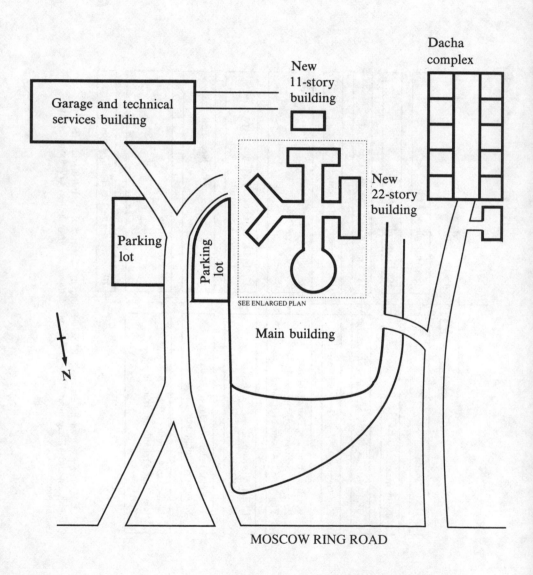

New
11-story
building

Dacha
complex

Garage and technical
services building

New
22-story
building

Parking
lot

Parking
lot

SEE ENLARGED PLAN

N

Main building

MOSCOW RING ROAD

KGB FIRST CHIEF DIRECTORATE (FOREIGN INTELLIGENCE) HEADQUARTERS, YASENEVO—MAIN BUILDING

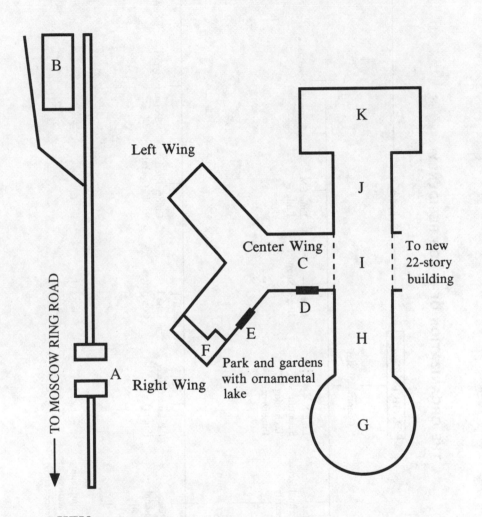

KEY

A   Entrance gate
B   Technical services building
C   Main building
D   Main entrance
E   Entrance for the "leadership"
F   2nd-floor offices occupied by the "leadership"
G   Assembly hall
H   General library
I   1st-floor canteen
J   Polyclinic
K   Sports complex with swimming pool

THE ORGANIZATION OF A KGB RESIDENCY

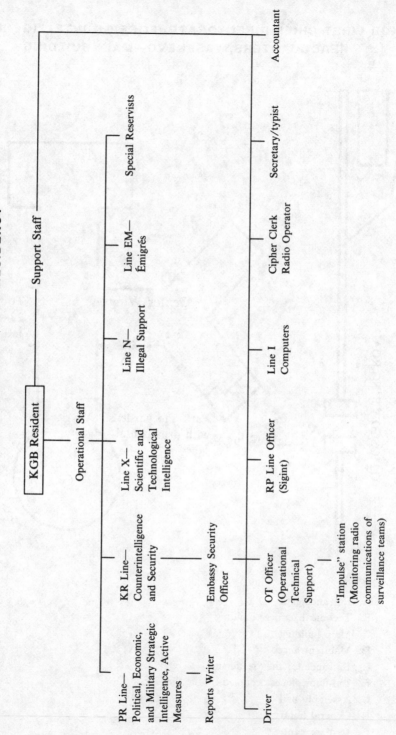

Appendix D
KGB Residents in the United States and Abroad

Most of the lists that follow derive from detailed research by Gordievsky on KGB battle order carried out between 1974 and 1985. In some cases his knowledge of individual career patterns, combined with study of diplomatic lists, has enabled him to identify residents appointed since 1985. For example, Ivan Semyonovich Gromakov, posted to Washington in 1987, is too senior a figure to have occupied a lesser post than resident. *Asterisks* indicate gaps in Gordievsky's knowledge.

KGB Residents in the United States

Washington, DC

Vasili Mikhailovich Zarubin (*alias* Zubilin)	1942–44
Grigori Grigorievich Dolbin	1946–48
Georgi Aleksandrovich Sokolov	1948–49
Aleksandr Semyonovich Panyushkin (also Soviet ambassador)	1949–50
Nikolai Alekseevich Vladykin	1950–54
	***
Aleksandr Semyonovich Feklisov (*alias* Fomin)	1960–64

Pavel Pavlovich Lukyanov	1964–65
Boris Aleksandrovich Solomatin	1966–68
Mikhail Korneevich Polonik	1968–75
Dmitri Ivanovich Yakushkin	1975–82
Stanislav Andreevich Androsov	1982–86
Ivan Semyonovich Gromakov	1987–

New York

Gaik Badalovich Ovakimyan	1933–41
Ivan Dmitrievich Borisov	1946–48 and 1949–50

***

Boris Semyonovich Ivanov	1962–64
Nikolai Panteleymonovich Kulebyakin	1966–68
Vikenti Pavlovich Sobolev	1969–71
Boris Aleksandrovich Solomatin	1971–75
Yuri Ivanovich Drozdov	1975–79
Vladimir Mikhailovich Kazakov	1979–85
Yuri Anatolyevich Antipov (acting resident)	1986–87

San Francisco

Vladimir Petrovich Pronin	1973–77
Gennadi Ivanovich Vasilyev	1977–83
Lev Nikolayevich Zaitsev	1983–86

KGB Residents in London

Aron Vaclavovich Shuster	?1934–38
Ivan Andreevich Chichayev	1941–43
Konstantin Mikhailovich Kukin	1943–47
Nikolai Borisovich Rodin (*alias* Korovin)	1947–52
Georgi Mikhailovich Zhivotovsky (acting resident)	1952–53

Sergei Leonidovich Tikhvinsky	1953–55
Yuri Ivanovich Modin (acting resident)	1955–56
Nikolai Borisovich Rodin (*alias* Korovin)	1956–61
Nikolai Borisovich Litvinov (acting resident)	1961–62
Nikolai Grigoryevich Bagrichev	1962–64
Mikhail Timofeevich Chizhov	1964–66
Mikhail Ivanovich Lopatin (acting resident)	1966–67
Yuri Nikolayevich Voronin	1967–71
Leonid Alekseevich Rogov (acting resident)	1971
Yevgeni Ivanovich Lazebny (*alias* Dontsov)	1971–72
Yakov Konstantinovich Lukasevics (*alias* Bukashev)	1972–80
Arkadi Vasilyevich Guk	1980–84
Leonid Yefremovich Nikitenko (acting resident)	1984–85
Oleg Antonovich Gordievsky (resident-designate)	1985

KGB Residents in Dublin

Mikhail Konstantinovich Shadrin	1974–78
Gennadi Aleksandrovich Salin	1980–83
Mikhail Sergeevich Smirnov (acting resident)	1983–85
Vladimir Vasilyevich Minderov	1985–

KGB Residents in Paris

Ivan Ivanovich Agayants (*alias* Avalov)	1947–49
Aleksei Alekseevich Krokhin	1950–54
Mikhail Stepanovich Tsymbal (*alias* Rogov)	1954–59
Anatoli Ivanovich Lazarev	1959–66
Aleksei Alekseevich Krokhin	1966–71
Ivan Petrovich Kislyak	1972–77

Nikolai Nikolayevich Chetverikov   1977–83
  After Chetverikov's expulsion in 1983, with forty-six other KGB and
  GRU officers, the residency had for a period only an acting head.

Anatoli Viktorovich Khramtsov   1986–

KGB Residents in Bonn

Yuri Nikolayevich Granov   1964–66

Yuri Nikandrovich Vorontsov   1966–69

Ivan Ivanovich Zaitsev   1969–72

                                                         ***

Yuri Stepanovich Yakovlev   1977–80
(possibly resident)

Yevgeni Izotovich Shishkin   1981–89

KGB Residents in Rome

Gurgen Semyonovich Agayan   1966–71

Gennadi Fyodorovich Borzov   1971–76

Boris Aleksandrovich Solomatin   1976–82

Georgi Aleksandrovich Orlov   1982–86

Valentin Antonovich Akimov   1987–

KGB Residents in Copenhagen

Pavel Kuzmich Revizorov   1953–56

Yuri Vladimirovich Bakey   1957–59

Boris Grigorievich Zhuravlyov   1959–64

Leonid Sergeevich Zaitsev   1964–69

Anatoli Aleksandrovich Danilov   1969–73

Alfred Fyodorovich Mogilevtchik   1973–76

Mikhail Petrovich Lyubimov   1976–80

Nikolai Petrovich Gribin   1980–84

Nikolai Aleksandrovich Shatskikh   1984–

KGB Residents in Oslo

Aleksandr S. Alyokhin	1948–52
Ivan Aleksandrovich Teterin	1954–57
Bogdan Andreevich Dubensky	1957–62
Aleksandr Nikolayevich Startsev	1962–66
Leonid Ilyich Lepyoshkin	1966–71
Viktor Fyodorovich Grushko	1971–72
Gennadi Fyodorovich Titov	1972–77
Leonid Alekseevich Makarov	1977–81
Gennadi Yakovlevich Sevryugin	1981–87
Lev Sergeevich Koshlyakov	1987–

KGB Residents in Stockholm

Ivan Dmitrievich Borisov	1957–60
Nikolai Viktorovich Statskevich	1961–64
Kapiton Ivanovich Parfyonov	1964–69
Yevgeni Ivanovich Gergel (acting resident)	1969–70
Dmitri Andreevich Svetanko (acting resident)	1970–71
Nikolai Viktorovich Statskevich	1971–75
Lev Nikolayevich Shapkin	1975–78
Vladimir Petrovich Koretsky	1978–82
Nikolai Sergeevich Seliverstov	1982–87
Igor Leonidovich Nikiforov	1987–

KGB Residents in Canada

Sergei Leontyevich Rudchenko	1951–53
Vasili Nikolayevich Shitarev	1953–56
Pyotr Pavlovich Borisov	1961–64
Konstantin Kirillovich Drobnitsa	1964–68

Illen Nikolayevich Petrovsky   1969–73

Nikolai Mikhailovich Talanov   1973–78

Vladimir Ivanovich Mechulayev   1978–82

Aleksandr Alekseevich Metelkin   1982–84

Sergei Aleksandrovich Labur   1984–89

Leonid Y. Ponomarenko (?)   1989–

KGB Residents in Australia

Semyon Ivanovich Makarov   1943–49

Valentin Matveevich Mikhailov   1949–51
(*alias* Sadovnikov)

Ivan Mikhailovich Pakhomov   1951–52
(acting resident)

Vladimir Mikhailovich Petrov   1952–54
(temporary resident)

                                                                   ***

Vladimir Aleksandrovich Alekseev   1967–70
(possibly resident)

Vladimir Yevgenyevich Tulayev   1970–74

Geronti Pavlovich Lazovik   1974–77

Lev Sergeevich Koshlyakov   1977–84

Yuri Pavlovich Yartsev   1985–89

KGB Residents in New Zealand

Vasili Petrovich Urenev   1946–52

Georgi Mikhailovich Sokolov   1953–56

Yevgeni Ivanovich Gergel   1956–61

Vladislav Sergeevich Andreev   1961–62

Vladimir Borisovich Koshelev   1962–65

Gennadi Yevlampievich Shlyapnikov   1965–68

Yuri Timofeevich Drozhin   1968–74

Dmitri Aleksandrovich Razgovorov   1974

Yuri Nikolayevich Obukhov	1974–77
Nikolai Aleksandrovich Shatskikh	1977–82
Sergei Sergeevich Budnik	1982–87

KGB Residents in India

Pavel Dmitrievich Yerzin	1947–52
	***
Radomir Georgievich Bogdanov	1957–67
Dmitri Aleksandrovich Yerokhin	1967–70
Yakov Prokofyevich Medyanik	1970–75
Leonid Vladimirovich Shebarshin	1975–77
Gennadi Afanasyevich Vaulin	1977–81
Aleksandr Iosifovich Lysenko	1981–87?
Feliks Ivanovich Tumakhovich	1988–

KGB Residents in Japan

Grigori Grigorievich Dolbin	1942–45
Grigori Pavlovich Kasparov	1949–52
Aleksandr Fyodorovich Nosenko	1954–?
Anatoli Anatolievich Rozanov	1957–60
Pyotr Andreevich Vygonny (possibly resident)	1960–63
Georgi Petrovich Pokrovsky (possibly resident)	1964–69
Yuri Ivanovich Popov	1969–73
Dmitri Aleksandrovich Yerokhin	1973–75
Oleg Aleksandrovich Guryanov	1976–79
Anatoli Nikolayevich Babkin (possibly resident)	1980–83
Aleksandr Aleksandrovich Shaposhnikov	1983–85
	***
Nikolai Nikolayevich Borisov	1988–

Notes

Abbreviations Used in the Notes

AAC   Australian Archives, Canberra
FBI   Freedom of Information Act Archive, Federal Bureau of
      Investigation, Washington, DC
NAW   National Archives, Washington, DC
PRO   Public Record Office, Kew, Surrey
SWB   BBC, *Summary of World Broadcasts*

Introduction

1. Christopher Andrew, *Secret Service: The Making of the British Intelligence Community* (London: Heinemann, 1985), 1st ed., p. 499; *Her Majesty's Secret Service: The Making of the British Intelligence Community* (New York: Viking, 1986), 1st ed., p. 499. In 1990 KGB Major-General Oleg Danilovich Kalygin, a former head of FCD Directorate K (counterintelligence), publicly revealed for the first time, to the wrath of the KGB leadership, that defection and penetration had become a more serious problem for the KGB than for the CIA. Interview in *Moscow News,* 1990, no. 25.

2. Interview with Philby by Phillip Knightley in *Sunday Times,* section C, 20 March and 10 April 1988. Christopher Andrew, "More Unreliable Memoirs From 'General' Philby," *Daily Telegraph,* 15 April 1988.

3. Kim Philby, *My Silent War* (London: Panther Books, 1969), p. 17.

4. It is fair to add that the two best-known literary mole hunters of the 1980s, Chapman Pincher and Nigel West, though mistakenly concentrating their fire on,

665

respectively, Sir Roger Hollis and his deputy, Graham Mitchell, also unmasked a number of genuine Soviet agents. The first chapter of our forthcoming book, *The Magnificent Five,* will explore some of the false trails that confused the mole hunt. In the early 1980s Andrew also followed one false trail. Having discovered that the German *Fünfergruppen* that inspired Guy Burgess to form a Cambridge "ring of five" in 1933–34 did not always have five members, and that Cambridge provided more than five recruits to the KGB, he began to doubt whether the term "Fifth Man" had much significance. His doubts were strengthened by skepticism about accounts of the defection of Burgess and Maclean in 1951 that mistakenly posited the involvement of a Fifth Man. Not until Andrew met Gordievsky did he learn that by the Second World War the KGB had christened its five ablest Cambridge recruits the Five (later the Magnificent Five), and that there was indeed a Fifth Man whose exploits ranked in importance with those of the other four, though he played no part in the flight of Burgess and Maclean.

5. Hollis was, in reality, a staunch anti-Communist who, even in the middle of World War II, was issuing urgent warnings that Stalin could not be trusted and predicting that "Once Russia is safe and out of the battle, our Communists will seize every chance to make trouble, as they did in the past." See Sheila Kerr, "Roger Hollis and the Dangers of the Anglo-Soviet Treaty of 1942," *Intelligence and National Security,* vol. V (1990), no. 3.

Chapter 1. Tsarist Origins (1565–1917)

1. N. V. Riasanovsky, *A History of Russia,* 4th ed. (Oxford University Press, 1984), pp. 148–55. Ronald Hingley, *The Russian Secret Police* (London: Hutchinson, 1970), pp. 1–4.

2. Richard Pipes, *Russia under the Old Regime* (Harmondsworth: Penguin, 1974), pp. 129–30.

3. Unless otherwise indicated, our account of the Third Section is based on Sidney Monas, *The Third Section* (Cambridge, Mass.: Harvard University Press, 1961) and P. S. Squire, *The Third Department* (Cambridge University Press, 1968).

4. Alexander Herzen, *My Past and Thoughts,* trans. Constance Garnett (London: Chatto & Windus, 1968), vol. II, pp. 441–42.

5. Pipes, *Russia,* pp. 294–95.

6. Ibid., pp. 297ff. Hingley, *Secret Police,* ch. 3.

7. Pipes, *Russia,* ch. 11. Hingley, *Secret Police,* ch. 4.

8. Hingley, *Secret Police,* pp. 92–93.

9. A. T. Vasilyev, *The Ochrana* (London: Harrap, 1930), ch. 6.

10. Hans Rogger, *Russia in the Age of Modernisation and Revolution 1881–1917* (London: Longman, 1983), pp. 199–206. Hingley, *Secret Police,* pp. 92–94.

11. Gordievsky.

12. Gordievsky.

13. Hingley, *Secret Police,* p. 79.

14. Richard J. Johnson, "Zagranichnaya Agentura: The Tsarist Political Police in Europe," *Journal of Contemporary History,* 1972, nos. 1–2.

15. "La police russe en France," 29 June 1914, Archives Nationales, Paris, F 7 14,605.

16. Norman Cohn, *Warrant for Genocide* (London: Eyre & Spottiswoode, 1967), pp. 78–79. Hingley, *Secret Police,* pp. 80–81.

17. Johnson, "Zagranichnaya Agentura."

18. "La police russe en France," 29 June 1914.

19. "Les polices étrangères en France," 19 June 1914, Archives Nationales, Paris, F 7 14,605.

20. Johnson, "Zagranichnaya Agentura."

21. "La police russe en France," 29 June 1914.

22. Cohn, *Warrant for Genocide,* p. 79. Hingley, *Secret Police,* p. 80.

23. "La police russe en France," 29 June 1914.

24. Cohn, *Warrant for Genocide,* pp. 76–86, 113.

25. Christopher Andrew, *Théophile Delcassé and the Making of the Entente Cordiale* (London: Macmillan, 1968), pp. 130–31, 239, 241.

26. Christopher Andrew, *Secret Service: The Making of the British Intelligence Community* (London: Heinemann, 1985), pp. 3, 85ff.

27. Vasilyev, *Ochrana,* ch. 5.

28. Hingley, *Secret Police,* p. 114.

29. David Kahn, *The Codebreakers* (New York: Macmillan, 1967), pp. 614–21.

30. Christopher Andrew, "Déchiffrement et diplomatie: le cabinet noir du Quai d'Orsay sous la Troisième République," *Relations Internationales,* 1976, no. 5.

31. Kahn, *Codebreakers,* p. 621.

32. Minute by Hardinge on Spring Rice to Grey, 28 Feb. 1906, secret despatch no. 151, PRO FO 371/123/7670.

33. Hardinge to Sanderson, 3 June 1904, private, Lansdowne Papers, PRO FO 800/115.

34. Hardinge's discovery was recalled in Spring Rice to Grey, 12 April 1906, secret despatch no. 263, PRO FO 371/123/12817. The founder of the secret department is identified only as "a man who had served as chief of the Russian police at Paris." Only Rachkovsky fits that description. His successor as head of the Foreign Agency, Ratayev, remained in Paris until 1905.

35. Spring Rice to Grey, 28 Feb. 1906, secret despatch no. 151, PRO FO 371/123/7670. Spring Rice to Grey, 12 April 1906, secret despatch no. 263, PRO FO 371/123/12817.

36. See, for example, the numerous intercepts in the four series of Russian documents in German translation edited by Otto Hoetsch, *Die Internationalen Beziehungen im Zeitalter des Imperialismus* (Berlin, 1933–42). There is still no study of the influence of sigint on Tsarist foreign policy. Two otherwise excellent recent studies of Tsarist foreign policy by William C. Fuller, Jr. ("The Russian Empire," see n. 42) and D. C. B. Lieven (*Russia and the Origins of the First World War* [London: Macmillan, 1983]) do not even mention sigint.

37. Lamsdorff to Osten Sacken, no. 27, 10 Jan. 1902, quoting extracts from German decrypts. Archives du Ministère des Affaires Etrangères, Paris, Nelidov Papers.

38. David Kahn, "Codebreaking in World War I and II: The Major Successes and Failures, Their Causes and Their Effects," in Christopher Andrew and David N. Dilks (eds.), *The Missing Dimension: Governments and Intelligence Communities in the Twentieth Century* (London: Macmillan, 1984), pp. 138–39. Though prewar Britain had no sigint, the Indian Raj had a small agency for its own purposes.

39. Andrew, "Déchiffrement et diplomatie," p. 51ff.

40. The latest German intercept published in Hoetsch, *Die Internationalen Beziehungen,* is for 1912.

41. Andrew, "Déchiffrement et diplomatie," p. 53. Both France and Russia were, however, able to decrypt German diplomatic traffic during the war.

42. William C. Fuller, Jr., "The Russian Empire," in Ernest R. May (ed.), *Knowing One's Enemies* (Princeton University Press, 1984).

43. Ian Armour, "Colonel Redl: Fact and Fantasy," *Intelligence and National Security,* vol. II (1987), no. 1.

44. Kahn, *Codebreakers,* pp. 622–28.

45. Christopher Andrew, "France and the German Menace," in May (ed.), *Knowing One's Enemies,* p. 133.

46. A. G. Raffalovitch, *L'abominable vénalité de la presse* (Paris, 1921). René

Girault, *Emprunts russes et investissements français en Russie 1887–1914* (Paris, 1973). Andrew, *Delcassé,* pp. 245–46.

47. According to Oleg Kalygin, head of FCD Directorate K (counterintelligence) for most of the 1970s and deputy head of the Leningrad KGB from 1980 to 1987, the KGB within the Soviet Union "is still using the instructions on how to handle agents that were written by the Tsarist police department." Interview in *Komsomolskaya Pravda,* 20 June 1990.

48. Robert Chadwell Williams, *The Other Bolsheviks* (Bloomington and Indianapolis: Indiana University Press, 1986), pp. 120–21, 154–55.

49. Stefan T. Possony, *Lenin: The Compulsive Revolutionary,* rev. Brit. ed. (London: Allen & Unwin, 1966), p. 142.

50. Bertram D. Wolfe, *Three Who Made a Revolution* (Harmondsworth: Penguin, 1966), pp. 535–36.

51. Our analysis of Malinovsky's career is based on R. C. Elwood, *Roman Malinovsky: A Life Without a Cause* (Newtonville, Mass.: Oriental Research Partners, 1977) and Wolfe, *Three Who Made a Revolution,* ch. 31.

52. Tsuyoshi Hasegawa, *The February Revolution: Petrograd, 1917* (Seattle: University of Washington Press, 1981), p. 201.

53. Ibid., p. 201.

54. Vasilyev, *Ochrana,* pp. 229, 249–50.

Chapter 2. The Cheka, Counterrevolution, and the "Lockhart Conspiracy" (1917–21)

1. See illustration in first section of photographs. Some other KGB emblems continue to show both shield and sword.

2. Gordievsky.

3. E. H. Carr, *The Bolshevik Revolution 1917–1923* (London: Macmillan, 1953), vol. III, ch. 21.

4. V. I. Lenin, *The State and Revolution* (London: Allen & Unwin, 1919), ch. 5, pts. 2 and 3.

5. George Leggett, *The Cheka: Lenin's Political Police* (Oxford University Press, 1981), ch. 1.

6. V. Andrianov, "Knight of the Revolution," *Pravda,* 10 Sept. 1987.

7. Leggett, *Cheka,* pp. 22ff.

8. "Dzerzhinsky on Himself" and extracts from his correspondence in *20 Let VChK-OGPU-NKVD* (Moscow: OGIZ, 1938), pp. 20–23. Andrianov, "Knight of the Revolution."

9. Leggett, *Cheka,* pp. 26–27.

10. Ibid., pp. 250ff.

11. Fyodor Timofeevich Fomin, *Zapiski Starogo Chekista,* 2nd ed. (Moscow: Politizdat, 1964).

12. Speech of 2 July 1926, *20 Let VChK-OGPU-NKVD,* p. 24.

13. *Pravda,* 11 Sept. 1987.

14. Interview by Christopher Andrew with the KGB defector Pyotr Deryabin, 25 Nov. 1987.

15. "Terror to Our Enemies, Glory to Our Fatherland," *20 Let VChK-OGPU-NKVD.*

16. See below, p. 342.

17. Gordievsky.

18. Extract from Sovnarkom minutes, 20 Dec. 1917, in *20 Let VChK-OGPU-NKVD.*

19. C. K. Tsvigun et al. (eds.), *V. I. Lenin i VChK: Sbornik documentov (1917–1922 gg)* (Moscow: Izdatelstvo Politicheskoi Literatury, 1975), especially no. 52.

20. Leggett, *Cheka*, pp. 54–55.

21. Ibid., p. 114.

22. Yakov Khristoforovich Peters, "Vospominaniya o rabote v VChK v pervyi god revolutsii," in *Proletarskaya Revoliutsia*, 1924, no. 10 (33).

23. Leggett, *Cheka*, ch. 123, p. 255.

24. Ibid., pp. 34, 219–20.

25. Peters, "Vospominaniya."

26. Leggett, *Cheka*, pp. 280–81.

27. Sergei Zakharovich Ostryakov, *Voyennye Chekisty* (Moscow: Voyenizdat, 1979), ch. 1.

28. Evan Mawdsley, *The Russian Civil War* (London: Allen & Unwin, 1987).

29. Ibid., p. 53. Leggett, *Cheka*, p. 102.

30. Tsvigun et al. (eds.), *Lenin i VChK*, no. 48.

31. Ostryakov, *Voyennye Chekisty*, ch. 1.

32. Speech by Lenin, 23 December 1921. Tsvigun et al. (eds.), *Lenin i VChK*, pp. 543–44.

33. Leggett, *Cheka*, pp. 73, 293.

34. Ibid., ch. 4.

35. Ibid. John J. Dziak, *Chekisty* (Lexington, Mass.: Lexington Books, 1987), p. 13.

36. Tsvigun et al. (eds.), *Lenin i VChK*, no. 198.

37. Christopher Andrew, *Secret Service: The Making of the British Intelligence Community* (London: Heinemann, 1985), pp. 212–13.

38. Ibid., chs. 2, 4, and 6.

39. Ibid., pp. 83–84.

40. "Richard Deacon," *A History of the British Secret Service* (London: Frederick Muller, 1969), pp. 139–42, 175.

41. Andrew, *Secret Service*, pp. 83–84, 214. Robert Bruce Lockhart, *Memoirs of a British Agent*, 2nd ed. (London/New York: Putnam, 1934), pp. 276–77.

42. Ostryakov, *Voyennye Chekisty*, Introduction and ch. 1. Another Soviet historian finds it "scarcely credible" that Reilly "was born in Odessa with the name of Rosenblum." Fyodor Volkov, *Secrets from Whitehall and Downing Street* (Moscow: Progress Publishers, 1986), p. 33.

43. Gordievsky.

44. Lockhart, *British Agent*, p. 323.

45. Kim Philby, *My Silent War* (London: Panther Books, 1969), p. 30.

46. G. A. Hill, *Go Spy the Land* (London: Cassell, 1932), quotation from p. 193.

47. G. A. Hill, Secret 29-page Report on Work Done in Russia, 26 November 1918, PRO FO 371/3350.

48. Leggett, *Cheka*, p. 419, n. 104.

49. Philby, *My Silent War*, p. 30.

50. Hill, *Go Spy the Land*, pp. 196–97.

51. Richard K. Debo, "Lockhart Plot or Dzerzhinskii Plot?," *Journal of Modern History*, vol. XLIII (1971), pp. 428–31. S. G. Reilly, *The Adventures of Sydney Reilly, Britain's Master Spy* (London: E. Mathews & Marrot, 1931), p. 21.

52. Richard H. Ullman, *Anglo–Soviet Relations 1917–1921* (Princeton University Press, 1961–72), vol. I, ch. 8.

53. Ibid., pp. 285–86.

54. Lockhart, *British Agent*, pp. 314–15, misdates the meeting and wrongly suggests that Berzin rather than Sprogis was present (see Debo, "Lockhart Plot or Dzerzhinskii Plot?," p. 434). Hill records Reilly's first meeting with Lockhart and the

Lettish agents provocateurs in Moscow as occurring "in the second week of August," almost certainly immediately following Berzin's and Sprogis's first encounter with Lockhart, "Report on Work Done in Russia," fols. 32–33, PRO FO 371/3350.

55. Debo, "Lockhart Plot or Dzerzhinskii Plot?," pp. 432–36. Lockhart, *British Agent,* p. 314.

56. Hill, "Report on Work Done in Russia," fols. 37–38, PRO FO 371/3350. Hill and Reilly of course believed that the safe house was provided by the Letts.

57. Leggett, *Cheka,* p. 281.

58. Ibid., p. 282.

59. Hill, "Report on Work Done in Russia," fols. 38–39, PRO FO 371/3350.

60. Leggett, *Cheka,* ch. 6.

61. Ostryakov, *Voyennye Chekisty,* ch. 1.

62. Lockhart, *British Agent,* pp. 317–19.

63. Peters, "Vospominaniya."

64. Lockhart, *British Agent,* pp. 319–20.

65. Ibid., p. 320.

66. Account given by Reilly to Hill, "Report on Work Done in Russia," fol. 41, PRO FO 371/3350.

67. *The Times,* 24 October 1918. Richard K. Debo, *Revolution and Survival: The Foreign Policy of Soviet Russia 1917–18* (Liverpool University Press, 1979), p. 361.

68. Hill, "Report on Work Done in Russia," fol. 39, PRO FO 371/3350.

69. *Izvestia,* 3 September 1918. Jane Degras (ed.), *Documents on Soviet Foreign Policy* (London: Oxford University Press, 1951), vol. I, pp. 98–99.

70. Lockhart, *British Agent,* pp. 324–26.

71. Leggett, *Cheka,* p. 283.

72. Hill, "Report on Work Done in Russia," fol. 38, PRO FO 371/3350.

73. Lockhart, *British Agent,* p. 322. Hill, *Go Spy The Land,* p. 238.

74. Hill, "Report on Work Done in Russia," fol. 42, PRO FO 371/3350.

75. Lockhart, *British Agent,* ch. 10.

76. Peters, "Vospominaniya."

77. Andrew, *Secret Service,* pp. 218–19. Leggett, *Cheka* p. 283.

78. Ostryakov, *Voyennye Chekisty,* ch. 1.

79. See below, pp. 93ff.

80. Tsvigun et al. (eds.), *Lenin i VChK,* nos. 286, 295.

81. Ostryakov, *Voyennye Chekisty,* ch. 1.

82. Leggett, *Cheka,* p. 349.

83. Ibid., Appendix C.

84. Tsvigun et al. (eds.), *Lenin i VChK,* p. 545.

85. Leggett, *Cheka,* ch. 15. Amy W. Knight, *The KGB: Police and Politics in the Soviet Union* (London: Unwin Hyman, 1988), pp. 14–15.

Chapter 3. Foreign Intelligence and "Active Measures" in the Dzerzhinsky Era (1919–27)

1. W. T. Angress, "The Takeover that Remained in Limbo: The German Experience 1918–1923," in Thomas Hammond (ed.), *The Anatomy of Communist Takeovers* (New Haven, Conn.: Yale University Press, 1975), p. 162.

2. J. P. Nettl, *Rosa Luxemburg,* 2 vols. (London: Oxford University Press, 1966).

3. Branko Lazitch and Milorad M. Drachkovitch, *Lenin and the Comintern,* vol. I (Stanford: Hoover Institution Press, 1972), pp. 214–15. Aino Kuusinen, *Before and After Stalin* (London: Michael Joseph 1974), pp. 35–36

4. E. H. Carr, *The Bolshevik Revolution 1917–1923,* vol. III (London: Macmillan, 1953), pp. 128ff.

5. Lazitch and Drachkovitch, *Lenin and the Comintern*, vol. I, pp. 167–93.

6. Dan N. Jacobs, *Borodin* (Cambridge, Mass.: Harvard University Press, 1981), p. 75.

7. Christopher Andrew, *Secret Service: The Making of the British Intelligence Community* (London: Heinemann, 1985), p. 244.

8. Lazitch and Drachkovitch, *Lenin and the Comintern*, vol. I, pp. 182–98.

9. Jane Degras (ed.), *The Communist International 1919–1942. Documents*, vol. I (London: Oxford University Press, 1956), pp. 166–72.

10. Geoffrey Hosking, *A History of the Soviet Union* (London: Fontana, 1985), p. 101.

11. Henry M. Pelling, *The British Communist Party*, 2nd ed. (London: A. & C. Black, 1975), pp. 11, 17–18, 29.

12. Lazitch and Drachkovitch, *Lenin and the Comintern*, vol. I, p. 141.

13. Branko Lazitch, "Two Instruments of Control by the Comintern: The Emissaries of the ECCI and the Party Representatives in Moscow," in Milorad M. Drachkovitch and Branko Lazitch (eds.), *The Comintern: Historical Highlights.* (New York: Praeger, 1966), p. 49.

14. Lazitch and Drachkovitch, *Lenin and the Comintern*, vol. I, pp. 158, 454.

15. Ibid., ch. 10.

16. Elizabeth Poretsky, *Our Own People* (London: Oxford University Press, 1969), p. 53n.

17. Kuusinen, *Before and After Stalin*, p. 20.

18. Francis Meynell, *My Lives* (London: Bodley Head, 1971), pp. 128–31.

19. Jacobs, *Borodin*, pp. 61–65, 81, 97.

20. Lazitch and Drachkovitch, *Lenin and the Comintern*, vol. I, ch. 11. Angress, "Takeover," pp. 176–82.

21. Paul Avrich, *Kronstadt 1921* (Princeton University Press, 1971).

22. S. K. Tsvigun et al. (eds.), *V. I. Lenin i VChK: Sbornik documentov (1917–1922 gg)* (Moscow: Izdatelstvo Politicheskoi Literatury, 1975), no. 390, pp. 440–42.

23. Richard H. Ullman, *Anglo–Soviet Relations, 1917–1921*, vol. III (Princeton University Press, 1972) gives the best account of these negotiations.

24. Ibid., p. 97.

25. George Leggett: *The Cheka: Lenin's Political Police* (Oxford University Press, 1981), pp. 298–99.

26. Tsvigun et al. (eds.), *Lenin i VChK*, no. 390.

27. Ullman, *Anglo–Soviet Relations*, vol. III, ch. 3.

28. Tsvigun et al. (eds.), *Lenin i VChK*, no. 390.

29. Hugh Brogan, *The Life of Arthur Ransome* (London: Jonathan Cape, 1984), pp. 223, 197.

30. Ibid., pp. 213, 253.

31. Ibid., pp. 218, 221.

32. On Ransome's contacts with Sir Basil Thomson, see ibid., pp. 234–35, 244.

33. See, e.g., Ransome's diary for 12 Oct., 3 Nov. 1922, 16 June 1923; Ransome Papers, Brotherton Library, University of Leeds.

34. The small number of addresses and telephone numbers recorded at the beginning of Ransome's 1924 diary included those of Klyshko in Moscow. Ibid.

35. Tsvigun et al. (eds.), *Lenin i VChK*, no. 390.

36. Brogan, *Ransome*, pp. 163–65.

37. Ransome subsequently claimed that "it was impossible to take Paul Dukes seriously enough to dislike him." Rupert Hart-Davis (ed.), *The Autobiography of Arthur Ransome* (London: Jonathan Cape, 1976), pp. 262–63.

38. Tsvigun et al. (eds.), *Lenin i VChK*, no. 390.

39. Ibid.

40. Ibid.

41. Hart-Davis (ed.), *Autobiography of Arthur Ransome,* pp. 309–11.

42. Ransome diary entries for 8–11 May 1923. His diary is entirely blank for the period from 15–21 May; Ransome Papers, Brotherton Library, University of Leeds.

43. Hart-Davis (ed.), *Autobiography of Arthur Ransome,* pp. 309–11. Ransome's diary for 23 May 1923 describes the encounter between Hodgson and Litvinov as a "decisive meeting"; Ransome papers, Brotherton Library, University of Leeds.

44. Hart-Davis (ed.), *Autobiography of Arthur Ransome,* p. 317. Later in 1924 Ransome told the *Manchester Guardian* that he had had enough of living in Eastern Europe and returned to England. Over the next few years he continued as a political correspondent, traveling to the Middle East and China, and paying one final visit to Moscow in 1928. Then, in 1929, he resigned from the *Guardian* and gave up journalism to live in the Lake District and concentrate on his increasingly successful career as a children's novelist.

45. Andrew, *Secret Service,* p. 261.

46. P. William Filby, "Bletchley Park and Berkeley Street," *Intelligence and National Security,* vol. III (1988), no. 2, p. 280.

47. W. F. Friedman, "Six Lectures on Cryptology," p. 18, NAW RG457 SRH-004.

48. Filby, "Bletchley Park and Berkeley Street," p. 280.

49. Ullman, *Anglo–Soviet Relations,* vol. III, passim. Andrew, *Secret Service,* pp. 266–74.

50. Andrew, *Secret Service,* pp. 273–96, 312, 315–17. Raskolnikov later perished in the Great Terror.

51. Leggett, *Cheka,* p. 299.

52. Andrew, *Secret Service,* pp. 306–07.

53. Georgi Agabekov, *OGPU* (New York: Brentano's, 1931), p. 271.

54. Leggett, *Cheka,* p. 458. Gary R. Waxmonsky, "Police and Politics in Soviet Society 1921–1928," unpublished Ph.D. thesis (Princeton University, 1982), pp. 373–74.

55. Gordievsky.

56. Agabekov, *OGPU,* pp. 12–13.

57. Kuusinen, *Before and After Stalin,* pp. 40ff. Poretsky, *Our Own People,* pp. 53ff. Walter Krivitsky, *I Was Stalin's Agent* (London: Hamish Hamilton, 1939), pp. 79ff.

58. See below, pp. 190ff.

59. Babette Gross, *Willi Münzenberg: A Political Biography* (Ann Arbor: Michigan University Press, 1974), p. 217. Krivitsky, *Stalin's Agent,* pp. 79–80.

60. Gross, *Münzenberg,* p. 217.

61. Arthur Koestler, *The Invisible Writing,* Danube ed. (London: Hutchinson, 1969), p. 253.

62. Ibid. Gross, *Münzenberg,* p. 120.

63. R. N. Carew-Hunt, "Willi Muenzenberg," in David Footman (ed.), *International Communism,* St. Antony's Papers, no. 9 (London: Chatto & Windus, 1960), p. 87.

64. A police raid in 1931 on the Berlin headquarters of the League Against Imperialism, founded by Münzenberg in 1927, found documents dealing with an intelligence network in several countries. Ibid., p. 77.

65. Agabekov, *OGPU,* p. 272. Kuusinen, *Before and After Stalin,* p. 40. Leggett, *Cheka,* p. 458.

66. Branko Lazitch and Milorad M. Drachkovitch, *Biographical Dictionary of the Comintern,* rev. ed. (Stanford: Hoover Institution Press, 1986), entries for Pyatnitsky and Trilisser.

67. Kuusinen, *Before and After Stalin,* pp. 61–62.

68. Angress, "Takeover," p. 186.

69. Boris Bajanov, *Bajanov révèle Staline: souvenirs d'un ancien secrétaire de Staline* (Paris: Gallimard, 1979), pp. 62–64. Bajanov was Secretary of the Politburo in 1923.

70. Ibid., pp. 64–66. Some confirmation of Unshlikht's role in the "German October" is provided by his leading part in 1928, together with Pyatnitsky and others, in commissioning a manual on armed insurrection based on detailed studies of the risings in Hamburg in 1923, Reval in 1924, and China in 1926–7. A. Neuberg, *Armed Insurrection* (London: NLB, 1970), pp. 9, 11.

71. Kuusinen, *Before and After Stalin,* p. 62.

72. Ibid., pp. 63–66.

73. Angress, "Takeover," p. 190.

74. There was one further, smaller-scale attempt to launch a revolution at Reval, the capital of Estonia, on 1 December 1924. The initiative was taken by Zinoviev (later accused of trying to strengthen his position in the leadership struggle after Lenin's death by orchestrating a successful insurrection) who was misled by overoptimistic Estonian Communists in Moscow and Leningrad into believing that Estonian workers would follow the Communists' revolutionary lead. They did not do so and the rising was brutally crushed in a single day. Neuberg, *Armed Insurrection,* pp. 11–12. Kuusinen, *Before and After Stalin,* p. 66.

75. Leggett, *Cheka,* pp. 443–44.

76. Gordievsky.

77. Gordievsky.

78. Leggett, *Cheka,* p. 294.

79. Gordievsky.

80. Agabekov, *OGPU,* p. 45.

81. Gordievsky. On Birk's role in the Trust, see Natalie Grant, "Deception on a Grand Scale," *Journal of Intelligence and Counterintelligence,* vol. I (1986–88), no. 4, p. 87.

82. Hodgson to Curzon, 29 May 1922, PRO FO 371/8216 N5429.

83. Hodgson to Litvinov, 24 and 31 May 1924, PRO FO 371/10495 N4868/ 2140/38.

84. Hodgson to MacDonald, 26 May and 9 June 1924, ibid.

85. Hodgson to MacDonald, 22 Aug. 1924, cited in memorandum "Soviet Espionage on British Mission in Moscow," 7 Oct. 1924, ibid.

86. Agabekov, *OGPU,* p. 33. Agabekov was head of the section that dealt with Apresov's correspondence.

87. Strang, minute of 25 April 1927, on Lampson to Foreign Office, 22 April 1927, no. 756, PRO FO 371/12500 F3967. Lampson to Foreign Office, 28 April 1927, no. 796, PRO FO 371/12500 F4134.

88. Andrew, *Secret Service,* pp. 402–09.

89. "Instructions for the Enlistment of Secret Co-Workers in Foreign General Consulates (British, American, Japanese)," 4 April 1927, PRO FO 371/12501 F6532.

90. See, e.g., Agabekov, *OGPU,* p. 35.

91. Leggett, *Cheka,* pp. 232, 446.

92. Gordon Brook-Shepherd, *The Storm Petrels* (London: Collins, 1977), p. 104.

93. Andrew, *Secret Service,* p. 407.

94. See below, pp. 111–12.

95. Kuusinen, *Before and After Stalin,* p. 73.

96. Andrew, *Secret Service,* p. 302.

97. Kuusinen, *Before and After Stalin,* p. 74.

98. Ibid., pp. 76–77.

99. Andrew, *Secret Service,* p. 335. After a number of disagreements Roy was expelled from the Comintern in 1929.

100. Kuusinen, *Before and After Stalin,* pp. 71–72.

101. Andrew, *Secret Service,* pp. 309–10.

102. Ibid., pp. 311, 319.

103. Kuusinen, *Before and After Stalin,* p. 51.

104. Andrew, *Secret Service,* pp. 312–13.

105. Kuusinen, *Before and After Stalin,* pp. 51–52.

106. Ibid.

107. Gordievsky.

108. Leonard D. Gerson, *The Secret Police in Lenin's Russia* (Philadelphia: Temple University Press, 1976), pp. 234–35.

109. S. P. Melgounov, *The Red Terror in Russia* (London: Dent, 1925), p. 253.

110. Tsvigun et al. (eds.), *Lenin i VChK,* no. 437.

111. Gordievsky.

112. Leggett, *Cheka,* p. 295.

113. David Golinkov, *The Secret War Against Soviet Russia* (Moscow: Progress Publishers, 1981), pp. 90–91.

114. Andrew, *Secret Service,* p. 288. Robin Bruce Lockhart, *Ace of Spies: A Biography of Sidney Reilly* (London: Hodder & Stoughton, 1967), pp. 101–08.

115. Leggett, *Cheka,* p. 295.

116. Ibid., pp. 295–96.

117. Golinkov, *Secret War,* p. 91.

118. Andrew, *Secret Service,* pp. 290–91.

119. Winston S. Churchill, *Great Contemporaries* (London: Odhams, 1947), p. 101.

120. Golinkov, *Secret War,* pp. 91–93.

121. Ibid., p. 93.

122. Andrew, *Secret Service,* pp. 313–14. Michael Kettle, *Sidney Reilly: The True Story* (London: Corgi, 1983), ch. 7.

123. Golinkov, *Secret War,* pp. 93–96.

124. Grant, "Deception on a Grand Scale," pp. 51–59. Sergei Zacharovich Ostryakov, *Voyennye Chekisty* (Moscow: Voyenizdat, 1979), ch. 2, s. IV.

125. Grant, "Deception on a Grand Scale," p. 64n. "Trest," Melgunov MSS no. 103, gruppa 18, papka 10, London School of Economics. V. Sidorov, "Once again about The Trust: the role played by M. V. Zakharchenko-Schultz," *Golos Zarubezhya,* 1987, nos. 45–46.

126. Gordievsky.

127. Grant, "Deception on a Grand Scale," pp. 56–58. Ostryakov, *Voyennye Chekisty,* ch. 2, s IV.

128. Gordievsky.

129. Ostryakov, *Voyennye Chekisty,* ch. 2, s. IV.

130. Grant, "Deception on a Grand Scale," p. 53.

131. Andrew, *Secret Service,* p. 286.

132. Ibid.

133. Ibid., p. 314. Lockhart, *Ace of Spies,* pp. 131–35. Kettle, *Sidney Reilly,* pp. 131–36.

134. Andrew, *Secret Service,* p. 315. S. G. Reilly, *The Adventures of Sidney Reilly, Britain's Master Spy* (London: E. Mathews & Marrot, 1931), pp. 180–81.

135. Gordievsky.

136. Reilly, *Adventures of Sidney Reilly,* pp. 194–98 (with facsimile of Reilly's letter of 29 Sept. 1925).

137. Gordievsky. Cf. letters from "Commander E." (Ernest Boyce) to Pepita Reilly published in Reilly, *Adventures of Sidney Reilly,* pp. 189–94.

138. Golinkov, *Secret War,* pp. 96–101. Gordievsky.

139. Reilly, *Adventures of Sidney Reilly,* pp. 209–14.

140. Ibid., pp. 214–15.

141. Ibid., pp. 225–47.

142. Gordievsky.

143. Grant, "Deception on a Grand Scale," p. 70.

144. Reilly, *Adventures of Sidney Reilly*, pp. 253ff, contains a facsimile of Zakharchenko-Schultz's letter, written in French. The English translation published in the text contains some errors, including the transliteration of Artuzov.

145. Ibid., pp. 255–56.

146. Grant, "Deception on a Grand Scale," pp. 68–69, 72.

147. Unattributable interview.

148. Reilly, *Adventures of Sidney Reilly*, pp. 257–59.

149. *Pravda*, 6 July 1927.

150. Ostryakov, *Voyennye Chekisty*, ch. 2, s. IV.

Chapter 4. Stalin and Spy Mania (1926–38)

1. Fyodor Timofeevich Fomin, *Zapiski Starogo Chekista*, 2nd ed. (Moscow: Politizdat, 1964).

2. Robert M. Slusser, "Chekist Leaders from Dzerzhinsky to Yezhov: Variations on a Theme," paper to 88th Annual Meeting of American Historical Association: copy in Hoover Institution, Stanford, Calif.

3. Boris Souvarine, *Stalin: A Critical Survey of Bolshevism* (London: Secker & Warburg, 1939), p. 425.

4. Georgi Agabekov, *OGPU* (New York: Brentano's, 1931) p. 256. Fomin, *Zapiski Starogo Chekista*, pp. 128ff.

5. Fomin, *Zapiski Starogo Chekista*, pp. 128ff.

6. Leon Trotsky, *My Life* (Gloucester, Mass.: P. Smith, 1970), pp. 448–50.

7. Fomin, *Zapiski Starogo Chekista*, pp. 128ff. Agabekov, *OGPU*, p. 256. Slusser, "Chekist Leaders." Teodor Gladkov and Mikhail Smirnov, *Menzhinsky* (Moscow: Molodaya Gvardiya 1969).

8. Agabekov, *OGPU*, pp. 256–57. A. M. Larina, "The Unforgettable," *Znamya*, October 1988.

9. Alexander Orlov, *The Secret History of Stalin's Crimes* (London: Jarrolds, 1954), p. 311. Like many memoirs, Orlov's contain a mixture of relatively reliable firsthand observation and secondhand gossip of varying reliability. His description of Yagoda in the summer of 1936 is based on firsthand observation.

10. Stephen F. Cohen, *Bukharin and the Bolshevik Revolution 1888–1938* (New York: Oxford University Press, 1980), pp. 288, 448.

11. Larina, "The Unforgettable."

12. Gary R. Waxmonsky, "Police and Politics in Soviet Society, 1921–1928," unpublished Ph.D. thesis (Princeton University 1982), pp. 373–74.

13. Agabekov, *OGPU*, pp. 256–57. Orlov, *Secret History*, p. 260.

14. David J. Dallin, *Soviet Espionage* (New Haven, Conn.: Yale University Press, 1955), p. 40. Christopher Andrew, *Secret Service: The Making of the British Intelligence Community* (London: Heinemann, 1985) pp. 330–32.

15. PRO FO 371/12500 and 12501.

16. Andrew, *Secret Service*, pp. 331–33.

17. E. H. Carr, *Foundations of a Planned Economy* (London: Macmillan, 1978), vol. III, chs. 84, 85.

18. Andrew, *Secret Service*, pp. 321–33.

19. R. C. Tucker and S. F. Cohen (eds.), *The Great Purge Trial* (New York: Grosset & Dunlap, 1965), p. 683.

20. Agabekov, *OGPU*, pp. 122–23.

21. Andrew, *Secret Service*, p. 332.

22. Article by Stalin of 23 July 1927 in Jane Degras (ed.), *Documents on Soviet Foreign Policy,* vol. II (London: Oxford University Press, 1952), pp. 233–35.

23. Ibid., pp. 236–37.

24. Orlov, *Secret History,* p. 311. Orlov claimed to be reporting a case of which he had direct knowledge.

25. Leonard Schapiro, *The Communist Party of the Soviet Union,* 2nd rev. ed. (London: Methuen, 1970), ch. 16.

26. Isaac Deutscher, *The Prophet Unarmed: Trotsky 1921–1928* (London: Oxford University Press, 1959), pp. 393–94.

27. Isaac Deutscher, *The Prophet Outcast: Trotsky 1929–1940* (London: Oxford University Press, 1963), pp. 1–3. Jean van Heijenoort, *With Trotsky in Exile* (Cambridge, Mass.: Harvard University Press, 1978), ch. 1, p. 154.

28. Kendall E. Bailes, *Technology and Society Under Lenin and Stalin* (Princeton University Press, 1978), pp. 73–77.

29. Eugene Lyons, *Assignment in Utopia* (London: Harrap, 1938), ch. 6.

30. Bailes, *Technology and Society,* pp. 87–88.

31. Gordievsky. Grigorenko's history is not to be confused with the classified history of the FCD completed in 1980.

32. Sergei Zakharovich Ostryakov, *Voyennye Chekisty* (Moscow: Voyenizdat, 1979), ch. 2.

33. Andrew, *Secret Service,* pp. 177–80.

34. Ibid., pp. 477–80.

35. Hiroaki Kuromiya, *Stalin's Industrial Revolution* (Cambridge University Press, 1988), pp. 14–17. Geoffrey Hosking, *A History of the Soviet Union* (London: Fontana, 1985), pp. 149–50.

36. Petro G. Grigorenko, *Memoirs,* trans. T. P. Whitney (London: Harvill Press, 1983), pp. 28, 98–99.

37. Kuromiya, *Stalin's Industrial Revolution,* pp. 110–115.

38. Amy W. Knight, *The KGB: Police and Politics in the Soviet Union* (London: Unwin Hyman, 1988), pp. 20–21. Martin McCauley, *The Soviet Union Since 1917* (London: Longman, 1981), pp. 72–74.

39. Report to the 16th Party Congress, 27 June 1930, in Degras (ed.), *Documents on Soviet Foreign Policy,* vol. II, pp. 444–45.

40. Jonathan Haslam, *Soviet Foreign Policy 1930–33* (London: Macmillan, 1983), ch. 4.

41. Reports to Central Executive Committee, 5 January 1931, and to 6th Soviet Congress, 6 March 1931, in Degras (ed.), *Documents on Soviet Foreign Policy,* vol. II, pp. 467, 473.

42. Lyons, *Assignment in Utopia,* pp. 357–58.

43. *Protsess "Prompartii," 25 noiabria–7 dekabria 1930 g. Stenogramma sudebnogo protsessa i materialov, priobshchennye k delu* (Moscow: People's Commissariat of Justice of the USSR, 1931).

44. Lyons, *Assignment in Utopia,* pp. 370–78.

45. Ostryakov, *Voyennye Chekisty,* ch. 2.

46. Roy Medvedev, *Let History Judge* (London: Macmillan, 1972), p. 127.

47. Kuromiya, *Stalin's Industrial Revolution,* pp. 171–72.

48. Lyons, *Assignment in Utopia,* p. 379.

49. Kuromiya, *Stalin's Industrial Revolution,* pp. 274–76.

50. Lyons, *Assignment in Utopia,* pp. 561–71. Andrew, *Secret Service,* pp. 355–56.

51. Robert Conquest, *The Harvest of Sorrow* (London: Hutchinson, 1986), pt. II. Lev Kopelev, *The Education of a True Believer* (London: Wildwood House, 1981). Alex de Jonge, *Stalin and the Shaping of the Soviet Union* (London: Collins, 1986), chs. 28, 29.

52. Isaac Deutscher, *Stalin: A Political Biography* (New York: Vintage Books, 1962), p. 325.

53. Conquest, *Harvest of Sorrow,* p. 233.

54. Ibid., pp. 242–43, 269.

55. Ibid., p. 240.

56. Ibid., pp. 232, 257, 327.

57. Ibid., ch. 17.

58. Boris Nicolaevsky, *Power and the Soviet Elite* (New York: Praeger, 1965), pp. 18–19.

59. Victor Sergei, *Memoirs of a Revolutionary, 1901–1941* (London: Oxford University Press, 1963) p. 259.

60. *Izvestia,* 1989, no. 6. *Ogonek,* 1989, no. 15.

61. J. Arch Getty, *Origins of the Great Purges* (Cambridge University Press, 1985), pp. 119–21. Getty seems to us to overstate the real extent of Trotsky's "clandestine organisation inside the USSR." See below, pp. 156ff.

62. See below, pp. 135–36.

63. Jonathan Haslam, "Political Opposition to Stalin and the Origins of the Terror in Russia, 1932–1936," *Historical Journal,* vol. XX (1986), p. 398. Hosking, *History of the Soviet Union,* pp. 184–85.

64. Haslam, "Political Opposition to Stalin," p. 402.

65. Ibid., pp. 402–07. De Jonge, *Stalin,* ch. 30.

66. Leonid Radzhishovsky, "December 1," *Moscow News,* 1988, no. 48.

67. Knight, *KGB,* pp. 24–26.

68. "Comrade Stalin's personal secretariat," the "Secret Department" and the "Special Sector" were originally three different organs within the central chancellery, but fused together in the early 1930s. Niels Erik Rosenfeldt, *Knowledge and Power: The Role of Stalin's Secret Chancellery in the Soviet System of Government* (Copenhagen: Rosenkilde & Bagge, 1978).

69. Aleksandr Orlov, *Handbook of Intelligence and Guerilla Warfare* (Ann Arbor, Mich.: University of Michigan Press, 1963), p. 187.

70. Rosenfeldt, *Knowledge and Power,* pp. 131–32.

71. Gordievsky. There was no support among those in the KGB with whom he discussed the case for the theory that Zaporozhets acted without the knowledge of Medved.

72. Extract from Khrushchev's memoirs published in *Ogonek,* 1989, no. 28. Medvedev, *Let History Judge,* pp. 159–61.

73. Bertram D. Wolfe (ed.), *Khrushchev and Stalin's Ghost: Text, Background and Meaning of Khrushchev's Secret Report to the Twentieth Congress on the Night of February 24–25, 1956* (London: Atlantic Press, 1957), p. 128.

74. Orlov, *Secret History,* p. 74.

75. Medvedev, *Let History Judge,* pp. 161–65.

76. Larina, "The Unforgettable."

77. Haslam, "Opposition to Stalin," p. 409.

78. Medvedev, *Let History Judge,* p. 166–67.

79. Deutscher, *Prophet Outcast,* pp. 326–29.

80. Though granted initially for one year, the powers were extended indefinitely in June 1937. Medvedev, *Let History Judge,* p. 393.

81. Haslam, "Opposition to Stalin," pp. 416–17.

82. *Report of Court Proceedings in the Case of the Trotskyite/Zinovievite Terrorist Centre* (Moscow: People's Commissariat of Justice of the USSR, 1936).

83. Haslam, "Opposition to Stalin," p. 418.

84. Orlov, *Secret History,* pp. 261–63. Orlov had firsthand experience of Yagoda's "amazing vanity" during the few months before his dismissal.

85. Wolfe (ed.), *Khrushchev and Stalin's Ghost,* p. 130.

86. Orlov, *Secret History,* ch. 12, pp. 260–62. Robert Conquest, *Inside Stalin's Secret Police: NKVD Politics 1936–1939* (London: Macmillan, 1985), pp. 22–23.

87. *Report of Court Proceedings in the Case of the Anti-Soviet Trotskyite Centre* (Moscow: People's Commissariat of Justice of the USSR, 1937).

88. Walter Krivitsky, *I Was Stalin's Agent* (London: Hamish Hamilton, 1939), pp. 166–70. Krivitsky's account, written by a ghostwriter, almost certainly derives chiefly from Slutsky, with whom he was in close contact.

89. Ibid., p. 171.

90. Conquest, *Inside Stalin's Secret Police,* pp. 14–25.

91. Orlov, *Secret History,* pp. 237–38. Since all other commissars of State Security grades 1 and 2 were shot, it seems unlikely that Slutsky died from natural causes.

92. Gordievsky.

93. Robert Conquest, *The Great Terror: Stalin's Purge of the Thirties* (London: Macmillan, 1968), ch. 7. Krivitsky, *I Was Stalin's Agent,* p. 253.

94. Orlov, *Secret History,* p. 242.

95. F. N. Kovalev, "Documents from the Soviet Plenipotentiary Representation in Prague Relating to the 'Tukhachevsky Affair,' " *Vestnik,* no. 8 (42), 1 May 1989.

96. Jonathan Lewis and Phillip Whitehead, *Stalin: A Time for Judgement* (London: Methuen, 1990), p. 109.

97. Conquest, *Great Terror.* Conquest, *Inside Stalin's Secret Police.* On the number purged in the armed forces, see *Pravda,* 22 June 1989.

98. Nadezhda Mandelstam, *Hope against Hope* (London: Collins, 1971), pp. 75–76. Idem, *Hope Abandoned* (London: Collins, 1974).

99. Lev Razgon, "The Executioner's Song," *Moscow News,* 1988, no. 48. Zenon Poznyak, "Kuropaty," *Moscow News,* 1988, no. 41.

100. Branko Lazitch, "Stalin's Massacre of the Foreign Communist Leaders" in Milorad M. Drachkovitch and Branko Lazitch (eds.), *The Comintern: Historical Highlights* (New York: Praeger, 1966).

101. Tucker and Cohen (eds.), *The Great Purge Trial.*

102. Ibid.

103. Interview with Sir Fitzroy Maclean, *Timewatch,* BBC2, December 1988.

104. Gordievsky.

105. Mikhail Shreider, "Ivanovo, 1937," *Moscow News,* 1988, no. 48.

106. Gordievsky.

107. *Izvestia,* 15 February 1939. Degras, *Documents on Soviet Foreign Policy* vol. III (1953), pp. 273–75.

108. *20 Let VChK-OGPU-NKVD* (Moscow: OGIZ, 1938).

109. S. K. Tsvigun et al. (eds), *V. I. Lenin i VChK: Sbornik documentov (1917–1922 gg)* (Moscow: Izdatelstvo Politicheskoi Literatury, 1975), p. 369.

110. Degras (ed.), *Documents on Soviet Foreign Policy,* vol. III, p. 273.

111. Wolfe (ed.), *Khrushchev and Stalin's Ghost,* p. 158.

112. Medvedev, *Let History Judge,* p. 333.

113. A. Pavlov and Z. Fedotova, "Consultation," *Literaturnaya Gazeta,* no. 32 (5253), 2 August 1989.

114. "Terror to Our Enemies, Glory to Our Fatherland," *Pravda,* 20 Dec. 1938.

115. Medvedev, *Let History Judge,* p. 339.

116. Orlov, *Secret History,* pp. 221–22.

117. De Jonge, *Stalin,* p. 365.

118. O. V. Khlevnyuk, "The Year 1937–Opposition to the Repressions," *Kommunist,* 1989, no. 18. R. V. Ivanov-Razumnik, *The Memoirs of Ivanov-Razumnik* (London: Oxford University Press, 1965), p. 342. Robert W. Thurston, "Fear and Belief in

the USSR's 'Great Terror': Response to Arrest 1935–1939," *Slavic Review,* Summer 1986, pp. 226–27.

119. De Jonge, *Stalin,* pp. 349–51. Evgenia Ginsburg, *Into the Whirlwind* (London, 1967), pp. 20–21.

120. Conquest, *Great Terror,* pp. 499–513.

121. Mikhail Gorokhov, "From the NKVD to the Polish Army," Dallin Collection, Bakhmeteff Archive, Columbia University.

122. Victor Kravchenko, *I Chose Freedom* (New York: Scribner's, 1946), p. 232. Thurston, "Fear and Belief," p. 228.

123. Elizabeth Poretsky, *Our Own People* (London: Oxford University Press, 1969), pp. 110, 149.

Chapter 5. "Enemies of the People" Abroad (1929–40)

1. Gordievsky was responsible for preparing the section dealing with FCD Third Department countries (Britain, Ireland, Scandinavia, Australasia). The classified history of the FCD completed in 1980 is not to be confused with Grigorenko's general history of the KGB as a whole (also classified), finished in 1978. See above, p. 118.

2. Marina Grey, *Le général meurt à minuit* (Paris: Plon, 1981), chs. 4, 10, 17. Leonid Mlechin, "A Minister in Emigration: Hitherto Unknown Pages in the History of the Soviet Intelligence Service," *New Times,* 1990, nos. 18–20, draws on material from the KGB archives that adds to, and in some instances corrects, Marina Grey's pioneering account of the operation against Kutepov.

3. Grey, *Le général meurt à minuit,* pp. 42–44, 88.

4. All KGB foreign assassinations have to be approved by the Politburo—or did until the KGB virtually ceased this form of "special operations." In the Stalin era such decisions were sometimes taken by Stalin personally.

5. Grey, *Le général meurt à minuit,* chs. 1, 14. Mlechin, "A Minister in Emigration," pt. 3, *New Times,* 1990, no. 20, p. 38. Report of Sûreté investigation in *The Times,* 25 March 1930.

6. Mlechin, "A Minister in Emigration," pt. 3, *New Times,* 1990, no. 20, p. 38.

7. Grey, *Le général meurt à minuit,* pp. 83–84. A. Shneider, *Zapiski starogo moskvicha* (Moscow, 1966), pp. 118–19. Mikhail Heller and Aleksandr Nekrich, *Utopia in Power* (New York: Summit Books, 1986), p. 313.

8. *Krasnaya Zvezda,* 22 Sept. 1965. John J. Dziak, *Chekisty: A History of the KGB* (Lexington, Mass: Lexington Books, 1988), p. 99.

9. Grey, *Le général meurt à minuit,* ch. 20.

10. Ibid., ch. 22, pp. 224–26.

11. Mlechin, "A Minister in Emigration," pt. 2, *New Times,* 1990, no. 19.

12. Gordievsky.

13. Isaac Deutscher, *The Prophet Outcast: Trotsky 1929–40,* (London: Oxford University Press, 1963), pp. 25–26. Georgi Vereeken, *The GPU in the Trotskyist Movement* (London: New Park Publications, 1976), ch. 2. Herbet Romerstein and Stanislav Levchenko, *The KGB Against the "Main Enemy"* (Lexington, Mass.: Lexington Books, 1989), pp. 155ff, ch. 10.

14. Sergei Zakharovich Ostryakov, *Voyennye Chekisty* (Moscow: Voyenizdat, 1979), ch. 2.

15. Georgi Agabekov, *OGPU* (New York: Brentano's, 1931), pp. 202–03, 207–08, 219–21, 238–40. Elizabeth Poretsky, *Our Own People* (London: Oxford University Press, 1969), pp. 146–47. Alexander Orlov, *The Secret History of Stalin's Crimes* (London: Jarrolds, 1954), pp. 200–03. There are minor discrepancies between these accounts, based on varying degrees of personal knowledge. All, however, agree on Blyumkin's meeting with Trotsky, Gorskaya's involvement, and Blyumkin's execution.

The official KGB version of the Blyumkin affair (the only one to give the date of his execution) is summarized in Ostryakov, *Voyennye Chekisty.*

16. Leonard Schapiro, *The Communist Party of the Soviet Union,* 2nd rev. ed. (London: Methuen, 1970), p. 307

17. Deutscher, *Prophet Outcast,* pp. 81–82, 277–78.

18. Vereeken, *GPU in the Trotskyist Movement,* chs. 2, 5.

19. Deutscher, *Prophet Outcast,* pp. 125–26.

20. Trotsky's peregrinations are chronicled in detail in Deutscher, *Prophet Outcast.*

21. J. Arch Getty, *Origins of the Great Purges* (Cambridge University Press, 1985), p. 119.

22. Deutscher, *Prophet Outcast,* pp. 347–48. Vereeken, *GPU in the Trotskyist Movement,* ch. 1.

23. Orlov, *Secret History,* pp. 229–34.

24. Hugh Thomas, *The Spanish Civil War,* 3rd rev. ed. (London: Hamish Hamilton, 1977), ch. 27. Jonathan Haslam, *The Soviet Union and the Struggle for Collective Security 1933–39* (London: Macmillan, 1984), ch. 7. R. Dan Richardson, *Comintern Army* (Lexington, Ky.: University Press of Kentucky, 1982), chs. 4, 5, 6.

25. Walter Krivitsky, *I Was Stalin's Agent* (London: Hamish Hamilton, 1939), p. 101.

26. Haslam, *Struggle for Collective Security,* p. 116.

27. Thomas, *Spanish Civil War,* pp. 460–61. W. H. Auden, *Spain* (London: Faber, 1937).

28. Thomas, *Spanish Civil War,* p. 454. Krivitsky, *Stalin's Agent,* pp. 113–14.

29. Thomas, *Spanish Civil War,* pp. 457–59. David J. Dallin, *Soviet Espionage* (New Haven, Conn.: Yale University Press, 1955), p. 47. Ruth Fischer, *Stalin and German Communism* (London: Oxford University Press, 1949), p. 500. Branko Lazitch and Milorad M. Drachkovitch, *Biographical Dictionary of the Comintern,* rev. ed. (Stanford: Hoover Institution Press, 1986).

30. For a good survey of the war from the vantage point of the International Brigades (to whom it is dedicated), see Paul Preston, *The Spanish Civil War, 1936–39* (London: Weidenfeld & Nicolson, 1986).

31. Poretsky, *Our Own People,* p. 211.

32. Preston, *Spanish Civil War,* p. 137.

33. Vereeken, *GPU in the Trotskyist Movement,* ch. 12.

34. Thomas, *Spanish Civil War,* pp. 706–09.

35. Ibid., p. 669.

36. Auguste Lecoeur, *Le partisan* (Paris: Flammarion, 1963), p. 72.

37. Richardson, *Comintern Army,* pp. 174–75.

38. Allen Weinstein, *Perjury: The Hiss–Chambers Case* (New York: Knopf, 1978), pp. 174–75.

39. Poretsky, *Our Own People,* pp. 1–3, chs. 9, 10. Krivitsky, *Stalin's Agent,* ch. 8. The two accounts are in general accord.

40. Krivitsky, *Stalin's Agent,* pp. 235–36, 260–01.

41. Grey, *Le général meurt à minuit,* pp. 222–23, chs. 15–19.

42. Miller's execution was admitted only in 1990. Mlechin, "A Minister in Emigration," pt. 1, *New Times,* 1990, no. 18, p. 37; pt. 3, *New Times,* 1990, no. 20, p. 38.

43. Grey, *Le général meurt à minuit,* ch. 31.

44. Orlov, *Secret History,* pp. 333–34.

45. In 1940 Münzenberg's body was found hanging from a tree in the French countryside; he had almost certainly been murdered by the NKVD. Krivitsky was found dead in a Washington hotel room in 1941; the official verdict was suicide. Orlov survived under a new identity in exile in North America.

46. Krivitsky, *Stalin's Agent,* pp. 290–91.

47. Deutscher, *Prophet Outcast*, pp. 394–97.

48. Interview by Christopher Andrew with Pyotr Deryabin, 25 Nov. 1987. Pyotr Deryabin and Frank Gibney, *The Secret World*, rev. ed. (New York: Ballantine Books, 1982), pp. 159–60, describes the postwar functioning of the Kamera.

49. Deutscher, *Prophet Outcast*, pp. 405–08. Poretsky, *Our Own People*, p. 265. Jean van Heijenoort, *With Trotsky in Exile* (Cambridge, Mass.: Harvard University Press, 1978), p. 129.

50. Deutscher, *Prophet Outcast*, pp. 419–20.

51. Ibid., pp. 420–26.

52. Gordievsky.

53. Robert Conquest, *The Great Terror: Stalin's Purge of the Thirties* (London: Macmillan, 1968), ch. 13.

54. Svetlana Alliluyeva, *Only One Year* (London: Hutchinson, 1969).

55. Sergei Shchirov, Hero of the Soviet Union and husband of one of Beria's victims, who lost his reason and his hero's medal in the gulag after Beria abducted and raped his wife, was posthumously rehabilitated in 1988. *Guardian*, 20 Oct. 1988.

56. Deutscher, *Prophet Outcast*, p. 482.

57. Van Heijenoort, *With Trotsky*, p. 132.

58. Gordievsky. On the Blyumkin liquidation, see above, p. 155.

59. Nikolai Khokhlov, *In the Name of Conscience* (London: Frederick Muller, 1960), p. 42.

60. Isaac Don Levine, *The Mind of an Assassin* (London: Weidenfeld & Nicolson, 1959), pp. 32–35.

61. See above, pp. 161–62.

62. "Secret. V. M. Petrov: Intelligence Report. Assassination of Trotsky," 2 May 1955, Records of Petrov's debriefing, AAC, CRS A6283/XR1/9, fol. 128.

63. Levine, *Mind of an Assassin*, chs. 7–10.

64. Vladimir Petrov reported during his debriefing that the KGB file "showed clearly that Trotsky's assassination was a planned operation directed from NKVD headquarters and that its organization on the American continent was in the hands of the NKVD Residency in the Soviet Consulate-General in New York." AAC, CRS A6283/XR1/9, fol. 128.

65. Unless otherwise indicated, our account of Trotsky's assassination is based on Deutscher, *Prophet Outcast*, ch. 5, and Levine, *Mind of an Assassin*.

66. Vladimir and Evdokia Petrova, *Empire of Fear* (London: André Deutsch, 1956), pp. 80–82. Petrov debriefing, "Miscellaneous Soviet Intelligence Personalities," AAC, CRS A6283/XR1/8, fol. 84.

67. AAC, CRS A6283/XR1/9, fol. 128. See n. 62.

68. Note by Enrique Castro Delgado on conversation with Caridad Mercader, in Levine, *Mind of an Assassin*, pp. 216–22.

69. Gordievsky discounts claims that Mercader (or Ramón López as he called himself after his arrival in Moscow) was made Hero of the Soviet Union, though he might well have received this award had he arrived while Stalin was alive. On his years in Moscow see Juan Cobo, "Trotsky's Assassin: Executioner or Victim?," *Moscow News*, 1989, no. 12. In the mid-1970s Mercader left Moscow for Cuba where he died in 1978. His widow returned to bury his ashes in Moscow's Kuntsevo cemetery. There is a photograph of his grave in *Moscow News*, 1989, no. 26.

Chapter 6. Sigint, Agent Penetration and the Magnificent Five from Cambridge (1930–39)

1. Gordievsky.

2. George Leggett, *The Cheka: Lenin's Political Police* (Oxford University Press,

1981), p. 301. Elizabeth Poretsky: *Our Own People* (London: Oxford University Press, 1969), pp. 211–12. Walter Krivitsky, *I Was Stalin's Agent* (London: Hamish Hamilton, 1939), pp. 115–18. Victor Suvorov, *Soviet Military Intelligence* (London: Hamish Hamilton, 1984), pp. 21–22. Robert Conquest, *The Great Terror: Stalin's Purge of the Thirties* (London: Macmillan, 1968), p. 230. John J. Dziak, *Chekisty* (Lexington, Mass.: Lexington Books, 1987), p. 15. There are minor discrepancies in these brief accounts of Berzin's career; we have followed the dates given by Leggett.

3. "Mrs Petrov's Statement Concerning Her Past Intelligence Work," 15 May 1954, AAC, CRS A6283/XR1/14.

4. Vladimir and Evdokia Petrova, *Empire of Fear* (London: André Deutsch, 1956), pp. 129–31.

5. "Mrs Petrov's Statement . . ." AAC, CRS A6283/XR1/14.

6. Poretsky, *Our Own People,* p. 1. Interview by Christopher Andrew with Yuri Rastvorov, October 1987. Further information from Gordievsky.

7. Gordievsky.

8. After his arrest in 1941, Sorge claimed in a memoir written in prison that the Fourth Department had the primary responsibility for foreign intelligence collection: "[The NKVD] collects secret information but is concerned chiefly with counter-espionage, anti-Soviet organisations, and observation of ideological tendencies in foreign countries." This statement reflected OGPU priorities when Sorge left Moscow in the spring of 1933; he returned to Moscow only once, for a few weeks in the summer of 1935. Sorge's memoir is published in Charles A. Willoughby, *Sorge: Soviet Master Spy* (London: William Kimber, 1952); the quotation above is from p. 139.

9. Hede Massing, *This Deception* (New York: Ivy Books, 1987), p. 59.

10. See, in addition to Sorge's own memoir, F. W. Deakin and G. R. Storry, *The Case of Richard Sorge* (New York: Harper & Row, 1964) and Gordon W. Prange et al., *Target Tokyo: The Story of the Sorge Spy Ring* (New York: McGraw-Hill, 1985).

11. Prange et al., *Target Tokyo,* p. 43.

12. Jane Degras (ed.), *Documents on Soviet Foreign Policy* (London: Oxford University Press, 1953), vol. III, pp. 48ff. Adam B. Ulam, *Expansion and Coexistence: Soviet Foreign Policy 1917–1973* (New York: Holt, Rinehart, 1974), pp. 200–08.

13. Willoughby, *Sorge:* p. 162.

14. Richard Storry, *A History of Modern Japan* (Harmondsworth: Penguin, 1960), ch. 8.

15. Massing, *This Deception,* pp. 59–60.

16. Deakin and Storry, *Sorge.* Prange et al., *Target Tokyo.*

17. B. V. A. Röling and C. F. Rüter (eds.), *The Tokyo Judgement: The International Military Tribunal for the Far East* (Amsterdam: APA University Press, 1977), vol. I, ch. 6. Jonathan Haslam, *Soviet Foreign Policy, 1930–33* (London: Macmillan, 1983), ch. 7.

18. Haslam, *Soviet Foreign Policy, 1930–33,* pp. 86–89.

19. "The Soviet Union and Japan," *Izvestia,* 4 March 1932.

20. Christopher Andrew, "Codebreakers and Foreign Offices: The French, British and American Experience," pp. 49–51, in Christopher Andrew and David N. Dilks (eds.), *The Missing Dimension: Governments and Intelligence Communities in the Twentieth Century* (London: Macmillan, 1984). Herbert Yardley, *The American Black Chamber* (London: Faber, 1931).

21. Röling and Rüter (eds.), *Tokyo Judgement,* vol. I, p. 312.

22. Krivitsky, *Stalin's Agent,* pp. 32–36. This account is confirmed by the widow of Krivitsky's close friend and fellow NKVD officer, Ignace Poretsky (alias Reiss). Mrs. Poretsky's memoirs identify a number of exaggerations in Krivitsky's memoirs for which his ghostwriter is probably chiefly responsible. On this occasion, however, she writes that Krivitsky "unaccountably" understates "his greatest coup." The under-

statement may derive from his ghostwriter's lack of grasp, two years before Pearl Harbor, of the significance of sigint. Poretsky, *Our Own People,* p. 71.

23. Speech by Litvinov on 23 November 1936. Degras (ed.), *Documents on Soviet Foreign Policy,* vol. III, p. 224.

24. Ibid.

25. Krivitsky, *Stalin's Agent,* p. 36.

26. Unless otherwise indicated, our account of the Oldham case is based on William F. Corson and Robert T. Crowley, *The New KGB,* "updated" Quill ed. (New York: William Morrow, 1986), pp. 40–68. Their account is based largely on American sources and intelligence debriefings that conceal Oldham's identity. Perhaps because the Oldham case has never been officially admitted in Britain, he is referred to throughout as "Scott." The place and date of "Scott's" suicide in the Corson and Crowley account identify him as Oldham.

27. Gordievsky identifies "Hans" as Galleni.

28. Information to Christopher Andrew from retired Dutch intelligence officers; further information from Gordievsky. A slightly different version of some of the story appears in Gordon Brook-Shepherd, *The Storm Petrels* (London: Collins, 1977), pp. 174–77.

29. Donald Cameron Watt, "[John] Herbert King: A Soviet Source in the Foreign Office," *Intelligence and National Security,* vol. III, no. 4 (1988), p. 62.

30. Igor Cornelissen, *De GPOe op de Overtoom* (Amsterdam: Van Gennep, 1989), pp. 156–57.

31. Information to Christopher Andrew from retired Dutch intelligence officers (one of whom was involved in later investigations of the Pieck case); further information from Gordievsky. Cf. Brook-Shepherd, *Storm Petrels,* pp. 174–79 and Cornelissen, *De GPOe op de Overtoom,* p. 158.

32. Gordievsky.

33. Gordievsky.

34. Press conference, 20 Nov. 1979, reported in the press the following day.

35. C. W. Guillebaud, "Politics and the Undergraduate in Oxford and Cambridge," *Cambridge Review,* 26 Jan. 1934.

36. Kim Philby, *My Silent War* (London: Panther Books, 1969), p. 15.

37. Paul Hollander, *Political Pilgrims* (Oxford University Press, 1981), p. 102.

38. Ibid., p. 105.

39. See above, pp. 81ff.

40. Babette Gross, *Willi Münzenberg: A Political Biography* (Ann Arbor: Michigan University Press, 1974), p. 240.

41. Ibid., pp. 241–42. Arthur Koestler, *The Invisible Writing,* Danube ed. (London: Hutchinson, 1969), pp. 242–43.

42. Published in Britain by Victor Gollancz in 1933.

43. Koestler, *Invisible Writing,* p. 243.

44. Ronald W. Clark, *Einstein: The Life and Times* (London: Hodder & Stoughton, 1973), p. 463.

45. *Brown Book,* p. 9.

46. Koestler, *Invisible Writing,* p. 243.

47. Gross, *Münzenberg,* p. 311.

48. Koestler, *Invisible Writing,* pp. 254ff.

49. Alexander Abusch, Epilogue (*Nachwort*) to reprint of *Braunbuch über Reichstagbrand und Hitlerterror* (Frankfurt/Main: Röderberg-Verlag, 1978).

50. Garfield Hays, cited in Fritz Tobias, *The Reichstag Fire: Legend and Truth* (London: Secker & Warburg, 1963).

51. The fabrication of evidence is discussed in Christopher Andrew and Harold James, "Willi Münzenberg, the Reichstag Fire and the Conversion of Innocents," in

David Charters and Maurice Tugwell (eds.), *Deception in East–West Relations* (London: Pergamon-Brassey, 1990).

52. Tobias, *Reichstag Fire.*

53. On Calic and his committee, see *Die Zeit* dossier, September–October 1979. Cf. E. Calic (ed.), *Der Reichstagbrand: Eine Wissenschaftliche Dokumentation,* Band II (Munich: K. G. Saur Verlag, 1978).

54. Gross, *Münzenberg,* p. 251.

55. See D. N. Pritt, *From Right to Left* (London: Lawrence & Wishart, 1985), esp. chs. 5, 7, 9, 12.

56. Foreign Office minutes of 14 Dec. 1933, PRO FO 371/16755.

57. *The Times,* 14 Sept. 1933.

58. *The Times,* 15 Sept. 1933.

59. Koestler, *Invisible Writing,* p. 244.

60. P. Stojanoff, *Reichstagbrand: Die Prozesse in London und Leipzig* (Vienna: Europa Verlag, 1966), p. 183.

61. *The Times,* 21 Sept. 1933.

62. Tobias, *Reichstag Fire,* p. 228.

63. *The Second Brown Book of the Hitler Terror* (London: Bodley Head, 1934). Andrew and James, "Münzenberg, the Reichstag Fire and the Conversion of Innocents."

64. Catherine Károlyi, *A Life Together* (London: Allen & Unwin, 1961), pp. 298–99.

65. John Costello, *Mask of Treachery* (London: Collins, 1988), pp. 164–67, 197–98.

66. Christopher Andrew, "F. H. Hinsley and the Cambridge Moles: Two Patterns of Intelligence Recruitment," in Richard Langhorne (ed.), *Diplomacy and Intelligence during the Second World War: Essays in Honour of F. H. Hinsley* (Cambridge University Press, 1985), p. 25.

67. Koestler, *Invisible Writing,* p. 28–30.

68. Michael Kater, *The Nazi Party: A Social Profile of Members and Leaders 1919–1945* (Oxford: Basil Blackwell, 1983), pp. 81–83.

69. Ernst Henri, "The Revolutionary Movement in Nazi Germany: (1) The Groups of Five ('Fünfergruppen')," *New Statesman & Nation,* 5 Aug. 1933.

70. Ibid.

71. Editor's introduction, ibid.

72. London: Dent, 1934.

73. *The Times,* cited in 1939 edition of Ernst Henri, *Hitler Over Europe?* (London: Dent), p. 292.

74. Henri, *Hitler Over Europe?,* pp. 299–300.

75. Andrew, "F. H. Hinsley and the Cambridge Moles," p. 26.

76. Private information to Christopher Andrew.

77. *New Statesman & Nation,* 7 April 1934.

78. Gordievsky.

79. Tape-recorded interviews with Henri in 1988 by Robin Bruce Lockhart (son of Sir Robert Bruce Lockhart, whose career is discussed in ch. 2) summarized in letters from Robin Bruce Lockhart to Christopher Andrew of 21 Nov. 1988 and 18 March 1989.

80. Interview with Edith Cobbett by Christopher Andrew on 18 March 1981. Ms. Cobbett did not realize Henri's involvement in espionage while she was working with him.

81. Ernst Henry [*sic*], *Stop Terrorism!* (Moscow: Novosti, 1982), pp. 32–33, 195.

82. Bruce Lockhart interviews (see n. 79).

83. Phillip Knightley, *Philby: KGB Master Spy* (London: André Deutsch, 1988), ch. 1.

84. Introduction to Andrew and Dilks, *Missing Dimension,* p. 5.

85. Knightley, *Philby,* ch. 2. Philby, *My Silent War,* introduction.

86. Bruce Page, David Leitch and Phillip Knightley, *Philby: The Spy Who Betrayed a Generation* (London: Sphere Books, 1977), ch. 5.

87. Knightley, *Philby,* p. 45.

88. Gordievsky.

89. Alexander Orlov, *The Secret History of Stalin's Crimes* (London: Jarrolds, 1954), pp. 235–37.

90. Massing, *This Deception,* pp. 116–18.

91. Poretsky, *Our Own People,* pp. 214–15. Cornelissen, *De GPOe op de Overtoom,* ch. 11.

92. Massing, *This Deception,* p. 117.

93. Knightley, *Philby,* pp. 39–43.

94. Page, Leitch and Knightley, *Philby,* p. 86.

95. Gordievsky.

96. "Nationale für ordentliche Hörer der philosophischen Fakultät": entries for Arnold Deutsch, 1923–27; "Rigorosenakt des Arnold Deutsch," no. 9929, 1928 (including CV by Deutsch); records of Deutsch's Ph.D. examination 1928 (University of Vienna Archives).

97. William M. Johnston, *The Austrian Mind* (Berkeley: University of California Press, 1983), pp. 188–92. "Nationale für ordentliche Hörer," entry for Deutsch, summer semester 1926.

98. See the university records referred to in n. 96. Police records for 1934 refer to Deutsch as *Konfessionslos* (see n. 100).

99. Wilhelm Reich, *Sexualerregung und Sexualbefriedigung,* the first publication in the series *Schriften der Sozialistischen Gesellschaft für Sexualberatung und Sexualforschung in Wien* carries the note "Copyright 1929 by Münster-Verlag (Dr Arnold Deutsch), Wien II." On Reich, see Myron Sharaf, *Fury on Earth: A Biography of Wilhelm Reich* (London: André Deutsch, 1983).

100. Police reports on Deutsch, 25 March 1934 and 27 April 1934, ref.: Z1.38.Z.g.P./34, Dokumentationsarchiv des Österreichischen Widerstandes, Vienna.

101. Gordievsky.

102. The birth certificate of his daughter, born at Chelsea Hospital for Women on 21 May 1936, gives Deutsch's occupation as "university lecturer" and the address of the Deutsch family as 7 Lawn Road Flats. London University Archives contain no record of Deutsch as either lecturer or research student but he may well have carried out part-time teaching or independent research unrecorded there.

103. Knightley, *Philby,* pp. 44–46. In his conversations with Knightley, Philby never identified any of his controllers by name.

104. Gordievsky.

105. Andrew Boyle, *The Climate of Treason* (London: Hutchinson, 1979), pp. 78–85.

106. Tom Driberg, *Guy Burgess: A Portrait with Background* (London: Weidenfeld & Nicolson, 1956), pp. 17–18. Costello, *Mask of Treachery,* p. 208.

107. Goronwy Rees, *A Chapter of Accidents* (London: Chatto & Windus, 1971), pp. 110–11.

108. Driberg, *Burgess,* ch. 1.

109. Ibid., pp. 15–17.

110. Rees, *Chapter of Accidents,* pp. 110–14.

111. Barrie Penrose and Simon Freeman, *Conspiracy of Silence* (London: Grafton Books, 1986), p. 69. Costello, *Mask of Treachery,* p. 50. The second Christian name of Blunt's father is usually wrongly stated to have been "Vere."

112. Anthony Blunt, "From Bloomsbury to Marxism," *Studio International,* November 1973, p. 164.

113. Penrose and Freeman, *Conspiracy of Silence,* pp. 32–34.

114. Blunt, "From Bloomsbury to Marxism," pp. 166–67.

115. University of Cambridge Archives. The Cambridge Mathematical Tripos, then as now, did not distinguish between upper and lower second-class honors. Blunt's Part I results in Modern Languages have commonly been misstated.

116. Costello, *Mask of Treachery,* pp. 190–94.

117. Penrose and Freeman, *Conspiracy of Silence,* p. 45.

118. Costello, *Mask of Treachery,* p. 190.

119. V. G. Lawford, *Bound for Diplomacy* (London: John Murray, 1963), pp. 141–42 (written long before Blunt's exposure as a Soviet agent).

120. Rees, *Chapter of Accidents,* pp. 110–14.

121. Blunt, "From Bloomsbury to Marxism," p. 167.

122. Driberg, *Burgess,* p. 34.

123. Blunt, "From Bloomsbury to Marxism," p. 167.

124. Ibid. Penrose and Freeman, *Conspiracy of Silence,* p. 107. In a press conference after his exposure in 1979, Blunt claimed that he "became a communist and more particularly a Marxist in 1935–36." That, however, was the date not of his conversion to Marxism but at which he began active intelligence work for the Russians.

125. The best study of Maclean is Robert Cecil, *A Divided Life* (London: Bodley Head, 1988).

126. *The Granta,* 8 Nov. 1933.

127. Driberg, *Burgess,* pp. 16–17.

128. Knightley, *Philby,* p. 45.

129. Rees, *Chapter of Accidents,* p. 131.

130. Gordievsky. Burgess later told Rees that he met his controller, whom he did not identify, "at regular intervals in an East End café." Rees, *Chapter of Accidents,* p. 145.

131. Knightley, *Philby,* p. 48.

132. Driberg, *Burgess,* ch. 2.

133. Michael Straight, *After Long Silence* (London: Collins, 1983), p. 94.

134. Ibid., p. 95.

135. Gordievsky.

136. Knightley, *Philby,* p. 48.

137. See below, pp. 401–2.

138. Cecil, *Divided Life,* pp. 36–39.

139. Boyle, *Climate of Treason,* p. 114.

140. The location of the meetings with Deutsch is revealed in Rees, *Chapter of Accidents,* p. 145.

141. Driberg, *Burgess,* p. 23.

142. Penrose and Freeman, *Conspiracy of Silence,* p. 143.

143. Rees, *Chapter of Accidents,* pp. 122–23. Straight, *After Long Silence,* pp. 94–95.

144. Straight, *After Long Silence,* p. 142.

145. Wendy Steiner, "Scholarship and its Affiliations: Wendy Steiner on the Blunt Case," *London Review of Books,* 30 March 1989.

146. Michael Straight, interviewed by Christopher Andrew in pt. 3 of the BBC Radio 4 documentary series, *The Profession of Intelligence,* first broadcast 16 Aug. 1981.

147. Gordievsky.

148. University of Glasgow Archives.

149. University of Cambridge and Trinity College Archives.

150. Penrose and Freeman, *Conspiracy of Silence,* pp. 369–71.

151. Nigel West, *Molehunt* (London: Weidenfeld & Nicolson, 1987), p. 26.

152. University of Cambridge and Trinity College Archives. John Colville, *The Fringes of Power* (London: Hodder & Stoughton, 1985), p. 30n.

153. Gordievsky.

154. Massing, *This Deception,* pp. 117–18.

155. Gordievsky.

156. Cecil, *Divided Life,* pp. 42–49. There are numerous minutes by the young Maclean on the Spanish Civil War in, e.g., PRO FO 371/21283–90.

157. Gordievsky.

158. Foreign Office to Phipps, 11 March 1938, Phipps Papers, Churchill College Archives Centre, Cambridge, PHPP 2/21.

159. Lord Gladwyn, interviewed by Christopher Andrew on *Timewatch,* BBC 2, 10 July 1984.

160. Minute by Cairncross, 23 March 1937, PRO FO 371/21287 W5214. Minutes by Cairncross and Maclean sometimes appear on the same file. See, e.g., PRO FO 371/21289 W7016.

161. Penrose and Freeman, *Conspiracy of Silence,* p. 527. Colville, *Fringes of Power,* pp. 30ff.

162. Gordievsky.

163. Christopher Andrew, *Secret Service: The Making of the British Intelligence Community* (London: Heinemann, 1985), p. 408. Filmed report on the Cambridge moles by Christopher Andrew on *Timewatch,* BBC2, 27 July 1983.

164. Straight, *After Long Silence,* p. 143.

165. Chapman Pincher, *Traitors* (London: Sidgwick & Jackson, 1987), p. 123.

166. Costello, *Mask of Treachery,* p. 405. Straight, *After Long Silence,* p. 105.

167. Knightley, *Philby,* pp. 51–52.

168. Philby, *My Silent War,* pp. 19, 102.

169. Gordievsky. Several NKVD recruits were given similar missions at the same time as Philby. According to Foreign Office files, three agents posing as anti-Communists entered Spain early in 1937 "with the object of assassinating General Franco," Sir H. Chilton to FO, 16 Feb. 1937 (seen by Maclean on 22 Feb.), PRO FO 371/21285 W3393.

170. Knightley, *Philby,* pp. 53–54.

171. Philby, *My Silent War,* pp. 19–21.

172. Knightley, *Philby,* ch. 5.

173. Gordievsky. Philby's brief involvement in an aborted mission to assassinate Franco was one of a number of episodes in his KGB career that he remained anxious to suppress during his Moscow exile. Cf. Knightley, *Philby,* p. 185.

174. Poretsky, *Our Own People,* pp. 213ff.

175. Orlov, *Secret History,* pp. 235–37.

176. Gordievsky.

177. Gordievsky.

178. Details of Miss Grey's meetings with Mr. Peters and the Stephenses were given at the police court hearing. Miss Grey was identified only as "Miss X." *The Times,* 4 Feb. 1938. Andrew, *Secret Service,* pp. 368, 370–71. Further information from Gordievsky on the identification of Peters and the Stephenses.

179. Gordievsky.

180. Andrew, *Secret Service,* pp. 370–71.

181. Gordievsky. A memorial tablet outside Deutsch's prewar apartment in Vienna, which records his role in the Resistance but not in the NKVD, confirms that he was executed by the SS in November 1942.

182. Gordievsky. Shortly before his arrest in January 1938, Glading complained to

Olga Grey that because of the failure of "Stephens" to return from Moscow and of anyone else to take his place, his funds were almost exhausted.

183. Gordievsky.

184. "Mrs. Petrov's Statement . . ." AAC, CRS A6283/XR1/14. Petrov, *Empire of Fear,* pp. 127, 129, 149.

185. Charles E. Bohlen, *Witness to History 1919–1969* (London: Weidenfeld & Nicolson, 1973), p. 34.

186. Ibid., p. 20.

187. An FBI report of 1940 refers to Kent's Russian mistress. In that year, by then employed as a code clerk at the London embassy, he was sentenced to seven years' imprisonment for passing classified documents to a pro-Nazi group. Ronald Kessler, *Moscow Station* (New York: Scribner's, 1989), p. 22. Anthony Masters, *The Man Who Was M* (Oxford: Basil Blackwell, 1984), ch. 6. Hayden B. Peake discusses the case in *Foreign Intelligence Literary Scene,* March/April 1986.

188. Bohlen, *Witness to History,* pp. 20, 15.

189. Ibid., pp. 44–45.

190. Unpublished "Memoirs of Ivan D. Yeaton USA (retd.), 1919–1953," pp. 11–15, 40, U.S. Army Military History Institute, Carlisle Barracks, Pa.

191. Ibid., pp. 21–22.

192. Bohlen, *Witness to History,* pp. 20–21.

193. "Memoirs of Ivan D. Yeaton," pp. 25–26. According to Bohlen, *Witness to History,* p. 72, "Our diplomatic code was not sophisticated" in 1939.

194. Kessler, *Moscow Station,* pp. 21–23.

195. "Memoirs of Ivan D Yeaton," p. 26.

196. Wellington A. Samouce, "I Do Understand the Russians," pp. 52–53, Samouce Papers, U.S. Army Military History Institute, Carlisle Barracks, Pa.

197. Unless otherwise indicated, our account of Chambers's career is based on Allen Weinstein, *Perjury: The Hiss-Chambers Case* (New York: Knopf, 1978).

198. Herbert Romerstein and Stanislav Levchenko, *The KGB Against the "Main Enemy"* (Lexington, Mass.: Lexington Books, 1989), pp. 76–79.

199. Weinstein, *Perjury,* p. 142.

200. Henry Julian Wadleigh, "Why I Spied for the Communists," pt. 7, *New York Post* Home News, 19 July 1949.

201. FBI 100-287685.

202. Romerstein and Levchenko, *The KGB Against the "Main Enemy,"* pp. 94–95.

203. Wadleigh, "Why I Spied for the Communists," pt. 4, *New York Post* Home News, 15 July 1949.

204. Weinstein, *Perjury,* pp. 241–63.

205. Wadleigh, "Why I Spied for the Communists," pt. 8, *New York Post* Home News, 20 July 1949.

206. Weinstein, *Perjury,* p. 261.

207. Wadleigh, "Why I Spied for the Communists," pt. 3, *New York Post* Home News, 14 July 1949.

208. Harry Rositzke, *The KGB: Eyes of Russia* (London: Sidgwick & Jackson, 1983), p. 55. Weinstein, *Perjury,* pp. 145–53.

209. Weinstein, *Perjury,* pp. 310–28.

210. See below, pp. 280–81.

Chapter 7. The Second World War (1939–41)

1. This interpretation of Hitler's policy is set out in greater detail in, *inter alia, The Fatal Attraction of Adolf Hitler* (BBC1, 21 April 1989), presented by Christopher Andrew.

2. Stalin's interpreter, Valentin Berezhkov, interviewed on Soviet TV, 12 May 1989; BBC, *SWB* 12 May 1989, SU/0464 C/1. Berezhkov was given a firsthand account of the Politburo meeting by Mikoyan. "I have no grounds for thinking that Comrade Mikoyan distorted that in any way," he told the interviewer.

3. John Erickson, "Threat Identification and Strategic Appraisal by the Soviet Union 1930–1941," in Ernest R. May (ed.), *Knowing One's Enemies* (Princeton University Press, 1984), p. 379.

4. Jonathan Haslam, *The Soviet Union and the Struggle for Collective Security 1933–39* (London: Macmillan, 1984), p. 127.

5. Walter Krivitsky, *I Was Stalin's Agent* (London: Hamish Hamilton, 1939), p. 22. Krivitsky's account is the more impressive for having been first published in the New York *Saturday Evening Post* several months before the conclusion of the Nazi–Soviet Pact at a time when the likelihood of such a pact was generally considered slim in the West. The Politburo discussion of the Night of the Long Knives and the Kandelaki mission, first reported by Krivitsky, have since been confirmed by other sources.

6. David J. Dallin, *Soviet Espionage* (New Haven, Conn.: Yale University Press, 1955), pp. 86–88. Branko Lazitch and Milorad M. Drachkovitch, *Biographical Dictionary of the Comintern,* rev. ed. (Stanford, Ca.: Hoover Institution Press, 1986).

7. Dallin, *Soviet Espionage,* pp. 92–99.

8. Robert Chadwell Williams, *Klaus Fuchs, Atom Spy* (Cambridge, Mass.: Harvard University Press, 1987), p. 14.

9. Dallin, *Soviet Espionage,* pp. 100–10.

10. Ibid., pp. 117–19.

11. Ibid., pp. 121–22. Louis Budenz, *This Is My Story* (New York: Whittlesey House, 1947), pp. 254–55.

12. Dallin, *Soviet Espionage,* pp. 122–23.

13. Lazitch and Drachkovitch, *Biographical Dictionary of the Comintern.*

14. See below pp. 306–7.

15. A. G. Denniston, "The Government Code and Cypher School Between the Wars," in Christopher Andrew (ed.), *Codebreaking and Signals Intelligence* (London: Frank Cass, 1986), p. 56.

16. Leopold Trepper's own story is told in *The Great Game* (London: Michael Joseph, 1977); the quotations are from ch. 2. Cf. Central Intelligence Agency, *The Rote Kapelle: The CIA's History of Soviet Intelligence and Espionage Networks in Western Europe 1936–1945* (Washington, DC: University Publications of America, 1984), pp. 13–55, 367–73.

17. Rado's career has been shrouded in numerous myths. The most reliable account is in CIA, *Rote Kapelle,* pp. 165–226, 334–38.

18. Gordon W. Prange et al., *Target Tokyo: The Story of the Sorge Spy Ring* (New York: McGraw-Hill, 1985), pp. 216–21. Harry Rositzke, *The KGB: Eyes of Russia* (London: Sidgwick & Jackson, 1983), p. 25.

19. I. A. Dementyeva, N. I. Agayants and Y. Y. Yankovlev, *Tovarishch Zorge* (Moscow: Sovetskaya Rossiya, 1965).

20. Prange et al., *Target Tokyo,* chs. 28, 32.

21. G. K. Zhukov, *The Memoirs of Marshal Zhukov* (London: Jonathan Cape, 1971), vol. I, p. 149.

22. Prange, *Target Tokyo,* p. 280.

23. *Final Report of the "Rote Kapelle" Case* (US Armed Forces Security Agency translation of captured German Security Police and Security Service report, "Abschlussbericht über den Fall Rote Kapelle," 22 March 1942), NAW RG 457 SRH-380, pp. 25, 43–4. CIA, *Rote Kapelle,* p. 232, suggests 1936 or 1937 as the date of von Scheliha's recruitment (the reference to 1934 on p. 348 may be a misprint). According

to the editors of Soviet diplomatic documents, von Scheliha was deceived into believing that he was working for "a Western intelligence agency." Donald Cameron Watt, *How War Came: The Immediate Origins of the Second World War 1938–1939* (London: Heinemann, 1989), p. 115.

24. Ernst Henri, *Hitler Over Europe?* (London: Dent, 1939), p. 265. Haslam, *Soviet Union and the Struggle for Collective Security,* appendix 2: "The Soviet Union and the Defence of Leningrad 1936–39."

25. Gordievsky wrote the sections of the history dealing with Britain, Ireland, Scandinavia, and Australasia.

26. Gordievsky interviewed Rybkina while working on the First Chief Directorate history.

27. Gordievsky.

28. Väinö Tanner, *The Winter War* (Stanford, Ca.: Stanford University Press, 1957), p. 3.

29. Petrov debrief, AAC, CRS A6283/XR1/80.

30. Gordievsky. Jews were the ethnic group most at risk during the purge of the Soviet intelligence services. Despite his anti-Semitism, however, Stalin spared some Jews of exceptional servility (like Kaganovich) or exceptional talent (like Litvinov).

31. Nikolai Tolstoy, *Stalin's Secret War* (London: Jonathan Cape, 1981), p. 127.

32. Tanner, *Winter War,* pp. 3–16.

33. Vsevolod Yezhnov, "An Anti-Hitler Coalition Before the War? Possibilities and Reality," *Literaturnaya Gazeta,* no. 17, 26 April 1989.

34. Petrov debrief AAC, CRS A6283/XR1/56. Vladimir and Evdokia Petrova, *Empire of Fear* (London: André Deutsch, 1956), p. 57.

35. Robert Conquest, *Inside Stalin's Secret Police: NKVD Politics 1936–1939* (London: Macmillan, 1985), p. 103.

36. Anthony Read and David Fisher, *The Deadly Embrace* (London: Michael Joseph, 1988), p. 466.

37. Ibid., p. 51. Watt, *How War Came,* pp. 117–18.

38. A. Roshchin, "Inside the Commissariat of Foreign Affairs on the Eve of the War," *Mezhdunarodnaya Zhizn,* April 1988.

39. *Pravda,* 1 September 1939. Haslam, *Soviet Union and the Struggle for Collective Security,* p. 201.

40. Donald Cameron Watt, "The Initiation of Talks Leading to the Nazi-Soviet Pact: An Historical Problem," in C. Abramsky and Beryl J. Williams (eds.), *Essays in Honour of E. H. Carr* (London: Macmillan, 1974).

41. Roshchin, "Inside the Commissariat of Foreign Affairs."

42. Martin Gilbert, *Winston S. Churchill,* vol. V (London: Heinemann, 1976), p. 1073.

43. J.-B. Duroselle, *La décadence, 1932–1939* (Paris: Imprimerie Nationale, 1979), pp. 416, 429.

44. Donald Cameron Watt, "[John] Herbert King: A Soviet Source in the Foreign Office," *Intelligence and National Security,* vol. III (1988), no. 4.

45. Ibid.

46. Read and Fisher, *Deadly Embrace,* pp. 256–59. John Toland, *Adolf Hitler* (New York: Doubleday, 1976), p. 548.

47. Read and Fisher, *Deadly Embrace,* pp. 337–40.

48. Tolstoy, *Stalin's Secret War,* pp. 117–20.

49. Strobe Talbott (ed./trans.), *Khrushchev Remembers* (London: Sphere Books, 1971), pp. 128–29.

50. Norman Davies, *God's Playground: A History of Poland,* vol. II (Oxford: Clarendon Press, 1981).

51. Interview with Margarete Buber-Neumann quoted in Read and Fisher, *Deadly*

Embrace, p. 432. Margarete Buber-Neumann, *Von Potsdam nach Moskau: Stationen Eines Irrweges* (Cologne: Hohenheim, 1981).

52. Davies, *God's Playground*, vol. II, pp. 448–52.

53. Article in the Polish weekly *Odrodzenie* cited in *Daily Telegraph*, 17 Feb. 1989.

54. Davies, *God's Playground*, vol. II, p. 452.

55. Gordievsky.

56. Tolstoy, *Stalin's Secret War*, pp. 129–34. Albert Seaton, *Stalin as Warlord* (London: Batsford, 1976), p. 90.

57. Tolstoy, *Stalin's Secret War*, pp. 135–36.

58. Evidence from Soviet POWs, cited in Jukka L. Mäkelä, *Hemligt Krig* (Stockholm, 1968), p. 10; Carl O. Nordling, *Defence or Imperialism?* (Uppsala: Universitet Reprocentralen HSC, 1984), p. 54.

59. Tolstoy, *Stalin's Secret War*, p. 137.

60. Tanner, *Winter War*, pp. 101–06.

61. Gordievsky.

62. Professor Mikhail Semiryaga, quoted in "The Road to World War Two," *Moscow News*, 1988, no. 36.

63. Talbott (ed./trans.), *Khrushchev Remembers*, pp. 153–54.

64. Tolstoy, *Stalin's Secret War*, p. 143.

65. Read and Fisher, *Deadly Embrace*, p. 462.

66. Tolstoy, *Stalin's Secret War*, p. 188.

67. Ibid., p. 189. *Izvestia*, 16 May 1941.

68. Read and Fisher, *Deadly Embrace*, pp. 467–78.

69. Ibid., p. 468. Tolstoy, *Stalin's Secret War*, pp. 192–96.

70. Read and Fisher, *Deadly Embrace*, p. 537. Tolstoy, *Stalin's Secret War*, pp. 206–07.

71. Milan Hauner, *Hitler: A Chronology of His Life and Times* (London: Macmillan, 1983), p. 156.

72. See photograph in Read and Fisher, *Deadly Embrace*, following p. 496.

73. Davies, *God's Playground*, vol. II, p. 444.

74. Dmitri Volkogonov, "On the Eve of War," *Pravda*, 20 June 1988.

75. Martin Gilbert, *The Second World War* (London: Weidenfeld & Nicolson, 1989), p. 179. Tolstoy, *Stalin's Secret War*, pp. 209–12.

76. Gordievsky. Cf. Trepper, *Great Game*, p. 92; Dallin, *Soviet Espionage*, p. 138.

77. Ismail Akhmedov, *In and Out of Stalin's GRU* (London: Arms & Armour Press, 1984), pp. 139, 143.

78. Auswärtiges Amt, Bonn: Handakten Ritter, Akten betr. Russland Bd.1–2: Aktennotiz Ritter, 20 July 1941. (We are grateful to Dr C. G. Mackay for this reference.)

79. Akhmedov, *In and Out of Stalin's GRU*, pp. 140, 145.

80. CIA, *Rote Kapelle*, pp. 275–76.

81. Ibid., pp. 146–50, 288–89. Dallin, *Soviet Espionage*, pp. 234ff.

82. Trepper, *Great Game*, p. 122.

83. *Final Report of the "Rote Kapelle" Case*, NAW RG 457 SRH-380, pp. 29–31, 37–38. CIA, *Rote Kapelle*, pp. 140–46, 353–54. Dallin, *Soviet Espionage*, pp. 238–44.

84. CIA, *Rote Kapelle*, pp. 144–45, 289, 353–54. Trepper, *Great Game*, pp. 122–24.

85. *Final Report of the "Rote Kapelle" Case*, NAW RG 457 SRH-380, p. 43. CIA, *Rote Kapelle*, pp. 151–52.

86. Trepper, *Great Game*, ch. 5. The oft-repeated claim that Rudolf Roessler (code name Lucy) gave Moscow advance warning of Barbarossa via Rado's Swiss network is false. Rachel Duebendorfer (Sissy) who ran Lucy through a cut-out, Christiane Schneider (Taylor), did not make contact with either until the late summer of 1942. CIA, *Rote Kapelle*, pp. 173ff.

87. Akhmedov, *In and Out of Stalin's GRU*, p. 127.

88. Ibid., p. 132. On Golikov's purge of some of his best officers, see the comments by Professor Vyacheslav Dashichev in Vladimir Petrov (ed.), *June 22, 1941: Soviet Historians and the German Invasion* (Columbia, SC: University of South Carolina Press, 1968), p. 254.

89. Akhmedov, *In and Out of Stalin's GRU*, pp. 133–34.

90. Conquest, *Inside Stalin's Secret Police*, p. 175.

91. N. N. Krasnov, *The Hidden Russia: My Ten Years as a Slave Labourer* (New York: Holt, Rinehart, 1960), pp. 67ff.

92. Nicholas Nyaradi, *My Ringside Seat in Moscow* (New York: Crowell, 1953), p. 56.

93. Gordievsky. On the recruitment of the two hundred, see A. Baidakov, "Facts on Intelligence. From the Archives of the Security Organs of the Soviet Union," *Pravda,* 9 May 1989.

94. Gordievsky.

95. Volkogonov, "On the Eve of War."

96. Petrov (ed.), *"June 22 1941,"* p. 181.

97. Ibid., pp. 250–51 (comments of G. A. Deborin).

98. Interview with Fitin quoted in Baidakov, "Facts on Intelligence."

99. G. K. Zhukov, *The Memoirs of Marshal Zhukov,* vol. I, p. 229.

100. Petrov (ed.), *"June 22 1941,"* pp. 253–54.

101. Barton Whaley, *Codeword Barbarossa* (Cambridge, Mass.: MIT Press, 1974), pp. 24–25. Gabriel Gorodetsky, *Stafford Cripps' Mission to Moscow 1940–42* (Cambridge University Press, 1984), ch. 2.

102. This crucial period in Cairncross's career has, remarkably, hitherto escaped attention. Sadly, the Hankey Papers in the Churchill College Archive Center at Cambridge contain few specific references to Cairncross. Only a few pages of Hankey's diary survive for this period; surviving correspondence is almost exclusively with major public figures and Hankey's family.

103. On Hankey's ministerial responsibilities and access to documents, see Stephen Roskill, *Hankey: Man of Secrets,* vol. III (London: Collins, 1974).

104. Gordievsky.

105. G. L. Clutton to Cairncross, 6 June 1941; Sir Alexander Cadogan to Hankey, 17 June 1941, Hankey Papers, Churchill College Archive Center, Cambridge, CCAC HNKY 4/33.

106. Winston S. Churchill, *The Second World War,* vol. III (London: Cassell, 1950), pp. 319–23. Gorodetsky, *Cripps' Mission to Moscow,* pp. 118–25.

107. Akhmedov, *In and Out of Stalin's GRU,* pp. 136–37.

108. Whaley, *Codeword Barbarossa,* p. 260.

109. Petrov (ed.), *"June 22 1941,"* pp. 190–91. Over a quarter of a century later, some leading Soviet historians were still insisting that the British government "undertook negotiations" with Hess after his landing "for provocative purposes . . . pushing Germany to attack the USSR." Ibid., pp. 291–92. Cf. Churchill, *Second World War,* vol. III, pp. 44–49. The same conspiracy theory was still being publicly peddled by the KGB in 1990 in a television documentary on Philby, *Cutting Edge,* Channel 4, 14 May 1990.

110. Gilbert, *Second World War,* p. 181. The *Timewatch* documentary, *Hess: An Edge of Conspiracy* (BBC2, 17 Jan. 1990), presented by Christopher Andrew, examined some of the Hess conspiracy theories.

111. Petrov (ed.), *"June 22 1941,"* p. 295.

112. "Letter from 'An Historical Optimist,'" *Druzhba Narodov,* March 1988. This previously unpublished letter was written by Semyon Rostovsky, alias Ernst Henri (or

Ghenri) to Ilya Ehrenburg on 30 May 1965. Henri told Ehrenburg: "If you don't wish to believe Hilger, ask Petrov."

113. Georgi Kumanev, "The 22nd at Dawn," *Pravda,* 22 June 1989.

114. "Letter from 'An Historical Optimist.' "

115. Whaley, *Codeword Barbarossa,* pp. 223–24, 241–43.

116. Dementyeva, Agayants and Yakovlev, *Tovarishch Zorge.*

117. Prange et al., *Target Tokyo,* chs. 42–47.

118. Baidakov, "Facts on Intelligence."

119. Trepper, *Great Game,* pp. 126–28.

120. F. H. Hinsley et al., *British Intelligence in the Second World War* (London: HMSO, 1979–88), vol. I, p. 470.

121. See above, p. 262.

122. Hinsley et al., *British Intelligence in the Second World War,* vol. I, ch. 14. Christopher Andrew, *Secret Service: The Making of the British Intelligence Community* (London: Heinemann, 1985), pp. 484–85.

123. Whaley, *Codeword Barbarossa,* pp. 226–45.

124. Petrov (ed.), *"June 22 1941,"* p. 183.

125. Ibid., pp. 200–23. John Erickson, *The Road to Stalingrad* (London: Panther Books, 1985), ch. 3.

Chapter 8. The Great Patriotic War (1941–45)

1. I. A. Dementyeva, N. I. Agayants and Y. Y. Yakovlev, *Tovarishch Zorge* (Moscow: Sovetskaya Rossiya, 1965). Gordon Prange et al., *Target Tokyo: The Story of the Sorge Spy Ring* (New York: McGraw-Hill, 1985), chs. 49–59.

2. A. Baidakov, "Facts on Intelligence. From the Archives of the Security Organs of the Soviet Union," *Pravda,* 9 May 1989, quotes four Japanese intercepts for the period November 1941 to March 1942. In keeping with normal Soviet practice he does not identify these as sigint (still a taboo subject in the U.S.S.R.) but says: "They are from one source only, and their value is indisputable."

3. Interview by Christopher Andrew with Yuri Rastvorov, who worked in the wartime Fifth Directorate, November 1987.

4. John Erickson, *The Road to Stalingrad* (London: Panther Books, 1985), p. 329.

5. Cathy Porter and Mark Jones, *Moscow in World War Two* (London: Chatto & Windus, 1987), ch. 5.

6. Nikolai Pavlenko, "The History of the War Is Still to Be Written," *Ogonek,* 1989, no. 25. Nikolai Pavlenko, "Tragedy and Triumph of the Red Army," *Moscow News,* 1989, no. 19. Pavlenko reveals that the section of Zhukov's memoirs dealing with this episode was censored before publication.

7. Amy W. Knight, *The KGB: Police and Politics in the Soviet Union* (London: Unwin Hyman, 1988), pp. 34–35.

8. See the articles by Pavlenko cited in n. 6. In an interview on Soviet TV on 29 April 1988 the lawyer G. A. Terekhov described his discussions with Stotenov about the approach to Germany after Beria's arrest in 1953. BBC, *SWB,* 2 May 1988, SU/0140 B/4.

9. Pavlenko, "The History of the War Is Still to Be Written."

10. Ibid.

11. L. Kolosov, "Immortality of Those Who Have Fallen," p. 3, *Izvestia,* 10 Oct. 1969.

12. *Final Report on the "Rote Kapelle" Case* (U.S. Armed Forces Security Agency translation of captured German Security Police and Security Service Report, "Abschlussbericht über den Fall Rote Kapelle, 22 March 1942"), NAW RG 457 SRH-380.

13. Ibid. On the fate of the captured code book, see below, pp. 284–85.

14. CIA, *The Rote Kapelle: The CIA's History of Soviet Intelligence and Espionage Networks in Western Europe 1936–1945* (Washington, D.C.: University Publications of America, 1984), pp. 140–41. Kolosov, "Immortality of Those Who Have Fallen," pt. 3.

15. *Final Report on the "Rote Kapelle" Case,* pp. 33–34, NAW RG 457 SRH-380. David J. Dallin, *Soviet Espionage* (New Haven, Conn.: Yale University Press, 1955), pp. 249–50.

16. See above, pp. 238–39.

17. Leopold Trepper, *The Great Game* (Michael Joseph, 1977), p. 133.

18. See above, pp. 275–76.

19. Trepper, *Great Game,* p. 133.

20. Erickson, *Road to Stalingrad,* pp. 483–85.

21. CIA, *Rote Kapelle,* pp. 105–11. Dallin, *Soviet Espionage,* pp. 163–64. Trepper gives his own version of events in *The Great Game.*

22. CIA, *Rote Kapelle,* pp. 165–93.

23. Anthony Read and David Fisher, *Operation Lucy* (London: Hodder & Stoughton, 1980). For the contrary view, see F. H. Hinsley et al., *British Intelligence in the Second World War* (London: HMSO, 1979–88), vol. II, p. 4, and Phillip Knightley, *The Second Oldest Profession* (London: André Deutsch, 1986), p. 204.

24. CIA, *Rote Kapelle,* pp. 222–26, 344–45.

25. Ibid., pp. 176–77, 344–45.

26. We are indebted on this subject to the pioneering research of Dr. David Glantz, and in particular to his paper to the Fourth U.S. Army War College International Conference on Intelligence and Strategy, May 1989, "The Role of Intelligence in Soviet Military Strategy During the Second World War."

27. Erickson, *Road to Stalingrad,* p. 639.

28. Geoff Jukes, "The Soviets and 'Ultra,' " *Intelligence and National Security,* vol. III (1988), no. 2.

29. On Hankey's career in 1941–42, see Stephen Roskill, *Hankey: Man of Secrets,* vol. III (London: Collins, 1974), chs. 14, 15.

30. Gordievsky.

31. Allen Weinstein, *Perjury: The Hiss-Chambers Case* (New York: Knopf, 1978), pp. 314–32, 340–42. On the interwar background, see above, pp. 228ff.

32. Robert J. Lamphere, *The FBI-KGB War: A Special Agent's Story* (New York: Berkley Books, 1987), pp. 24ff. Hayden Peake, Afterword to Elizabeth Bentley, *Out of Bondage* (New York: Ballantine Books, 1988), p. 231.

33. Bentley, *Out of Bondage,* pp. 103–06, 113–15. On the reliability of Bentley's account, see Hayden Peake's well-documented 115-page Afterword. Herbert Romerstein and Stanislav Levchenko, *The KGB Against the "Main Enemy"* (Lexington, Mass.: Lexington Books, 1989), ch. 7, adds some further details.

34. Bentley, *Out of Bondage,* pp. 68–69.

35. Ibid., p. 171 and passim.

36. Ibid., p. 110.

37. Ibid., pp. 121–22.

38. Record of meeting between General Deane and Captain Waere with General Fitin and Colonel Graur, 11 Nov. 1944, NAW RG 334, Military Mission to Moscow, Box 18.

39. Bentley, *Out of Bondage,* pp. 122, 165. Romerstein and Levchenko, *KGB Against the "Main Enemy,"* pp. 106–08.

40. Bentley, *Out of Bondage,* passim. Romerstein and Levchenko, *KGB Against the "Main Enemy,"* pp. 106–08.

41. Peter Wright claimed that the Venona decrypts revealed fourteen Soviet agents

"operating in or close to OSS" at HQ and in the field (*Spycatcher* [New York: Viking, 1987], p. 182).

42. Bentley, *Out of Bondage,* pp. 125–27; and Afterword by Peake, pp. 255–57.

43. Lamphere, *FBI-KGB War,* p. 86.

44. Romerstein and Levchenko, *KGB Against the "Main Enemy,"* pp. 111–12.

45. Lamphere, *FBI-KGB War,* p. 86.

46. G. Edward Buxton (acting Director OSS) to General Deane, 5 Jan. 1945, NAW RG 334, U.S. Military Mission in Moscow, Box 18.

47. Fitin to Deane; Deane to Fitin, 15 Feb. 1945, ibid.

48. Lamphere, *FBI-KGB War,* pp. 87ff.

49. Gordievsky. Thomas Powers, "Spook of Spooks," *New York Review of Books,* 17 Aug. 1989, gives Hiss's code name.

50. Weinstein, *Perjury,* pp. 349–51.

51. See above, p. 281.

52. Gordievsky.

53. Michael Straight, *After Long Silence* (London: Collins, 1983), p. 129.

54. Gordievsky.

55. Straight, *After Long Silence,* p. 143.

56. Bentley, *Out of Bondage,* pp. 161–71.

57. Gordievsky.

58. Robert E. Sherwood, *Roosevelt and Hopkins: An Intimate History* (New York: Grosset & Dunlap, 1950), p. 17.

59. Dwight W. Tuttle, *Harry L. Hopkins and Anglo–American–Soviet Relations, 1941–1945* (New York: Garland, 1983), p. 32.

60. Gordievsky.

61. Sherwood, *Roosevelt and Hopkins,* p. 325.

62. Ibid., p. 870. See below, p. 338.

63. Gordievsky.

64. Sherwood, *Roosevelt and Hopkins,* p. 318.

65. Tuttle, *Hopkins and Anglo–American–Soviet Relations,* p. 92.

66. Gordievsky.

67. Tuttle, *Hopkins and Anglo–American-Soviet Relations,* pp. 103–04.

68. Harry L. Hopkins, "The Inside Story of My Meeting with Stalin," *American Magazine,* Dec. 1941. Sherwood, *Roosevelt and Hopkins,* pp. 326–30.

69. Sherwood, *Roosevelt and Hopkins,* pp. 343–45.

70. Tuttle, *Hopkins and Anglo–American–Soviet Relations,* p. 105. Elliott Roosevelt, *As He Saw It* (New York: Duell, Sloan & Pearce, 1946), p. 22.

71. Review by Walter Trohan, chief of Washington Bureau, *Chicago Tribune,* of Sherwood, *Roosevelt and Hopkins;* "Memoirs of Ivan D. Yeaton, U.S.A. (retd), 1919–1953," Appendix 4, U.S. Army Military History Institute, Carlisle Barracks, Pa.

72. "Memoirs of Ivan D. Yeaton," pp. 37–38.

73. Warren Kimball, " 'They Don't Come Out Where You Expect': Roosevelt Reacts to the German–Soviet War" (forthcoming). There were significant differences between Steinhardt's account of a discussion between Hopkins and Molotov, and that given by Hopkins to Roosevelt. According to Steinhardt, in defiance of his instructions Hopkins gave Molotov an explicit assurance that the U.S. would respond if Japan attacked the U.S.S.R. Tuttle, *Hopkins and Anglo–American–Soviet Relations,* p. 102.

74. Gordievsky.

75. "Memoirs of Ivan D. Yeaton," pp. 38, 46, Appendix 4. Sherwood, *Roosevelt and Hopkins,* p. 396.

76. George McJimsey, *Harry Hopkins: Ally of the Poor and Defender of Democracy* (Cambridge, Mass.: Harvard University Press, 1987), p. 189.

77. Interview with Henderson cited in William F. Corson and Robert T. Crowley, *The New KGB,* updated Quill ed. (New York: William Morrow, 1986), p. 447.

78. Tuttle, *Hopkins and Anglo–American–Soviet Relations,* p. 105.

79. Ibid., pp. 212–13.

80. M. R. D. Foot, *SOE in France* (London: HMSO, 1966), pp. 1–6.

81. W. J. West, *Truth Betrayed* (London: Duckworth, 1987), ch. 6.

82. Ibid., pp. 62–64. Goronwy Rees, *A Chapter of Accidents* (London: Chatto & Windus, 1971), pp. 132–33. John Costello, *Mask of Treachery* (London: Collins, 1988), pp. 320–22.

83. See above, p. 214. Rees, *Chapter of Accidents,* pp. 132–33.

84. Tom Driberg, *Guy Burgess: A Portrait with Background* (London: Weidenfeld & Nicolson, 1956), pp. 40–41.

85. Gordievsky. Cf. Wright, *Spycatcher,* p. 228.

86. West, *Truth Betrayed,* p. 118.

87. Kim Philby, *My Silent War* (London: Panther Books, 1969), p. 26.

88. Foot, *SOE in France,* pp. 1–6.

89. Philby, *My Silent War,* pp. 23–24.

90. A. G. Denniston to T. J. Wilson (FO), 3 Sept. 1939, PRO FO 366/1059 X9173.

91. Philby, *My Silent War,* p. 24.

92. Ibid., pp. 24–29.

93. Gordievsky. The Kensington location of some of Gorsky's meetings with agents was revealed in a KGB-sponsored documentary on Philby, *Cutting Edge,* Channel 4, 14 May 1990.

94. Evidence from the 1954 KGB defector Pyotr Deryabin in Pyotr Deryabin and Frank Gibney, *The Secret World,* rev. ed. (New York: Ballantine Books, 1982), pp. 117–18.

95. Bentley, *Out of Bondage,* pp. 173–77.

96. Interview with Blunt cited in Robert Cecil, *A Divided Life* (London: Bodley Head, 1988), p. 66.

97. Note on Blunt's KGB file seen by Gordievsky.

98. Philby, *My Silent War,* pp. 31–35.

99. Ibid., p. 41.

100. *Cutting Edge,* Channel 4, 14 May 1990. On the Hess flight, see above, p. 263.

101. Philby, *My Silent War,* pp. 38–41.

102. David Martin, "James Klugmann, SOE-Cairo and the Mihailovich Deception," in David Charters and Maurice Tugwell (eds.), *Deception in East-West Relations* (London: Pergamon-Brassey, 1990). Klugmann did not in our view exert a decisive influence on Whitehall's decision to back Tito rather than Mihailovich. That decision was inspired chiefly by Tito's greater military effectiveness.

103. M.R.D. Foot, *SOE* (London: BBC, 1984), p. 47.

104. Ibid., pp. 145–46.

105. Philby, *My Silent War,* pp. 46–48.

106. Ibid., p. 61.

107. Phillip Knightley, *Philby: KGB Master Spy* (London: André Deutsch, 1988), pp. 105–10.

108. Ibid., pp. 123–25. Philby, *My Silent War,* pp. 92–93. Robert Cecil, "The Cambridge Comintern," in Christopher Andrew and David N. Dilks (eds.), *The Missing Dimension: Governments and Intelligence Communities in the Twentieth Century* (London: Macmillan, 1984), p. 179.

109. Gordievsky.

110. Barrie Penrose and Simon Freeman, *Conspiracy of Silence* (London: Grafton Books, 1986), pp. 212–21. The Intelligence Corps Museum at Ashford, Kent, contains

a brief record of Blunt's attendance at Minley Manor and a group photograph of those who took the course.

111. Penrose and Freeman, *Conspiracy of Silence,* pp. 221, 249–51. Costello, *Mask of Treachery,* pp. 370–72, 396–97. Cecil, "Cambridge Comintern," pp. 177–78.

112. Gordievsky.

113. Gordievsky.

114. Gordievsky.

115. Gordievsky.

116. Gordievsky.

117. Costello, *Mask of Treachery,* pp. 406–08.

118. Wright, *Spycatcher,* pp. 281–82. Nigel West, *Molehunt* (London: Weidenfeld & Nicolson, 1987), pp. 48–61.

119. Gordievsky.

120. Gordievsky.

121. Peter Calvocoressi, *Top Secret Ultra* (London: Cassell, 1980), p. 94. Hinsley et al., *British Intelligence in the Second World War,* vol. II, p. 59.

122. Hinsley et al., *British Intelligence in the Second World War,* vol. II, pp. 58–66.

123. Calvocoressi, *Top Secret Ultra,* p. 94.

124. Hinsley et al., *British Intelligence in the Second World War,* vol. II, pp. 58–66.

125. Gordievsky.

126. Cairncross debriefing, cited by Chapman Pincher, *Too Secret Too Long* (London: NEL, 1985), p. 396.

127. Ibid.

128. Hinsley et al., *British Intelligence in the Second World War,* vol. II, pp. 624, 764–65.

129. Gordievsky. Philby also provided intelligence before Kursk, but the claim in 1990 by KGB Major General Vasili Alekseevich Dajdalov that Philby was the major supplier of sigint ("There was nothing like it in the history of war!") is clearly unreliable. *Cutting Edge,* Channel 4, 14 May 1990.

130. Pincher, *Too Secret Too Long,* p. 396 (confirmed by Gordievsky). On the Soviet air attacks, see Janusz Piekalkiewicz, *Operation "Citadel"* (Novato, Ca.: Presidio Press, 1988), p. 94.

131. Gordievsky.

132. Jukes, "The Soviets and 'Ultra,' " pp. 239–40.

133. Pierre Accoce and Pierre Quet, *The Lucy Ring* (London: W. H. Allen, 1967). Read and Fisher, *Operation Lucy.*

134. Dallin, *Soviet Espionage,* p. 197. CIA, *Rote Kapelle,* p. 222.

135. Timothy P. Mulligan, "Spies, Ciphers and 'Zitadelle': Intelligence and the Battle of Kursk, 1943," *Journal of Contemporary History,* vol. XXII (1987), no. 2, pp. 236–40.

136. F. H. Hinsley, "British Intelligence in the Second World War," in Christopher Andrew and Jeremy Noakes (eds.), *Intelligence and International Relations 1900–1945* (Exeter: Exeter University Press, 1987), pp. 210–11.

137. Mulligan, "Spies, Ciphers and 'Zitadelle,' " p. 249.

138. Jukes, "The Soviets and 'Ultra,' " pp. 237–38.

139. David Kahn, *The Codebreakers* (New York: Macmillan, 1967), p. 649. Mulligan, "Spies, Ciphers and 'Zitadelle,' " p. 249.

140. Letter from Ralph Erskine in *Intelligence and National Security,* vol. III (1988), no. 4, pp. 184–85.

141. Major General A. Palii, "Radio-Electronic Combat in the Course of the War," *Voyenno-Istorichesky Zhurnal,* 1977, no. 5. David R. Beachley, "Soviet radio-electronic combat in World War Two," *Military Review,* vol. LXI (1981), no. 3.

142. Mulligan, "Spies, Ciphers and 'Zitadelle,' " pp. 245–46, 250–52.

143. Ibid., pp. 248–49.

144. Glantz, "The Role of Intelligence in Soviet Military Strategy," p. 159.

145. V. F. Nekrasov, "The contribution of the internal forces to the cause of the victory of the Soviet people in the Great Patriotic War," *Voyenno-Istorichesky Zhurnal,* 1985, no. 9.

146. John J. Dziak, *Chekisty: A History of the KGB* (Lexington, Mass.: Lexington Books, 1988), pp. 113–14. Erickson, *Road to Stalingrad,* pp. 517–18.

147. Nikolai Y. Khokhlov, *In the Name of Conscience* (London: Frederick Muller, 1960), pp. 30ff.

148. Ibid., p. 42. See above, p. 168.

149. *Front bez liniy fronta* (Moscow, 1965). Mulligan, "Spies, Ciphers and 'Zitadelle,' " pp. 251–52.

150. Major General V. N. Andrianov, "Partisan Reconnaissance during the Years of the Great Patriotic War," *Voyenno-Istorichesky Zhurnal,* 1986, no. 8.

151. John Erickson, *The Road to Berlin* (London: Weidenfeld & Nicolson, 1983), pp. 114–15.

152. Andrianov, "Partisan Reconnaissance."

153. Mulligan, "Spies, Ciphers and 'Zitadelle,' " p. 250.

154. Excerpt from captured German documents in Office of Naval Intelligence, "Espionage–Sabotage–Conspiracy. German and Russian Operations 1940 to 1945," p. 51, NAW RG 242, Box 70.

155. Cairncross was for a time joint-secretary of the Scientific Advisory Committee (Defence Services Panel) chaired by Hankey; S.A.C. (D.P.)(41)4, PRO CAB 90/8. On Hankey's role on the Scientific Advisory Committee and Tube Alloys Consultative Committee, see Roskill, *Hankey,* vol. III, pp. 487–93, 522–25.

156. A. I. Iovrysh, I. D. Morokhov, and S. K. Ivanov, *A-Bomba* (Moscow: Nauka, 1980), p. 377. David Holloway, *The Soviet Union and the Arms Race* (New Haven, Conn.: Yale University Press, 1983), p. 17.

157. David Holloway, "Entering the Nuclear Arms Race: The Soviet Decision to Build the Atomic Bomb, 1939–45," *Social Studies of Science,* vol. XI (1981), pp. 172–77.

158. A number of debriefings of Fuchs are now available at the FBI under the Freedom of Information Act. The fullest, 38 pages long, dated 26 July 1950, and conducted from 20 May to 2 June 1950 by Hugh M. Clegg and Robert J. Lamphere, is in FBI File 65-58805, vol. 38. The best biography is Robert Chadwell Williams, *Klaus Fuchs, Atom Spy* (Cambridge, Mass.: Harvard University Press, 1987).

159. In the course of his debriefing Fuchs identified the Soviet embassy as the location of one of his meetings with Kremer but did not say which. FBI 65-58805, vol. 38, p. 6.

160. Williams, *Fuchs,* pp. 59–61.

161. FBI 65-58805, vol. 38, p. 7.

162. Margaret Gowing, *Britain and Atomic Energy* (London: HMSO, 1964), pp. 65–68, 394–436.

163. Williams, *Fuchs,* pp. 41–45.

164. Ibid., ch. 6.

165. FBI 65-58805, file 38, p. 7.

166. FBI 65-58805, file 40, p. 5.

167. FBI 65-58805, file 38, p. 9.

168. FBI 65-58805, file 40.

169. Williams, *Fuchs,* pp. 75–82.

170. Report in *Bulletin of Atomic Scientists,* quoted in *Sunday Times,* 14 January 1990, section C.

171. Ronald Radosh and Joyce Milton, *The Rosenberg File* (London: Weidenfeld & Nicolson, 1983), ch. 3 and p. 212.

172. Harry Rositzke, *The KGB: The Story of the Sorge Spy Ring* (New York: McGraw-Hill, 1985), pp. 44–45.

173. Cecil, *Divided Life,* p. 77.

174. *The Defection of Igor Guzenko,* reprint of Canadian Royal Commission report of 27 June 1946, 3 vols. (Laguna Hills, Ca.: Aegean Park Press, 1984). On May, see especially vol. II, pp. 447–57. See also H. Montgomery Hyde, *The Atom Bomb Spies* (London: Hamish Hamilton, 1980).

175. *Defection of Igor Guzenko,* vol. II, p. 456; vol. I, p. 95.

176. The Canadian Royal Commission identified fourteen who had passed secrets to the Russians by name, and gave the unidentified code names of five others. Ibid., vol. III, p. 685.

177. Ibid., pp. 617–19.

178. Ibid.

179. Gordievsky. See Hyde, *Atom Bomb Spies,* pp. 125–42.

180. See above, p. 219.

181. Andrew Boyle, *The Climate of Treason* (London: Hutchinson, 1979), p. 300.

182. Cecil, *Divided Life,* p. 67.

183. Ibid., pp. 4–5.

184. Peter Hennessy and Kathleen Townsend, "The documentary spoor of Burgess and Maclean," *Intelligence and National Security,* vol. II (1987), no. 2, pp. 292–93. William Clark, "Cabinet secrecy, collective responsibility and the British public's right to know about and participate in foreign policy-making," in Thomas M. Franck and Edward Weisband (eds.), *Secrecy and Foreign Policy* (Oxford: Oxford University Press, 1974), pp. 202–03.

185. Gordievsky.

186. See above, pp. 286–87.

187. Bentley, *Out of Bondage,* pp. 173, 184, 200–02.

188. Ibid., ch. 12.

189. Bradley F. Smith, *The Shadow Warriors* (London: André Deutsch, 1983), p. 324. Philby, *My Silent War,* p. 32.

190. Philby, *My Silent War,* p. 30. On Hill's earlier adventures in Soviet Russia, see above, pp. 54ff.

191. Smith, *Shadow Warriors,* p. 335.

192. See above, p. 54.

193. Smith, *Shadow Warriors,* pp. 335–36.

194. Foot, *SOE,* p. 149.

195. Gordievsky.

196. Gordievsky recalls Chichayev, then a white-haired veteran, addressing a meeting in the First Chief Directorate Memory Room. Unlike Kukin, however, his portrait does not hang there.

197. František Moravec, *Master of Spies* (London: Bodley Head, 1975), pp. 233–43.

198. "Memorandum of Conversation at the Commissariat for Internal Affairs," 27 Dec. 1943, NAW RG 334, Military Mission to Moscow, Box 18.

199. Harriman to Roosevelt, telegram, 17 March 1944, ibid.

200. Smith, *Shadow Warriors,* pp. 339–46.

201. Donovan to Deane, 29 Aug. 1944, NAW RG 334, Military Mission to Moscow, Box 18.

202. See the records of the Military Mission to Moscow, ibid.

203. Fitin to Deane, 27 Sept. 1944, ibid.

204. Smith, *Shadow Warriors,* pp. 350–52.

205. "Principal Heads of SOE Contact with NKVD and Results Thereof," n.d.

[1944], PRO FO 371/47709. The first official Soviet military mission to Tito in February 1944 had arrived in gliders escorted by the RAF. Erickson, *Road to Berlin,* p. 339.

206. *The Times* obituary, 7 Nov. 1980. Sarah Gainham, "Smolka 'the Spy': A Letter from Vienna," *Encounter,* Dec. 1984.

207. Gordievsky.

208. H. P. Smolka, *Forty Thousand Against the Arctic: Russia's Polar Empire,* rev. ed. (London: Hutchinson, 1938), pp. 162, 274–75, 278.

209. W. J. West, *The Truth About Hollis* (London: Duckworth, 1989), p. 47. Gainham, "Smolka 'the Spy.' "

210. Gordievsky.

211. West, *Hollis,* p. 48.

212. Ministry of Information, Policy Committee minutes, 4 Sept. 1941, PRO INF 1/676.

213. Grubb to Leigh Ashton and Stevens, 29 Sept. 1941, PRO INF 1/147.

214. H. P. Smollett, "Policy on Russian Propaganda" [early Oct. 1941], ibid.

215. Smollett to Elizabeth Monroe, 20 March 1942, ibid.

216. Maisky to Bracken, 4 Nov. 1941, PRO INF 1/676.

217. Gordievsky.

218. Sargent to Grubb, 9 May 1942, PRO FO 371/32921/N 2523. We are grateful to Ms Sheila Kerr for this reference.

219. Smollett, "Policy on Russian Propaganda" [early Oct. 1941], PRO INF 1/147.

220. Ibid.

221. Ian McLaine, *Ministry of Morale* (London: Allen & Unwin, 1979), pp. 202–03.

222. Desmond Morton to Bracken, 16 Jan. 1942, PRO INF 1/677.

223. West, *Hollis,* pp. 107–08.

224. Smollett to Aynsley, 9 Oct. 1941, PRO INF 1/147.

225. Burgess, "Draft Suggestions for Talks on Russia," 15 July 1941. BBC Written Archives Centre, R51/520/1: first quoted in Christopher Andrew's filmed report on the Cambridge moles for *Timewatch,* BBC2, 27 July 1983 (producer: Robert Marshall); text in West, *Truth Betrayed,* pp. 59–61.

226. An extract from Henri's talk was included in Christopher Andrew's filmed report cited in n. 225.

227. West, *Hollis,* pp. 73–75.

228. McLaine, *Ministry of Morale,* p. 209.

229. Jane Degras (ed.), *The Communist International 1919–1943. Documents* (London: Oxford University Press, 1965), vol. III, pp. 476–77.

230. H. P. Smollett, "Arguments to Counter the Ideological Fear of 'Bolshevism,' " Feb. 1943, in W. J. West (ed.), *Orwell: The War Commentaries* (London: Duckworth, 1985), pp. 20ff.

231. Hugh Thomas, *Armed Truce: The Beginnings of the Cold War* (London: Hamish Hamilton, 1986), p. 67.

232. David N. Dilks (ed.), *The Diaries of Alexander Cadogan O.M. 1938–1945* (London: Cassell, 1971), p. 579. Martin Gilbert, *Winston S. Churchill,* vol. VII (London: Heinemann, 1986), pp. 568–69.

233. See above, pp. 287–90.

234. Cordell Hull, *The Memoirs of Cordell Hull* (New York: Macmillan, 1948), vol. II, p. 1249.

235. Lord Moran, *Winston Churchill: The Struggle for Survival 1940–1965* (London: Constable, 1966) p. 132.

236. Charles E. Bohlen, *Witness to History 1919–1969* (London: Weidenfeld & Nicolson, 1973), p. 148.

237. Thomas, *Armed Truce,* pp. 170–71.

238. Dilks (ed.), *Cadogan Diaries* p. 582.

239. Tuttle, *Hopkins and Anglo–American–Soviet Relations,* pp. 225–56.

240. Adam B. Ulam, *Expansion and Coexistence: Soviet Foreign Policy 1917–1973* (New York: Holt, Rinehart, 1974), p. 354.

241. Alex de Jonge, *Stalin and the Shaping of the Soviet Union* (London: Collins, 1986), p. 437. Sherwood, *Roosevelt and Hopkins,* p. 804.

242. Vojtech Mastny, *Russia's Road to the Cold War* (New York: Columbia University Press, 1979), pp. 132–39.

243. Allen Weinstein, *Perjury: The Hiss–Chambers Case* (New York: Knopf, 1978), pp. 352–54.

244. Tuttle, *Hopkins and Anglo–American–Soviet Relations,* pp. 242, 249.

245. Dilks (ed.), *Cadogan Diaries,* p. 703.

246. Joan Bright Astley, *The Inner Circle* (London: Hutchinson, 1971), p. 189.

247. Ibid., ch. 12 and p. 223. Richard Collier, *The War That Stalin Won* (London: Hamish Hamilton, 1983), pp. 237–39. Martin Gilbert, *Churchill,* vol. VII, p. 1182.

248. Bentley identified five other agents who worked in the U.S. Treasury at various times.

249. David Rees, *Harry Dexter White: A Study in Paradox* (New York: Macmillan, 1973).

250. Ibid., chs. 15–17.

251. Bentley, *Out of Bondage,* p. 166. Romerstein and Levchenko, *KGB Against the "Main Enemy,"* pp. 110–11.

252. Dilks (ed.), *Cadogan Diaries,* pp. 707–08.

253. Ibid., pp. 708–09.

254. Sherwood, *Roosevelt and Hopkins,* p. 860.

255. Ibid., p. 870.

256. De Jonge, *Stalin,* p. 485.

257. Thomas M. Campbell and George C. Herring (eds.), *The Diaries of Edward R. Stettinius Jr., 1943–1946* (New York: New Viewpoints, 1975), p. 416.

258. Collier, *War That Stalin Won,* p. 238.

259. J. W. Russell (Rome) to P. Mason (FO), 2 Oct. 1952, PRO FO 371/100826 NS 1023/29/G; H. A. F. Hohler (FO) to P. F. Grey (Moscow), ibid., N 31023/34/G. We are grateful for these references to Professor John Gaddis.

260. Ulam, *Expansion and Coexistence,* p. 377n.

261. Minute by R. A. Sykes, 23 Oct. 1952, PRO FO 371/100826 NS 1023/29/G.

Chapter 9. The Takeover of Eastern Europe (1944–48)

1. Amy W. Knight, *KGB: Police and Politics in the Soviet Union* (London: Unwin Hyman, 1988), pp. 35–36. John J. Dziak, *Chekisty: A History of the KGB* (Lexington, Mass.: Lexington Books, 1988), pp. 125–26. Strobe Talbott (ed./trans.), *Khrushchev Remembers* (London: Sphere Books, 1971), vol. I, p. 256. Besides Stalin, those envious of Beria's empire-building included Zhdanov, the Leningrad Party boss.

2. Interview by Christopher Andrew with Pyotr Deryabin, 25 Nov. 1987. Deriabin recalls the postwar disappearance of the Dzerzhinsky exhibit from the MGB officers' club, but is uncertain of the exact date (which he believes was before 1947) and the person responsible.

3. Sergei Zakharovich Ostryakov, *Voyennye Chekisty* (Moscow: Voyenizdat, 1979), ch. 3, p. IV.

4. Vladimir and Evdokia Petrova, *Empire of Fear* (London: André Deutsch, 1956), pp. 98–99.

5. Robert W. Stephan, "Death to Spies: The Story of Smersh," MA thesis, American University, Washington, DC, 1984, pp. 61–64.

6. Nikolai Tolstoy, *Stalin's Secret War* (London: Jonathan Cape, 1981), ch. 17.

Hugh Thomas, *Armed Truce: The Beginnings of the Cold War* (London: Hamish Hamilton, 1986), pp. 220-21.

7. Ostryakov, *Voyennye Chekisty,* p. 256.

8. Thomas, *Armed Truce,* p. 220. Tolstoy, *Stalin's Secret War,* ch. 17.

9. Nicholas Nyaradi, *My Ringside Seat in Moscow* (New York: Crowell, 1953), p. 155.

10. Stephan, "Death to Spies," pp. 150ff.

11. Ostryakov, *Voyennye Chekisty,* p. 205. Knight, *KGB,* p. 258.

12. Milovan Djilas, *Conversations with Stalin* (London: Rupert Hart-Davis, 1962), p. 105.

13. George H. Hodos, *Show Trials: Stalinist Purges in Eastern Europe, 1948-1954* (New York: Praeger, 1987), p. 40.

14. Djilas, *Conversations with Stalin,* pp. 15-16.

15. Stanislaw Mikolajczyk, *The Pattern of Soviet Domination* (London: Sampson Low, Marston & Co, 1949), p. 112.

16. See above, p. 141.

17. Hodos, *Show Trials,* pp. 137-38.

18. Jacques Rupnik, *The Other Europe* (London: Weidenfeld & Nicolson, 1988), p. 85, quoting document smuggled out of Warsaw archives in the 1970s.

19. Alex de Jonge, *Stalin and the Shaping of the Soviet Union* (London: Collins, 1986), ch. 45. Norman Davies, *God's Playground: A History of Poland* (Oxford: Clarendon Press, 1981), vol. II, pp. 472-80.

20. Gordievsky. On Serov's background, see Ilya Dzhirkvelov, *Secret Servant* (London: Collins, 1987), pp. 146-47, and William F. Corson and Robert T. Crowley, *The New KGB,* "updated" Quill ed. (New York: William Morrow, 1986), p. 248.

21. See the reports from SOE and others in PRO FO 371/47709.

22. Davies, *God's Playground,* vol. II, pp. 479-80.

23. Arthur Bliss Lane, *I Saw Freedom Betrayed* (London: Regency Publications, 1949), pp. 105-06.

24. Gordievsky.

25. PPR Politburo minutes, 17 Dec. 1944: in Antony Polonsky and Boleslaw Drukier (eds.), *The Beginnings of Communist Rule in Poland* (Routledge & Kegan Paul, 1980), pp. 396-99. There were later admissions that Red Army "debauchery" was "turning people against the Soviet Union." Ibid., p. 429.

26. Berling to Gomulka, 20 Sept. 1956, in J. Nowak, "Sprawa gen. Berlinga," *Zeszyćy Historyczne,* vol. XXXVII (1976), p. 39. John Coutouvidis and Jaime Reynolds, *Poland 1939-1947* (Leicester University Press, 1986), pp. 167-68.

27. Minutes of PPR Central Committee Plenum, 20-21 May 1945, in Polonsky and Drukier (eds.), *Beginnings of Communist Rule,* pp. 424-42.

28. The classic analysis of this three-stage political evolution is in Hugh Seton-Watson, *The East European Revolution* (London: Methuen, 1956).

29. Harry S. Truman, *Memoirs: 1945, Year of Decisions,* Signet ed. (New York: New American Library, 1965), p. 99.

30. Dwight W. Tuttle, *Harry L. Hopkins and Anglo–American–Soviet Relations 1941-1945* (New York: Garland, 1983), p. 277.

31. Gordievsky.

32. Robert E. Sherwood, *Roosevelt and Hopkins: An Intimate History* (New York: Grosset & Dunlap, 1950), pp. 885-86.

33. Tuttle, *Hopkins and Anglo–American–Soviet Relations,* pp. 275-76.

34. Herbert Feis, *Between War and Peace* (Princeton University Press, 1960), pp. 83-84.

35. Sherwood, *Roosevelt and Hopkins,* pp. 888-89. Feis, *Between War and Peace,* p. 98.

36. Vojtech Mastny, *Russia's Road to the Cold War* (New York: Columbia University Press, 1979), pp. 284–85.

37. *Foreign Relations of the United States: The Conference of Berlin (The Potsdam Conference)* (Washington, DC: U.S. Government Printing Office, 1960).

38. Ibid. Mastny, *Russia's Road,* pp. 286–87.

39. Tuttle, *Hopkins and Anglo–American–Soviet Relations,* pp. 289–91.

40. Gordievsky.

41. Tuttle, *Hopkins and Anglo–American–Soviet Relations,* p. 300. Mastny, *Russia's Road,* p. 287.

42. Lane, *Freedom Betrayed,* p. 111.

43. Gordievsky.

44. Lane, *Freedom Betrayed,* pp. 177–83.

45. Gordievsky.

46. Harry Rositzke, *The KGB: Eyes of Russia* (London: Sidgwick & Jackson, 1983), pp. 126–27. Further information from Gordievsky.

47. David J. Dallin, *Soviet Espionage* (New Haven, Conn.: Yale University Press, 1955), pp. 330–31.

48. Mikolajczyk, *Pattern of Soviet Domination,* p. 87. Stalin's comment is often wrongly applied to Poland.

49. Gordievsky. Branko Lazitch and Milorad M. Drachkovitch, *Biographical Dictionary of the Comintern,* rev. ed. (Stanford, Ca.: Hoover Institution Press, 1986).

50. Wolfgang Leonhard, *Child of the Revolution* (London: Collins, 1957), p. 303. Leonhard accompanied Ulbricht back to Germany from Moscow.

51. Thomas, *Armed Truce,* p. 347.

52. Erich Ollenhauer, *A bis Z* (Bonn: 1969), p.550. Martin McCauley, "East Germany," in McCauley (ed.), *Communist Power in Europe 1944–1949* (London: Macmillan, 1977).

53. Hans W. Schoenberg, "The Partition of Germany and the Neutralization of Austria," in Thomas Hammond (ed.), *The Anatomy of Communist Takeovers* (New Haven, Conn.: Yale University Press, 1975).

54. Dallin, *Soviet Espionage,* p. 332.

55. Ibid., pp. 364ff.

56. Cf. above, p. 351.

57. Ghita Ionescu, *Communism in Rumania 1944–1962* (London: Oxford University Press, 1964), pp. 79–81. Hodos, *Show Trials,* pp. 94–95.

58. Ionescu, *Communism in Rumania,* pp. 103ff, 186.

59. Robert R. King, *History of the Romanian Communist Party* (Stanford, Ca.: Hoover Institution Press, 1980), p. 92.

60. Petrov debrief, 29 Sept. 1954, AAC, CRS A6283/XR1/144. Cf. Anatoli Golitsyn, *New Lies for Old* (New York: Dodd, Mead, 1984), p. 185.

61. Gordievsky. Fedichkin was later resident in Rome, using the alias Yakovlev, from 1951 to 1955.

62. Joseph Rothschild, *The Communist Party of Bulgaria: Origins and Development, 1883–1936* (New York: Columbia University Press, 1971).

63. Nissan Oren, *Bulgarian Communism: The Road to Power 1934–1944* (New York: Columbia University Press, 1971).

64. Adam B. Ulam, *Titoism and the Cominform* (Cambridge, Mass.: Harvard University Press, 1952), pp. 91–93. Milovan Djilas, *Tito: The Story from the Inside* (London: Weidenfeld & Nicolson, 1981), p. 35.

65. Nissan Oren, "A Revolution Administered: The Sovietization of Bulgaria," in Hammond (ed.), *Anatomy of Communist Takeovers.* Joseph Rothschild, *Return to Diversity: A Political History of East Central Europe Since World War II* (New York: Oxford University Press, 1989), pp. 114–19.

66. Nyaradi, *Ringside Seat,* p. 51.

67. *Társadalmi Szelme,* April 1952: quoted in William Shawcross, *Crime and Compromise* (London: Weidenfeld & Nicolson, 1974), p. 56.

68. Nyaradi, *Ringside Seat,* pp. 276–77.

69. Béla Szász, *Volunteers for the Gallows* (London: Chatto & Windus, 1971).

70. Paul Ignotus, "The First Two Communist Takeovers of Hungary: 1919 and 1948," in Hammond (ed.), *Anatomy of Communist Takeovers.*

71. Róbert Gábor, quoted in Charles Gati, *Hungary and the Soviet Bloc* (Durham, NC: Duke University Press, 1986), p. 23n.

72. Ibid., pp. 88, 119–20, 130n.

73. Pavel Tigrid, "The Prague Coup: The Elegant Takeover," in Hammond (ed.), *Anatomy of Communist Takeovers,* pp. 419–20.

74. Karel Kaplan, *The Short March: The Communist Takeover in Czechoslovakia 1945–1948* (London: C. Hurst & Co., 1987), p. 135. Kaplan's study is based on Czechoslovak Party and state archives listed in his source references.

75. Ibid., pp. 137–38.

76. Tigrid, "The Prague Coup," pp. 414–15.

77. Kaplan, *Short March,* pp. 138–39.

78. Ibid., pp. 140–46, ch. 8.

79. Ibid., pp. 157–66, 175.

80. Ibid., ch. 14.

81. Djilas, *Tito,* p. 29.

82. Milovan Djilas, *Rise and Fall* (London: Macmillan, 1985), pp. 106–07.

83. Ibid., pp. 82–83, 105–06.

84. Thomas, *Armed Truce,* pp. 298ff.

85. Djilas, *Rise and Fall,* pp. 32, 83–86, 408.

86. Ibid., pp. 84–85, 92, 95, 98–99, 105–06. Vladimir Dedijer, *Tito Speaks: His Self-Portrait and Struggle with Stalin* (London: Weidenfeld & Nicolson, 1953), p. 268.

87. Thomas, *Armed Truce,* pp. 298ff. Djilas, *Rise and Fall,* pp. 35–38.

88. Djilas, *Tito,* p. 71.

89. Nora Beloff, *Tito's Flawed Legacy* (London: Victor Gollancz, 1985), pp. 133–34, 140–41.

90. Ulam, *Titoism and the Cominform.*

91. Ibid. Djilas, *Rise and Fall,* chs. 14, 15. Djilas, *Tito,* pp. 84–87. Beloff, *Tito's Flawed Legacy,* pp. 145–46.

92. Stephen Clissold, *Djilas: The Progress of a Revolutionary* (Hounslow: Maurice Temple-Smith, 1983), pp. 175–78. Djilas, *Conversations with Stalin,* pp. 144–47. Hodos, *Show Trials,* pp. 6–8. N. C. Pano, *The People's Republic of Albania* (Baltimore: Johns Hopkins University Press, 1968), pp. 47–68.

93. Hodos, *Show Trials,* pp. 9–12. Pano, *Albania,* pp. 81–87.

Chapter 10. Cold War: The Stalinist Phase (1945–53)

1. Gordievsky.

2. Gordievsky.

3. Interview with Colonel "Tar" Robertson, quoted in Chapman Pincher, *Too Secret Too Long* (London: NEL, 1985), p. 351.

4. Ibid., pp. 353–54.

5. Gordievsky.

6. Information from David Footman cited in Pincher, *Too Secret Too Long,* p. 397 (which misdates Cairncross's departure from Bletchley Park).

7. See above, pp. 319–20, 334.

8. Elizabeth Bentley, *Out of Bondage* (New York: Ballantine Books, 1988), chs. 11, 12 and Afterword by Hayden Peake.

9. On the Guzenko case, see Robert Bothwell and J. L. Granatstein (eds.), *The Guzenko Transcripts* (Ottawa: Deneau, n.d.); John Sawatsky, *Guzenko: The Untold Story* (Toronto: Macmillan, 1985); H. Montgomery Hyde, *The Atom Bomb Spies* (London: Hamish Hamilton, 1980), chs. 1, 2; Gordon Brook-Shepherd, *The Storm Birds* (London: Weidenfeld & Nicolson, 1988), ch. 2.

10. James Barros, "Alger Hiss and Harry Dexter White: The Canadian Connection," *Orbis,* vol. XXI (1977), no. 3.

11. Gordievsky.

12. The most reliable account of this episode, we believe, is Brook-Shepherd's *Storm Birds,* ch. 4, which corrects a number of inventions by Philby. The two agents within the Foreign Office referred to by Volkov were, in all probability, Burgess and Maclean. The seven in the intelligence services doubtless included Philby, Blunt, Cairncross, Long and Klugmann. Candidates for the other two wartime moles are Cedric Belfrage, who worked for two years during the Second World War for British Security Coordination in New York, and an SOE officer who cannot be publicly identified.

13. Kim Philby, *My Silent War* (London: Panther Books, 1969), pp. 114–15.

14. Brook-Shepherd, *Storm Birds,* pp. 42–43.

15. Phillip Knightley, *Philby: KGB Master Spy* (London: André Deutsch, 1988), p. 138.

16. Gordievsky.

17. Philby, *My Silent War,* p. 120.

18. Gordievsky.

19. Brook-Shepherd, *Storm Birds,* ch. 4. Gordievsky.

20. See above, pp. 283–84. Though not the code book used for communications between the Center and NKGB residencies in the West, it was of similar construction.

21. Interview by Christopher Andrew with retired NSA official. Gordievsky has no information on the cipher officer's fate.

22. Robert J. Lamphere, *The FBI-KGB War: A Special Agent's Story* (New York: Berkley Books, 1987), pp. 80–82.

23. Ibid., p. 84.

24. David Martin, *Wilderness of Mirrors* (New York: Ballantine Books, 1981), p. 46. Peter Wright, *Spycatcher* (New York: Viking, 1987), p. 184. Confirmed to Christopher Andrew in unattributable U.S. interviews.

25. Wright, *Spycatcher,* p. 185.

26. Christopher Andrew, "The Growth of the Australian Intelligence Community and the Anglo-American Connection," *Intelligence and National Security,* vol. IV (1989), no. 2, pp. 227ff. Robert Manne, *The Petrov Affair: Politics and Espionage* (Sydney: Pergamon, 1987), ch. 12.

27. Gordievsky.

28. A Lavrentyeva, "Stroiteli novogo mira," *V Mire Knig,* 1970, no. 4. David Holloway, "Entering the Nuclear Arms Race: The Soviet Decision to Build the Atomic Bomb, 1939–45," *Social Studies of Science,* vol. XI (1981), pp. 183–84.

29. "They Awakened the Genie" (interview with Professor Golovin and unpublished extracts from his biography of Kurchatov), *Moscow News,* 1989, no. 41.

30. P. L. Kapitsa (ed. Pavel Rubinin), *Pisma o nauke* (Moscow: Moskovsky Rabochy, 1989). David Holloway, "The Scientist and the Tyrant," *New York Review of Books,* 1 March 1990. Beria had his revenge: in 1946 Kapitsa was dismissed from the directorship of his research institute.

31. D. M. Ladd (FBI), memo to Hoover, 26 June 1951. Hoover added the minute, "I was always required to have an escort." FBI 100-374183, referrals file, p. 31.

32. AEC to Hoover, 10 July 1951, ibid., fols 9–10. "Atomic Energy Matters with

Which Donald Maclean Was Concerned As First Secretary, British Embassy, Washington DC," n.d., FBI 100-374183, serial 1-137.

33. "They Awakened the Genie," *Moscow News*, 1989, no. 41.

34. Ibid.

35. Lamphere, *FBI-KGB War*, ch. 9.

36. Hyde, *Atom Bomb Spies*, ch. 3.

37. Ibid., pp. 126–27.

38. Gordievsky.

39. Lamphere, *FBI-KGB War*, pp. 183–92.

40. Hyde, *Atom Bomb Spies*, chs. 4 and 5.

41. Gordievsky.

42. Our main source for the history and organization of the KI is a twenty-four-page paper prepared from information provided by the Petrovs, "The Committee of Information (KI) 1947–1951," 17 Nov. 1954, AAC, CRS A 6283/XR1/56.

43. Ilya Dzhirkvelov, *Secret Servant* (London: Collins, 1987), p. 138.

44. Gordievsky.

45. Dzhirkvelov, *Secret Servant*, p. 64.

46. Interview by Christopher Andrew with Yuri Nosenko, 15 Nov. 1987.

47. "The Committee of Information (KI) 1947–1951," 17 Nov. 1954, AAC, CRS A6283/XR1/56.

48. Andrei Gromyko, *Memories* (London: Hutchinson, 1989), pp. 318–19.

49. "The Committee of Information (KI) 1947–1951," AAC, CRS A 6283/XR1/56. The exact sequence (though not the identity) of KI chairmen is unclear. The Petrovs were confident that Molotov was the first and Zorin the last. But it is possible that Molotov handed over the chairmanship to Malik toward the end of his term as Foreign Minister, that Vyshinsky took over from Malik and was succeeded by Zorin.

50. Interview by Christopher Andrew with Yuri Nosenko, 15 Nov. 1987.

51. Tom Bower, *The Red Web* (London: Aurum, 1989), pp. 46–47, 59–62.

52. Ibid., pp. 72–79.

53. Ibid., pp. 97–103, 114–18, 123, 139–40. Anthony Cavendish, *Inside Intelligence* (London: privately printed, 1987), ch. 7.

54. Bower, *Red Web*, pp. 119, 165. See above, p. 103.

55. Gordievsky.

56. Quoted in Bower, *Red Web*, pp. 190–91.

57. Gordievsky.

58. BBC, *SWB, Poland*, 1 January 1953. Thomas Powers, *The Man Who Kept the Secrets: Richard Helms and the CIA* (London: Weidenfeld & Nicolson, 1979), pp. 40–45. Edward Jay Epstein, *Deception: The Invisible War Between the KGB and the CIA* (New York: Simon & Schuster, 1989), pp. 34–39.

59. Ever since the Second World War, KGB "active measures" have sought to portray Ukrainian partisans as former Nazi collaborators. The horrors of mass deportations, man-made famine and the Terror in the 1930s had, unsurprisingly, led many Ukrainians to welcome the Germans as liberators in 1941. Hitler, however, regarded them as *Untermenschen*.

60. Philby, *My Silent War*, p. 145.

61. Harry Rositzke, *The KGB: Eyes of Russia* (London: Sidgwick & Jackson, 1983), p. 134.

62. Gordievsky.

63. Ibid., ch. 9. Ismail Akhmedov, *In and Out of Stalin's GRU* (London: Arms & Armour Press, 1984), ch. 10.

64. Nicholas Bethell, *The Great Betrayal* (London: Hodder & Stoughton, 1984).

65. Philby, *My Silent War*, pp. 144–45.

66. Unattributable interview by Christopher Andrew in the United States.

67. Philby, *My Silent War,* p. 146.

68. Gordievsky. According to the Petrovs, Kukin remained head of the KI First Directorate until late 1950. AAC, CRS A 6238/XR1/56.

69. Gordievsky.

70. Robert Cecil, *A Divided Life* (London: Bodley Head, 1988), p. 88.

71. Affidavit sworn by Vladimir Petrov, 29 March 1956, AAC, CRS A 1209/60/769. Petrov had been acting resident in Canberra from 1952–1954. Less reliable accounts of his revelations appeared in the press. Additional information on Kislitsyn from Gordievsky.

72. Andrew Boyle, *The Climate of Treason* (London: Hutchinson, 1979), pp. 305, 341, 346. Goronwy Rees, *A Chapter of Accidents* (London: Chatto & Windus, 1971), p. 164.

73. Christopher Mayhew, *Time to Explain* (London: Hutchinson, 1987), p. 109.

74. Boyle, *Climate of Treason,* pp. 347–48.

75. Gordievsky.

76. Peter Hennessy and Kathleen Townsend, "The documentary spoor of Burgess and Maclean," *Intelligence and National Security,* vol. II (1987), no. 2.

77. Rees, *Chapter of Accidents,* p. 7. Barrie Penrose and Simon Freeman, *Conspiracy of Silence* (London: Grafton Books, 1986), pp. 324–27.

78. Gordievsky.

79. Cecil, *Divided Life,* chs. 6, 7.

80. *The Times,* 2 Jan. 1981.

81. Minute by Maclean, 21 Dec. 1950, PRO FO 371/81613 AU 1013/52.

82. Cecil, *Divided Life,* p. 123.

83. See his warnings to Italian Communists in *Osteuropa,* no. 10, October 1970, cited in George Kennan, *Memoirs 1950–1963* (New York: Pantheon Books, 1983), p. 94.

84. David Dimbleby and David Reynolds, *An Ocean Apart* (London: BBC/Hodder & Stoughton, 1988), p. 190.

85. Cecil, *Divided Life,* p. 123.

86. Philby, *My Silent War,* pp. 152–53.

87. Cecil, *Divided Life,* pp. 117–18.

88. Philby, *My Silent War,* p. 152.

89. Ibid., p. 153.

90. Cecil, *Divided Life,* p. 118.

91. Philby, *My Silent War,* pp. 155–56.

92. Martin, *Wilderness of Mirrors,* p. 51.

93. Philby, *My Silent War,* p. 156. The KGB's claim in 1990 that Burgess's escapades were preplanned (*Cutting Edge,* Channel 4, 14 May 1990) is unconvincing.

94. Gordievsky.

95. Philby, *My Silent War,* p. 154. Costello, *Mask of Treachery,* pp. 545–46.

96. Knightley, *Philby,* pp. 177–78.

97. Gordievsky.

98. Cecil, *Divided Life,* pp. 135ff.

99. Gordievsky.

100. Cecil, *Divided Life,* pp. 135–44.

101. Gordievsky.

102. Penrose and Freeman, *Conspiracy of Silence,* pp. 357–58.

103. Gordievsky.

104. P. M. Rossiter to Cairncross, 14 Mar. 1947, PRO T 225/13 B.A.T. (49), 2nd Meeting, 19 Dec. 1949; PRO T 225/117.

105. Penrose and Freeman, *Conspiracy of Silence,* pp. 369–70. John Colville, *The*

Fringes of Power (London: Hodder & Stoughton, 1985), pp. 30ff. Pincher, *Too Secret Too Long,* pp. 394–95. Wright, *Spycatcher,* pp. 219–23.

106. Press conference, 20 Nov. 1979.

107. Philby, *My Silent War,* pp. 151–52, 157–59.

108. Interview by Christopher Andrew with James MacCargar, 11 Dec. 1987.

109. Philby, *My Silent War,* pp. 167–70.

110. Knightley, *Philby,* pp. 184–85.

111. Costello, *Mask of Treachery,* p. 569.

112. "Soviet State Security Service Foreign Intelligence Operational Techniques ('Legal' Residency System)" based on debriefing of the Petrovs, 18 May 1955, Section VII, AAC, CRS A 6283/XR1/9.

113. See above, p. 208. Watson obituary in *King's College Calendar,* 1983. Wright, *Spycatcher,* pp. 190–93. Further information from Gordievsky.

114. Gordievsky.

115. H. Montgomery Hyde, *George Blake, Superspy* (London: Constable, 1987).

116. Gordievsky.

117. Hyde, *Blake,* pp. 39–40. Kuzmich, the first MGB officer to interrogate Blake, later defected.

118. "Miscellaneous Soviet Personalities who have served abroad," 29 Sept. 1954, AAC, CRS A 6283/XR1/144. It is certain that these documents were not sigint intercepts, which were closely guarded and would never have been left lying around.

119. Ibid. Additional information from Gordievsky. Krokhin's name is misspelled in the Petrov debrief as Krahin.

120. Cf. Thierry Wolton, *Le KGB en France* (Paris: Bernard Grasset, 1986), pp. 125–34).

121. Ibid., pp. 167–77. Further information from Gordievsky. See below, pp. 444–45.

122. Heinz Höhne and Hermann Zolling, *The General Was a Spy* (London: Pan Books, 1972), ch. 12. See below, pp. 448–49.

123. George H. Hodos, *Show Trials: Stalinist Purges in Eastern Europe, 1948–1954* (New York: Praeger, 1987), pp. 35, 28.

124. Unless otherwise indicated, our account of Field's career is based on Flora Lewis, *The Man Who Disappeared: The Strange History of Noel Field* (London: Arthur Barker, 1965) and Allen Weinstein, *Perjury: The Hiss–Chambers Case* (New York: Knopf, 1978), pp. 198–206.

125. Richard Harris Smith, *OSS: The Secret History of America's First Central Intelligence Agency* (Berkeley: University of California Press, 1972), pp. 227–28.

126. Lewis, *The Man Who Disappeared,* pp. 160, 191.

127. Karel Kaplan, *Dans les archives du Comité Central* (Paris: Albin Michel, 1978), pp. 145–47.

128. Hodos, *Show Trials,* p. 170.

129. Derek Kartun, *Tito's Plot Against Europe: The Story of the Rajk Conspiracy* (London: Lawrence & Wishart, 1949), p. 22.

130. Lewis, *The Man Who Disappeared,* p. 119.

131. Milovan Djilas, *Rise and Fall* (London: Macmillan, 1985), pp. 128–29.

132. Kádár's account of the meeting is contained in the biography by László Gyurkó, *Arcképvázlat történelmi háttérrel* (Budapest, 1982), pp. 180–81; and in the "introductory biography" by Gyurkó to János Kádár, *Selected Speeches and Interviews* (Oxford: Pergamon Press, 1985), pp. 71–72.

133. Hodos, *Show Trials,* ch. 5, p. 39.

134. Interview with Kádár in *Magyarorszag,* 19 May 1989.

135. Béla Szász, *Volunteers for the Gallows* (London: Chatto & Windus, 1971), pp. 71, 105, 108ff, 138ff, 172.

136. "Who Are You, Vladimir Farkas?," *Magyar Nemzet,* 3 Nov. 1988.

137. Interview in *Magyarorszag,* 19 May 1989.

138. Hodos, *Show Trials,* pp. 48–49.

139. *László Rajk and His Accomplices Before the People's Court* (Budapest, 1949). Rajk and two of the defendants were sentenced to hanging by the People's Court. Two others were referred to a military tribunal who sentenced them to firing squads.

140. Hodos, *Show Trials,* pp. 49–50.

141. Gordievsky.

142. Hodos, *Show Trials,* pp. 65–66.

143. Jiří Pelikán (ed.), *The Czechoslovak Political Trials, 1950–1954* (London: Macdonald, 1971).

144. Karel Kaplan, *Procès politiques à Prague* (Brussels: Editions Complexe, 1980), p. 45.

145. Dzhirkvelov, *Secret Servant,* pp. 246–49. Further information on the careers of Otrashchenko and Korotkov was provided by the Petrovs; AAC, CRS A6283/XR1/56, 143, 144.

146. Strobe Talbott (ed./trans.), *Khrushchev Remembers* (London: Sphere Books, 1971), vol. I, pp. 260–62.

147. Ibid., p. 263.

148. Dzhirkvelov, *Secret Servant,* p. 250.

149. Meir Cotic, *The Prague Trial* (New York: Herzl Press/Cornwall Books, 1987), p. 97. In 1990 Boyarsky was exposed in *Moscow News* as a sadist who had "relished beating people up," personally tortured women as well as men, and embezzled StB funds. Yevgenia Albat, "Will There Be an End to the Lubyanka?," *Moscow News,* 1990, no. 10.

150. Kaplan, *Procès politiques,* p. 45.

151. An official Czechoslovak report in 1963 described Keppert as notorious for "rabid anti-Semitism." Pelikán (ed.), *Czechoslovak Political Trials,* pp. 101–02. Cotic, *Prague Trial,* p. 219.

152. Pelikán (ed.), *Czechoslovak Political Trials,* pp. 102–03. Cotic, *Prague Trial,* p. 219.

153. Pelikán (ed.), *Czechoslovak Political Trials,* p. 103.

154. Interview by Christopher Andrew with Pyotr Deryabin, 25 November 1987. Deriabin was present at Khrushchev's speech in the officers' club. He recalls the date of the speech as September 1951. Some other accounts put Abakumov's arrest at up to two months later.

155. Amy W. Knight, *KGB: Police and Politics in the Soviet Union,* (London: Unwin Hyman, 1988), p. 36.

156. Pelikán (ed.), *Czechoslovak Political Trials,* pp. 106–07.

157. Cotic, *Prague Trial,* p. 12.

158. Gordievsky.

159. Gordievsky.

160. Talbott (ed./trans.), *Khrushchev Remembers,* vol. I, pp. 282–87. Alex de Jonge, *Stalin and the Shaping of the Soviet Union* (London: Collins, 1986), pp. 500–03.

161. Hodos, *Show Trials,* p. 66.

162. Cotic, *Prague Trial,* p. 144.

163. Talbott (ed./trans.), *Khrushchev Remembers,* vol. I., ch. 8. De Jonge, *Stalin,* ch. 49.

164. N. Barsukov, "On the Way to the 20th Congress," *Pravda,* 10 Nov. 1989.

165. "I *was* attached to him," Khrushchev admitted, ". . . I wept sincerely over Stalin's death." Talbott (ed./trans.), *Khrushchev Remembers,* vol. I, pp. 322–23.

166. Knight, *KGB,* pp. 47, 51, 70.

167. Roy Medvedev, "N. S. Khrushchev's Political Biography," *Druzhba Narodov,* July 1989.

168. Gordievsky.

Chapter 11. The Cold War After Stalin (1953–63)

1. N. Barsukov, "On the Way to the 20th Congress," *Pravda,* 10 Nov. 1989. After Stalin's death the Presidium was reduced in size to ten; in 1966 it was to be replaced by the old Politburo.

2. During the year from March 1953 to March 1954 when the MGB was absorbed by the MVD, the Foreign Directorate, previously the First Chief Directorate, became the Second; the Counter-Intelligence Directorate, previously the Second, became the First.

3. Interview with Pyotr Deryabin by Christopher Andrew, 25 Nov. 1987. Deriabin's account of the recall of residents to Moscow is confirmed by Yuri Nosenko (interview with Christopher Andrew, 15 Nov. 1987).

4. Roy Medvedev, "N. S. Khrushchev's Political Biography," *Druzhba Narodov,* July 1989.

5. Andrei Gromyko, *Memories* (London: Hutchinson, 1989), p. 318.

6. Medvedev, "Khrushchev's Political Biography." Strobe Talbott (ed./trans.), *Khrushchev Remembers* (London: Sphere Books, 1971), vol. I, pp. 321–26.

7. Pyotr Deryabin and Frank Gibney, The *Secret World,* rev. ed. (New York: Ballantine Books, 1982), p. 200.

8. Fyodor Burlatsky, "Khrushchev: Sketches for a Political Portrait," *Literaturnaya Gazeta,* 24 Feb. 1988. Malenkov, to whom Khrushchev's later recollections rarely did justice, probably played a less feeble part than Khrushchev claimed. Cf. Marshal Kirill. S. Moskalenko, "Beria's Arrest," *Moscow News,* 1990, no. 23.

9. Moskalenko, "Beria's Arrest." Medvedev, "Khrushchev's Political Biography."

10. Gordievsky.

11. Interview with "Merited Lawyer" G. A. Terekhov on Soviet TV, 29 April 1988; BBC, *SWB,* SU/0140 B/4, 2 May 1988.

12. Interview with Pyotr Deryabin by Christopher Andrew, 25 Nov. 1987.

13. Gordievsky. On Panyushkin's career, see also Petrov debrief, AAC, CRS A6283/XR1/56.

14. Nikolai Y. Khokhlov, *In the Name of Conscience* (London: Frederick Muller, 1960), p. 201.

15. Interview with Pyotr Deryabin by Christopher Andrew, 25 Nov. 1987.

16. Khokhlov, *In the Name of Conscience,* pt. III.

17. Interviews by Christopher Andrew with Yuri Rastvorov, Oct. 1987, and Pyotr Deryabin, 25 Nov. 1987.

18. Talbott (ed./trans.), *Khrushchev Remembers,* vol. I, p. 338.

19. Sándor Kopácsi, *Au nom de la classe ouvrière* (Paris: Editions Robert Laffont, 1979), p. 24. The claims in William F. Corson and Robert T. Crowley, *The New KGB* (New York: William Morrow, 1986), pp. 265–69, that Andropov was also KGB resident and that Viktor Chebrikov, another future KGB chairman, was also at the Budapest embassy are mistaken.

20. Amy W. Knight, *The KGB: Police and Politics in the Soviet Union* (London: Unwin Hyman, 1988), p. 123.

21. Interview with Kryuchkov, *New Times,* 1989, no. 32.

22. TV interview with Kryuchkov, 24 June 1989, BBC, *SWB,* SU/0496/B/1.

23. Gordievsky.

24. Joseph Rothschild, *Return to Diversity: A Political History of East Central Europe Since World War II* (New York: Oxford University Press, 1989), pp. 156–58.

25. On the course of the Revolution, see United Nations, *Report of the Special Committee on the Problem of Hungary* (New York, 1957).

26. Kopácsi, *Au nom de la classe ouvrière,* pp. 119–22.

27. Talbott (ed./trans.), *Khrushchev Remembers,* vol. I, p. 418.

28. Gordievsky.

29. Charles Gati, *Hungary and the Soviet Bloc* (Durham, NC: Duke University Press, 1986), pp. 144–47.

30. Arkadi N. Shevchenko, *Breaking with Moscow* (New York: Ballantine Books, 1985), p. 104.

31. Gati, *Hungary and the Soviet Bloc,* pp. 148–49.

32. UN, *Report of the Special Committee.*

33. Gordievsky.

34. Account given by Maléter to Kopácsi. *Au nom de la classe ouvrière,* pp. 247–88. The allegation that Maléter was arrested while at a banquet arranged by Andropov is mistaken. See Zhores Medvedev, *Andropov: His Life and Death,* rev. ed. (Oxford: Basil Blackwell, 1984), p. 37.

35. Béla K. Király, "Military Aspects," in Béla K. Király and Paul Jónás (eds.), *The Hungarian Revolution of 1956 in Retrospect* (New York: Columbia University Press, 1978), p. 70.

36. Kopácsi, *Au nom de la classe ouvrière,* pp. 240–41, 270.

37. Ibid., pp. 277–78, 306.

38. Tibor Méray, "The Trial of Imre Nagy," in Király and Jónás (eds.), *The Hungarian Revolution in Retrospect.* Selected parts of the transcript were later published: filmed extracts of the trial were also shown.

39. *The Counter-Revolutionary Conspiracy of Imre Nagy and His Accomplices* (Budapest: Information Bureau of the Council of Ministers, 1958), pp. 13–18, 108–29.

40. Khokhlov, *In the Name of Conscience,* p. 201.

41. Gordievsky. Knight, *KGB,* p. 122. Anatoli Golitsyn, *New Lies for Old* (New York: Dodd, Mead, 1984), pp. 185–86.

42. Gordievsky.

43. Gordievsky.

44. Golitsyn, *New Lies for Old,* pp. 283–87.

45. Andrei Gromyko, *Memories.*

46. Gordievsky.

47. Gordievsky.

48. Kim Philby, *My Silent War* (London: Panther Books, 1969), p. 171. Hollis was then deputy director general of MI5 and Graham Mitchell director of counterespionage. Had either been, as mistakenly alleged, a Soviet spy, Modin would scarcely have been quite so preoccupied with the threat from the Security Service.

49. Chapman Pincher, *Too Secret Too Long* (London: NEL, 1985), p. 355.

50. Gordievsky.

51. Philby, *My Silent War,* p. 151.

52. Vladimir and Evdokia Petrova, *Empire of Fear* (London: André Deutsch, 1956), ch. 23.

53. Philby, *My Silent War,* ch. 13.

54. Phillip Knightley, *Philby: KGB Master Spy* (London: André Deutsch, 1988), pp. 148–49.

55. Andrew, *Secret Service,* p. 496.

56. Gordievsky.

57. Peter Wright, *Spycatcher* (New York: Viking, 1987) pp. 172–73.

58. Knightley, *Philby,* ch. 15.

59. Gordievsky.

60. Unattributable interview by Christopher Andrew with former CIA officer.

61. David Martin, *Wilderness of Mirrors* (New York: Ballantine Books, 1981), pp. 74–90, 101–06. John Ranelagh, *The Agency* (London: Weidenfeld & Nicolson, 1986), pp. 288–96.

62. H. Montgomery Hyde, *George Blake, Superspy* (London: Constable, 1987), pp. 47–49.

63. Gordievsky was among those who attended the trial. He dismisses claims that Popov was tortured to death as an example to others.

64. In the four years between Rodin's two terms as resident, Georgi Mikhailovich Zhivotovsky served as acting resident, 1952–53; Sergei Leonidovich Tikhvinsky was resident 1953–55, then recalled by the Center; Yuri Modin served as acting resident 1955–56. Gordievsky.

65. Gordievsky.

66. Gordievsky.

67. John Vassall, *Vassall* (London: Sidgwick & Jackson, 1975).

68. Gordievsky.

69. Wright, *Spycatcher,* pp. 166–67. Gordievsky.

70. Gordievsky.

71. The KGB version of Molody's career appears in a volume prepared, with Philby's help, by active measures specialists in the First Chief Directorate: Gordon Lonsdale, *Spy* (London: Neville Spearman, 1965).

72. Gordievsky.

73. Valeri Agranovsky, "Profession: Foreigner," *Znamya,* Sept. 1988: a much franker account of Molody, based on interviews with him, than the KGB ghostwritten version of his memoirs, Lonsdale, *Spy.*

74. Agranovsky, "Profession: Foreigner."

75. Gordievsky.

76. Gordievsky.

77. Wright, *Spycatcher,* pp. 137–38. Harry Rositzke, *The KGB: Eyes of Russia* (London: Sidgwick & Jackson, 1983) pp. 76–77.

78. Wright, *Spycatcher,* pp. 128ff.

79. Harry Houghton, *Operation Portland: The Autobiography of a Spy* (London: Rupert Hart-Davis, 1972).

80. Lonsdale, *Spy,* pp. 87, 118.

81. Gordievsky. There is a brief description of Molody's funeral in Agranovsky, "Profession: Foreigner."

82. See above, p. 406.

83. Thierry Wolton, *Le KGB en France* (Paris: Bernard Grasset, 1986), pp. 167–72.

84. John Barron, *KGB Today: The Hidden Hand* (London: Hodder & Stoughton, 1984), ch. 9. Additional information from Gordievsky who met both Tsymbal and Lazarev when they headed Directorate S (Illegals) in the 1960s and 1970s.

85. Barron, *KGB Today,* pp. 376–418. Gordievsky confirms that this meeting took place.

86. Roger Faligot and Pascal Krop, *La Piscine: The French Secret Service Since 1944* (Oxford: Basil Blackwell, 1989), pp. 213–21.

87. CIA, *The Rote Kapelle: The CIA's History of Soviet Intelligence and Espionage Networks in Western Europe 1936–1945* (Washington, DC: University Publications of America, 1979), pp. 82, 99–100, identifies Robinson as the controller of André Labarthe (code-named Jérome). Wright, *Spycatcher,* p. 239, reveals that Labarthe was identified as a Soviet agent from Venona decrypts. This has been confirmed to Christopher

Andrew by two retired intelligence officers in North America with former access to the Venona traffic.

88. Brief details of Labarthe's career appear in *Dictionnaire Commentée de l'Oeuvre du Général de Gaulle* (Paris: Plon, 1975).

89. Wolton, *Le KGB en France,* p. 168.

90. Wright, *Spycatcher,* p. 239: confirmed to Christopher Andrew by the sources referred to in n. 87. Cot's career as a Soviet agent does not, of course, reflect in any way on the distinguished political career of his son, Jean-Pierre Cot.

91. Robert Young, *In Command of France* (Cambridge, Mass: Harvard University Press, 1978), p. 174. Anthony Adamthwaite, *France and the Coming of the Second World War* (London: Frank Cass, 1977), pp. 235–36. Jacques Chastenet, *Le Déclin de la Troisième République 1931–1938* (Paris: Hachette, 1962), p. 168.

92. Unattributable interview with retired American intelligence officer.

93. J. B. Duroselle, *La décadence, 1932–1939* (Paris: Imprimerie Nationale, 1979), p. 474.

94. Unattributable interviews with retired American intelligence officers.

95. *Washington Post,* 25 June 1944. Wolton, *Le KGB en France,* p. 202.

96. Philip M. Williams, *French Politicians and Elections 1951–1969* (Cambridge University Press, 1970), p. 13.

97. Wright, *Spycatcher,* pp. 240–41. Labarthe died in 1970—not, as Wright claims, in the middle of the DST interrogation.

98. Heinz Höhne and Hermann Zolling, *The General Was a Spy* (London: Pan Books, 1972), pp. 182–83. Anthony Glees, *The Secrets of the Service* (London: Jonathan Cape, 1987), pp. 229–44.

99. Felfe's own unreliable account of his career is in Heinz Felfe, *Im Dienst des Gegners* (Hamburg, 1986). Cf. Höhne and Zolling, *The General Was a Spy,* pp. 221–29.

100. Rositzke, *KGB,* pp. 189–94.

101. Jefferson Adams, "Crisis and Resurgence: East German State Security," *International Journal of Intelligence and Counterintelligence,* vol. II (1988), no. 4.

102. Corson and Crowley, *New KGB,* pp. 258–62.

103. "Enthüllungen über die Spionage in Bundesgebiet," in *Bulletin des Presse- und Informationsamtes des Bundesregierung,* no. 100, 6 June 1959, p. 980. We are grateful for this reference to Professor Jefferson Adams.

104. Rositzke, *KGB,* pp. 182ff.

105. Interviews by Christopher Andrew with Yuri Rastvorov, Pyotr Deryabin and Yuri Nosenko. Petrov debrief, AAC, CRS A6283/XR1/56.

106. Cf. above, pp. 226–28.

107. George F. Kennan, *Memoirs 1950–1963* (New York: Pantheon, 1983), pp. 117–18.

108. See above, p. 228.

109. Kennan, *Memoirs,* vol. II, pp. 154–57. Kennan was declared persona non grata in October 1952, though chiefly for reasons unconnected with the bugging incident.

110. Richard Harris Smith, "The First Moscow Station: An Espionage Footnote to Cold War History," *International Journal of Intelligence and Counterintelligence,* vol. III (1989), no. 3. Peer de Silva, *Sub Rosa: The CIA and the Uses of Intelligence* (New York: Times Books, 1978), p. 68. Ronald Kessler, *Moscow Station* (New York: Scribner's, 1989), p. 35.

111. Charles E. Bohlen, *Witness to History 1919–1969* (London: Weidenfeld & Nicolson, 1973) p. 346.

112. Ibid., p. 345.

113. Interview with Yuri Nosenko by Christopher Andrew, 15 Nov. 1987.

114. Bohlen, *Witness to History,* p. 345. Kessler, *Moscow Station,* p. 28.

115. Barron, *KGB Today*, pp. 169–82. Interview with Yuri Nosenko by Christopher Andrew, 15 Nov. 1987.

116. Interview with Yuri Nosenko by Christopher Andrew, 15 Nov. 1987.

117. Interview with Yuri Nosenko.

118. See above, pp. 174ff.

119. Interview with Stan Levchenko by Christopher Andrew, Nov. 1987.

120. Barron, *KGB Today*, pp. 16–17.

121. Ilya Dzhirkvelov, *Secret Servant* (London: Collins, 1987), pp. 211–14.

122. Interviews with Yuri Nosenko, 15 Nov. 1987, and Pyotr Deryabin, 25 Nov. 1987.

123. According to a retired CIA officer, the French were warned about "their terrible comsec" after the foundation of NATO, because of Anglo-American fears of its vulnerability to KGB and GRU attack.

124. Wright, *Spycatcher*, p. 118.

125. Wolton, *Le KGB en France*, pp. 242–43.

126. Interviews with Yuri Rastvorov, Pyotr Deryabin and Yuri Nosenko.

127. Interviews with Deriabin and Nosenko.

128. Anatoli Golitsyn, *New Lies for Old* (New York: Dodd, Mead, 1984), pp. 46–48. Though we are unconvinced by the elaborate conspiracy theories constructed by Golitsyn after his defection in December 1961, we regard his earlier recollections as generally reliable. At certain points Gordievsky is able to provide corroboration.

129. Knight, *KGB*, pp. 64–65.

130. Unattributable U.S. interview.

131. Interview with Yuri Nosenko, 15 Nov. 1987.

132. Knight, *KGB*, pp. 55–57.

133. Yuri Nosenko interview, 15 Nov. 1987. Nosenko came into contact with the Special Section and Seleznyov when he rejoined the First (American) Department of the Second Chief Directorate in January 1960. His first priority, he was instructed, was "work against cipher clerks."

134. James Bamford, *The Puzzle Palace* (Boston: Houghton Mifflin, 1982), pp. 133–45.

135. Edward Jay Epstein, *Deception: The Invisible War Between the KGB and the CIA* (New York: Simon & Schuster, 1989), pp. 173–74.

136. Unattributable U.S. interviews. Christopher Andrew's information on this point differs from that of Epstein (*Deception*, p. 174), who believes that Dunlap had been a KGB agent since 1957, "having been compromised and recruited in Turkey." It was, however, only in the summer of 1960 that Dunlap's life-style, thanks to Soviet funds, suddenly improved dramatically. Gordievsky has no information on the Dunlap case.

137. Bamford, *Puzzle Palace*, pp. 151–53.

138. Ibid., pp. 153–54.

139. Barron, *KGB: The Secret Work of Soviet Secret Agents* (London: Bantam Books, 1974), ch. 10. Additional information from Yuri Nosenko, 15 Nov. 1987. Previous accounts of Johnson's espionage wrongly attribute his arrest to information from his wife, which, in fact, came from Nosenko after his defection. Nosenko's role is confirmed by a retired U.S. intelligence officer with personal knowledge of the case.

140. Golitsyn, *New Lies for Old*, pp. 50–51. The Disinformation Department in the KI, headed by Andrei Graur, had a total staff of only about five (AAC, CRS A6283/XR1/56). Once in the West, Golitsyn developed a bizarre conspiracy theory that interpreted all apparent tensions within the Soviet bloc—among them the Sino-Soviet split, the Prague Spring, and the rise of Solidarity in Poland—as parts of a gigantic deception devised by Agayants and his successors. Sadly, his theory convinced a number of conspiracy theorists in Western intelligence services.

141. AAC, CRS A6283/XR1/56 and 144.

142. Wolton, *Le KGB en France*, pp. 204–05.

143. Barron, *KGB*, pp. 234–36.

144. Golitsyn, *New Lies for Old*, pp. 48–50. Gordievsky is able to corroborate the main features of this account of the meeting.

145. See above, pp. 426–27.

146. Barron, *KGB*, p. 421. Department Thirteen was officially described as "attached to the FCD": a designation intended to indicate a greater degree of independence than that possessed by other FCD departments (Gordievsky).

147. The fullest account of Stashinsky's career is Karl Anders, *Murder to Order* (London: Ampersand, 1965). Stashinsky brought with him on his defection an official "Service Testimonial," attributing the award of the Order of the Red Banner to his "successful contribution to the solution of an important problem."

148. Anders, *Murder to Order*, p. 107.

149. See below, pp. 574–75.

150. Gordievsky. Cf. Timothy Ashby, *The Bear in the Backyard: Moscow's Caribbean Strategy* (Lexington, Mass: Lexington Books, 1987), chs. 1, 2.

151. Recent literature on Castro is ably analyzed in Malcolm Deas, "Spectacle of the Rats and Owls," *London Review of Books*, 2 June 1988.

152. Gordievsky.

153. Ashby, *Bear in the Backyard*, pp. 22–26.

154. Jan Sejna, *We Will Bury You* (London: Sidgwick & Jackson, 1982), pp. 45–50. General Sejna was in charge of arrangements for Raúl Castro's visit.

155. Gordievsky. The account of the first meeting between Shitov and Castro is by Nuñez Jiménez, who was present. Tad Szulc, *Fidel: A Critical Portrait* (London: Hutchinson, 1987), pp. 408–09.

156. Ashby, *Bear in the Backyard*, pp. 28–29.

157. Gordievsky.

158. Gordievsky.

159. Arnold L. Horelick, *The Cuban Missile Crisis: An Analysis of Soviet Calculations and Behavior* (Santa Monica: Rand Corporation, 1963), p. 53.

160. Shevchenko, *Breaking with Moscow*, p. 154.

161. The most reliable account of the Penkovsky episode, in our view, is Gordon Brook-Shepherd, *The Storm Birds* (London: Weidenfeld & Nicolson, 1988) chs. 9, 10.

162. Ibid, p. 135.

163. Peter S. Usowski, "John McCone and the Cuban Missile Crisis: A Persistent Approach to the Intelligence-Policy Relationship," *International Journal of Intelligence and Counterintelligence*, vol. II (1988), no. 4.

164. Bolshakov was first publicly identified as a KGB officer by Ilya Dzhirkvelov in "KGB 'Back Channel' Documented," *Disinformation*, Summer 1989, no. 12. The identification is confirmed by Gordievsky.

165. Georgi Bolshakov, "The Hot Line," *New Times*, 1989, nos. 4–6.

166. Edwin O. Guthman and Jeffrey Shulman (eds.), *Robert Kennedy in His Own Words: The Unpublished Recollections of the Kennedy Years* (New York: Bantam Books, 1988), pp. 258–61.

167. Bolshakov, "Hot Line," *New Times*, 1989, no. 4.

168. Bolshakov, "Hot Line," *New Times*, 1989, nos. 5–6.

169. James G. Blight and David A. Welch (eds.), *On the Brink: Americans and Soviets Re-Assess the Cuban Missile Crisis* (New York: Hill & Wang, 1989), p. 248.

170. Bolshakov, "Hot Line," *New Times*, 1989, no. 6.

171. Gordievsky.

172. David Detzer, *The Brink: Cuban Missile Crisis 1962* (New York: Crowell,

1979), pp. 236–37. Arthur M. Schlesinger Jr., *A Thousand Days* (Boston: Houghton Mifflin, 1965), p. 827.

173. Gordievsky.

174. Nosenko interview, 15 Nov. 1987. Cf. Brook-Shepherd, *Storm Birds,* ch. 10.

175. Desmond Ball and Robert Windren, "Soviet Signals Intelligence (Sigint): Organisation and Management," *Intelligence and National Security,* vol. IV (1989), no. 4.

176. Nosenko interview, 15 Nov. 1987. (Sasha is not to be confused with a less important American Sasha recruited in the early 1950s.) Nosenko's account of Sasha's career has been confirmed to Christopher Andrew by a retired U.S. government official. Because of fears in the CIA that Nosenko was a plant—fears which led to his incarceration for three years—his lead on Sasha was not followed up until after his interrogation. Sasha, by then a major, was interrogated and fully investigated; his service career was brought to an end. But the evidence against him was insufficient for prosecution.

177. Nosenko interview, 15 Nov. 1987.

178. Dzhirkvelov, *Secret Servant,* pp. 65, 147.

Chapter 12. The Brezhnev Era: The East, the Third World, and the West (1964–72/73)

1. Gordievsky.

2. Sergei Nikitovich Khrushchev's memoirs of his father's fall from power were serialized in *Ogonek* in 1988.

3. Aleksei Adzhubei, "Retracing an Anniversary from Contemporary History," *Ogonek,* October 1989.

4. See the account by Khrushchev's son serialized in *Ogonek* in 1988.

5. Amy W. Knight, *The KGB: Police and Politics in the Soviet Union* (London: Unwin Hyman, 1988), pp. 65–69, 79ff. Geoffrey Hosking, *A History of the Soviet Union* (London: Fontana, 1985), ch. 13.

6. Zhores Medvedev, *Andropov: His Life and Death,* rev. ed. (Oxford: Basil Blackwell, 1984), pp. 46ff.

7. Aleksandr Solzhenitsyn, *The Oak and the Calf* (London: Collins, 1980), p. 102.

8. Medvedev, *Andropov,* p. 55. *Evening Standard,* 16 May 1967.

9. K. Svetitsky and S. Sokolov, "I would cope with any work," *Ogonek,* June 1989.

10. Medvedev, *Andropov,* p. 56.

11. Svetitsky and Sokolov, "I would cope with any work," *Ogonek,* June 1989.

12. Hosking, *History of the Soviet Union,* pp. 423–24, 450.

13. Adzhubei, "Retracing an Anniversary."

14. Gordievsky.

15. Zdeněk Mlynář, "That August of 1968," *Moscow News,* 1989, no. 50.

16. Gordievsky.

17. František August and David Rees, *Red Star over Prague* (London: Sherwood Press, 1984), pp. 125–29.

18. Gordievsky. His sources on KGB operations during the Prague Spring included the Center's veteran Czechoslovak expert in the mid-1980s, Anatoli Rusakov, who was posted to Prague in 1968.

19. Gordievsky.

20. August and Rees, *Red Star over Prague,* p. 128.

21. Interviews with Kalygin in *Komsomolskaya Pravda,* 20 June 1990, and *Moscow News,* 1990, no. 25.

22. Knight, *KGB,* pp. 292–93.

23. August and Rees, *Red Star over Prague,* pp. 127–28. Karen Dawisha, *The*

Kremlin and the Prague Spring (Berkeley, Ca.: University of California Press, 1984), p. 205.

24. Dawisha, *Kremlin and the Prague Spring,* pp. 236–38.
25. Ibid., pp. xi, 360ff.
26. Andrei Gromyko, *Memories* (London: Hutchinson, 1989), pp. 202–03.
27. Gordievsky.
28. Gordievsky.
29. Dawisha, *Kremlin and the Prague Spring,* pp. 319–20. August and Rees, *Red Star over Prague,* pp. 134–35.
30. Gordievsky.
31. Dawisha, *Kremlin and the Prague Spring,* chs. 12, 13.
32. *Pravda,* 19 Oct. 1968.
33. Solzhenitsyn, *The Oak and the Calf,* p. 220.
34. Dawisha, *Kremlin and the Prague Spring,* p. 217. *Pravda,* 19 July 1968.
35. Adzhubei, "Retracing an Anniversary."
36. Medvedev, *Andropov,* pp. 66–67.
37. Gordievsky.
38. Hosking, *History of the Soviet Union,* pp. 425–26. Richard Owen, *Crisis in the Kremlin* (London: Victor Gollancz, 1986), p. 91.
39. Gordievsky.
40. Gordievsky.
41. Gordievsky.
42. Philip Short, *The Dragon and the Bear* (London: Hodder & Stoughton, 1982), p. 148.
43. Ibid., p. 188.
44. Gordievsky.
45. There are vivid descriptions of the Cultural Revolution, viewed from two differing political perspectives, in Short, *Dragon and the Bear,* and Jean Esmein, *The Chinese Cultural Revolution* (London: André Deutsch, 1975).
46. Gordievsky.
47. Robin Edmonds, *Soviet Foreign Policy: The Brezhnev Years* (Oxford University Press, 1983), pp. 48–49. John Barron, *KGB: The Secret Work of Soviet Secret Agents* (London: Bantam Books, 1974), p. 243.
48. Gordievsky.
49. Barron, *KGB,* p. 243.
50. Gordievsky.
51. Gamal Abdel Nasser, *The Philosophy of the Revolution* (Cairo, 1954), p. 41.
52. On the development of Nasser's relations with the Soviet Union, see Mohamed Heikal, *Sphinx and Commissar* (London: Collins, 1978); and Karen Dawisha, *Soviet Foreign Policy Towards Egypt* (London: Macmillan, 1979), chs. 2, 3.
53. Anwar el-Sadat, *In Search of Identity* (London: Collins, 1978), p. 154. The CIA approach was doubtless reported to the KGB by Sani Sharaf, and probably by others also.
54. Gordievsky.
55. Dawisha, *Soviet Foreign Policy Towards Egypt,* chs. 2, 3.
56. Barron, *KGB,* pp. 69–73. Vladimir Sakharov, *High Treason* (New York: Ballantine Books, 1981), p. 193. Gamal Hammad, *The Hidden Government in the Era of Abdel Nasser* (in Arabic: Cairo, 1986), generally supports the evidence of Barron and Sakharov.
57. Gordievsky.
58. On Sharaf's phone-tapping see Sadat, *In Search of Identity,* p. 216.
59. Heikal, *Sphinx and Commissar,* pp. 226–27. Sharaf added a long quotation from "the great leader Lenin."

60. See Sergei Khrushchev's memoirs, serialized in *Ogonek*, 1988.
61. Gordievsky.
62. Gordievsky.
63. Robert Stephens, *Nasser: A Political Biography* (New York: Simon & Schuster, 1971), ch. 18.
64. Gordievsky.
65. Mohamed Heikal, *The Road to Ramadan* (London: Collins, 1975), pp. 83ff.
66. Gordievsky. Golubev later became first deputy head of Directorate K with the rank of general. His subsequent exploits included helping to poison Georgi Markov in 1978 and interrogating Gordievsky in 1985. See above, p. 11, and below, p. 645.
67. Heikal, *Sphinx and Commissar*, pp. 282–83.
68. Gromyko, *Memories*, p. 270.
69. Heikal, *Sphinx and Commissar*, p. 216.
70. Sadat, *In Search of Identity*, p. 206.
71. Ibid., pp. 223–25.
72. Gordievsky.
73. Sakharov, *High Treason*. See also Barron, *KGB*, ch. 2.
74. Gordievsky. Heikal, *Sphinx and Commissar*, chs. 14, 15.
75. B. N. Mullik, *The Chinese Betrayal* (Bombay: Allied Publishers, 1971), p. 110.
76. B. N. Mullik, *My Years with Nehru 1948–1964* (Bombay: Allied Publishers, 1972), pp. 60–61.
77. Jawaharlal Nehru, *The Discovery of India* (New York: John Day, 1946), p. 17.
78. Alexander Gorev, *Jawaharlal Nehru* (Moscow: Novosti, 1989), pp. 37, 48.
79. Gordievsky.
80. Ilya Dzhirkvelov, *Secret Servant* (London: Collins, 1987), p. 303.
81. Press reports of speech to parliament by Home Minister Chavan on 13 Dec. 1967, revealing Modin's role in the forgery campaign.
82. Barron, *KGB*, p. 237.
83. See below, p. 630.
84. John Barron, *KGB Today: The Hidden Hand* (London: Hodder & Stoughton, 1984), pp. 43, 271ff. Clive Rose, *The Soviet Propaganda Network* (London: Pinter, 1989), pp. 57–58.
85. Richard H. Shultz and Roy Godson, *Dezinformatsia: Active Measures in Soviet Strategy* (Oxford: Pergamon-Brassey, 1984), p. 124.
86. Rose, *Soviet Propaganda Network*, pp. 57–79. Other leading Soviet international front organizations included the Afro-Asian People's Solidarity Organization, Christian Peace Conference, International Association of Democratic Lawyers, International Federation of Resistance Fighters, International Institute for Peace, International Organization of Journalists, International Radio and Television Organization, International Union of Students, Women's International Democratic Federation, World Federation of Democratic Youth, World Federation of Scientific Workers, World Federation of Teachers, World Federation of Trade Unions.
87. Shultz and Godson, *Dezinformatsia*, p. 125.
88. Gordievsky.
89. On the treaty negotiations, see S. Nihal Singh, *The Yogi and the Bear* (London: Mansell, 1986), ch. 5; and Robert C. Horn, *Soviet-Indian Relations: Issues and Influence* (New York: Praeger, 1982), chs. 2, 3.
90. T. N. Kaul, *Reminiscences Discreet and Indiscreet* (New Delhi: Lancers, 1982), p. 255.
91. As a Novosti pamphlet acknowledges: "Given the situation on the Indian subcontinent, the Treaty was regarded everywhere as Soviet backing for Indira Gandhi's government." Alexander Gorev, *Indira Gandhi* (Moscow: Novosti, 1989), p. 40.

92. Singh, *The Yogi and the Bear,* pp. 89–96. Horn, *Soviet-Indian Relations,* p. 73.

93. Barron, *KGB Today,* p. 106; and Gordievsky.

94. Gordievsky.

95. Singh, *The Yogi and the Bear,* p. 235.

96. Daniel Patrick Moynihan, *A Dangerous Place* (London: Secker & Warburg, 1979), p. 41.

97. Singh, *The Yogi and the Bear,* pp. 245, 313.

98. Gordievsky.

99. Gordievsky.

100. Gordievsky.

101. Hugh Thomas, *The Cuban Revolution* (New York: Harper & Row, 1977), pp. 701–02, 719–20.

102. *Granma,* 28 and 30 Jan. 1968: quoted in Paul D. Bethel, *The Losers* (New Rochelle, NY: Arlington House, 1969), pp. 546–47.

103. Timothy Ashby, *The Bear in the Backyard: Moscow's Caribbean Strategy* (Lexington, Mass.: Lexington Books, 1987), p. 46. Bethel, *The Losers,* p. 551.

104. Gordievsky.

105. Thomas, *Cuban Revolution,* pp. 701–02, 719–20. Ashby, *Bear in the Backyard,* pp. 50–51.

106. U.S. Congress, Senate Committee on the Judiciary, *The Role of Cuba in International Terrorism and Subversion* (Washington, DC, 1982). Ashby, *Bear in the Backyard,* pp. 57ff. Further information from Gordievsky.

107. Thomas, *Cuban Revolution,* p. 657.

108. Gordievsky.

109. John Ranelagh, *The Agency* (London: Weidenfeld & Nicolson, 1986), p. 520.

110. Gordievsky.

111. Edmonds, *Soviet Foreign Policy: The Brezhnev Years,* pp. 116–17.

112. Gordievsky.

113. See, e.g., Mikhail Belyat, *Salvador Allende* (Moscow: Novosti, 1988).

114. H. Michael Erisman, *Cuba's International Relations* (Boulder/London: Westview, 1985), chs. 2, 3.

115. *Granma Weekly Review,* 16 Sept. 1973.

116. See below, pp. 554ff.

117. Paul Thomas, *Le KGB en Belgique* (Brussels: Editions J. M. Collet, 1987), pp. 89–100.

118. Josef Frolik, *The Frolik Defection* (London: Leo Cooper, 1975).

119. Harry Rositzke, *The KGB: Eyes of Russia* (London: Sidgwick & Jackson, 1983), pp. 196, 183–84.

120. Jefferson Adams, "East Bloc Intelligence in the FRG 1968–1986," paper to 1989 London Convention of the International Studies Association. See pp. 449–50.

121. Gordievsky. Chizhov's abrupt return to Moscow in 1966 was due to a brain hemorrhage.

122. Frolik, *Frolik Defection,* p. 82.

123. Nigel West, *A Matter of Trust* (London: Weidenfeld & Nicolson, 1982), p. 171. Gordon Brook-Shepherd, *The Storm Birds* (London: Weidenfeld & Nicolson, 1988), p. 198.

124. Gordievsky.

125. West, *A Matter of Trust,* pp. 115–19.

126. Ibid., pp. 130–31. Peter Wright, *Spycatcher* (New York: Viking, 1987), pp. 239–40.

127. Gordievsky.

128. Report of the Security Commission, June 1965, *Cmnd.* 2722 (1965). Gor-

dievsky is confident this was a GRU case. Cf. Chapman Pincher, *Too Secret Too Long* (London: NEL, 1985), pp. 421–23. West, *A Matter of Trust,* pp. 127–29.

129. Report of the Security Commission, Nov. 1968, *Cmnd.* 3856 (1968). West, *A Matter of Trust,* pp. 161–62. Pincher, *Too Secret Too Long,* p. 463.

130. Report of the Security Commission, May 1973, *Cmnd.* 5362 (1973).

131. Frolik, *Frolik Defection,* pp. 42–46. August and Rees, *Red Star over Prague,* pp. 90–91. West, *A Matter of Trust,* p. 165. Pincher, *Too Secret Too Long,* p. 468.

132. Frolik, *Frolik Defection,* pp. 58, 96–97.

133. Pincher, *Too Secret Too Long,* pp. 465–66.

134. Frolik, *Frolik Defection,* p. 98.

135. Wright, *Spycatcher,* p. 362.

136. John Stonehouse, *Ralph* (London: Jonathan Cape, 1982).

137. Chapman Pincher, *Their Trade Is Treachery* (London: Sidgwick & Jackson, 1981), pp. 198–205. Wright, *Spycatcher,* p. 361. Christopher Andrew, *Secret Service: The Making of the British Intelligence Community* (London: Heinemann, 1985), p. 369.

138. Frolik, *Frolik Defection,* p. 97.

139. V as in "Victor," not the Roman numeral 5.

140. Barron, *KGB,* pp. 110, 431ff. Idem, "They Spied for the Free World," *Reader's Digest,* May 1985. Pincher, *Too Secret Too Long,* pp. 488–90. Brook-Shepherd, *Storm Birds,* pp. 197–99.

141. Gordievsky.

142. Report of the Security Commission, May 1983, *Cmnd.* 8876 (1983), p. 13.

143. John Barron, *Breaking the Ring* (New York: Avon Books, 1988), pp. 153ff.

144. *Cmnd.* 8876 (1983), ch. 6.

145. Gordievsky.

146. Pincher, *Too Secret Too Long,* p. 558.

147. *Cmnd.* 8876 (1983).

148. Howard Blum, *I Pledge Allegiance* (New York: Simon & Schuster, 1987), p. 72.

149. Barron, *Breaking the Ring,* pp. 59–61.

150. Ibid., pp. 38, 153–58. Blum, *I Pledge Allegiance,* chs. 7, 8, 9.

151. See above, pp. 483–84.

152. See above, pp. 459, 517–18. Nigel West, *GCHQ* (London: Weidenfeld & Nicolson, 1986), p. 249.

153. Gordievsky.

154. Barron, *Breaking the Ring,* pp. 140–41.

155. Gordievsky.

156. *Cmnd.* 8876 (1983), ch. 5.

157. Barron, *Breaking the Ring,* ch. 9.

158. *Cmnd.* 8876 (1983).

159. Gordievsky.

160. Pincher, *Too Secret Too Long,* pp. 558–60 (quoting, inter alia, "NSA source"). West, *GCHQ,* pp. 250–55. Barron, *KGB Today,* pp. 230–32.

161. Gordievsky. *Cmnd.* 8876 (1983).

162. Barron, *Breaking the Ring,* pp. 23ff.

163. Ibid., p. 176.

Chapter 13. The Decline and Fall of Détente (1972–84)

1. Gordievsky.

2. Gordievsky.

3. Gordievsky.

4. *New Times,* 1989, no. 32.

5. Ibid.

6. Gordievsky.

7. Gordievsky, see below, pp. 541–43.

8. Adam B. Ulam, *Dangerous Relations* (New York: Oxford University Press, 1984), ch. 2.

9. Gordievsky.

10. Arkadi N. Shevchenko, *Breaking with Moscow* (New York: Ballantine Books, 1985), p. 375.

11. Ibid., pp. 256–62.

12. Andrei Gromyko, *Memories* (London: Hutchinson, 1989), p. 282.

13. Shevchenko, *Breaking with Moscow,* pp. 368ff.

14. Gromyko, *Memories,* p. 288.

15. Ulam, *Dangerous Relations,* pp. 166–68.

16. Gordievsky.

17. Ulam, *Dangerous Relations,* pp. 200–02. Shevchenko, *Breaking with Moscow,* p. 398.

18. Gromyko, *Memories,* p. 291.

19. Gordievsky.

20. Gordievsky. *Washington Post,* 2 Jan. 1982.

21. Gordievsky.

22. Gordievsky.

23. Gordievsky.

24. Gordievsky.

25. Gordievsky.

26. Karen Dawisha, *Soviet Foreign Policy Towards Egypt* (London: Macmillan, 1979), pp. 71–77.

27. Gordievsky.

28. A. A. Gromyko and B. N. Ponomarev (eds.), *Soviet Foreign Policy 1917–1980* (Moscow: Progress Publishers, 1981), vol. II, pp. 607–08.

29. Gromyko, *Memories,* pp. 222–23.

30. Gordievsky.

31. *Pravda,* 21 Sept. 1978.

32. Gordievsky.

33. *Washington Post,* 28 Nov. 1974. Roberta C. Goren, "The Soviet Attitude and Policy to International Terrorism," Ph.D. thesis (London School of Economics, 1982), p. 237.

34. Gordievsky.

35. Ion Mihai Pacepa, *Red Horizons* (Washington, DC: Regnery Gateway, 1987), ch. 1; interview with Pacepa by Christopher Andrew, Oct. 1987.

36. Gordievsky.

37. Gordievsky.

38. Christopher Dobson and Ronald Payne, *War Without End: The Terrorists: An Intelligence Dossier* (London: Sphere Books, 1987), pp. 172–82.

39. The 1981 report was one of a number captured by the Israelis. James Adams, *The Financing of Terror* (London: NEL, 1988), pp. 48–49.

40. Richard H. Shultz Jr., *The Soviet Union and Revolutionary Warfare* (Stanford Press: Hoover Institution, 1988), p. 89.

41. Gordievsky.

42. Gordievsky.

43. Gordievsky.

44. Gromyko, *Memories,* p. 274.

45. Gordievsky.

46. Gordievsky. In May 1990 the PDRY abandoned Marxism-Leninism and

merged with its northern neighbor, the Yemen Arab Republic, to form the Yemeni Republic. *Sunday Times,* 27 May 1990.

47. Gordievsky.

48. David Blundy and Andrew Lycett, *Qaddafi and the Libyan Revolution* (London: Weidenfeld & Nicolson, 1987).

49. Gordievsky.

50. Gordievsky. See also Tae-Hwan Kwak et al. (eds.), *The Two Koreas in World Politics* (Seoul: Kyungnam University Press, 1983).

51. Shultz, *Soviet Union and Revolutionary Warfare,* pp. 118ff.

52. Shevchenko, *Breaking with Moscow,* pp. 363–65.

53. Gordievsky.

54. Irving Kaplan (ed.), *Angola: A Country Study,* 2nd ed. (Washington, DC: U.S. Government Printing Office, 1979), Preface, chs. 3 and 4. Alexander R. Alexiev, "The Soviet Stake in Angola: Origins, Evolution, Prospects," in Dennis L. Bark (ed.), *The Red Orchestra,* vol. II: *The Case of Africa* (Stanford: Hoover Institution Press, 1988).

55. Gordievsky.

56. Gordievsky.

57. Thomas H. Henriksen, "The People's Republic of Mozambique," in Bark, *Red Orchestra,* vol. II.

58. Gordievsky.

59. Harold D. Nelson (ed.), *Mozambique: A Country Study,* 3rd ed. (Washington, DC: U.S. Government Printing Office, 1985), pp. 279–80.

60. Gordievsky.

61. Gordievsky.

62. Keith Somerville, "The Soviet Union and Zimbabwe: The Liberation Struggle and After," in R. Craig Nation and Mark V. Kauppi, *The Soviet Impact in Africa* (Lexington, Mass.: D. C. Heath, 1984).

63. Joshua Nkomo, *Nkomo: The Story of My Life* (London: Methuen, 1984), pp. 175–76.

64. Gordievsky.

65. Joachim Krause, "Soviet Arms Transfers to Sub-Saharan Africa," in Nation and Kauppi (eds.), *The Soviet Impact in Africa.*

66. Haggai Erlich, "The Soviet Union and Ethiopia: The Misreading of *Politica Scioana* and *Politica Tigrina,*" in Bark (ed.), *Red Orchestra,* vol. II. Harold D. Nelson and Irving Kaplan (eds.), *Ethiopia: A Country Study,* 3rd ed. (Washington, DC: U.S. Government Printing Office, 1981), pp. 261–63.

67. Gordievsky.

68. Gordievsky.

69. U.S. Senate, 97th Congress, 2nd Session, Report of the Chairman of the Subcommittee on Security and Terrorism, *Soviet, East German and Cuban Involvement in Fomenting Terrorism in Southern Africa* (Washington, DC, 1982). "South Africa: The Party Faithful," in *Africa Confidential,* vol. XXXI (1990), no. 1.

70. Gordievsky.

71. Gordievsky.

72. Gordievsky.

73. Gordievsky.

74. Gordievsky.

75. Gordievsky.

76. Tad Szulc, *Fidel: A Critical Portrait* (London: Hutchinson, 1987), pp. 533–34.

77. Herbert Romerstein, "Some Insights Derived from the Grenada Documents," in Bark (ed.), *Red Orchestra,* vol. I: "Instruments of Soviet Policy in Latin America and the Caribbean" (Stanford: Hoover Institution Press, 1986).

78. Gordievsky.

79. "Inside Communist Nicaragua: The Miguel Bolaños Transcripts," Heritage Foundation, *Backgrounder,* vol. I, pp. 78–79.

80. See the aerial photograph and map in Desmond Ball, *Soviet Signals Intelligence (Sigint),* Canberra Papers on Strategy and Defence, no. 47 (Canberra: Australian National University, 1989), pp. 31–35.

81. Robert A. Pastor, *Condemned to Repetition: The United States and Nicaragua* (Princeton University Press, 1987), ch. 12.

82. Gordievsky.

83. Ball, *Soviet Signals Intelligence,* pp. 27–29.

84. Gordievsky.

85. Gordievsky.

86. Gordievsky.

87. Gordievsky.

88. Ørnulf Tofte, *Spaneren* (Oslo: Gyldendal Norsk Forlag, 1987), pp. 130–53.

89. Gordievsky.

90. Tofte, *Spaneren,* pp. 130–53.

91. Gordievsky.

92. Tofte, *Spaneren,* p. 154.

93. Ibid., pp. 154–74. William Shawcross, "The New Model for the Perfect Spy," *The Spectator,* 7 June 1986.

94. Gordievsky.

95. Tofte, *Spaneren,* pp. 154–74. Shawcross, "New Model for the Perfect Spy." *Aftenposten* (Oslo), 5 March 1985, 30 April 1985.

96. Shawcross, "New Model for the Perfect Spy."

97. Ibid. Tofte, *Spaneren,* pp. 154–74.

98. Gordievsky.

99. Tofte, *Spaneren,* pp. 169–71.

100. Gordievsky.

101. See above, pp. 432–34.

102. Gordievsky helped prepare the annual reports on Finland from 1979 to 1981.

103. Ahti Karjalainen and Jukka Tarkka, *Presidentin Ministeri* (Helsinki: Otava, 1989), pp. 236–42.

104. Gordievsky.

105. Gordievsky.

106. Vladimir Kuzichkin, "Coups and Killings in Kabul," *Time,* 22 Nov. 1982. Kuzichkin defected from the FCD Directorate S (Illegals) in 1982.

107. Ulam, *Dangerous Relations,* p. 256.

108. Gordievsky.

109. Kuzichkin, "Coups and Killings in Kabul." John Barron, *KGB Today: The Hidden Hand* (London: Hodder & Stoughton, 1984), pp. 15–16, 447–48. The attempt to poison Amin is confirmed by Artem Borovik, "The Hidden War," *Ogonek,* 1989, no. 46, which cites the evidence of Amin's widow.

110. Gordievsky. Oleg Kalygin, then head of FCD Directorate K, was present at a meeting of senior FCD and GRU officers in August 1979 at which Kryuchkov declared, "Andropov is against our military involvement." But, according to Kalygin, Andropov "later became party to the decision to intervene." Interview with Kalygin, *Moscow News,* 1990, no. 25.

111. Borovik, "The Hidden War."

112. Gordievsky.

113. Kuzichkin, "Coups and Killings in Kabul."

114. *International Herald Tribune,* 24 Oct. 1989.

115. Kuzichkin, "Coups and Killings in Kabul."

116. Gordievsky.

117. Kuzichkin, "Coups and Killings in Kabul."

118. Ulam, *Dangerous Relations,* pp. 256–57.

119. Borovik, "The Hidden War."

120. Gordievsky.

121. Borovik, "The Hidden War."

122. *Sunday Times,* 10 April 1988.

123. Kuzichkin, "Coups and Killings in Kabul."

124. Gordievsky.

125. Gordievsky.

126. Amnesty International, *Afghanistan: Torture of Political Prisoners* (London: Amnesty International, 1986), p. 6.

127. Ibid., passim.

128. Oleg Kalygin, "Intelligence and Foreign Policy," *International Affairs* (Moscow), June 1989, p. 61.

129. Gordievsky.

130. Gordievsky.

131. Gordievsky.

132. Kevin Ruane, *The Polish Challenge* (London: BBC, 1982), p. 134.

133. Gordievsky.

134. Gordievsky.

135. Timothy Garton Ash, *The Polish Revolution: Solidarity 1980–82* (London: Jonathan Cape, 1983). Neal Ascherson, *The Struggles for Poland* (London: Michael Joseph, 1987), chs. 8, 9. Ruane, *Polish Challenge.*

136. Gordievsky.

137. Gordievsky.

138. Alexander M. Haig Jr., *Caveat* (London: Weidenfeld & Nicolson, 1984), p. 247.

139. Gordievsky.

140. Haig, *Caveat,* ch. 6.

141. Ibid., p. 219. David Dimbleby and David Reynolds, *An Ocean Apart* (London: BBC/Hodder & Stoughton, 1988), pp. 308, 317.

142. Gordievsky.

143. Gordievsky.

144. Gordievsky. On Fedorchuk's appointment, see also Jeremy R. Azrael, *The KGB in Kremlin Politics* (Los Angeles: Rand/UCLA, 1989), pp. 28–29.

145. Gordievsky.

146. Gordievsky.

147. Gordievsky.

148. Gordievsky.

149. *Pravda,* 28 Oct. 1982.

150. Geoffrey Hosking, *A History of the Soviet Union* (London: Fontana, 1985), pp. 450–51.

151. Gordievsky.

152. Gordievsky.

153. Gordievsky.

154. Gordievsky.

155. Seymour M. Hersh, *The Target Is Destroyed* (London: Faber, 1986), p. 16.

156. Gordievsky.

157. Gordievsky.

158. Gordievsky.

159. Gordievsky.

160. Gordievsky.

161. Hersh, *The Target Is Destroyed,* chs. 5–8.

162. Jonathan Haslam, "The KAL Shootdown (1983) and the State of Soviet Air Defence," *Intelligence and National Security,* vol. III (1988), no. 4.

163. Gordievsky.

164. Hersh, *The Target Is Destroyed.*

165. Gordievsky.

166. Gordievsky.

167. Hersh, *The Target Is Destroyed.*

168. Gordievsky.

169. *The World This Weekend,* BBC Radio 4, 18 Sept. 1983.

170. Gordievsky.

171. Hersh, *The Target Is Destroyed,* chs. 9–14.

172. Gordievsky.

173. R. W. Johnson, *Shootdown: The Verdict on KAL 007* (London: Chatto & Windus, 1986), Foreword.

174. Hersh, *The Target Is Destroyed,* pp. 190–91.

175. Gromyko, *Memories,* pp. 296–300.

176. Hersh, *The Target Is Destroyed,* p. 176.

177. Gordievsky.

178. Johnson, *Shootdown,* p. 106.

179. Gordievsky.

180. Gordievsky.

181. Gordievsky.

182. Gordievsky.

183. Gordievsky.

184. Gordievsky.

185. Gordievsky.

186. Gordievsky.

187. Gordievsky.

188. Gordievsky.

189. Gordievsky.

Chapter 14. The Gorbachev Era 1985–

1. Gordievsky.

2. Gordievsky.

3. Gordievsky.

4. Gordievsky.

5. Desmond Ball, *Soviet Signals Intelligence (Sigint),* Canberra Papers on Strategy and Defence, no. 47 (Canberra: Australian National University, 1989). Desmond Ball and Robert Windren, "Soviet Signals Intelligence (Sigint): Organization and Management," *Intelligence and National Security,* vol. IV (1989), no. 4.

6. Gordievsky.

7. *Time,* 10 July 1989. Cf. Ronald Kessler, *Moscow Station* (New York: Scribner's, 1989).

8. Ball, *Soviet Signals Intelligence,* pp. 131ff. Robert Woodward, *Veil: The Secret Wars of the CIA 1981–1987* (New York: Simon & Schuster, 1987), chs. 23, 24. On Operation Ivy Bells, cf. the interview with Chebrikov in *Pravda,* 2 Sept. 1988.

9. Gordievsky.

10. Gordievsky.

11. BBC, *SWB,* SU/0708 B/3, 9 March 1990. "KGB Without Secrets," *Trud,* 23 Feb. 1990.

12. Gordievsky.

13. Gordievsky.

14. Gordievsky.
15. Gordievsky.
16. Gordievsky.
17. BBC, *SWB*, SU/0606 C2/9, 6 Nov. 1989.
18. Gordievsky.
19. Gordievsky.
20. Gordievsky.
21. Gordievsky.
22. Gordievsky.
23. Shebarshin was first publicly identified by Tass as "head of Soviet foreign intelligence" on 28 Feb. 1990; BBC, *SWB*, SU/0703 A1/7. It was, however, possible to deduce his appointment earlier from the news of his promotion to the rank of KGB deputy chairman; *Pravda*, 15 March 1989.
24. Gordievsky.
25. BBC, *SWB*, SU/0708 B/3, 9 March 1990.
26. Gordievsky.
27. For the intelligence supplied by Farewell, see Philip Hanson, *Soviet Industrial Espionage: Some New Information* (London: RIIA, 1987); U.S. Government, *Soviet Acquisition of Militarily Significant Western Technology: An Update*, September 1985. Though probably shot in 1983, Farewell's execution was not announced in the Center until January 1985. Gordievsky was visiting Moscow at the time.
28. Gordon Brook-Shepherd, *The Storm Birds* (London: Weidenfeld & Nicolson, 1988), p. 260.
29. Hanson, *Soviet Industrial Espionage*, pp. 10, 23.
30. Christopher Andrew, "New Look Russia: Same Old Spies," *Daily Telegraph*, 23 May 1989. *International Herald Tribune*, 22 Feb. 1990. *Daily Telegraph*, 5 March 1990.
31. Ernest Gellner, Introduction to Oleg Glebov and John Crowfoot (eds.), *The Soviet Empire: Its Nations Speak Out* (London: Harwood Academic, 1989).
32. *Pravda*, 11 Sept. 1987.
33. Christopher Andrew, "How the KGB plans to come in from the cold," *Daily Telegraph*, 28 Dec. 1988.
34. Televised report to 19th All-Union CPSU Conference, 28 June 1988, BBC, *SWB*, SU/0191 C/21, 30 June 1988.
35. *Mezhdunarodnaya Zhizn*, Oct. 1988.
36. TV interview, 24 June 1989. BBC, *SWB*, SU/0496 B/1, 30 June 1989.
37. Interview in *New Times*, 1989, no. 32.
38. Supreme Soviet Hearings, 14 July 1989. BBC, *SWB*, SU/0513 C/1-6, 20 July 1989. Tass report, 14 June 1990.
39. Interview with Shebarshin, *Pravda*, 22 April 1990.
40. Gordievsky.
41. Herbert Romerstein, *Soviet Active Measures and Propaganda*, Mackenzie Institute Paper no. 17 (Toronto, 1989), pp. 14-15, 25-26. WPC, *Peace Courier*, 1989, no. 4.
42. USIA, *Recent Appearances of Soviet Disinformation*, 6 Oct. 1989. USIA, *Soviet Active Measures in the Era of Glasnost*, March 1988. Todd Leventhal (USIA), "An Overview of Soviet Active Measures, Operations and Instrumentalities," draft conference paper, Oct. 1989.
43. U.S. Department of State, *Soviet Influence Activities: A Report on Active Measures and Propaganda*, Aug. 1987.
44. USIA, *Recent Appearances of Soviet Disinformation*, 6 Oct. 1989.
45. *Monkey Business. AIDS: The Africa Story*, Channel 4, 22 Jan. 1990. *New Worker*, 2 Feb. 1990.

46. USIA, *Recent Appearances of Soviet Disinformation,* 6 Oct. 1989.

47. Gordievsky.

48. Christopher Dobson and Ronald Payne, *War Without End: The Terrorists: An Intelligence Dossier* (London: Sphere Books, 1987), p. 192.

49. Gordievsky.

50. Gordievsky.

51. Gordievsky.

52. Interview in *New Times,* 1989, no. 32.

53. *Daily Telegraph,* 5 Dec. 1988.

54. Interview in *New Times,* 1989, no. 32.

55. *Daily Telegraph,* 5 Dec. 1988, and other press reports.

56. Televised interview, 24 June 1989. BBC, *SWB,* SU/0496 B/1, 30 June 1989.

57. Speech to Supreme Soviet, 14 July 1989. BBC, *SWB,* SU/0513 C/1, 20 July 1989. Cf. interview in *New Times,* 1989, no. 32.

58. *Izvestia,* 27 Oct. 1989.

59. Interview with Shcherbak, broadcast 26 Oct. 1989. BBC, *SWB,* SU/0601/A1/3, 31 Oct. 1989.

60. Interview in *New Times,* 1989, no. 32.

61. Oleg Kalygin, "Intelligence and Foreign Policy," *International Affairs,* June 1989.

62. See above, pp. 541–43.

63. Mikhail Lyubimov, "From Intelligence War to Information Exchange," *Moscow News,* 1989, no. 9.

64. "Moscow Diary," *Moscow News,* 1990, no. 15.

65. Interview with Kalygin, *Moscow News,* 1990, no. 25.

66. Kalygin, "Intelligence and Foreign Policy."

67. Interview with Kalygin, *Komsomolskaya Pravda,* 20 June 1990. The KGB retaliated by stripping Kalygin of his major-general's rank and beginning a campaign of character assassination against him; see statement by KGB Public Relations Department in *Pravda,* 23 June 1990.

68. Gordievsky.

69. On the Pope's visits to Poland, see Neil Ascherson, *The Struggles for Poland* (London: Michael Joseph, 1987), pp. 198–99, 226.

70. Gordievsky.

71. Gordievsky.

72. Gordievsky.

73. Gordievsky.

74. Unattributable interview in USA by Christopher Andrew.

75. BBC, *SWB,* SU/0477 C/18, 8 June 1989.

76. BBC, *SWB,* SU/0679 B/10, 3 Feb. 1990.

77. "What's Behind the KGB's Figures?," *Moscow News,* 1990, nos. 8–9. Christopher Andrew, "Can the KGB ever escape the horrors of its past?," *Daily Telegraph,* 7 June 1989.

78. "Katyn: A Difficult Road to the Truth," *Moscow News,* 1990, no. 16.

79. BBC, *SWB,* SU/0590 A1/1–4, 18 Oct. 1989.

80. Gordievsky.

81. See above, pp. 503ff.

82. *Counterpoint,* vol. V, no. 8, Jan. 1990.

83. *New Times,* 1989, no. 22.

84. Gordievsky.

85. Unattributable interview by Christopher Andrew with a reliable American intelligence source, citing Yurchenko.

Bibliography

A. Unpublished Sources

Detailed references to documents consulted in American, Australian, Austrian, British, French, and German archives are given in the notes. Documents in the Public Record Office and other Crown copyright material are quoted by permission of the Controller of HM Stationery Office. KGB archives, the most important unpublished source for this volume, remain closed; see the article on these archives by Oleg Gordievsky in *Intelligence and National Security,* vol. VI (1991) no. 1.

B. Published Sources

Books and articles listed here are limited to those cited in the notes. The two most important Soviet works on the KGB referred to in the text and notes remain unpublished and highly classified: the in-house history of the KGB completed in 1978 under the direction of General Grigori Fyodorovich Grigorenko, and the history of the First Chief Directorate completed in 1980, of which Gordievsky was one of the authors. During the early years of the Gorbachev era, much of the most important Soviet writing on KGB history appeared as articles in newspapers and periodicals. These articles are listed here. References to other magazine and newspaper articles, to broadcasts, and to parliamentary reports and debates, appear only in the notes. Titles of articles in Russian periodicals are given in English translation.

Abramsky, C., and Beryl J. Williams, eds. *Essays in Honour of E. H. Carr.* London: Macmillan, 1974.

Accoce, Pierre, and Pierre Quet. *The Lucy Ring.* London: W. H. Allen, 1967.

Adams, James. *The Financing of Terror.* London: NEL, 1988.

Adams, Jefferson. "Crisis and Resurgence: East German State Security," *International Journal of Intelligence and Counterintelligence,* vol. II (1988), no. 4.

Adamthwaite, Anthony. *France and the Coming of the Second World War.* London: Frank Cass, 1977.

Adzhubei, Aleksei. "Retracing an Anniversary from Contemporary History," *Ogonek,* Oct. 1989.

Agabekov, Georgi. *OGPU.* New York: Brentano's, 1931.

Agranovsky, Valeri. "Profession: Foreigner," *Znamya,* Sept. 1988.

Akhmedov, Ismail. *In and Out of Stalin's GRU.* London: Arms & Armour Press, 1984.

Alexiev, Alexander R. "The Soviet Stake in Angola: Origins, Evolution, Prospects," in Dennis L. Bark (ed.), *The Red Orchestra,* vol. II: *The Case of Africa.* Stanford, Ca.: Hoover Institution Press, 1988.

Alliluyeva, Svetlana. *Only One Year.* London: Hutchinson, 1969.

Amnesty International. *Afghanistan: Torture of Political Prisoners.* London: Amnesty International, 1986.

Anders, Karl. *Murder to Order.* London: Ampersand, 1965.

Andrew, Christopher. *Théophile Delcassé and the Making of the Entente Cordiale.* London: Macmillan, 1968.

———. "Déchiffrement et diplomatie: le cabinet noir du Quai d'Orsay sous la Troisième République," *Relations Internationales,* 1976, no. 5.

———. "Codebreakers and Foreign Offices: The French, British and American Experience," in Christopher Andrew and David N. Dilks (eds.), *The Missing Dimension: Governments and Intelligence Communities in the Twentieth Century.* London: Macmillan, 1984.

———. "France and the German Menace," in Ernest R. May (ed.), *Knowing One's Enemies.* Princeton University Press, 1984.

———. *Secret Service: The Making of the British Intelligence Community,* 1st ed. London: Heinemann, 1985.

———. "F. H. Hinsley and the Cambridge Moles: Two Patterns of Intelligence Recruitment," in Richard Langhorne (ed.), *Diplomacy and Intelligence During the Second World War: Essays in Honour of F. H. Hinsley.* Cambridge University Press, 1985.

———, ed. *Codebreaking and Signals Intelligence.* London: Frank Cass, 1986.

———. "The Growth of the Australian Intelligence Community and the Anglo-American Connection," *Intelligence and National Security,* vol. IV (1989), no. 2.

———, and David N. Dilks, eds. *The Missing Dimension: Governments and Intelligence Communities in the Twentieth Century.* London: Macmillan, 1984.

———, and Harold James. "Willi Münzenberg, the Reichstag Fire and the Conversion of Innocents," in David Charters and Maurice Tugwell (eds.), *Deception in East-West Relations.* London: Pergamon-Brassey, 1990.

———, and Jeremy Noakes, eds. *Intelligence and International Relations.* Exeter University Press, 1987.

Andrianov, V. N. "Partisan Reconnaissance during the Years of the Great Patriotic War," *Voyenno-Istorichesky Zhurnal,* 1986, no. 8.

Angress, W. T. "The Takeover that Remained in Limbo: The German Experience 1918–1923," in Thomas Hammond (ed.), *The Anatomy of Communist Takeovers.* New Haven, Conn.: Yale University Press, 1975.

Armour, Ian. "Colonel Redl: Fact and Fantasy," *Intelligence and National Security,* vol. II (1987), no. 1.

Ascherson, Neal. *The Struggles for Poland.* London: Michael Joseph, 1987.

Ash, Timothy Garton. *The Polish Revolution: Solidarity 1980–82.* London: Jonathan Cape, 1983.

Ashby, Timothy. *The Bear in the Backyard: Moscow's Caribbean Strategy.* Lexington, Mass.: Lexington Books, 1987.

Astley, Joan Bright. *The Inner Circle.* London: Hutchinson, 1971.

Auden, W. H. *Spain.* London: Faber, 1937.

August, František, and David Rees. *Red Star over Prague.* London: Sherwood Press, 1984.

Avrich, Paul. *Kronstadt 1921.* Princeton University Press, 1971.

Azrael, Jeremy R. *The KGB in Kremlin Politics.* Los Angeles: Rand/UCLA, 1989.

Baidakov, A. "Facts on Intelligence. From the Archives of the Security Organs of the Soviet Union," *Pravda,* 9 May 1989.

Bailes, Kendall E. *Technology and Society under Lenin and Stalin.* Princeton University Press, 1978.

Bajanov, Boris. *Bajanov révèle Staline: souvenirs d'un ancien secrétaire de Staline.* Paris: Gallimard, 1979.

Ball, Desmond. *Soviet Signals Intelligence (Sigint).* Canberra Papers on Strategy and Defence, no. 47. Canberra: Australian National University, 1989.

———, and Robert Windren. "Soviet Signals Intelligence (Sigint): Organisation and Management," *Intelligence and National Security,* vol. IV (1989), no. 4.

Bamford, James. *The Puzzle Palace.* Boston: Houghton Mifflin, 1982.

Bark, Dennis L. (ed.). *The Red Orchestra,* vol. II: *The Case of Africa.* Stanford, Ca.: Hoover Institution Press, 1988.

Barron, John. *KGB: The Secret Work of Soviet Secret Agents.* London: Bantam Books, 1974.

———. *KGB Today: The Hidden Hand.* London: Hodder & Stoughton, 1984.

———. *Breaking the Ring.* New York: Avon Books, 1988.

Barsukov, N. "On the Way to the 20th Congress," *Pravda,* 10 Nov. 1989.

Beachley, David R. "Soviet radio-electronic combat in World War Two," *Military Review,* vol. LXI (1981), no. 3.

Beloff, Nora. *Tito's Flawed Legacy.* London: Victor Gollancz, 1985.

Belyat, Mikhail. *Salvador Allende.* Moscow: Novosti, 1988.

Bentley, Elizabeth. *Out of Bondage.* New York: Ballantine Books, 1988.

Bethel, Paul D. *The Losers.* New Rochelle, N.Y.: Arlington House, 1969.

Bethell, Nicholas. *The Great Betrayal.* London: Hodder & Stoughton, 1984.

Blight, James G., and David A. Welch (eds.). *On the Brink: Americans and Soviets Re-Assess the Cuban Missile Crisis.* New York: Hill & Wang, 1989.

Blum, Howard. *I Pledge Allegiance.* New York: Simon & Schuster, 1987.

Blundy, David, and Andrew Lycett. *Qaddafi and the Libyan Revolution.* London: Weidenfeld & Nicolson, 1987.

Blunt, Anthony. "From Bloomsbury to Marxism," *Studio International,* Nov. 1973.

Bohlen, Charles E. *Witness to History, 1919–1969.* London: Weidenfeld & Nicolson, 1973.

Bolshakov, Georgi. "The Hot Line," *New Times,* 1989, nos. 4–6.

Borovik, Artem. "The Hidden War," *Ogonek,* 1989, no. 46.

Bothwell, Robert, and J. L. Granatstein (eds.). *The Guzenko Transcripts.* Ottowa: Deneau, n.d.

Bower, Tom. *The Red Web*. London: Aurum, 1989.

Boyle, Andrew. *The Climate of Treason*. London: Hutchinson, 1979.

Braunbuch über Reichstagbrand und Hitlerterror. Frankfurt/Main: Röderberg Verlag, 1978.

Brogan, Hugh. *The Life of Arthur Ransome*. London: Jonathan Cape, 1984.

Brook-Shepherd, Gordon. *The Storm Petrels*. London: Collins, 1977.

———. *The Storm Birds*. London: Weidenfeld & Nicolson, 1988.

Brown Book on the Hitler Terror and the Burning of the Reichstag. London: Victor Gollancz, 1933.

Buber-Neumann, Margarete. *Von Potsdam nach Moskau: Stationen Eines Irrweges.* Cologne: Hohenheim, 1981.

Budenz, Louis. *This Is My Story*. New York: Whittlesey House, 1947.

Burlatsky, Fyodor. "Khrushchev: Sketches for a Political Portrait," *Literaturnaya Gazeta,* 24 Feb. 1988.

Calic, E. (ed.). *Der Reichstagbrand: Eine Wissenschaftliche Dokumentation.* Band II. Munich: K. G. Saur Verlag, 1978.

Calvocoressi, Peter. *Top Secret Ultra*. London: Cassell, 1980.

Campbell, Thomas M., and George C. Herring (eds.). *The Diaries of Edward R. Stettinius Jr., 1943–1946.* New York: New Viewpoints, 1975.

Canadian Royal Commission. *The Defection of Igor Guzenko*. Reprint of report of 27 June 1946, 3 vols. Laguna Hills, Ca.: Aegean Park Press, 1984.

Carew-Hunt, R. N. "Willi Muenzenberg," in David Footman (ed.), *International Communism.* St. Antony's Papers, no. 9. London: Chatto & Windus, 1960.

Carr, E. H. *The Bolshevik Revolution 1917–1923,* vol. III. London: Macmillan, 1953.

———. *Foundations of a Planned Economy,* vol. III. London: Macmillan, 1978.

Cavendish, Anthony. *Inside Intelligence*. London: privately printed, 1987.

Cecil, Robert. "The Cambridge Comintern," in Christopher Andrew and David N. Dilks (eds.), *The Missing Dimension*. London: Macmillan, 1984.

———. *A Divided Life*. London: Bodley Head, 1988.

Central Intelligence Agency, *The Rote Kapelle: The CIA's History of Soviet Intelligence and Espionage Networks in Western Europe, 1936–1945.* Washington, DC: University Publications of America, 1984.

Charters, David, and Maurice Tugwell (eds.). *Deception in East-West Relations.* London: Pergamon-Brassey, 1990.

Chastenet, Jacques. *Le Déclin de la Troisième République 1931–1938.* Paris: Hachette, 1962.

Churchill, Winston S. *Great Contemporaries*. London: Odhams, 1947.

———. *The Second World War,* vol. III. London: Cassell, 1950.

Clark, Ronald W. *Einstein: The Life and Times*. London: Hodder & Stoughton, 1973.

Clark, William. "Cabinet secrecy, collective responsibility and the British public's right to know about and participate in foreign policy-making," in Thomas M. Franck and Edward Weisband (eds.), *Secrecy and Foreign Policy*. Oxford University Press, 1974.

Clissold, Stephen. *Djilas: The Progress of a Revolutionary*. Hounslow: Maurice Temple-Smith, 1983.

Cohen, Stephen F. *Bukharin and the Bolshevik Revolution 1888–1938.* New York: Oxford University Press, 1980.

Cohn, Norman. *Warrant for Genocide*. London: Eyre & Spottiswoode, 1967.

Collier, Richard. *The War that Stalin Won*. London: Hamish Hamilton, 1983.

Colville, John. *The Fringes of Power*. London: Hodder & Stoughton, 1985.

Conquest, Robert. *The Great Terror: Stalin's Purge of the Thirties*. London: Macmillan, 1968.

———. *Inside Stalin's Secret Police: NKVD Politics 1936–1939.* London: Macmillan, 1985.

————. *The Harvest of Sorrow.* London: Hutchinson, 1986.

Cornelissen, Igor. *De GPOe op de Overtoom.* Amsterdam: Van Gennep, 1989.

Corson, William F., and Robert T. Crowley. *The New KGB,* 'updated' Quill ed. New York: William Morrow, 1986.

Costello, John. *Mask of Treachery.* London: Collins, 1988.

Cotic, Meir. *The Prague Trial.* New York: Herzl Press/Cornwall Books, 1987.

The Counter-Revolutionary Conspiracy of Imre Nagy and his Accomplices. Budapest: Information Bureau of the Council of Ministers, 1958.

Coutouvidis, John, and Jaime Reynolds. *Poland 1939–1947.* Leicester University Press, 1986.

Dallin, David J. *Soviet Espionage.* New Haven, Conn.: Yale University Press, 1955.

Davies, Norman. *God's Playground: A History of Poland,* vol. II. Oxford: Clarendon Press, 1981.

Dawisha, Karen. *Soviet Foreign Policy Towards Egypt.* London: Macmillan, 1979.

————. *The Kremlin and the Prague Spring.* Berkeley, Ca.: University of California Press, 1984.

Deacon, Richard. *A History of the British Secret Service.* London: Frederick Muller, 1969.

Deakin, F. W., and G. R. Storry. *The Case of Richard Sorge.* New York: Harper & Row, 1964.

Debo, Richard K. "Lockhart Plot or Dzerzhinskii Plot?" *Journal of Modern History,* vol. XLIII, 1971.

————. *Revolution and Survival: The Foreign Policy of Soviet Russia 1917–18.* Liverpool University Press, 1979.

Dedijer, Vladimir. *Tito Speaks: His Self-Portrait and Struggle with Stalin.* London: Weidenfeld & Nicolson, 1953.

Degras, Jane (ed.). *Documents on Soviet Foreign Policy,* vol. I: 1951, vol. II: 1952, vol. III: 1953. London: Oxford University Press.

————, ed. *The Communist International 1919–1942. Documents,* vol. I: 1956, vol. III: 1965. London: Oxford University Press.

Jonge, Alex de. *Stalin and the Shaping of the Soviet Union.* London: Collins, 1986.

Dementyeva, I. A., N. I. Agayants and Y. Y. Yakovlev. *Tovarishch Zorge.* Moscow: Sovetskaya Rossiya, 1965.

Denniston, A. G. "The Government Code and Cypher School Between the Wars," in Christopher Andrew (ed.), *Codebreaking and Signals Intelligence.* London: Frank Cass, 1986.

Deryabin, Pyotr, and Frank Gibney. *The Secret World,* rev. ed. New York: Ballantine Books, 1982.

de Silva, Peer. *Sub Rosa: The CIA and the Uses of Intelligence.* New York: Times Books, 1978.

Detzer, David. *The Brink: Cuban Missile Crisis 1962.* New York: Crowell, 1979.

Deutscher, Isaac. *The Prophet Unarmed: Trotsky 1921–1928.* London: Oxford University Press, 1959.

————. *Stalin: A Political Biography.* New York: Vintage Books, 1962.

————. *The Prophet Outcast: Trotsky 1929–1940.* London: Oxford University Press, 1963.

Dictionnaire Commentée de l'Oeuvre du Général de Gaulle. Paris: Plon, 1975.

Dilks, David N. (ed.). *The Diaries of Alexander Cadogan O. M., 1938–1945.* London: Cassell, 1971.

Dimbleby, David, and David Reynolds. *An Ocean Apart.* London: BBC/Hodder & Stoughton, 1988.

Djilas, Milovan. *Conversations with Stalin.* London: Rupert Hart-Davis, 1962.

————. *Tito: The Story from the Inside.* London: Weidenfeld & Nicolson, 1981.

————. *Rise and Fall.* London: Macmillan, 1985.

Dobson, Christopher, and Ronald Payne. *War Without End: The Terrorists: An Intelligence Dossier.* London: Sphere Books, 1987.

Drachkovitch, Milorad M., and Branko Lazitch (eds.). *The Comintern: Historical Highlights.* New York: Praeger, 1966.

Driberg, Tom. *Guy Burgess: A Portrait with Background.* London: Weidenfeld & Nicolson, 1956.

Duroselle, J.-B. *La décadence, 1932–1939.* Paris: Imprimerie Nationale, 1979.

Dzhirkvelov, Ilya. *Secret Servant.* London: Collins, 1987.

Dziak, John J. *Chekisty.* Lexington, Mass.: Lexington Books, 1987.

Edmonds, Robin. *Soviet Foreign Policy: The Brezhnev Years.* Oxford University Press, 1983.

Elwood, R. C. *Roman Malinovsky: A Life without a Cause.* Newtonville, Mass.: Oriental Research Partners, 1977.

Epstein, Edward Jay. *Deception: The Invisible War Between the KGB and the CIA.* New York: Simon & Schuster, 1989.

Erickson, John. *The Road to Berlin.* London: Weidenfeld & Nicolson, 1983.

————. "Threat Identification and Strategic Appraisal by the Soviet Union 1930–1941," in Ernest R. May (ed.), *Knowing One's Enemies.* Princeton University Press, 1984.

————. *The Road to Stalingrad.* London: Panther Books, 1985.

Erisman, H. Michael. *Cuba's International Relations.* Boulder, Col./London: Westview, 1985.

Erlich, Haggai. "The Soviet Union and Ethiopia: The Misreading of *Politica Scioana* and *Politica Tigrina,*" in Dennis L. Bark (ed.), *The Red Orchestra.* vol. II: *The Case of Africa.* Stanford, Ca.: Hoover Institution Press, 1988.

Esmein, Jean. *The Chinese Cultural Revolution.* London: André Deutsch, 1975.

Faligot, Roger, and Pascal Krop. *La Piscine: The French Secret Service Since 1944.* Oxford: Basil Blackwell, 1989.

Feis, Herbert. *Between War and Peace.* Princeton University Press, 1960.

Felfe, Heinz. *Im Dienst des Gegners.* Hamburg, 1986.

Filby, P. William. "Bletchley Park and Berkeley Street," *Intelligence and National Security,* vol. III (1988), no. 2.

Fischer, Ruth. *Stalin and German Communism.* London: Oxford University Press, 1949.

Fomin, Fyodor Timofeevich. *Zapiski Starogo Chekista.* 2nd ed. Moscow: Politizdat, 1964.

Foot, M. R. D. *SOE in France.* London: HMSO, 1966.

————. *SOE.* London: BBC, 1984.

Footman, David (ed.). *International Communism.* St Antony's Papers, no. 9. London: Chatto & Windus, 1960.

Franck, Thomas M., and Edward Weisband (eds.). *Secrecy and Foreign Policy.* Oxford University Press, 1974.

Frolik, Josef. *The Frolik Defection.* London: Leo Cooper, 1975.

Fuller, Jr., William C. "The Russian Empire," in Ernest R. May (ed.), *Knowing One's Enemies.* Princeton University Press, 1984.

Gati, Charles. *Hungary and the Soviet Bloc.* Durham, N.C.: Duke University Press, 1986.

Gellner, Ernest. Introduction to Oleg Glebov and John Crowfoot (eds.), *The Soviet Empire: Its Nations Speak Out.* London: Harwood Academic, 1989.

Gerson, Leonard D. *The Secret Police in Lenin's Russia.* Philadelphia: Temple University Press, 1976.

Getty, J. Arch. *Origins of the Great Purges.* Cambridge University Press, 1985.

Gilbert, Martin. *Winston S. Churchill,* vol. V: 1976, vol. VII: 1986. London: Heinemann.

———. *The Second World War.* London: Weidenfeld & Nicolson, 1989.

Ginsburg, Evgenia. *Into the Whirlwind.* London: 1967.

Girault, René. *Emprunts russes et investissements français en Russie 1887–1914.* Paris: 1973.

Gladkov, Teodor, and Mikhail Smirnov. *Menzhinsky.* Moscow: Molodaya Gvardiya, 1969.

Glantz, David. "The Role of Intelligence in Soviet Military Strategy During the Second World War," paper to Fourth U.S. Army War College International Conference on Intelligence and Strategy, May 1989.

Glebov, Oleg, and John Crowfoot (eds.). *The Soviet Empire: Its Nations Speak Out.* London: Harwood Academic, 1989.

Glees, Anthony. *The Secrets of the Service.* London: Jonathan Cape, 1987.

Golinkov, David. *The Secret War Against Soviet Russia.* Moscow: Progress Publishers, 1981.

Golitsyn, Anatoli. *New Lies for Old.* New York: Dodd, Mead, 1984.

Golovin, Igor. "They Awakened the Genie," *Moscow News,* 1989, no. 41.

Gorev, Alexander. *Indira Gandhi.* Moscow: Novosti, 1989.

———. *Jawaharlal Nehru.* Moscow: Novosti, 1989.

Gorodetsky, Gabriel. *Stafford Cripps' Mission to Moscow 1940–42.* Cambridge University Press, 1984.

Gowing, Margaret. *Britain and Atomic Energy.* London: HMSO, 1964.

Grant, Natalie. "Deception on a Grand Scale," *Journal of Intelligence and Counterintelligence,* vol. I (1986–8), no. 4.

Grey, Marina. *Le général meurt à minuit.* Paris: Plon, 1981.

Grigorenko, Petro G. *Memoirs.* trans. T.P. Whitney. London: Harvill Press, 1983.

Gromyko, A. A., and B. N. Ponomarev (eds.). *Soviet Foreign Policy 1917–1980.* Moscow: Progress Publishers, 1981.

Gromyko, Andrei. *Memories.* London: Hutchinson, 1989.

Gross, Babette. *Willi Münzenberg: A Political Biography.* Ann Arbor, Mich.: Michigan University Press, 1974.

Guillebaud, C. W. "Politics and the Undergraduate in Oxford and Cambridge," *Cambridge Review,* 26 Jan. 1934.

Guthman, Edwin O., and Jeffrey Shulman (eds.). *Robert Kennedy in His Own Words: The Unpublished Recollections of the Kennedy Years.* New York: Bantam Books, 1988.

Gyurkó, László. *Arcképvázlat történélmi háttérrel.* Budapest, 1982.

Haig, Jr., Alexander M. *Caveat.* London: Weidenfeld & Nicolson, 1984.

Hammad, Gamal. *The Hidden Government in the Era of Abdel Nasser.* in Arabic: Cairo, 1986.

Hammond, Thomas (ed.). *The Anatomy of Communist Takeovers.* New Haven, Conn.: Yale University Press, 1975.

Hanson, Philip. *Soviet Industrial Espionage: Some New Information.* London: RIIA, 1987.

Hart-Davis, Rupert (ed.). *The Autobiography of Arthur Ransome.* London: Jonathan Cape, 1976.

Hasegawa, Tsuyoshi. *The February Revolution: Petrograd, 1917.* Seattle: University of Washington Press, 1981.

Haslam, Jonathan. *Soviet Foreign Policy 1930–33.* London: Macmillan, 1983.

———. *The Soviet Union and the Struggle for Collective Security 1933–39.* London: Macmillan, 1984.

————. "Political Opposition to Stalin and the Origins of the Terror in Russia, 1932–1936," *Historical Journal,* vol. XX (1986).

————. "The KAL Shootdown (1983) and the State of Soviet Air Defence," *Intelligence and National Security,* vol. III (1988), no. 4.

Hauner, Milan. *Hitler: A Chronology of His Life and Times.* London: Macmillan, 1983.

Heijenoort, Jean van. *With Trotsky in Exile.* Cambridge, Mass.: Harvard University Press, 1978.

Heikal, Mohamed. *The Road to Ramadan.* London: Collins, 1975.

————. *Sphinx and Commissar.* London: Collins, 1978.

Heller, Mikhail, and Aleksandr Nekrich. *Utopia in Power.* New York: Summit Books, 1986.

Hennessy, Peter, and Kathleen Townsend. "The documentary spoor of Burgess and Maclean," *Intelligence and National Security,* vol. II (1987), no. 2.

Henri, Ernst. "The Revolutionary Movement in Nazi Germany: (I) The Groups of Five (Fünfergruppen)," *New Statesman & Nation,* 5 Aug. 1933.

————. *Hitler Over Europe?* London: Dent, 1934; 2nd ed. (1939).

————. "Letter from 'An Historical Optimist'," *Druzhba Narodov,* March 1988.

Henriksen, Thomas H. "The People's Republic of Mozambique," in Dennis L. Bark (ed.), *The Red Orchestra,* vol. II: *The Case of Africa.* Stanford, Ca.: Hoover Institution Press, 1988.

Henry, Ernst *(sic). Stop Terrorism!* Moscow: Novosti, 1982.

Hersh, Seymour M. *The Target Is Destroyed.* London: Faber, 1986.

Herzen, Alexander. *My Past and Thoughts.* trans. Constance Garnett, vol. II. London: Chatto & Windus, 1968.

Hill, G. A. *Go Spy the Land.* London: Cassell, 1932.

Hingley, Ronald. *The Russian Secret Police.* London: Hutchinson, 1970.

Hinsley, F. H., et al. *British Intelligence in the Second World War.* 3 vols. London: HMSO, 1979–88.

————. "British Intelligence in the Second World War," in Christopher Andrew and Jeremy Noakes (eds.), *Intelligence and International Relations 1900–1945.* Exeter University Press, 1987.

Hodos, George H. *Show Trials: Stalinist Purges in Eastern Europe 1948–1954.* New York: Praeger, 1987.

Hoetsch, Otto. *Die Internationalen Beziehungen im Zeitalter des Imperialismus.* Berlin, 1933–42.

Höhne, Heinz, and Hermann Zolling. *The General Was a Spy.* London: Pan Books, 1972.

Hollander, Paul. *Political Pilgrims.* Oxford University Press, 1981.

Holloway, David. "Entering the Nuclear Arms Race: The Soviet Decision to Build the Atomic Bomb, 1939–45," *Social Studies of Science,* vol. XI (1981).

Hopkins, Harry L. "The Inside Story of My Meeting with Stalin," *American Magazine,* Dec. 1941.

Horelick, Arnold L. *The Cuban Missile Crisis: An Analysis of Soviet Calculations and Behaviour.* Santa Monica, Ca.: Rand Corporation, 1963.

Horn, Robert C. *Soviet-Indian Relations: Issues and Influence.* New York: Praeger, 1982.

Hosking, Geoffrey. *A History of the Soviet Union.* London: Fontana, 1985.

Houghton, Harry. *Operation Portland: The Autobiography of a Spy.* London: Rupert Hart-Davis, 1972.

Hull, Cordell. *The Memoirs of Cordell Hull,* vol. II. New York: Macmillan, 1948.

Hyde, H. Montgomery. *The Atom Bomb Spies.* London: Hamish Hamilton, 1980.

————. *George Blake, Superspy.* London: Constable, 1987.

Ignotus, Paul. "The First Two Communist Takeovers of Hungary: 1919 and 1948," in

Thomas Hammond (ed.), *The Anatomy of Communist Takeovers.* New Haven, Conn.: Yale University Press, 1975.

Ionescu, Ghita. *Communism in Rumania 1944–1962.* London: Oxford University Press, 1964.

Iovrysh, A. I., I. D. Morokhov and S. K. Ivanov. *A-Bomba.* Moscow: Nauka, 1980.

Ivanov-Razumnik, R. V. *The Memoirs of Ivanov-Razumnik.* London: Oxford University Press, 1965.

Jacobs, Dan N. *Borodin.* Cambridge, Mass.: Harvard University Press, 1981.

Johnson, Richard J. "Zagranichnaya Agentura: The Tsarist Political Police in Europe," *Journal of Contemporary History,* 1972, nos. 1–2.

Johnson, R. W. *Shootdown: The Verdict on KAL 007.* London: Chatto & Windus, 1986.

Johnston, William M. *The Austrian Mind.* Berkeley, Ca.: University of California Press, 1983.

Jukes, Geoff. "The Soviets and 'Ultra'," *Intelligence and National Security,* vol. III (1988), no. 2.

Kádár, János. *Selected Speeches and Interviews.* Oxford: Pergamon Press, 1985.

Kahn, David. *The Codebreakers.* New York: Macmillan, 1967.

———. "Codebreaking in World War I and II: The Major Successes and Failures, Their Causes and Their Effects," in Christopher Andrew and David N. Dilks (eds.), *The Missing Dimension: Governments and Intelligence Communities in the Twentieth Century.* London: Macmillan, 1984.

Kalygin, Oleg. "Intelligence and Foreign Policy," *International Affairs,* Moscow: June 1989.

Kapitsa, P. L. (ed. Pavel Rubinin). *Pisma o nauke.* Moscow: Moskovsky Rabochy, 1989.

Kaplan, Irving (ed.). *Angola: A Country Study,* 2nd ed. Washington, DC: U.S. Government Printing Office, 1979.

Kaplan, Karel. *Dans les archives du Comité Central.* Paris: Albin Michel, 1978.

———. *Procès politiques à Prague.* Brussels: Editions Complexe, 1980.

———. *The Short March: The Communist Takeover in Czechoslovakia 1945–1948.* London: C. Hurst & Co., 1987.

Karjalainen, Ahti, and Jukka Tarkka. *Presidentin Ministeri.* Helsinki: Otava, 1989.

Károlyi, Catherine. *A Life Together.* London: Allen & Unwin, 1961.

Kartun, Derek. *Tito's Plot against Europe: The Story of the Rajk Conspiracy.* London: Lawrence & Wishart, 1949.

Kater, Michael. *The Nazi Party: A Social Profile of Members and Leaders 1919–1945.* Oxford: Basil Blackwell, 1983.

Kaul, T. N. *Reminiscences Discreet and Indiscreet.* New Delhi: Lancers, 1982.

Kennan, George. *Memoirs 1950–1963.* New York: Pantheon Books, 1983.

Kerr, Sheila. "Roger Hollis and the Dangers of the Anglo-Soviet Treaty of 1942," *Intelligence and National Security,* vol. V (1990), no. 3.

Kessler, Ronald. *Moscow Station.* New York: Scribner's, 1989.

Kettle, Michael. *Sidney Reilly: The True Story.* London: Corgi, 1983.

Khlevnyuk, O. V. "The Year 1937—Opposition to the Repressions," *Kommunist,* 1989, no. 18.

Khokhlov, Nikolai Y. *In the Name of Conscience.* London: Frederick Muller, 1960.

Khrushchev, Sergei Nikitovich. "The Plot to Oust Khrushchev," *Ogonek,* 1988.

Kimball, Warren. " 'They Don't Come Out Where You Expect': Roosevelt Reacts to the German-Soviet War" (forthcoming).

King, Robert R. *History of the Romanian Communist Party.* Stanford, Ca.: Hoover Institution Press, 1980.

Király, Béla K. "Military Aspects," in Béla K. Király and Paul Jónás (eds.), *The*

Hungarian Revolution in 1956 in Retrospect. New York: Columbia University Press, 1978.

Knight, Amy W. *The KGB: Police and Politics in the Soviet Union.* London: Unwin Hyman, 1988.

Knightley, Phillip. *The Second Oldest Profession.* London: André Deutsch, 1986.

————. *Philby: KGB Master Spy.* London: André Deutsch, 1988.

Koestler, Arthur. *The Invisible Writing.* Danube ed. London: Hutchinson, 1969.

Kolosov, L. "Immortality of Those Who Have Fallen," *Izvestia,* 8–10 Oct. 1969.

Kopácsi, Sándor. *Au nom de la classe ouvrière.* Paris: Editions Robert Laffont, 1979.

Kopelev, Lev. *The Education of a True Believer.* London: Wildwood House, 1981.

Kovalev, F. N. "Documents from the Soviet Plenipotentiary Representation in Prague Relating to the 'Tukhachevsky Affair'," *Vestnik,* no. 8 (42).

Krasnov, N. N. *The Hidden Russia: My Ten Years as a Slave Labourer.* New York: Holt, Rinehart, 1960.

Krause, Joachim. "Soviet Arms Transfers to Sub-Saharan Africa," in R. Craig Nation and Mark V. Kauppi, *The Soviet Impact in Africa.* Lexington, Mass.: D. C. Heath, 1984.

Kravchenko, Viktor. *I Chose Freedom.* New York: Scribner's, 1946.

Krivitsky, Walter. *I Was Stalin's Agent.* London: Hamish Hamilton, 1939.

Kryuchkov, V. A. "An Objective View of the World," *Mezhdunarodnaya Zhizn,* Oct. 1988.

Kumanev, Georgi. "The 22nd at Dawn," *Pravda,* 22 June 1989.

Kuromiya, Hiroaki. *Stalin's Industrial Revolution.* Cambridge University Press, 1988.

Kuusinen, Aino. *Before and After Stalin.* London: Michael Joseph, 1974.

Kuzichkin, Vladimir. "Coups and Killings in Kabul," *Time,* 22 Nov. 1982.

Kwak, Tae-Hwan, et al. (eds.). *The Two Koreas in World Politics.* Seoul: Kyungnam University Press, 1983.

Lamphere, Robert J. *The FBI-KGB War: A Special Agent's Story.* New York: Berkley Books, 1987.

Lane, Arthur Bliss. *I Saw Freedom Betrayed.* London: Regency Publications, 1949.

Langhorne, Richard (ed.). *Diplomacy and Intelligence During the Second World War: Essays in Honour of F. H. Hinsley.* Cambridge University Press, 1985.

Larina, A. M. "The Unforgettable," *Znamya,* Oct. 1988.

Lavrentyeva, A. "Stroiteli novogo mira," *V. Mire Knig,* 1970, no. 4.

László Rajk and His Accomplices before the People's Court. Budapest, 1949.

Lawford, V. G. *Bound for Diplomacy.* London: John Murray, 1963.

Lazitch, Branko. "Stalin's Massacre of the Foreign Communist Leaders" and "Two Instruments of Control by the Comintern: The Emissaries of the ECCI and the Party Representatives in Moscow," in Milorad M. Drachkovitch and Branko Lazitch (eds.), *The Comintern: Historical Highlights.* New York: Praeger, 1966.

————, and Milorad M. Drachkovitch. *Lenin and the Comintern,* vol. I. Stanford, Ca.: Hoover Institution Press, 1972.

————, and Milorad M. Drachkovitch. *Biographical Dictionary of the Comintern.* rev. ed. Stanford, Ca.: Hoover Institution Press, 1986.

Lecoeur, Auguste. *Le partisan.* Paris: Flammarion, 1963.

Leggett, George. *The Cheka: Lenin's Political Police.* Oxford University Press, 1981.

Lenin, V. I. *The State and Revolution.* London: Allen & Unwin, 1919.

Leonhard, Wolfgang. *Child of the Revolution.* London: Collins, 1957.

Levine, Isaac Don. *The Mind of an Assassin.* London: Weidenfeld & Nicolson, 1959.

Lewis, Flora. *The Man Who Disappeared: The Strange History of Noel Field.* London: Arthur Barker, 1965.

Lewis, Jonathan, and Phillip Whitehead. *Stalin: A Time for Judgement.* London: Methuen, 1990.

Lieven, D. C. B. *Russia and the Origins of the First World War.* London: Macmillan, 1983.

Lockhart, Robert Bruce. *Memoirs of a British Agent,* 2nd ed. London/New York: Putnam, 1934.

——. *Ace of Spies: A Biography of Sidney Reilly.* London: Hodder & Stoughton, 1967.

Lonsdale, Gordon. *Spy.* London: Neville Spearman, 1965.

Lyons, Eugene. *Assignment in Utopia.* London: Harrap, 1938.

McCauley, Martin (ed.). *Communist Power in Europe 1944–1949.* London: Macmillan, 1977.

——. "East Germany," in McCauley (ed.), *Communist Power in Europe 1944–1949.* London: Macmillan, 1977.

——. *The Soviet Union Since 1917.* London: Longman, 1981.

McJimsey, George. *Harry Hopkins: Ally of the Poor and Defender of Democracy.* Cambridge, Mass.: Harvard University Press, 1987.

McLaine, Ian. *Ministry of Morale.* London: Allen & Unwin, 1979.

Mäkelä, Jukka L. *Hemligt Krig.* Stockholm, 1968.

Mandelstam, Nadezhda. *Hope Against Hope.* London: Collins, 1971.

——. *Hope Abandoned.* London: Collins, 1974.

Manne, Robert. *The Petrov Affair: Politics and Espionage.* Sydney: Pergamon, 1987.

Martin, David. "James Klugmann, SOE-Cairo and the Mihailović Deception," in David Charters and Maurice Tugwell (eds.), *Deception in East-West Relations.* London: Pergamon-Brassey, 1990.

——. *Wilderness of Mirrors.* New York: Ballantine Books, 1981.

Massing, Hede. *This Deception.* New York: Ivy Books, 1987.

Masters, Anthony. *The Man Who Was M.* Oxford: Basil Blackwell, 1984.

Mastny, Vojtech. *Russia's Road to the Cold War.* New York: Columbia University Press, 1979.

Mawdsley, Evan. *The Russian Civil War.* London: Allen & Unwin, 1987.

May, Ernest R. (ed.). *Knowing One's Enemies.* Princeton University Press, 1984.

Mayhew, Christopher. *Time to Explain.* London: Hutchinson, 1987.

Medvedev, Roy. *Let History Judge.* London: Macmillan, 1972.

——. "N. S. Khrushchev's Political Biography," *Druzhba Narodov,* July 1989.

Medvedev, Zhores. *Andropov: His Life and Death,* rev. ed. Oxford: Basil Blackwell, 1984.

Melgounov, S. P. *The Red Terror in Russia.* London: Dent, 1925.

Méray, Tibor. "The Trial of Imré Nagy," in Béla K. Király and Paul Jónás (eds.), *The Hungarian Revolution of 1956 in Retrospect.* New York: Columbia University Press, 1978.

Meynell, Francis. *My Lives.* London: Bodley Head, 1971.

Mikolajczyk, Stanislaw. *The Pattern of Soviet Domination.* London: Sampson Low, Marston, 1949.

Mlechin, Leonid. "A Minister in Emigration: Hitherto Unknown Pages in the History of the Soviet Intelligence Service," *New Times,* 1990, nos. 18–20.

Monas, Sidney. *The Third Section.* Cambridge, Mass.: Harvard University Press, 1961.

Moran, Lord. *Winston Churchill: The Struggle for Survival 1940–1965.* London: Constable, 1966.

Moravec, František. *Master of Spies.* London: Bodley Head, 1975.

Moskalenko, Kirill S. "Beria's Arrest," *Moscow News,* 1990, no. 23.

Moynihan, Daniel Patrick. *A Dangerous Place.* London: Secker & Warburg, 1979.

Mulligan, Timothy P. "Spies, Ciphers and 'Zitadelle': Intelligence and the Battle of Kursk, 1943," *Journal of Contemporary History,* vol. XXII (1987), no. 2.

Mullik, B. N. *The Chinese Betrayal.* Bombay: Allied Publishers, 1971.

————. *My Years with Nehru 1948–1964.* Bombay: Allied Publishers, 1972.

Nasser, Gamal Abdel. *The Philosophy of the Revolution.* Cairo, 1954.

Nation, R. Craig, and Mark V. Kauppi. *The Soviet Impact in Africa.* Lexington, Mass.: D. C. Heath, 1984.

Nehru, Jawaharlal. *The Discovery of India.* New York: John Day, 1946.

Nekrasov, V. F. "The contribution of the internal forces to the cause of the victory of the Soviet people in the Great Patriotic War," *Voyenno-Istorichesky Zhurnal,* 1985, no. 9.

Nelson, Harold D. (ed.). *Mozambique: A Country Study,* 3rd ed. Washington, DC: U.S. Government Printing Office, 1985.

————, and Irving Kaplan (eds.). *Ethiopia: A Country Study,* 3rd ed. Washington, DC: U.S. Government Printing Office, 1981.

Nettl, J. P. *Rosa Luxemburg.* 2 vols. London: Oxford University Press, 1966.

Neuberg, A. *Armed Insurrection.* London: NLB, 1970.

Nicolaevsky, Boris. *Power and the Soviet Elite.* New York: Praeger, 1965.

Nkomo, Joshua. *Nkomo: The Story of My Life.* London: Methuen, 1984.

Nordling, Carl O. *Defence or Imperialism?* Uppsala: Universitet Reprocentralen HSC, 1984.

Novak, J. "Sprawa gen. Berlinga," *Zeszyćy Historyczne,* vol. XXXVII (1976).

Nyaradi, Nicholas. *My Ringside Seat in Moscow.* New York: Crowell, 1953.

Ollenhauer, Erich. *A biz Z.* Bonn, 1969.

Oren, Nissan. *Bulgarian Communism: The Road to Power 1934–1944.* New York: Columbia University Press, 1971.

————. "A Revolution Administered: The Sovietization of Bulgaria," in Thomas Hammond (ed.), *The Anatomy of Communist Takeovers.* New Haven, Conn.: Yale University Press, 1975.

Orlov, Alexander. *The Secret History of Stalin's Crimes.* London: Jarrolds, 1954.

————. *Handbook of Intelligence and Guerilla Warfare.* Ann Arbor, Mich.: University of Michigan Press, 1963.

Ostryakov, Sergei Zakharovich. *Voyennye Chekisty.* Moscow: Voyenizdat, 1979.

Owen, Richard. *Crisis in the Kremlin.* London: Victor Gollancz, 1986.

Pacepa, Ion Mihai. *Red Horizons.* Washington, DC: Regnery Gateway, 1987.

Page, Bruce, David Leitch and Phillip Knightley. *Philby: The Spy Who Betrayed a Generation.* London: Sphere Books, 1977.

Palii, A. "Radio-Electronic Combat in the Course of the War," *Voyenno-Istorichesky Zhurnal,* 1977, no. 4.

Pano, N. C. *The People's Republic of Albania.* Baltimore, Md.: Johns Hopkins University Press, 1968.

Pastor, Robert A. *Condemned to Repetition: The United States and Nicaragua.* Princeton University Press, 1987.

Pavlenko, Nikolai. "The History of the War Is Still to Be Written," *Ogonek,* 1989, no. 25.

Pavlov, A., and Z. Fedotova. "Consultation," *Literaturnaya Gazeta,* 1989, no. 32 (5253).

Pelikán, Jiří (ed.). *The Czechoslovak Political Trials, 1950–1954.* London: Macdonald, 1971.

Pelling, Henry M. *The British Communist Party.* 2nd ed. London: A. & C. Black, 1975.

Penrose, Barrie, and Simon Freeman. *Conspiracy of Silence.* London: Grafton Books, 1986.

Peters, Yakov Khristoforovich. "Vospominaniya o rabote v VChK v pervyi god revolutsii," *Proletarskaya Revoliutsia,* 1924, no. 10 (33).

Petrov, Vladimir (ed.). *'June 22 1941': Soviet Historians and the German Invasion.* Columbia, S.C.: University of South Carolina Press, 1968.

Petrov, Vladimir and Evdokia. *Empire of Fear.* London: André Deutsch, 1956.

Philby, Kim. *My Silent War.* London: Panther Books, 1969.

Piekalkiewicz, Janusz. *Operation 'Citadel'.* Novato, Ca.: Presidio Press, 1988.

Pincher, Chapman. *Their Trade is Treachery.* London: Sidgwick & Jackson, 1981.

————. *Too Secret Too Long.* London: NEL, 1985.

————. *Traitors.* London: Sidgwick & Jackson, 1987.

Pipes, Richard. *Russia Under the Old Regime.* Harmondsworth: Penguin, 1974.

Polonsky, Antony, and Boleslaw Drukier (eds.). *The Beginnings of Communist Rule in Poland.* Routledge & Kegan Paul, 1980.

Poretsky, Elizabeth. *Our Own People.* London: Oxford University Press, 1969.

Porter, Cathy, and Mark Jones. *Moscow in World War Two.* London: Chatto & Windus, 1987.

Possony, Stefan T. *Lenin: The Compulsive Revolutionary,* rev. Brit. ed. London: Allen & Unwin, 1966.

Powers, Thomas. *The Man Who Kept the Secrets: Richard Helms and the CIA.* London: Weidenfeld & Nicolson, 1979.

Prange, Gordon W., et al. *Target Tokyo: The Story of the Sorge Spy Ring.* New York: McGraw Hill, 1985.

Preston, Paul. *The Spanish Civil War, 1936–39.* London: Weidenfeld & Nicolson, 1986.

Pritt, D. N. *From Right to Left.* London: Lawrence & Wishart, 1985.

Protsess "Promparty," 25 noiabria-7 dekabria 1930g. Stenogramma sudebnogo protsessa i materialov, priobshchennye k delu. Moscow: People's Commissariat of Justice, 1931.

Radosh, Ronald, and Joyce Milton. *The Rosenberg File.* London: Weidenfeld & Nicolson, 1983.

Radzhishorsky, Leonid. "December 1," *Moscow News,* 1988, no. 48.

Raffalovitch, A. G. *L'abominable vénalité de la presse.* Paris, 1921.

László Rajk and His Accomplices Before the People's Court. Budapest, 1949.

Ranelagh, John. *The Agency.* London: Weidenfeld & Nicolson, 1986.

Read, Anthony, and David Fisher. *Operation Lucy.* London: Hodder & Stoughton, 1980.

————, and David Fisher. *The Deadly Embrace.* London: Michael Joseph, 1988.

Rees, David. *Harry Dexter White: A Study in Paradox.* New York: Macmillan, 1973.

Rees, Goronwy. *A Chapter of Accidents.* London: Chatto & Windus, 1971.

Reich, Wilhelm. *Sexualerregung und Sexualbefriedigung.* Vienna: Münster Verlag, 1929.

Reilly, S. G. *The Adventures of Sidney Reilly, Britain's Master Spy.* London: E. Mathews & Marrot, 1931.

Report of Court Proceedings in the Case of the Trotskyite—Zinovievite Terrorist Centre. Moscow: People's Commissariat of Justice, 1936.

Report of Court Proceedings in the Case of the Anti-Soviet Trotskyite Centre. Moscow: People's Commissariat of Justice, 1937.

Riasanovsky, N. V. *A History of Russia,* 4th ed. Oxford University Press, 1984.

Richardson, R. Dan. *Comintern Army.* Lexington, Ky.: University Press of Kentucky, 1982.

Rogger, Hans. *Russia in the Age of Modernisation and Revolution 1881–1917.* London: Longman, 1983.

Röling, B. V. A., and C. F. Rüter (eds.). *The Tokyo Judgement: The International Military Tribunal for the Far East.* Amsterdam: APA University Press, 1977.

Romerstein, Herbert. "Some Insights Derived from the Grenada Documents," in Dennis L. Bark (ed.), *The Red Orchestra,* vol. I: *Instruments of Policy in Latin America and the Caribbean.* Stanford, Ca.: Hoover Institution Press, 1986.

———. *Soviet Active Measures and Propaganda.* Mackenzie Institute Paper no. 17 Toronto, 1989.

———, and Stanislav Levchenko. *The KGB Against the 'Main Enemy'.* Lexington, Mass.: Lexington Books, 1989.

Roosevelt, Elliott. *As He Saw It.* New York: Duell, Sloan & Pearce, 1946.

Rose, Clive. *The Soviet Propaganda Network.* London: Pinter, 1989.

Rosenfeldt, Niels Erik. *Knowledge and Power: The Role of Stalin's Secret Chancellery in the Soviet System of Government.* Copenhagen: Rosenkilde & Bagge, 1978.

Roshchin, A. "Inside the Commissariat of Foreign Affairs on the Eve of the War," *Mezhdunarodnaya Zhizn,* April 1988.

Rositzke, Harry. *The KGB: Eyes of Russia.* London: Sidgwick & Jackson, 1983.

Roskill, Stephen. *Hankey: Man of Secrets,* vol. III. London: Collins, 1974.

Rothschild, Joseph. *The Communist Party of Bulgaria: Origins and Development, 1883–1936.* New York: Columbia University Press, 1971.

———. *Return to Diversity: A Political History of East Central Europe since World War II.* New York: Oxford University Press, 1989.

Ruane, Kevin. *The Polish Challenge.* London: BBC, 1982.

Rupnik, Jacques. *The Other Europe.* London: Weidenfeld & Nicolson, 1988.

el-Sadat, Anwar. *In Search of Identity.* London: Collins, 1978.

Sakharov, Vladimir. *High Treason.* New York: Ballantine Books, 1981.

Sawatsky, John. *Guzenko: The Untold Story.* Toronto: Macmillan, 1985.

Schapiro, Leonard. *The Communist Party of the Soviet Union,* 2nd rev. ed. London: Methuen, 1970.

Schlesinger, Jr., Arthur M. *A Thousand Days.* Boston: Houghton Mifflin, 1965.

Schoenberg, Hans W. "The Partition of Germany and the Neutralization of Austria," in Thomas Hammond (ed.), *The Anatomy of Communist Takeovers.* New Haven, Conn.: Yale University Press, 1975.

Seaton, Albert. *Stalin as Warlord.* London: Batsford, 1976.

The Second Brown Book of the Hitler Terror. London: Bodley Head, 1934.

Sejna, Jan. *We Will Bury You.* London: Sidgwick & Jackson, 1982.

Sergei, Victor. *Memoirs of a Revolutionary 1901–1941.* London: Oxford University Press, 1963.

Seton-Watson, Hugh. *The East European Revolution.* London: Methuen, 1956.

Sharaf, Myron. *Fury on Earth: A Biography of Wilhelm Reich.* London: André Deutsch, 1983.

Shawcross, William. *Crime and Compromise.* London: Weidenfeld & Nicolson, 1974.

Sherwood, Robert E. *Roosevelt and Hopkins: An Intimate History.* New York: Grosset & Dunlap, 1950.

Shevchenko, Arkadi N. *Breaking with Moscow.* New York: Ballantine Books, 1985.

Shneider, A. *Zapiski starogo moskvicha.* Moscow, 1966.

Short, Philip. *The Dragon and the Bear.* London: Hodder & Stoughton, 1982.

Shultz, Jr., Richard H. *The Soviet Union and Revolutionary Warfare.* Stanford, Ca.: Hoover Institution Press, 1988.

Shultz, Richard H., and Roy Godson. *Dezinformatsia: Active Measures in Soviet Strategy.* Oxford: Pergamon-Brassey, 1984.

Sidorov, V. "Once again about The Trust: the role played by M. V. Zakharchenko-Schultz," *Golos Zarubezhya,* 1987, nos. 45–6.

Singh, S. Nihal. *The Yogi and the Bear.* London: Mansell, 1986.

Smith, Bradley F. *The Shadow Warriors.* London: André Deutsch, 1983.

Smith, Richard Harris. *OSS: The Secret History of America's First Central Intelligence Agency.* Berkeley, Ca.: University of California Press, 1972.

———. "The First Moscow Station: An Espionage Footnote to Cold War History," *International Journal of Intelligence and Counterintelligence,* vol. III (1989), no. 3.

Smolka, H. P. *Forty Thousand Against the Arctic: Russia's Polar Empire,* rev. ed. London: Hutchinson, 1938.

Solzhenitsyn, Aleksandr. *The Oak and the Calf.* London: Collins, 1980.

Somerville, Keith. "The Soviet Union and Zimbabwe: The Liberation Struggle and After," in R. Craig Nation and Mark V. Kauppi, *The Soviet Impact in Africa.* Lexington, Mass.: D. C. Heath, 1984.

Souvarine, Boris. *Stalin: A Critical Survey of Bolshevism.* London: Secker & Warburg, 1939.

Squire, P. S. *The Third Department.* Cambridge University Press, 1968.

Stephan, Robert W. "Death to Spies: The Story of Smersh." MA dissertation, American University, Washington, DC, 1984.

Stephens, Robert. *Nasser: A Political Biography.* New York: Simon & Schuster, 1971.

Stojanoff, P. *Reichstagbrand: Die Prozesse in London und Leipzig.* Vienna: Europa Verlag, 1966.

Stonehouse, John. *Ralph.* London: Jonathan Cape, 1982.

Storry, Richard. *A History of Modern Japan.* Harmondsworth: Penguin, 1960.

Straight, Michael. *After Long Silence.* London: Collins, 1983.

Suvorov, Victor. *Soviet Military Intelligence.* London: Hamish Hamilton, 1984.

Svetitsky, K., and S. Sokolov. "I Would Cope With Any Work," *Ogonek,* June 1989.

Szász, Béla. *Volunteers for the Gallows.* London: Chatto & Windus, 1971.

Szulc, Tad. *Fidel: A Critical Portrait.* London: Hutchinson, 1987.

Talbott, Strobe (ed./trans.). *Khrushchev Remembers.* London: Sphere Books, 1971.

Tanner, Väinö. *The Winter War.* Stanford, Ca.: Stanford University Press, 1957.

Thomas, Hugh. *The Cuban Revolution.* New York: Harper & Row, 1977.

———. *The Spanish Civil War,* 3rd rev. ed. London: Hamish Hamilton, 1977.

———. *Armed Truce: The Beginnings of the Cold War.* London: Hamish Hamilton, 1986.

Thomas, Paul. *Le KGB en Belgique.* Brussels: Editions J. M. Collet, 1987.

Thurston, Robert W. "Fear and Belief in the USSR's 'Great Terror': Response to Arrest 1935–1939," *Slavic Review,* Summer 1986.

Tigrid, Pavel. "The Prague Coup: The Elegant Takeover," in Thomas Hammond (ed.), *The Anatomy of Communist Takeovers.* New Haven, Conn.: Yale University Press, 1975.

Tobias, Fritz. *The Reichstag Fire: Legend and Truth.* London: Secker & Warburg, 1963.

Tofte, Ørnulf. *Spaneren.* Oslo: Gyldendal Norsk Forlag, 1987.

Toland, John. *Adolf Hitler.* New York: Doubleday, 1976.

Tolstoy, Nikolai. *Stalin's Secret War.* London: Jonathan Cape, 1981.

Trepper, Leopold. *The Great Game.* London: Michael Joseph, 1977.

Trotsky, Leon. *My Life.* Gloucester, Mass.: P. Smith, 1970.

Truman, Harry S. *Memoirs: 1945, Year of Decisions.* Signet ed. New York: New American Library, 1965.

Tsvigun, S. K., et al. (eds.). *V. I. Lenin i VChK: Sbornik documentov (1917–1922 gg).* Moscow: Izdatelstvo Politicheskoi Literatury, 1975.

Tucker, R. C., and S. F. Cohen (eds.). *The Great Purge Trial.* New York: Grosset & Dunlap, 1965.

Tuttle, Dwight W. *Harry L. Hopkins and Anglo-American-Soviet Relations, 1941–1945.* New York: Garland, 1983.

20 Let VChK-OGPU-NKVD. Moscow: OGIZ, 1938.

Ulam, Adam B. *Titoism and the Cominform.* Cambridge, Mass.: Harvard University Press, 1952.

———. *Expansion and Coexistence: Soviet Foreign Policy 1917–1973.* New York: Holt Rinehart, 1974.

————. *Dangerous Relations.* New York: Oxford University Press, 1984.

Ullman, Richard H. *Anglo-Soviet Relations.* 1917–1921, vol. I: 1961, vol. III: 1972. Princeton University Press.

Usowski, Peter S. "John McCone and the Cuban Missile Crisis: A Persistent Approach to the Intelligence-Policy Relationship," *International Journal of Intelligence and Counterintelligence,* vol. II (1988), no. 4.

Vasilyev, A. T. *The Ochrana.* London: Harrap, 1930.

Vassall, John. *Vassall.* London: Sidgwick & Jackson, 1975.

Vereeken, Georgi. *The GPU in the Trotskyist Movement.* London: New York Publications, 1976.

Vezhnov, Vsevolod. "An Anti-Hitler Coalition Before the War? Possibilities and Reality," *Literaturnaya Gazeta,* 1989, no. 17.

Volkogonov, Dmitri. "On the Eve of War," *Pravda,* 20 June 1988.

Volkov, Fyodor. *Secrets from Whitehall and Downing Street.* Moscow: Progress Publishers, 1986.

Wadleigh, Julian. "Why I Spied for the Communists," *New York Post,* 12–20 July 1949.

Watt, Donald Cameron. "The Initiation of Talks Leading to the Nazi-Soviet Pact: An Historical Problem," in C. Abramsky and Beryl J. Williams (eds.), *Essays in Honour of E. H. Carr.* London: Macmillan, 1974.

————. "[John] Herbert King: A Soviet Source in the Foreign Office," *Intelligence and National Security,* vol. III (1988), no. 4.

————. *How War Came: The Immediate Origins of the Second World War 1938–1939.* London: Heinemann, 1989.

Waxmonsky, Gary R. "Police and Politics in Soviet Society, 1921–1929." Unpublished PhD thesis, Princeton University, 1982.

Weinstein, Allen. *Perjury: The Hiss-Chambers Case.* New York: Knopf, 1978.

West, Nigel. *A Matter of Trust.* London: Weidenfeld & Nicolson, 1982.

————. *GCHQ.* London: Weidenfeld & Nicolson, 1986.

————. *Molehunt.* London: Weidenfeld & Nicolson, 1987.

West, W. J. (ed.). *Orwell: The War Commentaries.* London: Duckworth, 1985.

————. *Truth Betrayed.* London: Duckworth, 1987.

————. *The Truth About Hollis.* London: Duckworth, 1989.

Whaley, Barton. *Codeword Barbarossa.* Cambridge, Mass.: MIT Press, 1974.

Williams, Philip M. *French Politicians and Elections 1951–1969.* Cambridge University Press, 1970.

Williams, Robert Chadwell. *The Other Bolsheviks.* Bloomington and Indianapolis: Indiana University Press, 1986.

————. *Klaus Fuchs, Atom Spy.* Cambridge, Mass.: Harvard University Press, 1987.

Willoughby, Charles A. *Sorge: Soviet Master Spy.* London: William Kimber, 1952.

Wolfe, Bertram D. (ed.). *Khrushchev and Stalin's Ghost: Text, Background and Meaning of Khrushchev's Secret Report to the Twentieth Congress on the Night of February 24–25 1956.* London: Atlantic Press, 1957.

Wolfe, Bertram D. *Three Who Made a Revolution.* Harmondsworth: Penguin, 1966.

Wolton, Thierry. *Le KGB en France.* Paris: Bernard Grasset, 1986.

Woodward, Robert. *Veil: The Secret Wars of the CIA 1981–1987.* New York: Simon & Schuster, 1987.

Wright, Peter. *Spycatcher.* New York: Viking, 1987.

Yardley, Herbert. *The American Black Chamber.* London: Faber, 1931.

Young, Robert. *In Command of France.* Cambridge, Mass.: Harvard University Press, 1978.

Zhukov, G. K. *The Memoirs of Marshal Zhukov.* London: Jonathan Cape, 1971.

Index

745